Adolescent
Development
and
Behavior

Adolescent Development and Behavior

Second Edition

JEROME B. DUSEK

Syracuse University

PRENTICE HALL Englewood Cliffs, New Jersey 07632

Dusek, Jerome B.
   Adolescent development and behavior / Jerome B. Dusek. — 2nd ed.
    p.   cm.
   Includes bibliographical references and indexes.
   ISBN 0-13-009119-7
   1. Adolescent psychology. I. Title.
BF724.D84 1991
155.5—dc20

                           90-49229
                             CIP

Acquisitions editor: Charlyce Jones Owen
Editorial/production supervision and
  interior design: Barbara Reilly
Cover design: Mike Fender
Cover photo: Billy E. Barnes/Uniphoto
Prepress buyer: Debra Kesar
Manufacturing buyer: Mary Ann Gloriande
Photo research: Lisa Kinne

© 1991, 1987 by Prentice-Hall, Inc.
A Division of Simon & Schuster
Englewood Cliffs, New Jersey 07632

Printed in the United States of America
10 9 8 7 6 5 4 3 2 1

ISBN   0-13-009119-7

Prentice-Hall International (UK) Limited, *London*
Prentice-Hall of Australia Pty. Limited, *Sydney*
Prentice-Hall Canada Inc., *Toronto*
Prentice-Hall Hispanoamericana, S.A., *Mexico*
Prentice-Hall of India Private Limited, *New Delhi*
Prentice-Hall of Japan, Inc., *Tokyo*
Simon & Schuster Asia Pte. Ltd., *Singapore*
Editora Prentice-Hall do Brasil, Ltda., *Rio de Janeiro*

Dedication

To Kennedy T. Hill, my advisor,
mentor, and friend. He taught me to
appreciate the advantages of studying
development and gave me an appreciation for
the importance of doing so. No student could
have been introduced to developmental
psychology by a better colleague.

Contents

Preface

Adolescence is exciting! It also is a period of development we all have experienced and, for better or worse, remember. That fact makes it an especially interesting period for college students, and their parents, to study and examine. It also makes it a very interesting topic about which to research and write.

We all harbor a variety of stereotypes about adolescents: They are moody and going through "stages" (Adolescence is, after all, a period of storm and stress); They don't care much about their family—they reside in their own world; They all believe that adults are incapable of appreciating their cares, concerns, and worries. What I like to call "myths" about adolescence, such as these, abound. I hope this text will serve to dispel some, if not all, of them.

By exploring the nature of adolescent development and the forces that shape it I hope we all can gain a better insight into the developmental period bridging childhood and adult self-realization. Hence, this text is written with an eye toward research that objectively describes the important influences shaping the nature of adolescence in both our own, and other, cultures.

A second purpose of this text is more subtle. Although not a primer on "how to raise an adolescent," a good deal of the material presented is pertinent to this issue. Be you a parent or future parent, there is a host of information relevant to the rearing of ad-olescents—and children in general. I hope that those of you who read this text will find helpful hints on dealing with the nuances of adolescent development as you encounter them in your own lives.

You will note that the material in the text is based on research documented by a great number of individuals. It is through research that we learn the general trends, which constitute the "truth" of adolescent development. That is how scientific discourse interacts with the "real world." By basing the observations in this text on scientific research I have tried to divorce opinion from fact. Don't let the science get in your way. Facts are facts! On the other hand, whether you are a student or a parent, remember that each adolescent is an individual, growing in a unique environment. I sincerely hope that that uniqueness has been adequately reflected throughout the text. Keeping it in mind will help round out the general trends discussed.

I wish to thank a number of people who have helped make this text possible. Thanks to the thousands of students who have shared with me their own student perspective on adolescence. Thanks, too, to the many researchers who have investigated the many facets of adolescent development. Without their contributions this and other similar texts would offer no more than personal opinion and conjecture. The following six reviewers of the manuscript of this book contributed many helpful suggestions: Joan Cannon, R.G. Gaddis, Arthur Glover, Lillian Grayson, William Moses, and James Thomas. I hope I have done justice to their contributions. Finally, thanks to my son, David. I love him. He has taught me more about adolescence than any research articles ever could.

Adolescent Development and Behavior

Introduction to Adolescence

1

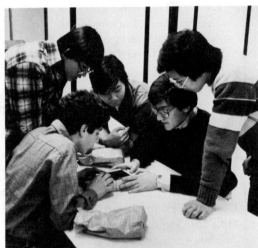

CHAPTER OUTLINE

MAJOR ISSUES ADDRESSED

INTRODUCTION

As a student in a course dealing with adolescent psychology, you are in a unique position—you have lived, or are living, in the period of development you are studying. Many of your own experiences will add a personal tone to the material you will read in this book and study throughout the course. On the one hand, this is a benefit. It will help you organize and remember information and will make the content appear more "real" to you. It also may help you gain insight into your own development.

On the other hand, there is an important liability in drawing on your own experiences as you read the text. You assuredly will find that aspects of your development will not completely match what is described. In this regard, a caution is in order—do not compare yourself too closely to the averages discussed in the text and presented in the tables. You are the product of a unique environment, unique home and parents, and unique personality. Therefore you *should* expect to find that some of your experiences will not coincide exactly with what is described, because the *general trends* summarized over unique experiences are the stuff of science.

In order to describe accurately the major trends in, and influences on, adolescent development, we rely on research findings. In your introductory psychology class you probably were exposed briefly to early, pre-scientific writings about the psychology of human behavior. In these writings one finds many ideas and opinions. Agreement on basic principles of psychology was reached, not by scientific methodology, but by debate (Boring, 1950; Elder, 1980; Kessen, 1965; Muuss, 1988). Hence, achieving a consensus about the critical factors in the development of human behavior was difficult, if not impossible.

This way of describing the important aspects of adolescent development may be seen in the writings of some of the early philosophers and scientists who wrote about adolescents. Each had a different view of the most important aspect of development during the years we now call adolescence. Plato, for example, emphasized the emergence of rational and logical thought. He felt the change in thinking signaled the time to teach science and mathematics as opposed to music or art. Aristotle, who called the years from 14 to 21 young manhood, emphasized the adolescent's ability to make choices, perhaps a precursor to our current view of adolescence as a time of independence strivings. As a final example, consider the ideas of G. S. Hall, the founder of developmental psychology, who viewed adolescence as a period of storm and stress, a time of conflict and upheaval. He explained adolescent behavior as reflecting the emotional difficulty of this stage of development.

All the above perspectives were largely, if not exclusively, based on subjective opinion, not on objective data. As psychology in general (Boring, 1950) and the study of adolescence in particular (Muuss, 1988; Elder, 1980; Sisson, Hersen, & Van Hasselt, 1987) became more "scientific," some of these views were supported and others shunted aside. For example, it was found that adolescence was a time of important cognitive change, but, for most, not a time of extreme storm and stress. Through the use of the scientific approach, and only that approach, was it possible to eliminate subjective observation in favor of objectively discovered data; it was possible to replace myth and speculation with fact.

What is described in the text are average trends, in a sense, trends in development of the average adolescent. This is done because research findings deal primarily with aspects of development that influence most, but maybe not all, adolescents. Hence, generalizations from such research allow a description of average development but ignore the unique development experienced by the sin-

3

gle individual. This is necessary because we cannot have a separate psychology for each and every adolescent. We must have a more economical view. Therefore, you should fill in the individual component by drawing on your unique developmental history. You may be surprised to learn that the combined approach—individual and average—leads to greater knowledge and insight than either alone.

Estimating the Size of the Adolescent Population

There is a tendency when studying developmental epochs to ignore the number of people composing that portion of the life cycle. Although we cannot determine precise numbers of adolescents, because census data are reported in rough age groupings, we can estimate the size of the adolescent population in the United States.

The total population of the United States in 1986 was approximately 241 million people (U.S. Bureau of the Census, 1989). In the age range 10 to 19, which encompasses most of those whom we would label adolescents, there were approximately 36 million people. The adolescent portion of the population, then, represented about 14% (one of every seven people) of the total population of the United States. Clearly, the study of adolescence concerns a very sizable group of people. It was you a few years ago, and your friends, and your friends' friends.

DEFINITION OF CRITICAL TERMS IN ADOLESCENT PSYCHOLOGY

The term *adolescence* comes from the Latin verb *adolescere*, which means "to grow up" or "to grow to maturity." As it is commonly used by psychologists, and as it shall be used in this text, it means somewhat more than the physiological development implied by the original Latin verb. In psychology, **adolescence** is the bridge between childhood

and adulthood. It is the stage in which the individual is required to adapt and adjust childhood behaviors to the adult forms that are considered acceptable in his or her culture. Hence, as we shall use the term, adolescence refers not only to biological growth, but also to social growth within a cultural framework.

Puberty is the term used to denote the point in time when an individual reaches sexual maturity and becomes capable of bearing offspring and reproducing the species. Puberty, then, is a much more specific term than adolescence.

Pubescence, the term generally used to refer to the approximately two-year period that precedes puberty, is the period when physiological changes that lead to the development of both primary and secondary sex characteristics take place. Pubescence occurs during late childhood and early adolescence, with puberty occurring somewhat later. Pubescence refers to the relatively massive physiological changes occurring during the growth spurt that is completed in the early teen years for most girls and in the mid-teen years for most boys. This growth includes changes in height, weight, exercise tolerance, and other, more subtle changes in physiological functioning. The specific physiological and psychological aspects of these physical growth phenomena are discussed in Chapter 3.

In addition to the highly individualistic physiological and physical correlates of adolescence, there are also important social and cultural determinants. For example, in some cultures adolescence, as such, does not even occur. Instead, a *puberty rite ceremony*, or *rite of passage*, marks the end of childhood and the immediate beginning of adulthood. In such cultures, we may consider adolescence to be an extremely short period of time, virtually the time from the beginning to the end of the puberty rite, or we may consider that these cultures have no adolescent period of development at all.

It should be clear that defining adoles-

BOX 1–1 **Are College Students Adolescents?**

As explained in the text, adolescence is a difficult stage of development to define. This is especially true for the endpoint of adolescence—or the entrance into adulthood. It is the defining characteristics of adulthood that lead to the interesting question of college students being adolescents. Adults, in a general sense, are viewed as being economically, emotionally, and socially independent of their original family and parents. In addition, adults often are viewed as better able than adolescents to accept responsibility, plan for the future, and behave in a mature manner. All of these characteristics are nebulous and difficult to define.

Consider the circumstances of a typical 14- or 15-year-old. This person is in a school setting, economically dependent on the family, emotionally immature, not able to accept complete responsibility for all his or her actions, and not employed full-time. These characteristics are reminiscent of those that describe children. A major difference between adolescents and children, however, is the level of physical development. Adolescents' physical development is much closer to adults' than to children's. And, on the other dimensions mentioned above, adolescents are more advanced toward adulthood than are children.

Now, consider an average adult. The typical adult is economically independent of his or her parents, relatively emotionally mature, able to plan for the future, capable of accepting responsibility, and usually employed. To be sure, not all adults fit this mold, and those who do may not fit it all the time. Nonetheless, these distinctions differentiate adults and adolescents.

Now consider the typical high school student who has recently become a college student. Although many may work to earn some of their expenses, they likely are dependent on their parents for some economic support. They need not, or do not, accept many responsibilities with which adults must deal. Responsibility for sexual behavior, e.g., pregnancy, or for providing food, clothing, and shelter for a family, are some examples. Although most college students are emotionally and socially much more mature than children or younger adolescents, they are likely less so than many adults.

This example raises several interesting points. First, it demonstrates what Erikson has called the rolelessness of adolescence—the adolescent is neither child nor adult. Second, it suggests that many college students are very similar to adolescents, and, indeed, might well be considered adolescents.

No doubt some of these students will object to being described as adolescent, even though certain adolescent characteristics may aptly describe them. Perhaps their concerns can be allayed by our pointing out that we must consider transitions into adulthood individually. The first transition is biological; other transitions are completed, in no as yet identified order, throughout the adolescent years. Hence, one may indeed be economically independent, socially or emotionally mature, or able to accept and deal with adult-type responsibilities. However, because we do not achieve all these competencies at the same time, we exhibit vestiges of adulthood and adolescence.

Are college students adolescents? In some ways, such as economically, their dependence on parents and family, the artificiality of their general environment, and the like, yes. In some ways, such as biological maturity, ability to make long-range decisions, and perhaps in other ways, no. And, of course, some college students are more, or less, advanced toward adulthood than others. Where do you stand?

cence is a difficult task. Defining the start of adolescence presents no particular problem: psychologists, in general, agree that adolescence starts with the physical changes that occur during pubescence.

It is more difficult, however, to define the end of adolescence, namely, *maturity*. Usually maturity refers to the age or stage of life when a person is considered to be fully developed physically, emotionally, socially, and intellectually. However, people do not mature in all these areas at the same rate.

Hence, as a scientific term, maturity is very inadequate. And the term *adulthood* is perhaps even less readily definable.

To help clarify, we usually assume that maturity is reached when one is engaging in the socially defined roles of typical adults in the society. These include voting, economic independence, completing education, and perhaps marrying and parenting, among others. Although this definition of maturity also presents problems (for example, how to classify college students—see Box 1–1 on p. 5), it is a reasonable set of bases on which to define the end of adolescence.

Hence, we shall define adolescence as that span in time which is bounded at the lower end by the beginnings of the physiological changes accompanying pubescence and bounded at the upper end by the assumption of various adulthood roles. Because we acquire these roles at different ages we become adults in stages; we "lose" our adolescence gradually.

Age Does Not Define Adolescence. You may wonder why we have not taken an age approach and defined adolescence as a stage beginning with the onset of puberty and ending at the age of 18, the age at which the federal government considers an individual an adult. Or you may wonder why we did not define adolescence as a developmental stage encompassed by the teen-age years. Certainly adoption of either of these alternatives would appear to make our definitional problems disappear.

However, there are several reasons why we have elected not to use age-graded definitions. First, there is considerable variation (approximately four years) in the age of onset of pubescence. This variability would not be recognized in an age-related definition. In addition, the 18-year-old is still likely to be in school, or at least not engaged in full-time employment or other kinds of activities that are "adult" in nature. Second, age is not a psychological variable, in any case. It is simply a measure of time and is only a very rough index of the experiences one encounters that are critical to psychological development. Hence, age is probably not a good index or defining characteristic of the adolescent period because it does not encompass the complete range of important psychological changes that accompany what we mean by adolescence. Finally, to restrict adolescence to the teen-age years is to ignore the fact that many individuals (for example, college students) remain in adolescent roles into the early twenties.

WHY AN ADOLESCENT STAGE OF DEVELOPMENT?

In this section we describe how adolescence as we know it came into being and how it changes as the society changes.

The Evolution of Adolescence

Adolescence as we know it today is, in many ways, a relatively new phenomenon. In fact, the stage of adolescence has undergone a social, evolutionary transition throughout recorded history (Kett, 1977; Elder, 1980); adolescence is a product of social age categories, institutions established for youth, and general social change.

A number of social conditions have exerted a significant influence on the development of the stage of life we call adolescence. One important influence was the urbanization/industrialization of the nation. During our rural/agricultural years children were considered to be merely miniature adults (Kessen, 1965; Kett, 1977). They were expected to work on the farm, take apprenticeships, and behave as adults. Often, children and adolescents were, in comparison to modern standards, abused. They worked in mines, factories, and sweat shops for long hours and very little pay. A predominant aspect of the rearing philosophy was to prepare the child for an adult job through work experiences. Formal

BOX 1–2   Developmental Tasks of Adolescence

Robert Havighurst (1951) coined the term **developmental task** to describe the individual's accomplishment of certain social abilities or attitudes related to development. Developmental tasks are skills, knowledge, functions, or attitudes that an individual must acquire at various stages during his lifetime in order to adjust successfully to the more difficult roles and tasks that lie before him. Developmental tasks are acquired through physical maturation, social fulfillment, and personal effort. Successful mastery of developmental tasks produces a well-adjusted individual who should be competent and capable of dealing with future levels of development. Failure to acquire these developmental skills can often result in maladjustment, increased anxiety, and an inability to deal with the more difficult tasks to come. Finally, Havighurst believes that the developmental tasks of any given stage are sequential in nature; that is, each task is a prerequisite for each succeeding task.

The optimal time for each task to be mastered is, to some degree, biologically determined. Havighurst believes that there is a critical period of time during which the individual should master each of the various developmental tasks for that particular age and stage of development. Although Havighurst points out that the kinds of developmental tasks through which the individual must proceed may differ from culture to culture, he notes that biologically determined tasks are more likely to be culturally universal than are tasks that have a strong cultural component. With respect to adolescence, Havighurst has noted nine major tasks:

1. Accepting one's physical makeup and acquiring a masculine or feminine sex role.
2. Developing appropriate relations with age mates of both sexes.
3. Becoming emotionally independent of parents and other adults.
4. Achieving the assurance that one will become economically independent.
5. Determining and preparing for a career and entering the job market.
6. Developing the cognitive skills and concepts necessary for social competence.
7. Understanding and achieving socially responsible behavior.
8. Preparing for marriage and family.
9. Acquiring values that are harmonious with an appropriate scientific world-picture.

As you can see, tasks 1, 2, and 8 have a strong biological basis and should be relatively universal, with the specific kinds of behaviors varying according to cultural influences. Tasks 3, 5, and 6 are somewhat biological, but their basis in biology is less obvious. Again, however, these tasks should be relatively universal. Tasks 4, 7, and 9 have no obvious biological basis and might be characteristic of some cultures but not others.

Thornburg (1970–71) reexamined Havighurst's tasks in light of changes that might be occurring in physical, cultural, or personal aspects of adolescence in more recent years. He discerned that some tasks are now more difficult to master. For example, preparing for and entering the job market is more difficult now than 35 years ago. As a result, adolescence is now longer and more complex than it used to be, and adolescents face more difficulties in becoming adults than did their parents. In turn, this may mean that today's parents have more problems in understanding the nature of adolescence than did their own parents, which may contribute to intergenerational (parent-adolescent) conflict. It also means that socializing adolescents, as in teaching them to become responsible adults, may be more difficult.

schooling was available for the elite but not the masses. Adolescence, as we know it, did not exist.

With increasing urbanization during the late 1800s and throughout the 1900s, increasing numbers of youth grew up in urban areas. As a result, a number of social and legal events occurred that impacted dramatically on the nature of adolescence. Child labor laws took children and adolescents out of the factories. Other laws (for example, criminal), defined special conditions for youngsters up to the age of 16 or 18. And it was during the late 1800s and early 1900s that a very major factor in the evolution of adolescence occurred—mandated mass public education.

The impact of placing large numbers of youth in the educational system contributed to the nature of adolescence in several ways. First, it established a formal separation of youth from the adult world. As discussed in a later chapter, the school is the setting of the youth culture. Second, schooling forced contact with peers. Indeed, adolescents spend more time with peers than with parents. Perhaps more than any other single factor, required schooling has formalized adolescence not only through the setting and peer contact, but also because of youth activities associated with the school setting.

To be sure, this very brief history does not do justice to the many factors that have contributed to the evolution of adolescence. However, it serves to point out that the nature of adolescence depends on the merging of a variety of cultural circumstances. As these circumstances change, so, too, will the nature of adolescence. Adolescence, then, is a continually changing stage of development. As a bridge between childhood and adulthood, it will reflect changing social standards for those age periods as well.

Adolescence as a Special Transition

In all of the above perspectives, adolescence is viewed as a transition period, a time of change. It is the one developmental period that formally is known as a transition, specifically, between childhood and adulthood. There are several reasons for singling out adolescence as an especially important transition period (Coleman, 1989; Hamburg & Takanishi, 1989).

First, with the exception of infancy, biological changes occur more rapidly than at any other point in the life span. These changes are relatively obvious signals that the individual is approaching adulthood. As a result of these biological changes, others' expectations for the individual's behavior change, and the individual's views of the self change. Hence, the biological changes of adolescence have important consequences for both social and personal development.

Second, and as you may suspect from the above, adolescence presents a unique opportunity to study the impact of biological change on social behavior. To be sure, biological changes in other parts of the life span, particularly the late adulthood years, also relate to changes in social behavior. However, the changes that occur during adolescence are unique in signaling entrance into the adult social world. Hence, one major aspect of development during the adolescent years is the uniqueness of the relation between biological change, and especially the rate of such change, and social and personal development.

Finally, a number of important qualitative changes occur during the adolescent years. The adolescent becomes capable of reproduction. Changes in cognition, peer relations, moral thinking, and the like, occur. In each instance, the result is a greater similarity to adulthood than childhood. In these ways, then, adolescents are much more adultlike than childlike. The qualitative transitions that occur are significant indicators of adulthood. The study of adolescent development, then, is critical to understanding development during the adult years, the longest of our life epochs.

A special word about the transitions of

adolescence is in order. It is very important to realize that we do not pass through all the transitions at the same time. And, to date, there is no evidence of any general sequence in the order of completing the transitions. Hence, each of us enters adulthood status in one or more spheres before we do in others. As a result, it is difficult, if not nearly impossible, to distinguish adolescents from adults in many ways. As an example, consider the question posed in Box 1–1: Are college students adolescents? It is the difficulty in defining the transitions, and measuring progress toward them, that makes for problems in defining the end of adolescence.

The transitions of adolescence involve virtually every sphere of adulthood roles. They occur as a result of continually changing and developing roles and tasks. And, they take place over an extended period of time. Havighurst (1951; see Box 1–2 on p. 7) has attempted to elucidate the specific nature of these transitions in his discussion of developmental tasks.

PERSPECTIVES ON ADOLESCENCE

The Social View of Adolescence

From a societal perspective, we can view adolescence as an important period of development during which children acquire the skills and attitudes that will help them become appropriately adjusted adults who can contribute to society in meaningful ways. Although this may seem somewhat illusory because we do not really know in any concrete sense what an effective and appropriately adjusted individual is, adolescents must learn behaviors that are within the broad range of what we call normal behavior.

One reason for this view of adolescence as a transitional stage is that today's adolescents are not required to play an adultlike role in society. For the most part, they are not needed or wanted in the job market (Campbell, 1969). By keeping adolescents out of the job market, society guarantees a greater number of jobs for its adult members.

A second reason is that it takes a good deal of time to acquire the training and skills necessary to function in our complex adult society. For example, of the occupations available in our culture only about 5 percent are for unskilled labor. Adolescence, then, is a period of time during which the individual may obtain the skills and training necessary to prepare for a vocation (Campbell, 1969).

A third important societal reason for having an adolescent period of development is that it allows the individual to learn other, non-work-related adult activities and skills (Martineau, 1966). Society suffers unless its adult members are well prepared for their marital, parental, and civic roles. Because our society is becoming increasingly complex, the learning of these roles is more difficult than in previous generations. The lengthening of the period of adolescence in modern times is in part a response to these complexities. However, just as the individual needs time to learn complex and changing adulthood roles, so too must society provide the supporting structure for these new roles; for example, relatively widespread and economical child-care facilities are needed today because of changing sex roles for women. Today's adolescents, both male and female, are told that they should try to reach their greatest possible potential. Yet society has not provided all of the necessary supports for that achievement. Hence, the development of society and the development of the individual are somewhat out of phase. This can produce frustration for both the individual and society.

Developmental-Psychology Viewpoint of Adolescence

From the point of view of developmental psychology, adolescence is a period of time for experimentation with a variety of adulthood roles and the determination of a realistic sense of the self (Campbell, 1969; Emmerich, 1973; Ahammer, 1973). One may determine whether to be a leader or follower, an active athlete or passive observer, and experiment with a host of other roles that relate to how one views oneself (for example, intelligent, valuable, sickly). Since adolescents do not have to accept the degree of responsibility that adults do when they take on various roles, the long-term consequences of trying out a role and having it fail are not very great (Martineau, 1966). It is hoped that the adolescent will develop a good notion of the degree to which various kinds of social roles and social situations are "comfortable."

The above suggests that adolescence is a time when one may ask and begin to answer the question "Who am I?" (Campbell, 1969),

Adolescence is a time for asking and answering the question, "Who am I?"

and to acquire relatively stable personality characteristics (Nesselroade & Baltes, 1974). This question involves concerns about careers, values, goals, and the like, as well as comparisons to others. If the individual is intellectually developed enough to ask the "Who am I?" question, and free enough from family identity to answer the question in a sense that is more meaningful than "I am Johnny," that person has taken a large step toward defining the self in appropriate and meaningful ways (Wylie, 1974, 1979). Such an individual should be able to demonstrate a good deal of maturity and learn what it means to behave in an adultlike fashion.

This view is different from the societal reasons for adolescence because it is more personal. Here, we are suggesting that the adolescent may try out a variety of adult roles to determine the kind of adult to be. The broad and vaguely defined notion of adulthood requires that we try out various behaviors before we can find the ones with which we feel comfortable. Adolescence gives us the time to do this.

Biological Perspective of Adolescence

We have noted the importance of biological changes in adolescent development. The biological changes that accompany adolescence occur earlier than either the intellectual changes or the social changes. Sex differences in the rate of biological growth may be responsible for differences in adult expectations for the behavior of adolescent females and males. Girls often are expected to behave more like adults than are boys. Similarly, timing of maturation—whether one is an early or late maturer—is related to social interactions with parents, other adults such as teachers, and peers. Early physical maturers often are treated as more socially and emotionally mature than they are, which may result in their being expected to behave in ways that are unreasonable. As discussed in Chapter 3, this may have lasting effects on personality development.

These biological influences are intimately related to the social and developmental factors discussed above (Richards & Petersen, 1987). From a general socialization point of view, then, adolescence is a time during which psychosocial learning can catch up to the biological-developmental changes that have occurred previously. The adolescent period gives the individual time to learn the social behaviors and to acquire and become comfortable with the psychological characteristics that are appropriate to a biologically mature person. By having this time period to "catch up," the individual can better integrate his social behaviors with the biological changes that influence the behaviors and expectations of others toward him.

The Intellectual-Competency View of Adolescence

The adolescent, unlike the child, is capable of abstract thinking (formal operations). The importance of a number of related aspects of such thinking (Elkind, 1967b, 1968, 1978a, 1978b; Looft, 1972) are discussed in Chapter 4. We need only mention here that changes in intellectual development allow the individual to interpret the social environment in ways not previously possible. The adolescent becomes capable of understanding the thought processes of others and of interacting with the environment in new and different ways. Changes in moral thinking and in views of the self also occur as a result of these cognitive advances. The increased cognitive competence of the adolescent also changes the way the adolescent will feel about the biological and developmental changes that we detailed above. The adolescent becomes capable of understanding the broader meaning and importance of these changes for behavior and development. This is not to say that abstract thinking itself causes these changes; it simply gives the individual an alternative way of viewing social realities that he or she may, but not necessarily will, use. From this perspective, then, adolescence is viewed as a time during which the individual learns to cope with formal operational thinking, and the consequences of that thinking as they relate to social development and to interaction with parents, teachers, peers, and others who have a significant impact on the socialization process.

CULTURE AND ADOLESCENCE

Adolescence occurs within a cultural context. In addition, it takes place within a specific time frame for each individual. Your adolescence, that of your parents, and that of your children will share certain commonalities, such as biological growth, but will be unique in other respects, such as music likes and dislikes. In addition, the experience of adolescence in the United States is different from that in England, Australia, the Soviet Union, China, and other industrialized and nonindustrialized countries. Institutional and societal values and mores impact on the meaning of the various transitions during adolescence, making the experience of adolescence peculiar to the broader social order. We will concentrate on describing trends in "typical" adolescence in the United States and will describe differences in these trends in other cultures where enough is known to do so.

Of course, there is not *one* American culture; there are many variations linked to social class, ethnic group, religious group, and the like. Although adolescents in each of these groups share certain common values and experiences, they also have their particular individualistic perspectives of what adolescence means. Adolescents who grow up in poverty conditions have a different adolescence than do those who grow up in middle- or upper-class families, be they white, black, Hispanic, Asian, or Native American. In turn, each of these ethnic groups has a history and value system that, while overlapping that of the typical middle-class in America, reflects a different cultural heritage, which means that being an adolescent entails differing experiences for those in these groups. Although researchers are attempting to identify the importance of these differing individual characteristics, with the exception of being black or growing up in poverty, little is known of how these factors influence becoming an adolescent.

What we shall attempt to do is describe the general trends of adolescence. Your own personal circumstances may lead you to a slightly different picture in some instances because you are black or Asian, first or second generation, Jewish or Catholic, and the like. Your personal experiences, then, will help you round out the meaning of adolescence by giving you a unique perspective of the more general trends. Do not be distressed that your adolescent experience may differ from that described in the text. That is to be expected because our stress is on general trends, not particular individual growth and development. You no doubt will find that there is "truth" in what you read about adolescents in general, and that the differences you experienced in your adolescence do not invalidate the general trends discussed in the text.

RESEARCHING ADOLESCENCE

We have stressed that we shall be describing the "typical" adolescent experience. We learn about the nature of that experience by conducting research. As noted above, it is research, or observation of the topic of interest, that allows us to describe development in an objective manner, relatively free of opinion.

The observations that are of interest are derived from various theories, best guesses, about how various influences affect development. These observations may be done through questionnaires, direct observation of adolescents in some naturalistic setting, or in the laboratory. For example, suppose we were interested in whether being an early maturer was related to aspects of peer relations. We could take a group of students and ask them if they were or were not early maturers and obtain a measure of their peer popularity in order to examine the relationship. Or, we could observe fifth-grade students in school situations and infer their peer popularity through their interactions with peers—say, in the playground. Finally, we could bring groups of fifth graders into the laboratory and have them interact in some predetermined situation while we observe them. Each method has its virtues and

Adolescents from different cultural and ethnic backgrounds share common experiences but also find unique aspects to their adolescence.

drawbacks. However, the important point is that our conclusions about any relation between early or late maturity and peer relations are based not on our individual experience or opinion, but on objective observation. Hence, what we find is more likely to be a good representation of what the "truth" is.

The evaluation of our observations and the methods by which they are made involve statistics and research design. These concerns are discussed in the Appendix to the text. Throughout the text we have drawn on examples of research to support the statements of general trends in adolescent development. That is why you will see citations to the researchers who have done the observations. Differences in techniques of observation, differences in measurement of the behavior under study—for example, asking people if they were early maturers vs. measuring maturity level through X-rays of bones—and the like may lead to somewhat different conclusions. That should *not* distress you. We have attempted to present the most consistent evidence available.

Finally, some of the research you will read about is very recent while other research was conducted 20, 30, or more years ago. In part, this reflects the changing interests of researchers. New topics of interest and importance arise—such as studying the impact on development of being an adolescent with a depressed mother. Other topics become resolved or uninteresting—for example, adolescent conformity to peers. In order to provide a sound and thorough treatment we draw on both the newer and the older research.

SUMMARY

Adolescence is a transition period between childhood and adulthood, a time when the child can acquire the social, emotional and personal skills necessary to enter the adult world of the society. Although all stages of life may be considered transitions, adolescence is a special transition because of the qualitative changes which occur.

Adolescence begins with the biological changes preceding the growth spurt and ends when the individual reaches adult status. Confusion about entering adulthood results from not attaining adult status in all spheres of development at the same time. Hence, adolescence has been described as a period of rolelessness, and adolescents as being neither child nor adult.

Adolescence evolves within a cultural setting, because the nature of the transition depends on the natures of childhood and adulthood, which vary across cultures. Moreover, as a culture changes, the nature of adolescence will change. In the United States, several major factors that have influenced the type of adolescence we have are industrialization and universal mandated public education.

To understand adolescence, then, requires studying the biological, cultural, and social factors that influence it. Some aspects of adolescence are universal, such as the biological changes of pubescence. Others—for example, the length of adolescence or the nature of the puberty rite—are not. Nearly all cultures, however, have a set of developmental tasks that must be mastered during adolescence in order to prepare the individual for adulthood. To the degree that the adolescent develops a relatively stable, positive, and constructive self concept, he or she should emerge from adolescence as a well-adjusted and well-socialized adult. This requires a well-integrated view of the various roles of the individual. Adolescence is a time during which the individual may begin to integrate various views of the self in meaningful and constructive ways.

Given the complex nature of the various influences on adolescent development, it is clear that, when we study adolescent development, we are really studying interactions between parents, peers, teachers, the social structure, and the developing individual characteristics of the adolescent. Obviously, this an arduous and difficult task and no single theory, or perhaps even any set of theories, can detail all the causes of the developmental changes that occur in adolescence. To accommodate this complexity, we have chosen to detail development in a series of chapters that deal with various important influences on the adolescent's development. Hence, we shall discuss adolescent social development with respect to parents, peers, the school, and other social institutions, and from the perspective of the adolescent with respect to moral development, self-concept, and vocational development. In addition, biological and intellectual changes are discussed, both in their own right, and as they relate to other aspects of adolescent development.

GLOSSARY

Adolescence.   The developmental period between childhood and adulthood.

Developmental task.   In Havighurst's view, a psychological or social milestone in development, the successful mastery of which prepares the individual for future development.

Puberty.   The period reached when the individual becomes capable of reproducing the species.

Pubescence.   The several year period prior to puberty when hormonal changes are beginning and the growth spurt is starting.

SUGGESTED READINGS

ADAMS, J. F. (1980). Adolescents in an age of acceleration. In J. F. Adams (Ed.), *Understanding adolescence: Current developments in adolescent psychology* (4th ed.). Boston: Allyn & Bacon.

Adams discusses issues surrounding the definition of adolescence. He then surveys areas of adolescent development and discusses the nature and importance of adult-adolescent interactions, particularly within the context of intergenerational differences in patterns of growing up.

AUSUBEL, D., MONTEMAYOR, R., & SVAJIAN, P. (1977). *Theory and problems of adolescent development* (2nd ed.). New York: Grune & Stratton.

Ausubel presents a discussion of the role of adolescence in the development of the individual. Major perspectives are briefly elaborated and important personal concerns are elucidated.

BANDURA, A. (1964). The stormy decade: Fact or fiction. *Psychology in the Schools, 1,* 224–231.

After surveying several aspects of adolescent development, Bandura suggests that at least part of the stress and conflict adolescents experience may be due to cultural expectations and self-fulfilling prophecies.

ELDER, G. (1980). Adolescence in historical perspective. In J. Adelson (Ed.), *Handbook of adolescent psychology*. New York: John Wiley & Sons.

Elder gives an excellent discussion of the historical perspective of the evolution of adolescence in the United States. His historical analysis is enlightening and points out the cultural bases of the adolescent period of development.

SISSON, L. A., HERSEN, M., & VAN HASSELT, V. B. (1987). Historical perspectives. In V. B. Van Hasselt & M. Hersen (Eds.), *Handbook of adolescent psychology*. New York: Pergamon Press.

This chapter is an excellent brief introduction into the history of the study of adolescence in the United States. The authors detail difficulties in defining adolescence and describe the scientific study of adolescence.

Theories
of
Adolescence

2

Chapter Outline

Major Issues Addressed

INTRODUCTION

In this chapter we shall discuss a number of theories of adolescent development. Some are primarily of historical interest and others are of more current concern. Before we do that, however, we discuss the role that theories play in psychological research. Often it appears to students that psychologists are interested in theories only for their own sake. However, theories serve an important function in the explanation of behavior.

DEFINITION OF THEORY

A **theory** is simply a statement, or a group of statements, that attempts to explain some event. In psychology that event is behavior. For our purposes, it is the behavior exhibited by adolescents. In a sense, a theory is a model of why some particular behavior, as opposed to some other kind of behavior, occurs; or, putting it in a slightly different way, a theory describes the factors that produce or cause some piece of behavior. Hence, theories about language development, mathematics, atomic particles, or personality development all have the same basic function. They all are attempts to explain why and how some behavior occurs. Such explanation helps us understand an event and predict when it will happen.

Our interest, of course, is in understanding adolescence and adolescent behavior. Questions of interest in this vein include the following:

Why does adolescence exist?

Is adolescence really a stressful period in the life span?

When does adolescence start and when does it end?

Why do independence strivings increase during adolescence?

What is the cause of changes in parent-adolescent relations and how can we make adjustments easier?

Like your own musings about issues such as these, the theoretical perspectives discussed in this chapter all are attempts to explain important questions of this type. As you can see, then, theories are not just for the scientist; they also are attempts to deal with the concerns of parents, adolescents, and young adults like you.

The Relation of Theory to Research

An important aspect of any theory is that it must be testable. A theory that cannot be subjected to experimental tests is relatively useless because its validity, that is, its accuracy as a model for describing development, can never be ascertained. But if **hypotheses** —best guesses as to the causes of behavior—derived from a theory can be tested and are supported by research, the theory gains in truth value. Each time a set of hypotheses from a particular theory is supported by research we have more confidence that the theory is a reasonable explanation of the behavior under investigation. If a theory generates hypotheses that are not supported by experimentation, we lose confidence in that theory as an adequate explanation of behavior. In such cases, we may either alter the theory or completely abandon it in favor of an alternative theory.

Psychologists use a variety of techniques to conduct research and test theories of development. The most widely utilized research designs are the *cross sectional* and *longitudinal*. In the cross-sectional study, individuals are tested one time. For example, we might be interested in the development of sex roles. And we might hypothesize that older adolescents will have less stereotyped sex roles because they understand sex roles differently due to their cognitive development. To test this hypothesis, we might give a questionnaire to adolescents in the age groups 12, 14, 16, and 18, and then compare sex roles as a function of age level of the adolescent. The age *differences*, if there are any, would either substantiate our hypothesis or indicate that our hypothesis is incorrect. As an alternative, we could conduct a longitudinal study, in which we repeatedly survey the same group of adolescents as they mature. Hence, we would have them complete the questionnaire when they were 12, again when they were 14, and so forth. In this instance, we would be measuring *age changes*, as opposed to age differences, because we have the same people involved in the research at each time period.

The study of age differences versus age changes is central to developmental psychology. As is detailed in the appendix, the study of age differences through the use of the cross sectional design is relatively easy and cheap. However, age differences may reflect developmental trends very different from those obtained through the use of longitudinal research aimed at measuring age changes in development. For example, we might find through cross-sectional research that younger adolescents (ages 12 and 14) have less rigid views of sex roles than do older adolescents (ages 16 and 18). A longitudinal study, on the other hand, might reveal that older adolescents have less rigid sex roles. Which set of findings reveals the "true" developmental trend? To determine the answer is not simple. As is noted in the appendix, it may be that cohort and time-of-measurement differences account for the discrepant findings.

A cohort is a group of people born in the same year. Suppose we conducted the above study in the early to mid-1960s. We might find that the cross-sectional and longitudinal studies both led to the conclusion that older adolescents had more rigid, stereotyped sex roles. This would be consistent with the general tenor of our times. Men were considered the workers, women were viewed as being responsible for running the household and taking care of the children. Were we to conduct the studies in the early to mid-1970s, however, we might find that the cross-sectional study showed greater rigidity among the older adolescents and that the

longitudinal study demonstrated less rigid sex roles at all ages. We could reasonably expect this because in the cross-sectional study the older adolescents were born earlier than the younger and lived through different "social times" than the younger adolescents. In the longitudinal study, the age changes (as opposed to differences) would reflect living through the same "social times."

Consider the well-publicized sexual freedom of today's adolescents. We find, as discussed in Chapter 8, that prevailing attitudes of adolescents about sexuality are different now than they were a generation ago. Hence, there is, in fact, a greater incidence of adolescent sexual intercourse today than a generation ago. This change is reflected in time-of-measurement effects in research designs. With rapid social change, we might well expect that cross-sectional and longitudinal studies of adolescent development might come to different conclusions because of cohort and time-of-measurement effects. Because the nature of adolescence is so tied to social conditions, psychologists interested in the study of adolescence must be aware of the impact of social factors and changes in society on the adolescent. Adolescents who grow up at different times may well have different views about any particular issue. That tells us that we must exercise caution in interpreting the results of research because we must consider the degree to which the topic under study is susceptible to the "social times." In addition, we must evaluate the topic of study to decide if cross-sectional research gives the most valid and reasonable picture of developmental trends.

We shall talk about testing theories by experimentation throughout this textbook. Research, then, is critical to our understanding of adolescent psychology because it is the way we validate or invalidate theories about adolescent development. Research also allows us to test alternative theories in order to compare their relative value for explaining development.

The Functions of Theories

Theories serve several major functions. *One function is to integrate information about behavior.* The more information a theory integrates, the greater its applicability. A word of caution is in order, however: a broad theory is not necessarily a good one. Theories that are broad may seem to incorporate a great deal of information but not explain behavioral development as adequately as theories that focus on narrower ranges of behavior.

Most theories tend to be relatively small in scope. Generally speaking, any given theory will deal only with very specific forms of behavior, for example, the effects of various child-rearing techniques on dependency and aggression. How, then, can we hope to learn how and why adolescents behave the way they do? The obvious answer to this question is that by looking at the theories for various aspects of development, we can put together a picture of the causes of adolescent development. In effect, this is what psychologists do—and what we will do below when we examine the underlying themes of adolescent development. We should state here that the adequacy of a theory, large or small, can be determined only by the results of experimental testing of hypotheses derived from it. *That leads to the second function of theories: to predict new events.*

By generating testable hypotheses, theories predict new events. That is, by closely examining a theory and deriving hypotheses from it, one should be able to predict that given a certain set of circumstances a certain kind of behavior should occur. This behavior may be "new" in the sense that it may not have been previously observed or considered. Hence, theories predict, through their statements, when a specific event will occur; that is, what conditions (factors) will cause some behavior.

The final function of a theory is to explain some piece or aspect of behavior or development. The issues involved in this notion are complex; but, for our purposes, the following should be sufficient.

To explain a behavior means that we can list its causes; that is, we can tell why the behavior occurs. Looking at the issue in another way, we can determine the conditions that will produce a specific behavior. Consider the following argument. If a theory predicts that conditions x, y, and z should produce some particular piece of behavior, and if we reproduce x, y, and z in an experiment and the predicted behavior occurs, then we can argue that x, y, and z are the determinants (causes) of that behavior. This is a prediction of behavior. Explaining behavior is simply the reverse of the coin; in other words, it simply involves listing the conditions (causes) under which a piece of behavior will occur. Hence, explanation involves stating the conditions that underlie the occurrence of some event.

THE ROLE OF THEORIES IN EXPLAINING ADOLESCENT DEVELOPMENT

Drawing on our definition of adolescent development and our discussion of the nature and functions of theories, it should be clear that the major functions of theories of adolescent development are (1) to describe the biological changes that accompany adolescence and how they affect adolescent development and (2) to explain the cultural-psychological factors that relate to the adolescent period of development. Therefore, a comprehensive theory of adolescence must take into account physical, psychological, cognitive, and social factors.

Perhaps the complexity of integrating these various influences is in part responsible for the lack of a well-articulated and unified theory of adolescent development. Obviously, explaining the impact of biological hormonal changes on behavior, and integrating that with the impact of psychological and social changes in behavior is an extremely difficult task. Nevertheless, whenever such interrelationships do exist, we will try to point them out so you will gain a more complete understanding of the multifaceted nature of the causes of adolescent development.

THEORIES OF ADOLESCENCE

For convenience, we have grouped the theories into those that take a biological, psychodynamic, social-learning, cognitive-developmental, or historical perspective of development during the adolescent years. We do this for convenience of presentation, because these orientations span the most important perspectives on adolescent development.

Biologically more mature adolescents play different roles than do biologically less mature adolescents.

Biological Theories

Perhaps the earliest sign of impending entrance into adolescence is the biological change undergone by the child. The changes are relatively obvious to parents, the child, siblings, and others. And the physical changes carry with them expectations for changes in behavior, such as acting "more grown up." It is not surprising, then, that considerable theorizing has centered on the importance of biological changes for explaining aspects of adolescent development.

The beginning of the scientific study of adolescence was marked by the publication of G. Stanley Hall's pioneering work, a monumental two-volume text entitled *Adolescence*, in 1904. Hall's thinking about psychological development was significantly influenced by Charles Darwin's *On the Origin of Species* (1859). From Darwin's writings, Hall formulated his notion of recapitulation, which stated that the experiential history of the species became part of the genetic structure of the individual organism, and thereby was passed on from generation to generation. Similarly, Hall believed that the development of the organism mirrored the

development of the species; that is, Hall believed that the individual developed in a series of stages that corresponded to the stages passed through by mankind in its development. He believed that ontogeny (the development of the individual organism) recapitulated phylogeny (the development of the species). As a result, Hall formulated a *stage theory* of human development.

Infancy, which extended from birth to age 4, reflected the animal stage of human development, when the species was walking on four legs. The infant acquires the sensorimotor skills necessary for survival. The years 4 to 8 represented the childhood stage and recapitulated the hunting/fishing ancestry of humans. Modern-day vestiges of this stage are seen in such children's games as hide-and-seek, and in building hiding places reminiscent of human's cave-dwelling history. The next stage, youth, occurred between the ages of 8 and 12; it reflected the life of savagery, in which rote-learned behaviors were necessary for survival. Adolescence is the next stage, and lasts through the early to mid-20s. It corresponds to a time when the human race was in a period of rapid transition. As detailed below, Hall viewed this stage as one of storm and stress because of the rapid and often turbulent changes that occurred. Adolescence is followed by the stage of maturity, reflecting the current social order.

Although Hall paid lip service to cultural and situational determinants of behavior, his major thesis was that genetically determined physiological factors controlled and directed the development and growth of the organism. As the organism matured, its behavior changed inevitably in a pattern set down in its genetic material. This influence of maturation was assumed to occur in any kind of environmental or sociocultural context.

Hall's belief, then, was that biological development exerted a direct influence on human behavior, an effect not tempered by environmental conditions such as the social structure, parental values and child-rearing techniques, peer relations, or cultural interpretations of the biological changes. Biology determined the course of development.

Although a number of hypotheses based on Hall's theorizing have been disproved by current research evidence in genetics and developmental psychology, his thinking shaped and focused the study of adolescence for many years. Therefore, it will be instructive to review his theorizing in some detail in order to gain a historical perspective on the issues that are viewed, even today, as important in any discussion of adolescent development.

Perhaps the most influential of Hall's concepts was his view of adolescence as a period of storm and stress (*Sturm und Drang*). In Hall's *recapitulation theory*, adolescence corresponds to the period when the human race was in a turbulent and transitional stage, as noted above. Although even today there are those who argue in favor of Hall's stress description, the evidence that adolescence is a period of storm and stress is not convincing. For example, IQ test reliability does not drop at adolescence, there is no strong evidence for emotional instability during the

adolescent period, and data on various socialization aspects of adolescence do not indicate that there are rapid changes in personality or social relations during the adolescent period. Rather, adolescence seems to represent a series of slowly evolving changes in a number of aspects of development. For some adolescents there may indeed be periods of storm and stress, as there may well be for some individuals at any point in the life span. On the whole, however, storm and stress does not appear to be an apt or appropriate description of adolescent development.

Why, then, does this notion persist? Although the answer is not simple, the following factors suggest why people continue to believe in the storm-and-stress view of adolescence. First, many parents view adolescence as a period of storm and stress because it is difficult for parents to let go of their adolescent children, to permit them to become independent. Hence, parents may become defensive in their reactions to, and views of, adolescence. Perhaps, as some have suggested, parents project the feelings of conflict and confusion they experience when their children become independent onto the adolescent, rather than themselves, and therefore view the adolescent as the one who "is going through a period of storm and stress." Second, the media does much to promote the storm-and-stress view of adolescence. Think of the number of television programs that deal with runaways, juvenile gangs, drug addicts, and teen-age prostitutes. It is no wonder that many are tempted to generalize from these specific instances to the adolescent population as a whole. Obviously, this is both unfair and unrealistic. What we are suggesting here—and it will be a theme that occurs in other places in the text—is that the view of adolescence as a period of storm and stress is a label put on adolescents by adults. Perhaps adults view adolescents as going through a period of storm and stress, but apparently the adolescent does not agree. It should be clear that one must be careful in interpreting adult views of adolescence, because they are written by adults and not adolescents. Were adolescents writing about themselves, perhaps views such as storm and stress would not appear.

Coleman (1978) has helped clarify the storm-and-stress concept of adolescence by pointing out that the various stresses on the adolescent do not all occur at the same time. Hence, the adolescent deals with one or two stressful events, which lessens their stress, before dealing with other stresses. His focal theory, which is detailed in Box 2–1, reminds us that adolescence occurs over a number of years. Because we tend to compress the time frame of adolescence when we think about or discuss it, we lose sight of the time frame. As we shall see in future chapters, the stresses of adolescence—adjusting to biological changes, learning about dating, making vocational choices—occur at different points in the time frame. Hence, adolescence is likely no more stressful than adulthood, or perhaps even childhood.

A second aspect of Hall's theory that is

BOX 2–1   **Is Adolescence a Period of Storm and Stress?**

There is no doubt that adolescence is a period of change in many ways. The most obvious changes are biological. But, other changes of importance also occur—friendship patterns change; there is initially an increase in conformity; pressure to learn new social roles and rules is exerted; and many important decisions, for example, about curricula, college attendance, career choice, etc., are made. Parents, peers, teachers, and society in general exert considerable pressure on the adolescent to "grow up." It is no wonder that a popular stereotype of adolescence is that it is a time of extreme stress.

Coleman (1978), however, points out that the results of the vast majority of research on adolescent development lead to the conclusion that adolescence is not an especially stressful time in the life span. He shows that evidence from research on the generation gap, conformity, and other areas contradicts the storm-and-stress concept. Moreover, he notes that conflict with parents tend to be over mundane, trivial issues for the most part. Although some adolescents may experience extreme stress, most adolescents, most of the time, do not. During much of the adolescent years, most adolescents get along well with parents, cope with school demands, and adjust well to changing social demands. Clearly, there is a contradiction between the popular and empirical views of adolescence.

Coleman suggests a "focal" theory that can help resolve the controversy. According to the focal theory, the peak age of concern for various stressful situations differs. Various issues come into focus at different ages. Although there is some overlap, it is unlikely that several peak at the same time. Hence, adolescents deal first with biological change, later with dating, and even later with career plans. The process of adaptation involves dealing basically with one issue at a time, resolving it, and then facing the next issue. Only rarely are there concentrations of two or more issues. In other words, the processes of growth into adult status occur over a number of years, basically gradually, not all in a short time.

One implication of the focal theory is that we must be cautious in our views of adolescence. The concerns of adolescents are real, but no more so than the concerns of adults or children. All stages of life contain their stresses, with which we must deal. Adolescence is simply no exception.

A second implication concerns our perspective of adolescence. We must avoid the tendency to collapse the time frame of adolescence. Our retrospective views will lead us to perceive adolescence as occurring over a relatively shorter period of time than is the case. We must continually realize that adolescence lasts six, seven, ten, or more years for some people. The stresses and decisions we face occur over this entire period. They are not lumped into a year or two, as they may in retrospect appear to be.

important for understanding modern-day thinking about adolescence is that adolescence represents a time of rapid change in most, if not all, aspects of the young person's personality. Hall's notion was that the adult who emerged from adolescence was altogether different from the child who entered it. In other words, Hall believed that development from childhood through adolescence was relatively discontinuous. The evidence on this issue is somewhat more in Hall's favor. The physical changes in adolescence, for example, are quite different from the kind of physical development that characterizes childhood. Perhaps because physical growth is such a visible and obvious rapid change, it has been generalized to other spheres of adolescent development. There are also some changes that occur relatively rapidly in the social sphere. For example, cross-sex friendships decline throughout late childhood until about the age of 12, when the curve reflecting choices of cross-sex friends begins to rise again. Piaget has noted that adolescence also brings a change in intellectual development—from concrete to formal operational thinking. The change is not abrupt, but nevertheless clearly there.

For most kinds of behavior, however, the changes that occur in adolescence are relatively gradual and continuous. Although current-day theorists would agree with this statement, the popular conception of adolescence is one in which rapid discontinuous changes are thought to be the norm. Perhaps these views persist because there is some tangible evidence for that kind of change, such as physical growth. Also, because it may be difficult for parents to deal with an adolescent who feels grown-up and is demanding the rights of an adult, they may believe that their child changed "overnight," when in fact the change has been a relatively continuous one.

Ausubel (1954), another biological theorist, has noted two kinds of change that occur in adolescence that are critical for an understanding of adolescent development. First, there is biological change, particularly as represented by the new sex drive that the adolescent experiences. This new drive is considered to be the first since infancy that must be socialized. Second, there is psychosocial change. For Ausubel, this change means becoming independent. Adolescents must learn to function psychologically and socially on their own, apart from their former adult caretakers.

In order to explicate the importance of these two changes, Ausubel discusses the impact of both psychobiological and psychosocial changes in development. **Psychobiological** aspects of development refer to those psychological factors that are consequences of biological change. For example, the psychological reactions to pubescence are extremely complex and include both societal perspectives and expectations and the adolescent's interpretation of physical and psychological changes. Psychobiological aspects are also relatively universal, since they occur in all cultures. However, cultural factors will determine to some degree the manner in which psychobiological aspects of adolescence emerge.

Psychosocial change refers to the changes, personal and social, that are due to cultural factors. Psychosocial changes tend to be more specific in nature, for example, cultural differences in terms of pre- and post-adolescent sexual behavior. Hence, for Ausubel there are important biological changes that occur in adolescence, particularly the new sex drive. In addition, however, culturally determined psychosocial changes also occur, in part as a function of the biological changes. Although this appears on the surface to be no different from the notions espoused by the cultural anthropologists discussed below, Ausubel, unlike the cultural anthropologists, pays more than lip service to the biological *and* cultural determinants of development. For example, both are important in the expression (culturally based) of sexual behavior (due in part to the increased sex drive). Another example of the interaction of biological and sociocultural influences on development is independence strivings. The adolescent grows larger, more experienced, and more competent and knows it, and others must learn to adapt and react to these changes and the demands for independence the adolescent exerts, in part, because of these changes.

Certain historical trends in the study of adolescence originated with these maturational theorists. For example, the study of the relation between physiological development, particularly physical growth and hormonal effects, and behavior was strongly emphasized by them and is a major consideration in current studies of adolescence. Chapter 3 deals exclusively with the biological changes that occur in adolescence and the relation of these changes to behavior. There we shall explore the available evidence linking biology to adolescent behavior.

Psychodynamic Theories

The psychodynamic view of adolescence, or any other period of development, rests on several fundamental principles (Adelson & Doehrman, 1980). First, psychodynamic theories are historical in nature. That is, from this perspective we can understand the adolescent's current behavior only through reference to his or her past experiences and personal history. By knowing something of the adolescent's developmental history (for example, how he or she was reared), we can gain a better understanding of current behavior, such as vocational choice.

Second, psychodynamic theories are steeped in instinct theory. During adolescence, this emphasis has been translated into a focus on drives, such as the sex drive, that are viewed as increasing in strength. In this context, the emphasis has been on the study of defenses against the increases in drives. This perspective of adolescent development

is well illustrated in the writings of Anna Freud (1948, 1958).

Anna Freud, the daughter of Sigmund Freud, attempted to spell out some of the dynamics of the psychoanalytic point of view (A. Freud, 1948) of adolescent development. Her view is that the behavior of adolescents is due to a sudden upsurge of sexuality which, in turn, is due to the biological changes that occur during pubescence. Hence, maturational factors (biological change) directly influence psychological functioning. The increase in sexuality brings about a recurrence of the Oedipal situation, which once again must be resolved. However, this time the resolution is through attraction to opposite-sex peers. Because of the increase in sexuality, the adolescent is viewed as being in a state of stress not very different from the stress created by the original Oedipal situation. This stress produces anxiety, which, in turn, must be defended against.

Defense mechanisms, which protect the individual from experiencing the anxiety associated with a stressful situation, also restore psychological equilibrium to the individual. Hence, defense mechanisms can be a useful and adaptive means of coping with stress. Examples of defense mechanisms include repression (keeping anxiety-producing impulses from consciousness), denial (insisting that some aspect of psychological reality does not exist), withdrawal (flight—mental or physical—from unpleasant situations), and regression (reverting to behaviors characteristic of an earlier stage of development). According to Anna Freud, the most important defense mechanisms for understanding adolescent behavior are asceticism and intellectualism. The former refers to attempts to deny completely the existence of instinctual drives, such as the sex drive, in order not to give in to them. Carried to extremes this may include the eating, sleeping, and other basic drives related to physical needs. Intellectualism refers to an abstract, impersonal evaluation of important issues in a manner implying they are not conflicts for the individual. Hence, discussions of free love, the existence of God, and the like, may represent the adolescent's way of dealing with deep-seated personal conflicts. Given the adolescent's increased cognitive abilities, intellectualization probably represents, in part, a practicing of abstract thinking.

Although we will not go into a detailed discussion of defense mechanisms, perhaps a simple example will help illustrate how they work. One defense mechanism associated with an increase or upsurge in sexuality is to avoid contact with opposite-sex individuals. Of course, this is a maladaptive form of behavior because it cuts off meaningful social relationships. An alternative to denial is to develop appropriate relations with opposite-sex peers, a hoped-for development in adolescence. Clearly, psychoanalytic theorists, and especially Anna Freud, believe that the kind of defense the individual uses, that is, the way the individual relieves the anxiety produced by stress, relates to the kind of psychological behaviors that the individual will demonstrate.

By using defense mechanisms, the individual reduces the anxiety associated with the drive and satisfies immediate needs. However, frequent use of defense mechanisms may result in unsatisfactory interpersonal relationships because they stunt personal growth and increase social distance between the individual and others.

More contemporary psychodynamic views of adolescence take the perspective that adolescence occurs in a series of stages (Adelson & Doehrman, 1980). Each stage is presumed to have its own major emphasis and relation to psychodynamic processes. Blos (1962, 1967, 1972, 1974), who views adolescence as adjustment to sexual and biological maturation, divides adolescence into the latency, early adolescent, adolescent, late adolescent, and postadolescent stages. Each stage has a unique major emphasis.

During the latency phase, sexual inhibition is prevalent as the ego and superego control the instincts. This phase ends with puberty and the concomitant increase in the sex drive. It is in this phase that defenses against the instincts come to the fore. In early adolescence there is an emphasis on same-sex friendships and the peer group. There is an adoption of values that oppose those of the parents. Because parental values are no longer seen as absolutely correct and right, the superego and ego are weakened and, in extreme cases, delinquency behaviors may emerge. During adolescence, heterosexual love relationships emerge, and there is an increased interest in the self. The major focus of late adolescence is the "Who am I?" question. Self-esteem becomes stable, and a firm sex-role identity is established. The end result is the emergence of a firm personality in the young adulthood years.

Finally, postadolescence involves completing the goals set for the self, including entrance into the adulthood roles of marriage and parenthood. Each sex further develops the sex-role image, including that of being a mother or father. During this time the ego becomes stabilized, and instinctual conflicts are diminished.

Another attempt to modify Sigmund Freud's conceptualizations to fit the nature of adolescent development may be found in Erik Erikson's writings. In his best-known work, *Childhood and Society* (1963), Erikson modified and elaborated the Freudian theory of psychosexual development in an attempt to apply those concepts to development during the adolescent years. His expansion of Freudian theory shifted the emphasis of psychoanalytic theories of adolescent development from the sexual nature of the stages of development to a type of psychosocial developmental pattern. The core concept Erikson uses to discuss adolescent development is the acquisition of ego identity, the person's sense of who and what he is, his evaluation of self. Since cultures determine to some degree how ego identity will be established, Erikson's psychoanalytic theory pays much more attention to cultural determinants of behavior than did the original Freudian theory.

Erikson views development as occurring within a series of psychosocial stages that are in part biologically determined (Table 2–1). His epigenetic principle is simply that anything that grows must grow according to a preset genetic plan. Hence, for Erikson, the development of the human organism is partially genetically determined. However, the individual's culture will influence the ways in which the genetically determined aspects of development will emerge within the series of psychosocial crises.

Each crisis has two possible outcomes, each denoted by one of the poles of the crisis. If the more positive and healthy resolution is worked out, that quality becomes part of the ego and further healthy development will be facilitated. If the less desirable outcome is the result of the crisis, that quality is incorporated into the ego and will interfere with further healthy development. In other words, resolutions of the crises of the stages are interdependent. Less optimal development of a given crisis may result in psychopathology and less optimal resolution of subsequent stages. Finally, each crisis is continually present, and subject to recur, but is most pronounced at a particular age. For example, the identity crisis is most pronounced during middle adolescence, but recurs with changing life roles, such as becoming a worker, a spouse, a parent, and the like.

Erikson, like other theorists (for example, Lewin, 1935, 1939), views adolescence as a marginal time of self-identity. The adolescent is seen as being in a poorly defined role, neither child nor adult. This lack of specificity in role definition leads to a disruption of self-concept and identity, leading to the Identity vs. Identity confusion crisis identified by Erikson. As with all of Erikson's crises, the crisis is always present and is never completely resolved, but its most pure form occurs in the adolescent years. Continual redefinition of the identity occurs throughout the life span. However, assuming that the identity versus identity confusion crisis is resolved with reasonable success during adolescence, then the individual will move into the adult stages of development and their corresponding crises with a firm identity. If the individual does not solve the adolescent identity crisis successfully, there will be maldevelopment of the ego. As a result, resolution of the crises of adulthood will be more difficult and perhaps less successful. Like Freud, then, Erikson includes both a continually evolving personality and the concept of maldevelopment in his theory.

For Erikson, both cultural and social factors play important roles in dealing with psychosocial conflicts; for example, in times of rapid social change, resolving conflicts will be much more difficult than in times when there is relatively little change.

In his discussions of identity formation, Erikson stresses the importance of developing a vocational identity and a personal philosophy of life. Formation of the former requires adolescents to come to grips with their own talents, abilities, and opportunities (for example, the likelihood of attending college or some other postsecondary training). Developing a

TABLE 2–1 **Erikson's Eight Stages of Development**

Developmental Period	Basic Crisis
1. Infancy	Trust vs. mistrust
2. Early childhood	Autonomy vs. shame and doubt
3. Preschool age	Initiative vs. guilt
4. School age	Industry vs. inferiority
5. Adolescence	Identity vs. identity confusion
6. Young adulthood	Intimacy vs. isolation
7. Adulthood	Generativity vs. stagnation
8. Senescence	Ego integrity vs. despair

(Source: Adapted from Erikson, E. K. [1963]. *Childhood and society*. New York: W. W. Norton & Co., Inc.)

philosophy of life, including religious and political beliefs, provides the adolescent with a frame of reference for evaluating and coping with life events; it also helps the adolescent make choices and guides the adolescent's behavior. It allows the adolescent to have a sense of continuity over time, linking the self to the past and to the future.

If the adolescent is not capable of forming a coherent and acceptable identity, self-doubt, role diffusion, and indulgence in self-destructive activities may result. In turn, these poor images of the self may relate to maldevelopment such as juvenile delinquency and personality aberrations.

As you can see, then, Erikson equally stresses biogenetic and social cultural factors in adolescent development. Erikson believes that both physiological and cultural factors exert important influences on the unfolding of the various stages of development. Both must be understood in order to accurately describe adolescent development.

Marcia (1966, 1967, 1980) has refined Erikson's conceptualizations of adolescent identity formation. Marcia views identity as a continually changing organization of one's own attitudes, values, beliefs, and the like. A well developed identity gives one a sense of one's strengths and uniqueness. A less well developed identity results in one's not being able to define strengths and weaknesses, and not having a well-articulated sense of self. It is during adolescence that the cognitive competence is achieved to evaluate and integrate in a meaningful manner the physical and social changes that have occurred. Such an integration sets the stage for continual changes in the content of identity through the adulthood years, for identity structures are dynamic, not static. For Marcia, identity formation involves the adoption of a sexual orientation, a set of values and ideals, and a vocational direction.

By examining commitment to occupation and ideology and the presence or absence of a decision-making period, that is, a crisis, Marcia has identified four identity statuses: identity achievement, foreclosure, identity diffusion, moratorium. **Identity achievers** have experienced a period of decision making and are now committed to an occupation and to a set of ideological values, all of which are primarily self-chosen. That is, the person has worked through his or her concerns in these areas and has made certain choices. These people have strength in their convictions and are adaptive and well adjusted. **Foreclosures** are also committed to a vocation and an ideological stance, but at least in part their choices have been made by others and not self-chosen. For example, parents who push their children into entering a vocation they themselves may have desired run the risk of rearing offspring who will have a foreclosed identity status, resulting perhaps in the child being rigid, dogmatic, and conforming. **Identity diffusions** evidence no commitment to an occupation or ideological stance, although they may have experienced a decision-making period. They may appear to be carefree, charming people, or they may appear psychopathic. **Moratoriums** are those who are *in a crisis* about occupational or ideological decisions. They are wrestling with the decisions that lead to a commitment in one or both of these areas. This stage is a prerequisite to identity achievements; it represents the period of questioning.

In these psychodynamic views of adolescence, we see an emphasis on aspects of personality development in general, and identity issues in particular. By examining the nature of personality development during adolescence, these theorists attempt to explain adolescent behavior as resulting from child rearing and a developmental history of interacting with the larger social order. They all, to a degree, view adolescence as a period of adjustment, or perhaps maladjustment, leading the individual into adulthood. The quality of coping during the adolescent years determines to a significant extent how well the person will adapt to adulthood roles and responsibilities.

Cognitive-Developmental Theories

Several times above we noted that the adolescent was viewed as evaluating some event, making some decisions, or evaluating some experience. Of course, such terms connote thinking and point to the potential importance of cognitive components in the description of adolescent development. Although there is no cognitive-developmental theorist who has focused exclusively on the adolescent years, the writings of several are highly pertinent to our obtaining a well-rounded picture of development during the adolescent years.

Jean Piaget developed a theory of cognitive development that is instructive. Piaget (for example, 1952) proposed that intelligence develops in stages and reflects the emergence of biological predispositions as well as cultural influences. Because we detail Piaget's theory in depth in Chapter 4, we shall give just a brief description of it here.

Piaget argues that from infancy through adulthood all humans *function* cognitively in the same fashion. In other words, the way in which intelligence works is age-invariant. However, Piaget argues that there are stages of cognitive development that reflect qualitative differences in the *structure* of an individual's intelligence from infancy through adulthood. Structures, which are reflected in the individual's behavior, determine intellectual competencies. Since structures change with age and with social interaction, competencies change, too. During adolescence the highest level of cognition, formal operational thinking, is reached.

Although, in reality, he views intelligence as progressing continuously from a less to a more complex nature, Piaget prefers to speak of stages of development in order to highlight what he feels are important changes through which intelligence develops. The various stages of intelligence are labeled sensory-motor (from birth to about 2 years of age), preoperational (from 2 to approximately 7 years of age), concrete operational (from 7 to approximately 11 years of age), and formal operational (abstract thinking), which represents the epitome of intellectual development. Although these age norms are only rough indicators of intellectual development, one may see that early adolescence is characterized by concrete operational thinking, whereas later adolescence is characterized by formal operational thinking. In other words, the adolescent years span a change in cognitive development which, as we shall see when we discuss the theorizing of Lawrence Kohlberg, relates to the way in which the individual perceives the external world.

Given the intellectual changes that occur during the adolescent stage of development, it is perhaps important to note that formal operational thinking is thinking in the abstract. Therefore, as adolescents become capable of formal operational thinking, their cognitive abilities as well as their views about the external world change. In addition, adolescents are capable of not only asking, but also of coming up with some answers to such abstract questions as "Who am I?". As we have already discussed, and as we shall detail throughout the text, this is an extremely important issue in adolescent development. Hence, it appears that Piaget's notions about cognitive development, which are based on a biological predisposition interacting with cultural demands, relate to certain aspects of adolescent behavior.

To give you some idea of how changes in intellectual development might relate to adolescent views toward the social environment, we shall discuss the research and theorizing of Lawrence Kohlberg. Again, we shall do this only briefly at this point since we shall deal with moral development in detail in a later chapter. Kohlberg (1969) has taken Piaget's theory of intellectual development and built around it a theory of moral development which assumes that moral thinking changes in conjunction with changes in cognitive competencies. Like Piaget, Kohlberg is a stage theorist; he believes that the stages of moral development are universal in that they should appear in the same sequence in all cultures. Since cognition progresses through a sequence of stages, moral thinking must, too. Hence, moral development, like cognitive development, has a maturational underpinning that is indirectly biogenetically based by its ties to cognition.

For Kohlberg, however, the age at which a particular stage of moral development will appear depends largely on cultural determinants. In other words, Kohlberg believes that intelligence, as defined by Piaget, acts as a backdrop upon which social behaviors are judged and evaluated. Through this process of judgment and evaluation, the individual is presumed to evolve views of the social order that progress through a series of stages relating to moral development.

During the adolescent years, the individual is assumed to develop to the level of moral thinking that is dominant within the society. For now, it is sufficient to note that understanding of the social order may change developmentally and may achieve adult levels during the adolescent years. In part this is achieved by role taking (Selman, 1976), which is promoted by peer interaction. Role taking helps the adolescent become capable of taking another's perspective.

During adolescence, then, cognitive competence reaches a peak, and this relates to moral thinking (Marcia's commitment to an ideology) and social perspective taking (developing views of the social order). By examining the relationships between cognitive development and other behaviors, then, we can gain some insight into adolescent peer relations, personality development, and idealism in viewing sociopolitical systems. Indeed, it may well be that the changes in cognitive competence during adolescence are the keystones to understanding much of adolescent behavior.

Social-Learning Theories

In the cognitive-developmental theoretical views we see an emphasis on the relation between individual development and the social context. As many researchers have noted, adolescence takes place within the confines of a society, a social structure. The nature of this social structure defines what is expected of adolescents and what is allowable behavior. Moreover, it is the social structure that defines the tasks of adolescence (Havighurst, 1951, 1972). In other words, the society in which the adolescent grows up has a very significant impact on the adolescent. This point was brought home most directly and forcefully first by cultural anthropologists who have studied adolescents and, more recently, by social learning theorists, who espouse the importance of setting conditions, reinforcers, and contexts in the study of development.

The writings of the cultural anthropologists largely challenge the writings of Hall, Freud, and others who theorized that there was a strong biological basis to adolescent development. The major contribution of cultural anthropology vis-à-vis adolescence was in demonstrating that the developmental patterns found in Western cultures were not necessarily found in all cultures. This focus is particularly true in the early writings of cultural anthropologists, which viewed social factors as the primary determinants of behavior. More recent writings show greater recognition of the importance of physical and genetic factors in development. Nevertheless, cultural anthropologists generally discuss the importance of physiological change *within different cultures*. It appears that for cultural anthropologists the role of physiological change is one that is culturally determined and is still not important in its own right. Therefore, even though cultural anthropologists do acknowledge physiological change, the role of this change is still assumed to be critically determined by the

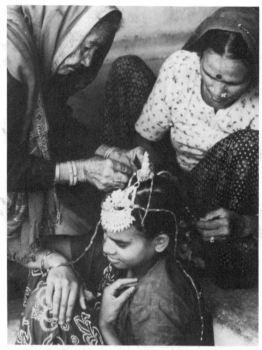

The duration and meaning of adolescence depends heavily on the culture in which it is occurring.

cultural context in which the change occurs. Culture, then, is the overriding factor in development.

Social-learning theorists, too, emphasize the role of the culture and the environment in explaining development. In addition, they also play down the importance of biological determinants of behavior. Social-learning theorists believe that people form their thoughts, feelings, and actions from observing and imitating what they perceive to be the thoughts, feelings, and actions of others.

The two most influential cultural anthropologists who have written about adolescent development are Margaret Mead and Ruth Benedict. Mead's *Coming of Age in Samoa* (1950) and *Growing Up in New Guinea* (1953) are two field studies of the effects of culture on adolescent development. The major point of Mead's writings is that in order to

understand the development and unfolding of human behavior, one must look seriously at the role of cultural institutions in the formation of behavior. This sort of research, conducted in cultures with religious, economic, and social institutions quite different from ours, led to the notions of *cultural determinism* and *cultural relativism*; that is, different cultures produce different kinds of personalities.

As an example of cultural relativism, consider Mead's (1950) description of adolescence in Samoa. She described the Samoan culture as characterized by a patience and gentleness that did not pressure individuals with regard to sexual or religious conflicts. She noted that adolescents and their parents did not experience serious disagreements. She underscored the sharp contrast in these patterns and those found in American culture. As a result, Mead argued that cultural norms dictated an easygoing, smooth transition through adolescence and into adulthood, even with regard to such concerns as sexual behavior; the experimentation with and expression of sexual behavior, Mead noted, met with no guilt, shame, or social sanction. Mead went on to argue that nurture, that is, cultural conditioning, was the key to explaining diversity in the adolescent experience. The nature of adolescence is dictated by cultural norms, mores, and values and will differ from one culture to another, or within a culture over time, because of differences in norms, mores, and values.

Although Mead's work stood for many years as a primary example of anthropological field study, Freeman (1983), who lived in Samoa for six years, provided a sharp contrast to Mead's description of Samoan culture. He found the Samoan culture to be much more Western in philosophy, fostering violence, competition, and guilt. And, he did so on the basis of official documents and meetings that were closed to Mead. As a result, Freeman devastated Mead's descriptions of Samoan life. Nonetheless, the preponderance of anthropological and other evidence continues to support the notion that sociocultural factors are at least as important to understanding adolescence as are biological changes. This is exemplified in the writing of another anthropologist, Ruth Benedict.

Ruth Benedict (1938) has spelled out several ways in which cultures affect the unfolding of human behavior. Benedict argues that the impact of culture on development is mediated by differences or similarities that exist between the roles of childhood and adulthood in different cultures. In some cultures, the roles played by children and adults are not very different. However, in others, such as ours, there are large role differences. Benedict's point is that cultures vary both in the degree of continuity in child-adult roles and in the nature of the transition from childhood to adulthood. If the transition from childhood to adulthood behaviors occurs in a socially and legally defined discontinuous manner, then the developmental patterns underlying transitions from childhood to adulthood will differ from those found in cultures in which the transitions from childhood to adulthood are relatively continuous. Benedict notes that in Western cultures there are a number of discontinuities in allowable child and adult behaviors. Hence, children must learn new behaviors and must unlearn childhood behaviors in order to become adults. In other cultures, the roles played by children and adults are not very different; hence, the child need not unlearn childhood behaviors and learn adulthood behaviors in the transition from childhood to adulthood.

According to Benedict, the transitions in developmental roles are particularly difficult during adolescence. When the differences in cultural expectations for adult and childhood behaviors are broad-ranging, the adolescent may experience conflict because of the redefinition and confusion of essential roles and behaviors. Benedict's major thesis is that discontinuity in childhood and adulthood roles produces emotional strain which,

in turn, produces conflict within the adolescent. On the other hand, cultural conditioning that is continuous will produce a smooth and gradual growth from childhood to adulthood with relatively little conflict.

There are a number of examples that will help make Benedict's point clear. In our culture, children—and to a large extent adolescents—are not expected to work, to contribute to the welfare of the community. In other cultures, however, children are expected to contribute to the development of the community with "worklike" behavior. The role of sexuality in childhood, adolescence, and adulthood is also very different in Westernized cultures than it is in many others. In the United States, for example, the traditional view is that one must wait until marriage to learn and engage in sexual behavior, whereas in other cultures, children as well as adolescents are allowed to engage in sexual behaviors and, indeed, may be encouraged to do so. Cultural conditioning, then, determines the form of transition during adolescence and the degree to which it will be difficult.

Benedict (1938) has identified three dimensions of continuity versus discontinuity that are important for understanding adolescent development:

1. Responsible versus nonresponsible role status;
2. Dominance versus submission;
3. Contrasted sexual roles.

An example of each as related to American adolescents will illustrate Benedict's assertion that cultural discontinuities such as we experience in our age-graded society increase the stress associated with the transition to adulthood.

The *responsible versus nonresponsible* dimension is illustrated by children and adolescents not being expected to work and contribute to the family's welfare, whereas such contributions are expected after graduation from high school, trade school, or college. At that point, the adolescent must assume a dramatically new and different role, as you will learn personally. In earlier times, when we lived in an agricultural society, the transition from nonresponsible to responsible roles was smoother, because children and adolescents were expected to contribute to family welfare according to their ability by doing various tasks on the farm. And, the importance of these tasks would increase with the child's or adolescent's competence. Hence, there was a continuity in the role of being responsible from childhood into adulthood. The chores performed by today's children and adolescents lack the direct contribution to family welfare. Hence, the transition to the role of being a responsible adult is more discontinuous today than previously, and is more discontinuous in our social system than in others. This discontinuity makes the transition to adulthood more difficult.

The independence strivings of adolescents are one illustration of the *dominance versus submission* dimension. In general, we do little to train our adolescents to be independent or to engage in appropriately dominant behavior, as in child rearing. Hence, adolescents in our society experience ambivalence, and at times difficulty, learning to be independent and assertive in appropriate ways. Some modes of parenting foster extreme dependence on parents and discourage the questioning of the dictates of either parents or other adults (see Chapter 10). As a result, the transition to being an appropriately dominant and assertive adult, as when supervising the work of others or rearing a child, is a more difficult transition than it need be.

Perhaps one of the most personal discontinuities for all of us is that involving *contrasting sexual roles*. In our culture, sexual experimentation is discouraged, and even illegal. The "official" stance is that one is not to engage in sexual behavior until one is married. Hence, one must "unlearn" adolescent values, attitudes, and roles—or experience a degree of guilt—and learn new

adulthood roles upon marriage, a clear discontinuity that may be very stressful.

The above examples illustrate Benedict's major point, namely, that discontinuities experienced during development can cause emotional strain and stress that make adolescence and the transition to adulthood roles and behaviors difficult. The greater the number of discontinuities the more difficult the transition to adulthood will be. We have not only social-role discontinuities but also legal ones defined by age—for drinking, voting, dropping out of school, getting married, and the like. These discontinuities not only add to the stress of the transition to adulthood but they also emphasize the role of societal/social factors in the evolution and nature of adolescence.

Modern-day attempts to explain cultural-environmental influences on adolescent development stem from social-learning theory. Social-learning theorists attempt to provide a theoretical description of social development based on concepts from stimulus-response (S-R) learning theory and theories of imitation and modeling. Cultural factors are assumed to shape social development by directly reinforcing desired behaviors and by providing models of socially appropriate behaviors. Through these two mechanisms people learn culturally acceptable behaviors.

The modeling aspects of social-learning theory set it apart from other theories that focus on cultural determinants of behavior. Although Mead and Benedict stress the reinforcing (S-R) consequences of social agents in shaping the behavior of the developing individual, social-learning theory goes beyond simple S-R learning principles and introduces modeling and imitation concepts. The cultural anthropologists and the social-learning theorists, then, share the same intent: to describe the environmental (cultural) factors that mold development.

Albert Bandura's theory will serve as our example because it is well detailed and representative of the various social-learning theories. Bandura outlined the basis for social-learning theory in several works (1969a, 1969b, 1973) and, in conjunction with Richard Walters (1959, 1963), discussed social-learning theory as it relates to problems of adolescent development.

According to Bandura, observation of a model may have any of several effects on the observer. One is to teach the observer an entirely new response, which Bandura calls a **modeling effect**. For example, a child may learn a new aggressive response by observing a model such as a boxer. A second function of observing a model is called an **inhibition disinhibition effect**. The observer perceives the consequences of a model's behavior. If the behavior is punished, it inhibits the observer from performing the same behavior. If the behavior is positively reinforced, it disinhibits. An example of an inhibiting effect is not being aggressive when a sibling has been punished for fighting. Finally, the observation of a model may have a **response-facilitation effect**. The response of the model acts as a cue to the observer to demonstrate a similar behavior already in his repertoire. For example, watching boxing may cause a child to become temporarily aggressive and very active. Of course, these processes apply to all types of learning, including problem solving and thinking behaviors, not just to the physical behaviors illustrated in our examples.

In conjunction with S-R learning, Bandura assumes that the effects of observing a model can account for the learning of nearly all social behavior. According to Bandura (1969a), the observed modeled stimulus is coded into a representational mediator that is retrieved and reproduced when the environmental cues are appropriate for that particular response. In other words, observational learning and imitation involve a number of internal and external psychological processes, such as attending processes, memory and retention processes, and physical reproduction abilities and motivation. A modeled behavior will not be acquired or learned if it is not attended to and discriminated from other kinds of responses. Bandura also notes a number of subprocesses that relate to the effects of modeling on the observer. These are outlined in Table 2–2.

It should be clear from our description that social-learning theory is quite different from the theories discussed previously. Social-learning theory is basically nondevelopmental; that is, the same psychological processes are assumed to operate in infants, children, adolescents, and adults. Hence, social-learning theories tend to be quite distinct from stage theories, in which differing psychological processes are assumed to operate at different developmental levels. Within social-learning theory, behavior is assumed to be determined primarily by social and situational contexts rather than maturational principles, making the concept of stages of development meaningless. In addition, there is very little by way of biological presumptions regarding behavioral expressions.

Because social-learning theory is nondevelopmental, one may ask what its contribution could possibly be to understanding adolescent development. This issue is discussed in an article by Bandura (1964) and in a monograph by Bandura and Walters (1959). Rather than assuming the unfolding of behavior in some predetermined developmental (maturational) pattern, social-learning theorists propose that adolescent development is due to cultural conditioning (much as the cultural anthropologists argue) and social expectations for certain kinds of behaviors. In discussing these notions, the social-learning theorists inevitably come back to an examination of the child's early learning experiences and the parents' child-rearing practices. In effect, social-learning theorists assume that adolescent behavior is simply the result of particular kinds of child-rearing practices. The notion here is that very few adolescents will exhibit deviant kinds of behaviors; most will exhibit behaviors that are in relative harmony with the kinds of behaviors they were taught in child-

TABLE 2–2 **The Mechanisms of Observational Learning**

Basic Concepts of the Theory	Modeled Stimuli	Internal Representation	Retrieval and Reproduction of Responses

Subprocesses influencing content and degree of observational learning. (The subprocesses are listed under the component they most directly influence.)	1. Attention processes
	  a. observer characteristics (sex, age)
	  b. prior discriminative observation training and experience (previous training and reinforcement for observational learning)
		2. Retention processes
		  a. overt practice
		  b. cover practice (mental rehearsal)
			3. Motor reproduction processes
			  a. response component availability (Does observer have the parts of the response in his behavioral repertoire?)
			  b. physical limits of observer (Can he physically do the behavior?)
			4. Incentive motivation processes
			  a. reinforcement to model
			  b. reinforcement to observer

hood. This thinking simply reflects the notion of social-learning theorists that there is continuity in human growth patterns and learning processes and that at no particular age level should there be broad changes in behavior that might be due to what we would call maturational development. Deviant development that emerges during the adolescent stage of life, then, is seen as a failure of socialization processes that were begun earlier in childhood. Children who are taught to behave adversely in stressful situations, who are taught to exhibit deviant behavior, or who did not learn to deal adequately with reality will, according to the social-learning theory view, exhibit similar kinds of behaviors in adolescence.

Our brief presentation of the social-learning view of adolescent development is intended to point out the role that the culture can play in adolescent development. The writings of the cultural anthropologists stress the importance of studying cultural factors such as religion and morality, the community, and the schools for a relatively complete perspective on adolescent development. Therefore, we have included chapters on these topics in the text. The social-learning theorists, too, have described the impact of environment on development, but at a more fine-grained level. They would have us explore cultural factors in depth in order to comprehend adolescent development. We shall have a number of occasions to draw on social-learning theory principles in the remainder of the text.

Historical Theories

Recently, researchers (Elder, 1980; Dragastin & Elder, 1975; Hill & Monks, 1977; Kett, 1977) have begun to examine adolescence within the context of social history. Although this perspective is more a description than a theory, it provides valuable insight into the evolution of adolescence. In a sense, this perspective is similar to the cultural anthropologists' view of adolescence. The cultural anthropologists point out that adolescence differs from culture to culture, because of different expectations, levels of technology, and other factors. The historical perspective examines adolescence within the context of historical changes in a single culture.

At the most basic level, the general notion is to examine how changes in the culture impact on the nature of adolescence. By looking at how changes in length of formal education, occurrences such as the Depression, transfer of socialization from parents to societal institutions, and the like, relate to generational differences in the nature of adolescence, we can study transitions in the nature of adolescence. What this perspective has shown, in part, is that adolescent behavior is more dependent on position in the social structure than upon age. In a very real sense, this type of theorizing and research

As global cultural changes (e.g., technological advances) occur, the experience of adolescence changes.

is truly ecological. That is, it relates development to "real life" events and studies development in naturally occurring environmental circumstances.

An example will help make the virtue of this approach more clear. Elder (1980) has considered the change in socialization influence of the family post–World War II. Prior to the war, the family was the major influence on socialization. Following the war, the school and the peer group, because of the greater increase in school size and length of time in school, became more salient. The major impetus was the increase in average school size, which doubled between the 1930s and 1960s. This increase in size resulted in an increase in influence of peers, partly because large schools offered less opportunity and fewer social rewards, such as recognition of leadership by peers, to the individual student (Barker, 1964); most students could not be members of sports teams, honor societies, and the like. In addition, the division of schools into elementary (K–6), junior high (7–9), and high school (10–12) helped establish lower boundaries for adolescence through age segregation. These, and other changes in the schooling of children, resulted in a shifting of socialization away from parents and toward peers and the school atmosphere.

As another example of this approach, Elder (1974) describes the effects of growing up during the Great Depression. The individuals Elder studied were in their late childhood and early adolescence during the Great Depression, and he was interested in determining the impact of that experience on later life. He found that the effects of the Depression were moderated by the social status of the family in which the youngster grew up. As adults, middle-class boys from families that suffered serious financial setbacks were psychologically more healthy, had stronger drive, and were employed in more prestigious jobs than their counterparts whose families did not suffer such serious hardships. In contrast, among boys from lower socioeconomic status, economic hardship was a detriment; boys whose families suffered greatly obtained less education and held lower-status jobs as adults. Girls from middle-class families that suffered economic hardship were more likely to assume household roles, to get less education, and to be more likely to prefer the homemaker role than was the case for their counterparts.

This type of analysis has the advantage of allowing us to place aspects of adolescent development into a historical perspective. This historical approach is well illustrated in Kett's (1977) work tracing the social evolution of adolescence (Box 2–2). Research of this type points to the critical importance of the milieu within which adolescence occurs. In order to understand adolescence, then, we must also look at the role of cultural institutions, such as the school, and events that may influence its expression.

BOX 2–2   The Social Evolution of Adolescence

In his work, *Rites of Passage*, Kett (1977) traced the relationship between social, religious, political, and economic events and changes since the late 1700s in conceptualizations of children and their place in society. Although we cannot summarize his entire treatise here, a few examples will not only point out the richness to be found in his work, but will illustrate the importance of considering cultural/historical events in the discussion of adolescence.

One interesting perspective is the social role played by children in the late 1700s and early 1800s. Until about age 7, both boys and girls were in the care of women and were viewed in some ways as a hindrance. This care also involved education, such as it was, for women taught the schools. Once the farming season began, however, the male children no longer attended school because they were needed for working the farm. In other words, male children were expected at an early age to contribute to the family's welfare by working. In effect, male children were expected to earn their way. Thereafter, school was attended only in winter months. Relatively permanent entrance into the work force was often achieved by age 11 or 12. Contrast this pattern with your own experience. In all likelihood, you have been attending school since age 5 or 6, working for the most part in the summer only. And, for most of you, this work was for your own spending money. Few of you were expected to work for your keep, as were children in the 1800s.

Leaving home was also a different experience than yours. Although some children left home for formal schooling, this was a rare occurrence. Much more frequent was the "farming out" of a child as early as age 12 or 13. In these instances, the father might farm out a son. The father would receive a small amount of money. The son would be bound to work, for example, at farming, in a factory, in a store, or at a trade, for room and board. After completing an agreed-upon length of time, often until he was 21, the son was free to return to the family and might receive some money from his master. In general, the concept here was a twofold one. First, the son's family had one fewer child to feed and clothe. Assuming there were sufficient children for the family's needs, the family benefited from this arrangement. Second, in some instances, the child could learn a trade or become an apprentice, both of which were of benefit to the child.

This treatment of children is no doubt foreign to you, but this is because it reflects a view of children very different from the current dominant perspective. A hint of this can be gained from looking at definitions of age groups during these times. "Infancy," unlike today, was applied to those aged 6 or 7 or less, "childhood" applied to those up to age 16 or so, and "youth" to those up to ages in the mid-20s. These terms carried with them much more than simple age meaning, including work responsibilities, training for vocations, and expectations for schooling. These connotations of the terms are, in part, illustrated above. So, when did the era of adolescence akin to the way we know it begin?

Kett cites information indicating that adolescence began to occur in Europe and America between 1900 and 1920. The lower boundary, or entrance into the stage of adolescence, was indexed by biological change. Biological processes became indicators for social transitions. The upper boundary, entrance into adulthood roles, increasingly stretched as adolescents remained in school longer and as other social factors delayed entrance into adulthood roles.

In part, the evolution of adolescence was a result of industrialization and urbanization. These events kept youth out of the job market, contributed to the formalization of increasing lengths of time in schooling, and segregated youth from adult roles. In part, adolescence emerged as a result of changes in the nature of the family. The modal family unit was extended, not nuclear. Moreover, trends toward having fewer children spaced more closely meant all children in a family might be teens at the same time. This trend contributed to generational distance, specifically between parent and offspring. Finally, social institutions of a secular nature, such as the Boy Scouts or YMCA, the emergence of child labor laws, and the availability of mass education contributed to the identification of a separate group within the society. Adolescence, then, was the (unintentional) product of a host of social, economic, political, and legal changes in the society.

The importance of Kett's work to us is that it shows how changes in the society, at many levels—religious, social, economic, academic, vocational—coalesced to change perceptions of, and opportunities for, youngsters. The lesson of this message, of course, lies in our understanding that adolescence, perhaps more than any other stage in development, is subject to change. Adolescence is a social evolutionary phenomenon. Part of the difficulties you may have had with your parents stem from the different nature of adolescence for your parents and for you. In turn, as social changes occur over the years, your children, who will be adolescents sometime around the year 2010, will have an adolescent experience different from yours.

AN ECLECTIC APPROACH

As you no doubt can discern, the various theoretical focuses discussed above span a number of different perspectives of adolescence. It likely is also obvious that none is all-inclusive. That is, no theory tells us all we want to know, or explains all that needs explaining. This is not unusual; the same comments may be made about the other developmental epochs. How, then, can we conceptualize adolescence from the theoretical perspectives we have discussed? The answer lies in taking an integrative and eclectic perspective, a view that takes the most useful aspects of the other views. Here, we shall attempt to integrate the various theoretical perspectives and derive an eclectic view using the best of each of the types of theories discussed.

Let us start with the contribution of the cognitive-developmental theorists. As we noted above, the cognitive-developmental theorists have tried to describe, first, the course of cognitive development and, second, the relation between cognitive development and other aspects of development. Hence, we learn that adolescence is a time during which cognitive functioning reaches a peak in the sense of becoming mature, namely, competent in abstract thinking ability. We also see that the change from concrete to formal operational thinking results in the adolescent viewing the social world in new and different ways that were not previously possible. Hence, the adolescent, in contrast to the child, develops sophisticated and abstract views of morality, in part because of increased role-taking ability. As we shall see in later chapters, the change in cognitive competence from childhood to adolescence also relates to aspects of personality development, peer relations, self-concept and political thinking.

Because formal operational thinking is content-free, that is, it is a *way* of thinking about any given concern, it represents a way of perceiving all the aspects of the world around us. It is a backdrop upon which we perceive and evaluate all that happens to and around us. In our eclectic approach, then, cognitive competence plays an important and unique role, both descriptively and explanatorily. Adolescents behave the way they do, in part, because of the ability to use formal operational thinking.

The other perspectives of adolescent development now take form. The importance of biological changes is less in the changes *per se* than in the meaning of the changes to the individual and to others. This meaning will depend on cultural standards which, in turn, reflect changing cultural norms.

The importance of the social-learning and historical perspectives is also clarified. What we learn from these views is important because they describe the current expectations for behavior and allow interpretations of behavior within current social standards. Hence, we become better able to understand and explain cultural and subcultural differences in the nature of adolescence. These variations reflect the different interpretations of cultural standards held by adolescents growing up in different environmental settings. Why do adolescents in the North and South, or in large cities and rural areas, differ in their behavior? In part, at least, because the adolescents in these different settings are living under different subcultural rules. They must interpret the rules around them and behave in that manner. The historical approach tells us whence come the current standards and why. The social-learning theorists tell us how the current standards are taught and enforced. The key, however, remains the cognitive backdrop upon which social standards are recognized, interpreted, and understood.

The psychodynamic approaches also fit comfortably within our eclectic framework. The emphases of these approaches are, in general, on personal aspects of development. The interpretations the adolescent makes of his or her fit to parents, peers, and other social interaction situations determine to a significant degree aspects of self-concept and personality predispositions.

In our eclectic approach, then, we have a cognizing adolescent interpreting social rules, and changes and differences in them, within the context of a cultural, subcultural, and developmental history. Variations in adolescence across generations and between strata within a generation come from the differences in historical precedence and current standards as perceived by the adolescent.

The emphases of the various theoretical orientations have, to a significant degree, focused research endeavors concerning adolescent development. The chapters that follow reflect major concerns addressed by theorists discussed above.

SUMMARY

Theories are statements about the factors that cause some form of behavior to occur. As such, they are critical to our understanding of the causes of various aspects of development. In order to determine the accuracy of a theory, that theory must produce hypotheses that can be tested by experiments. If a theory is supported by the findings of the research, we can use it to integrate information about behavior and to predict when, and under what conditions, new behaviors should occur. These are the major functions of any theory. In adolescence, this translates into explaining the importance and impact of the biological changes and social behaviors that occur.

There are five major theoretical orientations that contribute to our understanding of adolescence. From the biological approach we gain an understanding of the importance of physical change as related to adolescent behavior. The biological theorists emphasize the changes in drive level that occur as a result of puberty.

The psychodynamic theorists also emphasize drive changes. Anna Freud focuses on maldevelopment resulting from defenses against drive increases. However, more current theorists stress aspects of personality organization and self-concept development. In all instances, the focus is on individual adjustment during a time of significant change.

The cognitive-developmental theorists study the nature of thinking processes as they evolve during the adolescent years. Some, such as Kohlberg, emphasize the relation between changes in thinking and conceptualizations of the social environment. From this perspective it is clear that adolescent perceptions of the society change as cognition changes.

The social-learning theorists stress the importance of cultural factors in the shaping of adolescence. They note that cultural standards determine both the nature and importance of the changes that signal the introduction of adolescence. Hence, they help us understand how and why adolescence differs from culture to culture. The historical approach, though not really a theory, plays the important role of explaining the evolution of adolescence both across and within cultures over time. By examining the historical basis of adolescence we can better understand how and why it occurs as it does.

An eclectic perspective takes cognitive change as the foundation for the impact of the other changes on the adolescent. As cognitive changes allow new interpretations of the social world, the individual will develop new understandings of his or her role in the society. This new perspective will depend on the nature of the society, the person's developmental history, and the history of the society.

GLOSSARY

Disinhibition effect. In social learning, the reinforcement experienced by a model that may serve to cause an observer to exhibit some behavior that he or she otherwise would not perform.

Foreclosure. In Marcia's theory, the identity type in which a commitment has been made but without a period of questioning.

Hypothesis. A "best guess" as to the causes of some event tested through research.

Identity achiever. In Marcia's theory, an individual who has had a period of questioning and then made a commitment to the factors defining an identity.

Identity diffusions. In Marcia's theory, those who have not faced a period of questioning or made a commitment.

Inhibition effect. In social-learning theory, the reinforcement consequences to a model that may cause an observer not to exhibit a behavior that he or she might otherwise perform.

Modeling effect. In social-learning theory, learning a new and novel behavior or behavioral sequence through observation of a model.

Moratorium. In Marcia's theory, a state of being in a period of questioning or crisis with regard to issues defining identity.

Psychobiological. The impact of biological factors on psychological behaviors.

Psychosocial. In Erikson's theory, a crisis involving the individual's development with respect to social roles.

Response-facilitation effect. In social-learning theory, observation of a model acts as a cue to the observer to emit a similar behavior already in the observer's repertoire.

Theory. A statement or group of statements that attempt to explain some event and predict new events.

SUGGESTED READINGS

DRAGASTIN, S., & ELDER, G. (1975). *Adolescence in the life cycle*. New York: John Wiley & Sons.

A number of prominent authorities in the field contributed to chapters in this book about the many facets of adolescence. Chapters cover biological change, the effects of social institutions and expectations, and family and peer relations.

ELDER, G. (1974). *Children of the great depression*. Chicago: University of Chicago Press.

Elder presents an interesting study of the effects of environmental events, specifically the depression experience, on the development of adult personality. Emphasis on the experiencing of social events is related to aspects of development.

HAVIGHURST, R. J. (1972). *Developmental tasks and education* (3rd ed.). New York: David McKay.

Havighurst discusses developmental tasks across the life span and relates them to the role and nature of education.

HILL, J., & MONKS, F. (1977). *Adolescence and youth in prospect*. Surrey, England: IPC Science and Technology Press.

This book has a very interesting and readable collection of papers about many aspects of adolescence. A major emphasis is not only on existing knowledge but on directions for research to further our understanding of the many facets of adolescence.

KETT, J. (1977). *Rites of passage*. New York: Basic Books.

Kett presents an excellent, thorough historical perspective of the emergence of adolescence as we know it. The nature and impact of cultural evolution is merged with the evolution of the concept of adolescence.

MUUSS, R. E. (1988). *Theories of adolescence* (5th ed.). New York: Random House.

In Chapter 2, Muuss presents an excellent historical analysis of the roots of theorizing about the nature of adolescence.

VAN HASSELT, V. B., & HERSEN, M. (1987). *Handbook of adolescent psychology*. New York: Pergamon Press.

Chapters 2 through 6 present comprehensive summaries of the major theoretical approaches to adolescent development.

Biological Change
and
Adolescent
Development

3

difference between inner and outer clocks. A final and extreme example of the need for perceiving an ordered day and night cycle is seen in the traditional brainwashing technique of leaving a light constantly burning in a room containing no source of exterior stimulation. This procedure causes psychological stress that stems directly from disorders in the body's sense of time; that is, the body reacts to the constant "daylight" with hormonal and neural imbalances that cause behavioral symptoms as the individual struggles to maintain some semblance of time.

The Biological Clock in Humans

In humans, the master plan, that is, the biological clock, begins at conception. Physical development unfolds in a predetermined sequence beginning with a fertilized egg and ending approximately nine months later with a new human whose life systems can function independently of its mother's. We ___ t hasten to add, however, that even ___ levelopment is subject to environ- ___ ences—the fertilized egg devel- ___ according to a genetic plan but ___ t to environmental influences, ___ hegative ones called **teratogens** ___ , 1973). In other words, the fer- ___ egg cell inherits not only a genetic ___ lelopment but also an environ-

The H ___ Individual ___ Sex Differences in Ka ___ Major Physical Change ___ ert an effect only if Secular Trends in Phys ___ posed to them at a Psychological Effects of ___ ppment or if they Psychological Effects of B ___ d delivery (for by the mother).

___ gen, ___ n measles) for ___ mple, is pre ___ nt a ___ he first three months after conception ___ can produce malformed body structures beca ___ e a ___ body structures are not completely for ___ d. Once some organ or limb is formed, it is le ss likely that a teratogen can result in malformatic n, alth ___ ugh it may result in malfunction of ___ n o ___ g ___ Maternal drug use, alcoh ___ consum ___

tion, smoking, diet, emotional state, and exposure to radiation are examples of common teratogens (Stechler, 1973).

Although the above listing may indicate that teratogens are basically external, that is not the case. In the absence of the hormone **testosterone** a male fetus may be genetically male (for example, XY sex chromosome) but may lack aspects (for example, internal genitals, penis) of male sexual organs (Money & Ehrhardt, 1972). Teratogenic effects, then, may result from external or internal environmental factors.

As the above demonstrates, then, the normal course of development is dictated by biological factors. However, we cannot neglect the importance of environmental influences on development. We wish to emphasize this point here so you do not lose sight of the importance of environmental influences on adolescent development. Clearly, we cannot speak only of biological or environmental influences. We always must consider the interactive effects of both on development.

Onset of Puberty

The reasons for the onset ___ iological events leading to pubert ___ growth spurt remain, to a frustr ___ ificant degree, unknown (cf. Gru ___ ave, & Mayer, 1974; Katchadouria ___ At the start of puberty, a combined ___ d hormonal signal, sent to the hyp ___ alamus (Katchadourian, 1977), causes th ___ body to become more sensitive to certain h ___ ones. This increased sensitivity results in i ___ ased physical growth and sexual deve ___ ent, perhaps because levels of hormo ___ rigi- nally not sufficient to evoke ph ___ gical changes now do so. As a resul ___ body begins its spurt of growth tow ard ___ phys- ical maturity.

One factor that may be related to the ___ set of pubertal events is a critical we ___ (Frish, 1974, 19 ___ 3). Frish reports th ___ girls, puberta ___ onset ocurs at abo ___ pounds (30 kg), peak veloc ___ of ___ at about 87 pounds (39 kg), and menarche at about 105 pounds (47 kg), regardless of age. In other words, pubertal events are related more closely to body weight than to age. The reason for this relationship, Frish (1974, 1983), argues, lies in changes in metabolic rate, which decrease the sensitivity of the hypothalamus to estrogen. The decreased sensitivity results in an increase in "normal" estrogen levels sufficiently high to result, for example, in menarche. As we shall see below, increased estrogen levels also promote growth. Similar procedures may operate in males.

Although Frish's exposition seems straightforward and has the appeal of simplicity, we must point out that the "triggering" of puberty no doubt is much more complex (Grumbach et al., 1974a; Katchadourian, 1977). As we shall see, many hormones are involved. For the present time, then, we can only echo the professionals in the field and state that we cannot yet decipher the exact mechanisms causing the onset of the growth spurt and puberty.

The Termination of Puberty

Our lack of knowledge about the onset of puberty is far surpassed by our inability to explain its termination. As we shall see below, epiphyseal closure, the development of real bone tissue in place of cartilage, is one result of the growth spurt that is manifested in cessation of growth. Although it may appear obvious, therefore, that growth should stop, it is unclear why hormone levels stabilize and other aspects of the growth spurt cease. Richards and Petersen (1987) note that there is virtually no literature detailing why or how the growth events of puberty terminate.

GLANDS AND HORMONES

The physical changes that we see, and the growth to mature reproductive capability, are the result of the influence of hormones. Hormones are chemical substances that influence cells. They are secreted by endocrine (ductless) glands directly into the blood stream. Hormones are produced in one part of the body and are carried by the blood stream to another part of the body where they exert their effect on target tissues. For example, gonadotrophic hormones are produced in the pituitary gland and travel through the bloodstream to act on the gonads, that is, the ovaries and testes.

It is through the actions of hormones that we enter the growth spurt and change into physically mature adults. The influence of hormones also causes our reproductive systems to mature, allowing us to become capable of reproducing the species. It should be apparent that both these processes begin at conception (Grumbach, Roth, Kaplan, & Kelch, 1974b). The growth changes at the start of adolescence are simply a continuation of the earlier growth of the individual. Indeed, sexual maturation may be conceptualized in much the same manner. No new sexual systems are created during adolescence—puberty takes place within existing biological systems that have been present since prenatal development. Puberty, then, is simply a maturing of existing biological structures.

Endocrine Glands

There are several endocrine systems, for example, the hypothalamus-pituitary, gonadal, adrenal (Grumbach et al., 1974a, 1974b; Katchadourian, 1977). The **endocrine glands** that play the major role in adolescence are depicted in Figure 3–1.

It may be helpful to discuss briefly how the endocrine glands secrete hormones. The rate of secretion of hormones is controlled by a complicated negative feedback system, a system that *turns off* production of a hormone when a specific level is reached (Grumbach et al., 1974a, 1974b; Katchadourian, 1977). The major controlling system is the

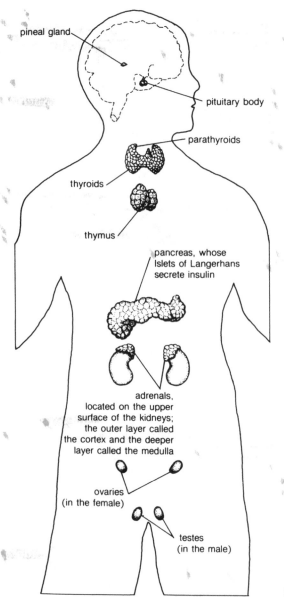

FIGURE 3–1   **The Endocrine System**

hypothalamic pituitary system. When a hormonal deficiency is detected, the **hypothalamus** secretes releasing factors keyed to initiate secretion of particular hormones. These releasing factors travel the blood stream to the anterior pituitary gland where they, in turn, stimulate the production of pituitary trophic hormones, each of which has a target organ it is programmed to activate. Activation of the target organ results in the production of the hormone detected to be at a low level. When the level of the hormone becomes optimal, the pituitary, through the hypothalamus, maintains that level. As we noted above, some (cf. Grumbach et al., 1974a, 1974b; Katchadourian, 1977) researchers have speculated that a change in the sensitivity of the hypothalamus results in its allowing higher levels of hormones, which is responsible for the onset of puberty.

The Functions of Hormones

Hormones fulfill three major functions in the body (Gold, 1968; Grumbach et al., 1974a). *One function is known as morphogenesis, that is, the determination of organ shape and structure (morphology).* The action of hormones on specific components of the body causes changes in overall body shape and structure. Specific examples of this aspect of hormonal function are the development of the gonads and the primary and secondary sex characteristics and bone and skeletal growth.

The second major influence of hormones on the body is that of the integration of autonomic functions and instinctual behavior patterns of a species. For example, the action of certain glands, such as the gonads and breasts, produces relatively set patterns of behavior within a species, for example, mating and nursing behavior. Although the concept of instinctual behavior in humans was formerly well accepted (e.g., McDougall, 1908), it is now questioned. Perhaps the best way to consider relatively stable specific traits in humans, such as mating and child-rearing behavior, is as biological predispositions for certain responses that are tempered by environmental influences. For example, while caring for the young is a universal pattern of behavior in humans, the manner in which this activity is carried out varies. A Melanesian mother may carry her baby with her in a body sling at all times, whereas a Western mother (or father, with our changing roles)

will leave an infant to its own devices for hours at a time. Both are exhibiting child-caring behavior. The differences are environmentally or socioculturally determined.

The final major hormonal function is that of regulation. Hormones are in part responsible for maintaining the integrity of the internal environment of the organism. For example, maintaining appropriate extracellular water levels and salt balance are regulatory functions of hormones.

As you can see, then, hormones are critical to both body formation and function. They trigger aspects of development and maintain body integrity. When they are out of balance, abnormal development, or maldevelopment, can occur (cf. Grumbach et al., 1974a, 1974b; Katchadourian, 1977; Kriepe & Strauss, 1989; Rees & Trahms, 1989; Riddle & Cho, 1989). For example, two- to three-year-old children may enter puberty due to abnormal functioning of the hormonal system (Cutler et al., 1983).

The study of hormones is, therefore, critical to our understanding of development, particularly during adolescence when hormones exert very real and observable effects on the individual.

Some Major Hormones

There are some two dozen hormones that exert various influences on us (Katchadourian, 1977). It is far beyond our scope to discuss the specific role each plays during puberty. Therefore, we shall briefly detail only the functions of several of the major hormones involved in the final growth to adult physique. Those interested in a more complete treatment will find Katchadourian's work very readable and informative.

Human Growth Hormone (HGH). **HGH** is produced by the anterior (front) portion of the pituitary gland. It is a trophic hormone, that is, it is a hormone that stimulates a target organ to respond in some way. HGH fosters the development of protoplasm and skeletal growth, plays a vital role in glucose and fat metabolism, and, in general, fosters growth. Its specific role in pubertal growth remains something of a mystery (Grumbach et al., 1974a), however. That it is critical may be seen from studies of its underproduction, which results in dwarfism, and its overproduction, which results in giantism (Connell et al., 1971; Grumbach et al., 1974a).

The major hormones affecting the development during the growth spurt are the **steroids**, the hormones produced by the gonads. The three major hormones of this type pertinent to our discussion are **testosterone**, **estrogen**, and **progesterone**. These three hormones are present in all of us, that is, we all have both male and female hormones. This occurs because these three hormones are also produced by the adrenal cortex, the outer part of the adrenal gland (Katchadourian, 1977). Where the two sexes differ is in the concentration of each hormone. These hormones are known as "sex hormones" because they are produced primarily by the gonads and because they strongly affect primary and secondary sex characteristic development. The male hormones are called androgens. There is no comparable term to describe the collection of female hormones.

Testosterone. Testosterone, and other **androgens**, are produced in the male by the interstitial, or Leydig, cells in the testes. In females, testosterone is produced mainly by the adrenal cortex, although the ovaries produce some androgens that can be changed into testosterone (Katchadourian, 1977). The low concentration of testosterone in children increases dramatically during puberty in boys, the blood level amount increasing between 10- and 20-fold. The major effect of testosterone is to promote growth of the reproductive system and the muscles. Hence, it is both a sex hormone and a growth hormone, and has the major responsibility for the pubertal changes in males. It is responsible for the change in voice, the development of secondary sex characteristics, and contributes to making the skin susceptible to acne. It also increases growth in height and hastens epiphyseal closure. There is then, a paradox. Small amounts of testosterone, such as are present in children, promote growth; large amounts, as during the growth spurt, hasten the cessation of growth. In girls, the androgens contribute to the growth of body hair and to the general aspects of the growth spurt.

Psychological effects of testosterone and the other androgens include an increase in the sex drive in males. Androgens may play a similar role in women, although this is less clear (Katchadourian, 1977). There is also some evidence (Katchadourian, 1977) of a correlation between androgen level and aggression in lower animals and in humans.

Estrogen. Estrogen is produced by the ovarian follicles (Graafian follicles). Its level increases in both males and females during the growth spurt, but the increase is much greater in females. In many ways it functions in females much as testosterone does in males. Hence, it contributes to muscle growth and the growth in height, development of the secondary sex characteristics, epiphyseal closure, and body fat distribution. Although it performs this function in females, its function in males remains unclear (Katchadourian, 1977).

Estrogen also has the effect of increasing the sex drive in females (Jones, Shainberg, & Byer, 1975). It is unclear if estrogen has any other direct psychological effects.

Progesterone. Although progesterone is secreted by the ovarian follicles, it is mainly produced by the remains of the follicle, called the **corpus luteum**, after the egg cell is released. This accounts for the increase in progesterone level after ovulation, and is the direct cause of the increase in body temperature following ovulation. If the egg cell is fertilized, the corpus luteum is retained and the progesterone level remains high. Progesterone serves several functions in the body, including producing changes in the uterus to facilitate implantation of the fertilized egg, stimulating breast development, aiding in the initiation of the menstrual cycle, and maintaining pregnancy once it occurs.

During puberty, the production of estrogen and progesterone takes on a cyclic pattern, resulting in the menstrual cycle. The cycles are generally quite irregular during puberty, and can be quite variable (in length) even in adulthood.

Again, we must note that other hormones play important roles during the growth spurt. However, these are the major hormones responsible for physical and sexual development. As you can see, the growth and functioning of the human body are complex, with many changes occurring at the same time. Although the changes do not occur over night, they do occur rapidly, and they are noticeable. Following a discussion of growth during the pubertal years, we shall examine some of the psychological consequences of this rapidity of growth.

PHYSICAL GROWTH DURING ADOLESCENCE

During about the first 10 years of life, boys and girls grow at about the same rate (Katchadourian, 1977). At birth, boys are about 29 percent and girls 31 percent, of final mature height. At age 10, boys are about 78 percent and girls 84 percent of final adult height. Girls reach final adult height about age 17, and boys at about age 19. Keep in mind that these are averages—some will grow faster and some slower.

These sex differences in growth rates are evident throughout the childhood and adolescent years. Starting at birth, a general maturity factor appears to favor girls in motor, cognitive, and sexual development. This difference apparently begins as early as fetal life and is probably due to the mother's immunological system acting against the Y chromosome, or the relative smallness of the

Y compared to the X chromosome. At birth, boys are approximately 4 weeks behind girls in development. From then until adulthood they remain behind: in maturational age, a boy is 20 percent behind a girl of the same chronological age (Tanner, 1970; see also Faust, 1977). As is obvious, then, girls enter the final phases of physical growth, that is, the growth spurt, ahead of boys by about 2½ years.

The Growth Spurt

The growth spurt, which is illustrated for height in Figure 3–2, may be characterized as an acceleration and then deceleration of skeletal (and other) growth. Girls may enter the growth spurt as early as 9½ or as late as 15. The average girl enters the growth spurt at about 10½, reaches the peak year of growth at about age 12, and completes the growth spurt by age 14. The average girl reaches **menarche** (first menstrual cycle) at about 12.8 years (Faust, 1977). Boys may enter the growth spurt as early as 10½ or as late as 16. The average boy starts the growth spurt at about 12½ years, reaches a peak at

During the early and middle adolescent years, girls are more physically mature than boys because they enter the growth spurt at an earlier age.

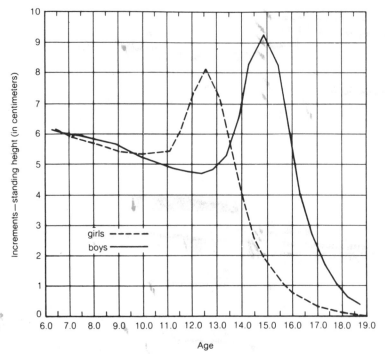

FIGURE 3–2   **Average Annual Increments in Height of Boys and Girls**
(Source: Adapted from Shuttleworth, F.K. [1939]. The physical and mental growth of girls and boys age six to nineteen in relation to age at maximum growth. *Monographs of the Society for Research in Child Development*, 4 [serial no. 22], 16.)

about age 14, and completes the growth spurt by age 16 (Tanner, 1970).

Although girls enter and complete the growth spurt earlier than boys, there are some aspects of physical growth that favor boys. Boys gain more height (average 21.1 cm or 8.3 in) during the growth-spurt years than do girls (average 19.6 cm or 7.7 in). And, boys grow more during the peak year (average 10.4 cm or 4.1 in) than do girls (average 9 cm or 3.5 in).

Despite these sex differences, there are a number of similarities in growth patterns for the two sexes (Faust, 1977). For each sex, the average duration of the growth spurt is about 2.8 years. The shortest duration for the growth spurt is about 1.9 years for boys and 1.5 years for girls; the longest duration

is about 4 years for both sexes. Finally, as may be seen in Table 3–1, sequencing of growth trends, specifically for pubertal growth, is the same for the two sexes (Botella-Llusia, 1973; Faust, 1977; Tanner, 1970). In other words, there are both sex-specific and species-specific patterns of growth.

You may well wonder about the origin of these sex differences. Katchadourian (1977) interpreted them in a historical/evolutional manner. In effect, her argument is that males have been selected for certain traits (for example, physical strength and prowess) and females for others. Later entrance by males into the growth spurt contributes, in part, to their greater size and strength. Entering the growth spurt relatively early

TABLE 3–1 **Chronology of Pubertal Growth Changes**

Age	Female	Age	Male
10–12	Critical phase in internal organ structural growth; equivocal morphology	12–13	Critical phase in internal organ structural growth; equivocal morphology
11–12	Initial development of breast and pelvis	13–14	Initial pubic hair growth, juvenile type
12–13	Initial pubic hair growth; juvenile type	14–15	Intensification of thoracic and muscular development
13–14	Initial axillary hair growth	14–15	Initial axillary growth
13–14	Menarche	14–16	Increase in size of genital organs
15–18	Completion of definitive female shape and psyche	16–18	Beginning of frank facial hair growth
		19–22	Completion of male shape and psyche

(Source: Botella-Llusia, J. [1973]. *Endocrinology of women.* Philadelphia: W. B. Saunders, p. 342.) Reprinted by permission of W.B. Saunders and the author.

may optimize the length of females' child bearing years. In the hunting culture of our early years as a species, both trends may have been adaptive and may have contributed to survival of the species. No doubt, these biological differences contributed to sex role differentiation (Hoffman, 1977). Of course, in today's society, differences in physical strength are no reason for sex discrimination in roles, jobs, or prestige (see Hoffman, 1977, and Katchadourian, 1977 for a discussion of these issues).

As you can surmise from the above, there are individual differences in entrance into, and exit from, the growth spurt. In other words, some adolescents are relatively early maturers and some are relatively late maturers. Indeed, the differences between groups of early and late maturers can be so great that early maturers may be completely grown before late maturers enter the growth spurt. In other words, early and late maturers, who are of the same age, are in very different portions of the growth cycle (Faust, 1977). We explore below the psychological consequences of these differences in rates of growth.

Physical Changes during the Growth Spurt

The entire body, external and internal, undergoes considerable change during the growth spurt years. Some aspects of change are greater than others, and some have more psychological importance. We discuss only some of the changes. A more complete treatment may be found in Katchadourian (1977).

Height. Growth in height (see Figure 3–2), of course, is one of the more dramatic and observable changes that occur during the growth spurt. The rate of gain in height is very rapid, approximating that of the late infancy years (about age 2). Much of the growth in height is in the long bones of the legs and in trunk length (Katchadourian, 1977). The accelerated growth in the legs contributes to the stereotype of the gangling adolescent.

Growth in height ceases when the skeleton matures. This maturation is illustrated in Figure 3–3, which details bone growth in the hand. As the figure shows, bones grow not only longer but closer together as development progresses. The **epiphyses**, which are the cartilage tips of the long bones such as those found in the fingers and legs, grow together as skeletal maturity is achieved. As long as these epiphyses are open, the bones grow longer and the person grows taller. As estrogen or testosterone exerts its influence to foster bone growth over cartilage growth, the cessation of growth draws nearer, because only cartilage can grow and cause increases in height (Katchadourian, 1977). Indeed, the longer time males have for slow growth, that is, growth at the epiphyses, prior to entering the growth spurt is in part why they are taller, on the average, than females.

FIGURE 3–3 **Age and Sex Differences on Ossification of the Hand and Wrist**

(Source: Redrawn from an illustration in Shuttleworth, F. K., [1949]. The adolescent period: A pictorial atlas. *Monographs of the Society for Research in Child Development, 14*, serial no. 49. The original illustration was based on unpublished material of Nancy Bayley.)

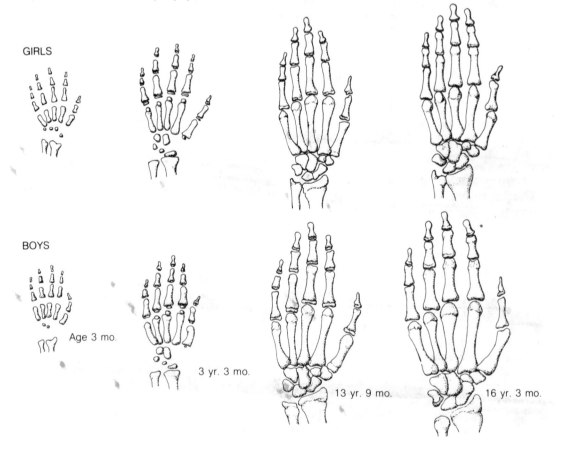

GIRLS

BOYS

Age 3 mo.   3 yr. 3 mo.   13 yr. 9 mo.   16 yr. 3 mo.

Weight. Gains in weight are due largely to nonskeletal growth, namely, muscle and fat growth. Boys have gained only about 55 percent, and girls 59 percent, of their adult weight by age 10 (Katchadourian, 1977). The growth curve for gain in weight is similar in shape to that for the gain in height (Tanner, Whitehouse, & Takaishi, 1966). Gain in weight is much more variable because of its reliance on diet.

Muscle Growth. Peak growth in musculature occurs about 3 months after the peak growth in stature (Katchadourian, 1977). Related to increases in muscle size are increases in strength. It is in this area that sex differences present at birth—for example, hand grip—become magnified. Male muscle cells increase by a factor of 14, female by a factor of 10, between ages 5 and 16.

Body Fat. Subcutaneous fat, that is, fat that is deposited directly under the skin, helps define body shape. At the onset of the growth spurt, there is a progressive loss of body fat, especially in boys, who generally experience a negative fat balance that contributes to their "string bean" look. The loss is not as great among girls, which results in their entering adulthood with more fat than boys. Moreover, females tend to "collect" subcutaneous fat in the region of the pelvis, breasts, upper back, upper arms, hips, and buttocks, which causes them to be more rounded. These differences are related to the sex differences in strength and athletic ability that emerge during the growth-spurt years; males have a greater muscle mass than do females (Grumbach et al., 1974a).

This sex difference in amount and distribution of body fat is responsible, in part, for the more muscular look of males. The fat layers of females cover the muscles, making their definition harder to see. Even female world-class athletes do not appear as muscular as their male counterparts, in part because of males' bigger muscles, and in part because of the fat layers accumulated by females.

Internal Changes. Virtually all internal organs increase in size and weight during the growth spurt. The heart doubles in size, lungs and respiratory capacity increase, exercise tolerance—the ability of the body to function under physical stress—increases. Brain growth, which is about 95 percent of adult weight by age 10, obviously is minimal.

Sexual Development. Sexual development includes development of both the primary and secondary sexual characteristics. Although this aspect of development parallels the other growth trends discussed above, it is unique in that it signals the emergence of reproductive maturity, a qualitative rather than quantitative change. The age ranges and relative developmental aspects of sexual maturity are illustrated in Figure 3–4.

In girls, the first visible sign of puberty is growth of the breasts. In the average girl this starts at about age 11 and is completed about age 15, the range of onset of growth being between 8 and 13 years, and the range of completion being between 13 and 18 years (Katchadourian, 1977). Although size and shape of the breasts have nothing to do with their capacity to nurse infants or respond to erotic stimulation, considerable psychological importance is attached to their development. It is not uncommon for a young woman to be concerned about whether her breasts will be the right size and shape, and a certain amount of self-consciousness and preoccupation is common. It is simply worth noting that one breast may develop faster than the other, and that if there are abnormalities in breast development, they usually can be corrected.

The appearance of pubic hair is usually the second sign of puberty in girls. It begins to grow between ages 11 and 12 and the adult pattern is achieved by about age 14.

The internal sexual organs—the ovaries, uterus, vagina, Fallopian tubes—all grow larger and increase in weight. The uterine wall becomes more muscular, as does the vagina. The ovaries, which are nearly com-

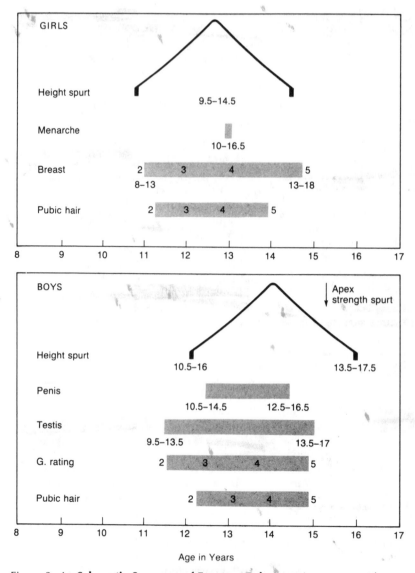

Age in Years

Figure 3–4 **Schematic Sequence of Events at Puberty.** An average girl (upper) and boy (lower) are represented. The range of ages within which each event charted may begin and end is given by the figures placed directly below its start and finish.

(Source: Tanner, J. M. [1974]. Sequence and tempo in the somatic changes in puberty. In Grumbach, M. M., Grave, G. D., & Mayor, F. E. [Eds.], *Control of the onset of puberty.* New York: John Wiley & Sons.)

pletely developed at birth, do not undergo dramatic change. A female is born with about 500,000 immature ova (egg cells) each of which may become mature later.

Menarche usually occurs two years after the start of breast development and after the peak growth spurt in height. The average age of menarche in the United States is 12.8 years, the range being between 9 and 18 years. Although there *usually* is a short period of sterility during the growth spurt, this should not be considered to amount to an effective contraceptive technique (Katchadourian, 1977).

In boys, pubertal onset is indicated by enlargement of the testes. This starts between the ages of 10 and 13½, and is accomplished between the ages of 14½ and 18. Testes produce sperm cells when the seminiferous tubules increase in size and their lining matures. Sperm cells are produced throughout the male's life. Unlike women, who produce no fertilizable eggs after menopause, males are capable of reproduction all their lives.

The prostate gland increases considerably in size during puberty. Its secretions account for much of the volume of semen during ejaculation. Some researchers (cf. Katchadourian, 1977) have equated ejaculation in males psychologically with menarche in females. It may be just as startling and unsettling. And, it signifies achievement of sexual maturity.

The penis and scrotum grow markedly about a year after the onset of testicular growth and the first appearance of pubic hair (between ages 10 and 15). Growth is completed between ages 13½ and 16½. The size and shape of the penis are unrelated to physique, race, sexual pleasure, etc. (Katchadourian, 1977).

A common pubertal event in males is a cracking of the voice. This results from a deepening of the voice due to enlargement of the larynx. Similarly, the appearance of facial and other body hair signals entrance into physical adulthood.

About 40 percent of boys experience some transient breast development (Katchadourian, 1977) for a short time during the growth spurt. In extremely rare cases, this breast enlargement may be pathological, that is, gynecomastia. In most males, it is a transient and normal event, however.

The Secular Trend

The term **secular trend** refers to generational differences in direction and magnitude of somatic (body) change (Meredith, 1963; Roche, 1979). For example, it is clear that, over recent generations, there has been an increase in final adult height of about an inch or so, more recent generations being taller (Hebbelinck, 1977; Meredith, 1963, 1976; Milani Comparetti, 1977; Roche, 1979). Other secular trends of a similar nature, for example, in body weight, are evi-

The secular trend has resulted in more recent generations of adolescents being taller than their parents' generation, on the average.

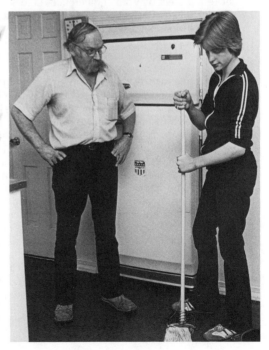

dent (See Box 3–1). These secular trends, which are most evident in Western industrialized nations (Roche, 1979), raise several interesting questions pertinent to our understanding of adolescence.

As may be seen in Figure 3–5, the secular trend in height is evidenced from ages 1–20, with the largest generational difference occurring during the adolescent years. Other evidence includes similar trends for weight (Meredith, 1963) and other measures of physical growth (Roche, 1979). In other words, the current generation of adolescents is more physically mature—in terms of height, weight, body build, age of menarche, and the like—than their parents were at a comparable age. This difference in rate and timing of growth may contribute to intergenerational (that is, parent-adolescent) conflict, because it may temper what it means to be an adolescent. Parents may be out of tune with the nature of adolescence, in part because of differences in rates of physical growth. Because physical growth character-

BOX 3–1   The Study of Secular Trends in Physical Growth

The study of secular trends in aspects of physical growth presents some unique methodological difficulties. First, major problems in finding presumably reliable measures of growth exist when we try to go back beyond the late 1800's (cf. Roche, 1979). Second, once data have been collected, they are at times difficult to interpret.

The interpretational difficulty stems from a variety of sources. Comparisons among studies are valid only to the degree that measures were taken in the same way. For example, weight may be measured with or without light clothing, and height may be measured to the nearest millimeter, centimeter, or last completed centimeter. Although these may appear to be trivial problems, causing only small differences between studies, it is important to note that secular trends themselves represent only small differences between successive generations. Hence, for example, the way measures of height are rounded off could either mask an existing secular trend or result in the conclusion that a secular trend exists when in fact none does.

Special problems are associated with birth date and age, each of which is critically important to the study of secular trends. Birth dates may come from multiple sources, some more accurate than others. Age may mean different things for different investigators: the year a person was in (for example, age 14 could mean anywhere in the range 14.0 to 14.99), or the exact age when the measures were taken, for example, on the birthday (Roche, 1979).

Despite these ambiguities, researchers have been able to establish secular trends for a number of physical measures. Aside from height (see text), clear secular trends exist for weight, body proportions, body fat, strength, rate of maturation, and age of entrance into the growth spurt. On a percentage basis, the intergenerational differences are relatively small but present.

Malina (1979) has reviewed a number of the factors that may have contributed to the secular trend. He has presented evidence indicating that there are two major determinants: nutritional advances and improvements in health care. Nutritional advances no doubt contribute to the secular trend by allowing more nearly optimal growth within the context of the genetic code. Malina argues, however, that nutritional increases are not the major cause of the secular trend because the trend has spread across all social class levels. Given the relation between social class and nutritional intake, this would be unexpected if nutrition were the major cause of the secular trend.

Malina argues that health care, specifically with regard to reduced infant and childhood mortality and morbidity, is the major cause of the secular trend. The elimination and control of diseases and infections not only allows more infants and children to survive, but also results in fewer insults to the organism and improves the chances for it reaching genetic potentials for growth.

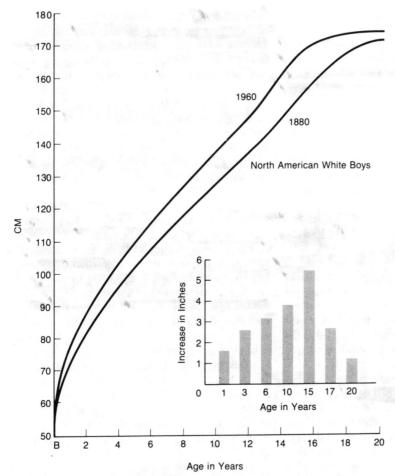

FIGURE 3–5 **Schematic Curves of Mean Stature for 1880 and 1960.**
Inset shows differences between the curves at selected ages.
(Source: Meredith, H. [1963]. Change in the stature and body weight of North
American boys during the last 80 years. In L. P. Lipsitt & C. C. Spiker [Eds.],
Advances in child development and behavior [Vol. 1]. New York: Academic
Press.)

istics are related to social behaviors, the social nature of adolescence for parents and
their adolescents may be very different.

There is some evidence that the secular
trend has ended in England, the United
States, Japan, and other developed countries
(Roche, 1979). Roche speculates that this is
a result of improvements in health care and
nutrition that allow genetic potential for optimal physical growth to operate. In other
words, the secular trend reflects environmental changes that interact with genetic potential. Indeed, if environmental conditions
were to change sufficiently, we could experience a secular trend opposite to that we
have experienced (Roche, 1979).

Influences on the Growth Spurt

The individual differences in age at entrance into, and progression through, the growth spurt make it clear that it is affected by both genetic and environmental factors. Genetic factors are evidenced by the species-specific trends noted above. In addition, some evidence indicates that identical twins enter the growth spurt at nearly identical ages, and that there is an increasing discrepancy in entrance into the growth spurt as genetic similarity decreases (Katchadourian, 1977).

Nutrition is an important environmental factor influencing pubertal growth. Malnutrition stunts growth and delays entrance into the growth spurt. Males are, in general, more susceptible to this negative influence than are females. Given this information about nutrition and the growth spurt, it should come as no surprise that less privileged adolescents enter puberty later and do not grow as much, probably because of nutritional deficits (Katchadourian, 1977).

Several other environmental influences affect pubertal growth. Illness may retard growth, but after the illness is over a catch up occurs, resulting in no permanent deficit. Although climate does not affect puberty, season of the year does. Height increases most in spring, weight in autumn. The mechanisms responsible for these effects are unknown at present.

PSYCHOLOGICAL ADJUSTMENT TO PHYSICAL GROWTH

As noted above, the growth rate during the growth spurt years is very rapid, being exceeded only by the rate of growth during the infancy years. In addition, it entails not only quantitative change, such as increases in body size, but also qualitative change, namely sexual maturity. These changes occur at different rates for individuals and, as we have seen, at different times for different generations. Despite these differences, the growth results in two basic effects: (1) the achievement of a mature adult physique and (2) the attainment of mature adult physical sex differences. The adolescent's adaptation to these changes has been the subject of research for a number of years (see Box 3–2).

Two aspects of physical change during the growth-spurt years are of potential importance in explaining psychological functioning. *Pubertal status* refers to the changes we all experience during maturation; it is reflected in measures of how physically mature, or developed, we are. *Pubertal timing* refers to the degree to which the pubertal changes coincide with the norm, the degree to which we are ahead of, or lag behind, the peer group. And, there are two models for explaining the relation between pubertal change and psychological functioning: the **direct-effects** model and the **mediated-effects** model (Petersen & Taylor, 1980; Richards & Petersen, 1987). Pubertal status effects may either be direct, as in the case of "distancing" (see Box 3–3) or premenstrual syndrome, or indirect, as in the case of reactions to menarche (discussed below). Pubertal timing effects, such as being an early or late maturer, are explained best by the mediated-effects model (Petersen, 1988).

Direct-Effects Model

According to this perspective, biological change directly results in psychological effects. In other words, direct causal linkages are hypothesized between biological change and psychological development. For example, hormones are known to affect mood states directly. And it has been shown that biological change causes changes in drives, such as the sex drive. These attributions regarding the importance of biological changes, of course, are reminiscent of some of the theories of adolescence discussed in Chapter 2 (for example, Hall, 1904; A. Freud, 1948).

Petersen and Taylor (1980) point out that

BOX 3-2 Relating Physical Growth to Psychological Development

At first blush, it appears that the study of physical growth is a relatively simple type of research to conduct. One need only measure height, for example, at various ages, and compute the gain from the previous measure, and one can describe the course of growth in height. This, in essence, is what was shown in Figure 3–2. Research of this type has proven very useful in advancing knowledge about the course of normal and abnormal physical growth.

This type of research is of little value in the study of the relationship between physical growth and psychological development, however. The major reason is that there is wide variation among adolescents in the age of occurrence of physical events, as we have described in the text. In other words, a measure other than chronological age is needed in order to relate physical changes to psychological development (cf. Eichorn, 1963; Zigler, 1963). It is for this reason that other measures were developed.

One measure that has proven useful is **skeletal age**, a measure of bone development (ossification) obtained from X-rays of the hand (see Figure 3–3) or knee. Adolescents' physical development may be classified along the dimension of completeness of bone growth. Then, measures of psychological development can be related to this measure of physical growth. In this way, comparisons of psychological development among people of the same, or different, chronological age may be made. As a result, psychological development can be related to physical growth without the confound of chronological age. This is what was done in the Berkeley Growth Studies, for example. Skeletal x-rays and a complete physical examination were given to the participants on their birthday and six months later, up to age 18. These measures were related to adult perceptions and peer ratings of various measures of psychological development, including self-concept, personality, social development, and the like (see text).

Other measures of physical growth also have been related to psychological development. Development of the secondary sex characteristics, changes in height growth, and age of menarche are examples of physical growth measures that have been related to measures of psychological development. Each of these measures is useful because the physical events of the growth spurt years are all positively correlated, as shown in Figure 3–4.

It was pointed out in Chapter 1 that age is not a useful component of a definition of adolescence. It is also not particularly useful in the study of the relation of biological change to psychological development, largely for the same reasons.

there is scant evidence supporting the direct-effects models. One area of support comes from the study of direct hormone effects on behavior. Recent advances in methods of measuring and otherwise doing research with hormones have facilitated this line of study.

Research on premenstrual tension indicates it has in part a hormonal basis (cf. Bardwick, 1971; Melges & Hamburg, 1977). About the 22nd day of the menstrual cycle, when the levels of both estrogen and progesterone are increasing substantially, a significant percentage of women (about 40 percent) experience an increased degree of moodiness, irritability, lowered self-esteem,

anxiety, and depression. These negative emotions and self-feelings generally are not as strong during the earlier days of the cycle. Keeping in mind that all of us at times are moody or feel poorly about ourselves, the important point is the dramatic and substantial nature of changes of this kind. These findings and the research on which they are based, have led some investigators to argue that hormone balances directly affect psychological behavior. Of course, sociocultural factors may also play a role (Melges & Hamburg, 1977).

In searching the literature, however, it is difficult to find clear demonstrations of direct biological effects on aspects of psycho-

BOX 3–3   **Pubertal Status and Adolescent Distancing**

One of the stereotypic beliefs about adolescence is that it is accompanied by an increase in conflict with parents. Researchers (e.g., Hill et al., 1985a, 1985b; Savin-Williams & Small, 1986; Steinberg, 1989) have begun to study the relation between the adolescent's pubertal status and degree of conflict in family relations. The findings of these studies indicate that pubertal status, *independent of age*, is indeed related to parent-adolescent conflict. More specifically, with increasing physical maturation, adolescents feel less close to their parents, and their feelings of emotional autonomy from parents increases. There also is an increase in feelings of dissatisfaction and conflict in offspring–parent relations. These feelings are stronger with respect to associations with mother than they are with respect to interactions with father. They are also more prevalent during the early to mid-adolescent years than later. Steinberg (1989) concludes that pubertal status, that is, physical maturation, facilitates the adolescent's strivings to become independent from the parents.

In discussing how we might explain the role of pubertal status, and not age, in these distancing behaviors, Steinberg (1989) proposes an evolutionary perspective that draws on research into social interactions in nonhuman primates and on anthropological evidence. Numerous examples exist of increased hostility in nonhuman primates between parents and offspring as the offspring enter puberty. These conflicts, in effect, drive the offspring away from the natal (family) group. Especially among monogamous species, this ensures mating outside the natal group; a violation of this norm would have serious consequences. In addition, there is evidence that leaving the natal group actually facilitates pubertal maturation, whereas staying in it retards the attaining of physical maturity. For example, among marmosets the presence of the mother inhibits ovulation among adolescent female offspring. When these females are removed from the natal group ovulation begins within about four weeks. Steinberg (1989) reports evidence of a similar depressive effect of the mother on the physical maturity of the adolescent daughter among humans.

To explain these findings, Steinberg (1989) outlines the possible role of evolutionary factors as being important in the increasing distance between adolescents and their parents. First, he notes that in humans the increased distancing during early adolescence, and the subsequent decline in such distancing during later adolescence, is consistent with findings for nonhumans. Second, he notes that historically we have had cultural institutions for separating adolescents and their parents. Hence, in the 1850s the practice of "placing out" adolescents at puberty (Kett, 1977), and the practice of *extrusion*—sending adolescents away from the family unit at puberty—which is practiced in a variety of cultures, are formalized means of separating the adolescent from the family unit.

Applying this line of reasoning to human adolescence, Steinberg suggests that the ultimate cause of increased adolescent–parent conflict during early adolescence may reflect the need to ensure that adolescents find mates outside the natal unit. With industrialization, improved health care and nutrition, and the like, we have seen adolescence lengthen because we mature at an earlier age and remain economically dependent on parents longer, than previously. Hence, the amount of time sexually mature adolescents remain in the family unit has increased substantially, which may contribute to prolonged periods of adolescent–parent conflict.

Steinberg's evolutionary analysis of adolescent–parent conflict is interesting and points out that such conflict, and particularly the increase of such conflict during the early to middle adolescent years, may actually be beneficial to the adolescent's development. The conflict may cause the adolescent to develop closer ties to age mates outside the family unit, which is beneficial to the species when reproduction occurs. Finally, this line of research points to the importance of pubertal status as a cause of adolescent behavior and highlights why age is not a particularly useful means of explaining adolescent development.

logical development. This has led many researchers to consider mediational factors in explaining links between biological changes and behavior (Richards & Petersen, 1987).

Mediated-Effects Models

In mediated-effects models, it is assumed that biological changes affect psychological events through both individualistic personal factors, called intervening variables, and sociocultural (contextual) factors, called moderator variables. In other words, the effects of biological change on psychological development and behavior are indirect, that is, mediated by other factors (Petersen & Taylor, 1980). For example, from this perspective, pubertal timing, that is, early, average, or late maturity, is important to the person not in its own right, but rather because of how the person, and others, perceive it, and because of cultural ascriptions and expectations for the timing of rates of growth.

Researchers have examined many biological changes and the mediating factors that make them important to understanding development. Biological changes include timing of entrance into the growth spurt, hormone changes, somatic changes, and the attainment of reproductive capacity. Mediating mechanisms include thoughts, attitudes, and feelings about body changes, acceptance of gender, attitudes about growing up, conflict with parents or peers, cultural standards of physical growth, societal norms for rates of growth, changes in social practices related to physical development, and the like (Petersen & Taylor, 1980; Richards & Petersen, 1987).

According to this formulation, the adolescent's cognitions and value systems are important for understanding the effects of biological change on the adolescent. Adolescents interpret the meaning and importance of the biological changes, the reactions of others to them—before and after the change—and how the change fits sociocul-

tural norms (Clausen, 1975). In other words, being an early, average, or late maturer does not directly affect the adolescent. Rather, it is the adolescent's *interpretation* of the timing of entrance into pubertal changes that is important. This interpretation rests on the adolescent's cognition of how fast or slowly he or she is maturing, how others, such as parents and peers, react to this timing, what the sociocultural norms for entrance into puberty are, and the like.

For example, late maturers *may* see themselves as being treated as less grown-up than their agemates and, therefore, *may* develop negative self-concepts and feelings about their body. The adolescent's cognitions mediate the effect of biological change.

An advantage of the mediated-effects models over the direct-effects models is that they allow explanation of individual differences in the effects of biological change on psychological development. Adolescents growing up in different cultures or subcultures may react differently to the same biological change. And adolescents within the same sociocultural context may react differently as a result of different rearing experiences, different interpretations of the biological event, or different interpretations of the behavior of others. This type of analysis is not possible from the direct-effects perspective because it is assumed that biological changes influence everyone in the same way. No allowance is made for individual differences.

Early versus Late Maturity

As stated earlier in the chapter, the time of onset of the growth spurt, as well as the actual rate of growth, varies widely among adolescents. These differences give rise to concomitant differences in personality development and social behavior that are important (Clausen, 1975).

Much of the research on the interactive effects of adolescent physical growth and personality development comes from the

Some adolescents enter the growth spurt years earlier than others. These differences in growth rates relate to social/behavioral differences.

Berkeley Growth Studies and the Oakland Growth Study. The researchers examined groups of adolescents of the same age and selected for study those who were either very early or extremely late maturers, usually the upper and lower 20 percent of the sample. Skeletal age was used as the method of assessing maturity. The social, emotional, and intellectual adjustment of these two groups was then assessed and compared. These surveys have been done separately with males and females because of differences in the psychological responses to these maturational variables. For clarity, we shall maintain this distinction in our discussion.

Early/Late Maturity in Boys. During the early and mid-adolescent years, early maturers are taller, heavier, more muscular, more advanced in pubic and axillary hair growth, and more sexually mature than late maturers. Late maturers, on the other hand, are characteristically long-legged, of slender build, and physically weaker than their same-age peers. There are several effects of the differences in physique evidenced in these two groups of individuals (Clausen, 1975).

Because of their precocious sexual and physical maturity, early maturers have the advantage of size, strength, and greater masculinity over late maturers. In our culture, which values physical attractiveness and competency, early maturers definitely have the edge over normal and late maturing adolescents purely on the basis of body build. For example, in most high schools, the athletes, who are predominantly early maturers, are the most popular and desirable boyfriends and leaders. These favorings by both peers and adults in the social sphere during the crucial adolescent years of self-concept formation have widespread psychological effects.

Behavioral differences are also readily apparent in comparisons between these two groups (Clausen, 1975). Adult ratings of male adolescents found that late maturers were consistently rated as less physically attractive, less masculine, less well-groomed, more childish, more attention-seeking, more tense, and less mature than early maturers (Jones & Bayley, 1950). Peer ratings of late maturers compared to early maturers found that late maturers were viewed as more restless, talkative, bossy, less self-assured, and less popular than their early-maturing classmates (Mussen & Jones, 1957). From these adult and peer ratings it can be seen that the extent of physical maturity readily elicits personality judgments from all the people with whom an individual comes into contact. Moreover, **early-maturing** boys are seen as having more positive social attributes than late maturers by both adults and peers. Finally, early-maturing boys perceive themselves as more attractive, because they are closer to physical maturity (Tobin-Richards, Boxer, & Petersen, 1983).

These social and personality judgments by others inevitably influence the adolescent's self-assessment and self-concept (Clausen, 1975). Using projective techniques, such as the Thematic Apperception Test (TAT) and the Rorschach Test, the researchers from the Berkeley Growth Studies found significant differences in self-evaluations between early and late maturing males. Late maturers consistently saw the central

figures/heroes as imbeciles or weaklings who were scorned by their parents or authorities. The hero was also described as someone incapable of solving his own problems and needing the help of others for an answer. The early maturers' themes, however, centered around potency, aggression, and positive self attributions (Mussen & Jones, 1957). The late maturers were more likely to hold negative or derogatory self-concepts than were the early maturers, a factor that was probably due to frustration of their strivings to be potent or strong. The feelings of inferiority generated in these individuals were found to carry over into adulthood, as we discuss below.

The late-maturing boy has negative experiences because he is usually treated like a child longer than others by being denied leadership and other adultlike responsibilities, which may seriously damage his self esteem (Clausen, 1975). His lack of development may hinder him in the classroom, in the locker room, and in the sports arena. Teachers may hesitate to attribute mature thoughts to him because of his immature physique. He may be singled out as a troublemaker because of his attention-seeking behavior, whether real or imaginary. His generally younger-looking stature, less mature muscle growth, and lower exercise tolerance and strength will prevent him from competing successfully with earlier maturers in physical contact sports, and indeed may hinder the development of social relationships with peers, particularly in the heterosexual sphere. The male late maturer may perform poorly in the classroom because, in many cases, imbalance in motor skills, such as lack of coordination and clumsiness, as well as concern about his worthiness, is accompanied by reading, writing, and attention deficits (Frisk et al., 1966). He may come to feel that he just can't measure up to anyone's standards. In fact, research (Jones, 1957, 1965; Peskin, 1967) has shown that the effects of differential treatment of early and late maturers may last 20 years or longer.

These early findings have been replicated in more recent research (e.g., Duncan et al., 1985; Petersen, 1985, 1988). The advantage of early-maturing boys with regard to self-concept and popularity among peers was evident. However, Duncan and colleagues (1985) reported that early-maturing boys were more likely to have problems at school, to be truants, and to engage in delinquent behavior.

Peskin (1967, 1973) has paid special attention to potential negative effects of being an early maturer. He notes that early maturers may not have a sufficient amount of time to develop values and views about oneself prior to coping with the biological changes of puberty. Hence, their pubertal experience may be more anxiety provoking. Peskin also reports that, during the initial stage of puberty, early maturers were more anxious, less intellectually curious, more somber, more submissive, less exploratory, and less active than their later-maturing counterparts. Hence, early maturity is filled not only with advantages but may also carry some disadvantages.

Despite some of the possible disadvantages of early maturity, there are definite assets, if one is a male. There is the possibility of heterosexual activity on an equal ground with normal-maturing girls of the same age, who have, on the average, a two-year head-start on boys. There is the possibility of successfully engaging in sports, and gaining peer acceptance from older, later maturing boys, as well as gaining a stable identity as an athlete throughout the difficult physical changes of adolescence.

Early/Late Maturity in Females. The situation is much different for early-maturing girls (Jones & Mussen, 1958). They are at the absolute lower age extreme of the initiation of the growth spurt—a very lonely position in which to find one's self. The early-maturing girl is faced with sudden physical changes that her peers are not as yet experiencing. This may intensify the effects of menarche, for example, or may bring added discipline, restrictions, and confusion that are burdens to the early-maturing girl (Bardwick, 1971). She may even be socially ostracized by her own age mates, who often view being "in phase" as important for social acceptance (Frisk et al., 1966; Petersen, 1988).

The early-maturing girl faces overall adjustment problems, not only with adults but also with her peers. She may seek the companionship of older individuals whose interests and problems are more similar to hers than are those of her prepubescent age-mates. She may come to see school as a childish waste of time because of her inability to interact emotionally with her classmates. The overall emotional deprivation may force an early-maturing girl into "going steady" or into an unwanted pregnancy in an effort to find emotional solace and a sense of belonging (Frisk et al., 1966). The early-maturing girl may be as much as five to six years ahead of normal-maturing boys and as much as two to three years ahead of her same-sex peers. She therefore finds herself with few peers with whom she can share the experience of newfound sexuality. In contrast to the early-maturing boy, for whom advantages are present, the early-maturing girl may face extreme stress.

The early-maturing girl must also deal with physical development and the hormonal aspects of her mature femininity without relatively close contact from peers having similar experiences (Clausen, 1975). The negative feelings many female adolescents have about menarche, for example, may further increase tenseness and discomfort. Girls of normal or late maturation levels may share their insecurities and questions with each other. The early maturer has no one, parents or peers, with whom to share the experience. Parents may greet her confidences with increased worrying and added restrictions; peers simply don't know what she is talking about.

In addition to these difficulties, the early-maturing girl is more prone to engaging in delinquency, using drugs and alcohol, and having problems in school, perhaps because she associates with older boys who introduce her to these activities (Aro & Taipale, 1987; Magnusson, Stattin, & Allen, 1986; Petersen, 1988). Whether a male or female, then, early maturity carries some detriments.

The late-maturing girl does not appear to be so handicapped, probably because girls enter pubescence approximatley two years ahead of boys of the same age. She may even appear to have the best of both worlds, because she enjoys a prolonged girlhood and emerges from puberty at the same time as her same-age male peers. She may have endured doubts about her female identity (Jones & Mussen, 1958), but they are all relatively successfully resolved in the reality of a first date or when members of the opposite sex find her attractive. She will also have the advantage of newness to the dating routine at a time when her early-maturing sisters may have tired of the "immature" activities of the newly matured males their own age. The early-maturing girl runs a greater risk of teen-age pregnancy or early marriage because of her need to date older males in order to find someone who has the same level of sexual need, experience, and drive that she has. Although these relationships may offer an early-maturing girl an opportunity to overcome her sense of difference and aloneness, they also may add to the sense of difference and questionable self-esteem if she should become pregnant (Frisk et al., 1966).

For females, being "on time" with respect to physical development is important to self-concept. Adolescent females who perceive themselves as on time as opposed to early or late maturers have better self-concepts. In addition, and consistent with our above comments, late-maturing females have a better self-concept than do early-maturing females. A particularly important specific physical component related to a positive self-concept is breast development (Tobin-

Richards et al., 1983; Brooks-Gunn & Warren, 1988, 1989), perhaps because of its positive stimulus value, both in reactions from others and in its signifying the start of physical development (Brooks-Gunn & Warren, 1988).

Overall, then, the most difficult personal and physical adjustments to biological change appear to be made by the early-maturing girl and the late-maturing boy, both of whom represent extreme points on the continuum of sexual maturity. However, any adolescent who experiences any sort of a developmental deviation experiences not only the psychosexual problems detailed above, but also very real psychosomatic disturbances, which may include tics, nail-biting, sleep and digestive problems, motor deficits, and unusual fatigue. These symptoms strongly suggest that perceived asynchrony in development may be a determining factor in physical as well as psychological problems and maldevelopment (Frisk et al., 1966).

Long-Term Effects. Studies of the long-term consequences of having been an early or late maturer are surprisingly rare (Jones & Mussen, 1958; Livson & Peskin, 1980; Peskin, 1973). At age 38, early-maturing males from the Berkeley Growth Studies rated themselves as more responsible, cooperative, warm, persistent, and as being looked on to play a leadership role. But they also rated themselves as more rigid and conforming (Jones & Mussen, 1958). Late maturers rated themselves as more rebellious, self-indulgent, impulsive, and childish, but also as more insightful and creative. These self-descriptions are very similar to the adult and peer ratings of these individuals during their adolescence, as described above. In addition, the late maturers held fewer jobs of responsibility (executive) and leadership, but they had happier and more successful marriages (Jones, 1965; Mussen & Jones, 1957).

Similar findings have been reported for 30-year-old females. The early-maturing females, who were under stress during adolescence, as adults were more self-directed, self-assured, and competent than were the late-maturing girls (Peskin, 1973). Although some evidence (Magnusson et al., 1986) shows deleterious long-term effects of being an early-maturing girl—for example, developing negative attitudes toward school and completing less education—it seems that the early-maturing female profits socially and intellectually from her early experiences.

This suggests that degree of physical maturity to a large extent determines societal expectations for the individual's behavior. For example, adults, in general, expect more mature and adultlike behavior from an early maturer than from a late maturer, perhaps because early maturers more closely resemble adults (Clausen, 1975). However, even the early-maturing, postpubertal adolescent lacks the cognitive and social maturity of an adult, and therefore may not be able to live up to these expectations. Conflicts between what is expected and what is possible may cause serious harm to the early maturer's self-esteem. For example, an early-maturing boy who is, say, president of his high school class, may bear the onus for class pranks the rest of his life because school authorities expected more from him than his younger-appearing classmates.

On the other hand, late maturers are expected to behave like children. An example is the 14-year-old whose parents force her to wear "little girl" clothes when she wants to dress like her more developed age mates. Again, then, expectations exist that are not necessarily congruent with the capacities of the individual. As we noted in Chapter 2, adults may place the source and cause of conflict and confusion about adolescence on the adolescent when, in fact, it rests on adult expectations that are inappropriate and out of phase with the adolescent's developmental level and associated competencies.

Perhaps some other examples of this dissonance between adult expectations and adolescent behavior are in order. Two cases that come readily to mind are a cognitively precocious teen-ager and the adolescent chess master. You have all read stories about 14- or 15-year-old geniuses who skip high school to attend college. These young students usually can meet adult expectations of academic achievement, but they are often social outcasts on the campus. They may do brilliant work in organic chemistry, but they are not potential dates, are unable to vote, and are not legally able to "blow off" after an exam at the local pub. The same set of circumstances holds true for the teen-age chess master who is a brilliant tactician on the chessboard but who is totally devoid of tact outside the game. He (the he's have received the most notoriety) has also been forced into an adult role by unrealistic overall expectations of his behavior. In both the above cases, adolescents are asked to meet behavioral standards that are impossibly severe considering their age and social experience. Although extreme, these examples point out the sorts of conflicts that exist for other early- and late-maturing adolescents.

The reproductive hormones, then, have dramatic psychological effects that have long-term consequences for adjustment well into adulthood. Adults, of course, should be aware of these individual differences and adapt their expectations for performance—behavioral, intellectual, and social—to the needs and capabilities of the individual adolescent in order to help him or her adjust to maturity. Unfortunately, this often does not happen (Clausen, 1975). The result can be conflict between the adolescent and adults. Although adults often "blame" this conflict on the adolescent, it is clear that adults contribute to adolescent confusion and conflict through their unrealistic and inappropriate expectations for, and reactions to, adolescent behavior. One determinant of these inappropriate adult expectations is adolescent physical growth rate.

Psychological Reactions to Menarche

Menarche, the onset of the menstrual cycle, is a signal of female physical maturity and fertility. As such, it is an important event in the lives of adolescent females. It would be surprising, indeed, if menarche did not have associated with it important psychological concomitants. Although answers are still being sought for many of the important questions concerning the psychological impact of menarche, some facts are available (see Greif & Ulman, 1982, and Brooks-Gunn, 1986, for thorough reviews).

Contrary to both theoretical and popular beliefs (cf. Greif & Ulman, 1982; Ruble & Brooks-Gunn, 1982; Brooks-Gunn & Ruble, 1982), menarche is apparently not an overly traumatic event for most adolescent girls. Ruble and Brooks-Gunn (1982), for example, report that adolescent girls indicate both positive and negative feelings about menarche. And, for postmenarchial girls, the negative aspects of menarche, particularly the physical symptoms, were not as severe as they expected them to be. Brooks-Gunn and Ruble (1982) suggest that premenarchial girls may attend more selectively to negative information, or may receive more negative than positive information, about menstruation and, hence, expect it to be more debilitating than in reality it is. Once the girl experiences menstruation firsthand, she is in a better position to understand both the positive and negative aspects of menstruation and develops a more balanced perspective of it.

An important aspect of the adolescent girl's feelings about menstruation seems to be how well she is prepared for it (Ruble & Brooks-Gunn, 1982; Brooks-Gunn & Ruble, 1982). In this context, preparation means the information the girl has had about menstruation. Brooks-Gunn and Ruble (1982) questioned girls about the sources from which they gained information about menstruation. The major sources of informa-

tion, as you might expect, were other females, particularly the girl's mother, and doctors. Males were not seen by the girls as a particularly useful source of information, and they were viewed as having negative perspectives of menstruation. It is interesting to note that those girls who indicated they had gained significant amounts of information from males also reported more debilitating and negative effects of menstruation than girls who learned less from male sources of information. It appears, then, that the type of information a girl acquires about menstruation is important in her perceptions of the event. Moreover, it is also clear that girls who know little of what to expect, that is, those who are not prepared for understanding menstruation, experience it as more unpleasant and debilitating.

Other aspects of the importance of menstruation for the psychological development of adolescent girls are scarce (Greif & Ulman, 1982). Some evidence (for example, Goldberg, Blumberg, & Kriger, 1982) indicates that postmenarchial girls respond more favorably to pictures of infants than adults. Although it has been argued that this type of finding results from increased interest on the part of the postmenarchial girl in future motherhood, Goldberg and others (1982) could find no evidence that this was the case. They suggest that postmenarchial girls' increased preference for pictures of infants over pictures of adults reflects the attention-getting features of infants. They further suggest that this may be a biological phenomenon, that is, biological changes at menarche sensitize the adolescent girl to infants. Such effects have clear value to the species, of course. However, much more research will need to be done before we can conclude that there is a biologically related preference for aspects of infants.

Postmenarchial girls are also somewhat more interested in their femininity than are premenarchial girls (cf. Greif & Ulman, 1982). They have a heightened awareness of their physical appearance and of cross-sex relationships. Postmenarchial girls also were more psychologically mature than premenarchial girls, as assessed by measures of figure drawing, general adjustment, and self-concept.

The psychological consequences of menarche and menstruation in general, are not well understood. Clearly, much still needs to be learned. However, we can conclude that the influence of menarche is present, and may have long-term effects. This seems especially true for the negative aspects of menstruation, particularly for those girls who experience this event very early relative to their peers, and for those who are not adequately informed about what to expect. We can conclude that, for some girls, menarche and menstruation are very significant negative events; fortunately, the percentage of girls for whom this is the case seems to be small. More generally, it appears that menstruation may initially be disconcerting and an inconvenience for many girls, but this is not a long-lived effect. As the girl has personal experience with menstruation, she is able to develop a more balanced view of the positive and negative aspects of it. As a result, it seems not to be as negative, or to have long-term negative influences, as some popular conceptualizations may suggest.

Body Type

As stated earlier, personality variables depend to some degree on the body shape and type of the individual, that is, adolescents' internal reactions to their external physical changes (Tanner, 1970). Sheldon (1940), a psychologist interested in the relationship between psychological characteristics and body type, categorized three distinct body types, each postulated to have a corresponding personality or temperament associated with it. (1) **Endomorphs** are soft, flabby persons with under-developed bones and muscles and a tendency toward fat. (2) **Mesomorphs** have a highly developed bone and muscle structure, a hard firm physique, and a tendency toward an athletic build. (3) **Ectomorphs** have linear and fragile bodies characterized by a flatness of chest and delicacy of bone structure; they are thin and slightly muscled, with a great deal of energy and a high metabolic rate but little strength.

Although it has some appeal, there are a number of problems with this approach to personality development. It seems simplistic; there are few pure body types; and the associated personality judgments are very subjective. However, Lindzey (1965) writes that Sheldon's theory of the relationship between somatotype and personality has some utility. His reasons center on the genetic argument that behavior and body structure may be jointly determined by genetic and environmental factors. For example, family and environmental factors, such as nutrition, that affect size may influence personality in the same manner as maturational aspects of sexuality and growth, such as early and late maturation, do. Lindzey also points out that physical handicaps such as diabetes and obesity produce personality types, and that while these are extreme cases, they do suggest that the physical characteristics of normal individuals affect their personality, emotions, and so forth. Finally, Lindzey acknowledges society's role in forcing personality-physique interactions by its tendency to typecast individuals based on physical aspects such as skin color, size, physique, and the like. However, this genetic component is always expressed in interactions with particular environments that may considerably alter its ultimate physical or behavioral presentation.

All these possibilities apply to overall growth and physical development. For example, certain cultures may value obesity. This value tends to detract from the negative feelings usually associated with this occurrence and to greatly increase positive self-esteem, because the person is conforming to sociocultural dictates. In another example, an adolescent boy who is not physically well developed may decide to excel at scholarly pursuits. However, this is not a cause-and-effect sequence. He may also embark on an Arnold Schwarzenegger weight-building program and become a Mr. Universe.

The importance of body type and maturity rate lies in the social behavior of others to the adolescent and in the adolescent's self-concept. Because body type and maturity rate are by and large genetically and hormonally controlled, there is little, if anything, the individual can do in the normal course of events to alter these biological aspects of development. Because our social structure, as well as that of other cultures, provides advantages to early-maturing individuals, biological factors have profound influences on psychological development.

A number of researchers have examined the relationship between body build (somatotype) and aspects of development. We summarize Clausen's (1975) review of this work.

By age 7 there is a clear preference for an athletic type of body build, that is, a muscular but neither fat nor thin build. Children and adolescents view the mesomorph as having leadership and athletic ability, and as being psychologically stable. There were fewer positive traits and views of endomorphs and ectomorphs. In turn, there is evidence that, in peer relations, mesomorphs tend to be more dominant and the other types of children tend to be more submissive and timid. In other words, the expectations of peers are, in one way or another, translated in the behavior of the group's members, some assuming dominant and others more passive roles within the group. Finally, some data (see Clausen, 1975) indicate that adolescent body build is related to personality ratings by adults when the individual was a child. Males who were ectomorphic at maturity were rated as infants as shy, not very active, and not very happy. Mature mesomorphs were rated just the opposite during their infancy years.

Peer relations were the most strongly re-lated to body build. The ectomorphs were viewed as seeking attention by nearly any means available, as being less knowledgeable about peer group functioning, as not being selective in making friends, and as being the butt of jokes. Although there are apparently some social class differences that temper these findings, for example, the effects just reported are much less strong in the middle social class levels, it appears that adolescents engage in a kind of self-fulfilling prophecy based on sociocultural standards for preferences in body build.

SUMMARY

The biological changes that occur during the early to mid-adolescent years are a result of the complex influences of hormones. The hormones are secreted by the endocrine glands, ductless glands that send their secretions directly into the blood stream. The hormones that are most important are testosterone, estrogen, and progesterone. Their levels increase considerably during adolescence and cause the growth spurt to final adult physique and sexual maturity.

Girls enter the growth spurt about 2½ years heads of boys, and complete the spurt earlier. But boys grow more during the growth-spurt years. Despite these sex differences, there are many similarities in growth-spurt development, including the duration of the spurt and the sequence of biological changes. More recent generations of adolescents evidence a secular trend such that they enter the growth spurt earlier, grow bigger, reach maturity sooner, and have an increased adult size. This secular trend, which seems to be ending in Western industrialized nations such as the United States, England, and Japan, seems to be due primarily to increased health care and nutritional advances.

The biological changes of puberty influence psychological development primarily through personal cognitions and sociocultural mediators. Hence, the negative effects of being a late maturer or an ectomorph reflect the adolescent's evaluations and attributions to both the self and the behavior of others toward the self. Of primary importance in this regard is the peer group. Adolescents, especially boys, who are late maturers or who deviate considerably from the preferred mesomorphic body build, tend to be viewed as more childish and are somewhat less accepted in the peer group. In addition, their own behavior reflects, to a degree, more childish modes of interacting with both peers and adults. Some evidence suggests these differences in the perceptions of others and the actual behavior of the individual may even be evident in the infancy and childhood years. Whatever the mechanisms, it is clear that biologically determined physical growth plays an important role in aspects of psychological development, such as personality.

Hypothalamus. A part of the brain that secretes hormones that affect the anterior pituitary and trigger the start of the growth spurt.

Mediated-Effects models. Attempts to explain the effect of biological factors on psychological development through reference to intermediary factors, such as cognitive, social, and cultural factors.

Menarche. The first menstrual period.

Mesomorph. A body type characterized by highly developed bones and muscles and a tendency toward an athletic physique.

Progesterone. A female hormone especially involved in preparing the uterus for a fertilized egg cell.

Secular trend. Intergenerational differences in direction and magnitude of somatic growth.

Skeletal age. Age determined on the basis of degree of bone ossification.

Steroids. A term referring to sex hormones.

Teratogen. An environmental influence that is harmful to the developing fetus.

Testosterone. The major male growth hormone.

GLOSSARY

Androgen. A general term meaning male sex hormone.

Corpus luteum. A temporary body organ formed when the egg cell separates from the ovary.

Direct-Effects model. Model or theory that explains how biological factors directly influence psychological development and behavior.

Ectomorph. A body type characterized by a thin build, slight muscles, and a high metabolic rate.

Endocrine glands. Glands that secrete hormones directly into the blood stream.

Endomorph. A body type characterized by softness, flabbiness, and underdeveloped bones and muscles.

Epiphyses. The cartilage tips of long bones.

Estrogen. The major female hormone responsible for growth.

Human growth hormone. A general growth facilitating hormone; no specific function during the growth spurt.

SUGGESTED READINGS

JONES, M. C., & BAYLEY, N. (1950). Physical maturing among boys as related to behavior. *Journal of Educational Psychology, 41*, 129–148.

This article deals with the overal effects of early and late maturation on the behavior of boys. The article explores the nature of physical growth factors and their correlation with specific positive or negative aspects of behavior.

JONES, M. C., & MUSSEN, P. H. (1958). Self-conceptions, motivations and interpersonal attitudes of early and late maturing girls. *Child Development, 29*, 491–501.

This study is closely related to that of Mussen and Jones and explores specific personality aspects of early and late maturing girls. The two studies present an interesting view of differential responses to physical stimuli by males and females.

MEREDITH, H. (1963). Change in the stature and

body weight of North American boys during the last 80 years. In L. P. Lipsitt & C. C. Spiker (Eds.), *Advances in child development and behavior* (vol. 1). New York: Academic Press.

Meredith presents a review of changes in height and weight that have led to the conclusion that there has been a secular trend in these two measures during the past 80 years.

PETERSEN, A. C. (1988). Adolescent development. In M. P. Rosenzweig & L. W. Porter (Eds.), *Annual review of psychology*. Palo Alto, CA: Annual Reviews, Inc.

Petersen presents a brief history of the development of the study of adolescence and then reviews contemporary research on adjustment, pubertal effects, family relations, and other areas of research.

RICHARDS, M., & PETERSEN, A. C. (1987). Biological theoretical models of adolescent development. In V. B. Van Hasselt & M. Hersen (Eds.), *Handbook of adolescent psychology*. New York: Pergamon Press.

The two contributing authors review the major biological models concerning adolescent development and relate biological development to a number of aspects of social/personality development.

STEINBERG, L. (1989). Pubertal maturation and parent-adolescent distance: An evolutionary perspective. In G. R. Adams, R. Montemayor, & T. P. Gullotta (Eds.), *Biology of adolescent behavior and development*. Newbury Park, CA: Sage Publications.

In this literature review, Steinberg presents a convincing argument for considering adolescent-parent conflict to be the result of evolutionary factors. His presentation is an excellent example of the integration of scientific evidence from multiple disciplines.

Intellectual and Cognitive Development in Adolescence

4

CHAPTER OUTLINE

MAJOR ISSUES ADDRESSED

Alternative Ways to Conceptualize Intelligence
Ways to Measure Intelligence
Intelligence as a Problem-Solving Ability
Developmental Trends in Intelligence
Adolescence as a Peak in Intellectual Development
Intelligence and Understanding Adolescence
Social Cognition and Adolescent Development

INTRODUCTION

In this chapter we discuss intellectual changes during the adolescent years. During adolescence the ability of the individual to learn, think, and make use of knowledge peaks. For example, IQ scores stabilize during adolescence (Honzik, Macfarlane, & Allen, 1948; Kaufman & Flaitz, 1987), allowing more reliable assessment of abilities. This allows us to better determine the degree to which intellectual development is influenced by environmental as opposed to genetic factors (Scarr, Webber, Weinberg, & Wittig, 1981; Kaufman & Flaitz, 1987). Similarly, during adolescence the facility of the individual to think abstractly, to consider multiple possibilities—for example, with regard to concerns over identity—and to think in a logical manner increases (Kaufman & Flaitz, 1987). To explore the importance of these changes for our understanding of adolescence we discuss both the quantitative (psychometric) and qualitative (structural) perspectives of the nature of intelligence.

WHAT IS INTELLIGENCE?

There is no simple definition of intelligence; there is not even a generally accepted one. For the purposes of the discussion that follows we need concern ourselves only with the fact that **intelligence** is usually defined in one of two ways: quantitatively (psychometrically) and qualitatively (structurally).

The quantitative approach typically defines intelligence as learning or problem-solving ability. Individuals are conceived of as having greater or lesser amounts of these particular abilities. Although there are alternatives to assessing these abilities (for example, Guilford, 1966, 1967), the typical way is the intelligence, or IQ, test. The IQ test produces a number (a score) representing the individual's relative standing in the population. Because IQ is a numerical representation, and people are assumed to possess more or less of it, we call it a quantitative measure of intelligence. The quantitative approach is nondevelopmental; that is, it assumes that the problem-solving abilities measured by IQ tests given at different ages are similar in nature. The only observable changes in an individual's IQ should be those due to errors in test construction, errors of measurement, or changes reflecting the particular motivational state of the person while taking the test. In fact, it is often assumed that IQ remains fixed forever. Obviously, this is not the case, as we will see when we look at the evidence presented below.

An alternative approach to conceptualizing intelligence is to look at it as a process that involves qualitative changes in cognition. In this case intelligence is defined by modes of "thinking"; that is, it is viewed as a construct relating to how the individual processes information from the environment. There are no simple tests for examining qualitative aspects of intelligence, although assessment procedures do exist for certain specific aspects of cognitive development, such as object permanence and conservation. Because the qualitative approach examines how individuals process environmental information at various stages in their lives, it has evolved into a developmental approach. That is, it is assumed that the individual processes environmental information differently during the various stages of intellectual development.

We must note at this point that neither approach denies the existence of the other. The quantitative approach does not deny that there may be different modes of thinking at different age levels, as witnessed, for example, by the different types of items on IQ tests designed for people of differing ages. Similarly, the qualitative approach does not deny quantitative differences in the development of the intellect. The two approaches are best viewed as the opposite sides of the same coin. Both are concerned with individual as well as group differences in the development of intelligence, but they differ with regard to the types of differences that are emphasized (Elkind, 1968, 1969). We shall discuss these issues in depth later in this chapter.

THE QUANTITATIVE APPROACH TO INTELLIGENCE

The quantitative approach to the study of intelligence dates back to the pioneering work of Alfred Binet, father of the intelligence test. In 1904 the French government commissioned Dr. Binet (a physician) to develop a test that would identify for a projected special school program those students who were not capable of profiting from the normal school curriculum. In collaboration with Simon, Binet developed a test that would pick out the students who did not have adequate learning capabilities. The original intelligence test, then, was designed to predict school success, and was not intended as anything more than an instrument for this purpose.

Because Binet's intent was to develop a test that would predict school performance, he chose to sample behaviors from a number of areas that related to school performance, such as perceptual-motor (hand-eye) coordination, memory, perception, verbal ability, and logical reasoning. He assumed that performance on tasks of this nature would reflect something of the child's general learning abilities. So that students with specific training and experiences would not be at an advantage, Binet tried to select tasks that would not reflect differences in background and motivation. He hoped that if items were picked in this way, he would obtain a more objective measure of intelligence.

The initial tests had activities that were graduated, with older children being expected to complete more complex tasks than younger children. Binet did not consider his test to be one assessing intelligence. Rather,

he viewed it as an index of academic readiness.

Binet's first test was published in 1905. In 1916, Lewis Terman, a psychologist at Stanford University, adapted Binet's test for use in the United States. This adapted test has become known as the Stanford-Binet intelligence test, after the university and the original test constructor. It was Terman who devised the **intelligence quotient**: IQ equals MA/CA × 100. In this formulation, IQ is a rate measure; that is, it reflects the child's rate of acquisition of presumably universally taught information (Zigler, 1967; Weir, 1967). CA is the child's chronological age. **MA** is the child's performance on the test measured as mental age units. Mental age, then, represents developmental level (Weir, 1967). People with higher IQs presumably learn things more quickly than people with lower IQs. In the same vein, people with high IQs are capable of demonstrating test performance well above their age, while people with low IQs perform below their age level. The classification systems that are often used to describe IQ levels are listed in Table 4–1.

Types of IQ Tests

There are two types of IQ tests. *Group tests* are of the paper-and-pencil variety. Al-

TABLE 4–1 **Classifications of Intelligence**

IQ	Classification	Percent Included
130 and above	Very superior	2.2
120–129	Superior	6.7
110–119	Bright normal	16.1
90–109	Average	50.0
80–89	Dull normal	16.1
70–79	Borderline	6.7
69 and below	Mental defective	2.2

(Source: Wechsler, D. [1955]. *Manual of the Wechsler Adult Intelligence Scale.* New York: Psychological Corporation.) Reproduced by permission from the *Wechsler Adult Intelligence Scale Revised.* Copyright © 1955, 1981 by The Psychological Corporation. All rights reserved.

though they are easy and cheap to administer they tap only limited behavior and are not particularly accurate. *Individually administered* tests, such as the Stanford-Binet and the Wechsler Intelligence Scale for Children-Revised (WISC-R), are more time-consuming and costly to administer, but they are more accurate and sample a wider variety of behavior. The WISC-R, for example, samples Information, Comprehension, Arithmetic, Block Design, Picture Arrangement, Object Assembly, and other skills. Assessment of differing types of skills reflects the perspective that there are qualitatively different types of intellectual abilities, despite the emphasis on the quantitative aspects of intellect.

As you can see, then, although the emphasis of the quantitative approach is on individual differences in intellectual functioning, virtually all tests involve qualitatively different subscales assessing alternative aspects of intellect. The quantitative approach incorporates qualitative aspects of intelligence into the general assessment instruments.

Cautions in Interpreting IQ Scores

First, an IQ score is not an absolute score; it represents a range of scores that allows only a rough estimate of ability. For example, an individual with an IQ of 95 can be considered within the normal range of intelligence, but the person's "real" IQ may be much higher or lower.

Second, IQ scores are not "real" in the sense of physical characteristics. IQ is what psychologists call a *hypothetical construct* that is useful in understanding behavior. Too often teachers, parents, and naive readers assume that IQ is fixed and real, like curly hair or long earlobes.

Third, we must take into account the debate about the number of kinds of intelligence. Spearman (1927) argued that there is only one general learning ability, which he labeled "**g**," for general intelligence. A num-

In the psychometric view of intelligence, performance on a standard test is compared to established norms.

ber of specific aspects to intelligence test performance, which he labeled "**s**" factors, were a result of the particular subtests used to measure "**g**." Each test measures "**g**" in a different way and produces an "**s**" factor related to the type of test. Specific factors, such as numberability, cloud our ability to get relatively pure estimates of "**g**" (intelligence).

Guilford's (1966, 1967) perspective is at the other extreme. Unlike Spearman, he does not believe that there is only one, overriding intellectual ability. Rather, he conceives intelligence to be a function of 120 different kinds of abilities, which he calls the *Structure of Intellect*. As a result, he does not believe that a single score, such as an IQ score, is a good descriptor of intellectual ability. Guilford prefers to examine a pattern of scores on a variety of tests in order to determine the intellectual competencies of children and adolescents. However, because tests have been developed for only about half the 120 abilities he postulates, the utility of the theory he advances remains to be seen.

The Nature/Nurture Controversy

Perhaps the most heated controversy concerning intelligence tasks has revolved around attempts to determine the degree to which intelligence is inherited versus learned. This debate has a long history, dating back to the initial studies of Galton (1883) in England and continuing up to modern-day investigations. Although this is an important issue in developmental psychology, generally speaking it is far too complex for a detailed exposition in this particular text. However, we shall discuss some of the relevant research because it is important to an understanding of adolescent development.

The study of the relative contributions of genetics and environment to the development of intelligence is pursued by those interested in the field of developmental behavioral genetics, the study of individual differences in development through the use of behavioral genetic techniques of research (Plomin, 1983; Scarr & McCartney, 1983; Crnic & Pennington, 1987). In the current context, developmental behavioral geneticists attempt to answer the question of how genetic endowments and environmental contexts interact during development.

One way of examining the relative contributions of genetics and environment to intelligence has been to examine the correlations of intelligence test scores for people with differing degrees of genetic relationship and environmental similarity. For example, randomly pairing groups of individuals and correlating their IQ test scores should result in a zero correlation if the hypothesis that intelligence is primarily genetically determined is correct. By the same argument, identical twins should have nearly the same IQs—the correlation should be high and positive. Data from Erlenmeyer-Kimling and Jarvik (1963), who have summarized the results of a number of investigations of the correlation between IQ and degree of genetic relationship, suggest that intelligence is influenced by both genetic and environmental factors. For example, although identical twins have IQs that are more highly correlated ($r = .80$)

than fraternal twins ($r = .60$), the correlation for the identical twins is higher than that for siblings ($r = .50$), and, according to genetic theory, it should not be. (Statistical correlations are explained in the Appendix.) Similarly, the correlation between foster-parent and foster-child IQ scores is approximately .20, when, according to the theory, it should be zero. Hence, these data suggest IQ is influenced not only by genetic factors but also by environmental factors.

Contemporary approaches of this type are much more sophisticated (cf. Hay & O'Brien, 1983; Scarr & Weinberg, 1976, 1977, 1978, 1983; Scarr, Webber, Weinberg, & Wittig, 1981). The extensive research of Scarr and her colleagues has utilized the adoption model to assess the impact of environment on intellective functioning and personality development. Because adopted children are genetically different from each other and from their adoptive parents, in a group of adopted children, differences between children should reflect differences between their families, that is, should reflect environmental influences on development. Studying the development of adopted children, then, allows the assessment of en-

The degree to which intelligence is genetically or environmentally determined is an open issue.

vironmental impacts without the contaminating influences of genetics.

In one of the studies, Scarr and her colleagues (Grotevant, Scarr, & Weinberg, 1977; Scarr, Webber, Weinberg & Wittig, 1981) used the adoption approach to study environmental effects on adolescents' IQs, school achievements, personalities, and interests. Comparably designed research with children showed similarities between adopted children's IQs and those of their adoptive parents, and between adopted children's IQs and those of their siblings in the adoptive family (Scarr & Weinberg, 1983). The purpose of the adolescent adoption study was to determine if these similarities, indicating a relatively important influence of environment, continued through the adolescent years.

A total of 194 adolescents and young adults (age range 16–22) composed the adoptive sample; all were placed in adoptive families during the first year of life. Unlike the findings for the childhood study, the IQs of the adopted adolescents were not correlated with the IQs of their siblings, with whom they were raised for minimally 18 years. Moreover, the IQs of the adopted adolescents were only very minimally related to the educational level of the adoptive parents but were moderately related to the educational level of their biological parents, this correlation being as high as that between the adoptive parents and their biological children. Similar findings occurred in the domains of vocational interests, personalities, and attitudes. In other words, by the end of adolescence, the similarity between adopted children and their adoptive families had dissipated considerably; the influence of the environment on these measures was attenuated.

Scarr and Weinberg (1978, 1983; see also Scarr & McCartney, 1983) offered the following explanation for these unexpected findings. Adolescents, unlike young children, grow away from the influence of their families and have greater freedom in pur-

suing their own interests, likes, and choices. Hence, as siblings enter and grow through the adolescent years, they become less and less alike, in part because of biological factors. In other words, there is a genotype-environment interaction (Scarr & McCartney, 1983) resulting in biologically unrelated siblings developing differently. The adopted children build a world related to their own genotype. Because the genotype is different from that of their adopted siblings, they come to resemble them less and less. Biologically related siblings, on the other hand, build correlated niches, in part because of their shared genotype.

Although these findings appear to indicate that environment has little, if any, impact on development, Scarr and Weinberg (1983) caution that this is not the case. They point out that studies such as these help define environmental impacts to which various genotypes will respond. By identifying environmental influences that do affect genotypes, we can develop better intervention programs to alleviate deficits in development.

It was research on the deleterious effects of environmental deprivation and the beneficial effects of environmental stimulation that led to nursery school programs such as Head Start. The purpose of Head Start was to facilitate intellectual (IQ) development in children from deprived backgrounds in order to enhance their likelihood of success in the typical school curriculum. Other benefits, such as better ability to listen to and follow directions, also were stressed. Some benefits were found. Evidence on the effects of preschool programs for adolescent academic performance is just beginning to be published (see Box 4–1). The results of these follow-up studies indicate some benefits of the programs for the adolescent years.

What may we conclude with respect to the nature/nurture issue and intelligence, then? Obviously, there is no simple set of conclusions because the issues are very complex. The work of the developmental behavioral

BOX 4–1   **The Effects of Preschool Experiences on Preadolescents and Adolescents**

During the 1950s and 1960s, a number of preschool programs aimed at helping children from low income families become better prepared for school were started. The programs focused on improving IQ, social skills, and skills related to successful academic performance. The programs were of various types (for example, summer oriented, academic year) and children entered at various ages and spent varying amounts of time in the programs. In most instances, control groups composed of children from similar backgrounds, but not enrolled in preschool programs, were tested to allow evaluation of the effectiveness of the program. Although there is some evidence (cf. Miller & Bizzell, 1983) that programs of various types were differentially effective, it was generally found that, at least initially, children enrolled in the special programs fared better in school than control group children (e.g., Lazar & Darlington, 1982). In addition, the improvement in IQ experienced by the children in the program tended to last for several years.

An interesting set of questions concerns longterm effects of the preschool experience on these children from poverty backgrounds. Researchers have now investigated the effects of preschool experiences on preadolescents and adolescents (e.g., Lazar & Darlington, 1982). Lazar and Darlington (1982) report analyses based on subjects from 11 different preschool programs encompassing students still in school and students who have completed high school.

Some of the findings are of general interest. Students from the preschool programs were much less likely to be recommended for special class placement than control students (13.8 percent vs. 28.6 percent). They also were less likely to be retained in a grade level (25.4 percent vs. 44.1 percent). In other words, these children were better able to profit from school experiences and meet school demands than children from low income backgrounds who did not have the preschool experiences. This was evidenced in reading and mathematics achievement test scores through grade 6, with the preschool students having somewhat higher scores than the control students. Indeed, some researchers (Schweinhart & Weikart, 1978) have reported that preschool students outperformed control students on standardized achievement tests through the eighth grade.

Some of the results reported by Lazar and Darlington (1982) are particularly pertinent to issues in adolescent development. Although both preadolescent and adolescent preschool students expressed more positive achievement attitudes toward themselves than control children, the effect was significant only for the preadolescents (ages 9–13). Adolescent (ages 15–19), but not preadolescent, preschool students had a more positive view of their school performance than control students. Finally, the mothers of the preschool students had higher vocational aspirations for their children than did the mothers of the control students.

These results are particularly impressive when it is realized that the preschool experience was relatively short (a year or two) and occurred some time in the past. Apparently, the preschool experiences aided the children's development of self-confidence as well as their school performance. In addition, doing better in school will build self-esteem and likely lead to better achievement attitudes. These long-term effects of preschool intervention demonstrate that the programs influence important aspects of development during the adolescent years.

geneticists, however, suggests that the important question is not *how much* genetics and environment contribute to intelligence but rather *how* each contributes to intellectual development (Scarr & Weinberg, 1983; Scarr & McCartney, 1983), because it is clear that each does. Accepting the proposition that both heredity and environment are important, then, leads to questions of how to structure environments to best suit various genotypes and promote optimal development.

IQ AND ADOLESCENT DEVELOPMENT

We have now discussed several points related to the development of the IQ test as well as data concerning the nature of IQ test performance. It is now time to ask ourselves what these data can tell us about adolescent intellectual development.

IQ and School Performance

Most professional psychologists today would probably agree that the most valuable aspect of the intelligence test is its usefulness as a predictor of certain aspects of performance in school. This should not be surprising, because the intelligence test was devised to do just exactly that. Bond (1940) investigated the relationship between school performance and IQ test performance in a group of adolescent tenth graders. He reported that IQ correlated .73 with reading comprehension, .59 with English usage and with history, .54 with biology, .48 with geometry, and .43 with reading speed. Clearly, the IQ teset is a moderately good predictor of how well adolescents will do in school— partly because it was designed to do so and partly because the skills, knowledge, and motives that are necessary to do well on an IQ test are those that are also necessary to do well in school. We can use the IQ score, then, as a diagnostic tool to help determine the adolescent's ability to deal with the school curriculum (cf., Sattler, 1982).

IQ Changes during Development

As you might guess from some of our introductory comments, the IQ score does not remain stable throughout the individual's developmental history; it changes, although not necessarily in predictable ways. There are considerable data on changes in IQ, for both groups and individuals. These two kinds of data answer different questions about IQ test performance as it relates to development, and we shall review them separately.

IQ Change in Individuals. Since many people assume that an IQ score remains con-

stant throughout an individual's life, an IQ assigned to a child on the basis of a test administered in second, third, or fourth grade might be considered a final judgment of that child's intellectual ability, whether or not the individual's competencies change in adolescence or adulthood. Obviously, if intelligence does change as people grow and mature, this is an undesirable error. This is particularly true in light of research (Dusek, 1975) indicating that teachers' judgments about students' abilities carry on into new classrooms and grade levels. One teacher's unfair judgment could prove detrimental to the child's educational future for a number of years.

Dearborn and Rathney (1963) report some very interesting longitudinal data on fluctuations in IQ during the early and mid-adolescent years, ages 8 to 16. Some students who had relatively high IQ scores, one standard deviation above the mean, changed and ended up with scores that were lower, one standard deviation below the mean, than their initial IQs. On the other hand, another group of students who were quite variable initially, stabilized in terms of IQ and ended up with higher scores. Others (Honzick, Macfarlane, & Allen, 1948; Pinneau, 1961) have reported similar data.

The implication of these data is that one should not assume that an IQ score several years old accurately represents the individual's current level of cognitive functioning. Because of the importance that is commonly attached to IQ test scores, it is critical to use only recent scores for diagnostic purposes. There is clearly little stability in IQ test performance during the early to mid-adolescent years.

Group Changes in IQ Scores. One way to examine group changes in IQ test performance is to correlate scores between tests administered at different points in time. Honzick, Macfarlane, and Allen (1948) did exactly this with a large group of children. The IQs of the subjects were determined from 21 months through 18 years of age. The data for ages 6–18 presented in Table 4–2 show a trend toward higher correlations for tests administered in consecutive years than for tests administered two, three, four, or more years apart. The tests administered in childhood correlate moderately well with those given in early adolescence (age 10) but somewhat less well with those given in later adolescence (age 18). Even tests given at age 12 did not correlate very well with those given at age 18. These data, then, support the conclusion that using childhood IQ tests as an estimate of adolescent ability is not a sound practice. Moreover, even though these correlations are on the order of .7 or .8, they are not high enough to preclude marked changes in the IQs of individuals. A correlation of .8 accounts for only 64 percent of the variance in a measure. The data indicate that, as children get older, the IQ score becomes somewhat more stable. However, Bayley (1955) reports data indicating that predictions of adult IQs from adolescent IQs are much more valid than prediction of adult IQs from childhood IQs or adolescent IQs from childhood IQs. As these data demonstrate, then, IQ scores change and are quite variable.

The most extensive study of change in IQ over age was reported by McCall, Appelbaum, and Hogarty (1973). They report longitudinal data from a sample of 80 subjects (38 males and 42 females) tested 17 times between the ages of 2½ and 17. In general, they found that most of the subjects showed change in IQ test performance. However, as may be seen in Figure 4–1, there were several types of changes. The largest group (1) showed a generally slow increase in IQ. Group 2 subjects generally showed a decline in IQ. The trends for the other groups may be seen in Figure 4–1. Hence, although 45 percent of the subjects showed relative stability with slight increases in IQ, the remaining subjects were highly variable.

McCall and others (1973) conducted analyses to determine factors related to the dif-

TABLE 4–2 Correlations between Stanford-Binet IQ Scores Obtained during Childhood and Adolescence

Age	6	7	8	9	10	12	14
7	.82						
8	.77	.83					
9	.80	.82	.91				
10	.71	.77	.88	.90			
12	.74	.71	.85	.90	.87		
14	.67	.73	.85	.87	.85	.92	
18	.61	.71	.70	.76	.70	.76	.73

(Source: Adapted from Honzik, M. P., Macfarlane, J. W., & Allen, L. [1948]. The stability of mental test performance between two and eighteen years. *Journal of Experimental Education, 17,* 304–324.) Reprinted with permission of the Helen Dwight Reid Educational Foundation, 4000 Albermarle St., N.W., Washington, D.C. 20016. Copyright 1948 by DEMBAR Educational Research Services, Inc.

fering types of IQ patterns. They reported that children in groups 2 and 3, both of which showed declines in IQ during the childhood and early adolescent years, had parents who did not attempt to accelerate mature behavior, particularly mental and motor skills related to those tapped by IQ tests. These children also experienced either the most mild (group 2) or most severe (group 3) parental penalties (various forms of punishment).

What does this information on IQ tests tell us about adolescent cognitive development? First, it indicates that the adolescent will reach a peak in intellectual capabilities. These skills will probably not decline through the adulthood years. Certainly, too, the adolescent has capabilities which the younger child does not have. Intellectual competence, as measured by absolute skills, is quite different from IQ, which is a relative measure. Third, intelligence testing does not produce stable estimates of cognitive abilities. We must be continually aware of the individual's changing intellectual abilities and take that change into account whenever we use an IQ test to make judgments about an adolescent's capabilities.

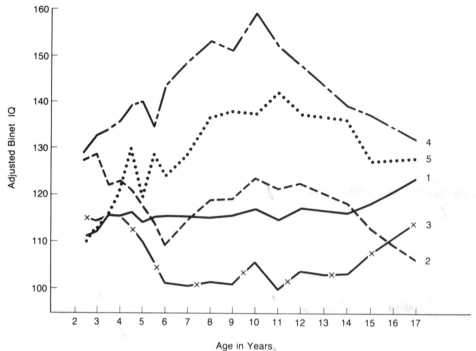

FIGURE 4–1 **Mean IQ (Adjusted for Differences between Binet Revision) over Age for the Five IQ Clusters**
(Source: McCall, R., Applebaum, M. & Hogarty, P. [1973]. Developmental changes in mental performance. *Monographs of the Society for Research in Child Development*, 38 [serial no. 150].)

These data are also very revealing in what they do not tell us. For example, by studying IQ growth and change in adolescence, we learn very little, if anything, of the nature of adolescent thought processes. Rather, we can only get some estimate of the relative standing of the adolescent vis-à-vis the peer group. Furthermore, because of the non-developmental nature of the quantitative model upon which IQ tests are constructed, it is not possible to make meaningful theoretical statements about IQ changes (development) over age. Rather, these changes are assumed to reflect motivational states of the individual or errors of measurement within the test or testing situation. From this approach, then, there is little of interest to study about adolescents from a develop-

mental perspective. As we noted, however, there are differences in the ways that adolescents attack problems, as well as differences in the items composing tests of intelligence over the preschool to adulthood years. Surely, this must mean that there is something of interest in the qualitative aspects of intelligence that might help us understand adolescent intellectual functioning. It is to these qualitative issues that we shall now direct ourselves.

THE QUALITATIVE DEVELOPMENT OF ADOLESCENT INTELLIGENCE

The study of intelligence from a qualitative perspective is based on the notion that the individual continually undergoes transitions

The qualitative approach to intellect is focused on the nature of thought processes and how they change with development.

in development that may be characterized as stages (Reese & Overton, 1970; Overton & Reese, 1973; Pepper, 1942). Further, it is assumed that people change from one stage to another and that these changes are qualitative in nature. Hence, intelligence is conceived as reflecting different qualitative modes of thinking. That is, the manner in which a preadolescent thinks is different from the manner in which an adolescent is capable of thinking. This difference cannot be quantified because it is a change in kind, not amount. Unlike the quantitative perspective, then, differences in intelligence reflect different modes of thinking—as we explain below—and not differences in amount of intellect.

Congruent with these notions is the perspective that intelligence develops in a sequence of stages, each representing a different mode of thinking. The basic emphasis, then, is not on differences in amount of intelligence but on the description of the qualities of the different modes of thinking that occur throughout development. Differences in the modes of thinking result from changes in cognitive structures, and it is these differences that define stages of development (Flavell, 1963, 1977; Kessen, 1970; Wohlwill, 1970).

Several aspects of stage theory are important. First, a stage theory does not imply that behavior develops in a step-by-step fashion. Rather, stage theorists argue that there are important qualitative differences in the behavior of the individual at different stages of development. There is no implication, then, that structures and, hence, behaviors, change abruptly; the use of the stage concept is simply to highlight different aspects of development. Second, age is not a good representation of stage (Kessen, 1970; Wohlwill, 1970). Individuals progress through various stages of development at different rates and, therefore, one might find two individuals of the same chronological age whose competencies reflect different structural development (stages). Finally, stage theory implies that all individuals progress through the same sequence of stages in the same order. In other words, everyone must pass through stage A before stage B and stage B before stage C, and so on.

Piaget's (1952) theory of intellectual development is an example of a qualitative view of intellectual development. Within this model, intelligence is seen as developing in sequential stages.

Piaget's Theory of Cognitive Development

There are three major theoretical concepts in Piaget's theory of cognitive development (Flavell, 1963). One is *content*, by which Piaget means behavior, either as action or as verbal explanation of thought processes. The second is *structure*, which is simply a set of cognitive operations for behaving in certain ways. Finally, there is *function*, which refers to adaptation and organization, the broad characteristics of intelligence that are the essence of intelligent behavior. Adaptation consists of two components: assimilation and accommodation. *Assimilation* is the cognitive structuring of environmental information and the incorporation of this information into existing

According to Piaget, regardless of age, we all function intellectually through the same mechanisms.

cognitive structures themselves. *Accommodation* is the change in, or adjustment made by, cognitive structures to receive this new incoming information. *Organization* means that every intelligent act occurs within the child's existing cognitive competencies.

As you can see in Table 4–3, functions produce structures which in turn result in content—specific kinds of behavior on the part of the individual (Flavell, 1963). Function refers to the broad aspects of intelligence that are the same for all people and remain constant across the life span. Hence, in Piaget's theory, infants, children, adolescents, and adults all function intellectually in the same way; that is, the intellect operates on environmental information (stimulation)

using the processes of assimilation and accommodation described above. Assimilation and accommodation work together. In order for assimilation of environmental information to occur, the cognitive structures must accommodate. Accommodation, in turn, allows for further assimilation. Accommodatory acts are continually being extended to new and different features of the environment. These newly accommodated-to events are then assimilated into the cognitive structures of the organism, thereby changing those structures to some degree and making further accommodatory acts possible. Finally, function is organized. By this, Piaget means that every assimilation-accommodation act assumes some kind of

TABLE 4–3 **Basic Concepts in Piaget's Theory of Intellectual Development**

Concepts	*Components*
Function	... Organization

|
produces
  |
	Adaptation
	   assimilation
	   accommodation
	   (age invariant)

Structures
  |
resulting
in
  |
	... Cognitive rules. They change with level of development; the structures themselves (and thereby the individual's level of development) are revealed by the content (behavior) they produce.

Content	... Overt or covert (thinking) behavior that reflects structural development. It changes with age.

structure or organization within which it takes place.

Through the assimilation and accommodation mechanisms the individual forms schemas, or cognitive structures (Flavell, 1963). It is to these structures that assimilated information is attached, and it is these structures that must accommodate to incoming information and change as a result of it. A structure has reference to a particular action sequence, or behavior. Cognitive structures are organized sequences of responding and, unlike function, are in continual states of change. These changes define the level of development of the individual. Cognitive development, or progress, is indexed by a change in structures; change occurs as a result of the effects of assimilation and accommodation.

Assimilation and accommodation are prompted by the mechanisms of equilibrium and disequilibrium. **Equilibrium** is a homeostasis between the individual's structures and sensory demands placed on the individual by the environment. If the individual's cognitive structures match environmental demands, a state of equilibrium exists between the individual and the environment. When environmental information does not match the individual's cognitive structures,

as when new problems are encountered, a state of disequilibrium exists. **Disequilibrium**, then, occurs when there is a mismatch between existing structures and environmental stimulation. This disequilibrium initiates the assimilation/accommodation mechanism as the individual tries to assimilate the new information and accommodate existing structures to it. Through the continuous process of equilibrium and disequilibrium, structures are changed and become more complex. This is how cognitive development progresses (Piaget, 1970). Moving from a state of structural disequilibrium to a new and higher state of equilibrium is what Piaget means by cognitive development. Because of the higher state of equilibrium, the individual is able to solve more complex problems, view experiences in new and different ways, advance higher order generalizations, and the like. In other words, the individual is more cognitively sophisticated.

By observing the behavior of individuals, we can determine what structures they are using, and thereby their level (stage) of cognitive functioning (see Box 4–2). Hence, behavior plays an important explanatory role in Piaget's theory.

Piaget has identified four stages of cognitive development: *sensorimotor* (birth to two

BOX 4–2 **Does Cognition Develop in Stages?**

Recently, theoreticians have begun to ask the question that is the title to this box (cf. Brainerd, 1978; Flavell, 1982). Flavell (1982), in his Presidential Address to the Society for Research in Child Development, framed the question in terms of the homogeneity versus heterogeneity of the mind. According to Flavell, a heterogeneous mind is one that is characterized by variability in complexity across situations. A homogeneous mind evidences similar complexity across situations; in Flavell's terms, it has a distinctive way of functioning regardless of the cognitive demands of various situations. To the extent the mind is relatively homogeneous, it is likely that it develops in a stagelike manner. To the extent it is heterogeneous, it is likely that it does not develop in a stagelike way (Flavell, 1982).

Heterogeneity of the mind could result from species-specific heredity, person-specific heredity, and person-specific environmental factors (Flavell, 1982). Species-specific hereditary influences reflect the evolution of the human species, particularly with regard to the functioning of the central nervous system. Some mental skills may emerge prior to others because of genetic programming. Person-specific hereditary factors are evidenced in differing abilities and aptitudes—mathematical and verbal, for example—that vary across persons. Some of us do better on one type of problem than on the other, giving the appearance of a heterogeneous mind. Finally, person-specific environmental factors are evidenced in educational and cultural experiences. The greater and more appropriate our experiences are for certain types of problems, the better we will do at them, as opposed to other problems for which we may have limited experiences on which to draw. Again, we would see evidence of heterogeneity in the mind. Flavell suggests the example of a child with high ability in computer-related areas, who has high interest in computers, and who has a parent who encourages this and is a computer scientist. The child's performance in computer work will likely exceed the child's performance in other areas of mental life. In other words, the child's mind is best conceptualized as heterogeneous—all areas of mental life do not evidence similar levels of development.

Homogeneity in mental life may result from limited mental capabilities at various ages. Flavell suggests, for example, that limited information processing capability may make the mind look similar across situational demands because the child can only hold so much information in the mind at one time. Homogeneity would also be evidenced by examining our approach to problem solving, for example. We tend to develop ways of dealing with various types of problems that are similar across situations. For example, consider the way you begin to study for a test in psychology, sociology, religion, or other college courses that are "reading" courses. Indeed, there are even similarities across domains. This general approach will harken to a homogeneous mind. Finally, Flavell (1982) suggests that for still unknown reasons, some children may develop in a more homogeneous manner than other children.

At present, we cannot determine if the mind is best viewed as homogeneous or heterogeneous. Indeed, Flavell suggests it may be a bit of both. In this instance, we may see a merging of the psychometric and cognitive approaches to the nature of intelligence. If this turns out to be the case, it will simply be a further demonstration that intelligence develops both qualitatively and quantitatively.

years), *preoperational* (2–7 years), *concrete operational* (7–11 years), and *formal operational* (11 and up). Although these age norms are only rough indicators of developmental level, it is clear that the periods of concrete and formal operational thinking are the ones that span the adolescent years of development. In the following paragraphs, we will discuss the earlier stages briefly, and the concrete and formal operational stages in depth.

Sensorimotor and Preoperational Thinking. To gain a firm and clear understanding of adolescent cognitive processes as described by Piaget, it will be helpful to review briefly the thinking processes of the infant and the child. The nonoperational (illogical) thinking of the infant and child provides an informative contrast to the adolescent's more advanced thought processes.

The basis of all intellectual behavior lies in sensorimotor intelligence. Sensorimotor development occurs from birth to about age 2. The infant lacks symbolic functions; a very young baby does not have the capability to make internal representations and, therefore, cannot evoke images of people or objects that are absent. This ability develops slowly during the sensorimotor period. Thinking initially is in terms of simple and then increasingly complex action-structures. The infant displays a relatively continuous movement from actions based on reflexive behavior to habits (of action) to intelligent behavior such as that exhibited by movements causing desired effects; for example, kicking a crib to make a mobile shake. Coordination of arms, legs, hands, eyes, mouth, and so forth, reflect sensorimotor assimilation as the infant builds increasingly complex sensorimotor cognitive structures. The infant's thought processes are action-oriented and egocentric; they are based on his own body and actions. As the infant slowly comes to recognize that he is simply an object among other objects, the egocentric nature of sensorimotor intelligence dissipates somewhat. Sensorimotor intelligence, then, organzies actions in terms of objects, space, time, and causality. However, this form of **cognition** is very much tied to the here and now, to immediately present objects and actions. As the infant slowly *decenters*, for example, comes to realize objects exist apart from his actions on them, a more firm grasp of the reality of the world is gained. In turn, his thought processes slowly develop representational capabilities.

During the preoperational period, two important developments occur. In the *preconceptional* substage (roughly ages 2 to 4),

the child acquires the ability to symbolize the external environment by means of internal "signifiers." The rapid development of language during this time is both a result of this symbolization ability as well as a contributor to it.

The *intuitive* substage (roughly ages 4 to 7 years) is so named because, although the child begins to use mental "operations," the principle behind the operations escapes the child. For example, the child may be capable of classifying objects but may not understand the principles underlying the classification.

Irreversibility is another characteristic of preoperational thought. The numerous experiments on conservation of matter, size, and shape illustrate this thought process. A 6-year-old who observes two balls of clay that are the same size will say there is the same amount of clay in them. If one is subsequently rolled into the shape of a hot dog, while the child is watching, the child will insist that one (the ball) has more clay in it than the other (the hot dog) because it is "fatter." In other words, the child's intellectual functioning is still perceptually bound. The child cannot refute the perceptual evidence with a mental operation, reversing the transformation on the clay, and see that the amount of clay has remained the same (conservation).

As we have briefly outlined, the young child's thought processes tend to be egocentric, bound up in the child's own actions and tied to the child's own point of view. In addition, they are limited somewhat by perception and hence are largely nonoperational.

Operational Thinking. **Operational thinking,** the use of logical thought processes, begins to emerge when the child is 7 to 8 years old. It is epitomized by an integrated cognitive system by which the individual organizes and cognitively manipulates the world around him. There are two stages of operational thinking: concrete and formal. The former covers the later childhood and pre-adolescent years and the latter the adolescent years.

During the *concrete operational period* (roughly ages 7 to 11) the child develops logical operations, that is logical thought processes, that can be applied to concrete problems. **Concrete**, here, refers to problems that are tied to reality, to the way things are, and to things that exist. The major limitation of concrete thinking is the inability of the individual to think in the abstract, or to think about the possible as well as the real. Because concrete thinking is logical (operational), it is not perceptually bound. When faced with a conservation problem, such as the two balls of clay problem, the concrete operational child denies the perceptual distortion by considering both length and height, and concludes that there is the same amount of clay in each shape because none was added and none was taken away. The operational child, then, makes logical conclusions based on cognitive operations as opposed to illogical conclusions based on perception.

Although children's thinking makes significant advances during the concrete operational period, advances that will be important throughout life, their thinking is still more limited than that of formal operational children. Concrete thought is, in effect, attached to reality; that is, it is attached to what exists as opposed to what is possible. The concrete operational child is stuck with the reality of the here and now as personally experienced and has difficulty dealing with hypothetical situations. Extending the solution of a problem to new and similar problems that have not been encountered is still relatively difficult. Finally, as Elkind (1968) has pointed out, the concrete operational child has difficulty dealing with problems with more than two dimensions. The operational system is simply not developed sufficiently to deal with problems that have many possible solutions or combinations of solutions. Thinking in the abstract, and being able to think of hypothetical situations with multiple solutions or multiple dimensions, is not a characteristic of concrete operational thinking.

It is in the area of *formal operational thinking* (ages 11 and up) that Piaget has most directly addressed the adolescent period of development. A major theme in Piaget's thinking is that the adolescent is capable of imagining the many possibilities inherent in a particular situation. The adolescent is not bound by the here and now, but is able to compensate mentally for transformations in reality and to develop the capability of dealing with abstract problem-solving situations. Elkind (1967a), in his summary of Inhelder and Piaget's (1958; Piaget & Inhelder, 1969) discussion of the critical features of the cognitive structures of adolescence, makes the following points. First, the adolescent uses combinatorial logic, dealing with many factors at the same time. Second, the adolescent uses a second symbol system (that is, symbols for symbols), which makes his or her thought much more flexible than that of younger adolescents or children. Third, the adolescent can deal with contrary-to-fact situations. In other words, the formal operational adolescent can deal with the possible as well as the real. Because it has important consequences for understanding adolescent behavior and personality development, we explore formal operational thinking in some depth. (See Box 4–3.)

Formal Operations and Adolescent Thinking

The period of **formal operations** is characterized by the ability to use both abstract and concrete thinking skills (Inhelder & Piaget, 1958). From ages 11 to 15 (early formal operations) abstract thinking still is cumbersome. Later, the difficulty is overcome as the adolescent becomes more facile with abstract thinking. Older adolescents can formulate complex and logical theories of social, political, and moral philosophy. They are able to

BOX 4–3   **The Universality of Formal Operational Thinking**

A general tendency is to conceive of formal operational thinking as being universal. That is, it is usually taken as a given that, during the early to middle adolescent years, all adolescents become facile with formal operational thinking.

Evidence bearing on this view suggests this is not the case (Keating, 1980; Neimark, 1975; Piaget, 1972). Researchers using the tasks devised by Inhelder and Piaget (1958) to assess formal operational thinking have reported that, on the average, only between 40 percent and 60 percent of college students and adults demonstrate successful performance (see Keating [1980] and Neimark [1975] for reviews). This evidence led Piaget (1972) to suggest that perhaps all people reached formal operations, but not at the same age. He also suggested that the influences of the social environment might affect rate of acquisition of formal operations. Finally, he suggested, as another alternative explanation for these findings, that specific abilities, aptitudes, and interests may determine how, or even if, we demonstrate formal operational competencies.

Dulit (1972) has proposed a branch model of cognitive development in which the first three stages proposed by Piaget's model are relatively universal and are affected only in a limited manner by cultural and educational influences. During adolescence, the individual may go on to develop strong formal operational problem-solving skills, which Dulit considers an optimal direction for growth, or the individual may develop problem-solving skills of different types, which he terms Standard and Inspirational. The former skills work well in coping with everyday situations but are less suited to solving novel problems. The latter reflect solving problems by intuitive leaps in logic. As Berzonsky (1978) has noted, this model allows for individual variation in adolescents' demonstration of formal operational skills and explains how cultural and educational experiences influence cognitive development. Formal operational thinking skills, then, may be much more affected by interests, aptitudes, and specific learning experiences and, hence, may not be demonstrated by everyone (Piaget, 1972; Dulit, 1972).

At first blush, the findings noted above might appear to invalidate or attenuate the importance of Piaget's theory. This is not the case, however. First, the stage characteristic of the theory is not disputed. And, formal operations still is considered to follow the other three stages. Second, there is no doubt that a stage of formal operations exists, even if as only one among several alternatives. Finally, Dulit's theorizing simply expands Piaget's theorizing, allowing for greater explanatory power because of the emphasis on individual differences. That this is of value cannot be questioned. Hence, as with any theory, new evidence adds strength and makes the theory applicable over a wider range of behavior.

conceptualize the possible as well as the real, that is, they can think about what *may be* as well as what *is* (Piaget, 1980; Keating, 1980; Neimark, 1975).

Formal operations allow the adolescent to combine propositions in order to confirm or disprove hypotheses through the isolation of the variables that cause some event. This form of thinking is *hypothetico-deductive* and is very much like the kind of thinking employed in science. It might be helpful at this point to describe an experiment illustrating this form of cognition.

The experiment we will use as an example was designed to allow the adolescent to dis-cover the factor(s) that affect the oscillation of a pendulum (Inhelder & Piaget, 1958). A pendulum was constructed by hanging an object on a string. The subject was shown how to change the length of the string, the weight of the object, and how to release the object from different heights with different degrees of force. The subject was asked to discover which of the four factors or combinations of them affected the rate of oscillation of the pendulum. The subject was then allowed to experiment with the materials in any way that was desired. Of course, Piaget was not particularly interested in whether or not the subject obtained the correct answer, but rather in the cognitive processes the subject used in solving the problem. These processes were inferred by observing the subject's behavior as he carried out the experiment.

The behavior of the preoperational child in the pendulum task is extremely haphazard and ineffectual. There is no real overall plan or pattern to the manipulations the child performs while trying to discover the factor(s) that cause the pendulum to swing more quickly. For example, some children try to determine if weight is a factor by using a long string with a heavy weight and a short string with a light weight. This procedure cannot tell anything of the role of either variable because both are being varied simultaneously. Moreover, children do not always report the results of their "experiments" accurately, perhaps because their expectations influence their observations and cause them to report what they expect rather than what they observe. As you might expect on the basis of such procedures and reporting, the preoperational child rarely comes to the correct conclusion that it is the length of the string that makes the difference. The child's inability to devise appropriate experiments and to observe and report the results accurately and objectively, as well as his inability to think logically about the results, precludes obtaining the correct solution.

The performance of the concrete operational child is considerably more accurate and reflects a much higher level of intellectual ability than that of the preoperational child. A number of concrete operational children can observe and report the results of this experiment. In fact, some even come up with the correct answer. However, most concrete operational children do not design the procedures of their "experiments" in such a way as to come to the correct conclusion. As with the preoperational child, varying both the length and weight of the string at the same time is quite common. The correct procedure, of course, is to vary only one of the two while keeping the other constant.

Only in that way is it possible to determine whether the variable being manipulated exerts any effect on the oscillation of the pendulum. The concrete operational child may also have difficulty drawing conclusions from the results that are observed, even though the results are correctly observed and reported. For example, Inhelder and Piaget (1958) report that one subject observed that a short but heavy pendulum swung more rapidly than a light but long one, and concluded that both length and weight were determining factors in the oscillation of the pendulum. Obviously, this is an incorrect conclusion, and it is incorrect partly because it is based on an incorrect procedure. Nevertheless, the logic the child used to arrive at the conclusion was consistent with what he observed.

The behavior of the formal operational adolescent is qualitatively quite different from the behavior of children in earlier stages of cognitive development or from concrete operational adolescents. For example, the "experiments" are adequately designed, the results accurately observed, and proper logical conclusions drawn from the observations. The formal operational adolescent is aware immediately that there are several possible determinants of the frequency of oscillation of the pendulum. The youngster realizes, furthermore, that any one of, or combination of, them may well be critical to determining the frequency. This type of realization is what Piaget refers to when he says that formal operations allow the imagining of purely hypothetical results. Before engaging in any experimentation, the adolescent is capable of conceiving all possible outcomes of the experiment. In fact, this individual may later go on to test for all possible outcomes in order to determine which factor or combination of factors affect the oscillation of the pendulum. An example might be testing a long string with light and heavy weights and testing a short string with the same light and heavy weights. In this way it is possible to see if string length makes a difference, if weight makes a difference, or if some combination of the two is the determinant. In other words, the adolescent begins with a hypothetical set of determinants, conducts experiments that are designed to test the hypotheses, and is capable of accurately observing, reporting, and drawing conclusions from the results of the experiments. Since the experiments are well conceived, the results accurately observed, and appropriate logical thinking applied to them, the adolescent is able to come to the correct conclusion on the basis of the data.

This behavior on the part of the adolescent demonstrates the hypothetico-deductive (if-then) nature of formal operational thinking. The adolescent is able to test hypotheses much as a scientist does. By experimenting with each of several potential influences, the adolescent is able to discover that the length of the string is the important variable: *if* the short string is used and the swing is fast, *then* a long string will swing more slowly.

The analysis of this example demonstrates the logical-thinking capabilities of the adolescent. To explain this process, Piaget (see Elkind, 1968; Flavell, 1963; Inhelder & Piaget, 1958) relies on concepts from formal logic theory. That is, Piaget attempts to explain the nature of adolescent thinking through explanations grounded in the tenets of logic theory. Hence, he invokes the concepts of conjunction, disjunction, identity, and the like to build a model to describe how formal operational thinking may be conceived. This model captures the essence of the adolescent's thought and the ways in which it differs from that of the concrete operational or preoperational child.

It does not necessarily describe the adolescent's performance, because many factors other than cognitive factors may be involved in the adolescent's actual performance on any given problem-solving task. Fatigue and boredom, for example, may cause the adolescent's performance to deteriorate. Competence, however, remains the same. Performance, then, is only an imperfect reflection of competence.

What, then, have we learned about adolescent thought processes from the foregoing discussion? First, we know that the adolescent is capable of dealing with the possible as well as the real. In fact, the real is only one particular instance of the possible. Consider, for example, the pendulum problem. The adolescent may correctly determine that short pendulums swing more quickly than long ones, but then may go on to test whether or not other factors are involved. The adolescent is capable of imagining that many factors might influence the swinging of the pendulum and that several interpretations of the data might be feasible; only after testing all these possibilities will he come to the conclusion that only length of the pendulum makes a difference. As we noted before, the adolescent's thought processes are hypothetico-deductive.

Observation of adolescent thinking also reveals that the structures of formal operational thinking can be applied to a variety of novel situations because they are content-free thinking structures. This makes the adolescent's thought processes extremely flexible, much more so than those of the concrete operational or preoperational child. Because adolescents can conceive of a number of possible alternatives to a problem before investigating the situation, they are less likely to be surprised or confused by outcomes that are unusual. The younger child is not capable of doing this, and, in fact, may not understand that certain unexpected or unusual occurrences might adequately represent reality. Recall the problems that the concrete operational and the preoperational child have in accurately observing, reporting, and drawing conclusions from results of experiments on the pendulum.

We must stress again that adolescent thought processes are *qualitatively* different from those of younger children. Indeed, they are extremely powerful ways of dealing with information coming from the environment. They are better because they can be applied successfully to a greater variety of problems than can the thought processes of the concrete or preoperational child. It is not surprising, then, that Piaget and others have attempted to relate formal operational thinking to other behavioral domains of adolescence. It is these relationships that we shall explore next.

Implications of Piaget's Theory for Adolescent Development

Piaget's theory of cognitive development has a number of implications for understanding adolescent development. In subsequent chapters, we shall look at the contributions of cognition to social, affective, and educational development. In the following paragraphs, we briefly highlight those contributions in order to stress the importance of the impact of Piaget's theory in all aspects of adolescent development.

Moral Development. Although Piaget (1932) has discussed and researched the role of cognition in adolescent moral development, Kohlberg's (1963a, 1969, 1976) theorizing has advanced our understanding of the relation of cognition to moral thinking to a greater degree. Kohlberg has formulated a stage theory of moral development that is related to and parallels the levels of cognition defined by Piaget. Since we shall discuss moral development in detail in a later chapter, it is sufficient to note here that Kohlberg believes that as cognitive competencies increase, the individual's capability for understanding increasingly complex and subtle moral issues also increases. The highest levels of moral thinking are reached when the individual becomes capable of formal operational thinking. In all likelihood, this is a result of the adolescent's newly found abilities to reason about various alternatives in problem-solving situations. The

content-free, formal operational structures and the logical abstract thinking processes reflected in them are applied to moral situations and result in increasing capabilities to deal with intricate moral issues.

Relations with Parents. Elkind (1967a, 1967b, 1968, 1970) notes that, by understanding the dynamics of formal operational thinking, we may gain insight into a number of adolescent social behaviors, including parent-child conflict. For example, the adolescent's ability to formulate hypotheses makes it possible for him to respond to parental demands with a list of possible alternatives. The rebelliousness of adolescence is due, in part, then, to an awareness of the difference between the possible and the real. Because adolescents often perceive a gap between the "ideal" and the real world, they may come to feel parents are hypocrites—professing one set of ideals and living by another.

As the adolescent enters the job market and joins the adult world with its various roles and responsiblities, the relatively pure cognitive approach to understanding society is replaced by a more realistic perspective. The adolescent then seems to work for improvement in the social order in a more effective and less militant way. The result is a more positive stance toward society and adults in general, and parents in particular (Elkind, 1967a, 1968). More than one individual has observed that as he grew older (and out of adolescence) his parents grew smarter.

Self-Concept and Identity. Current theorizing suggests a link between self-concept and identity development and cognition (cf. Dusek, Carter, & Levy, 1986; Damon & Hart, 1982; Brim, 1975, Epstein, 1973). For example, adolescent self-descriptions are more abstract than children's (e.g., Montemayor & Eisen, 1977; Guardo & Bohan, 1971; Emmerich, 1974), which seems to reflect the adolescent's emerging formal operational competence (Koocher, 1974).

Moreover, adolescents tend to use more personality traits in describing the self than do children (Mohr, 1978). During adolescence, then, conceptualizations of the self take a new turn as adolescents become capable of answering the "Who am I?" question in more substantive ways than do children. This change, no doubt, is related to the change from concrete to formal operational competence.

Egocentrism. Adolescents are not only capable of thinking about their own thoughts, but also of conceptualizing the thoughts of others. According to Elkind (1967b, 1978a, 1978b), it is this latter ability that is the foundation of adolescent **egocentrism**. The difficulty lies in the adolescent's inability to separate his or her own thoughts—and the events to which they are directed—from the thoughts of others. Since the adolescent is absorbed with thoughts about the self, he or she feels others must be too.

One consequence of this egocentrism is that adolescents feel they are "on stage," playing to an *imaginary audience*, with attention being continually focused on them. It is an imaginary audience because seldom is the adolescent's perception veridical. Because the adolescent feels on stage, and

therefore important, he begins to view his own thoughts and feelings as special and unique. This tendency Elkind(1967b, 1978a, 1978b) terms the *personal fable*. The imaginary audience, then, arises from a failure to differentiate objective and subjective aspects of reality, and the personal fable arises from the failure to differentiate the universal and particular aspects of reality (Elkind, 1978a). The imaginary audience leads adolescents to believe they are the center of everyone's thoughts and concerns; the personal fable leads adolescents to believe their thoughts and feelings are entirely unique, that no one has ever thought or felt as they do.

To date, Elkind's research (1967b; Elkind & Bowen, 1979) and that of others (for example, Enright, Lapsley, & Shukla, 1979; Enright & Sutterfield, 1980) has centered on the imaginary audience aspect of adolescent egocentrism. Elkind and Bowen (1979) developed the Imaginary Audience Scale (IAS) to measure this aspect of adolescent egocentrism. The scale assesses willingness to reveal relatively permanent aspects of the self (personality characteristics, for example), which Elkind and Bowen term the *abiding self*, and the momentary, nonpermanent aspects of the self (a poor haircut, for example), which they call *transient self* charac-

Egocentrism leads adolescents to believe everyone is as interested in their thoughts and feelings as they are.

teristics. They hypothesized that one effect of the imaginary audience would be to increase the adolescent's feelings of self-consciousness (high scores on the IAS) because of the tendency to view the self as being on stage.

Consistent with predictions, scores on the Imaginary Audience Scale increased from fourth, to sixth, to eighth grade and declined by twelfth grade. Females had higher scores than males, and scores were higher for the abiding self scale than for the transient self scale. Similar findings were reported by Enright and his colleagues (Enright et al., 1979; Enright & Sutterfield, 1980).

The developmental trend reported by Elkind and Bowen is interesting because it matches the general developmental trend in adolescent conformity to peers. It may be that adolescents conform in order not to stick out, that is, not to reveal the self. As the self-concept and identity become more firm and developed, and with continued peer interaction (Piaget, 1968) that helps the adolescent decenter (become less self-focused), egocentrism declines, which may result in the lower conformity to peers that occurs during the later high school years.

In this brief discussion of the relationship between formal operational thinking and adolescent development, we have tried to highlight how cognitive structures relate to the behavioral characteristics of adolescence. The abstract logical thinking processes encountered during adolescence allow the adolescent to understand the world, and events in the world, in new and different ways—ways not previously considered. In a sense, adolescence is when we first become capable of understanding that there are few, if any, absolutes in the political, social, and personal worlds in which we live. In part because of these new ways of viewing their experiences, adolescents begin to question political systems and social systems, the manner in which they are reared by their parents (which may contribute to some disagreements between adolescent and parent), and views of the self.

In a sense, cognitive developments contribute to independence strivings because they allow the adolescent to realize that his or her views *may* be as "correct" as the views of others.

SOCIAL COGNITION

The material reviewed earlier, particularly that dealing with moral development and the understanding of the social order, and that concerning egocentrism, suggests that cognitive processes play an important role in social behavior and understanding. The study of how the person comes to know, understand, and conceptualize the social world, and particularly other people, is termed **social cognition** (Shantz, 1975; Sherman, Judd, & Park, 1989). Hence, those interested in social cognition study how people perceive others, including their inner psychological states, and how they view the self in relation to others.

In general, research on social cognition involves the study of role taking, including studies on how we conceptualize what others see, feel, think, intend, and are like (Sherman et al., 1989). Social cognition involves psychological processes such as memory, attention, information processing, and the like (Sherman et al., 1989). As you may well surmise, the field of social cognition is very diverse. To date, very little research on social cognition has been done with adolescents. However, Selman (1976, 1980) has proposed a developmental model of social cognition that is pertinent to our study of adolescent development.

Selman's Model of Social Cognition

Based largely on the theorizing of Piaget concerning cognition and Kohlberg (1969, 1976) concerning moral thinking, Selman (1976, 1980) has proposed a stage theory of social cognition with a particular focus on aspects of role taking (Selman & Byrne,

1974). To assess the stage of role taking, Selman has developed a series of social dilemmas concerning four social domains: individual, friendship, peer group, and parent-child. After reading the dilemma, the subject answers a series of structured and less structured questions aimed at assessing understanding of the social domain. For example, in the area of friendships, the respondents answer questions aimed at assessing their conceptualizations of how and why friendships are formed, intimacy in friendships, reciprocity between friends, jealousy in friendships, resolving conflicts with friends, and how and why friendships break up. In the individual realm, issues assessed include understanding of the private (for example, thoughts) aspects of others, ability to comprehend the self, personality traits, and how people change. Issues assessed in the peer group realm are how and why groups form, group cohesion, conformity to the group, understanding of group norms, working within a group, the functions of the group leader, and why groups disband. In the parent-child relations area, issues addressed are why parents have children, emotional bonds between parent and child, obedience to the parents, the child's and parent's views of punishment, and conflict resolution between parent and child.

Selman (1976) has emphasized the structural aspects of the responses to the social dilemmas as opposed to their content. Content refers to the amount of social knowledge the child has acquired. Structure refers to the child's differentiation of the self from others and the child's ability to coordinate the self-perspective and the perspectives of others. Selman's analysis of responses to the dilemmas, then, allows him to determine the degree of social understanding (as opposed to knowledge) the child has acquired. It is this structural aspect of social cognition that defines the stage of development the child has achieved. Selman (1980) has identified five stages in the development of role taking.

The first stage is labeled *Egocentric Undifferentiated* (ages 3–4 to 6) because the child is unable to distinguish a personal perspective from another's point of view. Moreover, the child cannot comprehend that the personal perspective might be incorrect. Although children in this stage may well know that others have a different perspective of a social situation, they do not have the skills necessary to derive the other's possible perspective. The second stage, *Subjective Perspective Taking* (ages 6–9), is characterized by the ability to understand that the self and others may have different perspectives of a social situation, and that this may result in their thinking and feeling differently. However, the child still cannot view his or her own behavior from the perspective of others. Importantly, the child at this stage understands intentionality and realizes that others have their own unique psychological perspectives. Moreover, the child can infer others' thoughts and feelings to a degree. We see in this stage, then, the beginnings of social perspective taking. It is in the third stage, *Reciprocal Perspective Taking* (ages 8–9 to 12), that children become capable of making inferences about the perspectives of others, and come to realize how others may view them and their behavior. The preadolescent can relatively accurately take the perspective of others. But the preadolescent cannot take a more generalized (global) perspective of the self and others at the same time. The perspective taking in this stage is sequential—own view, other's view, et cetera.

The early adolescent is in the fourth stage, *Mutual Role Taking* (ages 10–11 to 15). These individuals can "step out of the situation" and take a wholistic perspective of a social situation, a perspective such as might be taken by a third party. The early adolescent, then, can coordinate his or her own perspective, and that of others. Hence, early adolescents can understand the mutual nature of social relationships. The early adolescent is able to take a neutral, objective perspective on social interactions, while at the same time being able to consider the

Social cognition involves understanding the various roles we all play.

self's perspective and that of the other person.

The final stage, characteristic of later adolescence and adulthood, is called *In-Depth and Societal Perspective Taking*. In this stage, the individual comes to understand the shared social system perspective of social situations. The social system perspective is understood to reflect group consensus, a consensus derived from many possible multiple mutual perpsectives. As a result, the adolescent and adult understand that there are many levels of social perspectives, and that one's psychological characteristics determine, in part, one's perspective. This stage of social role taking requires advanced formal operational thinking and may not be reached by all adolescents or adults because, as noted above, not all adolescents or adults reach the required level of formal operational thinking.

We see in Selman's theory the emergence of social understanding. It is during adolescence that the complexities of social understanding become expressed. An example taken from Selman's (1980) research will help clarify the development of social role taking. Consider the child's understanding of punishment by the parent. In the first stage, children know that punishment follows a misbehavior, but they cannot infer their parent's motives for punishing. In the second stage, children understand that parents punish to teach the child what is wrong and at times to protect the child ("Don't touch the hot stove!"). In other words, the child does infer motives for punishment. During the third stage, the preadolescent comes to realize that punishment at times instills fear (anxiety), which, when internalized, controls behavior. Preadolescents also realize that punishment is a form of communicating the parent's concern for the preadolescent's well-being. Adolescents, in the fourth stage, begin to view punishment as only one way, and probably not the best for them, of controlling behavior. But they also understand that parents have needs and personalities that must be expressed, and that punishment may serve such a need. Finally, during the last stage, the adolescent realizes that punishment may reflect an unconscious attempt on the part of the parent to psychologically control others.

As the example illustrates, role-taking skills become increasingly flexible. In part, this seems to be related to advances in cognitive development (Selman, 1976, 1980; Byrne, 1974). The scant available evidence indicates that Selman's stages in social perspective taking parallel Piaget's stages of cognitive development, with the last two stages reflecting initial formal operations and well-developed formal operations.

Byrne (1974) reported that some subjects may have reached a specific level of cognitive development but not the corresponding level of role taking. However, it was very unlikely that a particular level of role taking was reached without the corresponding stage of cognitive development being reached. In other words, cognitive devel-

BOX 4–4 **The Social-Cognition View of Adolescent Egocentrism**

An alternative perspective of the causes of adolescent egocentrism (Elkind, 1985; Lapsley, 1985; Lapsley, Milstead, Quintana, Flannery, & Buss, 1986; Lapsley & Murphy, 1985; Lapsley et al., 1988) is built on the suggestion that egocentrism can better be understood in the framework of social cognition. Drawing on Selman's (1980) theorizing, Lapsley and his colleagues suggest that the imaginary audience can best be conceptualized as an outgrowth of stage 3 perspective-taking skills. That is, the imaginary audience reflects the adolescents' considerations of others' reactions to them in imaginary situations (such as their death) in conjunction with formal operational thinking skills. In other words, they argue that the imaginary audience cannot occur without the ability to "step out" of the diadic relationship and mentally view the self–other interaction. The increase in self-consciousness, then, is the outcome of this process.

Lapsley and his colleagues explain the personal-fable construct in much the same manner. They note that stage 3 perspective taking includes the ability to self-reflect, that is, an awareness of self-awareness. This cognitive ability allows the adolescent mentally to remove the self from the background, to make the self stand out from the crowd. As a result, the adolescent gains a distorted view of his or her own individuality and importance.

Both Elkind (1967a, 1967b) and Lapsley (1985; Lapsley & Murphy, 1985) agree that role-taking experiences encountered in later adolescence are critical to the decline in imaginary-audience and personal-fable behavior. Lapsley and Murphy (1985) suggest that this is a result of the more powerful perspective-taking skills that emerge in stage 4 of Selman's theoretical model. When adolescents gain the ability to coordinate perspectives of the self in relation to others and the broader social system they come to realize that the self can be part of the background. Hence, imaginary audience (self-consciousness) and personal fable decline.

What we see in this alternative description of adolescent egocentrism is the important role played by both cognitive and social factors in the adolescent's development. To understand adolescent behavior fully we need to consider multiple determinants, in this case cognitive and social.

opmental competence seems to underlie role-taking skills, just as Selman has hypothesized.

An important question, of course, is the degree to which social cognition is related to social behavior. This was the focus of a study by Ford (1982), who tested ninth and twelfth graders. One of the findings Ford reported was that more socially competent adolescents were more facile in thinking about social situations, were better able to assess the consequences of their behavior for themselves and others, and were better able to devise strategies for dealing with social conflict. In addition, those adolescents who were better able to behave effectively in challenging social situations scored high in wanting to help others, wanting to get socially involved, and wanting to get along with peers and parents. Ford concludes, on the basis of these findings, that social cognition and social behavior are clearly related. It is interesting to note that the descriptions Ford's data allow match well with the theorizing of Selman (1976, 1980).

Social Cognition and Adolescence

The field of social cognition is an emerging one, and one that is, as noted above, very diversified. The degree to which research will help clarify the nature of adolescent development remains somewhat undefined. However, the available evidence is encouraging.

First, it is clear that there is a relationship between role-taking skills and cognitive development. Hence, Selman's (1976, 1980) theorizing and research expand our knowledge of the importance of cognitive development for adolescent behavior. We gain a more in-depth understanding of adolescent behavior by realizing this relationship. For example, adolescent-parent conflict may result in part from immature social perspective-taking skills on the part of the adolescent. Lapsley's interpretation of adolescent egocentrism is another example. (See Box 4–4 on p. 97.)

Second, and at a more global level, we can begin to understand how adolescents come to comprehend interpersonal relations by studying social cognition. As we watch children, preadolescents, and adolescents interact with peers, for example, or as we examine our own social relations with peers, we gain insight into peer group influences on the individual. The changing nature of adolescent friendships reflects the realization of individual differences in social perspective taking and the emerging understanding of others' internal need states and personalities. Both of these are aspects of social cognition.

QUALITATIVE VERSUS QUANTITATIVE INTELLECTUAL DEVELOPMENT

At this point a number of questions may come to mind. Which concept of intelligence is most useful for understanding adolescent development, the quantitative or the qualitative? Aren't quantitative and qualitative aspects of intelligence really the same thing? If not, how are they different? Although there are no simple, or even correct, answers to any of these questions, we shall in this last section try to give you some perspective from which to view the sticky issues revolving around the nature of intelligence.

Similarities in Psychometric and Piagetian Concepts of Intelligence

Elkind (1969) has noted several ways in which the psychometric (IQ) and Piagetian

concepts of intelligence are similar. First, both traditions have an interest in maturational aspects of intellectual development. We noted this in our discussion of qualitative differences in IQ test construction and in the general nature of Piagetian conceptualizations of the qualitative aspects of intellectual development.

Second, both the psychometric and Piagetian views consider intelligence to be rational. That is, both consider intelligence to be the capacity to deal effectively and rationally with the environment.

Differences in Psychometric and Piagetian Concepts of Intelligence

Genetic causality is one area in which the two approaches differ. The psychometric approach is, to put it very simply, based on the notion of chance gene combinations that result in a normal (bell-shaped) distribution curve of abilities within a given population. This approach, then, leads to issues about differences in amount of intelligence. Piagetian notions of genetic determinants of intelligence are not focused on random gene combinations but rather on the inheritance of certain brain functions that are organized. This organization produces similarities in the function (assimilation and accommodation) of intelligence and results in the invariant stage sequence through which intelligence develops.

In a real sense, the psychometric approach is concerned with interindividual differences, and the Piagetian approach with intraindividual changes in intelligence.

Intellectual growth is a second area in which the two approaches differ in perspective. The emphasis of the psychometric model is on the quantitative growth of intelligence, as assessed by correlations (predictions) of IQ scores taken at different ages. The Piagetian approach, on the other hand, emphasizes the qualitative development of intelligence from a less to a more complex mode of operation as the result of the formation of new mental structures. As we have already seen, IQ or MA scores tell us little more than that the adolescent can solve more problems than the child, a piece of information that has only limited uses. The Piagetian approach has a much broader set of implications for understanding adolescent behavior and development, as we have seen above. This distinction is in large part due to the developmental nature of the qualitative model.

The final difference Elkind notes in the two approaches is the way they treat the nature-nurture issue. The psychometric approach treats the relative contributions of nature and nurture in a statistical sense—the amount of variance in IQ scores attributable to nature or nurture. Heated debates (e.g., Jensen, 1969) have revolved around these concepts, and large-scale intervention programs such as Head Start have resulted. Piagetian views, on the other hand, speak of the inheritance of intellectual processes (assimilation and accommodation). The genetic endowment, then, is one of function. Nurture may influence the rate of intellectual development and even whether or not an individual or a societal group will reach formal operations (Piaget, 1972).

Examination of the similarities and differences in the two perspectives of intelligence highlight our opening suggestion that it is best to consider the two approaches as opposite sides of a single coin. Each tells us something of the nature of intelligence and, although they do so to differing degrees, each contributes to our understanding of adolescence.

SUMMARY

There are two prevailing views of the nature of intelligence. One view, the quantitative, or psychometric, conceives of intelligence as an ability. People are assumed to have more or less of this ability. Hence, an emphasis from this perspective has been in identifying individual differences in this ability. A sec-

ond emphasis has been that of the developmental behavioral geneticists, who have focussed their research efforts on identifying how genetic and environmental factors contribute to intelligence. The result of these efforts has shown that both environment and heredity are important contributors to intelligence.

A second type of research effort involves ascertaining the degree to which IQ changes during the course of development. It is now well established that IQ peaks during the adolescent years and remains stable through the adulthood years, declining only slightly during the aging years. There is, however, considerable change in IQ, with only about 45 percent of children and adolescents having an IQ that remains relatively stable from early childhood through adolescence.

The greatest utility of IQ scores seems to be for screening for educational purposes. IQ scores correlate moderately with performance on achievement tests and are a good predictor of ability to perform well in the traditional school curriculum. However, IQ scores tell us very little about adolescent development. This is because the quantitative approach is not a developmental perspective of intelligence.

The second perspective is the qualitative, or cognitive, developmental view of intelligence. Theorists of this persuasion view intelligence as changing in type as development progresses. Piaget, for example, has identified four stages through which intelligence progresses. The highest stage, formal operations, is reached during the adolescent years. With the emergence of formal operations the adolescent is able to think abstractly about many things and is able to consider the possible as well as the real. Although some debate centers on the stagelike nature of intellectual development and on the degree to which reaching formal operations is universal among the population, it is generally accepted that formal operations is, at least, one logical end point in cognitive development.

Research based on this perspective has focused on identifying the competencies (cognitive skills) that emerge with development. One such skill is social cognitive in nature. The field of social cognition is concerned with examining the importance of changing cognitive skills for aspects of social development, including the ability to take another person's point of view. Researchers have demonstrated that this ability changes from childhood to adolescence, with adolescents having a much more flexible and broad understanding of social interactions.

Another line of research is aimed at explaining how cognitive advances relate to adolescent personality development, including self-concept and egocentrism. With development, self-concept is viewed more abstractly. In addition, the type of egocentrism associated wtih adolescence reveals that the adolescent may have hesitancies about revealing aspects of the self. This hesitancy may be related to peer group conformity. In both instances, it has been demonstrated that an important underlying factor is the entrance into formal operational thinking.

In contrast to the quantitative approach, the evidence reveals that the qualitative approach contributes substantially to our understanding of adolescent development and behavior. We gain insights into adolescent relations with parents and peers, adolescent views of society, and adolescent personality development when we consider cognitive gains during adolescence.

It seems best to conclude that the two perspectives of intelligence are not contradictory, but are best viewed as complementary. Each tells us something different about intelligence because each has a different definition and emphasis on the issues involved in studying the intellect.

GLOSSARY

Cognition. The processes of knowing, perceiving, and evaluating events.

Concrete operations. In Piaget's theory, mental operations applied to real, as opposed to possible, events.

Disequilibrium. In Piaget's theory, a motivational mechanism resulting from an imbalance between how the individual interprets events and emerging new ways of understanding events.

Egocentrism. Extreme concern and interest in the self, often to the exclusion of interest in others.

Equilibrium. In Piaget's theory, a balance between the individual's cognitive competencies and the demands of the environment.

Formal operations. Abstract, logical thinking skills that can be applied to the real as well as the possible; if-then thinking.

"g." In Spearman's terms, overall general intelligence.

Intelligence. Intellectual ability.

IQ (intelligence quotient). A measure of intellectual capability derived by performance on a standardized test of intelligence.

MA (mental age). A developmental marker, based on performance on an intelligence test, of intellectual level or development.

Operational thinking. In Piaget's theory, logical thinking—either concrete or formal.

"s." According to Spearman, a specific factor (such as mathematical ability) involved in intelligence.

Social cognition. Cognitive skills applied to social situations.

SUGGESTED READINGS

Child Development, 1983, *54* (2), 253–435.

A portion of this volume is given over to a series of papers examining aspects of development from a developmental behavioral genetic perspective. Both data based and theory papers are presented, in readable form. Topics covered include personality, learning disabilities, temperament, and method/theory.

ELKIND, D. (1978). *The child's reality: three developmental themes.* Hillsdale, NJ: Lawrence Erlbaum.

Elkind discusses the development of religious, perceptual, and egocentric aspects of the child and adolescent. The chapter on egocentrism is particularly pertinent to those interested in adolescence.

ELKIND, D. (1970). *Children and adolescents: Interpretive essays on Jean Piaget.* New York: Oxford University Press.

In this short book Elkind discusses the nature of Piaget's theory and compares it to traditional (IQ) investigations of intellectual development. He also discusses the relationship of Piaget's theory to education and learning.

FLAVELL, J. (1982). On cognitive development. *Child Development, 53,* 1–10.

Flavell presents a brief discussion of issues involved in the question of the stage relatedness of cognitive development. This is a seminal paper written in a manner suitable for an audience of widely divergent backgrounds.

FLAVELL, J. (1977). *Cognitive development.* Englewood Cliffs, NJ: Prentice-Hall.

The author discusses Piaget's theory and research testing it. The discussion of social cognition during adolescence is particularly helpful in understanding the implications of Piaget's theory for adolescent development.

SHERMAN, S. J., JUDD, C. M., & PARK, B. (1989). Social cognition. In M. R. Rosenzweig & L. W. Porter (Eds.), *Annual review of psychology*, Vol. 40. Palo Alto, CA: Annual Reviews, Inc.

The authors review a number of areas in which research in social cognition is being conducted.

Moral Development in Adolescence

5

CHAPTER OUTLINE

MAJOR ISSUES ADDRESSED

Theoretical Perspectives on Moral Development
Socialization Influences and Moral Development
Universal Stages of Moral Thinking
Moral Thinking and Moral Behavior
The Development of Political Thinking
Adolescents' Changing Views of Religion

INTRODUCTION

All adolescents must construct a set of values that will help them function successfully as adult members of society; it is one of the developmental tasks of adolescence (Havighurst, 1951, 1972). This broad-ranging task, referred to as *moral development*, involves personal codes of social behavior. As the values of childhood are surrendered, adult values slowly emerge and solidify into a value system that guides interactions with others and the society for the remainder of the adolescent's life. In a sense, then, the study of moral development is the study of the socialization processes by which the adolescent becomes an adult.

Of course, the development of moral and value codes does not begin in adolescence. As we have noted many times, adolescence is a transition to adulthood. Our discussion, therefore, centers on transitions to adult modes of morality.

ADOLESCENCE AND MORAL DEVELOPMENT

Two major reasons exist for studying moral development during adolescence. First, the cognitive changes that occur during adolescence are related to moral development (for example, Colby, Kohlberg, Gibbs, & Lieberman, 1983; Kohlberg, 1963a, 1963b, 1969, 1976; Piaget, 1932). As we pointed out in the previous chapter, formal operational thinking allows the adolescent to interpret the social environment, including aspects of morality, in new and different ways.

Second, because adolescents are capable of devising new and idealistic social orders to which all are expected to conform (Windmiller, 1976), we may view them as moral philosophers. With further development a more balanced view of the social order is taken.

A number of researchers (for example, Feather, 1980; Hoffman, 1980; Mitchell,

1975) have noted other changes in moral development that point to the importance of adolescence as a transition stage in moral development.

First, unlike children, the adolescent is concerned with what is right as opposed to what is wrong, reflecting an emerging sense of justice. Second, adolescents become preoccupied with personal and social moral codes. As they gain the competency to understand alternative points of view, they see that moral codes are relative, not absolute. Finally, the above changes result in some conflict between moral conduct and moral thinking during adolescence.

WHAT IS MORALITY?

Early writing in the area of moral development was left to philosophers, who evolved three major doctrines of morality, each of which is represented in contemporary psychological theorizing (Hoffman, 1970). The **doctrine of original sin** assumed that parental intervention was necessary to save the child's soul. Current-day vestiges of this viewpoint may be found in theories of personality structure and the development of the conscience, or superego, which argue that the child internalizes parental standards of right and wrong.

The **doctrine of innate purity** argued that the child is basically moral, or pure, and that society, and especially adults, are corrupting influences. This view is represented in the theorizing of Piaget (1932), who argues that morality develops from the acquisition of autonomy emerging from the need to get along with peers. For Piaget, moral thinking develops through peer-to-peer interactions that lead to an understanding of rules. Piaget believes parents do not allow this autonomous thinking to develop because parent-child relationships are basically heteronomous, that is, the child is ruled by the parents. Hence, the parents retard moral development.

The third philosophical doctrine is the ***tabula rasa*** (blank slate) notion, which assumes that the child is neither innately pure nor corrupt but rather the product of environmental influences. The current-day representatives of this position are, of course, the learning theorists, who believe that development is the result of reinforcement and imitation mechanisms.

In addition to these differing philosophical and theoretical views regarding the origin of morality, we must keep in mind the distinctions between three concepts: systems of morality, moral behavior, and moral character. Although definitions of these concepts vary according to the theory or research being discussed, the following definitions are sufficiently broad to cover most instances. *Systems of morality* are evidenced in the rules that guide social and interpersonal behavior, and include rules (e.g., laws) that are written down as well as those that are not, such as treating others in a courteous manner. This broad definition includes all types of social behaviors, not just those we usually consider moral behavior; for example, this definition includes rules for behavior toward friends, teachers, and peers, as well as formally codified laws. From this perspective **moral behaviors** are those behaviors that are consistent with rules of morality. Hence, like moral systems, moral behaviors include social behaviors of all types. It should be noted at this point that this definition of moral behavior also includes behavior contrary to that expressed in the moral code. That is, immoral behavior is simply a subclass of moral behavior.

Moral character is a much more difficult concept to define, largely because it involves an individual's *motives* for behaving in a particular manner. The basic problem in defining moral character is to determine those personality dimensions that determine it and vary as a function of it. Moral knowledge, socialization, empathy, autonomy, and moral judgment are the major concepts defining moral character.

In order to have successful peer and adult relationships, the adolescent must learn the rules (morality) of the society and act in accordance with these rules (moral behavior or conduct). Individuals who successfully master these tasks are said to possess moral character.

Throughout this chapter, then, we will attempt to answer three major questions about moral development. First, how are moral rules internalized? Second, how are moral judgments made, and how do they change with development? Third, what is the relationship between internal moral standards and overt behaviors?

THEORIES OF MORAL DEVELOPMENT

Among psychologists, the writings of Freud and Piaget have had the greatest impact on research in moral development. Following their early works, there was little written about moral development. In the last two or three decades, however, there has been considerable research and theorizing about the processes underlying moral development.

Psychoanalytic Theory

According to the principles of psychoanalytic theory, morality is part of the individual's conscience, or superego. The acquisition of morality, then, is explained by the formation of the superego, which results from resolution of the Oedipal complex and identification with the same-sex parent (Freud, 1924). Society ensures its survival through this identification process by imposing its cultural standards, as represented by the parents' behaviors, attitudes, and aspirations, on the individual. Although the exact basis of identification is unclear, Freud's theorizing has stimulated considerable research into the effects of parental behavior on the child's moral development. The major research concerns have centered on moral character, the consistency of moral behavior across situations, and the role of parental disciplinary techniques in shaping moral behavior.

The Hartshorne and May Research. One implication of Freudian theory is that identification with a single individual should lead to the acquisition of highly consistent moral behaviors. This implication was tested by Hartshorne and May (1928–1930), who administered a series of tests to measure moral conduct in children and adolescents.

Briefly, Hartshorne and May administered tests to children and adolescents ages 8 to 16 to measure their resistance to the temptation to cheat in situations where it appeared they were not being observed. The most important findings were that (1) cheating behavior was normally distributed in the children and adolescents studied, and (2) cheating in one situation did not predict cheating in another situation. In other

Some research suggests that some adolescents have a tendency to violate rules on a consistent basis, although most follow rules of the social order.

words, the children could not be classified as "cheaters" or "noncheaters." Almost all the children cheated, but for some, the incidence of cheating varied according to the risk of being caught. Therefore, Hartshorne and May concluded that cheating was situationally determined and that there was not a general trait of honesty or morality as would be expected from Freudian theory.

However, when Burton (1963) reexamined the data for the best and most reliable tests he found a general "honesty" trait, indicating some consistency in honesty across tasks. Similar situations seemed to elicit similar cheating behavior. Going a step further, other researchers (e.g., Peck & Havighurst, 1960) have reported a trait of "outward conformity to rules," which seems to describe people. At one end of this dimension of honesty is the person who follows rules and regulations in a highly consistent manner. At the other end is the individual who regularly evades or violates social rules. A person's rule-following orientation remains stable from ages 10 to 17. In other words, Peck and Havighurst seem to have been able to classify people along a dimension of honesty, and that classification seems to have no developmental trends associated with it.

As we have seen, psychoanalytic theory relies heavily on the importance of identification. The identification process works, in part, because the child learns to feel guilt (a form of internal self-punishment) whenever he violates a parental prohibition or is tempted to do so. In order to avoid guilt, the child must behave in a manner consistent with the values or morals incorporated through identification with the parent. These standards become part of the child's own value and moral system and presumably guide behavior. Hence, it is not surprising that those at higher levels of moral development are less likely to cheat (Coady & Sawyer, 1986).

These psychoanalytic conceptualizations led to considerable research on a number of topics related to moral development, for example, the formation and effects of guilt, resistance to temptation, and the effects of parental discipline techniques. In general, investigators were looking for a relationship between parental discipline techniques and children's moral development. A number of indices of children's internalization of adult moral standards have been used: *resistance to temptation*, the degree to which a child will resist violating a standard when the chances of getting caught are remote or nonexistent; **guilt**, the intensity of the internal emotional response following transgression; *reactions to transgression*, the child's moral judgments about a transgression; and *confession*, admitting a transgression. Unfortunately, most of the research on these topics was done with children and very young adolescents. Nevertheless, a brief survey will be helpful in understanding the nature of adolescent moral development.

In a well-designed experiment, Hoffman and Saltzstein (1967) assessed the relationship between several measures of adolescent moral development and various forms of parental discipline and affection in a sample consisting of middle-class and lower-class boys and girls. All were seventh graders. Hoffman and Saltzstein made several predictions based on the different forms of discipline that parents might use. The types of disciplines studied were induction, power assertion, and love withdrawal. *Induction discipline* involves explaining to the child why a specific behavior was wrong and providing examples of alternative behaviors. *Power assertion* refers to the use, or threat of use, of physical punishment. *Love withdrawal* involves ignoring the child, isolating the child, or expressing dislike or disappointment toward the child. Hoffman and Saltzstein hypothesized that induction discipline techniques (that is, explaining why certain behaviors are unsatisfactory) would relate most strongly to moral development. This hypothesis was based on the fact that induction techniques, unlike power-assertive or love-withdrawal discipline techniques,

would provide the child with the knowledge that his behavior may be harmful to someone else, thereby capitalizing on his capacity for empathy and presumably motivating him to develop moral controls.

Measures of morality included guilt, **moral judgment**, how the adolescent reacted when caught doing something wrong, how considerate the adolescent was toward other adolescents, and identification with the same-sex parent. Parental disciplinary practices were obtained from reports by the adolescents and, for the middle-class adolescents, parent interviews. In sum, measures of both morality and parental discipline were obtained and related to each other.

The findings may be summarized as follows:

1. For middle-class children
   a. Maternal use of power assertion was consistently related to weak moral development.
   b. Maternal use of induction was consistently associated with advanced moral development.
   c. Maternal use of love withdrawal related negatively but infrequently to moral development.
   d. Paternal discipline techniques related infrequently and inconsistently to moral development.
   e. Parental affection related positively to moral development, much more so for the mother than the father.
2. For lower-class children
   a. There were few relationships between children's moral development and children's reports of parental discipline techniques. The relationships which were significant were inconsistent and inconclusive.
   b. There were few relationships between parental affection and moral development. The three significant relations were positive.

Other research supports these findings. Mothers' frequent use of power-assertion

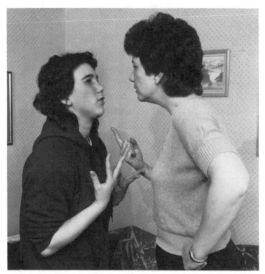

Power assertive discipline relates negatively to moral development; induction discipline fosters moral development.

discipline is related to weak moral development, whereas maternal induction and affection are associated with moral growth. It seems that induction techniques facilitate moral development because of their cognitive component, a component that is lacking in the other discipline techniques. The literature also supports Hoffman and Saltzstein's findings that love-withdrawal discipline does not relate to moral development.

The research also generally supports Hoffman and Saltzstein's findings about the importance of paternal discipline techniques. Few relationships between fathers' discipline techniques and moral development have been reported. Although fathers' discipline techniques are not related to moral development, fathers' presence is apparently important for boys. Boys from father-absent homes tend to score lower on indices of moral development than boys from father-present homes (Hoffman, 1970). There are two possible explanations for this finding. First, fathers may provide direct instruction for moral standards in nondisciplinary situations. Second, it may be that the father's disciplinary role is critical only in exceptional circumstances, for example, delinquency, since mothers handle most discipline situations. In either event, the role of the father in moral development is apparently not as important as that of the mother.

The social-class differences reported by Hoffman and Saltzstein have not been investigated in other studies, the majority of which have been conducted with middle-class children and adolescents. Hoffman (1970) conjectures that the basis of these social-class differences may lie in the predominantly power-assertive discipline techniques used in the lower-social-level families. To the extent that power assertion is the primary mode of discipline, it may reduce the relationships between other discipline techniques and moral development. In addition, the father tends to be the primary disciplinary agent in the lower-social-level families, thus diluting the mother's influence on moral development. As Hoffman (1970) suggests, one result may be that peers play a more prominent role in moral development for lower-class than for middle-class children.

Some other evidence (Parikh, 1980; Olejnik, 1980) supports and extends the findings relating to induction disciplinary techniques. Parikh tested eighth and tenth graders and their parents and reported that mothers', but not fathers', use of induction discipline was related to higher levels of moral judgment. This seemed to be the result of the interchange that occurs in this type of discipline: the reasoning that is involved stimulates thinking about moral issues. This reasoning was more likely to be used by parents who, themselves, were higher in level of moral reasoning.

Olejnik (1980) reported that college students with higher levels of moral reasoning perceived their mothers as using induction disciplinary techniques. Those of lower levels of moral judgment perceived their mothers as using power assertive disciplinary techniques. Moreover, those who perceived their mothers as using induction discipline, said they would do so with children when discussing the importance of telling the truth, obeying rules, and the like.

Because these "real life" investigations demonstrate the importance of parental discipline techniques in the development of morality, they lend credence to the psychoanalytic interpretation of moral development. Induction discipline apparently helps the child identify with and internalize the parent's moral values, as demonstrated in the relationship between adolescent moral behavior and earlier parental child-rearing techniques. It is important to keep in mind, however, that naturalistic/self-report data are often difficult to interpret in a cause-effect sense. Therefore, it is important to review laboratory research dealing with discipline effects and moral development. In these studies, the dependent variable is usually a measure of some overt behavior rather than some covert event such as guilt.

Since the experimental research relevant to our current discussion has been done with children, not adolescents, we shall simply summarize the findings. Considerable research on the timing of physical punishment has been done to test the hypothesis that physical punishment administered early in an undesirable behavior sequence will more effectively lower the probability of recurrence of the unwanted behavior. Research supports the hypothesis. Apparently, early punishment in the unwanted behavior sequence causes anxiety to become associated with the behavior and arouses avoidance responses preventing its recurrence. Punishment administered later in the behavioral sequence cannot have this effect. Since parents usually punish bad behavior after it has taken place, it is not surprising that physical punishment does not relate to moral behaviors, as demonstrated above.

Recall that the naturalistic evidence relating love withdrawal to moral development indicated a general lack of correspondence between the two measures. The experimental evidence also offers little support to the psychoanalytic hypothesis that anxiety over possible loss of parental love is a major factor in the child's internalization of parental values and standards. At this time, it must be concluded that love withdrawal does not reliably relate to moral development.

It is unfortunate that, at the current time, laboratory research on the relationship between induction discipline and moral behavior is rare. Research by Leizer and Rogers (1974) supports the naturalistic studies demonstrating that induction techniques are more effective than physical or verbal punishment. This was true both immediately and two weeks after the experiment was completed. But the research of LaVoie (1974) did not demonstrate this effect. In both studies resistance to deviation was the measure of morality used. Until further research on induction techniques is conducted, the issue must remain unresolved.

The findings of both naturalistic and experimental research on the relation between parental disciplinary techniques and moral development provide only partial support for the psychoanalytic theory of moral development. Power assertion appears not to promote moral development and love withdrawal seems to be inconsistently related to indices of moral development. Induction techniques do seem to promote moral development, although the evidence is not entirely clear.

With some reservation, then, it seems safe to conclude that adolescents who were raised as children by parents who used induction discipline likely would have higher levels of moral development. This should be true for both moral behavior and moral judgment. Part of the differences in the ways adolescents behave in "moral" situations—cheating, concerns about social moral issues, and views of right and wrong—likely reflect how they were disciplined during childhood.

Social-Learning Theory

Social-learning theory was discussed in detail in Chapter 2. From this perspective, the acquisition of moral behavior is accomplished through the same mechanisms as the acquisition of any other kind of behavior, namely, the process of direct tuition (Gewitz, 1969) or generalized imitation (Bandura, 1969b; Gewitz, 1969).

The bulk of the social-learning research on moral development deals with the internalization of moral standards. To social-learning theorists, however, it is imitation, not the psychoanalytic concept of identification, that is responsible for the acquisition of moral behavior. Learning theorists define identification as a continuous, ongoing process of response acquisition and modification resulting from direct tuition as well as simple observation of parents and other models. This is in direct contrast to the psychoanalytic view, in which identification is seen as a more or less passive process that is relatively complete by the age of 4 or 5. In addition, social-learning theory places less emphasis than psychoanalytic theory on the child's nurturant and punitive interactions with parents. Interactions with adults, in general, are seen as related to development. One implication of the social-learning-theory approach is that moral judgments should be relatively unrelated to age and modifiable through environmental intervention.

This implication was tested in a study by Bandura and MacDonald (1963). The subjects, boys aged 5 to 11, were separated into two groups, one of which exhibited primarily an objective and the other primarily a subjective moral orientation. (That is, the first group made moral judgments on the basis of damage done, and the second on the intentions of the transgressor.) The children in each of these two groups were further subdivided into three groups for the experiment. One group observed an adult model who expressed moral judgments counter to those of the children's orientation, and the children were verbally reinforced for imitating the model's responses. The second group observed the adult model but received no reinforcement for matching the model's responses. Children in the third group observed no models but were reinforced whenever they expressed moral judgments opposite to their dominant orientations. The dependent variable was the number of objective judgments made by subjectively oriented children and the number of subjective judgments made by objectively oriented children during the base (initial assessment) period, the experimental treatment period, and the immediate post-test period, which was conducted in a different social setting with the model and reinforcement procedures absent.

The findings may be summarized simply. Children who observed a model altered their moral judgments and matched those of the model regardless of the reinforcement contingencies. Children who did not observe a model, but were reinforced for moral judgments opposite to their primary orientation, tended not to change, especially if they were subjectively oriented children. These data suggest that children do learn moral behaviors from observing models, which lends credence to learning-theory interpretations of the acquisition of moral behavior.

Shifts in moral judgment have also been reported in several other experiments. In addition, in their study of adolescent moral development, LeFurgy and Woloshin (1969) reported shifts that lasted as long as three months. These experiments demonstrate that long-term moral judgments may be acquired and shaped by basic learning processes.

There are a number of additional types of research on morality generated from the social-learning-theory viewpoint. Resistance to transgression, aggression, self-reward, and delay of gratification are among the most researched areas. All these experiments demonstrate that aspects of moral behavior may be controlled by observation of a model.

In describing the observational learning/imitation process, researchers have identified a number of motivational factors related to children's moral behavior. In other words, notions of morality are based on external sanctions. Before the significance of this research can be adequately evaluated, however, it is necessary to consider the cognitive approaches of Piaget and Kohlberg.

The Cognitive-Developmental Approach to Moral Development

A cognitive-developmental approach to the analysis of moral development follows the principles spelled out in our discussion of general cognitive development (Chapter 4) and the cognitive-developmental approach to social development (Chapter 2). The emphasis of this approach is on the thought processes underlying moral development, which emerge in a sequence of stages much in the same manner as the stages of intellectual development. As development progresses, the moral thinking processes in each stage are integrated into those in the next higher stage, the emerging stage being an integration of the old and the new. The stages of development are passed through in an unvarying sequence, and age is not equivalent to stage.

Piaget (1932) and Kohlberg (1963a, 1963b; 1969, 1976) have been the chief advocates of the cognitive-developmental approach to analyzing the child's moral development.

Piaget's Theory. Piaget studied the development of two aspects of morality, the child's developing respect for rules of the social order and the child's developing sense of justice, in order to explicate the cognitive-developmental shifts underlying them.

Children's respect for rules of the social order was assessed by observing their conformity to the rules of the game of marbles.

Children were given some marbles and asked to explain how the game was played. Piaget then asked the children if they thought it would be fair to make up new rules. Responses to the latter question represented the child's understanding of the nature of rules (Flavell, 1963).

From investigations of this type, Piaget developed a stage theory of the child's conformity to, and understanding of, rules. Up to about age 3 (stage 1) the child plays with marbles in an apparently ruleless fashion, and, as might be expected, is unable to verbalize rules. In stage 2, from about age 3 to 5, the child imitates aspects of the rule-regulated behavior of older children, but play remains idiosyncratic and socially isolated until about 7 to 8 years of age (stage 3). At about this time the child regards rules as unchangeable, as though they were given by some divine source. New rules or changes in old rules are seen as unfair, even if all agree to them. After about age 11 to 12 (stage 4) children tend to alter rules to fit unique situations and may invent new rules to cover special circumstances. Rules are perceived as changeable and as the product of evolution during late childhood and early adolescence.

The child's developing sense of justice was measured by telling children stories about persons who engaged in various wrongdoings. The child was then asked why the acts were wrong or, in some instances, which of two acts was more wrong and why this was so. For example, in one of the stories, children were asked to judge who was "naughtier," a child who broke 15 cups through an unavoidable accident or a child who broke one cup while attempting to sneak some jam. As a second example, children were asked who was the guiltier of two girls, the one who stole a roll to give to a poor and hungry friend or the one who stole a (less costly) ribbon for herself.

On the basis of these investigations Piaget developed his notions of children's development of a sense of *retributive justice* (punishment). Younger children tended to employ *expiatory punishment*, in which the severity of punishment to the wrongdoer is in direct proportion to the seriousness of the offense, but not necessarily related to the offense. Older children seemed to feel that the punishment should fit the crime in some way so that the individual will better understand the consequences of his misdeed. The idea behind this form of punishment, which Piaget called *punishment by reciprocity*, is not the infliction of punishment *per se*, but rather the demonstration of the consequences of an act through punishment logically related to the misdeed (Flavell, 1963).

An example from Flavell will illustrate this point. Suppose a child fails to bring home food from the store after being requested to do so. A spanking would be an example of expiatory punishment. Reducing the size of the child's meal or refusing to do a favor for the child would be examples of punishment by reciprocity, the former because the child is responsible for the lack of food and the latter because the child refused to do a favor.

Combining all the evidence, Piaget determined there were two broad stages of moral development. In the first stage, variously termed *morality of constraint* or *moral realism*, one obeys rules because they are viewed as rigid and unalterable. Behaviors are viewed as either right or wrong, depending on the extent to which the behavior follows established social rules. Thus, younger children believe in what Piaget has termed *immanent justice*, that is, the notion that God will punish people for their misdeeds.

The older child operates according to a *morality of cooperation*. At this second stage of development, rules are viewed as being determined by reciprocal agreements depending upon the social circumstances. The child realizes that there is no absolute right or wrong. Notions of justice include considerations of the intentions of others. Following moral rules is viewed as being essential to the functioning of society. Punishment is viewed as being suited to the misdeed (pun-

ishment by reciprocity) rather than simply being dished out by authority.

Hoffman (1980) summarized Piaget's views of psychological mechanisms and processes underlying this conceptualization of moral development. Experience with peers is the primary influence on moral development. The reasoning behind this assertion is as follows. Peer interactions involve the kind of give and take that is necessary for moral development. Peer interactions are helpful in two ways. First, by sharing in decision making with peers, the child gains confidence in his or her ability to apply rules to specific situations and make decisions about changing rules. As a result, rules come to be viewed as flexible rather than rigid, as the result of agreement and cooperation between individuals sharing a common goal. Second, through various role-taking experiences with peers, the child learns that he or she thinks and feels about experiences in a way similar to one's peers, who in turn think and feel about things in a way similar to the child. This realization helps the youngster learn that rules are useful because they benefit the group. It also helps the child understand the motives behind the actions of others, and thereby allows the child to base moral judgments on intention rather than simply on overt behavior.

Research on Piaget's Theory. Hoffman (1970) carefully and critically reviewed the research stimulated by Piaget's theorizing and listed 21 experiments aimed at assessing the stages of development postulated by Piaget for five areas of moral development: (1) relativism of perspective versus absolutism, (2) objective view of punishment versus immanent justice, (3) intentions versus consequences, (4) relative versus expiatory justice, and (5) conformity to peer expectations versus obedience to adult authority. With one exception the findings supported Piaget's theoretical assertions and age trends for the traits listed. Although this is an impressive array of data, it is even more compelling in that the age trends were consistent for all intellectual levels, social classes, and races. The only limiting factor of Piaget's theory is that it may be applicable only to Western cultures (Hoffman, 1970).

At first glance, it seems that research of Bandura and MacDonald (1963) and Le-Furgy and Woloshin (1969), reviewed above, is damaging to Piaget's notions in several respects. First, the results suggest that the steps proposed by Piaget do not occur in an invariant sequence. Second, the findings call into question Piaget's contention that progress through the stages involves successive reorganization of cognitive content.

However, as Hoffman (1970) noted, the post-tests in these studies were constructed of items very similar in nature, and on the same moral dimension, as the items composing the pretest. Therefore, the findings may not reflect a real change in the subject's underlying notions about morality, but may merely reflect changes in overt responses to a particular moral dimension. Were the post-tests composed of items from a dimension different from the one used in pretesting and training, the results would argue more convincingly in favor of a change in underlying conceptualizations of morality. A second problem in the Bandura and MacDonald (1963) study is that both the model and the experimenter were adults, and one of them was always present. Since children are highly susceptible to social cues in an experimental situation (e.g., Dusek, 1971), it is quite possible the children simply gave the response they felt the adult wished them to give, a form of what is known as experimenter bias (Rosenthal, 1966). As a result, the social-learning research is inconclusive with respect to sequencing of the stages of moral development postulated by Piaget.

Finally, several investigations have tested Piaget's notion that peer interaction and role playing promote moral development. Moir (1974) administered the Kohlberg Moral Development Test described below and tests

of nonmoral role taking (for example, understanding the motives and feelings of others) to forty 11-year-old girls. The scores on the two tests were positively correlated, indicating that higher levels of moral thinking were associated with higher levels of role taking ability. Moir's results replicate those of others who demonstrated these effects for boys as well as girls. In addition, it seems that the ability to understand reciprocal interpersonal relations is necessary for moral development. The findings of these experiments strongly suggest that the child's developing ability to see things from another's perspective, a cognitive task, is a necessary precursor to the development of mature levels of moral thinking (Perlmutter & Shapiro, 1987).

Kohlberg's Theory of Moral Development. Kohlberg, like Piaget, argues that conceptualizations of morality develop in a way consistent with a cognitive-developmental approach (Kohlberg, 1963a, 1963b, 1969, 1976). Kohlberg's major interest is to examine and delineate the thought structures underlying moral judgments, that is, moral thought, not the content of moral responses. Kohlberg is interested in moral thought because he believes that all humans, children, adolescents, and adults, are moral philosophers. Kohlberg further assumes that children have a morality that is distinct and different from adult morality. The problem is to determine the psychological processes underlying the transition from the child's relatively immature morality to mature, adult forms of moral thought.

In his research Kohlberg interviewed a large number of boys and girls ranging from 6 to 16 years of age (Kohlberg, 1963b). During the interviews the children and adolescents heard 10 stories (see Table 5–1) in which a moral dilemma was posed. Kohlberg was not particularly interested in the specific alternatives selected, but rather in the reasons given for the choices. The reasons given reflect the subject's way of thinking about

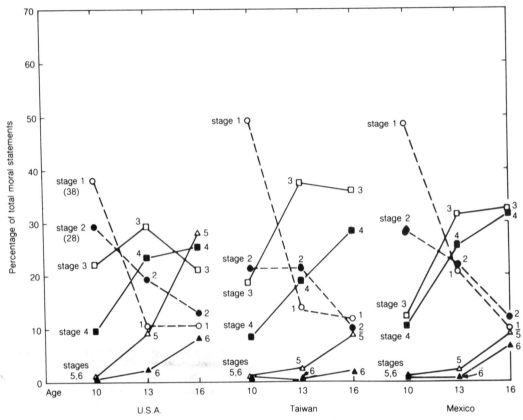

FIGURE 5–1   **Age Trends in Moral Judgment in Middle-Class Urban Boys in Three Nations (left) and Isolated Village Boys in Two Nations (right)**
(Source: Kohlberg, L. [1969]. Stage and sequence: The cognitive-developmental approach to socialization. In David A. Goslin [Ed.], *Handbook of socialization theory and research* [pp. 384–385]. Chicago: Rand McNally. Used by permission.)

the situation and, therefore, reveal the thought processes underlying moral development. The particular choices, on the other hand, reflect the content of moral values, which is not of primary interest to Kohlberg. The subjects' responses were scored according to the stage of moral development they reflected, and each subject was then classfied according to stage of moral development.

On the basis of responses to the questions such as those shown in Table 5–1, Kohlberg postulated three levels of moral development composed of a total of six stages (see Table 5–2). Kohlberg believed these stages represented a universal developmental sequence, were a result of cognitive conflict arising from development in cognitive abilities, and reflected level of sociomoral perspective or point of view that is the foundation of the formulation of moral judgments (Kohlberg, 1969, 1976; Colby, Kohlberg, Gibbs, & Lieberman, 1983). Column 1 in Table 5–2 is the listing of the stages in the developmental sequence, columns 2 and 3 reflect the cognitive organization concerning morality for each stage, and the last

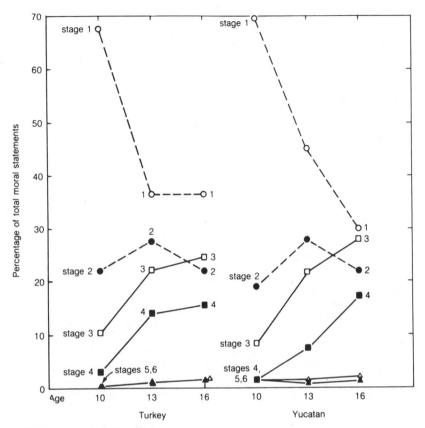

FIGURE 5–1   **(Continued)**

column states the sociomoral perspective of the stage. Following a description of each stage we examine research assessing the underlying assumptions of the theory.

The Preconventional Level. At this level of development, the child's concepts of good and bad, right and wrong, are determined by the physical consequences resulting from actions, that is, by rewards and punishments for specific behaviors, or by the perceived power of those in authority. In *stage 1* the physical consequences of an act completely determine its goodness or badness. There is an unquestioning deference to authority motivated by avoidance of punishment. In *stage 2* acts are defined as right if they are satisfying to the self or to others. There is

some indication of a concept of fairness and egalitarianism of a reciprocal nature, but it is of the naive "you do for me and I'll do for you" sort. It is not reciprocity based on justice.

The Conventional Level. At this level, the immediate physical consequences of an act become secondary to maintaining the accepted social order and living up to the expectations of others. Behavior at this level differs from that at the preceding level in that the child not only behaves in a manner consistent with the expectations of others (that is, in terms of their anticipated praise and blame), but also identifies with and incorporates the rules of others and respects their judgment. *Stage 3* is composed of a sort

TABLE 5–1 **Examples of the Moral Dilemma Stories Used by Kohlberg**

1. Joe's father promised Joe that he could go to camp if he earned the $50 for it, and then changed his mind and asked Joe to give him the money he had earned. Joe lied and said he had earned only $10 and went to camp using the other $40 he had made. Before he went he told his younger brother Alex about the money and about lying to their father. Should Alex tell their father?
2. In Europe, a woman was near death from a special kind of cancer. There was one drug that the doctors thought might save her. It was a form of radium that a druggist in the same town had recently discovered. The drug was expensive to make, but the druggist was charging 10 times what the drug cost him to make. He paid $200 for the radium and charged $2000 for a small dose of the drug. The sick woman's husband, Heinz, went to everyone he knew to borrow money, but he could only get together about $1000, which is half of what it cost. He told the druggist that his wife was dying and asked him to sell it cheaper or let him pay later. But the druggist said: "No, I discovered the drug and I'm going to make money from it." So Heinz got desperate and broke into the man's store to steal the drug for his wife. Should the husband have done that?

(Source: From Kohlberg, L. [1963]. The development of children's orientations toward a moral order: I. Sequence in the development of moral thought. *Vita Humana, 6,* 11–33.)

of "good boy" morality. Good and bad are defined by what pleases others. The child may well conform to the cultural stereotype of what is good and bad behavior, but begins to judge the behavior of others on the basis of their intentions to mean well. *Stage 4* may be characterized by a "law and order" orientation toward authority, rules, and maintenance of the social order. "Right" behavior is defined as doing one's duty, showing respect for authority, and maintaining the social order for its own sake. Though similar to stage 1, the stage 4 orientation differs because it includes a respect for an underlying moral order that is maintained by reward and punishment. At this stage, the individual also is able to understand that others have rights.

Postconventional or Principled Level. At this level, moral values and principles are defined according to equitable standards or rights, and the possibility of conflict between several socially accepted standards is realized. There is an effort to define morality in a manner distinct from the authority of groups and from the individual's identification with various groups and authority. *Stage 5* is characterized by defining morality in terms of mutually agreed-upon standards, that is, contracts. There is an emphasis upon the legal point of view, but with the knowledge that laws are formed on some rational basis and can be changed to fit changing social situations. This latter characteristic is an important distinction between stages 4 and 5. There is also an awareness that personal opinions are relative and that conflict can be resolved through a set of agreed-upon procedures. *Stage 6* is characterized by defining *right* according to a set of abstract, universal ethical principles, for example, the Golden Rule or the greatest good for the greatest number. The basic notion is that universal principles of justice, equality, and human rights do exist.

Stage Universality and Sequentiality

Some have criticized Kohlberg's claim that the stages of moral development are universal (see Perlmutter & Shapiro, 1987). The typical objection is that the claim is based on data from a relatively small number of cultures.

Kohlberg (1969) reported data for 10-, 13-, and 16-year-olds in the United States, Taiwan, Mexico, Turkey, and Yucatan. In Figure 5–1 the percentage of moral statements made by adolescents at the three age levels in each of these five cultures are plotted for each of the six stages. At age 10 in each country, the order of the stages is the same as the order in which they occur. That is, judgments are based on stage 1 and most often, stage 2 next most often, and so forth. In the United States, the

TABLE 5–2　**The Six Moral Stages Identified by Kohlberg**

Level and Stage	CONTENT OF STAGE		
	What Is Right	*Reasons for Doing Right*	*Social Perspective of Stage*
Level 1—Preconventional Stage 1— Heteronomous Morality	To avoid breaking rules backed by punishment, obedience for its own sake, and avoiding physical damage to persons and property.	Avoidance of punishment, and the superior power of authorities.	*Egocentric point of view.* Doesn't consider the interests of others or recognize that they differ from the actor's; doesn't relate two points of view. Actions are considered physically rather than in terms of psychological interests of others. Confusion of authority's perspective with one's own.
Stage 2— Individualism, Instrumental Purpose, and Exchange	Following rules only when it is to someone's immediate interest; acting to meet one's own interests and needs and letting others do the same. Right is also what's fair, what's an equal exchange, a deal, an agreement.	To serve one's own needs or interests in a world where you have to recognize that other people have their interests, too.	*Concrete individualistic perspective.* Aware that everybody has his own interest to pursue and these conflict, so that right is relative (in the concrete individualistic sense).
Level II—Conventional Stage 3—Mutual Interpersonal Expectations, Relationships, and Interpersonal Conformity	Living up to what is expected by people close to you or what people generally expect of people in your role as son, brother, friend, etc. "Being good" is important and means having good motives, showing concern about others. It also means keeping mutual relationships, such as trust, loyalty, respect, and gratitude.	The need to be a good person in your own eyes and those of others. Your caring for others. Belief in the Golden Rule. Desire to maintain rules and authority which support stereotypical good behavior.	*Perspective of the individual in relationships with other individuals.* Aware of shared feelings, agreements, and expectations which take primacy over individual interests. Relates points of view through the concrete Golden Rule, putting yourself in the other guy's shoes. Does not yet consider generalized system perspective.
Stage 4—Social System and Conscience	Fulfilling the actual duties to which you have agreed. Laws are to be upheld except in extreme cases where they conflict with other fixed social duties. Right is also contributing to society, the group, or institution.	To keep the institution going as a whole, to avoid the breakdown in the system "if everyone did it," or the imperative of conscience to meet one's defined obligations.	*Differentiates societal point of view from interpersonal agreement or motives.* Takes the point of view of the system that defines roles and rules. Considers individual relations in terms of place in the system.

117

TABLE 5–2 *Continued*

	CONTENT OF STAGE		
Level and Stage	*What Is Right*	*Reasons for Doing Right*	*Social Perspective of Stage*
Level III—Postconventional, or Principled Stage 5—Social Contract or Utility and Individual Rights	Being aware that people hold a variety of values and opinions, that most values and rules are relative to your group. These relative rules should usually be upheld, however, in the interest of impartiality and because they are the social contract. Some nonrelative values and rights like *life* and *liberty*, however, must be upheld in any society and regardless of majority opinion.	A sense of obligation to law because of one's social contract to make and abide by laws for the welfare of all and for the protection of all people's rights. A feeling of contractual commitment, freely entered upon, to family, friendship, trust, and work obligations. Concern that laws and duties be based on rational calculation of overall utility, "the greatest good for the greatest number."	*Prior-to-society perspective.* Perspective of a rational individual aware of values and rights prior to social attachments and contracts. Integrates perspectives by formal mechanisms of agreement, contract, objective impartiality, and due process. Considers moral and legal points of view; recognizes that they sometimes conflict and finds it difficult to integrate them.
Stage 6—Universal Ethical Principles	Following self-chosen ethical principles. Particular laws or social agreements are usually valid because they rest on such principles. When laws violate these principles, one acts in accordance with the principle. Principles are universal principles of justice: the equality of human rights and respect for the dignity of human beings as individual persons.	The belief as a rational person in the validity of universal moral principles, and a sense of personal commitment to them.	*Perspective of a moral point of view* from which social arrangements derive. Perspective is that of any rational individual recognizing the nature of morality or the fact that persons are ends in themselves and must be treated as such.

(Source: Adapted from Kohlberg, L. [1976]. Moral stages and moralization: The cognitive developmental approach. In T. Lickona [Ed.], *Moral development and behavior: Theory, research, and social issues.* New York: Holt, Rinehart & Winston.)

trend is toward judgments increasingly based on stages 3, 4, and 5. Stage 6 is used relatively infrequently. In all the other cultures, both stages 5 and 6 are used as a basis for judgments relatively infrequently.

Some other research lends credence to Kohlberg's claim of universality in the stages of moral judgment. Pirakh (1980), for example, compared moral development in U. S. and Indian adolescents, and White (1975) examined moral development in Bahamian children and early adolescents. Snarey, Reimer, and Kohlberg (1985) surveyed Israeli kibbutz adolescents. Finally, Ma (1988) investigated moral judgments in groups from Hong Kong, mainland China, and England. In all these studies, the clear finding is that moral judgments and reasoning develop in the sequence described by Kohlberg (see also Boyes & Walker, 1988; Walker, de Vries, & Trevethan, 1987). Adolescence is the time when moral reasoning at more advanced stages emerges.

Despite the fact that these data are complex and cannot be tied closely to specific cultural variations, they are consistent with Kohlberg's claim of stage universality. The cultural differences depicted in Figure 5–1, and found in other research, may reflect either or both of two factors.

First, individuals may not pass through the stages at the same rates. This may be true both within a single culture as well as across several cultures. Second, the demands imposed on individuals living in different cultures may cause them to proceed through the stages at different rates. Nonetheless, these surveys support Kohlberg's theory and demonstrate that mature forms of moral thinking coincide with adolescence.

The findings of these and other cross-sectional studies provide strong support for Kohlberg's claim that the stages of moral development are hierarchical in nature. However, the longitudinal study of the development of moral reasoning would provide even stronger support. The most extensive longitudinal study of moral reasoning levels was reported by Colby and others (1983), who retested subjects in Kohlberg's original sample six times over a 20-year interval. Over the course of the 20 years, no subject skipped a stage nor reverted to the use of a prior stage. Moreover, stage scores in childhood were positively correlated with stage scores in adulthood, indicating the progressive and long-term nature of moral reasoning. More recently, Walker (1989) reported the results of a two-

year longitudinal study of moral reasoning in children (grades 1 and 4), adolescents (grades 7 and 10), and their parents. Again, the findings supported the stage sequence postulated by Kohlberg, with higher stages of moral reasoning emerging with increasing age level.

Taken in total, the evidence supports the contention that moral reasoning and judgment develop in an identifiable sequence, with adolescence being the time when more advanced stages of moral thinking begin to emerge. Apparently, there are no important sex differences in this finding, either with respect to its sequence or ultimate stage of moral reasoning attained (see Box 5–1). Part of the reason that adolescence is the time when more advanced stages of moral reasoning begin to be observed seems to be due to the changes in cognitive development that occur at that time.

Cognitive Development and Moral Judgment

Researchers have examined two aspects of Piaget's and Kohlberg's claims that moral judgment and reasoning are related to aspects of cognitive development. One facet of these research efforts has been to determine if certain levels of cognitive development are related to moral reasoning. For example, must one be able to reason at the formal operational level—which is presumed to be characteristic of adolescents—in order to reason morally at the last two stages postulated by Kohlberg? The second aspect of research efforts has been aimed at exploring how cognitive conflict relates to development and progression through the stages of moral judgment.

Cognitive Stage and Moral Stage. Lee (1971) demonstrated what is perhaps the clearest relationship between cognition and moral development. The subjects of her study were 195 middle-class boys, 15 from each grade level, kindergarten through 12. The boys ranged from 5½ to 17 years of

BOX 5–1   Are There Sex Differences in Moral Reasoning?

Carol Gilligan, in her book *In a Different Voice* (1982), has strongly suggested that current theories of moral development are biased toward male perspectives of morality. She points out that contemporary as well as more historical perspectives of morality are based on the writings of men, not women. As a result, she claims, females are prone to score lower on tests of moral judgment because they view moral concerns through a different perspective. In addition, she points out that in contemporary culture a particular perspective—one emphasizing achievement, competition, and detached individualism—is considered more mentally healthy and appropriate.

Gilligan goes on to note that there may be at least two perspectives in approaching moral dilemmas. In the *justice* orientation the emphasis in moral reasoning is on individual rights and whether or not individuals are treated fairly. In the *care* perspective the emphasis is on attention to others' needs, with moral judgments being based on attachments to others. Clearly, the former perspectives is "male oriented" and the latter "female oriented" in nature, consistent with traditional sex roles. Current indices of moral reasoning give greater weight to the male-oriented perspectives of morality, those most consistent with the male sex role. As a result, Gilligan argues, females as a group are likely to seem to have lower levels of moral thinking than males because females are prone to looking at the world in a different manner.

As an example, consider the drug dilemma in Table 5–1—should Heinz have stolen the drug or not? From the justice perspective the issue concerns the rights of the individual—by stealing the drug Heinz was infringing on the rights of the druggist. From the caring perspective, the question is one of the druggist's lack of concern for the life of another human. These are two very different interpretations of the moral dilemma and, Gilligan points out, they are likely to be considered differentially by males and females. Given the formulation of Kohlberg's theory, if women take a caring perspective they are likely to score at a lower moral level than men, who are more likely to take a justice perspective.

Gilligan's critique of theories of moral development has stirred considerable debate and research (see Baumrind, 1986; Gilligan & Attanucci, 1988; Donenberg & Hoffman, 1988; Friedman, Robinson, & Friedman, 1987; Walker, 1986, 1989). The general findings of these studies are that there are no sex differences in moral judgment, whether the scoring scheme is based on Kohlberg's model or on an alternative one assessing moral judgments on the justice and care dimensions. In other words, it does not appear that current means of assessing moral reasoning are biased against females. In addition, it appears that both males and females are capable of making moral judgments on both the justice and care dimensions, although females may be more likely to use the latter dimension to make moral judgments.

An interesting finding is that educational level is related to level of moral development, but perhaps not in the same manner for males and females (Baumrind, 1986; Boldizar, Wilson, & Deemer, 1989). For males, both involvement in and dedication to educational goals were indirectly related to moral development. For females, they were directly related. Boldizar and colleagues suggest that institutional settings that are male oriented as opposed to being female oriented account for this sex difference. Males see the opportunity to advance in a male-dominated culture. For females, this is less likely.

Although the research does not bear out Gilligan's initial assertion of bias in assessments of moral judgment, her critique has led to important research on the bases of moral judgments that tie these judgments to broad-based cultural concerns such as sex roles. Her thinking has inspired studies that clarify the very complex nature of examining moral thinking and link moral thinking to other major research domains.

age. Lee first determined the Piagetian stage of cognitive development of the child by administering a series of conceptual tasks, for example, conservation of mass and conservation of liquid. Lee then administered Kohlberg's nine moral judgment stories, which were simplified for the younger children. The child's responses to each story were scored and the level of moral reasoning determined.

The results, although complex, demonstrated that cognitive level, independent of age, correlated highly with the level of moral reasoning. For example, concrete operational thinking predicted a decrease in level 1 (authority) moral reasoning, and formal operational thinking predicted an increase in level 4 (societal) moral reasoning.

Other researchers have provided evidence relating stages of moral development, as defined by Kohlberg, to levels of cognitive development. Tomlinson-Keasey and Keasey (1974) reported high correlations between cognitive development stage and moral thinking for both sixth-grade students and college students. Rowe and Marcia (1980) tested cognitive development and moral thinking in 18- to 26-year-olds. They found that only subjects at least at beginning formal operations had moral judgment levels in the higher stages. Walker (1980) tested fourth through seventh graders for level of moral development and level of cognitive development. He reported that, for students in level 2 of moral development, increases in moral development after exposure to role playing occurred only for students with at least beginning formal operations. Similar relationships between level of cognitive development and level of moral development have been reported by Krebs and Gillmore (1982) and Lutwak (1984).

The relationship between level of cognitive development and level of moral development probably has two bases. First, as we will discuss below, cognitive development is related to perspective taking about moral issues (for example, Colby et al., 1983). As can

be seen in Table 5–2, different sociomoral perspectives are associated with the different levels of moral development. It is likely that, as cognitive skills develop, perspective taking along moral lines changes, these changes being in part responsible for the relationship between cognitive and moral development.

Second, as we spelled out in Chapter 4, formal operational thinking allows the individual to consider the possible as well as the real. It also is the basis for abstract thinking. Examination of Table 5–2 shows that increases in moral development are associated with increasingly abstract concepts of justice.

Some research support for this link between cognitive and moral development is available. The research reviewed in the immediately preceding section shows that discussions of moral issues promote moral development only for those at least having beginning formal operations. Parikh (1980) reported that mothers with higher levels of moral development were more likely to engage their children in discussions of moral issues, thereby promoting understanding of these issues. Not surprisingly, these children had higher levels of moral development than did the children of mothers who did not engage their children in such discussions.

Finally, there is increasing evidence (Damon & Killen, 1982; Broughton, 1982; Berkowitz & Gibbs, 1983) that both contrived (as in experimental situations) and spontaneous (occurring in natural circumstances) discussions of moral issues are related to increases in moral development (Niles, 1986). It may be that discussions with peers who are at more advanced levels of moral thinking promote development in those who are less advanced.

It appears, then, that cognitive development is related to the development of concepts in the moral domain through two mechanisms. First, cognitive development allows one to perceive moral interactions from different perspectives. Second, with increasing ability to think and consider issues from an abstract perspective, one gains new insights into moral issues, such as the rights of others and the reasons for behaving rightly (see Table 5–2).

This is important to our understanding of adolescents because it helps explain their idealism, particularly with regard to understanding the nature of the social system and politics, and the "rules" of social interaction. Formal operational thinking allows the adolescent to consider the possibility that things might be different with different political systems because of the hypothetico-deductive (if-then) thinking that accompanies formal operational competence. Although likely egocentric in nature, adolescent thinking might simply, for example, lead to the idea that all countries should dispense with all nuclear weapons, thereby eliminating the threat of nuclear war. The adolescent might well not consider the possibility that some nation might cheat.

Similarly, the level of moral development is related to moral thinking about "real" as well as contrived dilemmas, such as those on Kohlberg's inventory (de Vries & Walker, 1986; Walker et al., 1987). In addition, moral thinking about current politically and morally sensitive issues such as capital punishment is related to moral thinking stage (de Vries & Walker, 1986), with more morally advanced adolescents being more opposed to capital punishment.

Cognitive Conflict and Moral Development. The reason that both contrived and spontaneous discussions of moral issues may facilitate stage transitions in moral development is that they may produce cognitive conflict between one's current moral structures (stage of moral reasoning) and one's own as well as others' opinions on moral issues (Walker, 1983). The disequilibrium resulting from the conflict, according to cognitive-developmental theory (Chapter 4; Turiel, 1974, 1977; Kohlberg, 1969, 1976),

stimulates structural change and, hence, change in moral thinking and judgment.

The role of cognitive conflict in moral stage transition was most clearly shown by Walker (1983). He exposed students in grades five through 7 to one of six experimental conditions in which two adults exhibited moral reasoning either one stage above the subject or at the subject's stage. In addition, the adults either were of the same or different opinions. Some subjects were given no treatment. The subjects were tested with Kohlberg's moral dilemmas both one week and seven weeks after hearing the adults. Students exposed to the conflict, especially when the adults had differing opinions, evidenced upward stage development in moral reasoning. Students exposed to reasoning and opinions at their own stage showed some change upward, but it was minimal. Those students not exposed to adult moral reasoning showed no change.

The results of this and other research are important for two reasons. First, they help clarify how transitions in our thinking about moral issues occur. By being exposed to various views and opinions, as well as to logically stated arguments, our thinking about moral issues is changed. Parents, then, can facilitate their offspring's moral development by engaging them in discussions of moral issues. Second, the findings demonstrate that moral thinking has a cognitive basis. Hence, advances in cognitive development should be related to advances in moral thinking. As many (for example, Colby et al., 1983) have pointed out, moral thinking is an expression of cognitive structures applied to a specific domain.

Role Taking and Moral Development

In our earlier discussion of Piaget's theorizing about morality we noted the important place of role taking in moral judgment development. The relationship between role taking and moral development has been described by Selman (1976). In essence, what

Selman suggests is that role-taking ability, which develops in a series of stages parallel to Piaget's stages of cognitive development, influences the child's understanding of the social world and how conflicts should be resolved. Moral judgments reflect the application of role taking to the moral domain, leading to views of how social conflicts should be resolved. Developments in role taking, or perspective taking, then, should precede developments in moral reasoning and judgment.

Kohlberg (1969, 1976; Colby et al., 1983) has noted that progression through the stages of moral development may be enhanced by role-taking opportunities because role taking allows the child to play various roles and to learn to take somebody else's point of view. This perspective, of course, is consistent with research, reviewed above, demonstrating that contrived and spontaneous discussions lead to increases in moral reasoning. Such discussions are, in effect, role-taking opportunities.

More direct evidence of the link between role taking and moral development comes from a number of studies. Moir (1974), for example, found that 11-year-old girls' level of moral reasoning was positively correlated with their role-taking ability, even when IQ was controlled. In other words, the relationship between role taking and moral judgment was not due to IQ. Arbuthnot (1975) had some children role-play in moral dilemma situations and had some children simply be exposed to the moral arguments. The children's level of moral thinking was assessed immediately and a week later. It was found that children who role-played showed increased levels of moral development on both post-tests, but that children simply exposed to the moral arguments did not change in level of moral thinking. Krebs and Gillmore (1982) found that role taking and moral development were moderately (.7) correlated. Finally, Walker (1980) found that adolescents' role-taking ability was closely related to their advancement from stage 2 to stage 3 moral thinking in an experimental situation.

Even more direct evidence on the importance of role taking and moral development was provided in a study by Keasey (1971). Keasey assessed boys' and girls' moral development and obtained measures of social participation for each individual. The social participation measures came from the child, peers, and teachers, and included measures of quantity (the number of clubs or social organizations to which the child belonged) and quality (for example, the number of leadership positions held). For all three

Playing various roles, such as group leader, promotes the development of moral thinking, according to Kohlberg.

sources of information, and for measures of both quantity and quality, greater participation was associated with higher levels of moral development. Although the issue of direction of causation is important here, the study nevertheless demonstrates a close link between role taking and moral development.

On the basis of evidence such as that provided in the studies reviewed above, a number of researchers have concluded that opportunities for role playing promote understanding of other's views, reduced egocentrism, and lead to advances in moral thinking. Indeed, some (for example, Rest, 1976; Selman, 1976) contend that cultural differences in progression through the stages of moral thinking may be the result of differing opportunities for role taking in various cultures. Less complex cultures may provide fewer opportunities for role taking than our industrialized, urban culture. Hence, progression through the stages of moral development may be slower and the predominant moral stage lower (see evidence presented above on cultural differences).

Moral Judgment and Behavior

It is natural at this point to raise the issue of the relationship between moral reasoning and moral behaviors. Is the above theorizing about the nature and development of moral reasoning applicable to explaining behavior other than verbal statements, or is it simply fodder for the theorists' grist mill?

Studying the relationship between moral reasoning and moral behavior is complex. One must not only identify levels of moral development, but must also choose a behavior that clearly falls in the moral domain. The latter is especially difficult because what one person considers an act in the moral domain may not be similarly considered by others. And, links between thinking and behavior may not be as direct as we might think.

One of the first studies relating moral thinking to moral behavior was conducted by Turiel and Rothman (1972), who examined the relationship between level of moral reasoning and behavior in 13-year-old boys. Two weeks after each boy's level of moral development was determined by his responses to six Kohlberg-type stories, each boy participated, along with two adults, as a "teacher" in a learning task. The task of these "teachers" was to read alternately a list of words to a third adult, who was then to spell the words. Each time a spelling error was made, poker chips (representing money) were taken away from the adult. The adult doing the spelling was a confederate who made a predetermined number of spelling errors. After six words had been presented, one of the two adults participating as a "teacher" said the experiment should be stopped. He presented an argument that was either one stage above (+ 1) or one stage below (− 1) the child's level of moral development. The second adult "teacher" presented a counter-argument either one stage below or one stage above the child's level of moral thinking. These two adults then left, presumably to resolve their conflict, and the child was given the choice of taking his turn or not participating. The reasons for each boy's choice were then assessed. A week later, a post-test was administered to again determine each boy's level of moral reasoning.

The results showed that the boys whose moral thinking level was at stage 2 or 3 continued the task regardless of the arguments presented. Boys functioning at stage 4 behaved in a manner consistent with the + 1 reasoning argument. That is, if the argument presented for stopping the experiment was one stage above the child's current level, the stage 4 child would stop, and vice versa. The behavioral choices of the stage 4 boys were subordinated to moral reasoning, the reasoning and behavior domains being integrated. This was not the case for the stage 2 and 3 boys. The post-test scores, however, revealed no long-term changes in moral reasoning as a function of the experimental situation.

This study is important for several reasons. First, the results clearly demonstrate a relationship between the two domains for stage 4 adolescent boys and suggest that there may be a progressive integration of the two domains prior to the child's reaching stage 4 moral thinking. The second important implication of the experiment stems from its failure to find lasting changes in level of moral reasoning. This is especially interesting for the stage 4 subjects whose behavior was definitely affected by the experimental situation. The importance of this finding lies the separation of behavioral choice and level of reasoning, and suggests that research from the social-learning approach (for example, Bandura & MacDonald, 1963) may not be demonstrating changes in the child's level of moral reasoning. Rather, the experimental manipulations may simply alter behavioral choices rather than the cognitive processes presumed by Kohlberg to underlie moral reasoning. The findings from the social-learning approach and those of Turiel and Rothman suggest that the conditioning procedures used in the former are more effective for altering behavioral choices than the procedures used by Turiel and Rothman, at least for boys in stages 2 and 3. There is no way at present to determine which procedure, if either, would be better for stage 4 subjects. This view is consistent with theorizing by Kohlberg about processes related to progression through the stages of moral development.

More recently, Weiss (1982) studied moral thinking as related to the actions of the self vs. the actions of others. The subjects were adolescents aged 16 to 18. The task was to determine if a wrongful act should be told to the parents of the character in the story involving the act. In one story, the adolescents answered as if they were the main character; in the other story, they answered about a fictitious other person. Two findings were important. First, moral reasoning was higher for the "other" than the "self" story. In other words, the adolescents were more likely to consider consequences to the self and use lower levels of moral reasoning when placing themselves in the context of the main character. Second, this discrepancy was not as large for those in stage 4 of moral reasoning as it was for those in lower stages. As in the Turiel and Rothman study, with increases in moral thinking, there was a closer relationship between moral reasoning and moral action. The findings of this study, then, point to an important aspect of studying the link between thinking and behavior in the moral domain; namely, that moral reasoning and action may be differentially related depending upon whether it is the self or someone else being judged.

Other researchers have shown that people reason about "real life" personal dilemmas in the same manner that they reason about the hypothetical dilemmas and that more developmentally advanced moral thinkers behave consistently with their thinking. Coady and Sawyer (1986), for example, have shown that more developmentally advanced moral thinkers are less likely to cheat, presumably because of their level of moral development. Similarly, those with higher levels of moral development are less likely to engage in antisocial behavior and are more likely to help others (Rest, 1983).

With the exception of delinquency (see Box 5–2), reviewers of the literature Blasi, 1980; Kupfersmid & Wonderly, 1980) find mixed support for a link between moral thinking and moral behavior. Kupfersmid and Wonderly (1980) offer several explanations for the paucity of positive evidence. First, they note that in few studies are there individuals at the highest levels of moral thinking. Hence, links between moral thinking and behavior may be difficult to find. Second, they note that the behaviors studied often are artificial. They suggest that the artificiality may produce positive findings in many instances. Were we to study moral be-

BOX 5—2 **Morality and Delinquency**

As detailed in the text, the study of morality and behavior is fraught with difficult problems. One line of investigation that researchers have pursued is the study of differences in moral judgments between delinquent and nondelinquent groups. The logic under which such research endeavors were undertaken was the possibility that delinquents were delayed in their moral reasoning judgments, this immaturity leading to their engaging in behaviors normally considered immoral.

Jurkovic (1980) has reviewed the literature on the relationship between moral reasoning and delinquent behavior. In one set of studies the moral reasoning of delinquents and nondelinquents was compared. In general, it was found that delinquents had a less mature level of moral reasoning than nondelinquents. In addition, it was found that the moral development of delinquents evidenced a developmental lag compared to the moral development of nondelinquents; that is, the older delinquents had higher levels of moral reasoning than the younger delinquents but those levels were comparable to nondelinquents who were chronologically younger. In other words, immature moral reasoning, in itself, cannot be considered the sole cause of delinquency.

Although adolescents who do not give up their premoral orientation while their peers are progressing in moral reasoning may well be at risk for engaging in behaviors considered delinquent, progressing to higher levels of moral thinking does not insulate the adolescent from engaging in delinquent behaviors.

Jurkovic (1980) suggests that moral thinking is only one of a complex of factors that determines the behavior in which we engage. Temperamental, biological, and personality factors are also important in delinquency. In addition, situational contexts are important in determining behavior. Finally, Jurkovic notes that delinquents may well rationalize their behavior with age-appropriate stage 3 or 4 moral judgments.

A study of Petronio (1980) is interesting in this light. He investigated the possibility that repeater delinquents of 13 to 17 years of age might have lower levels of moral reasoning than nonrepeaters. This possibility was based on the notion that repeat offenders may have an arrested moral development, making them more prone to engaging in delinquent acts. Surprisingly, however, he found that the repeater delinquents had a *higher* level of moral reasoning (stage 3) than the nonrepeaters (stage 2). Just as Jurkovic (1980) suggested, the repeater delinquents rationalized their behavior with age-appropriate moral standards. Petronio suggests they did this in an attempt to reduce their feelings and appearances of "badness."

Jurkovic (1980) draws several conclusions on the basis of the existing evidence. First, he concludes that the link between delinquency and low levels of moral thinking has not been shown to be very strong. Delinquents are as heterogeneous in their moral thinking as others. Second, he notes that, just as moral thinking is complexly related to other behaviors, the links between moral judgments and delinquency are also complex. Few, if any, behaviors, including delinquency, are determined by a single factor. Indeed, that is in part what makes predicting human behavior so difficult. Hence, attempts to increase the level of moral thinking ability of delinquents, which can be done (Niles, 1986), may not translate to reductions in delinquency.

havior in "real life" domains, such as work habits, returning found money, and income tax preparation, they state, we might well find different results. It seems that when individuals perceive that they may be hurt by behaving in a morally advanced manner they are less likely to do so (Sobesky, 1983).

Given the above evidence, it is not surprising that adolescents do not *always* behave at the moral level of which they are capable, virtually no one does. Adolescents will engage in delinquency (see Chapter 13), for example, in part because they feel they won't get caught (egocentrism; Chapter 4) and in part because they are more concerned about the self (see above). Although they may morally "know better," adolescents will engage in unprotected sexual intercourse. Situational factors, perceptions of the self, and the like are all important to explaining why adolescents behave the way they do.

An Integrated Theory of Moral Development

Any overview of the area of moral development must, of necessity, be somewhat incomplete. We have reviewed the theorizing and research representing the three major approaches to the topic—psychoanalytic, social-learning, and cognitive-developmental. The evidence notes the importance of peers, parents, and the culture in the formation of morality. In this overview, we shall attempt to integrate the theories into a coherent whole and demonstrate that they all contribute to a unique understanding of moral development.

The psychoanalytic view of moral development provided the original impetus for investigating the child's social environment vis-á-vis moral development. Hence, a considerable body of research on parent-child relationships, particularly with respect to discipline techniques, has accumulated. These data reveal significant relationships between parent-child interactions and moral development. These relationships are best explained by social-learning-theory principles, because of their demonstrated relationship to behavior.

As the adolescent's cognitive abilities mature, and he or she becomes exposed to an increasingly wider range of environmental encounters, the adolescent redefines notions about rules and authority learned from parents in a more rational and objective manner. With the advent of formal operational thinking the adolescent becomes a moral philosopher, capable of reasoning about moral issues at an abstract level. Moral judgments become based on higher principles than personal issues. Cognitive development fosters moral reasoning that *allows* higher levels of moral behavior. Whether or not these behaviors will occur depends on situ-

ational factors best represented by social-learning theory. Hence, our best explanation of moral development may include all three theoretical positions discussed earlier. In this way, we can begin to explain moral thinking, moral behavior, and internalization of standards in ways allowing us to understand their interrelationships.

MORAL EDUCATION

An important question at this point concerns how we learn moral values and behaviors. Historically, moral values have been viewed as being taught not only by parents but also by teachers. However, a continuing debate centers on the degree to which the school system should be involved in the teaching of morals. Questions center on what values should be taught, how they are best taught, and who should decide what should be taught (Perlmutter & Shapiro, 1987).

Regardless of how one feels about these issues, a bit of reflection reveals that the school system is a setting in which moral values are taught. Teachers set examples of fairness and honesty, consideration for others, the importance of behaving in a manner consistent with rules and regulations designed to benefit the whole, and the like. Peers present other value systems which must be considered in addition to one's own. From the time the students arrive at school until they leave, they are exposed to a host of values and ideals that fall within the realm of morality, even if there is no specific curriculum focused on the development of moral thinking and moral behavior.

Curricula and methods schools use to teach morality fall into three broad categories, each consistent with the theoretical perspectives of moral development discussed above: values clarification, behavior modification, and cognitive-developmental.

Values Clarification Curricula

The essential aspect of values clarification curricula is the determination of the **values** one holds dear and would be willing to stand up for (see Box 5–3). As you well know, adolescents ponder many issues that have a value orientation: When, if ever, should there be war?; What sexual values should I hold?; Why can't wealth be distributed more evenly so there would be no poor people?; Since many of my friends use drugs why shouldn't I?; What kind of person do I want to be?; etc.

The procedures used in values clarification do not focus on what the correct answer to these questions should be (Minuchin & Shapiro, 1983; Perlmutter & Shapiro, 1987)—the answers are subjective and individualistic. Rather, values clarification aims to help students learn the process of valuing and become aware of the values they hold. Students learn to weigh pros and cons and to consider the implications of making various choices. In this way, they become more sophisticated in how they think about the values they hold and how to think about values in general. Through direct teaching in how to analyze and refine one's values, and through the indirect learning that all of us experience, we come to hold personal values and to realize that there are individual differences we should appreciate. Values clarification curricula help make adolescents more aware of their values and provide mechanisms for thinking about values.

A variety of techniques is used in values clarification classes. One technique requires students to make forced choices of what they would rather be, for example, a loner or a person in lots of groups. Another procedure asks students to rank order world issues, such as poverty, national defense, and the like. By discussing the reasoning underlying the choices, students become more aware of how they think about issues and how they make choices about values.

In a sense, the values clarification curriculum, then, helps develop the individual. As you can see, the specific value contents are not of particular importance; the emphasis

is on how one may go about developing values by considering alternatives.

Behavior Modification and Moral Behaviors

As the name implies, behavior modification, which is based on the social learning perspective of moral development, has as its aim the training of moral behaviors. As opposed to teaching processes of value determination or moral judgment, the emphasis is on teaching children and adolescents to behave in what are considered morally correct ways. (Perlmutter & Shapiro, 1987).

One method used is to reward or punish specific behaviors directly. In effect, this is the practice parents use, especially with younger children but also with adolescents, to get them to behave in ways the parents wish. Hence, when parents withdraw a privilege because the adolescent has engaged in behaviors deemed undesirable, such as staying out too late, or allow special privileges because the adolescent has exhibited appropriate behavior, they are using behavior modification techniques to alter the adolescent's behavior along the lines they deem appropriate. Teachers, too, use such techniques to control the behavior of their students in the classroom—violation of school rules can have severe consequences.

A second technique that explains how social learning may be used to teach moral behavior revolves around adults as models for moral and ethical behavior. Parental behavior can set examples for how one should behave in a variety of circumstances. Similarly, teachers are models for fairness, rule following, responsibility, and the like. In this way, both parents and teachers are teaching moral behaviors—and at times they are at odds with each other.

Although behavior modification and modeling clearly are effective means of altering behavior, there are some criticisms of this means of teaching morality. First, in-

BOX 5–3 **Adolescent Values**

The importance of value clarification lies in the establishment of a system of values. As adolescents develop formal operational cognitive skills, these skills are applied to concerns of personal beliefs, as we discussed in Chapter 4. The value system resulting from these introspections is important for resolving moral conflicts because it provides a basis for decision making (Feather, 1980).

Four Most Important and Four Least Important Values in Five Groups of Male Students

			TERMINAL VALUES		
Rank of Value	United States	Canada	Australia	Israel	Papua New Guinea
1	Freedom	Freedom	Wisdom	A world at peace	A world at peace
2	Happiness	Happiness	True friendship	National security	Equality
3	Wisdom	Mature love	Freedom	Happiness	Freedom
4	Self-respect	Self-respect	A sense of accomplishment	Freedom	True friendship
15	Pleasure	A world of beauty	A world of beauty	A comfortable life	A sense of accomplishment
16	Salvation	Social recognition	Social recognition	Social recognition	Pleasure
17	National security	National security	National security	A world of beauty	Mature love
18	A world of beauty	Salvation	Salvation	Salvation	A world of beauty

			INSTRUMENTAL VALUES		
Rank of Value	United States	Canada	Australia	Israel	Papua New Guinea
1	Honest	Honest	Honest	Honest	Honest
2	Responsible	Responsible	Broad-minded	Responsible	Helpful
3	Ambitious	Loving	Responsible	Logical	Responsible
4	Broad-minded	Broad-minded	Loving	Capable	Ambitious
15	Cheerful	Imaginative	Imaginative	Clean	Independent
16	Polite	Polite	Polite	Imaginative	Clean
17	Clean	Clean	Clean	Obedient	Logical
18	Obedient	Obedient	Obedient	Forgiving	Imaginative

(Source: Feather, N.T. [1980]. Values in adolescence. In J. Adelson [Ed.], *Handbook of adolescent psychology.* New York: John Wiley & Sons.)

Rokeach (1973) divides values into two types: terminal, which reflect endstates of our existence, and instrumental, which relate to ways of behaving. He goes on to note that, although there likely are many more instrumental than terminal values, the numbers of each likely are much smaller than the number of other more specific beliefs and attitudes that we hold. The distinction between terminal and instrumental values and our other beliefs and attitudes is that the former two types of values are central to our belief system—our other beliefs and attitudes reflecting the more general core values. Changes in core values, then, will have widespread effects on our general belief system.

In one of the more extensive contemporary studies of the development of adolescent value systems, Feather (1975, 1980) examined college students' values by using Rokeach's (1973) Value

Survey. The survey lists 18 terminal and 18 instrumental values. The respondents are asked to rank each set of values in regard to the self.

Feather (1975, 1980) had male college students in five countries complete the survey, in order to examine cultural differences in value systems. Three countries (United States, Canada, Australia) were relatively affluent and two (Israel, Papua New Guinea) were not. The surveys were conducted in the late 1960s and early 1970s. The results of the survey are presented in the accompanying table for the four most important and four least important terminal and instrumental values, that is, for the values deemed most and least important on the basis of the responses to the survey.

Examination of the accompanying table shows similarities in the values of students from the three affluent countries. Nonetheless, there are differences reflecting the varying emphases of each country. For example, the high stress in the United States on achievement is present. The values of the Israeli students reflect the political climate of the Middle East. Finally, the Papua New Guinea students' values reflect the emergence into nationhood at the time the data were collected.

Because values are so closely tied to national perspectives and issues, it should not be surprising to find that as national tides change, so, too, do adolescent value structures. For example, it has been noted among college professors that students seem more task-oriented now than in the 1960s and 1970s, and that students seem to be more attuned to academics. Indeed, more recent data on adolescent interests (Bachman, Johnston, & O'Malley, 1980) show that this is the case.

consistencies in reinforcement teach conflicting messages. Second, there may well be differences in the behaviors deemed moral by parents and those deemed moral by teachers. Third, the behaviors taught as moral reflect the individualistic perspectives of those doing the teaching. As some critics have noted, there are few generally accepted moral behaviors. Most are viewed by many as reflecting single perspectives and very middle-class values that may not be applicable to everyone. Finally, behavior modification, in itself, does not teach *why* certain behaviors are preferable to others. Rather, adolescents need to be taught why certain behaviors are more moral than others so they can rely on this knowledge when moral choices must be made. This task is the *forte* of the final perspective on moral education.

Teaching Moral Reasoning

Curricula aimed at teaching the principles of moral reasoning are derived from Kohlberg's theory. The exemplary program was, indeed, established by Kohlberg in 1974. The emphasis in the program is on the dis-

cussion of realistic issues that arise in the school environment, with an emphasis on the importance of give and take, mutual caring, and group commitment (Kohlberg, 1980). In this system, the teacher is viewed as someone to facilitate discussion of moral issues, bringing out the importance of various alternatives for the larger community (the school). The aim is to have the students come to feel stronger responsibilities to the community, as in Kohlberg's stage 4 moral thinking. There is no attempt to get the students to begin to make moral judgments at stages 5 and 6, in part because it is apparent that relatively few people reason about moral issues at these levels.

Although programs vary among schools, in general they are also aimed at teaching moral behavior. For example, by discussing rules for conduct, the students not only became more aware of the reasons for rules but also begin to follow the rules more closely. To foster further coherence between moral reasoning and behavior, Kohlberg developed the Moral Atmosphere Interview (Higgins, Power, & Kohlberg, 1983). The interview is composed of dilemmas that involve social responsibiblity in the school setting. Students discuss alternative perspectives (recall the above discussion of the importance of role taking in moral development) and consequences of various actions (the idea being to judge one's choices in light of the impact on the community). Students encountering such a program were more attuned to behaving in accord with the rules determined to be beneficial to the community at large than students not experiencing the program.

As we can see from the above review, moral education is a daily event in the lives of adolescents. Parents, teachers, and peers all promote various aspects of moral thinking and behavior, as well as value development. To argue this should not go on in settings such as the school is, of course, to miss the point that it does go on, even if informally. To argue that the values taught are likely arbitrary or middle-class misses the point that there are some values to which we all agree. And, these values can, and are, being taught, either directly or indirectly, in public school settings.

The question of which technique of teaching morality is better is very difficult. One must, of necessity, opt for the procedure that not only teaches whatever is considered appropriate behavior, but also teaches the cognitive skills that allow an internalization of moral rules that can be applied to circumstances outside the realm of specifically taught behavior. In this regard, it appears that Kohlberg's scheme may prove, in the long run, most beneficial.

UNDERSTANDING THE SOCIAL ORDER: DEVELOPMENT OF RELIGIOUS AND POLITICAL THINKING

Just as cognitive and social influences interact to produce identifiable changes in adolescents' moral thinking, so too do they produce changes in views of religion, politics, and other aspects of the social order. Changes in these areas are a manifestation of the emergent changes in moral thinking, that is, thinking about the nature of the social order. Hence, they are appropriately discussed in a chapter on moral development. As will become apparent below, changes in the areas of religion and political thinking parallel those discussed above for moral thinking.

The Adolescent and Religion

The cognitive changes of adolescence trigger a questioning about the role of religion in the individual's life. Questions center on issues such as the role that religion should play in one's life, what it means to be religious, does one need to go to church or temple to be a religious person, and the like. Although some adolescents do, indeed, experience one form or another of what might be called a religious crisis (McAdams, Booth, & Selvik, 1981), most do not. Rather, for most adolescents, there is simply a renewed interest in religion as it begins to take on a more serious and personal meaning. As with other aspects of development, transitions in religious thinking are smooth and continuous, not abrupt.

Interest in Religion. Data on the degree to which adolescents view religion as important are somewhat scarce. Dusek and Monge (1974), in their study of adolescent interests, reported that "philosophy and religion" ranked quite low, between 9 and 14 on the 14-item checklist of interests, across grades 5 through 14. Only college freshmen ranked it as high as 9. In ratings of interest, religion was never more than average, that is, 4.0 on a 7.0 scale. These data, as well as others (Harris, 1959), indicate that the degree to which religion is viewed as interesting, important, or a "significant problem area" during adolescence is relatively low.

The most extensive investigation of aspects of adolescent religious interest was

During adolescence, views of the role of religion in one's life become more personal.

conducted by Kuhlen and Arnold (1944). A questionnaire on religious beliefs and problems was administered to 547 adolescents 12, 15, and 18 years old. The results indicated significant changes in beliefs across the adolescent years. The data generally support those discussed above. Religion was not viewed as a significant problem except by a relatively small percentage of adolescents.

Adolescents' Views of Religion. During adolescence the individual's views of religion change. As adolescents grow older, religion tends to become more a matter of personal conviction than external circumstance (Kuhlen & Arnold, 1944; Gallup & Poling, 1980; Harris, 1971). Although there is no evidence to indicate a repudiation of religious beliefs during the adolescent years, adolescents do come to view religion in a more personal and less dogmatic manner.

This was shown dramatically in a recent survey by Gallup and Poling (1980). The adolescents in this survey had little confidence in organized religion, and about 40 percent indicated that the honesty and ethical standards of the clergy were only average or less. Gallup and Poling suggest that this reflects a lack of confidence in organized religion. This may occur because organized religion is viewed as not changing with the times. Sorensen (1973) found that about half of 13-to 19-year-olds felt organized religion, as reflected in official church doctrine, was out of touch with the times and not as helpful as it might be to adolescents dealing with difficult personal issues in modern society.

The notion that views of religion are tied to the "social times" received considerable credence in a study conducted by Caplow and Bahr (1979). They surveyed the attitudes of adolescents in "Middletown," a community first surveyed 50 years earlier. Although the views on the purpose of religion, namely, to prepare one for the hereafter, changed little over the course of 50 years, a number of other views did. For example, far fewer adolescents believed the Bible was a sufficient guide for dealing with modern problems, that it was wrong to go to the movies on Sunday, and that Christianity was the one true religion. In turn, many more believed that evolution was a more accurate rendition of the origin of the human species than the Biblical account.

Religious Behavior. These changing views of adolescents are reflected in attendance at churches and in the view that religion is important in the lives of people. Harris's survey (1971) indicated that about 58 percent of high school students and 43 percent of college students regularly attended church. Other data report similar trends in church attendance across the adolescent years. Typically, girls attend church more frequently than boys, and better-educated adolescents attend church more frequently than less well educated adolescents. Since religious beliefs and practices are open to the same social influences as other forms of social behavior, one might suspect that parental involvement in religion should be related to adolescent religious views. This is indeed the case; if parents attend church regularly, their adolescent children do, too. This seems particularly true for Catholics, who have the highest rate of church attendance, and somewhat less true for Jews, who have the lowest attendance rates.

Some changes in religious behavior have been noted. Religion is losing its influence on the daily lives of the American people. The percentage of students feeling that religion is becoming less important in their daily lives increased during recent years. This is in direct contrast to the increases in the percentage of those who viewed religion as important between the Depression and the World War II years. Concurrent with this view is an increasing tendency to view religion more as a part of a philosophy of life and less as a means of personal salvation. Should this trend continue, it will become difficult to separate religious notions from notions of morality, as discussed above.

Cognition and Religious Views. The age changes in various views of religion, noted above, lead to the possibility that religious views are subject to reinterpretation as one develops cognitively. Some evidence, indeed, points in this direction.

The most relevant study linking cognitive development to perspectives of religion was reported by Elkind (1978a). Using an open-ended set of questions, he asked 5- to 14-year-olds about their views of religion. He compared the answers of those who were concrete operational and those who were formal operational. The concrete operational students were much less reflective and

personal in their views of religion. For example, they viewed going to church as a sign of one's religiosity, whereas the formal operational students argued religiosity was signified by one's ideological perspectives and personal beliefs about religious practices. In general, the data are consistent with the notion that, as one matures cognitively, the perspective of religion becomes both more personal and more abstract, as we have discussed above.

As the research points out, then, emerging cognitive capabilities along with existing social influences alter adolescent views of religion in a manner similar to the alterations that occur in moral thinking. As a result, adolescents view religion in a more abstract and personal way than children do. Their views are much more similar to those of adults. In some cases, however, parents and adolescents may clash on issues of religious observances, for example, attending services. This is much less likely to happen with children, who are not as able as adolescents to question the nature and role of religion.

Moral Development and Political Thinking

The study of political socialization is extremely complex (see Gallatin, 1980; Renshon, 1977; Sears, 1975, for general reviews), encompassing issues in political behavior (for example, voting), the acquisition of political values (for example, liberal versus conservative viewpoints), interpersonal relations (for example, the role of compromise in political decision making), and the understanding of the nature of the social order (for example, the roles of government and laws, community versus individual rights). It is far beyond our purpose to review all this material, as interesting as it is. Instead, we shall focus on concerns in the latter realm; specifically, we shall examine evidence on the link between moral development and political thinking within a cognitive-developmental frame-work. As a result, we focus on the adolescent's political (broadly conceived) thinking, that is, the adolescent's perception of political issues and understanding of the social order.

Sullivan (1970) has discussed the differences between moral and political development. Although the two are closely related, moral development is seen as being more general, as relating to both public and private thinking concerning interpersonal issues. Political thinking is more specific; it relates to thinking about the relationship between individuals and public institutions. Hence, it concerns the types of issues raised immediately above. From the developmental perspective, however, both are related to general progressions in cognitive development, which provide the underlying basis for examining their relationship in this chapter. From the cognitive-developmental perspective, then, the interesting questions revolve around the development of mature political thinking. In this regard, an important question is the degree to which changing cognitive competencies are related to the development of political thinking.

Of course, if the cognitive-developmental perspective on understanding of the social order is a fair approximation of reality, there should be a relationship between political thinking and moral development. This was the subject of an investigation conducted by Lonky, Reihman, and Serlin (1981). They had students in grades 8, 10, and 12 complete the Defining Issues Test (DIT; a measure of moral development) and answer questions concerning aspects of political thinking, values, and beliefs (for example, the nature of minority rights, equality of opportunity, social welfare, and the like). Subjects were then divided into two groups, low and high, on the basis of their answers on the DIT. Those evidencing more advanced moral thinking scored higher on all questions concerning political thinking than those with lower levels of moral development. The authors concluded that more mature and abstract political thinking was associated with higher levels of moral thinking, which in turn were associated with higher levels of cognitive development. The findings of this study, then, demonstrate a link between moral thinking and political thinking.

This relationship was also investigated by Joseph Adelson (Adelson, 1971, 1975; Adelson & O'Neil, 1966), who studied extensively the development of political thinking during the adolescent years. Generally speaking, during early adolescence, political thinking is concrete and personalized. Young adolescents view politics as involving either specific people or particular government agencies such as the police or the Congress. They tend to think political problems can be solved in highly concrete and simplistic ways. An authoritarian mode of behavior dominates their views; for example, punishment rather than rehabilitation is viewed as the remedy for crime. It is interesting to note how these views parallel Kohlberg's stages of moral thinking.

Other research shows a link between moral and political thinking. Conservative, liberal, and egalitarian political views correspond, respectively, to Kohlberg's last three stages (Simpson, 1987). Understanding the reasons for having government and laws and political organizations increases between ages 6 and 15 (Berti, 1988). This research indicates that moral and political thinking are intertwined, reflecting a common underlying basis, likely cognitive development.

In mid- or late adolescence political thinking takes on a different and mature tone. Older adolescents view political agencies as existing to protect the rights of people. Political and social problems can be solved by the mutual cooperation of individuals and social institutions. Perhaps most importantly, older adolescents have cognitive capabilities that allow them to think of the ramifications and implications of various kinds of decisions; they can see beyond the immediate consequences of social rules.

Older adolescents, then, demonstrate a reasoned and rational view of the development and nature, as well as function, of existing political systems. Notions such as political compromise (Furth & McConville, 1981; Berti, 1988:) the rights of the individual, the rights of the community, and the guarantees that political systems owe to individuals become important criteria for making political and social decisions. By 15 to 18 years of age, adolescent political views, that is, views about the nature of politics, are representative of those in the adult world. It seems it is no accident that 18 years of age represents the lower limit for voting rights. It is at this time that the individual's political thinking has matured in terms of realizing both short-term as well as long-term consequences of decisions, and can take into account the variety of circumstances that might legitimately influence, and be affected by, a given political decision.

Some examples from the research of Adelson and his colleagues will help to illustrate these changes. The ingeniously devised research asked adolescents in the United States, England, and West Germany to set up a political and legal system for an imaginary group of 1,000 people who ventured to an island in the Pacific. This approach was employed in order to avoid contamination of differing existing political systems in the cross-cultural research that was conducted. The responses of the adolescents were scored for views about the purpose of government, the utility of law, and the emergence of political entities such as political parties and offices. Views about the nature of justice and crime, individual and community rights and freedom, and the function of politicians and political entities were also examined.

Twelve-year-old adolescents viewed laws as ways to prevent people from engaging in illegal activities, a form of circular argument relating to punishment-obedience. The older adolescents viewed laws as ways to enforce the rights of the individual within the social order. Younger adolescents viewed fear of punishment as a primary motive for obeying the law. As you might expect from our discussion of Kohlberg's notions about the development of morality, the younger adolescents viewed things as either right or wrong, good or bad. The older adolescents on the other hand, were more likely to recommend remediation rather than punishment for lawbreakers. In addition, older adolescents understood the relativity of laws of particular times and circumstances. In this sense, they viewed laws as made by man for the good of man.

The emergence of political ideology parallels closely both Piaget's stages of cognitive development (see Chapter 4) and Kohlberg's notions of reciprocity of justice and contracts. As such, the development of political thinking represents another aspect of applied moral thinking.

SUMMARY

Early writing concerning morality was left to the philosophers, who developed three general perspectives. The doctrine of original sin led to the current psychoanalytic view, the doctrine of innate purity is the precursor of the cognitive-developmental perspective, and the *tabula rasa* notion is the basis for the learning-theory view of moral development.

The focus of the psychodynamic theorists is on the development of the superego, which is viewed as the internalization of societal standards of right and wrong. From this perspective, one develops a "character" that is either moral or immoral, in part as a result of the manner in which one is raised, and in part because of the nature of child-rearing practices. Social-learning theorists focus on moral behavior, which they view as resulting from both imitation and direct training by parents, teachers, and the society at large. This perspective has led to considerable research on the importance of child-rearing practices and the importance of models in the development of morality. The cognitive developmental perspective, in which it is assumed that morality develops in a sequence of stages that are universal, is focused on moral judgments as opposed to moral behavior. As a result, the research emphasis is on the relationship between cognitive development and moral thinking.

Each perspective has something to contribute to our understanding of moral development during the adolescent years. The conclusion that is appropriately reached is that adolescence is a critical time for transitions in moral behavior and judgment. Moral behavior is impacted by a variety of factors, including major socializing agents and cognitive development. To predict moral behavior requires information gleaned from all three perspectives.

In a general sense, moral development is related to other realms of development. More specifically, it is related to developments in religious and political thinking. As adolescents mature, their religious and political views become more personalized and abstract. They develop new views of the social order, that is, society and social institutions, that shape their views of religion and politics.

With development, religious views become more abstract, as do perspectives of what a religious person is. Church attendance declines, doubting of church doctrine increases, and the role of religion becomes more personalized with development through the adolescent years.

A similar phenomenon occurs with respect to political thinking. With development, adolescents come to more mature views of the reasons for laws, come to understand that the rights of the individual must be viewed within the context of the larger community, and begin to understand the complex interplay between political institutions and the individual.

Developments in these latter two realms, as in moral thinking generally, rest on advances in cognitive functioning. As the adolescent comes to think with formal operational skills he or she comes to view aspects of the social order in a more mature, adultlike fashion. Wrestling with both personal and social issues represents a maturing process adolescents experience as they grow into adulthood.

GLOSSARY

Doctrine of innate purity. The notion that the child is basically moral and pure and that society is a corrupting influence.

Doctrine of original sin. The notion that parental intervention is necessary in order to save the child's moral soul.

Guilt. An internal feeling that one experiences when breaking a rule or doing something that one should not do.

Moral behavior. Those behaviors that are consistent with rules of morality.

Moral judgment. An individual's judgment of why some behavior should or should not be done.

Tabula rasa. The concept that the child is born neither innately pure nor innately corrupt and is a product of environmental influence.

Values. The ideals and moral beliefs one holds about the proper way to behave.

SUGGESTED READINGS

ADELSON, J. (1972). The political imagination of the young adolescent. In J. Kagan & R. Coles (Eds.), *12 to 16: Early adolescence.* New York: W. W. Norton & Co., Inc.

The development of political thought is related to traditional areas of psychological development, such as motivation, cognition, and personality. There is a cogent discussion of political activism and rebellion among youth.

FEATHER, N. T. (1980). Values in Adolescence. In J. Adelson (Ed.), *Handbook of adolescent psychology* (pp. 247–294). New York: John Wiley & Sons.

Feather discusses a variety of influences on adolescent value system development. In addition, he presents evidence on the structure of values during the adolescent years.

GALLATIN, J. (1980). Political thinking in adolescence. In J. Adelson (Ed.), *Handbook of adolescent psychology* (pp. 344–382). New York: John Wiley & Sons.

The complexity of coming to grips with political issues, and the relationship between political and moral thinking, are captured well by Gallatin in this chapter. The historical review and the information about how adolescents develop thinking skills in the political arena are thorough.

KOHLBERG, L. (Ed.). (1987). *Child psychology and childhood education: A cognitive-developmental view.* New York: Longman.

This volume offers a number of articles that attempt to narrow the gap between theoreticians and practitioners. Various approaches to understanding moral developmental issues within the context of cognitive-developmental theory and application are presented.

KURTINES, W. M., & Gewirtz, J. L. (Eds.). (1987). *Moral development through social interaction.* New York: John Wiley & Sons.

The major emphasis of the papers in this edited volume is the shaping of moral development through social interaction. Many different concerns are discussed and related to both theory and research and everyday applications.

Self-Concept, Self-Esteem, and Identity

6

CHAPTER OUTLINE

MAJOR ISSUES ADDRESSED

The Complexity of the Self-Concept
Theories of Self-Concept Formation
Developmental Trends in Self-Concept and Identity
Influences on Self-Concept and Identity Development
The Importance of a Healthy Self-Concept
Changing the Self-Concept

INTRODUCTION

Perhaps no other psychological construct has received the theoretical and empirical attention that has been directed toward the self-concept. Just over 100 years ago, William James (1890) devoted an entire chapter of his *Principles of Psychology* to a description of the development of the self-concept. Since that time, hundreds of articles in the scientific literature and in the popular press have been devoted to issues concerning the self-concept. Major concerns have centered on issues related to self-concept development, how the self-concept changes as we mature, how we acquire a self-concept, and factors that influence self-concept.

More than any other single aspect of adolescent development, the self-concept, and related constructs such as self-esteem and identity, have been addressed within the context of the adolescent years. No doubt this is in large part a result of Erikson's (1959, 1963, 1968) very influential writings. He views adolescence as a time when the individual faces a crisis with regard to identity development.

In this chapter, we explore developmental trends in the self-concept and identity formation of adolescents. In so doing, we discuss influences on the nature of self-concept and identity. We also examine how self-concept and identity relate to other aspects of adolescent development.

DEFINING SELF-CONCEPT, SELF-ESTEEM, AND IDENTITY

There are nearly as many different definitions of the **self-concept** as there are individuals who have studied it. For William James (1890), the self was simply an object, like any other. In this sense, the self is whatever the individual feels belongs to the self, including the material self and the social self. James's *material self* referred to the individual's possessions, including the body. He re-

ferred to this as the "Me" aspect of the self. James's *social self* was concerned with the views the individual felt others held about that person. This aspect of the self he referred to as the "I" self. There was also an affective component associated with the self, the positive or negative views the individual held about the self. In more modern terms, this is called **self-esteem**.

Others (for example, Cooley, 1902; G. H. Mead, 1934) defined the self as that which was meant by the pronouns *I, me, mine,* and so forth. From this perspective, the self was all those feelings the individual had about the self. These feelings arise and develop from social interactions with others and from the individual's concern about how others react to him or her. By learning to view the self as others do, individuals learn to predict how others will react to them. As a result, the self-concept comes to regulate the individual's behaviors, particularly those that are social in nature.

Lecky (1945) and Snygg and Combs (1949) view the self-concept in terms of personality structures. For these researchers, the self-concept is the nucleus of the personality, an individual's constellation of traits and values.

McCandless (1970) viewed the self-concept as a learned perception, subject to environmental rewards and punishments as well as cognitive evaluations. As positive reinforcements to the individual are increased, the self-concept grows in esteem. The converse also is true. The self-concept is learned from experiences with success and failure; these experiences help the individual become aware of the limits of his or her competencies, which is critical in self-concept development. This awareness depends on cognitive evaluations.

Self-concept, then, may readily be defined as the way(s) in which we view ourselves. In this sense, it contains perspectives of our physical selves, ourself in various roles such as son or daughter, friend, relative, and other dimensions which are important to us.

140

Self-esteem is our evaluation of our self-concept. Part of our self-concept may include us as a student, and self-esteem would reflect how positively we view ourself as a student, for example, from good to poor. Self-esteem, then, represents the affective component of self-concept.

These definitions have several implications for our understanding of self-concept. First, it is now generally accepted that there is more than one self-concept and, hence, more than one self-esteem (e.g., Harter, 1989; Wylie, 1974, 1979). Although it is possible to measure global self-concept, researchers have found it more productive to view self-concept as multifaceted. Hence, they may study social and academic self-concept, for example, or even mathematic and verbal self-concept as components of academic self-concept (Marsh, Byrne, & Shavelson, 1988). Other researchers deal with the "real" self-concept (individuals' perceptions of themselves as they see themselves) and the "ideal" self-concept (individuals' perceptions of how they ideally would like to be). Still other investigators explore the importance of possible selves (see Box 6–1). The self-esteems associated with these various self-concepts may fluctuate with particular experiences; for example, attending a sport camp or participating in sports can increase one's sport self-concept (Anshel, Muller, & Owens, 1986; Smith, 1986). Similarly, doing poorly on an exam may decrease one's self-esteem with regard to academic self-concept. These refinements in how we conceive of the self-concept reflect not only the diversity of perspectives of those who study it, but also the centrality of self-concept to our everyday lives.

A second implication of current theorizing is that the self-concept serves several functions. These have been most succinctly summarized by McCandless (1970), who viewed the self-concept as having four major functions: self-evaluation; self-actualization (the striving to reach one's highest potential); determining whether behavior will be inner- or outer-directed; and predicting the activities in which one will engage. As McCandless views it, the self-concept has a motivational function that steers people into choosing lifestyles and behaviors that combine maximum chances of success with maximum rewards. Moreover, the self-concept directs one to engage in behavior that is socially sanctioned and to seek out social situations and deal with conflicts in ways consistent with the self-concept. An example of the latter may be found in discussions of the relationship between self-concept and vocational development, choices in the latter being guided by the former.

Finally, self-concept development can be viewed as a processes of building a theory about the self (Brim, 1975; Epstein, 1973). Through our everyday experiences we come to view ourselves in new and different ways. As a result, we come to formulate a perspective, a theory, of who we are that reflects our self-perceptions and evaluations of them.

Identity refers to one's values, beliefs, morals, and the like (Dusek, Carter, & Levy, 1986; Erikson, 1959, 1963; Grotevant, 1986, 1987; Marcia, 1980). It is a self-developed, internal, and ever-changing organization of one's attitudes and beliefs. It helps one identify one's strengths and weaknesses, and one's uniqueness, as well as similarity to others. Identity provides a sense of continuity of the self over time and a sense of integration of the self. During adolescence, the confluence of physical, cognitive, and social aspects of development allow one to construct this identity.

Identity development reflects a life-span process of exploration (Dusek, 1987; Grotevant, 1987), and it undergoes continual changes as we encounter new and different roles, such as worker, spouse, parent, and retiree. With each new role we again must explore our identity further and make adjustments dependent upon the new role. Change in identity is discussed later in this chapter, but for now it is important to note

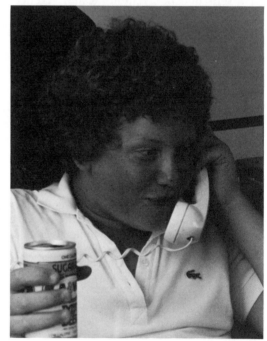

The self-concept is composed of many faces related to the various roles we play.

BOX 6–1   **Possible Selves**

As noted in the text, when the adolescent becomes capable of formal operational thinking, views of the self entail not only what the self is perceived to be but also what it might become. One consequence of this is that adolescents not only form perspectives of the self as they see the self, but they also form ideal selves, selves as they wish they might become, because they understand that there are a number of *possible selves*. Markus and her colleagues (e.g., Markus & Nurius, 1986) have explored the importance of possible selves.

Possible selves entail the selves we very much wish to become and the selves we very much wish to avoid becoming. Those we hope to become might include successful and rich, thin, or admired by others. Those we fear becoming might include delinquent or criminal, unhappy, or unemployed. In each instance, the possible self represents a cognitive representation of a potential self. As such, possible selves not only reflect what we have been, that is, the past, but also what we could be, the future. Although we might have a large number of possible selves, the ones we formulate reflect our particular developmental history of experiences. By striving to become a particular possible self, we influence our own future developmental history. Hence, possible selves serve as motivators for future behavior and provide a context for current evaluation of the self (self-esteem).

Markus and Nurius (1986) emphasize this motivational function of possible selves. Among other examples, they point out that positive possible selves may enhance recovery from life crises. Being able to view the self as happy, adjusted, and in control may facilitate recovering from extremely stressful life situations. Not having these possible selves available, Markus and Nurius suggest, may be determined because it may reflect a lack of incentives to progress, an inability to see the self in better circumstances.

Although much research is needed to determine if the construct of potential selves will endure, it represents an exciting potential link between aspects of self-understanding and motivation. What possible selves do you have? How do they affect your behavior? Simply consider your role as student. One possible self entails some vocational opportunity to which you aspire. In turn, the potential of reaching that possible self motivates you to study and work hard to achieve what is necessary for you to attain that possible self. What possible selves do you fear? These feared possible selves also motivate you, in this case perhaps to avoid behaving in certain ways (e.g., as a criminal).

As you consider your possible selves it becomes apparent that you have more than one self-concept. There are a number of "yous."

that identity formation is a continuous process of discovery about the self.

A very difficult problem consists of assessing self-concept and identity. As noted in Box 6–2, there are no generally accepted means of measuring either construct. As a result, what is meant by self-concept or identity depends to a large degree on the instrument used to measure it. Although this makes it difficult to assess developmental trends, in part because it is difficult to devise an assessment technique that is appropriate across a wide age range (for example, from age 5 to age 50), researchers have shown considerable creativity in their efforts. As a result, we are able to make some generalizations about the nature of self-understanding across the life span.

Self-Concept and Identity as Self-Understanding

The perspective presented above suggests that self-concept and identity are means of understanding the self (Dickstein, 1977; Damon & Hart, 1988; Harter, 1989). The general perspective, like the one William James proposed, is that the self is simply a concept to be known just as any other concept. Self-understanding, then, refers to how we come to know the self and how that knowledge changes with development. For example, it is now well-established that self-descriptions shift from being predominantly concrete during childhood to being primarily abstract during late adolescence (e.g., Montemayor & Eisen, 1977; Rosenberg, 1986). Hence, children tend to describe the self in terms of physical characteristics, likes and dislikes, and possessions, whereas adolescents are more likely to describe the self in terms of emotions, moods, motives, and beliefs that are not always overtly observable.

Selman (1980) has suggested a stage sequence in self-understanding that reflects the child's changing comprehension of both physical and psychological experience. Initially, the child fails to distinguish psychological and material experience. Hence, the child views the self only in physical terms. The distinction between internal psychological states and external physical states occurs during childhood. By about age 6, the child enters the second stage, realizing that psychological experience is distinct from physical experience. However, the child tends still to view the two as consistent with each other. At about age 8, the child enters the third stage, which is characterized by the knowledge that inner psychological reality

BOX 6—2   Assessing Self-Concept and Identity

There are no generally accepted means of assessing self-concept and identity (Wylie, 1974, 1979). Most measures have their own particular peculiarities and difficulties, and none are free from distortion and error.

Self-concept most often is measured by structured questionnaires, such as the Coopersmith Self-Esteem Inventory (CSEI; Coopersmith, 1967). The CSEI is composed of 58 items measuring self-esteem in four areas: social, home-parent, school, and general. Respondents read each of the statements and rate the degree to which the statements are like them on a scale ranging from "like me" to "unlike me." Scales such as this are applicable over a wide age range and are simple to administer and score.

Another popular method of assessing self-concept is through the use of the semantic differential. In this approach, bipolar adjective pairs (e.g., Bad–Good) are at the opposite ends of a line and the subject is instructed to put a check on the line to indicate how the self is perceived. Although simple to administer, the selection of adjective pairs may limit the components of the self that area assessed. For example, if none of the adjective pairs assess academically related self-perceptions, then no academic self-concept may be measured. Also, respondents may tend to answer in socially desirable ways.

The assessment of identity is more complicated and in some ways less refined than the assessment of self-concept. Marcia (1966) developed a popular, and often used, semi-structured interview to assess **identity status**. The questionnaire assesses whether or not the individual has experienced a crisis (a period of questioning) and made a commitment in the areas of vocation, politics, and religion (and sometimes sex roles). Subjects are then classified as *achieved, moratorium, foreclosed,* or *diffuse,* based on their responses. Other researchers have developed more structured questionnaires and inventories to assess identity status. As with measures of self-concept, however, there are limitations that make the assessment of identity difficult.

As with any personality measure, it is difficult to develop an assessment tool that is beyond reproach. To give you some feel for this problem, consider your answers to the question, "Who am I?" As you try to answer this question think about what you are doing. Are you trying only to give the good side of you—avoiding the negatives? This technique, a variant of the 20 Statements Test, is quite popular as a measure of self-concept with young children. As you analyze your means of responding to the question, you can see some of the pitfalls in the measurement of self-concept and identity.

and external physical reality do not need to coincide. The child comes to learn that conscious deception is possible, for example, that the "true self" (inner psychological) need not be accurately reflected in the outer self. Because the child can accurately separate inner and outer states he or she comes to understand the unique access the individual has to the self. During early adolescence, the individual learns self-awareness or self-reflection. As a result, the adolescent comes to realize that the inner psychological state is a filter or interpreter of experience, and indeed is a source of experience, for example, in attempts to mentally convince one's self of something. The adolescent at this stage believes the self has control over its own thoughts. The last stage, reached during the later adolescent years, is characterized by the understanding that there may be some nonconscious mental experiences that can influence thoughts and behaviors. During adolescence, then, the individual views the self largely in mental terms, as a manipulator of thoughts and actions.

The results of a study by Bernstein (1980) illustrate this sequence. He had 10-, 15-, and 20-year-olds answer three types of questions aimed at elucidating their self-conceptions. One type of question was aimed at exploring differentiation of the self-system, a second type at assessing abstractness of the view of the self-system, and the third type at integration of the self-system.

Bernstein reported that, in response to the first type of question, the 10-year-olds referred to concrete categories, behaviors, or situations, but that the adolescents responded in terms of personality characteristics, attitudes, and beliefs. With regard to the second type of question a similar trend occurred. The children linked their selves to individual concrete actions. The 15-year-olds viewed the self in thematic ways, that is, they indicated that certain types of behaviors were characteristic of them. The responses of the 20-year-olds were more abstract and complex, indicating a tendency to describe the self in ways allowing perception of consistency of actions that might even be divergent. For example, the oldest adolescents were able to justify helping one sibling with homework while at the same time not helping another because the latter really didn't need help.

The responses of the participants to the last type of question varied on a dimension of recognition and resolution of apparent contradictions in the self. The children tended to respond much as they had to the initial question, without apparent awareness of contradictions in self-description. The 15-year-olds recognized that they might behave in different ways in similar situations, that is, that there were apparent contradictions in their selves. But, they didn't know how to explain why they could behave like two different people. The late adolescents were able to understand the diversity in their selves and justify and coordinate it. They had a set of integrating principles that allowed them to understand that they might behave as different people in different but similar circumstances.

Bernstein's findings, then, indicate that our ability to organize self-conceptions around abstract belief systems emerges and increases during the adolescent years. Hence, adolescents are able to describe the self with regard to abstract personality dimensions and traits rather than just concrete physical and behavioral characteristics.

By examining more closely the particular attributes (contents) used to describe the self, Damon and Hart (1988) proposed that there are four developmental levels in self-descriptions. Further, they noted that at each level there may be behavioral, social, and psychological components to self-descriptions, but that these will be qualitatively different at each level. The levels reflect differing understandings of the self. In early childhood (level 1) the self is conceived as a group of separate categories and is described by reference to momentary emotional states, preferences, and physical descriptions. There is no particular sense of integration of the various aspects of the self. In middle to late childhood (level 2) the self begins to be defined in reference to others and with regard to normative standards. For example, at this level children may describe their skills as being better than, or not as good as, those of their friends. There is the beginning of a sense of integration of aspects of the self. We see the beginnings of viewing the self in social contexts. Level 3 (early adolescence) descriptions reflect the emerging importance placed on social interactions, as adolescents come to understand that they live in a highly social world. Hence, there is a preponderance of self-descriptions reflecting self-appeal and characteristics that are important in social interactions. During late adolescence (level 4) the self is described in terms of a system of beliefs, moral standards, and a philosophy of life. This level reflects the late adolescent's understanding of the self in a social order, or social system (society), consisting of mutually accepted and agreed upon codes of conduct.

Damon and Hart's (1988) description reflects the sequence of self-understanding we traverse from early childhood to late adolescence. At each level, new perspectives on the self come into being, but previous perspectives are not lost. Hence, even during late adolescence we may describe the self in concrete terms, although we also are likely to include moral beliefs and personal philosophies.

Self-Understanding and Cognitive Development

Both Selman's (1980) and Damon and Hart's (1988) descriptions of the developmental course of self-understanding, and research (e.g., Montemayor & Eisen, 1977) demonstrating a shift from concrete to abstract self-descriptions, suggest that the development of self-descriptions is influenced by emerging cognitive competencies. Indeed, this appears to be the case (Harter, 1989; Rosenberg, 1986).

The majority of those who have researched and theorized about the relations between self-descriptions and cognitive development have done so on the basis of Piaget's theory (see Chapter 4). Harter (1986, 1989) has summarized this work, which begins with the preoperational period of development. It was noted above that the young child's self-descriptions lack a sense of integration and coherence. This reflects the youngster's inability to generalize about the self, because the preoperational child does not have the requisite integrative cognitive operations. Hence, self-descriptions refer largely to the child's immediate experience (physical characteristics, likes and dislikes, possessions, etc.). Young children cannot make reference to inner psychological states because their cognition is bound to observable and often momentary events.

The emergence of concrete thinking skills allows the child to develop categories of events and to form sets of categories. When applied to the concept of self, the concrete operational child has the cognitive competence to group individual modes of behaving (e.g., liking sports, being strong, and being able to run fast) into higher-order generalizations, or traits (e.g., athletic). Hence, during middle childhood we see the emergence of trait descriptions of the self.

Formal operational processes allow the individual to consider the possible as well as the real, and to understand the unobservable as well as the observable. By mid- to late adolescence, then, the individual is able to think abstractly about the self, including the psychological, or inner, self. Hence, by late adolescence we can integrate trait labels into higher-order descriptions that are further removed from specific behaviors and that are more abstract than concrete in nature. For example, the traits *likable, outgoing, concerned about others*, and *enjoys doing things for others* might be grouped into the much more abstract category of *friendly*. On the one hand, such abilities allow us to conceive of the self in new and important ways. On the other hand, as Harter (1986, 1989) has noted, these more abstract traits are more open to distortion and may be less realistic.

Self-descriptions and self-understanding, be it self-concept or identity, then, rest in part on transitions in cognitive skills. Changes in these skills allow us to view the self in new and different ways. Indeed, it is very tempting to suggest that we experience an Eriksonian-like self-crisis during adolescence simply because we are able to do so. Just as we begin to examine the rest of the world in new ways during adolescence, we also begin to examine the self in new ways. Because abstract thinking allows us to see the possible as well as the real, we are able to view what we might be as well as what we are. This can result in confusion, a crisis, because we begin to understand that we have choices and can be many things. As we make choices and have new experiences we slowly develop a more firm concept of self and the crisis subsides. This suggests that there are other developmental changes in the self-concept and identity, the topic to which we next turn.

DEVELOPMENTAL TRENDS IN SELF-CONCEPT AND IDENTITY

Describing developmental trends in self-concept and identity has been a major concern of researchers. In part, this emphasis stems from theoretical concerns. A considerable body of research has accumulated from attempts to test the writings of Freud, Erikson, and others who argue that important changes in self-concept and identity occur during the adolescent years. In part, the interest stems from the desire to describe adequately how the self-concept develops from childhood through the adulthood years. One important reason for doing so is that self-concept is related to many other aspects of psychological development, for example, school achievement, cognitive development, and relations with parents. In this section, we discuss theoretical and methodological issues, and developmental trends in self-concept and identity development.

Theoretical Underpinnings

A number of theoreticians, most notably Erikson (1959, 1963, 1968), have suggested that the self-concept undergoes significant change during the adolescent years. For Erikson, this aspect of development was represented by the identity versus identity diffusion crisis. For Anna Freud (1948, 1958), it was represented by a recurrence of the Oedipal situation following the latency period. However conceptualized, the general perspective is that adolescence represents a time when our views of ourselves can be expected to change substantially. In other words, these theoreticians argue that self-concept development is not stable from childhood to adolescence.

The impetus for these expected changes lies primarily in biological change. The physiological and physical changes of puberty are suggested as the causes of self-concept and identity change. Because our bodies change physically, we are forced to re-evaluate our "self." Our physical competencies change as well, forcing us to consider these aspects of our self-perception. Our cognitive competencies change, too, during the early adolescent years (see Chapter 4), which causes us to evaluate ourselves differently, thereby causing a change in self-concept. In addition, changes in peer relations and interactions with parents, increases in independence strivings, and the like, may cause us to change our self-concept. To the degree that physical, cognitive, social, and interpersonal-relational behaviors are related to self-concept and identity, then, we might well expect measures of self-concept and identity to reveal changes during the adolescent years.

Methodological Issues

At first blush, it may appear to you that the study of change in self-concept should be relatively straightforward. One might have a group of adolescents complete one of the measures of self-concept or identity at time 1 and again at time 2, the difference in scores from the two testings being the measure of change. Or, one might administer a self-concept or identity measure to students of different ages, the differences in scores for different aged students being the measure of development. However, the measurement of development is not at all this simple. Rather, there are numerous methodological concerns that make measuring change much more difficult (for example, Harris, 1963; Wohlwill, 1973; McCall, 1979; McCall, Eichorn, & Hogarty, 1977). And, these issues are perhaps particularly pertinent to the investigation of developmental changes in self-concept (Dusek & Flaherty, 1981) and other aspects of adolescent personality development (Nesselroade & Baltes, 1974). We mention here only several of the more important methodological aspects of measuring change.

One important consideration in assessing change in self-concept during the adolescent years is the determination of the relative value of cross-sectional versus longitudinal designs for measuring development (cf. Dusek & Flaherty, 1981; McCarthy & Hoge, 1982). In cross-sectional designs, age differences are assessed, because subjects of different ages are compared. In longitudinal studies, age changes are measured, because the same group of subjects completes the instrument at two (or more) different points in time. It is now clear that cross-sectional studies do not accurately reflect developmental trends in adolescent self-concept (Dusek & Flaherty, 1981; McCarthy & Hoge, 1982). There are many complex reasons for this conclusion. For our purposes, however, the most pertinent are that cross-sectional comparisons are particularly subject to co-

hort effects (see Appendix) and to transitory fluctuations in self-regard. Therefore, the results of cross-sectional studies do not accurately reflect developmental trends in self-concept. As a result, we shall rely as much as possible on longitudinal studies in our discussion of self-concept and identity development.

Another important aspect of change is that it may occur qualitatively or quantitatively. Qualitative change would be evidenced by our viewing ourselves in different ways at different developmental periods. For example, as we noted above and shall detail below, adolescents have more abstract self-concepts than children or preadolescents. The way in which adolescents view the self is different, but not better or worse, than the way children or preadolescents view themselves. Quantitative change in self-concept would be evidenced by increases or decreases on some measure of self-concept, for example, the semantic differential. Adolescents may view themselves as more or less a leader, for example. If self-concept is shown to be qualitatively the same across developmental epochs, then it is considered to be continuous, as opposed to discontinuous. If there are no quantitative changes across developmental periods, self-concept is considered to be stable, as opposed to unstable.

Self-Concept/Self-Esteem Development

One of the first longitudinal investigations of self-concept during the adolescent years was conducted by Engel (1959), who tested 172 eighth and tenth grade students, retesting them two years later. The correlation of the scores for the two testings was .78, indicating relative stability but some change in self-concept over the two years of the study.

Carlson (1965) studied 49 students, 16 males and 33 females, in the sixth grade and then again in the senior year in high school. Girls showed an increase in social orientation, and boys showed an increase in personal orientation. These differences probably reflect cultural personality variables, but there were no significant sex differences in stability of self-concept. The size of the sample, however, precludes any definitive statements.

Constantinople (1969) conducted a longitudinal study of self-concept development with 952 college students. Part of the study included a six-week test-retest of self-concept with 150 subjects. The stability correlations ranged from .45 on the identity diffusion scale to .81 on the intimacy scale, with a median correlation of .70 over all scales. These correlations indicate a moderate degree of stability, but they are not particularly impressive because of the short time span between tests. Moreover, the subjects were clearly at the upper age range of adolescence, considerably older than adolescents experiencing important biological and social changes that might be related to changes in self-concept.

In these studies, only a global assessment of self-concept was obtained. As noted earlier, the self-concept is likely not unidimensional. Hence, assessment of multiple aspects of the self-concept seems warranted. A second difficulty with these studies is that there were either relatively short-term or very long-term spans between testings. Neither is desirable, the former because development may not yet have taken place, and the latter because it is not possible to measure fluctuations in development. Measuring self-concept at moderate time intervals, such as every six months or a year, is likely more appropriate for assessing developmental change. This was done in several studies.

Dusek and Flaherty (1981) tested 330 adolescents yearly over a three-year period with a semantic differential self-concept instrument measuring four aspects of self-concept (see Table 6–1). Achievement/leadership reflects the individual's feelings of competence and sense of being a striving, achieving person. Congeniality/sociability reflects the person's view of the self as a sociable, outgoing, and warm individual. Adjustment is the view of the self in a homeostatic balance with the environment. Sex role is the perception of sex-typing of the self. For all year-to-year comparisons, the correlations were statistically significant, ranging from about .4 to about .7. These correlations indicate a moderate to high degree of stability for each of the four aspects of self-concept across virtually the entire adolescent age span.

McCarthy and Hoge (1982) tested 1,970 students initially in grades 7, 9, and 11 and again a year later, with the Coopersmith Self-Esteem Inventory, which, as noted above, measures multiple aspects of the self-concept. They report slight increases with age (grade level) for each of the various aspects of the self-concept.

Finally, there is a series of very large-scale

TABLE 6–1 **Adjectives Describing Each Self-Concept Factor**

Achievement/ Leadership	Congeniality/Sociability	Adjustment	Sex Appropriateness of Self-Concept
confident-unsure	friendly-unfriendly	happy-sad	hard-soft
leader-follower	good-bad	healthy-sick	rugged-delicate
sharp-dull	kind-cruel	refreshed-tired	strong-weak
smart-dumb	nice-awful	relaxed-nervous	
success-failure		satisfied-dissatisfied	
superior-inferior		stable-unstable	
valuable-worthless		steady-shaky	

(Source: Derived from Dusek, J. [1978]. *The development of the self-concept in adolescents.* [Final Report, Grant No. RO1-HD-09094.] Washington, DC: National Institute of Education.)

longitudinal studies of self-concept development across the adolescent years (Bachman & O'Malley, 1977, 1986; O'Malley & Bachman, 1983; National Opinion Research Center, 1980). The sampling of subjects typically involved several grade levels and repeated testing every year or two, including post–high school years. Because of the large samples (numbering in the thousands) and the rigor of the design of the studies, including the use of national probability samples, the results of these types of investigations are highly reliable and provide important evidence concerning self-concept development.

O'Malley and Bachman (1983) have summarized the data from their own large-scale study and data from five other investigations. Their analyses indicate small and consistent increases in self-concept across the age range from 13 to 23 years. Although there was evidence of stability, they conclude that the overwhelming trend is toward increasing self-concept during the later adolescent and early adulthood years.

In examining the evidence presented above, it is clear that the self-concept does, indeed, change during the adolescent years. The results of these studies, and particularly the results of the latter studies (for example, Bachman & O'Malley, 1977; Nottelmann, 1987; O'Malley & Bachman, 1983), indicate the change is not large for most adolescents. Rather, the self-concept seems to change slowly and gradually. In other words, contrary to the suggestions of a number of theorists, there is no evidence to indicate that there is an upheaval or drastic change in self-concept during the adolescent years. As Dusek and Flaherty (1981) indicate, the person who enters adolescence is virtually the same as the person who emerges from it. We can expect, then, that adolescents' self-concepts will change to a degree, but that adolescents will not become different people during the course of the adolescent years.

A word of caution is in order. The data reported above are for groups of adolescents. That is, change was assessed not for individuals, but for groups of adolescents of the same age. It may well be that some individual adolescents undergo significant and dramatic change in self-concept during the course of the adolescent years. At present, however, it is not possible to determine ahead of time who these adolescents might be or how many adolescents may experience this large change.

The finding of relative stability of self-perceptions from mid-adolescence onward may seem at odds with your own experiences. No doubt, you have at one time or another felt either highly pleased or displeased with yourself; your view of yourself changed, perhaps dramatically and substantially. To reconcile these common experiences with the conclusions from the research cited above, we draw on the notions of Rosenberg (1986), who has noted that there are two types of self-esteem.

Barometric self-esteem reflects the fact that self-esteem is subject to moment-to-moment fluctuations, which may occur rapidly. For example, if you receive a poor test grade you may feel bad and your self-esteem, particularly with regard to academic performance, may be lowered. However, after some time, your academic self-esteem will increase to its former level. What you have experienced is an alteration of your barometric self-esteem. Rosenberg (1986) has suggested that early adolescence is a time of increased volatility of the barometric self-esteem, which may account for the common-sense perspective that adolescence is a time of rapid fluctuations in self-perceptions.

In contrast, your **baseline self-esteem** is not subject to moment-to-moment fluctuations. It is stable over time and is not influenced by immediate experiences. Hence, if you receive a poor test score your baseline self-esteem will not be affected. Indeed, your barometric self-esteem will recover in part because your baseline self-esteem is at odds with the momentary experience and will help you reassess it and your self. You know that you are a better student than your poor score shows you to be and the reason you know that is partly due to your baseline academic self-esteem.

The research reviewed above that shows stability of self-perceptions measured baseline self-esteem, which changes slowly and gradually. This stability in the context of slow and positive change is a result of the stability of the determinants of baseline self-esteem. Parental child-rearing techniques, overall school performance, and social class, for example, are unlikely to fluctuate widely. Because they remain relatively constant, and because they are important determinants of baseline self-esteem, baseline self-esteem does not change on a moment-to-moment basis. Hence, individuals with high self-esteem during adolescence are likely to be adults with high self-esteem.

Identity Development

Erikson's (1959, 1963, 1968) theorizing has stimulated research on identity development during adolescence. According to Erikson, the major crisis faced by the adolescent is identity versus identity diffusion. Optimal solution of this crisis is an important precursor to entering the adulthood years and their crises. More specifically, successful resolution of this crisis allows the individual to face the intimacy versus isolation crisis of the early adulthood years in good stead (see Box 6–3). Hence, studies of identity development are important not only to understanding adolescence but also to comprehending adulthood.

As Marcia (1980) has pointed out, however, there are no sufficient longitudinal studies of identity development. Although longitudinal studies of identity development during the college years exist, longitudinal research with younger adolescents is conspicuous by its relative absence. Marcia has estimated that an appropriate longitudinal study, that is, one involving subjects from sufficiently young age levels who are studied

sufficiently long enough to allow identity to solidify, would take between 20 and 25 years. Clearly, we are unlikely to see this type of study in the near future. Hence, we must rely on short-term longitudinal studies and on cross-sectional studies for describing developmental aspects of identity during the earlier adolescent years.

Marcia (1976) reported longitudinal data on identity development in 30 males whom he first tested in 1966 (Marcia, 1966). Forty-seven percent of the men changed identity status over the six-year time span between testings, with half this change being due to subjects initially in the moratorium status. Only 3 of the 16 subjects in the foreclosure and identity diffusion statuses changed to a higher status; eight of the 14 identity achiever and moratorium subjects moved to a lower status. Marcia suggests that achieving an identity during the college years may not result in continued identity achievement, and that not having achieved an identity during the college years is predictive of not having achieved one 6 years later.

Although this seems counterintuitive, Adams and Fitch (1982) provide a possible explanation. They suggest that the college atmosphere presents the individual with a milieu that prompts identity crises. Hence, it is reasonable to expect that some who are identity achieved will change during the course of their college years to a moratorium status. Moreover, it is very possible that the identity achieved during the college years is in some ways specific to the peculiar environment of the college life. Upon entering the noncollege world, the individual may well be expected to demonstrate some regression in identity status as a reconceptualization of identity within the noncollege atmosphere occurs. Some evidence (Munro & Adams, 1977) indicates that more noncollege than college youths are identity achieved, especially in the areas of religion and politics. Such evidence is consistent with the notion that identity continually develops (Erikson, 1963), perhaps changing with dif-

BOX 6–3 **Identity as Preparation for Intimacy** _____

According to Erikson (e.g., 1963) the initial crisis of adulthood is intimacy versus isolation. By intimacy Erikson meant acquiring the ability to commit oneself to intimate relationships with others. His emphasis was not so much on physical intimacy as it was on psychological intimacy; for example, revealing the true self, including one's aspirations, fears, and most deep feelings, to others. Isolation is evidenced by a readiness to alienate oneself from others, perhaps by harming those people who encroach on one's tenuous relations with others.

In order to establish intimate relations with others, one must first know who and what one is. This is why Erikson notes that the identity crisis occurs prior to the intimacy versus isolation crisis. If one is to reveal the inner self to others, one must know what that inner self is and have self-acceptance; for if one cannot accept the self, how can one ask others to accept it? Those who have not resolved the identity crisis within the optimal range have trouble developing intimate relationships, for they continually fear that they will reveal they have no firm sense of self. Although these adolescents may exhibit socially approved stereotypes consistent with a sense of identity, they cannot develop intimate relations involving revealing the true inner self (Dyk & Adams, 1988).

Some research has focused on the sequentiality of the identity and intimacy crises. Orlofsky, Marcia, & Lesser (1973) developed an intimacy-status interview and identified five intimacy statuses. *Isolates* have few relationships and none are intimate. *Stereotyped* individuals have friends but the relationships are superficial and tend to be self-serving. *Pseudointimates* appear to be committed to a single heterosexual relationship, but it does not involve genuine openness and mutuality of expression of feelings. *Preintimates* have a few truly intimate relationships involving openness and reciprocal acceptance. However, they are not committed to long-term relationships. *Intimates* are self-aware and relate to others in open and reciprocal relationships of some length. These relationships are mutually satisfying, not self-serving.

Orlofsky et al. (1973) tested late-adolescent males and reported that intimates tended to be identity achievers and that preintimates were predominantly moratoriums. Isolates tended to come from the diffusion identity status. Marcia (1976) replicated these findings, reporting that more identity achieved subjects were in the intimate and preintimate statuses, and that foreclosures and diffusions tended to be in the pseudointimate and stereotyped intimacy groups. Kacerguis and Adams (1980) also reported that, with increasing resolution of the identity crisis, there was an increase in intimacy. Moreover, they reported that occupational identity status was the major contributor to the relationship.

Hodgson and Fischer (1979) also measured identity status and intimacy status, and reported a sex difference in the relationship between the two constructs. They suggest that males may have an identity crisis concerning issues of competence and knowledge in the occupational, political, and religious realms. Females, they suggest, experience an identity crisis in the interpersonal realm. Successful resolution of the crisis revolves around the female satisfying herself and important others in this domain. In turn, they report that more females than males experienced high levels of intimacy. Finally, they suggest an androgynous identity path that involves identity development in all these areas. Both males and females who followed the androgynous path scored high in intimacy. Males following the masculine path tended to score low in intimacy, but females following the masculine path tended to score high in intimacy. No males followed the feminine identity path. Females following the feminine path tended to score high in intimacy. In general, females scored higher in intimacy than males.

Findings such as those reported above support Erikson's theorizing of the relationship between identity and intimacy and show the importance of the crises faced by adolescents as they prepare for adulthood. In this sense, then, adolescence clearly is a transition to adulthood.

A final point to note is that in Orlofsky's study (Orlofsky et al., 1973; Levitz-Jones & Orlofsky, 1985) only a few of the subjects had reached a mature identity status. This likely reflects Erikson's perspective that intimacy is a young-adulthood crisis that may take some time to resolve, perhaps because of changes in identity, as discussed in the text. To the extent that intimacy is related to identity, shifts in identity may cause reevaluation of aspects of intimacy.

152

ferent contextual demands. We would, then, except the regression reported by Marcia (1976) for identity achieved college students.

Although Marcia (1966, 1976) studied only males, Adams and Fitch (1982) reported changes in identity statuses for both male and female freshman, sophomore, and junior college students over a one-year period. They report that the patterns of change in identity status were very similar for the two genders, but that males had a more accelerated rate of growth, that is, they changed earlier than the females. This is an important finding in light of the suggestion (Marcia, 1980) that Erikson's theorizing may be a more appropriate description of male than female identity development. The issue of gender differences in identity development is complex (see Box 6–4) and in need of considerable research.

One of the more extensive studies of identity development was conducted by Archer (1982). Twenty males and 20 females at each of the grades, 6, 8, 10, and 12 completed a modified version of Marcia's (1966) identity status interview. Archer was interested in investigating developmental trends in the various identity status categories. She noted that the identity diffusion and foreclosure statuses were relatively developmentally immature (Marcia, 1976); in the former case, because the individual has not made a commitment to an identity and is not in the process of making one, and in the latter case, because the commitment to an identity is premature and made without appropriate exposure to various experiences which could alter it. She further suggested that the moratorium and identity achiever statuses were developmentally mature (Marcia, 1976). Moratorium individuals are looking to make a commitment, are obtaining information about possible choices, and are selecting among choices. This is developmentally mature because it immediately precedes identity achievement status. The identity achiever status is developmentally mature because these individuals have experienced

a crisis and have made a commitment to an identity. They have selected from the alternatives the one that best suits their individuality at the present time. Archer expected to find that, with increasing grade level, there would be fewer individuals in the less developmentally advanced statuses and more individuals in the developmentally advanced statuses.

The results were generally in line with the predictions. With increasing grade level, there were increases in achiever status. In other words, more of the older adolescents than younger adolescents were in the more developmentally mature identity statuses.

However, and somewhat surprisingly, the developmentally mature statuses accounted for relatively few individuals. Those in the moratorium and identity achiever status groups accounted for only 11 percent of the sixth graders, 13 percent of the eighth and tenth graders, and 19 percent of the twelfth graders. Hence, it appears that, during the early to mid-adolescent years, identity status is best characterized as developmentally immature. The largest number of identity achievers was in vocational plans and religious beliefs, and the largest number of moratoriums was in vocational plans. Identity diffusion was most apparent in political philosophy, and the foreclosure status was most evident in sex-role preference. These results held for both sexes. Apparently, a mature identity develops during the very late adolescent and early adulthood years.

Some evidence that identity achiever status occurs rather late in the adolescent years comes from both cross-sectional and longitudinal studies in which older adolescents and young adults were participants. Meilman (1979) studied 25 males each at ages 12, 15, 18, 21, and 24. He reported increases in achiever status and decreases in the diffusion and foreclosure statuses with increases in age. The transition to achiever status occurred in the 18- to 24-year-old age range. Meilman suggested, therefore, that the 18- to 24-year-old period was critical in identity development.

BOX 6–4 **Gender and Identity Development**

Recently (Adams & Jones, 1983; Waterman, 1982) there has been some discussion of sex differences in identity development during the late adolescent and early adulthood years. In part, theoretical advances in the areas of identity development (Marcia, 1980; Waterman, 1982; Adams & Jones, 1983; Grotevant & Thornbecke, 1982) and sex-role acquisition related to identity development (cf. Waterman, 1982; LaVoie, 1976; Matteson, 1977; Hodgson & Fischer, 1979) have fueled these concerns. In general, these researchers note that the traditional masculine and feminine sex roles have different emphases, with the masculine role stressing more heavily the instrumentality and achievement associated in Erikson's theory with the formation of an identity.

Some impetus for investigating the possibility of sex differences in identity achievement comes from methodological concerns (Matteson, 1977; Marcia, 1980; Waterman, 1982; Grotevant & Thornbecke, 1982). One set of criticisms is aimed directly at Marcia's (1966) instrument for measuring identity status. It is noted that the interview assesses crisis and commitment in occupational, political, and religious areas, and that the former two, and especially the first, may be more related to the traditional masculine sex role. Indeed, some evidence (Kacerguis & Adams, 1980; Grotevant & Thornbecke, 1982) indicates that occupational identity achievement may be more central to successful resolution of the identity crisis. As a result, it is argued, males may be more likely than females to appear identity achieved on the identity status interview.

These criticisms have resulted in an expansion of Marcia's interview by including assessment of crisis and commitment in areas central to the traditional female sex role. Grotevant and his co-workers (Grotevant & Thornbecke, 1982; Grotevant, Thornbecke, & Meyer, 1982) have assessed identity development not only in the occupational, political, and religious realms but also in the domains of dating, friendship, and sex roles.

Waterman (1982; see also Bourne, 1978a, 1978b) has reviewed the research findings on sex differences in identity status. His general conclusion is that sex differences are relatively rare, indicating that males and females evidence similar patterns of identity development in the various interview topic areas. However, he goes on to suggest that the identity statuses may have different psychological implications for males and females (Bourne, 1978a, 1978b; Marcia, 1980). Specifically, for both males and females, it appears that the identity achiever status reflects good adjustment and that the identity diffusion status indicates poor adjustment. Moratorium status males appear like identity achieved males and show better adjustment than males in the foreclosure and diffusion statuses. For females, the distinctions between the various identity status groups are not as clear; in some instances, identity achievers and moratoriums are similar and, in some instances, identity achievers and foreclosures are similar (Bourne, 1978a, 1978b).

It appears, then, that both males and females traverse the identity crisis in similar fashions. However, it may be that the identity statuses have different meanings for the two genders (Bourne, 1978a, 1978b). Specifically, given the traditional female sex role, a foreclosed status in which the girl makes a commitment based on the pressures and wishes of significant others, may, in effect, be a form of identity achievement. This clearly would not be the case for males given the traditional masculine role. However, until further research clarifies this issue, it must remain a hypothesis.

The considerable body of research on identity development during the college years, which cover the 18- to 24-year age range, bears directly on this point. The most extensive research on college student identity development has been carried out by Waterman and his colleagues (for example, Waterman & Waterman, 1971; Waterman, Geary, & Waterman, 1974; Waterman & Goldman, 1976). The general procedure in these studies was to have the students complete the identity status interview in the beginning of their freshman year and at the end of their senior year in college. Identity statuses and change in status were determined for the areas of occupation, religion, and politics. As one might expect on the basis of the vocational emphasis of college (Bourne, 1978a, 1978b), there was an increase in identity achievers for the vocational area. Although there was some evidence of an increase in identity achievers in the political area, there was no evidence of an increase in identity achievers in the religious area. These latter findings were not replicated entirely by Adams and Fitch (1982), who reported significant increases in identity achievers for religious beliefs and political ideologies. Hence, it appears that college attendance does influence identity in the vocational area. Change in the ideological areas, namely, religion and politics, however, is more problematic.

Montemayor and his colleagues (Montemayor, Brown, & Adams, 1985) have shown that the importance of the college years to identity development likely entails the entire college experience and not just the freshman year. They measured identity development in a group of students prior to their entering college and then again near the end of the freshman year. Consistent with the findings noted above, on the first testing half the subjects were identity diffuse and about 40 percent were moratorium. Only about 8 percent were identity achieved, the remaining 2 percent being foreclosed. Over the course of the freshman year, most remained diffuse or moratorium, or changed statuses from achieved or foreclosed to diffuse or moratorium. This pattern of shifts in identity status led Montemayor and his colleagues to conclude that the freshman-year college experience causes much questioning of identity issues but does not provide the environmental stability necessary to develop an identity. It seems, then, that it is during the later college years, perhaps after considerable experience in the general atmosphere of college, that identity stabilizes into what Meilman (1979) referred to as a *college-student identity.*

These data, then, poi⃠ of the later adolescent an⃠ years for identity developme⃠ indicate that structured experi⃠ critical to obtaining identity achie⃠ It may well be that identity achieve⃠ in ideological areas is attained later be⃠ experiences critical to such attainment a⃠ not encountered until the early adulthood years, when family relationships, vocational decisions, and other aspects of development are stabilized.

As with the measures of self-concept discussed above, then, identity does change during the adolescent, especially late adolescent, years. And, as near as we can tell from the limited longitudinal data, the change appears to be slow and gradual, not abrupt. In these studies of identity development, qualitative change is assessed. That is, change to an identity achiever status is not indicative of a change in amount of identity, but rather signals a change in kind of identity status. These studies, then, demonstrate qualitative change in adolescent self-views.

The data reviewed here also lend credence to Erikson's (1959, 1963, 1968) theorizing in demonstrating that there is a decision period involved in adopting an identity. Whether this decision period is best described as a "crisis" is questionable, however. Moreover, the data thus far available do not adequately address questions concerning transitions between stages and between identity statuses within a stage of Erikson's theory.

We can summarize the developmental studies of adolescent self-concept and identity development, then, by noting that the evidence indicates both quantitative and qualitative change. But, the change that occurs, and especially the quantitative change, does not support an "upheaval" concept of these aspects of adolescent development. Development of self-concept apparently is stable and continuous. On these measures, we remain basically the same person across

from a
ıtus is a
ınd one
olution.
ınsistent
ıpid and
Rather,
ns to be

CONCEPT DEVELOPMENT

As we noted at the beginning of this chapter, the development of the self-concept reflects the influence of a number of physical, social, and cognitive factors. Although at the present time it is not possible for us to specify all the determinants of self-concept development, researchers have identified some of the more important sources of influence.

Parental Influences

Research on parent effects on adolescent self-concept development has been conducted from two emphases. Some researchers have focused on attachment to parents and self-concept development. Others have examined family composition. And still others have examined parental child-rearing techniques, particularly as perceived by the adolescent, and how variations in child-rearing techniques relate to self-concept development.

A number of theorists (e.g., A. Freud, 1948; Erikson, 1959, 1963, 1968; Gewirtz, 1969) emphasize the importance of identification with the parent for the acquisition of appropriate social behavior. One prediction that may be made on the basis of such theorizing is that those adolescents who have a healthy identification with their parents will have more stable and mature self-concepts than those who do not. Data on the relationship between identification with the

For boys, identification with the father is an important aspect of self-concept development.

parents and adolescent self-concept development are scarce, however.

Some research (Howard, 1960) suggests that girls with either poor or excessive identification with their mothers have weak ego identities. Boys from the middle class tend to have higher self-esteem than boys from lower social classes, partially because fathers of middle-class boys tend to be more supportive. Rosenberg (1965) demonstrated that the closeness of the father-son relationship is highly related to self-esteem development in adolescent boys. Generally speaking, the data confirm the psychoanalytic notion that a high degree of positive relationship with the parents is crucial to the development of an adequate self-concept.

In his extensive study, Coopersmith (1967) studied the antecedents of self-esteem in fifth and sixth grade boys. One goal of his research was to assess the quality of the boys' parental relationships and relate these relationships to self-esteem development. High self-esteem boys were reared by parents who exhibited nearly complete acceptance of their offspring and who provided a home atmosphere that was understanding and tolerant. For example, there were definite limits of acceptable behavior; unacceptable behavior was appropriately punished. Individuals, both parents and children, were treated with respect and dignity, and the parents provided good adult models for their children. The respect that the parents showed toward their children was reciprocated by them, and at times led to strong conflict in the home. However, these conflicts were healthy, in that they provided an atmosphere which was conducive to growth for all members of the family. Greater degrees of permissiveness or harshness seemed to be related to a less highly developed self-esteem.

It is interesting to consider Coopersmith's findings in relation to material on parental effects discussed in a later chapter (for example, Elder, 1962, 1971). Elder's research leads to a relatively clear identification of parental types based on child-rearing philosophy. The data on parent–child and parent–adolescent relationships, which indicate especially poor relationships for autocratic, permissive, and laissez-faire (ignoring) parents, suggest the importance of parental types for self-concept development. Coopersmith's research substantiates this relationship, in part. Those characteristics of parent-offspring relationships that promote the development of good self-esteem, as identified by Coopersmith, are most likely to be found among democratic and equalitarian parent types.

More recently, Leiderman, Meldman, and Ritter (1989) have reported similar findings not only for white adolescents but also for black, Asian, and Hispanic adolescents.

It appears, then, that specific kinds of parental child-rearing practices are optimal for healthy psychological growth and development *vis-à-vis* the self.

The most extensive study of self-concept development in single-parent homes is from Rosenberg's (1965) observations. Two factors are critical to self-concept development in adolescents from single-parent homes: the age of the mother and the age of the child. Because it is rare to find a single-parent home in which the father has custody of the children, although there are some changes in this direction, Rosenberg's sample was limited to homes in which women had custody of the children. Generally speaking, the effects of the single-parent home on the child were lessened if the mother was slightly older than the average mother with children of a given age, partly because older women appear to deal more effectively with the stresses of a single-parent family.

In addition, the self-concepts of younger children were more adversely affected than were the self-concepts of older children. The greater degree of self-concept stability, as well as the older child's greater ability to cope with and understand new situations, apparently stands the older child in good stead. Similar findings occurred whether the single-parent home was caused by divorce or by death. As with other research (see Chapter 10), when the mother remarried, it appeared to have a negative effect on the development of self-esteem of the children, perhaps because of changes in the structure and rules of the household when a stranger entered the setting.

Recent research by Parish and his associates has examined self-concept development in intact, reconstituted (the mother remarried), and single-parent families in school-age (Parish & Taylor, 1979; Nunn & Parish, 1987) and college (Young & Parish,

1977) students. Young and Parish reported that college students who came from divorced families had lower self-esteem than college students who came from intact families. They suggest that the effects of parental divorce on the growing child may be long-term. Parish and Taylor replicated the earlier study with school-age children. In addition, they tested children whose mothers had remarried. They hypothesized that children in reconstituted families would have self-concepts more similar to children from intact families than to children from divorced families. The results were that the children from intact families had the highest self-concepts scores and the children from divorced families had the lowest self-concept scores. Although the scores of the children from reconstituted families were in the middle, they were much closer to the scores of children from divorced, than intact, families.

It appears, then, that divorce, or growing up in a single-parent family, may have detrimental effects on self-concept. Some evidence indicates that these influences are long-term and are not reduced by family reconstitution.

Several investigators have examined the relationship between adolescent self-concept or identity and the adolescent's perceptions of his or her parents' child-rearing techniques. The general strategy employed in these studies was to have the adolescents complete a measure of self-concept. In some research (for example, Leahy, 1981), parents completed a questionnaire detailing their child-rearing practices. In other research (for example, Litovsky & Dusek, 1985; Adams & Jones, 1983), the adolescents completed a questionnaire detailing their perceptions of their parents' child-rearing practices. This latter approach to assessing child-rearing techniques is based on the assumption that it is not what parents say they do in rearing their children, or the objective child-rearing practice *per se* that is important to the child's development, but rather the

child's perception of the parental behavior (Schaefer, 1965a, 1965b).

Leahy (1981) had tenth-grade males and females complete a 20-item self-concept questionnaire once for their real self and once for their ideal self. The adolescents' parents completed the Child-Rearing Practices Report, a measure of parent-adolescent interaction and child-rearing practices. Although few of the correlations between self-concept and measures of child rearing were statistically significant, there was some indication that, for boys, a lower real self-concept was related to a mother's maintaining boundaries between her son and others (for example, keeping the child away from others with different values and ideals). Boys' ideal self-concept was related to fathers' acceptance of the boy (for example, taking into account the boy's preferences when making plans for the family). Fathers who used considerable control and supervision (for example, those who feel children's play should be supervised by adults) and who felt ambivalent about the child's autonomy (for example, those who experience conflict between the child and themselves) had boys with greater discrepancies between ideal and real self-concepts, indicating poorer self-feelings.

Maternal support of initiative (for example, allowing the child to take chances and try new things) was related to a more positive real self-concept. Girls' positive ideal self-concept was related to fathers' emphasis on control and supervision and to mothers' authoritarian control of sex and aggression (for example, not allowing the child to get angry with her, feeling children should not be given sex information until they can understand everything). For girls, the disparity between real and ideal self-concepts was not related to the child-rearing measures.

In noting that parental practices seemed to have different influences on male and female adolescents, Leahy (1981) suggests that inhibiting initiative in males may not allow them to test their "self" and feel they are acquiring independence. On the other hand, controlling girls may influence them to develop in traditional feminine ways, which may positively influence their real self-concepts, but may be detrimental to their ideal self-concepts. (Bourne, 1978a, 1978b).

Litovsky and Dusek (1985) used a different approach in her study of the relationship between adolescent self-concept and child-rearing practices of parents. She tested males and females in grades 7, 8, and 9 with the Coopersmith Self-Esteem Inventory. She also had the students complete Schaefer's (1965a) Children's Report of Parental Behavior Inventory (CRPBI). The CRPBI is a questionnaire that requires the individual to read a short statement and indicate on a three-point scale (ranging from "a lot" to "a little" to "not at all") the degree to which the behavior was like their parent. The scale is completed twice, once for the mother and once for the father. The CRPBI measures three dimensions of child-rearing perceptions. The Acceptance/Rejection dimension reflects the degree to which the child perceives the parent as warm, loving, accepting, and supportive versus cold, detached, hostile, and uncaring. The Psychological Autonomy versus Psychological Control dimension reflects perceptions concerning

parents allowing autonomy, not being overprotective, and not using psychological means of controlling behavior (for example, guilt) versus feeling the parents are overbearing, intrusive, and high users of guilt and other psychological means of controlling the child's behavior. The third dimension is labeled Firm Control versus Lax Control, and reflects variations in the degree to which the parent makes rules and regulations and sets limits and rigidly enforces the rules, regulations, and limits.

The results were the same for male and female adolescents and across all three grade levels, but depended somewhat on gender of parent. Perceptions of mother's acceptance were positively related to self-concept, particularly on the Home-Parent subscale of the SEI. Adolescents who felt accepted and loved by their mothers had higher self-concepts than did those who felt less accepted or unwanted. High maternal use of psychological control was negatively related to self-concept. Adolescents who perceived their mothers as being intrusive, overprotective, and as using guilt to control their behavior had lower self-concepts. The perceptions of the mother on the third dimension, Firm Control versus Lax Control, were unrelated to adolescent self-concept.

Perceptions of fathers' child-rearing tech-

Parental acceptance is a critical factor in adolescent self-concept and identity development.

niques were related to self-concept in the same way for the first two dimensions. Hence, adolescents who perceived their fathers as warm and accepting, and who felt their fathers were not intrusive or guilt provoking, had higher self-concepts. However, the relationships between self-concept and perceptions of child-rearing were not as strong for father as they were for mother. Moreover, perceiving the father as not exerting excessive firm control was positively related to self-concept development. Adolescents who perceived their fathers as rigidly enforcing large numbers of rules had poorer self-concepts.

It appears that feeling wanted and loved by the parents is critical to adolescent self-concept formation. It is interesting to note that, although this is especially important in perceptions of the mother, it is also important to perceive the father as being loving and warm, a role that is somewhat at odds with traditional male roles. Feeling wanted may provide a sense of worth and value that is translated into a positive view of the self. Perceiving that one has a degree of autonomy, and perceiving the parents as not intrusive or over-protective, likely allows one to feel free to engage the environment, which may help build confidence and competence. The relationship between Firm Control versus Lax Control and self-concept for perceptions of father, and the absence of such a relationship in perceptions of mother, may reflect the generally greater rule making and enforcement typically done by fathers.

Although rules and regulations need to be made and enforced, allowing some flexibility allows the adolescent to learn competencies and feel confident and in control of his or her own life, no doubt an important aspect of a positive self-concept. The use of extreme rules and enforcement, on the other hand, may be stifling.

In one study (Adams & Jones, 1983), perceptions of parental child-rearing patterns were shown to relate to identity statuses.

Adams and Jones had female adolescents in grades 10, 11, and 12 complete an identity status questionnaire based on Marcia's (1966) interview procedure, and a brief (5 question) measure of perceptions of child rearing. Girls in the more advanced identity statuses, moratorium and identity-achieved, perceived their mothers as less controlling and regulating and more encouraging of freedom and independence than did girls in the less advanced identity statuses. Moreover, the moratorium and identity-achieved girls viewed their fathers as fair in their punishment, although they also viewed them as not very praising.

Adams and Jones (1983) suggest that identity achievement is fostered by parenting styles that promote autonomy and the learning of one's unique individuality. Girls in the diffused identity status viewed their mothers as extremely controlling and regulating *and*, paradoxically, as encouraging independence to a high degree. In addition, they perceived their fathers as unfair in discipline practices. Adams and Jones argue that diffused females may come from homes that encourage independence, but with little guidance, which may cause the girls to feel rejected. Foreclosed females viewed their mothers as somewhat controlling and regulating and as not allowing much freedom and independence. They perceived their fathers as highly praising and fair in discipline situations. Adams and Jones note that such parenting practices may not encourage the independent self-exploration necessary for the self-defined commitment involved in identity achievement.

Litovsky and Dusek (1988) examined specific child-rearing techniques, using the CRPBI, related to identity development in adolescents in grades 7 through 12. Those adolescents who perceived *both* parents as warm and accepting and who perceived *both* parents as low in the use of psychological control (e.g., guilt) had the higher identity scores. An important aspect of these findings is that it was perceiving acceptance by both parents and perceiving low use of guilt by both parents that was important. Having only one highly accepting parent is not enough, for example, to allow the adolescent to formulate an identity in an optimal manner. Both mothers and fathers are important.

These studies highlight the importance of child-rearing to self-concept and identity development. Making the child feel wanted, exerting control that indicates concern for the welfare of the child, and being fair in punishment seem to be optimal for self-concept and identity development. In all likelihood, this is because such practices allow the exploration and self-understanding that is necessary to learn one's competencies. As such, it promotes defining the self. Stifling the adolescent in these regards, or using extremes of these forms of child rearing, seems to result in less than optimal personal development.

Social Class Influences

The relationship between self-esteem and social class has been the subject of a number of investigations, but the nature of the relation remains somewhat unclear. Some evidence suggests that adolescents who are poor have weaker or less positive self-concepts than those who are relatively well off. Some researchers (e.g., Demo & Savin-Williams, 1983) have suggested this is a result of middle-class students doing better in school, their higher performance leading to higher self-esteem (Bachman & O'Malley, 1986; see Box 6–5).

There are, however, some data suggesting this difference may not be as dramatic or widespread as it appears on the surface. Trowbridge (1972), for example, reported that general, social and academic self-concepts did not differ between middle- and lower-class black and white males and females, although the middle-class groups were more positive on measures of home and parent relationships. Soares and Soares (1969, 1971, 1972) arrived at similar findings in their extensive studies of advantaged, compared to disadvantaged, adolescents. They found few differences in self-concept between either children or adolescents from advantaged versus disadvantaged backgrounds. In fact, in some of their findings, the disadvantaged adolescents presented a more favorable picture. For example, middle-class boys had lower self-esteem than middle-class girls, with the opposite being the case for the lower-class adolescents. In addition, although teachers thought more highly of the middle-class students, lower-class students did not perceive that the teachers felt this way. The conclusion we can draw is that lower social-class backgrounds do not necessarily produce a negative self-concept.

This finding should not be very surprising if one considers that middle-class homes and lower-class homes may have similar atmospheres, and that for both middle- and lower-class adolescents, home atmosphere was found to be a critical factor. A poor home atmosphere and poor relationship with parents are likely to produce a negative self-concept. Material possessions or quality of neighborhood are less likely to be a factor, especially if the home atmosphere is one conducive to self-growth. In other words, negative self-concepts and low self-esteems may emerge in either middle- or lower-class homes.

Filsinger (1980) has elaborated this contextual analysis of the relationship between self-concept and social class in a more fine-grained manner. His theorizing and research (for example, Filsinger & Anderson, 1982) have focused on the concept of self-efficacy, the feeling that one is capable of achieving some desired goal. In the present context, self-efficacy theory predicts that individuals interacting in social class contexts higher than their own are more likely to have high self-esteem and those interacting largely in social class contexts lower than their own are likely to have lower self-esteem. These predictions are based on the

BOX 6–5 Self-Concept and School Achievement

In general, measures of self-concept are positively correlated with grades earned in school and with achievement test performance. Those who have higher self-concepts get higher grades and do better on achievement tests than do children with lower self-concepts (Marsh, 1987). Moreover, high- and low-self-concept children behave differently in the classroom (Shiffler, Lynch-Sauer, & Nadelman, 1977). High-self-concept students evidence more task-oriented behavior (doing classroom work) and the low-self-concept students show more nondirected behavior (nontask behaviors, such as looking around and watching others).

Observations such as these have, of course, led to the investigation of the causal direction in the relationship between self-concept and school achievement. Self-enhancement theorists argue that the predominant causal sequence is from self-concept to school achievement. In other words, they believe that good self-concepts cause good school achievement and vice-versa. From this perspective, the initial responsibility of the school system should be to build strong, positive self-concepts in students. Then, it is argued, school achievement will be respectable. The reverse view is espoused by the skill-development theorists. These theorists believe that doing well in school results in self-concept enhancement and that doing poorly results in a lowering of the self-concept. With regard to educational philosophy, then, they would argue that the major role of the school system initially should be to develop solid educational skills, including academic and social skills, that will ensure adequate achievement and thereby promote a positive self-concept (cf. Calsyn & Kenny, 1977).

Evidence in support of each position is available. Shavelson and Bolus (1982), for example, reported that for a sample of seventh and eighth graders, self-concept was causally predominant over measures of school achievement. Calsyn and Kenny (1977), on the other hand, reported that for students in grades 8 through 12, academic achievement was causally predominant over self-concept. Finally, it appears that attempts to increase school achievement *via* programs aimed at self-concept enhancement have typically failed, perhaps because the self-concept enhancement procedures were faulty.

At the present time, it appears best to consider the causal relationship between self-concept and school achievement as reciprocal. There can be no doubt that feeling one is competent is important to school success. One need only listen to the reasons students give for not wishing to take certain types of courses. Often the major reason is "I don't do well in that (subject)." Clearly, this is an expression indicative of the causal importance of self-concept. In turn, it is also clear that doing well in a subject area promotes interest in the topic and the feeling that one can do well. To keep to the analogy, one can look at the reasons for wishing to enroll in courses in some area, including the often heard "I want to take (subject) because I like it and do well in it."

assumption that the social class level within which one acts influences the individual's views of self-competence.

To test these notions, Filsinger and Anderson (1982) had college students complete a self-esteem questionnaire and a questionnaire designed to assess their own social class and that of their best friend in high school. Correlations were then computed between self-esteem and (a) own social class, (b) best friend's social class, and (c) the difference between own and best friend's social class.

The correlation between own social class and self-esteem was not statistically significant, but those between self-esteem and best friend's social class and between self-esteem and the difference between social classes were statistically reliable. Filsinger and Anderson suggest that late adolescents gain a sense of social status and a feeling of competence from associating with close friends of higher social status, perhaps because they have greater confidence in themselves. Unfortunately the converse, that associating with best friends of lower social classes may be detrimental to feelings of self-competence, also is true.

Maturational Influences

Research on the relationship between biological development and self-concept is relatively rare (Clausen, 1975). Because there is a complete discussion of the influences of maturity rate on personality development in Chapter 3, we focus specifically on self-concept issues here.

Mussen and Jones (1957) studied self-concept in early- and late-maturing boys. They hypothesized that, because of the slower rate of physical growth, and the concomitant social disadvantages, late-maturing boys would have more negative self-views than early maturers. Their hypothesis was borne out. The late-maturing boys indicated more feelings of inadequacy than the early maturing boys, and they showed a generally negative self-concept. The early-maturing boys had more strong and positive self-concepts. Of course, physical maturation in and of itself cannot cause this difference. It is much more likely that society (in the form of differential expectations and behaviors), not biology, is the critical factor.

With respect to this issue, the late maturers felt rejected by their parents and other authority figures, were less likely to try to assert independence, had stronger underlying dependency needs, and were more sensitive about their personal feelings than were the early maturing boys. Recall our discussion of the effects of maturity rates on psychological development (see Chapter 3); one study found that, for boys, the negative effects of late maturity may last well into adulthood (Jones, 1965). Self-concepts of late maturers, then, may be expected to be somewhat negative and may interfere with choices of adult roles.

The self-concepts of early maturers may be stressed, too, although for a different set of reasons. Adults are likely to expect early-maturing adolescents to behave more like adults than like their peers (see Chapter 3) because of their physical growth. However, their psychological and social makeup is not that of an adult. Failure to measure up to these inappropriately high expectations may damage the developing self-concepts of early maturers (McCandless, 1970; Peskin, 1967). Hence, although early maturity is generally advantageous for boys, the issue is not completely black and white.

Jones and Mussen (1958) used the same techniques to study early versus late maturity effects on self-concept development in girls. Maturity rate was determined by X-rays. There were 16 early maturers and 18 late maturers. Jones and Mussen (1958) reported that, in general, the early-maturing girls were somewhat better adjusted, that is, viewed themselves more favorably, than the late-maturing girls. The early-maturing girls scored higher on total adjustment, family adjustment, and feelings of personal adequacy. The late maturers described themselves more in negative terms, and were more oriented toward seeking fame or prestige. It was interesting to note that far fewer differences emerged between early- and late-maturing girls than between early- and late-maturing boys.

Simmons and Blyth (1987) report that early-maturing girls may fare the worst in the relation of physical appearance and self-esteem. Because they are somewhat heavier and do not see themselves as having an ideal culturally stereotyped female figure, they tend to be the most dissatisfied with their body image. The result is, in part, a poorer self-image.

In explaining these maturity rate influences on self-concept, one must examine the social environment. It is likely that the way in which adolescents are treated, as noted above and as discussed in Chapter 3, by parents and others, mediates the effects of maturity rate on self-concept.

These findings suggest that physical attractiveness, in general, and not just matu-

Self-concept and school performance are positively correlated.

the self-concept is a theory of the self, leads to the possibility that development of self-concept is related to development of cognitive processes such as those discussed by Piaget (1952, 1968; Inhelder & Piaget, 1958).

We reviewed some evidence consistent with this suggestion above. It is clear that across the childhood and adolescent years there is an increase in the tendency to describe oneself in abstract terms. Moreover, there is evidence that this tendency increases as children gain facility with formal operational skills. Adolescents also tend to use more personality trait descriptors in elaborating conceptions of self. All these findings are consistent with the view that increasing cognitive competence is an underlying factor in self-concept development.

Further evidence comes from research relating self-concept to measures of school performance, including achievement test performance (see Box 6–5). It is well documented that there is a positive correlation between self-concept and performance in school and on standardized achievement tests. Students with higher self-concepts do better.

rity rate, is important to self-esteem. Indeed, some research indicates that physical appearance is the single most important component of global self-esteem. This is especially important for understanding the self-esteem of females, who report greater difficulty adjusting to pubertal changes than do adolescent males (Simmons & Blyth, 1987; Zumpf, 1989). This difficulty seems to cause a lowered self-esteem in adolescent females than in males (Zumpf, 1989).

Cognitive Influences

Consideration of Damon and Hart's (1982, 1988) notions regarding the self-concept as self-understanding, and Brim's (1975) and Epstein's (1973) suggestion that

IMPORTANCE OF A STRONG SELF-CONCEPT

Quite aside from theoretical concerns about describing the development of self-concept and determining factors that influence that development, the exploration of adolescent self-concept is important to understanding everyday aspects of adolescent behavior. Self-concept is pervasive, relating to many facets of adolescence, including general adjustment, vocational choices, and delinquency.

Self-Concept and Adjustment

People with low self-esteem exhibit more symptoms of unhealthy emotional development (for example, nervousness, insomnia, psychosomatic illness), than do individuals with high self-esteem (Harter, 1989). In part, this seems to reflect the low-self-concept person's feelings of poor self-worth (Rosenberg, 1986), which may cause these people to avoid social situations that are important in self-concept building.

Adolescents with low self-esteem are especially vulnerable to criticism and rejection because these reinforce their feelings of low self-worth and negative views of the self. Hence, low self-esteem adolescents tend to avoid social activities, including heterosexual relationships, which might result in rejection or failure. As a result, they often feel they cannot succeed in social situations. The vicious circle is then developed.

In this vein, researchers (e.g., Harter, 1989; Pfeffer, 1986; Rosenberg, 1986) have explored the role of self-esteem in adolescent depression and suicide. Adolescents with low self-esteem are prone to a depressive mood. In addition, they are less likely than their high-self-esteem counterparts to do well in activities that are important to them and their parents, such as school, which may lead them to feelings of helplessness—they can't satisfy themselves or their parents. These feelings of depression and helplessness are highly predictive of their considering suicide as their only answer. What is important in the current context is that at the center of the complex factors involved in suicide is poor self-esteem.

Self-Concept and Vocational Development

The relationship between vocational development and self-concept is detailed in Chapter 9, particularly with regard to Super's (1953; Super et al., 1957) theory of vocational development. Super believes the self-concept is intimately linked to vocational aspiration, choice, and satisfaction.

Those with higher self-concepts and self-esteem have higher vocational aspirations and make choices that are higher in status than those with lower self-concept or self-esteem. High-self-concept individuals choose occupations in which there is a demand for leadership and power, and avoid vocations in which they are subservient or dominated by others. Self-concept, then, seems to provide one directive influence on vocational decision making during the adolescent years.

Self-Concept and Delinquency

One popular approach to the study of juvenile delinquency is to examine and compare personality characteristics of delinquent and nondelinquent samples of adolescents. Generally speaking, studies have found that delinquents tend to be more socially assertive, hostile, destructive, and lacking in self-control than nondelinquents. It has been suggested that this behavioral pattern represents a defense against a negative or inadequate self-concept development resulting from frustration due to rejection (Ahlstrom & Havighurst, 1971; Conger & Miller, 1966). Delinquents perceive themselves in much the same way they are perceived by others—lazy, bad, and ignorant. They do not see themselves as desirable people, and they have relatively little respect for themselves. Differences along these dimensions seem to begin relatively early in life, with more serious behavioral manifestations of these differences appearing during adolescence.

The issue of causal direction in the relationship between self-concept and delinquency is very complicated (Harter, 1989; Kaplan, 1975; Rosenberg & Rosenberg, 1978; Bynner, O'Malley, & Bachman, 1981). One hypothesis is that engaging in delinquency causes one to have a lower self-concept because the individual comes to see the self negatively (Rosenberg & Rosenberg, 1978). The deliquent begins to see the self through the eyes of others and internalizes their negative feelings and attitudes toward him or her. Hence, delinquency is seen as the cause of lower self-concept.

An alternative hypothesis is that having a low self-concept or self-esteem causes one to engage in delinquent behavior. Kaplan (1975), for example, suggests that a build-up of negative feelings about the self due to inability to measure up to the standards of others causes some adolescents to seek the company of those who reject traditional standards in favor of alternative standards, often involving delinquency. By living up to the alternative standards, the individual gains the prestige that is unavailable in other contexts.

Bynner et al. (1981) suggest a third hypothesis, namely, that engaging in delinquent behavior acts to increase self-concept for those with an initially low self-concept. The difference between this and the previous hypothesis rests on the emphasis on an initial low self-concept. Hence, the positive relation between self-concept and delinquency reported in some studies should be evident only for those with low self-concepts.

A test of these three hypotheses was presented by Bynner et al. (1981). The longitudinal study involved nearly 1,500 boys tested in grades 10, 11, and 12, and one year after leaving school. The results for those who entered high school with relatively high self-concepts were different from the results for those who entered high school with relatively low self-concepts. For the high-self-concept group, there was no evidence that reductions in self-concept caused the boy to engage in delinquency. Indeed, there was some evidence that engaging in delinquency might reduce self-concept, although this was not a strong finding. For the low-self-concept group, the evidence indicated that engaging in delinquency increased self-concept. For low-self-esteem adolescents, then, delinquency offers a way to gain self-regard.

This is indeed a sad state of affairs. Delinquents caught and punished for delinquent behavior simply have the negative aspects of their self-concept reinforced. Being put in a juvenile detention home or, worse, in a prison is likely to lead to reaffirmation of their belief in their worthlessness. As a result juvenile delinquents are likely to believe that they cannot function as normal members of society and that the only doorway open to them is one of continued delinquency and crime. In all likelihood, early parental child-rearing practices, which form in part the child's views of the world, set the stage for the beginning of a delinquent personality pattern. Some research suggests that these early self-concepts are reinforced by teachers and peers, and leave the individual with a relatively firm but negative self-identity, which then gets expressed through attempts to achieve success through delinquent acts.

Changing the Self-Concept

It is clear that having a positive self-concept is advantageous and healthy. Yet, it also is clear that many adolescents do not have adequate self-concepts, and that this may contribute to emotional, educational, and behavioral problems. It behooves us, then, to investigate methods for changing poor self-concepts.

Some clues about how one might change the self-concept come from our earlier discussions of significant influences on self-concept development. Parental influences, for example, are important in the development of the self-concept. Creating a warm and more accepting, yet appropriately controlling, home atmosphere in which the child feels wanted can help improve the child's self-concept. Parents of adolescents with poor self-concepts would do well to provide this type of home atmosphere in order to increase their child's chances of adapting well to adult life.

Some researchers have attempted to improve self-concept through changes in school programs. The intent is to improve self-concept in order to improve school performance. Although some effects in the desired directions have been observed, the preponderance of the evidence is on the negative side. That is, to date, it has not been unequivocally demonstrated that alterations in the school environment significantly improve self-concept. However, at the individual classroom level, it is possible that the teacher can, through judicious use of rewards and praise, help the low-self-concept child both do better in school and improve self-concept (Curney, 1987).

Finally, in some cases, therapy of one type or another may be used in attempting to improve self-concept. For some individuals who have had a lifetime of denigrating experiences, this may be the only way in which to alter self-concept.

Of course, it is extremely important to keep in mind that even if the self-concept is improved, alterations in behavior may not occur, or may not occur immediately. The self-concept is only one of many influences on behavior and, in many instances, it may not be the primary one. Moreover, it is not at all clear that the self-concept is always a causal influence. It may be a result of some behavior.

SUMMARY

The self-concept is a complex self-perception that changes as the individual develops from childhood through the adolescent years. Early conceptualizations of the self-concept viewed it in a trait perspective. More contemporary psychologists see the self-concept as a theory of the self or in the context of self-understanding. As a result, the self-concept is seen in a developmental context stressing progressive changes with development, especially in the cognitive realm.

There are many different ways to measure the self-concept. Some are questionnaires that measure various aspects of identity, or the self-concept. Others are projective techniques, in which it is assumed that the individual "projects" the self into responses to vaguely defined stimuli. Regardless of the variety of measures, however, all seem to assess the same personality construct. Hence, information derived from experiments in which different measures were used may still be integrated.

The self-concept, which changes gradually across the adolescent years, is influenced by a variety of factors. Parental child-rearing techniques that are warm, firm but not strict, and that make the child feel wanted promote good self-concept. Being overindulgent, being too strict, and making the child feel unwanted foster poor self-concepts. Lower-social-class children and adolescents have poorer self-concepts than their middle-class peers. This seems to reflect differences in parental child-rearing techniques as well as more general effects associated with the general social relations of those in the lower economic strata. Early maturers tend to have more positive self-images than later maturers, particularly among males. This difference apparently is a result of different treatment by adults and peers, the advantages associated with being an early maturer, and the confidence early maturers gain by virtue of their relatively larger physique vis-à-vis peers. In addition, self-conceptions are related to aspects of cognitive development. With increasing cognitive competence, self-concepts become more abstract and complex.

Having a positive self-concept is important in many ways. Adolescents with stronger self-concepts are better adjusted psychologically, have higher career aspirations, and conform more appropriately to generally accepted social standards. Hence, they fare more successfully in the real world. The development of means to alter poor self-concepts might be useful for helping the adolescent become better adjusted, but other factors also must be taken into account if one wishes to alter the behavior of poor-self-concept adolescents, because the self-concept is only one factor determining behavior.

GLOSSARY

Barometric self-esteem. Self-esteem that is subject to moment-to-moment fluctuations as a result of immediate experiences.

Baseline self-esteem. A more permanent perspective of the self that is not subject to moment-to-moment fluctuations.

Identity. The constellation of one's values, morals, and beliefs that guides one's behavior.

Identity status. In Marcia's theory, one's state of identity development: achieved, diffuse, moratorium, or foreclosed.

Self-concept. One's perception of the self.

Self-esteem. One's evaluation, from positive to negative, of the self-concept.

SUGGESTED READINGS

COOPERSMITH, S. (1967). *The antecedents of self-esteem.* San Francisco: W. H. Freeman.

Coopersmith details his seminal investigation and relates aspects of self-concept to a variety of other measures. His introduction provides interesting background information and his summary illustrates the complexity of the issues involving self-concept development.

ERIKSON, E. (1963). *Childhood and society.* New York: W. W. Norton & Co., Inc.

In this book Erikson details his theory of personality development and indicates factors he feels are critical to that development.

KAPLAN, H. (1975). *Self attitudes and deviant behavior.* Pacific Palisades, CA.: Goodyear.

Kaplan discusses the relationship of self-concept to aspects of deviant behavior, including delinquency. He also presents important theoretical perspectives on the relationship of self-concept to delinquency.

MARCIA, J. (1980). Identity in adolescence. In J. Adelson (Ed.), *Handbook of adolescent psychology.* New York: John Wiley & Sons.

Marcia discusses his research on identity development and presents a review of the literature with suggestions for future research.

ROSENBERG, M. (1986). Self-concept from middle childhood through adolescence. In J. Suls & A. G. Greenwald (Eds.), *Psychological perspectives of the self* (Vol. 3). Hillsdale, NJ: Lawrence Erlbaum.

Rosenberg reviews a number of perspectives on the self and details how self-concept and self-esteem relate to a variety of adolescent behaviors.

Sex-Role Socialization

7

CHAPTER OUTLINE

MAJOR ISSUES ADDRESSED

Biological Contributions to Sex Differences in Behavior
Historical Basis of Sex Differences
The Nature of Psychological Androgyny
Current Changes in Sex-Role Stereotypes
Theories of Sex-Role Development
The Nature of Socialization

INTRODUCTION

One of the most important aspects of our self-concept and identity is our sex role, our view of our self within the context of societally defined roles related to gender. Sex roles are learned, starting in infancy, and continually develop throughout the life span (Eccles, 1987; Fagot & Leinbach, 1987). Sex roles are learned through the processes of socialization, just as other social behaviors. One purpose of this chapter is to describe the socialization processes involved in sex-role development.

A second purpose of this chapter is to describe sex-role development, and its consequences, during the adolescent years. It is during adolescence that many existing sex differences emerge (Eccles, 1987; Maccoby & Jacklin, 1974; Unger, 1979) and sex roles begin to stabilize. Adolescence, then, represents a unique opportunity to study the multifaceted socialization agents that affect sex-role development.

In our discussion we shall review several theories of sex-role socialization. These theories are attempts to describe how sex roles are learned and how various behaviors, attitudes, and values related to sex roles are acquired. In doing this task we shall examine sex-role development during adolescence and describe the important agents influencing that development. Prior to examining these issues, however, it will be helpful to describe general socialization processes.

THE NATURE OF SOCIALIZATION

Definition of Socialization

Socialization is a difficult term to define because it is used to describe *what, why*, and *how* the individual comes to behave in ways deemed appropriate by society. Because all human beings live in social systems that have rules and norms for behavior, everyone must learn to behave in ways deemed "ap-propriate" by the society. Although various cultures, and subcultures, differ with respect to the specific behaviors seen as appropriate, all have standards for what will and will not be tolerated. Members of the society learn these social rules, as well as how far the code may be stretched. Socialization, then, may be defined as the study of how individuals learn the knowledge and skills required for effective participation in the society (Brim, 1966).

Our knowledge about socialization processes comes from a number of diverse areas of inquiry, including anthropology, sociology, and psychology. As a result of differences in research emphases, the contributions of these fields provide a rich perspective of the factors that influence socialization. Not only do obviously important individuals (for example, parents, siblings, peers, and teachers) affect socialization, but so do the general cultural setting, the history of the society, and socially defined stereotypes of acceptable behavior.

This latter point is most clearly demonstrated in the area of sex roles. As we elaborate below, **sex roles** reflect prevailing societal stereotypes for male and female behavior. With changes in the nature of the society, we can expect changes in the nature of the sex-role stereotypes (L. Hoffman, 1977; Rabin, 1987). The stereotypes are taught by parents, peers, and other social agents and institutions. The task of those interested in studying socialization is to describe the manner in which the individual acquires the stereotypes and the nature of influence exerted by cultural agents and institutions.

Socialization and Adolescent Development

There are several important implications of our definition of socialization. First, socialization involves learning. Of necessity, then, we shall look to the utility of learning theory, especially social-learning theory, in

Adolescents take an active role in their socialization, including the task of "educating" their parents about what it means to be an adolescent.

describing how the individual comes to be socialized in sex-typed ways.

Second, socialization reflects cultural expectations and stereotypes. We expect children, adolescents, and adults to behave in specifiably different ways consistent with broad-based social stereotypes. We expect more mature behavior from adolescents than from children, for example. When adolescents engage in childish behavior, we likely express displeasure. Similarly, we may look askance at a male adolescent who behaves in a more feminine manner than that deemed appropriate, because the behavior is not consistent with established societal norms.

Socialization, then, involves an interaction between the individual and the conceptions of expected behavior for that person by socializing agents—parents, peers, the general social order. This is a dynamic interaction, with the role of socializer and socializee continually interchanging (Bell, 1968; Rheingold, 1969). For example, just as the parents socialize the adolescent, so too does the adolescent socialize the parents. As a general example, consider adolescent independence strivings. Adolescents "push" their parents for greater freedom and autonomy, and

their parents must learn to give it. By showing they can accept greater responsibility, adolescents "teach" their parents to give greater independence. It is the nature of this give-and-take process that is at the heart of much parent-adolescent conflict and stress. When one party, in either the role of socializer or socializee, violates too strongly the expectations of the other, then conflict can result. Goslin (1969) captured this perspective very well when he noted that role learning and role teaching always go hand in hand.

In the realm of sex-role learning the same interchanging of socialization roles occurs. As social expectations for sex-role-appropriate behavior change—for example, an adolescent female calling a boy for a date—adolescents must teach their parents the new norms. In turn, parents must allow differences in socially sex-typed behaviors. Because parents and children grew up in different cohorts, or generations, some aspects of sex-typed behavior will be different, while some will be the same. Adolescents and their parents, then, continually act as the role learner and role teacher for sex-typed behaviors.

This leads to the last important implication of our definition of socialization. Although the particular behaviors socialized may change from generation to generation, the psychological processes and mechanisms involved in explaining socialization remain the same across generations. During the past 15 to 20 years there have been changes in sex roles. As a result, different sex roles are being learned by today's adolescents from those that were learned by their parents when they, themselves, were adolescents. But the manner in which the sex roles were learned—from parents, peers, social institutions, and the like—remains the same. Although you and your parents learned different sex roles to some degree, the manner in which you learned them is the same.

In sum, socialization is a very complex phenomenon. Consider yourself as an example. You are either a male or a female, a son or daughter, probably a college student, from a particular social background, of a particular ethnic group, growing up in a particular social climate and time, with a particular set of beliefs, and the like. Psychologists interested in the study of socialization must try to explain how you became what you are by reference to your gender, the social roles you play, your personal background, and the prevailing sociocultural factors, including existing stereotypes, that impinged on you throughout your life.

SEX TYPING

Sex typing is the term used to refer to the individual's acquisition of the motives, attitudes, values, and behaviors regarded by the culture as masculine or feminine. Sex typing begins in infancy when children are labeled male or female and are treated differently as a function of the label. The parents, and others, begin to shape the child's behavior in accord with societal expectations for acceptable and expected behavior from males and females. During the childhood and adolescent years, the individual incorporates those behaviors considered appropriate to its sex. In this section we described sex-role stereotypes and sex differences in behavior.

In most cultures, the **male role** is viewed as an instrumental one. Males are considered to be controlling, independent, assertive, competitive, aggressive, and manipulative of the environment. The **female role** is seen as involving passivity, dependence, nurturance, nonaggressiveness, and warmth. The fact that these roles are reversed in some cultures (Barry, Bacon & Child, 1957; Block, 1973) indicates that humans are not biologically predestined to these roles and that an important aspect of sex-role acquisition is the historical context into which the culture places these roles. Moreover, such evidence indicates that, as

cultural expectations change, there will be a change in expected sex roles. The women's movement in the United States is an attempt to change sex roles away from their historical nature and is related to changes in the cultural context (see Box 7–1). This attempt at changing sex roles reflects the strong belief that socialization influences are the major factor in sex-role development.

Opposed to the cultural perspective is the thesis that at least some sex differences in behavior have a biological basis (Beach, 1958; Money, 1961; Money & Ehrhardt, 1972; Quadagno, Briscoe, & Quadagno, 1977). This research, which is reviewed below, reveals that there are biological (for example, hormonal) influences on behaviors (for example, aggressiveness) that are sex typed. However, the available evidence reveals that socializing influences interact with biological influences in the expression of sex-typed behaviors. Hence, it appears most wise not to take either extreme position, but rather to view sex roles and sex differences as reflecting the interactive influences of both biology and socialization.

Sex-Role Stereotypes

The traditional sex-role stereotypes are familiar to all of us. Both children and adults expect men to be independent, competitive, assertive, and masters of the environment. They expect women to be nurturant, passive, dependent, and nonaggressive. These different expectations reflect a cultural history of the human species. Indeed, at one time, the sex-role differences may well have been adaptive (L. Hoffman, 1977; Unger, 1979; Box 7–1). Recently, however, strong social forces have been at work to change these sex roles, and particularly the female sex role, because they no longer are viewed as necessary or adaptive, but rather as restrictive.

Several surveys of adolescents by Broverman and her colleagues (Broverman et al., 1970, 1972; Rosenkrantz, Vogel, Bee, Bro-

BOX 7–1 **The Historical Basis of Sex Differences**

There can be but little doubt that sex differences in behavior, which form the foundation of sex roles, have a historical basis in biological sex differences (e.g., L. Hoffman, 1977; Unger, 1979). The biological ability of females to bear and nurse infants is at the heart of the [child care, nurturant, home-oriented] basis of the female sex role. In turn, the greater physical strength and endurance of males is the foundation of the [provider, aggressor, protector] male sex role. Early in the history of humans, this division of roles likely served a useful function and aided survival of the species. As humans evolved and developed in increasingly complex social institutions, the necessity for the historical division of sex roles was eroded. Today, in contemporary American society, the initial bases for the historical differences in sex roles no longer exist. Hence, there has been considerable social and political pressure to no longer discriminate on the basis of sex.

In an interesting paper, Lois Hoffman (1977) has provided an insightful perspective of how technological and medical advances in American society have influenced family roles, and thereby, in part, eliminated the necessity for a number of differences in sex roles. In particular, she has noted that women are spending much less of their adult lives in mothering functions. In part, this is a result of increased use of contraception to prevent unwanted pregnancies and to allow the planning of desired pregnancies. In part, it is due to increased acceptance of female employment. And, in part, it reflects increases in life expectancy. Moreover, technological advances have made it possible for women to caste off the traditional homemaker role and pursue activities outside the home, because of freed-up time.

Rabin (1987) has provided a more critical view of this perspective. She notes, for example, that the time now saved because of technological advances is used up in other, different household chores, such as driving children to doctor appointments (because doctors no longer make house calls), standing in line at supermarkets, putting away groceries, and chauffeuring offspring to various after-school and out-of-school activities. In other words, Rabin argues, even in two-earner families the basic running of the household and its ancillary responsibilities falls on the female. Some of the time savings noted by Hoffman simply are not there. It seems that the long history of having females be responsible for day-to-day child and household care is stronger than the possibility for change.

One important implication of all this is that existing sex differences reflect the socialization of sex roles to a greater degree than they do biological differences. Historically, girls have been socialized for the motherhood role. That still seems to be the case, despite the increased socialization for instrumental roles. It still is expected that the wife will be responsible for the bulk of the routine operation of the household and of child care, even if she is employed outside the home. This state of affairs reflects the fact that although attitudes about female employment, for example, may have changed, behaviors have not, likely due to the long history of sociocultural conditioning of these sex differences.

This perspective of the evolution of sex roles does not deny that biological factors may be important contributors to sex differences. Rather, it is based on the notion that there is an interaction between biological and social factors in the evolution of sex differences and similarities. Sex differences and sex roles, then, may be seen to reflect not only biological differences, but also the evolution of culture.

verman, & Broverman, 1968) have examined the degree to which the historical sex-role stereotypes have changed. Initially, approximately 100 male and 100 female undergraduates listed the characteristics on which they thought men and women differed. The traits were put into a checklist that was completed by 74 male and 80 female college students. Of the 60 items on the list, 41 were identified as indicating sex-typed behavior—at least 75 percent of the students of each sex agreed the behavior was masculine or feminine. For example, being aggressive, independent, competitive, logical, adventurous, self-confident, ambitious, and not dependent were sex-typed masculine traits, with the reverse traits being sex-typed as feminine. In turn, being gentle, tactful, strong, in need of security, enjoying art and literature, and expressing tender feelings were sex-typed feminine traits, with the reverse traits being sex-typed as masculine. It is interesting to note that both males and females agreed on the traits most characteristic of an adult man or an adult woman. On the basis of these and other findings, Broverman et al. (1972) concluded that for both sexes and for various age groups, marital statuses, religious groups, and educational levels, there was general agreement on the characteristics defining the male and female sex roles. Moreover, it was generally found that across all these groupings, male traits were more highly valued than female traits.

Some researchers have studied change in sex-role stereotyping specifically during the adolescent and adulthood years. Urberg and LaBouvie-Vief (1976) reported that sex-role stereotyping was most prominent when ratings were made of opposite-sex persons. In other words, both adolescents and adults viewed individuals of their own sex as less stereotyped than persons of the opposite sex. The authors also reported that some previously sex-typed traits, for example, affiliation and achievement strivings, were not viewed as sex-typed by either the adolescents or adults. Urberg (1979) replicated these findings, but found that the twelfth graders held the most stereotyped views. Of interest, she found sex-role stereotyping no less strong than was found in the previous study. In other words, there was little evidence of cultural change in sex-role stereotypes.

Several other researchers provide evidence that cultural change in sex-role stereotypes is not widespread. Roper and LaBeff (1977), for example, compared the perspectives of parents and adolescents in 1934 with a comparable sample of parents and adolescents in 1974. They reported that both males and females held to the traditional belief that women should maintain strong ties to household management and child rearing. A stronger role of women in economic issues was evident, however. This latter trend was also noted by Albrecht, Bahr, and Chadwick (1979), who reported that younger adults (those under 30) held more positive views of women contributing to family income than did older adults. Again, however, there was a strong feeling that women still should hold a primary commitment to the traditional female child-care and household management roles. Veroff, Depner, Kulka, and Douvan (1980) reported that the findings from two national surveys (1957 and 1976) indicated that the greatest change in sex-role perspectives was for women's achievement motivation. As was reported by Urberg (1979), there was a tendency for women to be more achievement-oriented, particularly in terms of careers outside the home.

More recent research (Baber & Monaghan, 1988; O'Connell, Betz, & Kurth, 1989) shows that college females remain committed to the motherhood role and plan to stay at home with their children for some length of time (see Box 7–2). Additionally, Lewin and Tragos (1987) have shown that adolescents' stereotypes of the male and female sex role have not changed substantially over the past 25 years.

On the basis of these studies, we must conclude that the sex-role stereotypes of adolescents have undergone very little, if any, substantial change. The few documented changes—less stereotyping of achievement motivation and an increased desire for long-term careers—are important, however. These changes reveal a broadening of the female sex role into areas traditionally considered not only masculine but desirable. Therefore, they represent a convergence of sex-role stereotypes. Whether additional changes will occur, of course, remains for the future to answer. Changing strongly entrenched stereotypes is a difficult and likely

BOX 7–2   **Career and Motherhood Expectations of College Women**

With the increasing opportunities for outside-the-home employment of women, researchers have begun to explore the expectations of college women with regard to career and motherhood plans (Baber & Monaghan, 1988; O'Connell, Betz, & Kurth, 1989). In each instance, these researchers asked college women in either traditional (e.g., nursing) and nontraditional (e.g., engineering) career programs about their plans regarding balancing working outside the home and their role as mother.

Nearly all the women reported that they planned to work full time until their first child was born. This was true for both those entering traditional as well as nontraditional careers. Following the birth of their first child, however, only a minority said they planned to go back to work full time, although it was a sizable minority (ranging from 25% to 46%). Although there was a slightly greater percentage of women in nontraditional career paths who said they planned to return to work full time by the time their first child was a year old, the difference was not large.

Baber and Monaghan note that a substantial percentage of these women argue that they will take rather long maternity leaves, including some who state they will do so for a full year. However, these women seemed to have failed to consider that they may not have a job to which to return. Laws limit the amount of time one may take a maternity leave and still have the employer hold the job open, and most businesses have a maternity leave of only six weeks. As a result, the careers of these women are at risk. After six weeks their employers may have no jobs for them.

The findings of both these studies point out another interesting phenomenon. Although the percentage of women training to enter nontraditional careers has increased, no doubt due in part to changing sex-role stereotypes, these changes have not been translated into changing family plans. Even those women who have sufficiently overcome traditional sex-role stereotypes to train for nontraditional careers plan to play a rather traditional family role, at least for some period of time.

These studies point out the complexity of sex-role stereotypes and the degree to which assessment of change in them is complex. On measures of career training there clearly have been changes. But with regard to family life, changes have been minimal and slower in coming.

long-term process. In this context, it is important to note that, although there is greater acceptance of women working, as noted above, there is a continued feeling that women still should have the primary, and historically feminine, responsibility for child care and the day-to-day operations of the household. In other words, when women go to work they, more than men, have two jobs.

It is interesting to speculate about the importance of other cultural changes in the etiology of the documented changes in sex roles. The greater achievement strivings of females and acceptability of careers outside the home for females may reflect the increase in the proportion of working mothers (see Chapter 10 for a complete discussion of maternal employment). There is evidence to show that the daughters of working mothers have more flexible sex-role stereotypes and are more career-oriented. Moreover, they are more approving of mothers working than are daughters of mothers who do not work. The working mother provides an alternative model for her daughter. Changes in sex-role stereotypes, then, may be fostered by other changes in the society, such as the economic necessity of two incomes in the household, and reflect those changes.

Sex Differences in Behavior

Sex-role stereotypes, of course, reflect expected differences in behavior due to the sex of the individual. Although observed differences in behavior may not be consistent with sex-role stereotypes, the stereotypes still exist because they are based on historical precedent. For example, the stereotype of women being homemakers still exists even though half of women work outside the home.

The most extensive study of sex differences in behavior was published by Maccoby and Jacklin (1974). They reviewed research investigating sex differences in a variety of areas, including school learning, memory, perception, personality, and the like. They then summarized their findings by listing areas in which (1) stereotypes were not supported by experimental evidence, (2) real sex differences existed, and (3) questionable sex differences existed. Nonsupported beliefs included girls being more social and suggestible and boys being more analytic. Real sex differences existed for girls having greater verbal ability and boys excelling in visual-spatial ability. Questionable sex differences were found for activity level, dominance, and competitiveness, for example. More recent research has documented further some of these sex differences. For example, differences in spatial ability are well documented (e.g., Linn & Petersen, 1985; Tracy, 1987), as are sex differences in mathematics achievement (e.g., Feingold, 1988; Wentzel, 1988), although the basis of these differences is not well understood (see Box 7–3 on p. 178). No doubt, the reasons for these sex differences will be complex and will involve both biological and social factors.

PSYCHOLOGICAL ANDROGYNY

Historically, the study of sex-role stereotypes and sex differences in behavior has been based on the notion that masculinity and femininity are polar opposites. In other words, it has been assumed that the more feminine an individual perceived the self to be, the less masculine the self was perceived to be. More recent research and theorizing by Sandra Bem (1974, 1975, 1977, 1981) and

Janet Spence (Spence & Helmreich, 1978, 1979, 1981) has focused on the concept of psychological androgyny. Underlying this perspective is the view that masculinity and femininity are not polar opposites, but rather are relatively independent dimensions along which our behavior may differ. Each of us may have greater or lesser traditionally masculine *and* feminine characteristics.

Psychological **androgyny** refers to sex-role flexibility and adaptability. The major underlying assumption of this perspective of sex roles is that the individual may act in either a traditionally masculine or traditionally feminine manner, depending upon situational constraints and needs. One example Bem (1977) uses is the firing of an employee (which involves the stereotypical masculine traits of assertiveness and dominance) with sensitivity and understanding (which involves the stereotypical feminine traits of empathy and compassion). In this view, then, considerable emphasis is placed on the role of situational factors as determinants of our behavior. For example, becoming an expectant parent increases the femininity scores of both males and females and becoming a parent further increases the femininity scores of females, but reduces those of males (Abrahams, Feldman, & Nash, 1978). This latter finding may reflect the traditional sex-role stereotypes of expressivity (e.g., mothering) and instrumentality (being the provider).

Both Bem and Spence have argued that the androgynous sex role is the most adaptive because it allows the greatest behavioral flexibility. Those who are able to demonstrate either masculine or feminine behaviors, depending upon situational demands, are presumed to have an optimal sex role.

In order to measure psychological androgyny, Bem (1974) developed the Bem Sex Role Inventory (**BSRI**) and Spence (Spence, Helmreich, & Stapp, 1974) developed the Personal Attributes Questionnaire (**PAQ**). Each instrument is composed of sev-

BOX 7—3 **Sex Differences, Sex Roles, and Mathematics Achievement**

Sex differences in mathematical ability are well documented (Feingold, 1988; Wentzel, 1988). Boys are more likely than girls to choose mathematics courses as electives (Sherman & Fennema, 1977) and, although classroom performance of boys and girls in mathematics courses remains consistent across the high school years, standardized test score performance of females declines across the high school years, dropping below that of boys by grade 11 (Feingold, 1988; Wentzel, 1988). Although there is some evidence (Feingold, 1988) that sex differences in standardized test performance are diminishing in the earlier grade levels, the difference favoring boys in the later grade levels has remained constant for about the past 30 years. A number of potential causes of this sex difference have been investigated.

In attempting to determine the complex reasons for sex differences in mathematics, some researchers (e.g., Heller & Parsons, 1981; Parsons, Kaczala, & Meece, 1982; Eccles & Wigfield, 1985) have examined the role played by teacher-student interactions in the classroom on student expectancy for success in the study of mathematics. More specifically, they have focused on sex differences in the teacher's use of praise and criticism in the classroom.

Heller and Parsons (1981) observed teacher-student interactions in junior high school (grades 7 and 9) mathematics classes. In addition, teachers were asked to indicate how well they thought the students would do in an advanced mathematics course, and students were asked how well they thought they would do in both familiar and unfamiliar mathematics tasks. The researchers reported no sex differences in teacher use of praise and criticism and no sex differences in teacher expectancies for performance. However, girls had lower expectancies for success on unfamiliar mathematics tasks, which might be related to their hesitancy to enroll in mathematics when it is an elective.

Parsons et al. (1982) essentially replicated these findings in their study of teacher-student interactions in grades 5 to 9. However, they did report that girls had lower expectancies (self-concept of ability) when teachers praised high-expectancy boys (those they felt would do well in advanced math) but not girls. Parsons and colleagues also reported that praising high-expectancy girls had a positive effect on all girls. It seems that distributing praise and criticism similarly for both sexes and for both high- and low-expectancy children attenuates sex differences in student expectancies for mathematics success.

That teachers' use of praise and criticism plays some role in sex differences in mathematics achievement and student expectancies for success in mathematics seems clear on the basis of these studies. Equally clear is the fact that this is not a simple relationship. For example, the influence of the teacher may be different for children than for adolescents. Nonetheless, the data reveal that sex differences in mathematics achievement and self-concept of mathematics ability are determined in part by sex differences in student-teacher interaction.

Another line of research has focused on the role of parents (Eccles, Jacobs, Harold-Goldsmith, Jayaratne, & Yee, 1989; Raymond & Benbow, 1986; Yee & Eccles, 1988). The aim of this line of inquiry has been to investigate whether or not parents differentially encourage their adolescent males and females to excel in mathematics, and whether or not parents have differential expectations for males and females in mathematics. Although some evidence (Raymond & Benbow, 1986) indicates that parental encouragement and assessment of adolescents' performance in math is not differential for males and females, other evidence (Yee & Eccles, 1988; Eccles et al., 1989) indicates that parents hold differential expectations for young children's mathematics performance that are sex-typed in favor of boys. In addition, parents attribute boys' performance to ability and girls' performance to effort (Eccles et al., 1989).

The effort to identify the causes of sex differences in mathematics achievement seems to indicate that there are important socialization factors, reflecting prevailing sex-role stereotypes, which contribute to boys doing better than girls.

eral scales, one measuring masculine traits and one feminine traits. Individuals completing the scales indicate the degree to which each trait is characteristic of them. Their scores for masculine and feminine self-attributions are then calculated. By dividing the subjects at the median masculinity and femininity scores (see Appendix) four classifications of individuals are obtained. *Androgynous* individuals rate themselves high (above the median score) in both masculine and feminine traits. *Masculine* individuals rate themselves high on masculine traits and low (below the median) on feminine traits. *Feminine* individuals rate themselves low in masculinity and high on the feminine traits. **Undifferentiated** individuals rate themselves low on both masculine and feminine traits.

In contrast to measuring sex roles as traits, Orlofsky and colleagues (e.g., Orlofsky & O'Heron, 1987) have devised a sex-role scale that assesses self-perceptions in the domains of interests and behaviors in four areas: leisure activity preferences, vocational interests, social interaction, and marital, or primary relationship, behaviors. Evidence (Orlofsky & O'Heron, 1987; Whitley, 1988a) shows that the Sex Role Behavior Scale masculinity and femininity scores do not correlate highly with the masculinity and femininity scores from the trait measures, indicating they assess different aspects of sex roles, and that sex roles involve not only traits that are comparable to self-esteem, but also attitudes and behaviors that are different. Sex roles, in other words, seem to be more than simply traits.

Behavioral Evidence of Androgyny

Behavioral evidence in support of Bem's claim that an androgynous sex role leads to greater behavioral flexibility is relatively scarce. In her initial study, Bem (1975) reported that androgynous college students exhibited masculine independence and feminine playfulness in appropriate situations.

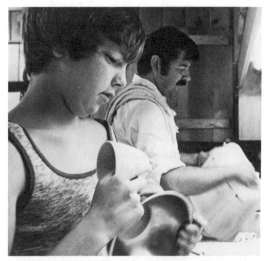

Androgynous individuals feel comfortable when performing either traditionally masculine or traditionally feminine roles.

In contrast, sex-typed individuals displayed traditionally sex-typed behavior in each situation. Russell (1978) reported that both androgynous and feminine fathers engaged in more day-to-day care of their children and played with their children more than did fathers who were in the masculine or undifferentiated sex-role categories. No differences were found for mothers in the four sex-role categories. Androgynous and feminine fathers, both of whom viewed themselves high in traditional feminine traits, were more nurturant and sensitive toward their children.

The most extensive study of the effectiveness of androgynous individuals relative to their nonandrogynous counterparts was reported by Baumrind (1982; see also Spence, 1982). The study involved 9-year-olds and their parents. The parents completed the BSRI in order to investigate the claim that androgynous parents rear children who are more competent and well-adjusted than traditionally sex-typed children. Data were gathered from naturalistic as well as structured observational situations, interviews, and standardized tests. For example, the children were observed in school and at home, structured situations with parents and children took place in the laboratory, and children and parents were interviewed. Parental child-rearing practices and attitudes were assessed.

Although there were many interesting results from this study, we summarize only those most closely pertinent to our concerns. Androgynous mothers tended to use more guilt induction in child rearing and androgynous fathers tended to be less firm with their children. Sex-typed fathers tended to be firm and demanding, and sex-typed mothers tended to be loving and highly involved with the activities of their children. Undifferentiated fathers did not differ from other fathers, but undifferentiated mothers were less nurturant and more punishing than other mothers. Parents who were cross-sex-typed (feminine fathers and masculine mothers) reared children with no characteristics that distinguished them from children whose parents were in the other groups.

Behavioral evidence linking sex roles and adolescent behavior also is very rare. One area in which there is some behavioral evidence, and an area very important to adolescent development, is sexual behavior. Researchers (Leary & Snell, 1988; Whitley, 1988b) have examined the relation between college students' sex roles and their sexual experience (whether or not they had engaged in sexual intercourse, number of sexual partners, and the like). For males, level of masculinity was positively related to sexual experience—those with higher masculinity scores had higher scores on the sexual experiences questionnaires. Level of femininity was unrelated to sexual experience for males. For females the general findings were somewhat more complex. Masculinity was related to sexual experience in both the Leary and Snell (1988) and Whitley (1988b) studies, but Leary and Snell found this was true only for females with low femininity scores. Femininity acted as a deterrent to

sexual behavior for females. Of course, these findings are consistent with sex-role stereotypes, with masculine individuals of both sexes, and androgynous males, but not females, having the greater sexual experience.

Until further behavioral evidence is available, any conclusions concerning the advantage of an androgynous sex role with regard to daily behaviors, child rearing, and the like must be tentative, particularly as it relates to the adolescent years. However, the scant evidence in existence is consistent with the suggestion that an androgynous sex role is related to greater behavioral flexibility.

Androgyny and Psychological Adjustment

A correlate of the behavioral flexibility hypothesis is that an androgynous sex role should be psychologically more healthy than sex-typed sex roles because the latter restrict psychological growth. To investigate this hypothesis, researchers have examined the relation between sex roles and various measures of psychological adjustment (see Dusek, 1987), primarily in college students. Some researchers have shown that androgynous individuals have higher self-concepts than masculine, feminine, or undifferentiated individuals. They argue that this is the case because of the more wide-ranging self-views, feelings of competence, and comfort with different situations that androgyny allows.

Other researchers (see Dusek, 1987) have argued that it is not the balance between high levels of masculinity and femininity that results in a more positive self-concept, but rather that it is simply high masculinity. The basis of this suggestion is that masculine traits are viewed as more desirable in our culture. These researchers provide evidence that androgynous and masculine subjects score equally high on measures of self-concept. Because the masculine individuals have relatively low femininity scores, while both groups have relatively high masculinity scores, the argument goes, it is high masculinity and not a balance of high masculinity and high femininity that is important to adjustment.

Because a variety of different self-concept measures were used in these studies, it is difficult to reconcile the divergent findings. Moreover, the self-concept measures used were global, overall assessments of the self. It is conceivable that the nature of the relationship between sex-role orientations and self-esteem depends on the specific aspect of self-esteem measured. To test this hypothesis, Flaherty and Dusek (1980) had college males and females complete the BSRI and a self-concept measure assessing four aspects of self-concept: Achievement/Leadership (a measure of the traditional masculine/instrumental role), Congeniality/Sociability (a measure of the traditional feminine/expressive role), Adjustment (a measure of homeostasis with the environment), and Masculinity/Femininity. The androgynous and masculine subjects scored highest on the instrumental scale, the androgynous and feminine subjects scored highest on the expressive aspect of the self-concept, the androgynous subjects had slightly (but not significantly) higher scores on the adjustment aspect of the self-concept, and the masculine subjects had the highest and the feminine subjects the lowest scores on Masculinity/Femininity, with the androgynous subjects having a middle score. Flaherty and Dusek (1980) concluded that during the late adolescent years the androgynous sex role was associated with higher levels of several aspects of self-esteem. Those with the traditional sex roles had more restricted self-concepts. These data, then, support those who argue the value of androgyny for psychological adjustment.

In general, the research relating sex-role orientation to measures of psychological adjustment has been conducted with college students. Ziegler, Dusek, and Carter (1984) used the same instruments and procedures as Flaherty and Dusek (1980) and tested adolescents in grades 6, 8, 10, and 12. They found the same relationships between self-esteem and sex-role orientation as those reported by Flaherty and Dusek (1980). Of interest, there were no grade level differences in these relationships. During the adolescent years, then, an androgynous sex role is associated with higher levels for several components of self-concept.

Another line of research relating sex roles to adjustment involves studying identity development in the four sex-role groups. According to Erikson (1963, 1968), it is during the late adolescent, specifically college, years that the greatest gains in identity occur (Bourne, 1978a, 1978b; Marcia, 1980; Waterman, 1982). Two aspects of identity that are particularly critical during these years are resolution of the identity versus identity diffusion and industry versus inferiority crises. Of course, an important aspect of identity is sex-role development. A firm identity involves a perspective of the self within the context of sex roles. In addition, achieving a sense of industry entails views of the self along traditional masculine/instrumental roles. Because androgynous individuals are presumed to have more flexible sex roles, it may be that they are more successful in resolving these crises.

In order to test this hypothesis, Della-Selva and Dusek (1984) had college students complete the BSRI and a measure of resolution of the identity versus identity diffusion and industry versus inferiority crises. They found that the androgynous subjects scored highest, the masculine and feminine subjects next highest, and the undifferentiated subjects lowest on resolution of the crises. Further, they demonstrated that it was the possession of high levels of masculinity *and* femininity that related to more successful resolution of the crises. Similar results were reported by Waterman and Whitbourne (1982) and by Glazer and Dusek (1985). In addition, in these latter two studies, it was demonstrated that the advantage of the androgynous sex role extended across all six of Erikson's crises. In other words, these studies provide clear evidence that an androgynous sex role is associated with more successful resolution of various crises faced in the course of childhood and adolescent development.

Finally, Dusek, Klemchuk, Hutchinson, and Bock (1989) have shown that more well-adjusted college students score higher on masculinity and femininity, lower on measures of depression and poor psychological adjustment, and higher on self-esteem than those who are less well-adjusted. These findings are consistent with the suggestion that an androgynous sex role is associated with better psychological adjustment.

The results of the research reported in this section leave little doubt that an androgynous sex role leads to optimal psychological adjustment, although much still needs to be learned. However, it should also be pointed out that a sex-typed sex-role leads to better adjustment than an undifferentiated sex role. In studies of self-concept (for example Flaherty & Dusek, 1980) and resolution of developmental crises (for example, Della-Selva & Dusek, 1984; Waterman & Whitbourne, 1982), undifferentiated subjects had by far the poorest adjustment. As Flaherty and Dusek (1980) noted, then, it may be best to be androgynous, but it is better to be sex-typed than undifferentiated. Although sex-typed roles have their disadvantages, it is important for a balanced perspective to realize that they are better than some alternatives.

Della Selva and Dusek (1984; see also Dusek, 1987) suggested that the important question was not whether it was masculinity or femininity that was responsible for better psychological adjustment, but rather how much each contributed to adjustment. In examining the research so as to address this question, Dusek (1987) found that the masculinity aspect of sex roles was more important than the femininity component, but that femininity was positively related to adjustment. This finding is consistent with an androgyny view as it relates to psychological

adjustment. However, it raises the question of why masculinity is more important than femininity with respect to adjustment.

The answer is complex, and not completely understood, but we can offer some insights. First, as noted above, masculine traits are viewed as more desirable, in general, than are feminine traits, and they are viewed as more valuable in our society. Second, some evidence exists to indicate that measures of self-concept assess more masculine, instrumental aspects of self-concept. Recall that Flaherty and Dusek (1980) found that for expressive aspects of self-concept, femininity was more strongly related to self-concept. Finally, there is evidence (Griffiths, Dusek, & Carey, 1988; Snel, Carey, & Dusek, 1988, 1989) that the manner in which we define and characterize maladjustment, such as depression, is based in part on traits that are more expressive (e.g., crying, feeling helpless) than instrumental (e.g., attacking a stressful situation). This seems to reflect the fact that in our society we reward instrumental traits to a greater degree than we do expressive ones. In other words, part of the reason that femininity may relate less strongly than masculinity to adjustment may be the result of the nature of our social order and the way we define adjustment and maladjustment.

Developmental Trends in Androgyny

An interesting question concerns developmental trends in sex-typing and androgyny. Hyde and Phillis (1979) had subjects aged 13 to 85 complete the BSRI in order to examine age differences in sex-role orientations. They reported that the proportion of androgynous males increased with age and that the proportion of androgynous females decreased with age. Ziegler and colleagues (1984) found a similar trend for adolescents in grades 6, 8, 10, and 12. For males, there was a trend toward androgyny; for females, there was a shift away from androgyny and toward a feminine sex role. To explain these age differences, they suggested that it is difficult for women to acquire masculine traits as they get older because those traits have a youthful tenor. Males, however, could acquire feminine traits relatively readily. For example, as males mature, acquiring the traditionally female traits of nurturance, caring for the feelings of others, and the like will stand them in good stead in their roles of husband and father. Antill (1983), for example, demonstrated that males who score high in femininity tend to have happier marriages than males who do not score as high. Hence, an increase in male androgyny should be expected because it is adaptive.

The most extensive investigation of age differences in sex-role orientation was undertaken by Spence and Helmreich (1979). They had high school students, college students and their parents, and a group of parents of first- and second-graders complete the Personal Attributes Questionnaire. Males had higher masculine scores, and fe-

With increasing age, males become more androgynous by acquiring traditionally feminine nuturant behaviors.

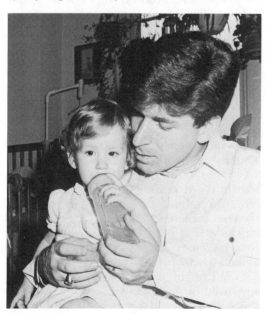

males higher feminine scores, on the PAQ. The *adult* males had higher masculinity scores than the younger males (whose scores were like those reported by Ziegler and others). There were no age trends on the femininity scale. Spence and Helmreich suggest that it may be adaptive for all people to become more instrumental with increasing age because of responsibilities for schooling, work, and the like. Males may find this easier because of the traditional masculine role. Females may not become more instrumental because the traditional feminine role holds them back.

Although the data concerning developmental trends in sex roles clearly are less than conclusive, they are suggestive of developmental changes consistent with traditionally held societal sex roles. The failure to find increases in androgynous orientations for females illustrates the detrimental effect of the feminine sex role.

THE BIOLOGICAL BASES OF SEX DIFFERENCES

Interest in biological influences on sex differences stems in part from our knowledge of prenatal and postnatal differences between the sexes. Males tend to be miscarried more often and are more susceptible to diseases throughout their lives. Female infants tend to be physically more mature at birth than male infants. Females walk and talk earlier and enter the growth spurt several years earlier than boys. These biological differences suggest the possibility that sex differences in behavior may have a biological link.

Research on the biological bases of human sex differences is not extensive. Some researchers (for example, Ehrhardt & Baker, 1973) have examined the relationship between hormones and sex-typed behavior, such as aggression (Tieger, 1980; Maccoby & Jacklin, 1980). A second approach (for example, Money, Hampson, & Hampson, 1955; Money & Ehrhardt, 1972) has been to examine how hereditary influences may be modified by social factors.

Hormones and Sex Differences

Some biological research on sex-role behaviors has focused on the effects of hormones (Beach, 1958; Money, 1961; Money & Ehrhardt, 1972; Tieger, 1980). The hormones of primary interest are estrogen, progesterone, and testosterone. The general notion has been to examine the activating function of the hormones; the presence or absence of the hormone may exert some influence on current behavior (Tieger, 1980). One specific hypothesis is that hormones absorbed prenatally may contribute to differences in behavior between the sexes. For example, injecting pregnant monkeys with testosterone (a male hormone) results in hermaphroditic female offspring who exhibit not only physiological alterations, but also show behavior patterns more similar to those of males than to those of females (Quadagno et al., 1977). Injecting male hormones into an infant monkey after birth does not alter its physical attributes but can result in changed behavioral patterns, including dominance and aggressive behavior (Tieger, 1980). Although some methodological difficulties in this research area lead to the necessity of drawing cautious conclusions, it does appear that research with animals demonstrates a link between hormones and behavior that in humans is called sex-typed (Quadagno et al., 1977; Tieger, 1980).

Research with humans is much less conclusive (Tieger, 1980; Maccoby & Jacklin, 1980), in part because of the ethical issues involved in research on hormonal reactions. We cannot in good conscience just randomly select children to be injected with hormones so we can observe the impact on their behavior. As a result, research has focused on "accidental" occurrences of hormone abnormalities.

Much of this research has involved aggressive behavior (Maccoby & Jacklin, 1974,

1980; Tieger, 1980) because males seem to be more aggressive than females across a variety of cultures. It has been hypothesized that the higher levels of testosterone in males may be linked to their greater aggressiveness and general activity level (Maccoby & Jacklin, 1974, 1980; Tieger, 1980; Quadagno et al., 1977).

Research with humans shows that male hormones masculinize the prenatal development of girls. Ehrhardt and Baker (1973) studied 17 fetally androgynized girls and their sisters, who served as a control group. The androgynized girls, who were exposed to excessive prenatal androgens because of genetic anomalies or because the mother took hormone therapy to help prevent possible miscarriage, exhibited masculinized behavior. They had a preference for outdoor sports, for example, and preferred to play with boys and showed little interest in doll play and other girlish activities. Both mothers and children rated these girls as having masculinized behaviors. In general, their behavior could be classified more readily as masculine rather than as feminine. It is important to note, however, that Ehrhardt and Baker (1973) found no evidence of increased fighting or aggressive attacking in these girls. Hence, they suggested that aggressiveness may be the wrong variable on which to try to measure biological influences on sex differences.

Ehrhardt and Baker (1974) replicated these findings for girls but also found that boys experiencing similar circumstances were more energetic and active than a matched control group of boys. However, they again found no evidence indicating the boys in the experimental group were more prone to fighting or engaging in other aggressive activities. It seems reasonable to conclude that prenatal exposure to androgens increases activity levels and perhaps some aspects of sex-typed behaviors, but does not relate to aggressiveness, at least as measured in these studies.

Some research has been conducted on the

effects of prenatal exposure to estrogen or progesterone (both are female hormones). Yalom, Green, and Fisk (1973) showed that teacher ratings of boys exposed to very high levels of estrogen or progesterone (their mothers were being treated for diabetes) indicated lower assertiveness at age 6 relative to a control group. These differences continued through age 16, perhaps because being less assertive causes others to treat one less assertively; in other words, it may not be solely a hormonal influence. Girls exposed to excesses of progesterone under similar circumstances tend to be less tomboyish and show increased preferences for feminine clothes.

Tieger (1980; see also Quadagno et al., 1977) has reviewed research on the hormonal basis of aggression in humans. He concluded that there is very little evidence to indicate that aggression is linked to hormones, although general activity level is. He and others (e.g., Quadagno et al., 1977) suggest that social influences—reacting to boys' greater physical size, responding to sex differences in activity level, behaving toward children in accord with social stereotypes—mediate biological influences on sex-typed behavior. Reacting differently to very young children may cause sex differences in aggression to appear early in children and may make it seem that aggression is biologically determined.

A direct assessment of the relation between testosterone levels and females' sex roles was reported by Baucom, Besch, and Callahan (1985). They found that androgynous and masculine females, those with higher masculinity scores, had higher levels of testosterone than did feminine females. Those with higher testosterone levels also saw themselves as being more instrumental (self-directed, action-oriented, etc.). Those with lower testosterone levels saw themselves as more expressive (nurturing, moody, etc.).

The data reviewed in this section point to the importance of considering biological factors when discussing sex differences in behavior as well as sex roles. Untangling the relative contributions of biology and social factors, however, remains a task for future researchers. In all likelihood, as we detail below, the most fruitful approach will be to look at interactions between the two types of influences.

Social Factors, Biology, and Sex Differences

That biological factors and social influences interact to foster sex differences in behavior cannot be disputed. The most extensive demonstration of such effects comes from the research of Money and his co-workers.

In one set of studies (Money et al., 1955; Money & Ehrhardt, 1972) Money and colleagues examined behavior in androgynized females. These girls had normal internal reproductive systems but abnormal external genitalia. Although they showed an interest in marriage and having children, and although they dated like other girls, they also behaved in ways typically considered more masculine, as in aggressive play and games. They learned, through cultural and social forces, to overcome the biological anomalies and play the feminine role.

In a second set of studies Money and Ehrhardt (1972) studied children who were assigned the incorrect sex at birth because of deceptive external genital anomalies. Babies with male chromosomal patterns were raised as girls, and babies with female chromosomal patterns were raised as boys. In all 19 cases, the child learned to behave in a manner consistent with the assigned sex, which was opposite to the chromosomal sex. Thus, socialization influences overrode biological attributes.

These data reinforce the conclusion, drawn above, that although there may be biological predispositions for certain sex differences in behavior, one cannot ignore the role played by social factors. Indeed, as Maccoby and Jacklin (1980) point out, in examining sex differences in behavior one must consider a variety of influences, including biological, social, and societal/cultural setting conditions. This point is brought home forcefully when one considers the topic of sex differences in aggression. Although more males than females tend to be highly aggressive, the overlap in the distributions of male and female aggressiveness is very substantial. In other words, even if there is a biological predisposition toward aggressiveness in males, most males do not behave in aggressive ways most of the time. Again, then, we see that the two sexes are more similar than different.

THEORIES OF SEX-ROLE DEVELOPMENT

As the above information demonstrates, sex differences in behavior cannot be attributed entirely to biological factors. Indeed, it appears that biological predispositions are highly malleable and can be altered substantially by social influences. Much research and theorizing has been focused on the description of how social influences act on the individual's behavior. At present, there are three theoretical perspectives that are attempts to explain socialization, including sex-role acquisition.

Psychodynamic Theories of Socialization

Freud's Theory. The first global and developmental theory of socialization was formulated by Sigmund Freud (1924, 1930, 1935; see also Chapter 2). Freud believed that sex-role acquisition occurred through identification with the same-sex parent, which, in turn, was a result of resolution of the Oedipal complex. By **identification**, Freud meant that the child took on the characteristics of the same-sex parent (see Figure 7–1). As a result, boys learned how to be males and girls learned how to be females by identifying with their fathers or mothers,

respectively (Bronfenbrenner, 1960). Put very simply, Freud believed that identification resulted in the development of a firm superego (conscience), which is the internal (mental) representation of societal standards of behavior, including sex-role behavior. Since the parent's values represent, to a greater or lesser degree, the values deemed acceptable by society in general, identification with the parent is critical to socialization. By identifying with the parent, the child and adolescent learn the rules and behavioral norms that society expects of them.

Because Freud assumed that primary sex-role identification took place in early childhood, his theory had little to say about either adolescent sex-typing in particular or socialization in general. The implications of Freudian theory for adolescent socialization rest on the importance it places on early childhood experiences. If these have long-term effects on personality development, they will affect the adolescent's behavior.

One problem with this approach is its lack of specificity about some of the factors that affect identification with, and modeling of, parents, such as situational contingencies and traits of the observer or the model. It also suggests a lack of flexibility in sex roles, because of the emphasis placed on early sex-role learning. In addition, Freud was unable to give serious consideration to the possibility of a biological basis for sex differences because relevant information was not available at that time. Finally, considerations of the role of cognition in social development were sketchy and largely ignored.

Erikson's Theory of Sex-Typing. Erikson (1963, 1968) has dealt with some of these problems in his cultural approach to psychoanalytic theorizing. In his discussion of the adolescent identity crisis, Erikson pointed out the important role of broad cultural influences on identity development, including sex-role learning. Erikson also believed there was a biological basis to sex-role development.

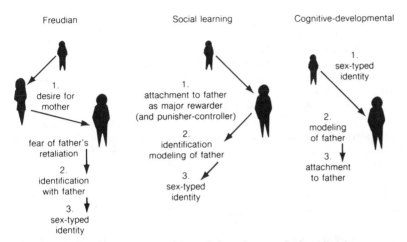

FIGURE 7–1   **Theoretical Sequences in Psychosexual Identification**
(Source: Kohlberg, L. [1966]. A cognitive-developmental analysis. Reprinted from
E.E. Maccoby [Ed.], *The development of sex differences.* Used with permission of
the publishers, Stanford University Press. Copyright © 1966 by the Board of
Trustees of the Leland Stanford Junior University.)

This latter point is stressed in Erikson's view that sex differences in behavior stem from anatomical differences between the sexes. More specifically, Erikson (1951) believed that personality and behavioral differences between the sexes reflected their different genital structures, an idea derived from Freud's view that human behavior is related to reproductive processes. Hence, Erikson argued that males are more intrusive and aggressive, and females passive, because of genital differences. To investigate this hypothesis Erikson gave 10-through 13-year-old boys and girls a variety of toys and building blocks and observed their play and the structures they constructed. The boys built tall buildings and their play was characterized by movement, aggressiveness, and openness. The girls tended to construct buildings that were enclosed and not very tall and their play was more static and passive. These differences in play, Erikson argued, reflected differences in the erectable and intrusive sex organs of males versus the female's intruded upon and more enclosed genitals.

However, a number of researchers (for example, Caplan, 1978) have pointed out difficulties with Erikson's view and it is now largely discounted as an accurate explanation of sex differences.

Social-Learning Theories of Socialization

The work of Robert Sears (1950; Sears, Maccoby, & Levin, 1957; Sears, Rau, & Alpert, 1965) was the first attempt to describe social behavior within a learning-theory framework. Sears's primary emphasis was on parental child-rearing practices. He was strongly influenced by Freud's theorizing and tried to translate Freudian theory into learning-theory terms. His basic thesis was that personality development in children was determined by the ways in which the child was raised, a tenet clearly taken from Freudian theory.

Sears's writings allow us to pick out several basic assumptions about the causes of behavior that fit not only his conceptualizations but also those of other social-learning theorists. One is that behavior is at once both the cause and the result of other behavior. For example, it is well known that individual differences in children, such as sex or temperament, cause parents to react differently toward the child from the first few days of life. Of course, the child's behavior is a response to adult behavior. Hence, socialization is a two-way process in which the behavior of the individual depends upon the behavior of other people, and in which the individual's behavior acts to elicit behavior from others.

Sears's second basic notion is that behavior is learned by reinforcement from those who share his environment. Because the child is reinforced for some behaviors and not reinforced, or perhaps even punished, for others, the child learns socially approved behaviors. If the same contingencies exist in the adolescent's world, similar behaviors will be exhibited in adolescence and adulthood.

More modern-day social-learning theories (for example, Gewirtz, 1969; Bandura, 1969a, 1969b) are based on the principles of classical and operant conditioning and imitation. In general, the notion is that human behavior is shaped through the use of reinforcement and punishment. Teaching children and adolescents appropriate social behavior through rewards and punishments is accomplished by positively reinforcing desired behavior and ignoring or punishing undesired behavior. Hence, desired behavior should increase in frequency and undesired behavior should decrease.

Humans are conditioned from infancy through childhood and even through adolescence to respond to environmental cues. Fagot and Leinbach (1989; see also Fagot & Leinbach, 1987), for example, found that parents who reinforced sex-typed behavior in their 18-month-olds reared children who learned sex-role labeling earlier (by age 27 months) and who at age 4 were more aware of sex-role discriminations. The parents of the early labelers "taught" their infants and young children to attend to and learn about sex roles.

A second way social behaviors are learned is through the process of imitation. Imitative learning occurs when the individual matches his behavior to the behavior of some other person (model). Imitative learning is itself a learned behavior. Gewirtz speaks of generalized imitation (for example, Gewirtz & Stingle, 1968), which is conceptualized as a learned tendency to imitate models, particularly if they are adults. In other words, by being reinforced for imitating, the child learns to imitate adults. These adults are primarily the parents during the child's early life. As the social world expands, however, the child and adolescent come to imitate other adults, for example, friends of their parents. Hence, imitative learning becomes generalized and is applied to a variety of models in a variety of circumstances. Identification with parents occurs, then, because of generalized imitation. It is no surprise that there are similarities in parent-offspring personality and behavior because offspring imitate their parents.

Bandura's (1969a, 1969b) social-learning theory was spelled out in detail in Chapter 2. Unlike the other social-learning theorists, he has detailed not only the mechanisms involved in the acquisition of responses by observing a model, but also the conditions under which imitation of a model's responses occurs. Together these two mechanisms explain a great deal about how a child is socialized and learns to behave in approved ways.

Social behaviors are acquired by observational learning and are imitated in appropriate circumstances. Like the other social-learning theorists, Bandura prefers to talk about behavioral similarity (imitation) rather than the ill-defined term *identification*. Behavioral similarity between the child and parent is what we mean by the term *identification*. By observing the parents, the child learns social behaviors. When the child behaves like the parent, we say the child has identified with the parent. This may occur with overt behaviors or with attitudes and

Parents act as models for sex-appropriate behavior, and thereby promote sex roles.

beliefs. Sex-role learning occurs when the child is taught (or imitates) the sex-typed behaviors of the same-sex parent. Such observational learning of sex-typed behaviors allows the child to learn the behavioral manifestations that we label sex role.

It may be helpful at this point to discuss briefly the many social models to which the adolescent is exposed in order to highlight the importance of modeling for adolescent social development. The first models that come to mind are the parents. The effects of parents as models for social development are as important in adolescence as in childhood (e.g., Campbell, 1969). The adolescent can learn how to behave in different social situations, such as weddings, football games, and formal parties, by observing the parents in these kinds of situations, as well as by direct parental training. In addition, the parents provide models for appropriate behaviors in a number of other social spheres, such as moral thinking and sex-role specific behaviors. It goes without saying, of course, that the parents are also instrumental in teaching specific kinds of behaviors through the use of operant conditioning. Generally speaking, too, parents are the

models for the adult social behaviors the adolescent is expected to acquire.

Other members of the family unit are also models for the adolescent. Older brothers and sisters, particularly, are important in introducing the young adolescent to the social world of the peer group. Although virtually no research exists on this issue, older siblings are highly important models for the adolescent because they engage in social activities and behaviors that are more similar to the adolescent's own than are those of the parent. This similarity should facilitate observational learning.

Other adults and peers are also important models (Campbell, 1969). In other words, through generalization processes, the adolescent will imitate other adults as well as peers because they exhibit behaviors similar to those of parents and siblings. In addition, generalized imitation theory (for example, Gewirtz, 1969; Gewirtz & Stingle, 1968) suggests that the adolescent will imitate these individuals because he or she has been taught to imitate people in general. Adolescent conformity may, in fact, be nothing more than extreme imitation of peers, although the reasons for that imitation may differ somewhat from the reasons for imitation under other circumstances.

From the social-learning perspective, sex-role learning is the result of direct training and observational learning (see Figure 7–1). Parental stereotypes of sex-appropriate behaviors may be reinforced as well as modeled by parents. As a result, boys and girls learn to behave in different ways because they are taught to behave in those ways, and because they see their parents behaving in sex-typed ways. Of equal importance, too, is the role played by other models and reinforcing agents, such as teachers, peers, other immediate and extended family members, and the media (Eron, Huesmann, Brice, Fischer, & Mermelstein, 1983; Carter, 1987; Fagot & Leinbach, 1987). The extensive investigations of the social-learning theorists and the application of learning theory to issues about development have underscored the importance of studying the role of modeling and environmental reinforcement contingencies for understanding sex-role development.

Cognitive-Developmental Theories of Socialization

The cognitive perspectives of sex-role learning emphasize the child's comprehension of and attention to the importance of gender and sex-role socialization. Drawing on Piaget's theory (see Chapter 4), Lawrence Kohlberg attempted to describe the role of cognitive development in sex-role learning.

Kohlberg contends that the child's cognitive representation of the external social world determines the child's basic sex-role learning. This view is predicated on Piaget's suggestion that intellectual development involves redefinitions of the world that, in turn, demand new ways of adapting and coping. Therefore, intellectual development is both an initiating force in social development and a facilitator of it (Kohlberg & Zigler, 1967). Kohlberg suggests that the developmental trends in sex-role learning start early in life with the child's self-categorization as a male or a female. Sex-typed preferences in children's activities and relationships are viewed as resulting from these initial judgments of gender identity. Boys, then, value masculine things, and girls value feminine things, because they are consistent with their conceived identities (Kohlberg & Zigler, 1967). A young girl engages in sex-appropriate behavior because she knows she's a girl and finds it rewarding to act like one. The social-learning theorists would say that the young girl exhibits sex-appropriate behavior because she wants rewards, which she gets for acting like a girl (see Figure 7–1).

Differential sex-role learning for adolescents follows the same pattern. The adolescent organizes his or her role learning according to gender identity. A result of this approach to sex-role learning is that changes in the sex-role image become possible as the child grows older because of developmental changes in cognition. Changes need not await environmental reinforcement contingencies, as in social-learning theory.

Kohlberg suggests that gender identity or categorization as a boy or a girl is a basic organizer of sex-role values and attitudes. Gender identity is a result of a cognitive judgment made by the child very early in development, and is subject to some aspects of change during childhood, adolescence, and adulthood (Kohlberg, 1966). According to Kohlberg, the progression of sex-role development is something as follows: I am a girl (boy), therefore I want to do girl's (boy's) things, and therefore the opportunity to do girl (boy) things is rewarding. This view is in direct contrast to the social-learning view, which states that the child wants rewards, receives rewards for sex-appropriate behavior, and, as a result, learns the appropriate sex-role behavior.

Kohlberg and Zigler (1967) tested these notions by measuring a number of aspects of sex-typing (e.g., verbal dependency, imitation of adults, sex-typing preferences) in children 4 to 8 years of age. They found that with development, boys become more same-sex oriented and more father oriented, while girls become less same-sex oriented and, although initially more mother oriented, become more father oriented. Kohlberg and Zigler interpreted these data as indicating the importance of changing cognitive competence as it relates to understanding of sex roles.

More contemporaneous cognitive attempts to explain sex-role development emphasize what Bem (1981) called *gender schema* (see also Martin & Halverson, 1981, 1987). A gender schema is a theory, a cognitive representation, of sexes, sex differences in behavior, and sex roles. Gender schemas function to regulate behavior (for example, by influencing goal setting), influence the information to which we attend (by highlighting the sex appropriateness of the behaviors to which we attend), and influence how we perceive our social world (through sex-typed lenses; Bem, 1981; Martin & Halverson, 1987). The general notion, here, is that as we grow we develop expectations and rules about the nature of the social world much the same way as we do about the physical world (e.g., Carter & Patterson, 1982; Levy & Carter, 1989). This was demonstrated clearly by Carter and Patterson (1982), who showed that children in grades K–8 increasingly understand that sex roles involve rules for behavior that are culturally determined and flexible. Gender schemas, then, act to filter the information we perceive from the external world, but little is known of how the schemas develop and the factors responsible for their development (Martin & Halverson, 1987). Sex-typed individuals are assumed to have gender schemas that emphasize examining incoming information in that manner, and that guide the individual to engage in opposite-sex behavior at low levels.

Eccles (1987) has elaborated the various cognitive developmental perspectives of sex roles into a life-span view of sex-role development. One basic assumption of this model is that sex-role transcendence—overcoming sex-role stereotyping—is the most developmentally mature sex-role perspective. Eccles views adolescence as an especially important time in the development of perspectives of sex roles. The cognitive changes that occur during early adolescence allow the individual to perceive the social order, including sex roles, in new and more flexible ways. Peer groups become more heterosexual in composition. And the identity crisis causes the individual to consider a number of critical issues—career plans, role as mother or father, being a spouse, and the like, that need to be resolved. According to Eccles, if the environment provides androgynous models the adolescent will progress toward sex-role transcendence. If the environment provides more traditional models the adolescent will develop a more traditional sex

role. It is important to make clear that sex-role transcendence does not mean the absence of sex roles, but rather the knowledge that they are arbitrary. Further, it means understanding that processing information and making judgments on the basis of gender schemata is limiting.

The cognitive-developmental theories by and large have been focused on development during the childhood years and have not provided much information for understanding adolescent sex-role development. But they do point to the importance of cognitive factors in sex-role development and make the important point that our understanding of sex roles is no different from our understanding of other systems of rules. Finally, researchers have shown that during childhood, and likely during adolescence, humans understand the arbitrariness of the sex-role schemata.

Comparison of Psychodynamic, Social-Learning, and Cognitive-Developmental Theories

Figure 7–1 depicts the psychodynamic, social-learning, and cognitive-developmental views of sex-role development. As you can see, the cognitive-developmental view is very nearly the opposite of the social-learning view, and both differ considerably from the Freudian view. The cognitive view contrasts with the psychoanalytic view in that identification with respect to sex is not fixed and established early in the child's life, but rather is a concept that changes with development. In addition, the social-learning view and the cognitive view agree that imitation is an important part of sex-role theory. However, Kohlberg reverses the sequence of the behaviors with his assumption that the child's cognitive awareness of sex roles determines the behaviors that should be adopted; the social-learning view is directly the reverse. Both direct reinforcement and imitation are relevant to the acquisition of sex-typed behaviors within the cognitive-developmental view, but both depend upon developmental changes that occur in cognition as well.

If you consider the nature of the cognitive changes that occur during the adolescent period (Chapter 4) it is not difficult to see that changes in perception of sex roles are quite possible from a cognitive-developmental view. The development of formal operations should allow the adolescent to restructure his or her former perceptions of an appropriate sex role. Although concrete operational thinking may be all that is required for the establishment of a firm sex role, formal operational thinking allows one to imagine hypothetical alternatives to traditional sex roles (for example, androgyny). As a result, cognitive developmental notions allow new ways to consider socialization phenomena, including changes in, and alternatives to, sex-role conceptualizations, and point up the importance of the cognitive dimensions in socialization. Of course, these possibilities exist only after entering adolescence.

Biology and Socialization Revisited

We discussed evidence regarding the direct effects of biology on socialization (see Chapter 3). In that discussion, we concluded that there likely was an interaction between social and biological factors in the emergence of sex differences, sex roles, and socialization. We now can list some specific examples directly pertinent to the study of adolescence. Each fits in the context of mediated effects models of the influence of biology on development, as discussed in Chapter 3.

First, the material on early and late maturity indicates the important role biological growth factors play in socialization. We have seen how other people's reactions and expectations of behavior depend somewhat on the physical characteristics of the adolescent. Adolescents who are out of phase with the norm will be expected to behave as older or younger than they are. In turn, their self-

concept (Wylie, 1961, 1974; Dusek & Flaherty, 1981), including their sex role and expectations for their own behavior, will be affected. For example, one may find a very young but relatively physically mature girl who feels her sex role must include various aspects of sexual behavior for which she is ill-equipped emotionally. In turn, a very late-maturing boy may be made to feel inadequate in the masculine sex role.

Second, today's adolescents reach physical maturity earlier than previous generations (the secular trend). Therefore, the parents and teachers of today's adolescents were less physically mature than today's adolescents at any given age of adolescence. Hence, they may be out of tune with the competencies of their children and students, treating them as younger than they are. This may make the task of socialization of adolescents more difficult than in previous generations, particularly since the "social times" have changed so much in recent years. Generational differences such as these make the task of both the socializer and the socialized more difficult because the pressures impinging on each may not be well understood by the other. Indeed, it may be harder to be an adolescent today and it may be harder to rear an adolescent.

Finally, since girls enter the growth spurt earlier and mature earlier than boys the same age, they are likely to be treated as older and more psychologically mature. Dating patterns and expected social behaviors for adolescent females and males are different; girls tend to date older boys and are expected to behave more like adults at an earlier age. Parents who treat their adolescents as adults and expect adult behaviors from them may be disappointed because of the lag between biological and social development. To stress one aspect of development over the other is inappropriate.

As you can see, in order to understand adolescent socialization, one must have a good grasp of the cognitive, physical, and social factors that influence it. All are important, and their interactive effects are critical in determining adolescent social behavior. The factors that might affect socialization in childhood are obvious. Certainly, the child's growth pattern, social experiences, and cognitive competencies all have some influence on how the parent treats the child. These same factors are as important—or perhaps even more important—at adolescence.

SUMMARY

Socialization refers to the acquisition of those behaviors considered appropriate by the society. An important aspect of adolescent socialization is the learning of sex-role stereotypes. Traditionally, the masculine role has been viewed as instrumental, and the feminine role has been viewed as expressive. Hence, the male sex role includes the traits of assertiveness, mastery, achievement, and aggressiveness. The female role includes the characteristics of passivity, warmth, and gentleness. Although these different roles may at one time have been adaptive, they no longer are considered essential to the species. As a result, there have been considerable pressures toward sex-role convergence, that is, toward males acquiring some of the traditionally feminine traits and females acquiring some of the traditionally masculine traits. Some evidence indicates that such changes in the traditional stereotypes are occurring, but the norm is still largely in the direction of the historical sex differences in behavior.

Current conceptualizations of sex roles do not consider masculinity and femininity to be polar opposites. Rather, the prevalent perspective is that any individual may possess both masculine and feminine traits, although to greater or lesser degrees. Hence, there are some individuals who are sextyped in the traditional vein, but others who are considered androgynous; that is, who view the self as being capable of expressing masculine or feminine traits to a high degree depending upon situational demands. Some theorists argue that the androgynous sex role leads to better psychological adjustment, for example, as measured by self-concept or self-esteem. Available evidence indicates this is the case, although behavioral evidence showing greater adaptability for androgynous individuals is very scant.

An important area in the study of sex roles is concerned with biological predispositions toward differences in behavior between the sexes. Research on biological influences on human sex differences is scarce. Some evidence reveals hormonal influences on sex-typed behavior, such as aggression. However, the preponderant conclusion is that although there may be biological differences between the sexes that lead to behavioral differences, social factors may alter the behavior and may be more influential than biological predispositions. Hence, although some evidence links aggression to the hormone testosterone, socialization influences cause most people, male and female, not to behave in aggressive manners most of the time.

There are three major theoretical approaches to the explanation of sex differences. Psychodynamic theories focus on identification with the same-sex parent, from whom sex-typed behaviors are learned. Social-learning theorists note the importance of direct training and the effects of models for the learning of sex-typed behavior. Cognitive-developmental theorists argue that sex differences in behavior reflect the abstraction of social rules from the environment. Each perspective has something to offer in the explanation of sex-role learning, and no one theory is preferred over the others.

Socialization during the adolescent years involves more than simply acquiring behaviors considered appropriate for one's gender. Adolescents must learn to handle independence, which parents must learn to give. Adolescents also wrestle with identity questions, issues related to sexual maturity, the learning of adult behavior, and other concerns pertinent to entering adulthood. The adolescent years, then, represent an important time for the transition to adulthood.

The adolescent is exposed to a number of important socializing influences from which both sex-typed behavior and more general social behavior are learned. Parents are the most important agents of socialization, in part because they have reared the individual for a long period of time. However, peers and other adults are also important to the adolescent's socialization. Finally, social institutions, such as the school and the media, influence to a significant degree the socialization of the adolescent.

GLOSSARY

Androgyny.   The perception of the self as having both masculine and feminine psychological characteristics to a large degree.

BSRI (Bem Sex Role Inventory).   A questionnaire used to assess one's perception of the self as possessing traditional masculine and feminine sex-role characteristics.

Femininity (female role).   In terms of sex roles, the sex role characterized by passivity, expressivity, and nonaggressiveness.

Identification.   In Freud's theory, taking on the characteristics and values of the same-sex parent.

Masculinity (male role).   In terms of sex roles, the sex role characterized by assertiveness, achievement, and independence.

PAQ (Personal Attributes Questionnaire).   A questionnaire to assess sex roles.

Sex role.   The cultural ascriptions of behaviors differentially by gender.

Sex typing.   The acquisition of sex-role behaviors.

Socialization.   A term referring to what, why, and how an individual comes to behave in the manners deemed appropriate by the society in which he or she lives.

Undifferentiated.   With regard to sex roles, the perception of the self as not possessing traditionally masculine or traditionally feminine sex roles to a large degree.

SUGGESTED READINGS

CAMPBELL, E. Q. (1969). Adolescent socialization. In D. A. Goslin (Ed.), *Handbook of socialization theory and research*. Chicago: Rand McNally.

Campbell presents a very readable discussion of the multiple factors involved in adolescent socialization.

CARTER, D. B. (Ed.). (1987). *Current conceptions of sex roles and sex typing*. New York: Praeger.

The chapters in this edited book present reviews of the major theoretical, methodological, and substantive issues involved in the study of sex roles.

COOK, E. P. (1985). *Psychological androgyny*. New York: Pergamon Press.

Cook provides a comprehensive introduction to androgyny theory. Substantive issues as well as measurement issues are discussed in a manner that does not require a high level of expertise.

MACCOBY, E., & JACKLIN, C. (1974). *The psychology of sex differences*. Stanford, CA: Stanford University Press.

Maccoby and Jacklin review over 1,400 studies involving sex differences in various aspects of behavior and psychological development. The conclusions they draw are at times controversial, but the review is thorough and provides considerable insight into the nature of sex differences.

SPENCE, J., & HELMREICH, R. (1978). *Masculinity and femininity: Their psychological dimensions, correlates, and antecedents*. Austin: University of Texas Press.

Spence and Helmreich discuss the nature of psychological androgyny and review research demonstrating its existence. They also present a cogent discussion of the antecedents of sex differences.

Adolescent Sexuality

8

CHAPTER OUTLINE

MAJOR ISSUES ADDRESSED

INTRODUCTION

Perhaps no single other event during the adolescent years has as dramatic or widespread effects as the realization of sexuality. In part, this is a result of physical changes —growth to adult physical maturity, development of secondary sexual characteristics, and the increase in the sex drive. In part, it is a result of social factors, including peer influences, parent values, moral and religious beliefs, pressures involved in dating, and stereotypes involving adolescents and sexuality. The biological changes and social influences cause the adolescent to begin to integrate sexuality into the self-concept. In a sense, a whole new dimension is added to the self, and this requires considerable adjustment. It is not surprising, then, that the adolescent's emerging sexuality causes adjustment problems, which might be severe for some.

Of course, emerging sexuality takes place not in a void but in the context of a variety of other personal and social changes. Cognitive changes allow the individual to evaluate aspects of sexuality differently from what was previously possible. Changing societal standards with regard to sexuality impact on the nature of adolescent adjustment to sexuality. In this chapter, we explore many facets of adolescents' sexual attitudes and behaviors and look toward relating these to personal and social factors.

ADOLESCENCE AND SEXUALITY

Both professional views, such as psychological and psychiatric perspectives of adolescence, and common stereotypes link the adolescent years and sexuality. Theoretical conceptualizations as well as everyday common concerns have been focused on many aspects of adolescent sexuality and on the effects of becoming sexual.

Sexuality in Theories of Adolescence

Theoretical conceptualizations describing adolescent interest in sexuality, and the importance of emerging sexuality for understanding adolescent development, have been present since Hall (1904) first wrote about adolescent development. Psychoanalysts such as Anna Freud (1948) have emphasized the sexual nature of human development and have specifically highlighted the upsurge in sexuality that occurs during the adolescent period of development. As we explained in Chapter 2, Anna Freud argued that the physiological changes occurring at puberty cause an increase in the sex drive that is reflected in a set of corresponding behavioral manifestations.

On the basis of this and other theorizing (Miller & Simon, 1980), one would suspect that there should be an increase in interest in sexuality, and behaviors related to sexuality, at adolescence. Indeed, popular stereotypes would have us believe that adolescents are consumed with interest in sexuality and that they spend very large portions of their time wondering about, and experimenting with, sexuality.

Adolescent Interest in Sexuality

The most extensive study of the relationship of interest in sexuality to other adolescent interests was conducted by Dusek (Dusek & Monge, 1974; Dusek, Kermis, & Monge, 1979). In the initial phase of the study, about 100 students in each of the grades 5, 7, 9, 11 and college were asked to list the things that they would like to know more about. It was stressed that the topics listed could be anything, and the listing was anonymous. In all, 31 different categories of interests were identified from the data, with five categories dealing specifically with aspects of sexuality: social diseases, birth control, sexual relations, dating, and love and marriage. The percentage of students who listed a topic included in one of the five sexuality categories is presented for each grade and sex in Table 8–1. As you can see, 35 percent of the seventh-grade males and 39 percent of the seventh-grade females mentioned an interest in sexual relations (Table 8–1). The data indicate that only a small percentage of the students expressed interest in "social diseases," "birth control," "dating," and "love and marriage." Hence, there is an increase in interest in "sexual relations" during adolescence, with approximately one-third of the males and females at the seventh-grade level indicating they would like to know more about it. Again, there is much less interest in topics dealing with other aspects of sexuality.

In the second phase of the study, the 31 categories of interests were combined to form 14 general topics of interest. New groups of participants in grades 5 to 12 were asked first to rank-order the topics in terms of how important they were to them (1 = most important) and then rate the topics on a seven-point scale with regard to degree of interest they had in the topic (7 = very highly interesting). There were about 100 participants in each grade level.

Interest in sexual relations and love and marriage remained at medium levels until the late adolescent years, interest in venereal disease remained low, as did interest in birth control, and interest in dating and going

steady was higher. In no instance was a topic related to sexuality the top-ranked topic or the topic receiving the highest interest score. This was true for all grades and both sexes (Kermis, Monge, & Dusek, 1975; Dusek, Kermis, & Monge, 1979). Although there were some sex differences in interest in the various topics of sexuality, such as female's greater interest in birth control, these were in line with traditional sex-role behaviors (cf. Maccoby & Jacklin, 1974).

The final analysis was aimed at investigating the stereotype that adolescents, and especially males, do not view sexual relations within the context of an affectional relationship. One popular stereotype of adolescents is that they tend to be interested in sex for sex's sake. In order to study this stereotype, Dusek and his colleagues factor-analyzed the interest ratings. Factor analysis is a statistical technique for grouping items, in this case topics of interest, that seem to "go together" in the responses of those completing a questionnaire. One factor included the items "love and marriage," "dating and going steady," and "sexual relations." A second factor included the items "venereal disease" and "birth control."

Two aspects of this analysis are important. First, contrary to the popular stereotype, the adolescents viewed sex within the context of a love relationship, and this was true for both the males and females. We

TABLE 8–1   **Percentage of Males and Females in Five Grade Levels Listing a Topic Related to Sexuality**

Topic	MALES					FEMALES				
	5	7	9	11	College	5	7	9	11	College
Social diseases	0	0	0	0	3	0	0	3	6	1
Birth control	0	0	0	1	10	0	0	3	6	20
Sexual relations	5	35	19	13	13	2	39	9	6	18
Dating	0	4	2	3	3	2	18	3	9	0
Love and marriage	0	0	0	3	3	0	9	9	6	8

(Source: Adapted from Dusek, J., & Monge, R. [1974]. Communicating population control facts to adolescents. Final report, Grant No. RO1-HD 06724, submitted to the National Institute of Child Health and Human Development, National Institutes of Health, U.S. Department of Health, Education, and Welfare.)

shall review below other data supporting the notion that this is a significant trend in present-day adolescent views of sexuality. Second, the adolescent males and females viewed several aspects of sexuality, namely, contraception and health risks, separately from sexual intercourse.

Several conclusions are warranted. First, these data suggest that sexuality and interest in sexual behavior are *not* a prime motivator of adolescents, contrary to popular stereotypes and to the theorizing of a number of individuals (e.g., A. Freud, 1948; Hall, 1904). Although adolescents have a definite interest in sexuality, there are also other topics of greater or equal interest and importance to them. Sexuality is only one interest in a hierarchy of various interests.

Second, the information on adolescent interests suggests that sex education programs in public schools should begin at least as early as the sixth grade, where both the perceived importance of, and interest in, sexual topics are relatively high. Traditionally, such programs are started later.

Third, the data indicate a rather distressing fact about how adolescents view several related components of sexuality. As you can see in Table 8–1, interest in venereal disease and birth control is not as high as interest in sexual relations. Given the epidemic nature of venereal disease among adolescents this is indeed unfortunate. Since the interest data were collected in a school district that does not have a sex education program, it is unlikely that the students had a great deal of information about venereal disease.

Similarly, interest in birth control does not correlate with interest in sexual relations. Perhaps this is because adolescents, who are not supposed to engage in sexual relations, feel little need for knowledge about birth control. On the other hand, the evidence (reviewed below) suggests that adolescents do, indeed, engage in sexual relations and therefore would certainly profit from knowledge about birth control (Zelnik & Kantner, 1972; Settlage, Baroff, & Cooper, 1974). These data support notions indicating that sex education, whether given in the school, the home, or through some other agency, needs to deal with a widely ranging but well-integrated set of issues in order to be optimally effective.

The Sex Drive

During the adolescent years there is an increase in the sex drive. This appears to be a relatively universal physiological phenomenon related to hormonal development (Udry, 1987). In males, the rapid rise in testosterone levels that occurs between ages 12 and 14 is associated with increases in the sex drive as measured by nocturnal emissions and masturbation (Higham, 1980).

In addition, the research of Udry and his colleagues (Smith, Udry, & Morris, 1985; Udry, Talbert, & Morris, 1986) has shown that boys with increased androgen levels are more likely to be sexually active than are boys with lower androgen levels. Similarly, more biologically mature younger boys were more likely to be sexually active than less mature but older boys. The same relationships did not hold for girls. Although increased androgen levels in females were associated with a greater interest in sex, social factors, such as an environment that is more discouraging of premarital sexual intercourse for females, exerted a strong influence on females' decision to engage in sex.

Although one must be cautious in ascribing causal influences to hormones—more mature males are more physically attractive to females—it does appear that hormones exert a rather direct and strong influence on the sexual behavior of boys. In girls, the influence of hormones seems to depend on the social context in which they are raised to a greater degree than it does in boys. Hence, to understand the causes of adolescent sexual behavior fully, we must consider both biological and sociocultural factors in interaction (see Box 8–1).

The Biosocial View of Adolescent Sexual Behavior

ically, biomedical and social scientists have explored the antecedents of adolescent sexual behavior independently. The biomedical research has focused on normal and abnormal physiological development and its implications for understanding adolescent sexual behavior. The study of the role of hormones in sexual behavior is one example. Social scientists have focused on the importance of social factors, such as peer and parent influences, that affect adolescent attitudes and behaviors in the realm of sexuality.

The research of Udry (see text) illustrates rather clearly that both biological and social factors need to be considered in interaction when attempting to explain adolescent sexual behavior. Udry's research, in part, has stimulated the formulation of explanations of adolescent sexual behavior that examine the influence of biological changes within cultural contexts—the biosocial perspective (see Smith, 1989).

According to this perspective, biological factors (hormones) influence adolescent sexual behavior in two ways. First, they directly influence sexual motivation through the increase in the sex drive. As noted in the text, increases in androgens in both males and females occur during adolescence and are related to increases in the sex drive and interest in sexuality. Second, hormones have an indirect influence on adolescent sexuality through their effect on physical appearance. Hormones are responsible for making us look more mature and therefore more appealing to the opposite sex (see Chapter 3).

Social factors are posited to operate through the encouragement or discouragement of having sexual involvement. Hence, social factors influence age of engaging in sexual intercourse, the acceptability of various forms of sexual expression, attitudes about sexuality, and appropriate sexual partners.

This perspective has the virtue of allowing us to understand individual differences in adolescent sexual behavior. For example, adolescents growing up in different subcultures experience the same hormonal influences. Differences in sexual behavior, then, rest in different subcultural standards, as represented by peer, parent, and media presentations of relevant cultural standards. Similarly, sex differences in sexual behavior may be related to differences in sex-role socialization, which also may differ from subculture to subculture. Age differences in rates of maturity become important because they reflect different levels of biological development and, hence, influences of hormones. From a practical perspective, this approach suggests that sex education, for example, should not be tied to grade level but rather to maturational level.

Perhaps more than any other biological drive, the sex drive is viewed as needing a considerable degree of socialization for the benefit of both the individual and the society. As a result, it is necessary that adolescents learn the appropriate and socially sanctioned behaviors with respect to dealing with the new (sex) drive they are experiencing. As Douvan and Adelson (1966) and other investigators (for example, Kinsey et al., 1953; Kinsey, Pomeroy, & Martin, 1948; Bardwick, 1971; Sorensen, 1973) have pointed out, there appears to be a sex difference in how male and female adolescents deal with the socialization of the sex drive as well as in how the sex drive affects the

individual. The basis of this sex difference, no doubt, lies not only in the nature of the sex drive but also in cultural conditioning (Maccoby & Jacklin, 1974).

The evidence seems to indicate that adolescent males require relatively direct expressions of the sex drive. Adolescent males engage in greater amounts of sexual activity, such as sexual intercourse or masturbation, than do females (Sorensen, 1973; Luckey & Nass, 1969). And, male attitudes about sexual behavior are more liberal than female attitudes (Douvan, 1970; Luckey & Nass, 1969; Sorensen, 1973; Miller & Simon, 1980). For example, males are more likely than females to agree that sex outside strong

The sex drive is present for both males and females, although sexual intercourse may have different meanings for males and females.

emotional involvement is acceptable (Haas, 1979; Sorensen, 1973). Adolescent males also are aroused to a greater degree than adolescent females by a wider variety of stimuli, such as erotic art or films (Miller & Simon, 1980).

The sex drive for girls is more diffuse and may be displaced into other areas and dealt with more indirectly (Douvan & Adelson, 1966; Masters & Johnson, 1966, 1970). Aspects of the quality of the relationship between the girl and her partner are very important for most expressions of adolescent female sexuality (Haas, 1979; Sorensen, 1973). A majority of adolescent females would agree that sexual intercourse is acceptable if the two people are in love and is not acceptable if the two people are not in a romantic relationship.

Females are less likely than males to list pleasure, pleasing their partner, and relieving sexual tension as reasons for having sex (Leigh, 1989). Males are more likely to list lust or pleasure, and females love or emotional involvement, as reasons for having sex (Whitley, 1989). As a result, sexual impulses are more likely to be integrated with other aspects of social-emotional development for girls, particularly within the context of overall heterosexual relationships.

These sex differences in integration of the sex drive are related to differences in several aspects of sexual behavior. Simon, Berger and Gagnon (1972) surveyed a national sample of college students about their sexual behavior. They reported that 46 percent of the males were *not* emotionally involved with their initial partner and only 31 percent had been in love with or planned to marry her. In contrast, only 5 percent of the females were not emotionally involved with their initial partner and 81 percent were in love with him, indicating the importance of a love relationship for an adolescent female engaging in sexual intercourse. Miller and Simon (1980) interpret these findings as indicating sex differences in the motivational structure underlying adolescent male and female willingness to engage in sexual intercourse.

They suggest that, for males, the rewards intrinsic to the act are more important than the relationship with the girl, at least for the initial partner in sexual intercourse. In part, they believe this translates into feelings of achievement by the self and others. In support of their argument, they noted that a third of the college males had sex with the initial partner only one time and another third five or fewer times. This would not be expected if the relationship were one of strong attachment. In addition, substantial percentages of males immediately talk with someone other than their partner about their experience (Kallen & Stephenson, 1982).

Miller and Simon (1980) paint a different picture in describing the motivational structure underlying adolescent females' willingness to engage in sexual intercourse. They suggest that, for the adolescent female, the partner rather than an audience or sense of achievement is critical in understanding sexual intercourse. The importance of the sense of the relationship to the adolescent female was evidenced in the fact that 29 percent of the college sample were still engaging in sexual intercourse with their initial partner and another third had sex with their initial partner between 6 and 20 times. In addition, a smaller percentage (14 percent) of females immediately discussed their sexual experience with someone other than their partner, although the percentage discussing their experience within a month (65 percent) was similar to the percentage of males doing so (71 percent) (Kallen & Stephenson, 1982).

Although for both males and females the initial sexual experience is likely to occur prior to marriage, the circumstances are different. The modal male will engage in his initial sexual intercourse with someone with whom he has no particular emotional attachment. He will have sex with her a few times and then never again. The modal female will be in love with her initial partner and will likely be planning to marry him. The relationship will last some period of time and may result in marriage.

Although these sex differences exist, as we detail below, there is a convergence in attitudes and behaviors for adolescent males and females. Hence, increasing percentages of males believe the nature of the relationship is a primary determinant of engaging in sexual intercourse, with casual sex—sex with someone with whom you are not emotionally involved—being less acceptable to

males than in previous generations (Sorensen, 1973; Kallen & Stephenson, 1982).

The reasons for these sex differences are not well understood, although a number of possible explanations have been offered. Cultural anthropologists such as Margaret Mead (1939a, 1939b) suggest that the physiological makeup of the male and female genital systems is related to sex differences in actual incidences of masturbation or other kinds of sexual activity during adolescence because males are more used to handling their genitals than are females. Others believe that basic physiological differences in sex drive may be responsible for the differential integration of sexuality into interpersonal relationships (for example, A. Freud, 1948)

There is no doubt that the differences in sexual behavior of males and females have a very strong cultural component, as reflected in what is taught the sexes and in restrictions, sanctions, and expected behaviors. Generally speaking, sexual behavior in our culture is much more restricted for females than for males. It may be that the culture teaches girls, but not boys, to integrate sexuality into the total personality. As a result, conditions must be almost perfect for girls to experience optimal arousal and sexual satisfaction (Simon & Gagnon, 1970). By almost perfect conditions, we mean a sexual environment that does not conflict with the values and "virtues" society has instilled in the girl. In part, this may account for the evidence indicating that boys, in general, are more readily aroused sexually by a wider range of stimuli, such as books or films, than are girls. The sanctions taught to boys do not preclude arousal under such conditions.

As a final comment, we must make it clear that, although there are sex differences in the degree to which stimuli arouse sexuality, as well as in the conditions eliciting sexual activity, the differences are neither as wide nor as definitively distinct as was once believed. There are definitely groups of females who can become more sexually excited by a wider range of stimuli than some groups of males. For example, more sexually experienced females may be more arousable than less sexually experienced or more inhibited males (Kinsey et al., 1953; Masters & Johnson, 1966, 1970).

Several conclusions can be made on the basis of the data reviewed in this section. Clearly the sex drive does exist, and adolescents are interested in knowing and finding out more about sexual behavior. This is true particularly with respect to actual sexual relations; it is less true for correlated issues such as birth control or venereal disease. But the data also point out that sexuality is not an overbearing interest in the adolescent population. Rather, it is only one interest in a well-balanced hierarchy of interests. Furthermore, these data demonstrate that interest in sexuality, although differential for males and females, affects the behavior of both of them. The differences in expression of sexuality during adolescence, as well as adulthood, are probably in part due to differences in the biological and hormonal makeup of the sexes and in part due to the different ways boys and girls are taught to behave sexually. These teachings will affect not only actual sexual behavior, but also attitudes toward sexuality and the integration of sexuality with other components of the personality. It does appear that girls are more successful than boys in achieving the desired integration. This, in turn, seems to relate to male-female differences in the degree to which sexual arousal is experienced from differing ranges of stimuli.

SEXUAL ATTITUDES OF ADOLESCENTS

Although biological factors no doubt are related to sexual behavior, the above discussion makes it clear that social factors cannot be ignored in the study of adolescent sexual behavior. Social influences determine appropriate behaviors and set the standards for what is considered right and wrong, allowed and disallowed. We should expect to find different standards in different cultures, and different standards in the same culture at different time points.

Cultural Differences in Sexual Socialization

The most obvious demonstration of cultural influences on sexual attitudes comes from cross-cultural comparisons (for example, Mead, 1939a, 1939b; Benedict, 1938; Ford & Beach, 1951; Luckey & Nass, 1969). Although a full discussion of cultural differences in sexual attitudes and behaviors is beyond the scope of this text (see Luckey & Nass, 1969 and Ford & Beach, 1951 for more complete discussions), a brief discussion of the diversity of differences in sexual behavior across cultures is instructive.

Some cultures are highly restrictive with regard to the information provided to, and the behaviors tolerated by, the unmarried. Sexual intercourse is forbidden until marriage or a rite of passage. Chaperones may be required for "dating" and the sexes may not be allowed to play together. Any sexual activity must be done in secret (Ford & Beach, 1951). In these cultures, sexual behavior represents what Benedict (1938) called a *discontinuity*.

Some societies are semirestrictive with regard to sexual behavior. The "official" attitude of the culture may be to prohibit premarital sexual intercourse, but the restrictions may not be very serious and may not be enforced with any vigor. Sexual behavior in these social systems is semidiscontinuous. This system seems to characterize the contemporary American scene. We do not segregate the sexes or require chaperones. We encourage dating, a vehicle that fosters sexual experimentation. And, we do not severely or publicly punish sexual behavior. Nonetheless, sexual behavior does occur under some wraps of secrecy, because we do "try" to discourage it.

Finally, in some societies sexual socialization may best be characterized as permissive. It is allowed and even encouraged in childhood, adolescence, and adulthood. There are few if any restrictions. In these societies, sexual behavior is continuous in Benedict's terminology.

Of course, within a culture there are wide variations in sexual attitudes and beliefs. For example, we have noted that males in our culture tend to hold more liberal attitudes and engage in more sexual behavior than do females. And, even within the gender groupings, there are wide individual differences in attitudes and behaviors. Hence, discussions of attitudinal and behavioral norms, although informative in a general sense, do not depict the whole range of individual differences in adolescent sexual behavior.

Adolescent Attitudes toward Sexuality

Although a popular stereotype of adolescent beliefs about sexual behavior entails the perspective that adolescents are very liberal and believe sex for sex's sake is acceptable, the data paint is very different picture. A number of researchers (e.g., Leigh, 1988; Whitler, 1988) have surveyed adolescents to determine their views and attitudes about sexual activities.

One generalization that emerges from these studies is that adolescents' views about the permissibility of various aspects of sexual behavior are related to the intensity and nature of the relationship between the individuals (Luckey & Nass, 1969; Sorensen, 1973; Kallen & Stephenson, 1982). In general, both male and female adolescents believe sexual intercourse is permissible if the couple are engaged (Luckey & Nass, 1969; Sorensen, 1973) or have a strong emotional commitment to each other (Sorensen, 1973; Kallen & Stephenson, 1982). In general, both male and female adolescents hold the view that the quality of the relationship is an important factor in the decision to have sexual intercourse although males tend to be somewhat more liberal than females in this matter. Moreover, it is very clear that both males and females agree that sex with someone you know only casually is not appropriate (Sorensen, 1973). Finally, some evidence indicates that the gender difference with regard to this issue is narrowing (Sorensen, 1973; Kallen & Stephenson, 1982). Most male and female adolescents now feel that sex for the sole enjoyment of it or for exploitation is inappropriate.

A second important factor in understanding adolescents' views about the permissibility of various aspects of sexual behavior is the age of the individuals (Luckey & Nass, 1969; Sorensen, 1973). In general, adolescents tend to agree that the older the individuals, the more reasonable it is for them to engage in various aspects of sexual behavior. This perspective was illustrated in Luckey and Nass's (1969) study of college students' attitudes about various aspects of sexual behavior. The students were asked about the type of relationship that should prevail before a male and female should consider coitus as personally and socially reasonable. The college students felt sexual intercourse was more permissible for older individuals, even if they were not engaged or tentatively engaged. The view of these students was that older people have greater freedom in deciding to have coitus, even if their relationship is not one of strong emotional involvement.

Sorensen's (1973) survey with adolescents aged 13 to 19 sheds some further light on this finding. Sorensen reported that, in general, older adolescents felt fewer restrictions on aspects of sexual behavior; that is, they tended to have more liberal views of many aspects of sexual behavior. The older adolescents, both male and female, agreed that they would do what they wanted to with regard to sex even if it violated social standards, felt less strongly that people must be in love to have sex (especially the males), felt less strongly that sex before marriage was wrong, and the like.

The trends discussed above seem to reflect, in part, changing social standards. Bell and Chaskes (1970) reported on the sexual behavior of coeds in 1958 and 1968. In 1958, 10 percent of the coeds had intercourse while dating, 15 percent while going steady, and 31 percent while engaged. The corresponding percentages for the 1968 sample were: 23, 28, and 39, respectively. Although the same pattern exists, the percentages indicate a lessening of stringent standards for coitus in the more recent sample.

The research discussed in this section clearly is contrary to the popular stereotype of adolescents believing in nondiscriminant sex. Indeed, we can best conclude this section by noting that adolescents rank having sex with many partners high among those goals considered *least* important (Haas, 1979; Sorensen, 1973). In general, most adolescents argue that they have sex in a mature perspective (Sorensen, 1973). When they do engage in sex, it is not indiscriminant, and it is viewed as a way of expressing feelings and emotions toward another individual.

Individual Differences in Attitudes

The attitudes described above apply to adolescents in general. Of course, there is variation among adolescents—some hold views very different from the average. The study of such individual differences is complicated, but enlightening. Sorensen (1973) has presented some data on individual differences in adolescents' views about sexuality based on his extensive interviews from a national sample of male and female adolescents aged 13 to 19. Sorensen identified two groups of adolescents, the serial monogamists and the sexual adventurers, who hold very different views concerning sex.

The **serial monogamists** were those adolescents who were engaging in sexual intercourse with a single steady partner. Although the individual may acquire a new partner at some time—hence the descriptor

serial—the individual does not engage in intercourse with a variety of partners during the same time period. About 40 percent of those in the sample who had had intercourse were in this group. The group was composed of 64 percent females and 36 percent males, and 80 percent of them were in the 16 to 19 age group.

The serial monogamists feel they love and are loved by their partners, although only 55 percent said they planned to marry or probably would marry their current partner. The monogamists believe in fidelity and other conventional values reminiscent of adult marriages. Nearly 90 percent find their sexual experiences satisfying, although they wish they and their parents could agree more closely about their sexual behavior. These adolescents get along reasonably well with their parents, have rather traditional religious and political beliefs, and, in effect, reflect the values of the traditional adult society.

The **sexual adventurers** were those who sought many sexual partners. Eighty percent of the adventurers were males and 69 percent were in the 16 to 19 age group. The adventurers had many more partners than the monogamists, but they engaged in sex less frequently. In addition, they were less likely than monogamists to find their sex life satisfying. The adventurers tended not to believe love was a prerequisite to sexual intercourse, and many agreed that they used sex in a reward/punishment manner with their partners. The general attitude was one of sex for sex's sake, not as an expression of affection or commitment to another person. The adventurers had somewhat unconventional attitudes toward religion, society, and their parents—with whom many (48 percent) said they did not get along very well. The sexual adventurers also tended to have their first sexual intercourse at an earlier age than the monogamists (59 percent versus 26 percent by age 14).

As is readily apparent, adolescents vary considerably in their views about sexuality.

About 21 percent of adolescents (28 percent of females and 15 percent of males) are serial monogamists. About 15 percent of adolescents (24 percent of males and 6 percent of females) are sexual adventurers. These data highlight the importance of not stereotyping adolescent attitudes concerning sexuality.

SEXUAL BEHAVIOR DURING ADOLESCENCE

There are widely varying conceptions of the extent to which adolescents engage in sexual behavior. These range from views suggesting that adolescents are either engaging in, or thinking about, sexual behavior virtually every spare moment to perspectives that deny adolescent sexuality. Of course, neither of these extreme positions reflects reality. In this section, we examine data concerning adolescent sexual intercourse and other sexual behaviors.

Several important and interesting questions have been asked by researchers of adolescent sexual behavior. One issue concerns gender differences in sexual behavior. Do the traditional sex differences still exist? A second issue concerns generational differences in the percentage of adolescents engaging in sexual intercourse. Is there a sexual revolution? A third matter of interest is the age at which adolescents begin to engage in sexual intercourse. Are adolescents experiencing sex sooner now than in previous generations?

Premarital Sexual Intercourse Experiences of Adolescents

No one today can doubt that significant percentages of adolescents engage in premarital intercourse. No doubt, this always has been the case. A number of interesting questions about adolescent premarital sexual intercourse have been asked.

Sex Differences. The Kinsey survey (1948, 1953) probably was the first serious attempt to investigate adolescent sexual behavior. Kinsey reported that approximately 55 percent of males had experienced sexual intercourse by age 15 but that only 3 percent of females had engaged in premarital intercourse by age 16 and only 20 percent by age 19.

More current research shows some changes over the past 35 years (Sorensen, 1973; Zelnik, Kim, & Kantner, 1979; Zelnik & Kantner, 1980). Eastman's (1972) data agreed with Kinsey's for males; 55 percent of males had engaged in premarital sexual intercourse. However, Eastman reported that 49 percent of females had engaged in premarital intercourse. Sorensen (1973) reported that 52 percent of his sample of 13- to 19-year-olds had engaged in premarital sexual intercourse. This included 59 percent of the males and 45 percent of the females. Zelnik and Kantner (1980) reported that in 1979, 50 percent of adolescent females aged 15 to 19 had engaged in premarital sexual intercourse at least once. Rogel, Zuehlke, and Petersen (1980) reported that 84 percent of their sample of 12- to 19-year-old girls were sexually active. Finally, Zelnik and Kantner (1980) reported that 70 percent of males aged 17 to 21 in 1979 had engaged in sexual intercourse at least once.

When compared to the information available from Kinsey's (1948, 1953) seminal studies, the above data show little change in male premarital sexual intercourse. It appears that since the 1940s, or in all likelihood earlier, about 70 percent of adolescent males engage in premarital sexual intercourse.

The data for adolescent females is different. It is very clear that there has been an increase in the percentage of adolescent females who have engaged in premarital sexual intercourse. If there is a sexual revolution, it is occurring for adolescent females.

Changes Over Time. The changes in adolescent premarital sexual behavior are well documented. One form of documentation consists of data on age at first intercourse. Eastman (1972) reported that by age 17, about 50 percent of males had engaged in premarital sexual intercourse. By age 18 to 19 about 50 percent of adolescent females had engaged in premarital sexual intercourse at least one time. In Sorensen's (1973) study, 53 percent of the males had engaged in sex by age 14 and 56 percent of the females had engaged in sex by age 15. Finally, in Zelnik and Kantner's (1980) study of females aged 15 to 19 the mean age of first intercourse in 1979 was 16.2 years. However, nearly 50 percent of unmarried 17-year-old females had engaged in sexual intercourse.

Information on age at first intercourse, then, indicates a decline; that is, adolescents, and especially females, are engaging in sexual intercourse at increasingly early ages. Rogel et al. (1980) indicate that the age range for first intercourse for females aged 12 to 19 was 9 to 18 years, with a median age of 15. This is especially interesting because it is the age group of 15 or under that is at the greatest risk of premarital pregnancy (Koenig & Zelnik, 1982). In 1979, the risk of pregnancy within 12 months of first engaging in premarital intercourse was 41 percent for the 15 and under age group of women (Koenig & Zelnik, 1982). Should the age for first intercourse continue to decline, we may expect to find increasing numbers of adolescent women becoming pregnant.

A second measure of change over time in adolescent sexual behavior is the study of sexual behavior at different points in time. Robinson, King and Balswick (1972) reported the percentage of male and female college students having had premarital intercourse in 1965 was 65 and 29, respectively. In 1970, the corresponding percentages were 65 and 37, an increase of 8 percent for the females. In Bell and Chaskes's (1970) 1958 sample, 28 percent of coeds had engaged in premarital coitus, but in their 1968 sample, 65 percent had experienced premarital intercourse.

Hofferth, Kahn, and Baldwin (1987) report a continuation of the trend for increased sexual intercourse for females into the 1980s. As may be seen in Table 8–2, the percent of 15- to 19-year-old females who have engaged in premarital sexual intercourse has risen steadily since 1971. By age 19 nearly three-quarters of females have engaged in premarital sexual intercourse—a percentage that matches that of adolescent males. And the increases have occurred at all the ages from 15 to 19.

Clear changes in adolescent sexual behavior are indexed by two types of measures. First, there are clear changes over time in the percentage of adolescents, and especially females, engaging in sexual intercourse. Second, adolescents are engaging in premarital sex at earlier ages.

Reactions to Becoming Sexual Some data are available on adolescents' reactions to becoming sexual. In general, adolescents find their sexual relations satisfying.

Sorensen (1973) studied adolescents' reactions to their first experience with sexual intercourse. Males indicated they felt excited (46 percent), happy (42 percent), satisfied (43 percent), and the like. Although some females indicated these same feelings, the females were more likely to feel afraid (63 percent), guilty (36 percent), worried (35 percent) and embarrassed (31 percent).

TABLE 8–2 **Percent of Females Who Have Engaged in Premarital Intercourse Over Time**

Age	*Year*			
	1971	1976	1979	1982
15–19	31.7	39.0	43.4	45.2
19	54.0	65.8	64.8	73.4

(Source: Hofferth, S. L., Kahn, J. R., & Baldwin, W. [1989]. Premarital sexual activity among U.S. teenage women over the past three decades. *Family Planning Perspectives, 19*, 46–53.)

Forty-one percent of males and 56 percent of females indicated intercourse strengthened their relationship with their partner, and about 70 percent were pleased their first experience was with that partner. Finally, over 80 percent of adolescents felt they got a lot of satisfaction out of their sex lives. Although adolescents are understandably somewhat apprehensive about their initial sexual intercourse encounter, then, they do find their sex lives satisfying.

Are Adolescents Promiscuous? The increases in adolescent sexual behavior, and the attention that behavior receives in the press and other media, has led to the stereotype of the promiscuous adolescent. Several types of information bear on this issue.

Previously we discussed adolescent perspectives of when it was and was not appropriate to engage in sexual relations. As you will recall, very few adolescents believe it is alright to have sex with casual friends; the large majority of adolescents believe that sex is "right" only when two people care deeply about each other. To the degree that attitudes and behavior are related, then, it would deny the notion of the promiscuous adolescent.

Reiss (1967) was among the first to assess the degree of relationship between attitudes toward sexuality and actual sexual behavior. He studied 248 college juniors and seniors and found that their current sexual behavior and their current attitudes were highly related. For example, of the 25 students who felt kissing was the acceptable standard, 64 percent engaged in kissing, 32 percent engaged in petting, and only 4 percent engaged in coitus. Of the 84 students who felt coitus was acceptable, 5 percent engaged only in kissing, 31 percent engaged in petting, and 64 percent engaged in coitus.

More recent evidence pertinent to the attitude/behavior relationship comes from a report by Shah and Zelnik (1981), who used data from Zelnik and Kantner's (1977, 1980) study of 15- to 19-year-old females. The girls

TABLE 8–3   Percentage of 15- to 19-Year-Old Women with Premarital Sexual Experience, by Respondents' Opinion on Premarital Sex

Respondents' Opinion on Premarital Sex	*Percent*
Acceptable	79.1
Acceptable if engaged	54.7
Never Acceptable	10.7

(Source: Adapted from Shah, F., & Zelnik, M. [1981]. Parent and peer influence on sexual behavior, contraceptive use, and pregnancy experience of young women. *Journal of Marriage and the Family, 43*, 339–348.)

were asked to indicate if premarital sexual intercourse was (1) acceptable even if there were no plans to marry, (2) acceptable only if there were plans to marry, or (3) never acceptable. The percentages of women in these three groups who engaged in sexual intercourse are presented in Table 8–3. As you can see, in general, attitudes and behavior were reasonably strongly related. Only 11 percent of those who said premarital intercourse was never acceptable had engaged in premarital sex, but 79 percent of those who felt premarital sex was acceptable even if marriage was not planned had engaged in premarital sex.

A second type of information, more directly related to the issue of promiscuity, concerns the number of sexual partners the adolescent has had. The data generally support the notion that adolescents are not promiscuous. Luckey and Nass (1969) report that over 70 percent of both males and females engaged in premarital intercourse with one partner with whom they are deeply involved emotionally. Very few females engage in one-night affairs (about 7 percent), although males do so to a somewhat higher degree (30 percent) (Luckey & Nass, 1969).

Sorensen (1973) reported that 76 percent of the sexually active adolescents in his sample engaged in sexual intercourse with only one partner in the month preceding the interview, and that 11 percent engaged in sex with only two partners in the prior month. In contrast, only 2 percent engaged in sex with 5 or more partners in the month prior to the interview. Among the monogamists, 92 percent engaged in sex with only one partner, the remaining 8 percent having sex with only two partners. A different pattern emerged for the sexual adventurers. Forty-seven percent engaged in sex with a single partner, 18 percent with two, 20 percent with three, 11 percent with four, and 4 percent with five or more partners during the preceding month.

Bell and Coughey (1980) report that although substantial percentages of college women have sexual intercourse, there is no evidence of an increase in the number of partners they have. In 1968, 44 percent of college females surveyed had sexual intercourse with only one partner, and only 22 percent had sex with five or more partners. The comparable percentages for a 1978 sample from the same university were 37 and 23, respectively. Hence, although more college women have engaged in sexual intercourse, they are not promiscuous. It seems that the first experience comes earlier, but it is not casual.

Although there are individual differences, then, it seems a fair generalization to conclude that, by and large, adolescents are not promiscuous. Rather, they engage in sex with discretion, with someone with whom they have a strong emotional relationship. This behavior, of course, is consistent with the attitude that sex for sex's sake is not appropriate (Sorensen, 1973).

Other Sexual Behaviors

Of course, premarital intercourse is not the only sexual behavior adolescents engage in. Petting and masturbation are the other two most frequently experienced sexual behaviors.

Petting. By age 16, over 90 percent of adolescent males and females have engaged in at least "light" petting, and before age 17 over 80 percent have engaged in "heavy"

petting (DeLamater & MacCorquodale, 1979). Moreover, the evidence seems to verify the "common sense" lore that there is a sequence in sexual behaviors leading to intercourse: necking, French kissing, petting, intercourse.

As with intercourse, petting is more prevalent and occurs at younger ages today. Robinson, King, and Balswick (1972) report that in 1965 71.3 percent of college males and 34.3 percent of college females had engaged in heavy petting. The comparable figures for students in the same college in 1970 were 79.3 percent for males and 59.7 percent for females. The more recent data indicate a continual increase in heavy petting, and at younger ages.

Masturbation. In the initial studies of masturbation, Kinsey and his associates (Kinsey et al., 1948, 1953) found that masturbation was more common among males than females. By age 15, over 80 percent of boys had masturbated, that percentage increasing to about 90 percent by age 20. The percentages for girls were much lower, being approximately 17 percent and 30 percent, respectively.

More recent data (e.g., Sorensen, 1973; Haas, 1979) indicate that this sex difference is still present, although higher percentages of adolescent females report they have masturbated. Sorensen reported that, for his 13- to 19-year-olds, 58 percent of males and 39 percent of females had masturbated. Masturbation was more common for the older adolescents and, surprisingly, for the non-virgins. Finally, masturbation apparently is occurring earlier now than previously, and there is an increase at all age levels in the percentage of adolescents who masturbate (Kinsey et al., 1948, 1953; Sorensen, 1973; Haas, 1979).

Masturbation is a primary source of sexual gratification for adolescent males, and for an increasing percentage of adolescent females. In general, adolescents do not feel particularly guilty about masturbating (Sorensen, 1973). Masters and Johnson (1966, 1970) suggest that masturbation may provide the opportunity to learn sexual responses, and some of Sorensen's adolescents agreed. Although previous generations of adolescents may well have grown up with unnecessary guilt born of falsehoods about the consequences of masturbation, large percentages of today's adolescents do not have these feelings about masturbating (Sorensen, 1973; Masters & Johnson, 1970). At present, most adolescents (approximately 80 percent) feel that masturbation is an acceptable sexual behavior.

INFLUENCES ON ADOLESCENT SEXUAL BEHAVIOR

We have already noted that a majority of adolescents engage in premarital sexual intercourse. However, a substantial minority do not.

Reasons for Not Engaging in Sex

We already have discussed above some reasons for not engaging in sexual intercourse. Specifically, we already know that some adolescents have yet to enter into a relationship with someone with whom they feel such strong attachment that they will consider engaging in sex (Sorensen, 1973). Sorensen reports that about 55 percent of both male and female sexually inexperienced adolescents—those with no sexual contact other than kissing—said they were not ready for sex and that they had not yet found a person with whom they wanted to have sex.

College students cite a variety of reasons for not engaging in sex (Miller & Simon, 1980). Both males and females who do not engage in sex state they have moral concerns (65 percent) and fear pregnancy (63 percent). Females also state that they fear parental disapproval (60 percent) and have concerns for their reputation (55 percent).

Males cite an unwilling partner (55 percent) as a major reason for not engaging in sex, although 43 percent also note fear of parental disapproval and 40 percent fear for their reputation. Other data (Leigh, 1989) support these findings.

A final factor of importance in whether or not coitus will occur is the prior experience of the individuals, and especially of the female. Peplau, Rubin, and Hill (1977) studied 231 college couples. They reported that coitus was least likely if both were virgins, but it was a virtual certainty if neither was a virgin *or* if the female was not a virgin. They go on to suggest that it is the female who determines if sex will occur, a notion that is consistent with males' statements that a primary reason for not having sex is an unwilling partner.

Parent and Peer Influences

The most extensive study of the relative influences of parents and peers on adolescent sexual behavior was reported by Shah and Zelnik (1981). The subjects in the study were 2,193 females aged 15 to 19. The participants were asked whether their views about college, career plans, sex before marriage, making lots of money, and having an abortion were like those of their (a) parents, (b) friends, (c) both, or (d) neither. They were also asked their opinions about sex prior to marriage, and indicated if it was (a) permissible even if the couple had no plans to marry, (b) permissible only if the couple had plans to marry, or (c) never permissible. These questions allowed the determination of the degree to which the adolescent's beliefs were like those of the parents, the peers, both or neither, and which exerted the greater influence on the adolescents' views of sex.

Of the females who believed premarital sex was acceptable, 64 percent felt their views about sex were like those of their friends and only seven percent felt their views about sex were like those of their parents. In contrast, of those who felt premarital sex was never acceptable, only 33 percent felt their views were like their parents.

To understand these data more fully, it is helpful to look at the adolescent women's views of similarity to parents and friends on some of the other issues. The data for views about college, careers, and making money indicated that the women felt their views were much like those of their parents or both their parents and friends. In other words, there was not simply a bias toward feeling one's views were more like those of friends than parents. Clearly, the subject matter within which the judgment was made was relevant. Shah and Zelnik (1981) suggest these data indicate that, with regard to premarital sexual behavior, a substantial percentage of adolescent females face a real conflict between the values expressed by their parents and those espoused by their peers.

This conflict is illustrated most clearly by the data presented in Table 8–4. As you can see quite readily, sexual experience is relatively highly related to perceptions of how one's views relate to those of the parents or the peers. Conflict in parent and peer values is demonstrated by the fact that the relationships are not perfect. For example, 26 percent of adolescent females who felt their perspectives were like those of their parents

TABLE 8–4 **Percentage of 15- to 19-Year-Old Females with Premarital Sexual Experience, by Similarity of Views on Sex to Significant Others**

Views on Sex Similar to	Percent
Parents	26.0
Friends	59.4
Both	36.2
Neither	44.2
All	47.5

(Source: Adapted from Shah, F., & Zelnik, M. [1981]. Parent and peer influence on sexual behavior, contraceptive use, and pregnancy experience of young women. *Journal of Marriage and the Family, 43*, 339–348.)

had engaged in premarital sexual intercourse. In turn, 41 percent of adolescent females who perceived their views were like those of their peers had not engaged in premarital sexual intercourse.

More current research (Moore, Peterson, & Furstenberg, 1986) also demonstrates that parental influences on adolescent sexual behavior are minimal. Adolescents whose parents discuss sex with them, or whose parents keep a tight rein on their activities, are no more or less likely to engage in premarital sex. Similar evidence (Eisen & Zellman, 1987) indicates that attending sex education classes does not promote or discourage adolescents from engaging in sexual intercourse.

It appears that adolescents may discuss aspects of sexuality with parents and learn their views. The same may be true for sex education classes. But the factors related to having sex may be more contextually and situationally controlled. An examination of the reasons that adolescents give for having sex or not having sex supports this distinction. The feeling of wanting to please one's potential partner, for example, may be a stronger motivator for behavior than knowing that one's parents might disapprove.

CONTRACEPTION, PREGNANCY, AND SEXUALLY TRANSMITTED DISEASES

As the above data demonstrate, substantial percentages of adolescents engage in premarital sexual intercourse. And the percentage of younger adolescents doing so is increasing. However, adolescents by and large do not guard against pregnancy with regularity, resulting in a large number of premarital pregnancies in the adolescent population.

Contraceptive Use

A well-established finding is that adolescents engage in sex without the benefit of

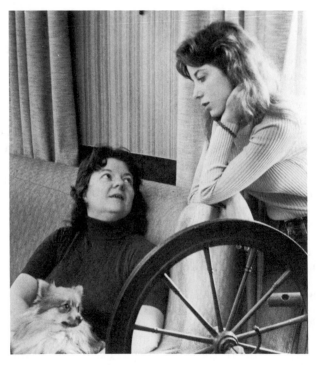

Adolescents who feel they have views more similar to those of their parents than their peers are less likely to engage in premarital sexual intercourse.

contraception (Sorensen, 1973; Zelnik, Kim, & Kantner, 1979; Zelnik & Kantner, 1980; Shah & Zelnik, 1981). Although one might expect that the initial sexual intercourse may occur without the benefit of contraception, subsequent intercourse, which may be more "planned" or "expected," could involve the use of contraception.

First Intercourse. Sorensen (1973) reported that 55 percent of adolescents (49 percent of males and 63 percent of females) did not use contraception during their first intercourse. In 32 percent of the instances either the boy (28 percent) or the girl (37 percent) used some form of contraception. (In the remaining instances the boy did not, and he was unsure if the girl did or did not.) As you might expect, use at first intercourse was higher for older (45 percent) than younger (26 percent) adolescent females, with lack of use showing the reverse trend. This was an interesting finding because

about 86 percent of the females felt that contraception was their responsibility.

Zelnik and Kantner (1980) report more recent data and demonstrate some changes from the mid- to late 1970s for adolescent women. In 1976, only 38 percent of adolescent women used some form of contraceptive the first time they engaged in sexual intercourse, but in 1979 some 49 percent said they did. Hence, there is some evidence that adolescent females' contraceptive use at first intercourse increased during the 1970s. More recent evidence (see Davidson & Haviland, 1989a), however, indicates no further change during the 1980s for 15- to 19-year-olds in general, although older adolescents are increasingly using contraception at their first intercourse.

General Contraceptive Use. Use of contraception at other than the first intercourse is also low. Zelnik and Kantner (1980) reported that in 1976 approximately 29 percent of adolescent women always used contraception and another 36 percent sometimes used it. In 1979 the comparable percentages were 34 and 39, respectively. In turn, in 1976 about 36 percent of the women said they never used contraception, but this percentage was only 26 in 1979.

Although these recent changes imply more responsible sexual behavior, at least on the part of adolescent females, this is not entirely the case. Zelnik and Kantner (1980) report data on the specific contraceptive methods used by the women. In general, use of the most effective methods of contraception, such as the Pill and the IUD, declined between 1976 and 1979, and use of less effective methods, such as rhythm and withdrawal, increased.

Reasons for Not Using Contraception. Adolescents give a variety of reasons for not using contraception (Zelnik & Kantner, 1972, 1974, 1977, 1980; Zelnik, Kim, & Kantner, 1979; Sorensen, 1973; Shah & Zelnik, 1981). Some adolescents indicate they do not know about contraceptive techniques or devices, and others indicate they want to

Although adolescents are knowledgeable about contraceptive materials, they generally do not use them when engaging in sexual intercourse.

get pregnant. In each case, however, the percentages are small, being about 5 percent (Sorensen, 1973; Zelnik & Kantner, 1972, 1974, 1980). About 70 percent of adolescent males and females believe that if the girl uses the Pill or other birth control, it means she is planning on having sex (Sorensen, 1973).

Because adolescents have a somewhat romantic view of sex as being spontaneous, they do not wish to have it seem planned. In addition, to plan for sex requires admitting you are a sexual person, a task that is difficult for adolescents, and especially younger ones, who are at the greatest risk of pregnancy (Shah & Zelnik, 1981; Zelnik & Kantner, 1977, 1980). In support of this analysis, Davidson and Haviland (1989a, 1989b) noted that the ability to accept one's sexuality increases the probability that the adolescent female will use some form of contraception. In addition, females who are in love and who have some sex education are more likely to be consistent contraceptive users (Chilman, 1973; Kantner & Zelnik, 1973; Zelnik & Kantner, 1977, 1978).

In part, adolescent females do not use contraception because they fear their parents will find out (Sorensen, 1973). Fifty-eight percent of Sorensen's female sample stated this reason. Health concerns, particularly with respect to the Pill, are also stated as reasons for not using contraceptives (Sorensen, 1973; Zelnik & Kantner, 1980; Zelnik et al., 1979). In all likelihood, awareness of health concerns accounts for the decrease in adolescent females' use of the Pill. As Rogel et al. (1980) note, there is a tendency to equate contraception with the Pill, which may account for the failure of some adolescents to use any contraception.

Gerrard (1987) has suggested that part of the reason for college students' failure to use contraception is attributable to what he calls *sex guilt*. Adolescents who feel guilty about having sex are less likely to use contraception, perhaps because their guilt prevents them from planning to use it or perhaps because planning to use it increases their guilt. Some evidence (Davidson & Haviland, 1989b) indicates that when sexuality is integrated into one's identity, contraceptive use increases, perhaps by reducing guilt associated with being sexually active.

Some reasons for not using contraception seem, from an adult perspective, to be very immature. For example, a substantial proportion of nonvirgin females (40 percent) agree that sometimes they don't care if they get pregnant, and a third of adolescents believe that if a girl doesn't want to get pregnant she won't, even if she has sex without contraception. And, 30 percent to 40 percent believe they won't get pregnant because they don't have sex often enough (Zelnik & Kantner, 1974, 1977, 1980; Sorensen, 1973). Of course, believing false notions such as these can lead the adolescent to suffer the consequences of premarital pregnancy.

Adolescent Pregnancy

Koenig and Zelnik (1982), who have studied the risk of premarital pregnancy among urban adolescent females, reported that in 1976, some 32 percent of sexually active adolescent females experienced a premarital pregnancy within two years of their first intercourse. This figure rose to 36 percent in 1979. The increase was due largely to the younger adolescents, those aged 15 or less. In 1976, some 27 percent of sexually active females aged 15 or less experienced a premarital pregnancy within two years of their initial intercourse. In 1979, 41 percent of this group had a premarital pregnancy within two years of initiating sexual intercourse. There was little change from 1976 to 1979 for adolescent females older than 15. It is reasonable to conclude that, if there is a continuation of the decline in average age of first intercourse, and if the frequency of engaging in sexual intercourse continues to increase, we shall see a continued increase in the percentage of adolescent females who

experienced a premarital pregnancy (Koenig & Zelnik, 1982).

Incidence of Premarital Pregnancy. Estimates of the number of premarital pregnancies among adolescents range up to a million or more a year (Zelnik et al., 1979). Zelnik et al. (1979) estimate that in 1976, 20 percent of sexually active adolescents had experienced a premarital pregnancy by 18.7 years of age. Approximately 16 percent of 15-year-olds, but 35 percent of 19-year-olds, are estimated to have had a pregnancy in 1976. (The difference in these percentages and those cited above is due to these not being restricted to the first two years after the start of intercourse.)

Zelnik and Kantner (1980) present information that the percentage of premarital pregnancies nearly doubled during the 1970s. In 1971, 9 percent of adolescent females experienced a premarital pregnancy. The comparable percentages were 13 and 16 for 1976 and 1979, respectively. Of interest, Zelnik and Kantner (1980) report that, during the same time period, the percentage of premaritally pregnant adolescents getting married declined. In 1971, 33 percent of premaritally pregnant adolescent women got married, the percentage doing so declining in 1976 (23 percent) and 1979 (16 percent). The percentage getting married in 1976 corresponds well with Sorensen's (1973) finding that 24 percent of males and 38 percent of females responded that if they were involved in a pregnancy, the couple should get married and have the baby.

As you might suspect, premarital pregnancy is not desired by most adolescents. In 1971, 24 percent of the adolescent women said they wanted to get pregnant, in 1976, the percentage was 25, and in 1979, it was 18. Of importance, however, was the fact that of those who got pregnant but did not want to, the vast majority (91 percent in 1971, 79 percent in 1976, and 68 percent in 1979) said they did not use contraception to avoid pregnancy.

Pregnancy Resolution. There are several resolutions to an adolescent premarital pregnancy. One is for the adolescent, whether married or not, to have the baby. Sorensen (1973) found that 60 percent of males and 70 percent of females believed the girl should have the baby and keep it. The males and females differed, however, in their feelings about raising the child. As noted above, having the baby and getting married was suggested by 24 percent of males and 38 percent of females. Having the baby and bringing it up alone was suggested by 18 percent of the females but only 7 percent of the males. Having the baby and counting on the baby's father to help rear it was expressed by 23 percent of the males but only 15 percent of the females. The resolution suggested by the highest percentage of males (30 percent) was abortion, but only 18 percent of females suggested this solution. These adolescents felt abortion was a reasonable alternative if neither person wanted the baby (55 percent of males and 45 percent of females), although 60 percent of the nonvirgin females said they themselves would not have an abortion because they did not believe in taking a life.

Despite these views, the data are clear in showing that there has been an increase in the percentage of adolescent females who have abortions (see Box 8–2). Zelnik and Kantner (1980) found that the percentage of adolescent females who had had an abortion was 23, 33, and 39 for 1971, 1976, and 1979, respectively. Clearly, abortion is an alternative used by substantial proportions of adolescent women in resolving an unwanted pregnancy.

Live births to premaritally pregnant adolescent women have showed a steady decline during the 1970s. The percent of live births for 1971, 1976, and 1979 was 67, 56, and 49, respectively. The resolution for the remaining pregnancies was either stillbirth or miscarriage—10 percent in 1971, 12 percent in 1976, and 14 percent in 1979. The increase in the latter figures probably reflects the increase in pregnancies for the younger adolescents, who run a higher risk of such outcomes because of poorer prenatal health care and nutrition.

The Adolescent Mother. Although previous conceptualizations of being an adolescent mother were in some ways overly pessimistic (see Furstenberg, Brooks-Gunn, & Morgan, 1987), it still is difficult and often results in a less bright future. Nor is it a particularly desirable situation for the adolescent father (see Box 8–3).

The pregnant adolescent is best described as outgoing and typical, not as maladjusted or deviant (Kane, Moan, & Bolling, 1974). Although some have psychological or emotional disturbances, most do not. They seem simply to be involved in an emotional and caring relationship that leads to sexual intercourse and pregnancy.

Some evidence indicates that pregnant adolescents come from homes characterized by conflict and stress, such as single-parent homes (Russ-Eft, Sprenger, & Beever, 1979). The latter may result from lowered control by the single parent over the adolescent's activity or from stronger intimacy needs (Ross, 1978) experienced by females growing up in a single-parent, mother-headed household. In addition, single-parent mothers themselves may present models for dating, and sexual behavior, that alter their daughters' perspective of sexuality.

The picture one gets, then, is of an adolescent girl who is relatively typical of others her age. However, she also is likely to come from a home that has some conflict and stress, which may increase her need to express affection to others outside the immediate family. She is not deviant in any standard use of the term.

Part of the difficulty encountered by pregnant adolescents lies in their completing their education, which relates to their employability. Many pregnant adolescents drop out of school and, therefore, are less likely

BOX 8–2   **Abortion and the Adolescent**

The issue of abortion is a complex one, involving legal constraints, moral and religious concerns, and personal freedoms. Moreover, abortion involves physical risks, including death of the woman—approximately 0.6 deaths occur for every 100,000 legal abortions (Centers for Disease Control, 1980). Abortion, then, although it is one of the most widely performed operations in the world, is not something to be taken lightly, for it has considerable physical and emotional consequences for the woman, her family and friends, her partner, and the society.

The type of procedure used for aborting the pregnancy depends on gestation age, the length of time the woman has been pregnant. For up to 12 weeks' gestation age, vacuum curettage is the most used procedure. In this procedure, a tube is inserted into the uterus and the pregnancy is aborted by suction. When the gestation age is more than 12 weeks, the abortion procedure involves either a dilatation and evacuation, in which the cervix is dilated and the fetal material is removed, or instillation, which involves inducing contractions. It is in part because of differences in these procedures that abortion at later gestation ages involves more difficulties and an increased risk to the mother. This is an especially important consideration with respect to adolescent abortion, because adolescents are much more likely than older women to obtain abortions after the first trimester of pregnancy. In 1978, 14 percent of abortions to women age 19 or younger were after the first trimester, compared to 7.4 percent for women 20 or older. Indeed, women 19 or younger accounted for about half the abortions performed after a gestation age of 16 weeks (Centers for Disease Control, 1980).

In 1978, 30 percent of women obtaining abortions were aged 19 or younger, 35 percent were women aged 20 to 24, and 35 percent were women older than 25. Translating the percentages to numbers indicates that, in 1978, there were approximately 189,000 legal abortions to adolescent females (Centers for Disease Control, 1980). Approximately 10 percent of these abortions were for females 15 or younger and 58 percent were for females 18 or 19.

The data for 1982 and 1983 (Henshaw, 1987) show substantial increases in adolescent abortions. For adolescents under age 15, there were 14,590 abortions in 1982 and 16,350 in 1983. For those in the 15 to 19 age range there were over 400,000 abortions annually, more than double the number in 1978. This represents about 40 percent of the pregnancies that occur in this age group. The remaining 55 percent of pregnancies are accounted for by stillbirths (10 percent), having the baby and keeping it (45 percent), or having the baby and putting it up for adoption (5 percent).

Do these statistics mean that adolescents are using abortion as a method of birth control? The answer to this question is unknown. What is clear is that substantial numbers of adolescents do not use other means of contraception, and this leads to their considering abortion.

to obtain the education and training that allow them to be competitive for reasonably high-paying jobs. In addition, about half are likely to experience another pregnancy within 36 months. Finally, if they do get married they are unlikely to receive child support (Box 8–3) and are more likely to see their marriages end in divorce.

What all this suggests is that poverty conditions are an important factor in determining the effects of adolescent pregnancy, both on the mother and the child. The concerns are complex. It turns out that babies born of nonpoverty adolescent mothers are very similar in their development to babies born of married mothers. The converse also is true. These data underscore the importance of economics in understanding the effects of adolescent pregnancy on the child.

On the other hand, adolescent females are not particularly skilled at mothering. Adolescent mothers are less communicative with their babies, and they engage in lowered levels of play and interaction with them (Culp, Culp, Osofsky, & Osofsky, 1989). They are less expressive, engage in poorer

BOX 8–3   **Adolescent Fathers**

Historically, the focus of interest in adolescent pregnancy has been on the mother. Hence, as discussed in the text, we know a good deal of information about adolescent mothers. For example, we know that they differ little from adolescent nonmothers in most ways. Only recently, with the work of Arthur Elster and Michael Lamb, have we come to investigate the characteristics of adolescent fathers.

In order to characterize the adolescent father, Elster, Lamb, and Tavare (1987) compared on a variety of measures a group of males who had fathered a child prior to the age of 19 with a comparable group of males who had not. The parents of adolescent fathers had less education than did the parents of adolescent non-fathers. In addition, prior to age 14, future adolescent fathers were more likely than subsequent non-fathers to have lived within single-parent or re-constituted homes. Those who fathered a child while an adolescent were more likely to have had school problems (to have been expelled or suspended), to have engaged in antisocial aggres-sion (fighting), used drugs, and to have had encounters with the police (stopped for, charged with, or convicted of a crime other than a driving violation). With some exceptions, these findings held for black, Hispanic, and non-black/non-Hispanic fathers. Because the samples involved came from a representative national sample of adolescent males, these findings indicate that, unlike adolescent mothers, about half of adolescent fathers are "atypical" on a number of aca-demic and social dimensions. Elster et al. (1987) suggest that the data indicate that adolescent fathers are less likely to profit from sex education programs, are less capable of assuming the responsibility of adulthood roles that come with fatherhood, and reflect a developmental history indicative of emotional and social difficulties.

Data such as these spurred a federal government investigation into the problem of adolescent pregnancy in general and adolescent fatherhood in particular (Smollar & Ooms, 1987). In addition to specifying general characteristics of adolescent fathers, such as those noted above, the findings of the investigation included a number of recommendations aimed at helping adolescent fathers meet their responsibilities to their children, to the adolescent mother, and to society. For example, while noting that adolescent fathers should be responsible financially for their children, the report also suggested that it would be necessary to provide means for adolescent fathers to acquire the skills leading to reasonable employment. This not only would allow the adolescent father to contribute to the support of his child, but would also allow him to develop the self-respect and esteem that come with being a contributor to society.

By focusing interest on the adolescent father we have come full circle in studying the impact of adolescent pregnancy. In the long run, the benefit of the information we gain and the policy that is made will aid the children, mothers, and fathers involved in adolescent pregnancy.

quality play, and generally interact at a qual-itatively lower level with their infants than do other mothers. As a result, the child's development does not progress at an opti-mal level.

The most basic difficulty seems to be economic in nature (Furstenberg, Brooks-Gunn, & Morgan, 1987). Adolescent moth-ers who can reenter the educational system fair well in the job market. Their children develop in a manner similar to children born of wedded mothers. This highlights the im-portance of weighing ethnic and economic factors when considering the impact of an adolescent mother on the child's develop-ment. In addition, maintaining an exclusive relationship with the child's father is desir-able (Russell, 1980) because this has the ben-efit of stabilizing the relationship with the father and of encouraging the father's in-teractions with the child.

Sexually Transmitted Diseases

The term *sexually transmitted diseases* refers to a variety of diseases transmitted from one

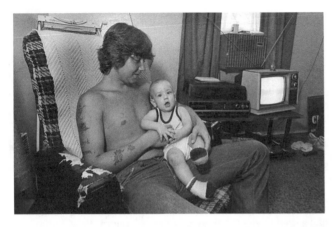

In order to allow adolescent fathers to be responsible for their children, we need programs to help them gain training allowing access to employment.

person to another through sexual intercourse, although it is known that one, **acquired immune deficiency syndrome (AIDS)**, can be transmitted in other ways such as through shared use of needles used for intravenous drugs.

Adolescents generally have heard about sexually transmitted diseases, and 75 percent believe it is a serious health problem (Sorensen, 1973). Most adolescents believe they should inform their partner immediately upon finding out they have a sexually transmitted disease, and about half say they would not have sex with someone who had had a sexually transmitted disease even though the person had been cured (Sorensen, 1973).

Although they are aware of the names of various sexually transmitted diseases, most adolescents do not know the symptoms of the diseases and, thus, are unlikely to recognize them when they occur. This is especially unfortunate in that for some diseases, such as **syphilis** and *herpes*, the symptoms may come and go, leading the adolescent to believe that he or she is not suffering from a very serious problem.

In general, sexually transmitted diseases are caused by bacteria or parasites. The most common among the adolescent population are **gonorrhea** and *herpes*, which can lead to disorders of the reproductive system, sterility, and other symptoms (headache, fever),

including in the case of herpes increased risk of cervical cancer and miscarriage.

Among the most serious sexually transmitted diseases is AIDS. This is so because AIDS has few if any initial symptoms and because the adolescent population is at high risk because of increased sexual activity and intravenous (IV) drug use (Millstein, 1989). Indeed, adolescents have the highest age-adjusted sexually transmitted diseases rates of all age groups studied, and this places them at an increased risk for AIDS. Again, this largely is due to homosexual activity within the context of shared IV drug use, and is especially important for understanding adolescent female exposure to AIDS.

The high degree of sexuality among the adolescent age group puts it at a high risk for AIDS because (1) sexual activity begins at a relatively early age, when individuals are likely limited in their ability to foresee realistic consequences of their activity, and (2) when condoms are unlikely to be used (condoms provide some protection against AIDS infection). In addition, adolescents represent a high-risk group if they fall into one or more of the following categories: being homeless, being a runaway, being an IV drug user, or being gay. Because AIDS has no overt symptoms of infection, at least initially, it is possible for the individual to become infected, infect others, and not know that treatment is needed. Again, given the high rate of sexual behavior among adolescents, this leads to the possibility that AIDS will become a major epidemic among the adolescent population even though it may not be detected (because of its long incubation period of up to 8 years) until the adolescents are young adults.

SEX EDUCATION

Sex education is a controversial topic. Parents tend to feel that sex education is not the function of the public school system. Libby (1970) reports that, although an overwhelming majority of the 125 parent couples he interviewed believed sex education in the schools was good and desirable, they wanted that education to focus on the "don'ts" of sexuality. It seems that when parents agree that sex education should be taught, they want it to stress traditional conservative values. Often, however, the adolescent wants to learn about alternative value systems. As a result, many adolescents feel that they are not getting adequate sexual education from any source, including the school, from which they had hoped to obtain it (Hunt, 1970; Harris, 1971).

School administrators, too, must face a variety of issues surrounding the controversy of sex education in the public school. Scales and Kirby (1983) found that both administrators and staff found fear of community opposition to be a very strong barrier to instituting sex education programs. Interestingly, they found few program characteristics or contents, such as discussing contraception or masturbation, to be perceived barriers.

Generally speaking, then, there are three interrelated issues that must be resolved in any decision to implement a sex education program (Baskin & Powers, 1969). First, the need for sex education classes in the public school curriculum must be established. Second, a decision must be made about whether the sex education classes are to be primarily biological in nature, or whether they will discuss sex in the context of personality and morals. Third, there are a number of critical issues regarding the construction of sex education classes; for example, what should be taught at the various age levels? Should the classes be co-ed or sexually segregated? Should the material be incorporated into existing courses or should a new course be established? Which teachers are best suited for teaching the material, and what age groups should receive instruction?

The Need for Sex Education

There is considerable evidence to support the need for sex education in the public schools (Di Clemente et al., 1989). Some argue it is desirable and necessary in light of the social problems presented by teen-age premarital pregnancy and increasing venereal disease rates. In support of this argument is survey information indicating that 50 percent of the high school girls who marry are pregnant, that 50 percent of high school students do not know venereal diseases are transmitted through sexual intercourse, and that only 10 percent of those who have actually been treated for venereal disease have adequate knowledge of the disease. Adolescents are very poorly informed about birth control and do not use it, as noted earlier. Many believe school programs should provide the information necessary to increase birth control and reduce venereal disease.

A slightly different point of view is held by those who believe that sex education is needed to help young people cope with the prevalence of sexuality in the mass media. Some authors believe that changes in the general culture, such as earlier dating ages and easy access to automobiles, have presented conditions conducive to sexual experimentation by individuals who have an inadequate knowledge of sexuality. Providing the knowledge, it is argued, may go a long way to help these individuals cope with sexuality in our culture and may take some of the pressures off individuals to experiment with sexuality because of curiosity born from lack of knowledge. Unbiased and accurate information should help adolescents cope with their anxieties about sexuality and help them understand individual differences in views toward sexuality. In turn, sexuality may be more readily integrated within the context of living, rather than being suddenly and anxiously thrust upon the individual at the time of marriage.

Perhaps the strongest plea for sex education programs in the public schools comes from those concerned with the quality of sex information obtained by children and adolescents (e.g., Andre, Frevert, & Schuchmann, 1989). Andre and colleagues note that the question is not whether youths will receive sex education but how—through peers, the mass media, or the schools. For the large majority of adolescents, the peer group and printed material are the primary sources of information regarding sexuality. Several investigations indicate that the information given by peers is often faulty and incomplete (Elias & Gebhard, 1969), and the information given by reliable sources is usually too biologically-physiologically oriented and imparted without interchange or discussion.

There are two interrelated questions here, each in need of an answer. First, where do adolescents actually get information about sexuality? Second, where would they prefer to get it? As we indicated above, there is considerable information about the answer to the first question, but very little about the second. In an extensive study, Angelino and Mech (1955) investigated the first sources of information regarding contraceptives, venereal disease, prostitution, masturbation, intercourse, and menstruation in 67 college females approximately 19 years of age. A checklist of first sources contained the following possible responses: female companions, mother, father, both parents, printed material, male companions, other relatives, school courses, other sources, and undecided. Information regarding contraception was obtained primarily from female companions ($n = 31$); venereal disease information was acquired by printed material ($n = 22$), mother ($n = 12$), and female companions ($n = 10$); information regarding prostitution was obtained primarily from female companions ($n = 24$) and printed material ($n = 27$). First information regarding sexual intercourse was obtained from the mother ($n = 20$) or female companions ($n = 19$). The only case in which the mother was a principal informer was in matters dealing with menstruation ($n = 48$). Similar findings were reported by Ehrmann (1960), Landis and Landis (1968), and Thornburg (1972) for relatively large samples of college students. In these surveys, peers were the primary sources of information about sexuality, although books contributed to information in some ways.

There are only a small number of studies investigating the first sources of sexual information for adolescent public school students. One of the earliest surveys was conducted by Ramsey (1943), who studied the acquisition of sex information in 10- to 20-year-old boys, 85 percent of whom were between the ages of 12 and 16. Ramsey also investigated the degree to which the students could deal with sex vocabularies. By age 14, 93 percent of the boys had obtained information about ejaculation, 100 percent knew that mothers were the origin of babies, 73 percent had information about nocturnal emissions, 86 percent knew about contraceptives, but only 38 percent knew about menstruation. Nearly 100 percent of the boys had information about masturbation, intercourse, and prostitution, but only 57 percent had any information about venereal disease. In general, most of the boys were introduced to sexual information before they reached the junior high level. In every one of these instances, the information was obtained from conversations with male companions. Mothers played a significant role only in providing information about the origins of babies (27.5 percent) and menstruation (20 percent). Fathers played virtually no role in the sexual education of their sons. In fact, 82 percent of the boys stated that their father had played no role at all in their sex education. Given parental dislike for sex education in the public schools, it was interesting to note that only 45 percent of the boys said the parents contributed at all to their sex education. Obviously, the parents of the boys in this study made little or no effort to teach sexuality to their children. Of course, in 1943 sexuality was a much more taboo subject than it is presently. In the apparently more open atmosphere of today, one might expect this to change. However, no such change in the degree of parental involvement in sex education is apparent.

Interesting results also emerged from Ramsey's vocabulary checklist, which was completed by 128 of the 291 boys. Although the boys had obtained a great deal of information about sexual behavior prior to high school, they were unfamiliar with the physiological terms, and even many of the nontechnical terms, used to describe that behavior. These boys would have had difficulty reading even the simplest sex education pamphlet.

Andre and colleagues (1989) investigated the sources of sex information among male and female college students. They found that written material was the most common source of information. In addition, they reported that nonvirgins used reading material more, perhaps because if they choose to engage in sex, adolescents seek out additional information. Hence, sexual involvement may lead to a lower relative use of parents as sources of sexual information.

Finally, DiClemente and colleagues (1989) demonstrated that school programs not only affect knowledge but also attitudes. Their particular concern was with knowledge and attitudes about AIDS. They found that both middle-school and high-school students exposed to minimal (three classes) instruction about AIDS not only learned more accurate information (e.g., AIDS cannot be contracted by casual contact with someone who is infected) but also became more tolerant of those who have AIDS (e.g., it is all right to attend school with them).

A number of conclusions may be drawn from the studies discussed above. It is very clear that peers play a major role in the adolescent's acquisition of sexual information. This is particularly true for boys, but also true for girls. The little material available also suggests that this information is quite often inaccurate and incomplete. Parents, and especially father, play only a minor role in transmitting information about sexuality. Similarly, teachers seem to be an untapped source of information about sexuality, quite probably because discussions of sexuality are viewed as inappropriate in the school setting. Books, magazines, and other types of literature can provide considerable information to adolescents, but they require a degree of sophistication and vocabulary that may be beyond many adolescents. Moreover, it is not possible to carry on a discussion or a question-and-answer session with a book. Hence, although used by sexually active adolescents (Andre et al., 1989), it is often an unsatisfactory source of information. Finally, a great deal of written material deals with the straightforward physiological or biological aspects of sexuality, and not with the more personal and social aspects. Hence, the adolescent is more or less stuck with the information available from peers.

As we noted above, there is a related issue that has not been researched very much, namely, *the sources to which adolescents feel they would go for information.* As part of their survey of adolescent interests, Dusek and Monge (1974; Dusek et al., 1979) asked adolescents to indicate whether or not they would go to each of 10 possible sources for information about each of the various topics of interest. The 10 sources are listed in Table 8–5. Several of the topics—"love and marriage," "birth control," "venereal disease," and "sexual relations and reproduction"—

TABLE 8–5 **Percentage of Male and Female Adolescents in Grades Five through College Who Would Seek Out Various Sources for Information about Each Topic**

Topic	Media	Same-Sex Friends	Mother	Doctors and Nurses	Siblings	Teachers	Opposite-Sex Friends	Father	Priests and Ministers	Books
					SOURCE					
Love and marriage										
males										
5th–8th	19	34	79	34	36	28	29	79	38	46
9th–12th	17	55	54	55	40	24	52	68	40	41
college	18	78	50	34	45	28	81	66	23	68
females										
5th–8th	13	48	94	34	38	23	20	60	24	33
9th–12th	14	60	82	44	44	24	46	58	35	48
college	16	86	83	36	54	30	71	56	17	33
Birth control										
males										
5th–8th	26	22	75	73	31	26	23	77	33	48
9th–12th	34	43	44	83	17	21	34	47	32	51
college	28	79	33	88	31	22	55	45	12	81
females										
5th–8th	23	41	84	73	18	14	15	52	18	50
9th–12th	35	56	65	79	30	20	21	27	32	63
college	23	87	53	94	41	13	33	17	5	76
Venereal disease										
males										
5th–8th	34	32	72	84	26	35	17	68	26	50
9th–12th	38	38	40	91	22	29	25	44	37	49
college	40	70	28	91	24	32	42	40	12	86
females										
5th–8th	35	53	79	84	28	33	20	67	21	46
9th–12th	46	55	48	85	28	27	17	26	33	68
college	30	65	47	93	37	22	31	24	9	80
Sexual relations and reproduction										
males										
5th–8th	22	40	69	59	36	15	28	74	17	38
9th–12th	33	50	48	73	33	23	36	56	31	34
college	29	88	36	79	25	30	77	53	14	88
females										
5th–8th	15	47	92	66	28	23	18	54	11	38
9th–12th	32	59	70	77	38	17	29	41	23	57
college	28	84	64	84	54	24	47	33	7	77

(Source: Adapted from Dusek, J., & Monge, R. [1974]. Communicating population control facts to adolescents. Final report, Grant No. RO1-HD 06724, submitted to the National Institute of Child Health and Human Development, National Institutes of Health, U.S. Department of Health, Education, and Welfare.)

deal specifically with sexuality. Table 8–5 lists the percentages of adolescent males and females in grades five through college who indicated they would seek out the various sources of information for each of these topics. As you can see, the mother and father are viewed by both boys and girls as someone to be sought out for information about love and marriage. However, same-sex friends are an even more important source of information for older adolescents. A similar trend was observed for information about birth control, but this time doctors and nurses are the first choice for both males and females. The same general trend held for venereal disease. With respect to sexual relations and reproduction, the percentage of adolescents who say that they would seek out their parents also declines with age. Doctors and nurses, peers (especially same-sex peers), and books and pamphlets all become more important with age.

A reasonable conclusion is that parents and teachers play a minor role in the sex education of adolescents and that peers play a major and significant role. This is unfortunate, since there is evidence (for example, Hunt, 1970; Dusek & Monge, 1974) of the poor reliability of information obtained from peers. As Gagnon and Simon (1969) and Simon (1969) noted, adolescents, if left to their own devices, will acquire the information that they want, even though that information may come from an inadequate, poorly informed source. Information of the sort presented above is in part responsible for the notion that the public school ought to undertake part of the responsibility of sex education.

Surveys of adolescents reveal that the majority wants sex education taught in the public schools, primarily as a separate and coeducational class (Hunt, 1970; Harris, 1971). Adolescents feel that they would get better and more valuable sex information from such classes, and that the opportunity to interact with knowledgeable teachers as they learn about sex would help them develop mature views about sexuality. Unlike their parents, they do not feel that discussing sex in the classroom will provoke increases in sexual behavior. Adolescents also feel that it would be less embarrassing to discuss sex information in a classroom atmosphere than it would be with their parents.

Adolescents also have very definite views about the content of sex education courses. Hunt (1970) surveyed 13- to 19-year-old girls to find out what they were taught in sex education courses and what they felt

Through sex education classes, adolescents gain significant amounts of accurate information about sexuality.

should be taught. As you might expect, most (over 80 percent) felt that the physiology of reproduction and pregnancy should be taught. Although a similar percentage were taught about the female reproductive system, only 68 percent were instructed about the male reproductive system and only 63 percent were taught about pregnancy. It may be, then, that sex education courses meet, or come close to meeting, girls' needs to learn about the physiology of reproduction. However, it was also clear that when it came to personal ethics or social issues, sex education classes did not meet the needs of a high percentage of girls. Ninety percent felt abortion should be discussed, but only 42 percent were exposed to information about abortion in their classes. Similarly, over 80 percent of the girls felt that information about venereal disease, loss of virginity, the male and female sex drives, infertility, impotence, contraception, masturbation, and homosexuality should be discussed. However, the percentage receiving any instruction about these topics ranged from only about 30 percent to 45 percent. Finally, the girls thought sex education classes should be separate courses—not part of phys ed classes or health courses—taught by teachers specifically trained in sex education.

Although it may seem that "the times have changed" since Hunt's survey, as we note below this appears not to be the case. Sex education courses still are very controversial, at least for parents, even though they do not promote sexual intercourse among adolescents (Eisen & Zellman, 1987), and as a result many adolescents do not receive even rudimentary sex education in the public school context.

Does Sex Education Make a Difference?

One might question whether or not students gain significant amounts of information from exposure to a sex education class. This was recently investigated by Monge, Dusek, and Lawless (1977) in a study involving 404 ninth-grade students, 193 of whom were enrolled in a six-week sex education course and 211 of whom were in a control group (that is, not enrolled in the course). Both sexes were represented in roughly equal numbers in the two groups. The course contained considerable content relating to adolescent sexuality; for example, sexual behavior, sexual development, and the physiology of reproduction. Students were given reading assignments and exposed to classroom presentations. Content dealing with birth control, physiology of sex organs, reproduction, venereal disease, premarital sexual relations, and pregnancy was included. A pretest was administered to half the experimental and half the control group on the first day of the sex education course. This was done in order to assess initial level of knowledge and allow measurement of gains in knowledge due to the course content. A post-test was administered six weeks later at the end of the course to all students involved in the study. Of the 50 items on the test, 24 dealt with specific aspects of sexuality: venereal disease (6 items), birth control

and reproduction (7 items), male physiology (6 items), female physiology (5 items).

The experimental and control group subjects who were pretested scored at equivalent levels, indicating that they had equivalent amounts of information on the 24 sexuality items at the start of the study. Neither group scored at a high level (mean score of 8), indicating a relatively low level of knowledge initially. Analysis of the post-test data revealed that the experimental group scored significantly higher than the control group, the experimental subjects getting 16 items correct and the control group getting 8. Furthermore, pretested subjects in the experimental group scored significantly higher than nonpretested subjects, indicating that a degree of sensitization toward the item content occurred because of the pretest. In all instances, the subjects in the experimental group acquired significantly more information about sexuality than the subjects who did not take the course (see Table 8–6). Although this is to be expected, it is interesting because it suggests that students enrolled in the course did not impart the information they received to their peers who were not enrolled in the course, even though the students knew each other and attended other classes together.

Other evidence (see Andre et al., 1989) indicates that adolescents gain significant amounts of information through sex edu-

TABLE 8–6 **Mean Scores of Experimental and Control Groups for Items Relating to Sexuality**

Topic	GROUP	
	Experimental	Control
Venereal disease	3.03	1.49
Female biology	3.90	2.64
Male biology	4.25	2.08
Birth control— reproduction	4.81	2.48

(Source: Monge, R., Dusek, J., & Lawless, J. [1977]. An evaluation of the acquisition of sexual information through a sex education class. *Journal of Sex Research, 13*, 170–184.)

cation courses. In addition, it does appear that having had a sex education course results in more liberal and tolerant views toward sexuality (cf. Kilmann et al., 1981), although it may be that those who are more liberal enroll in sex education courses. However, the available evidence (Eisen & Zellman, 1987; Kim & Zelnik, 1982) reveals no association between taking a sex education class and (a) engaging in premarital sex or (b) the frequency of premarital sex.

ADOLESCENCE AND HOMOSEXUALITY

In discussing homosexuality it is important to distinguish between homosexual experience and homosexuality. Homosexual experience refers to sexual experiences in the company of same-sex peers or adults. Homosexuality refers to the primary sexual orientation of the individual, one in which the individual prefers to have sexual relations with another of the same sex, and in fact seeks out this kind of sexual arrangement. Homosexual experiences are relatively common during adolescence, but homosexuality is much less common.

Sorensen (1973) reported that 90 percent of the adolescents in his sample had heard of homosexuality and that 9 percent indicated they had had a homosexual experience. In addition, 17 percent said they would consider having sex with a same-sex partner. However, their feelings about homosexuality were generally not positive. Only 40 percent agreed that if two girls (boys) wanted to have sex with each other it was okay. Two thirds felt it was right to have laws against homosexuality, and over 75 percent felt that homosexual sex was abnormal, disgusting, or immoral. It is interesting that these otherwise relatively liberal adolescents found homosexuality less a matter of choice.

Kinsey's data indicate that over 50 percent of adolescent boys and 30 percent of adolescent girls engaged in homosexual sex play as a child or early adolescent. The behaviors ranged from exhibitionism to mutual masturbation. The homosexual sex play may or may not have reached the point of orgasm. There was again a sex difference, with boys being more likely than girls to have experienced orgasmic release during homosexual experiences. Although these percentages are large, only a small number of adolescents go on to establish a primarily homosexual orientation in adulthood.

There were also complex age trends in Kinsey's data. Briefly, male homosexual experiences reach a peak of about 25 percent at age 10 and slowly decline to about 8 or 9 percent at age 45. Heterosexual responses show quite a different trend. They slowly increase across the adolescent years and reach a peak at about 30 years of age, when about 85 percent of males have a primarily heterosexual orientation.

One may look for the causes of homosexuality in either or both of two aspects of development. There is some evidence that the causes of homosexuality are primarily a function of interactions with other people, particularly the parents. From the opposite point of view, there is some evidence with respect to the hereditary nature of homosexuality. And Green (1980, 1987) suggests it is an interaction.

The most prevalent current view is that homosexuality results from the quality of the child's interaction with the parents. In other words, homosexuals are a product of interpersonal social relations and not of genetic material. The picture one gets of the parent-child relationships of homosexuals is that they were, at best, poor. Boys feel their mothers were domineering, overprotective, preferred them to their father, and made them feel dependent (Wyden, 1968a, 1968b). The fathers of homosexual boys are viewed as scorning them, as presenting poor role images, and as ignoring them or behaving as though they were not wanted (Allen, 1958, 1962; Bell, Weinberg, & Hammersmith, 1981). A similar picture emerges for female homosexuals, who view their fathers as weak (Bene, 1965), feel their parents are overly restrictive (Kaye, 1967; Schaeffer, 1969), and generally don't get along with either parent (Kenyon, 1968). Restricting girls' dating activities and instilling in them a fear of heterosexual relationships (because of the possibility of early pregnancy) seems to cause some girls to seek affection from same-sex individuals.

Particularly strong evidence with regard to the environmental basis for homosexuality comes from research by John Money and his colleagues (Ehrhardt & Money, 1967; Money, Ehrhardt, & Masica, 1968; Money, Hampson, & Hampson, 1955). In several investigations, Money studied the development of individuals who were assigned the incorrect sex at birth because abnormal prenatal development had transformed the appearance of the external genitalia. Some babies with a male chromosomal makeup were reared as girls, and some with a female chromosomal makeup were reared as boys. The sex role learned by the individuals was consistent with the *assigned* as opposed to chromosomal gender. In other words, social determinants were more important to sex-role learning than were constitutional factors.

These, as well as other data, suggest that a homosexual orientation is learned as a result of both direct and indirect conditioning. Girls may be taught to *fear* male company, and males may be taught to feel uncomfortable in the company of females. The only outlet for affection, then, is in homosexual relationships.

SUMMARY

In both theoretical conceptualizations and common sense views, sexuality is seen as an important aspect of adolescence. This seems to reflect the fact that it is during adolescence that sexuality emerges in an adult sense, although adolescents are not as consumed with interest in sexuality as common stereotypes would have us believe. Rather, interest in sexuality is simply one of a variety of interests in a hierarchy of adolescent interests. And, it is not the topic of the highest interest.

Another factor linking adolescence and sexuality is the increase in the sex drive that occurs during the adolescent years. Some evidence links the increase in the sex drive to hormonal changes, particularly in androgens, that occurs during adolescence. Other evidence reveals that the expression of the sex drive depends on cultural contexts. Hence, there are differences in males' and females' expressions of the sex drive, with males requiring a more direct means of expressing it.

The most recent evidence indicates that the majority of adolescents engage in premarital sexual intercourse. Although this is true of a larger percentage of males than females, the gap between the sexes is narrowing as larger percentages of females engage in premarital sexual intercourse. It also appears that during the 1970s and 1980s the average age of first intercourse declined. Another way in which the genders are becoming more similar is in the motivational structure underlying engaging in premarital sexual intercourse. Historically, females have tended to rely a great deal on the nature of the relationship in deciding to have intercourse. Hence, for females, the tradition has been that they do not engage in premarital intercourse unless they are in love with their partner. It now appears that this is becoming more true of males. Hence, most males now agree that casual sex is not reasonable, and that the quality of the relationship between the partners is an important aspect of premarital sexual relations.

This convergence on the part of males is not true for all, however. Some males, who might be called sexual adventurers, still hold to the standard of sex for the sheer pleasure of it. Others, labeled serial monogamists, tend to engage in sex only with partners with whom they are in love.

When adolescents do engage in sexual intercourse, they tend not to use contraceptive techniques, or to use ineffective ones. Hence, we find that up to a million children are born of unmarried adolescent women each year. These women face a variety of problems, including dropping out of school, having to take poor paying jobs, and other difficulties that make being an adolescent mother less than attractive.

There is some evidence that adequate sex education can alleviate some of these problems with adolescent sexual behavior. Adolescents clearly wish to have sex education taught in the public school curriculum. Those who have been exposed to a sex education course tend to be more responsible in their sexual behavior, at least with respect to consistent use of contraception.

GLOSSARY

AIDS (acquired immune deficiency syndrome).   A usually fatal disease, most often sexually transmitted, that attacks the body's immune system and thereby reduces the individual's ability to fight diseases and infections.

Gonorrhea.   A sexually transmitted disease that may lead to heart problems, blindness, or other physical problems.

Serial monogamist.   An adolescent who has sexual relations with a single, steady partner.

Sexual adventurer.   An adolescent who engages in sexual behavior, solely for the sake of sex, with multiple partners.

Syphilis.   A sexually transmitted disease that may lead to severe retardation, physical problems, or death.

SUGGESTED READINGS

FURSTENBERG, F., BROOKS-GUNN, J., & MORGAN, S. (1987). *Adolescent mothers in later life.* New York: Cambridge University Press.

The authors review information on the long-term effects of adolescent motherhood. They note areas in which the popular stereotypes do not apply and discuss means for reducing the negative impact on the mother and child of adolescent pregnancy.

GREEN, R. (1987). *The 'sissy boy' syndrome and the development of homosexuality.* New Haven, CT: Yale University Press.

Green explores the difficult and complex problem of explaining homosexuality. Both biological and social factors are examined for their contribution toward determining sexual preference.

SHAH, F., & ZELNIK, M. (1981). Parent and peer influence on sexual behavior, contraceptive use, and pregnancy experience of young women. *Journal of Marriage and the Family, 43,* 339–348.

This is an interesting article in which peer and parent influences on adolescent perspectives of sexuality are compared and contrasted. The large national sample makes the findings relatively valid for the entire adolescent population of 15- to 19-year-olds.

SMITH, E. A. (1989). A biosocial model of adolescent sexual behavior. In G. R. Adams, R. Montemayor, & T. P. Gullotta (Eds.), *Biology of adolescent behavior and development.* Newbury Park, CA: Sage Publications.

Smith presents evidence for the impact of both biological and social factors impacting on adolescent sexual behavior. He presents a model that incorporates the two influences in the determination of whether or not an adolescent will engage in premarital sex.

ZELNIK, M., & KANTNER, J. (1980). Sexual activity, contraceptive use and pregnancy among metropolitan-area teenagers: 1971–1979. *Family Planning Perspectives, 12,* 230–237.

The data demonstrate the types of changes in sexual behavior that occurred during the 1970s. This is one of the few articles that traces changes in adolescent sexual behavior.

Vocational Development

9

CHAPTER OUTLINE

MAJOR ISSUES ADDRESSED

Adolescent Interest in Work
The Benefits and Detriments of Part-Time Work
The Work Experiences of Adolescents
Employment Opportunities for Female Adolescents
Parental and Peer Influences on Vocational Development
Long-Range Vocational Planning
Individual Characteristics and Vocational Choice
Theories of Vocational Choice

INTRODUCTION

Planning and preparing for a vocation, which is one of the major developmental tasks encountered during the adolescent years, is a relatively recent development. Until the mid-1800s, children and adolescents were considered miniature or incompletely developed adults (Kessen, 1965; Kett, 1977). They often worked long hours on the family farm or in shops. Some, especially boys, were given as apprentices, for example, to blacksmiths, and worked for no money, the learning of the trade being their only reward (Kett, 1977). The learning of work skills occurred "on the job," with increasing demands placed on the youngster as he or she grew more physically and mentally capable of contributing further to the family or as an apprentice or a worker. Adolescents had little or no say in their choice of a vocation. Although the benefits of real vocational training were present for many adolescents, the choice of a vocation was made by others, usually the father. In effect, children and adolescents were viewed as a primary source of labor for, and an economic asset to, the family.

The advent of child labor laws took children and adolescents out of the workplace and set the stage for them to spend their days in school.

Owing to the passage of the first child labor laws (in Massachusetts in 1836), the nature of adolescent vocational decision making changed dramatically. The initial labor laws were protective, in that they defined working conditions and hours, set age limits for work in some areas, and later established job training programs for youth. Although passage of labor laws meant that many adolescents did not experience too much work too soon, it also meant that acquiring vocational training, outside working on the family farm or in the family business, was much more difficult. Younger adolescents were now prevented from acquiring skills by working in many jobs.

As Borow (1976) related, society began to function under the assumption that adolescents were not necessary to the labor force. In time, young people were viewed as a threat by older people who wanted jobs; and the lack of relevant work experiences kept young people out of the job market because they were not qualified for jobs requiring experience. In Benedict's (1938) terms, we came to view vocational development in a discontinuous manner, making it more difficult for the adolescent to make vocational decisions, and making the transition into adulthood more difficult (Steinberg, 1984).

Recent years have seen a change in attitudes (Steinberg, 1982, 1984) about the importance of work experience in the transition to adulthood. Career education programs, in which adolescents could gain some work experience while attending school, were aimed, in part, at easing the transition into adulthood while at the same time providing more meaning to school-learned material. Federally sponsored youth employment and training programs, which were aimed at low income, minority youth, had a similar goal. And, or course, part-time employment during the school years often was heralded as a means of giving the adolescent important experience in adjusting to the transition from the world of school to the world of work.

THE IMPORTANCE
OF VOCATIONAL CHOICE

There are a number of obvious reasons for studying how adolescents make vocational choices. First, it offers another opportunity to examine the ways in which the family, peers, school, and other social forces influence adolescent development. It also helps us understand something of the adolescent's views of the self, because vocational choices reflect, in part, the individual's assessment of his or her capabilities. Second, the study of vocational choices tells us something of the future the adolescent is likely to have. Job choice determines income, which in turn is related to the quality of the individual's life. Third, studying the processes of vocational choice during late adolescence helps us understand how vocations are chosen by people in general.

Adolescents' Interest in Future Work

Adolescents are well aware of the importance of their future vocations. Studies of adolescent interests (for example, Dusek & Monge, 1974; Dusek, Kermis, & Monge, 1979; Dusek, 1978; Freeberg & Rock, 1973) reveal that interest in future work slowly increases in rank from the late elementary school years to become the number one or two interest of adolescents from grade 10 through the college years. Although interest in future work is high, most adolescents have given relatively little thought to their vocational plans. Moreover, even those who have considered alternatives have little idea of the vocational skills they possess, the vocations for which they are suited, or the vocations that they would find interesting. Hence, they cannot make intelligent decisions about future work goals and cannot make long-term commitments toward an occupation. In effect, adolescents, like most people, make vocational choices in a haphazard and random way (Elder, 1971). Vocational training programs may help those considering entering skilled occupations. (Lambert & Mounce, 1987), but help for the remaining students is lacking. Although schools attempt to provide vocational counseling, the counselor is typically more concerned about, and more capable of dealing with, students planning to on to college than with students who need help making a vocational choice because they plan to enter the job market after high school.

Career education programs were initiated in part to deal with this problem (Fitzgerald, 1973). Career education programs allow adolescents to have work experience while still enrolled in school, through cooperative arrangements with various businesses, industries, and public institutions. It was hoped that such experience would be a forum for introducing students to varieties of vocations, thereby allowing students to make more informed career decisions and choices. Evaluations of career education programs (see Steinberg, 1982, 1984 for thorough reviews) indicate, however, at best limited success in this regard. Although students in career education programs are somewhat less likely to drop out of school, they learn no more than students not in career education programs. More to the point, students in career education programs tend to score higher than comparable students not in career education programs. on measures assessing desire to work, and they have enhanced career decision-making, job-hunting, and job-getting skills. However, these benefits of the programs dissipate several years after completing the program. Finally, there is no evidence that involvement in career education programs increases the employability of adolescents completing the programs. Hence, career education programs demonstrate some short-term benefits but no long-term advantages. Similar findings have emerged from evaluations of federally sponsored youth employment programs aimed at disadvantaged adolescents (Steinberg, 1982, 1984).

Despite efforts to integrate adolescents

into the work force in ways that will be meaningful in the long term, then, the problems of adolescent career decision making remain.

Developing a Vocational Identity

Some theorists (for example, Vandenberg, 1968) have argued that adolescence cannot end until the individual chooses a vocation and enters the adult work world. Although this may be a more rigid perspective than is desirable, it does point out the importance of work for an adult identity. From Erikson's (1964, 1968; see also Marcia, 1980) perspective, developing a view of the self in a vocational setting is critical to forming a mature adult identity. Hence, adolescent work experiences may be viewed as beneficial to identity formation, although too much pressure for vocational decisions too early may retard identity development.

Because the role of work in one's life is closely related to one's gender, it may be expected that males and females do not develop **vocational identities** in the same manner. Occupational identity may be a more salient issue for males and may be a less pressing issue for females because of its relation to traditional sex-role development. Patterns of relationships between occupational identity development and sex-role development were the subject of a study by Grotevant and Thornbecke (1982). They had high school juniors and seniors complete Marcia's identity status interview and a measure of sex-role orientation (Spence, Helmreich, & Stapp's [1974] Personal Attributes Questionnaire).

Although the males and the females had progressed equivalently toward achieving a vocational identity, they did so by different paths. For males, viewing the self as masculine, that is, having an instrumental orientation, enjoying acceptance of challenging tasks, and not being too concerned about the negative evaluations of others were related to higher levels of occupational identity. Occupational identity development for females was related to a willingness to work hard and to the avoidance of competition.

This study demonstrates that male and female adolescents come to achieve an occupational identity via different psychological routes. For males, sex-role concerns are intimately tied to vocational issues. For females no such direct link exists. This suggests that male and female adolescents go about achieving an occupational identity differently, and that adolescent work experiences may have different meanings for males and females.

Occupational identity formation, of course, is a very complex process. Havighurst (1964, 1972) highlighted this complexity by listing vocational choice and decision making as one of the important developmental tasks of adolescence.

The developmental task approach to vocational choice allows a life span study of the processes underlying vocational development. From a life span perspective, current vocational experiences are viewed as lesson plans for helping future generations as they approach various decision points with respect to vocational determination (Borow, 1966, 1976). Havighurst's perspective is illustrated in Table 9–1. The concept of being a future worker (via identification with parents) is integrated into the ego ideal first (ages 5–10). Between ages 10 and 15 the adolescent learns to budget time for school work, chores, and the like. These "work" responsibilities become primary, and play or leisure becomes secondary. The third stage results in the individual gaining actual work experience and learning something of the role of worker. During this stage, the individual prepares to become economically independent. Finally, being a productive worker allows one to progress up the employment ladder.

This developmental approach has certain advantages. For example, it makes it possible to study the continuing processes by which vocational training skills become integrated

TABLE 9–1 **Tasks of Vocational Development**

Age	Task
5–10	Identify with significant others—such as parents
10–15	Acquire work habits vs. other habits, such as play
15–25	Identify the self in work settings
25–40	Be a productive worker

into the individual's personality. As we noted in Chapter 1, an important question all adolescents must answer is "Who am I?" A closely related question is "What will I do with my life?" A significant part of the response to these questions involves the individual's identification with a particular vocation. In turn, an individual's particular personality characteristics determine to some extent the vocations that will be considered and entered (for example, Vandenberg, 1968). Individuals with different orientations seek out different kinds of vocations. Hence, for example, some individuals receive a great deal of satisfaction from helping others, and some seek personal self-satisfaction and recognition through achievement. Neither of these specific orientations, nor others that could be noted, is necessarily any better than another. The primary function of all of them is to provide the individual with optimal self-realization and self-fulfillment through appropriate occupational choices.

ADOLESCENT WORK EXPERIENCES

In many ways, studying adolescent work experiences entails the same considerations as the study of adult work experiences. Unemployment rates, what is looked for and seen as important in a job, job satisfaction, and the influence of the job on aspects of development are important factors in understanding both adolescent and adult employment. In addition, it is becoming increasingly evident that gender discrimination in adolescent employment mirrors that which exists in adult employment (see Box 9–1).

This perspective of adolescent employment is reflected in the types of questions and research done to increase our understanding of the effects of adolescent work experiences on development. Earlier research on adolescent employment was derived from a perspective of adolescent work easing the transition to adulthood. Hence, the major questions asked centered on the degree to which working increased responsibility, taught job-relevant skills, and the like. It is now realized that, although working may have some benefits, it may also entail

Sex discrimination in the work force begins during the adolescent years and teaches both female and male adolescents to expect such discrimination during adulthood.

BOX 9–1 **Does Sex Discrimination in Employment Begin in Adolescence?**

In recent years we all have been made aware of the problems of job discrimination on the basis of gender. It is well established that, on the average, adult women earn less money than do men, and that this is true even within the same broad occupational category (for example, professional). Women are clustered in lower-paying jobs and in lower-prestige jobs. Indeed, until recently, some professions have been virtually entirely closed to women.

Recently, researchers have become interested in studying sex discrimination in the adolescent work force (Greenberger & Steinberg, 1983). Initial information based on data collected by the Bureau of Labor Statistics and by the U.S. Census for in-school adolescents aged 14 and above indicates that more boys than girls are employed, boys work longer than girls, and there is sex segregation in the adolescent work place that is very similar to sex segregation in the adult workplace. For example, males are more likely to be employed as unskilled or skilled laborers while girls are more likely to be employed in child care or clerical jobs. In part as a result of this distribution of occupations, girls earn nearly a dollar less per hour than boys. Finally, even within the same job category, boys tend to make more money than girls.

Although it is tempting to attribute differences in hours worked and money earned to sex discrimination, Greenberger and Steinberg (1983) point out that the differences may be attributable to differences in job histories rather than gender. For example, if boys enter the work force at an earlier age than girls and have more experience working than do girls, it would be reasonable and logical to attribute differences in hours worked and money earned to differential work histories and not gender.

To study the relationship between adolescents' work histories and employment experiences, Greenberger and Steinberg (1983) surveyed nearly 1,900 adolescents, some of whom had had as many as three different part-time jobs. The questions asked of the adolescents concerned hours worked, hourly wage, how long the job had been held, and the like. They found that boys held their first job at a younger age than did girls. Age was clearly related to the job held, with older workers holding more formal jobs, such as working in a store or factory, and younger workers holding more jobs similar to the chores they do at home, such as babysitting, house cleaning, and newspaper delivery. In their first jobs, boys are more likely to work as laborers or recreation aids and girls are more likely to work as sales clerks or in child care. Similar trends were observed for the adolescents' second and third jobs. Although girls worked fewer hours on their first job, there was no sex difference in hourly wage. Girls did earn lower hourly wages than boys on their second and third jobs, however. Finally, there was no sex difference in change in wages when adolescents moved from one job to another.

In interpreting their findings, Greenberger and Steinberg (1983) note that, when they enter the labor force, adolescents are exposed to the same sex discrimination that exists in the adult labor force. The type of work open to male and female adolescents is different, the hours worked different, and, to some degree, the wages different. They go on to suggest that adolescent work experiences socialize the adolescent to expect differential employment opportunities as a function of gender once they enter the adult work force. Indeed, they note that early work training through doing chores around the house reflects sex discrimination, with boys and girls having different chores that reflect sex roles.

It appears, then, that the elimination of sex discrimination in the adult work force may be more difficult than imagined because of the socialization experiences males and females have with regard to working. These experiences may cause adolescents to expect and accept job discrimination, and may relate to the different occupations which they consider for adulthood. In order to expand the occupations considered by adolescents for their life's work, we may have to alter adolescent employment and adolescents' attitudes about part-time work.

some costs. Hence, the questions asked concern the types of jobs adolescents hold, how adolescents react to job pressures, the degree to which working facilitates (or not) the entrance into the adult job market, and how working in different settings, not just working *per se*, influences aspects of adolescent development (Greenberger & Steinberg, Final Report).

Adolescent Presence in the Work Force

Before examining statistics on the percentages of adolescents who are employed and unemployed, it is necessary that we wrestle with the difficult problem of defining what we mean by work. At first blush, this may appear to be a pseudoissue, for certainly we all know, for example, that making or serving food at a fast-food store is "work" and that going to a movie on Saturday night is not. As Steinberg (1984) points out, however, there are many activities in which adolescents engage that might not be so readily classified. One example he uses is that of mowing the lawn every week. We all would agree that mowing a neighbor's lawn for pay is work. But what about mowing the family lawn, even for pay. Is that work or is that something else?

To provide a perspective on work, Steinberg suggests we must look at the role the adolescent is playing. From this perspective, **work** is any activity that places the individual, subjectively or objectively, in the role of "worker" and takes the person out of the role of "student" or "family member." It makes no difference if the work is for pay or if it is voluntary as opposed to mandatory. Hence, the doing of household chores is not considered work, for the role the adolescent is playing is that of family member—all members of a family have chores to perform. However, working in a family business is not part of the family member role of son or daughter and, hence, is considered work.

Steinberg (1984) further notes that work entails the learning of a new role, that of

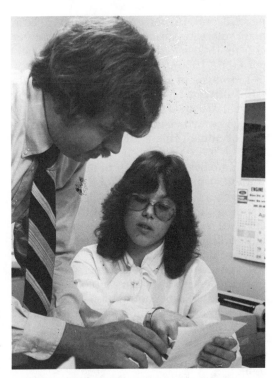

Part of working involves learning the role of "worker."

"worker," which has values and ideals that are somewhat unfamiliar to the adolescent. Other roles, such as son, daughter, sibling, and student, change during the course of adolescence; they are familiar because one has been those things for some time. The role of worker, then, may be the first new role acquired during the transition to adulthood.

Since 1940, when the Bureau of the Census first began reporting employment statistics for both in- and out-of-school teenagers, there has been a steady increase in the proportion of adolescents in the part-time work force and in the amount of time they work (Greenberger, Steinberg, Vaux, & McAuliffe, 1980; Steinberg, Greenberger, Garduque, & McAuliffe, 1982a). In 1940, about 4 percent of in-school male and 1 percent of in-school female 16-year-olds were employed. In 1970 these figures were 17 percent and 16 percent, respectively. Dramatic increases also occurred for younger (14- to 15-year-old) adolescents (Greenberger et al., 1980).

Employment rates based on census data (U.S. Bureau of the Census, 1987) for the years 1970 to 1986 are shown in Table 9–2. As may be seen, a substantial proportion of adolescents work at least part time. Indeed, it is estimated that, by the time they graduate, over 80 percent of all high school students will have held a job (Greenberger & Steinberg, Final Report). Clearly, understanding the impact, both positive and negative, of such work experiences is a very important component of understanding adolescent development.

Of course, not all adolescents who wish to work are able to do so. Unemployment rates in the adolescent population tend to be much higher than in the population at large. And, they tend to be much higher for younger than older adolescents and for black than for white adolescents (see Table 9–3).

As with adults, unemployment (Table 9–3) is higher during a recession (1975). As can also be seen, higher unemployment is evidenced among females than males and among blacks than whites.

In part, these statistics reflect general labor trends—adolescents do not have the skills for some jobs and usually are unable to take full-time jobs. In part, these unemployment statistics reflect socioeconomic background differences—disadvantaged youth have fewer educational opportunities even when educational background is equivalent to that of nondisadvantaged youth (Schulenberg, Vondracek, & Crouter, 1984). In a response to these needs, the federal government sponsored several types of job programs aimed at helping disadvantaged youth better prepare for the work place. We review the impact of these programs below, but it is important to note that the extent of these programs was not, and is not, sufficient to meet the employment needs of many minority or other disadvantaged adolescents.

TABLE 9–2 **Percent of Adolescents in Civilian Work Force, 1970–1986**

Sex	Age	1970	1975	1980	1985	1986
Male	16–17	47.0	48.6	50.1	45.1	45.3
	18–19	66.7	70.6	71.3	68.9	68.3
Female	16–17	34.9	40.2	43.6	42.1	43.7
	18–19	53.5	58.1	61.9	61.7	62.3

(Source: U.S. Bureau of the Census. [1987]. *Statistical abstract of the U.S., 1987* (108th ed.). Washington, DC: Government Printing Office.)

TABLE 9–3 **Adolescent Unemployment Rates, 1975–1986, for ages 16–19**

Sex	Race	1975	1980	1985	1986
All	All	19.8	17.8	18.6	18.3
Male	All	20.1	18.3	19.5	19.0
Female	All	19.7	17.2	17.6	17.6
	White	17.9	15.5	15.7	15.6
	Black	39.5	38.5	40.2	39.3

(Source: U.S. Bureau of the Census. [1987]. *Statistical abstract of the U.S. 1987* (108th ed.). Washington, DC: Government Printing Office.)

Not only are more adolescents working, but they are working longer. Between 1960 and 1970, the percent of inschool adolescents working more than 14 hours per week rose for both males (from 44 percent to 56 percent) and females (from 34 percent to 46 percent) (Steinberg, 1982; Steinberg et al., 1982a). Steinberg (1982; Steinberg et al., 1982a; Greenberger & Steinberg, Final Report) expresses severe reservations about this amount of work by in-school adolescents because it interferes with school performance. High school sophomores who work more than 15 hours per week, and juniors who work more than 20 hours per week, experience a drop in grade point average. Steinberg makes it clear that it is not working *per se* that hinders school performance, but working long hours. As amount of time working increases, school absences increase, enjoying school decreases, amount of time spent on homework decreases, and involvement in extracurricular activities diminishes. The drop in grade point average may well reflect both reduced study time and a lack of involvement in school that occur when adolescents spend too much time working.

Given the numbers of adolescents in the work force, and the amount of time they work, an interesting question is why so many choose to work as opposed to doing other things. Although adolescents give a variety of reasons for wishing to work, the most prevalent, not surprisingly, deal with making money, whether simply for spending or for saving, as for college expenses. Girls rate training and experience as somewhat more important than do boys, who rate automobile expenses as a more important reason than do girls. These sex differences, which are not as large as the similarities between the sexes in reasons for working (e.g., to help support the family, working in a family-owned business), likely reflect traditional sex roles.

More girls than boys may find part-time work, such as being a salesperson, of the variety they wish to do upon leaving school.

In addition, more girls than boys may not plan on attending college or entering a long-term career path.

This analysis is borne out by looking at the ways in which adolescents spend their money. Boys spend more money than girls in categories related to dating (gasoline, entertainment) and girls spend more money on categories related to femininity (grooming, cosmetics). The two sexes spend about equal amounts of money on records, cigarettes, books, and other non-sex-typed categories.

The emphasis on making money as the primary reason for working is quite consistent with adolescent independence strivings and likely reflects them. The money adolescents make, although not enough to allow them complete independence, helps them enjoy a certain degree of personal autonomy. They may even give up an allowance, clearly an expression of the desire to become more independent.

As adolescents mature with regard to developing an occupational identity, they begin to consider work values outside the realm of income. The most extensive research on older adolescents' work values has been conducted by Bachman and his associates (Bachman & Johnston, 1979; Bachman, Johnston, & O'Malley, 1980). One measure assessed what was viewed as important in a job. Approximately 90 percent of the large national sample listed having interesting work as important, approximately 75 percent wanted a job that would allow them to use their skills and abilities, and over 60 percent indicated they felt a job should allow you to see the results of what you do. In turn, only about 50 percent of college bound and 60 percent of non-college-bound seniors listed making a lot of money as important in a job (Bachman & Johnston, 1979). Similar results were found for a 1980 survey of high school seniors, who were asked to rank from not important to important a variety of job characteristics. Those characteristics that were ranked as "pretty important" or "very important" included seeing the results of one's work, having something interesting to do, good chances of advancement, the opportunity to help others, having a secure future, the chance to make friends, learning new skills, and not having to pretend to be someone you aren't. Those characteristics indicated as "not important" or only "a little important" included an easy pace of working, more than two weeks of vacation, and being free of supervision.

Although these older adolescents and young adults are interested in job security and income, they are also interested in the opportunity to make themselves better people and to develop as a person. They view a job as one type of experience that will make them well rounded, and as a setting in which they can employ their skills and talents. One may conclude they are not interested in working at just any old job, but rather want a job that will help them develop themselves. It is of interest to note that these values were shared nearly equally by those planning to attend college and by those with no college plans (or plans for less than four years of college). Concerns of quality of vocational experience, then, pervade the younger work force.

The degree to which one's occupation met these goals was the focus of a study done by Miller and Simon (1979). As part of a larger study of 18- to 49-year-olds, they surveyed both younger (18–22) and older (30–49) working men in order to measure their perceptions about what was important in a job and their perceptions about how well their jobs met these needs. Both younger and older workers shared views about what a job should provide, such as doing meaningful things, providing an opportunity to use one's mind and abilities, and receiving appreciation for a job well done. However, both groups reported that their current jobs did not live up to their hopes and aspirations with regard to these values. Only about 20

percent found their jobs were an excellent source for satisfying their vocational values.

The Positive and Negative Aspects of Adolescent Work Experiences

During the 1970s, there was considerable interest in utilizing the workplace as a forum for advancing adolescent development. Adolescents were perceived as disenchanted with formal school as a means of preparation for entrance into the world of work (Steinberg, 1982, 1984). There was an increased concern for the stresses of the transition between adolescence and adulthood. Integrating adolescents into the workplace was seen as a means of easing the transition into adulthood. In part because of the turbulence of the 1960s, adolescents were viewed as being too segregated from the mainstream of society, and work was seen as a means of better integrating and preparing adolescents for the adult world. Feeding into this set of influences was the increased dropout rate, illiteracy, and unemployment of disadvantaged adolescents. As a result, traditional educational programs were seen as not meeting the needs of many students, and alternative education programs, such as career development and youth employment programs (see Box 9–2), were established. The intent of these programs was to provide an educational setting and job experience that, it was hoped, would promote better career planning and employability than was possible through traditional educational programs. The upshot of these concerns was that integrating adolescents into the work force was perceived as providing them with positive experiences that would be beneficial in their adult lives.

Of course, part-time work has always been viewed as beneficial to adolescents. Parents, and others, have generally felt that by going to work adolescents gained in positive ways, such as those listed in Table 9–4. Until recently, concerns about possible negative

BOX 9–2 **The Effects of Career Education and Youth Employment Programs**

As a result of the social, political, and economic turbulence of the 1960s, the 1970s saw an increased emphasis on methods of integrating youth into the mainstream of adult society (Hamilton & Crouter, 1980; Steinberg, 1982). Prevailing views were that adolescents and youth were too alienated from adults, that schools were not adequately preparing young people to enter the adult world, and that the transition from adolescence to adulthood was too abrupt. In attempting to deal with these concerns, a number of private and government commissions (Hamilton & Crouter, 1980; Steinberg, 1982, 1984) suggested that furthering adolescent integration into the workplace could serve to better prepare adolescents for the world of work, promote intergenerational understanding, and ease the transition from adolescence to adulthood. One upshot of this perspective was the establishment of career education and youth employment and training programs, the former being devised by school districts and the latter by the federal government.

Although there are variations among the programs, the general idea was to supplement standard educational training with on-the-job experiences, often for school credit. Students were expected, and in some cases required, to attend classes part of the day and work another part of the day. It was hoped that mixing school and work experiences would aid the student's awareness of the relevance of school, and thereby increase school performance. Youth employment and training programs were aimed primarily at nonwhite disadvantaged youth. Federal government agencies spent over $3 billion between 1977 and 1980 on these programs. Career education programs were less restrictive in the definition of the target population, but the general goals were the same.

Evaluations of these programs (Hamilton & Crouter, 1980; Steinberg, 1982, 1984) have shown that they did not have the effects intended. Enrollment in these programs did not facilitate basic skill learning in school situations, although they may have kept some students from dropping out of school. The programs did facilitate the development of more positive attitudes about working, but these effects washed out soon after the student left the program. Most importantly, there is no evidence that students completing the programs were more employable, or employable in better jobs, than their counterparts who were not enrolled in the program.

The important issues, of course, concern the reasons the programs failed to deliver their promises. Steinberg (1982, 1984) suggests that, in part, the programs were doomed to failure because they were based on false premises. First, the jobs available to adolescents do not require the use of the skills typically taught in school, and do not require the learning of other cognitive skills, such as problem solving. Hence, he argues, they should not be expected to promote school learning or the teaching of additional cognitive skills. Second, he suggests there has been an overreaction to the disquiet of youth in the 1960s. Most middle-class adolescents are reasonably well educated and socialized and, as a result, are reasonably employable. Indeed, those entering the adult work force do not have difficulty finding jobs. Finally, Steinberg suggests that few adolescents are reluctant to accept adult roles and responsibilities, or are not prepared for adulthood. Today's adolescents are as committed to working, and have as positive attitudes about adulthood, as adolescents in previous generations. Hence, it is unlikely that early work experiences, even in structured programs such as career education and youth employment and training programs, could exert a substantial impact. The work experiences of adolescents are simply too narrow to exert an influence of any magnitude.

What, then, can be done to help adolescents acquire better jobs and be more employable when they enter the adult work force? Steinberg (1982, 1984) suggests the answer lies in education. Education, and specifically completing high school, is a much better predictor of employment than any form of early work experience, be it in a structured program or in naturally occurring circumstances. Substituting work experiences for academic training, in fact, may be doing adolescents a disservice. An increased emphasis on schooling and education, on the other hand, certainly will facilitate employability.

influences on the adolescent due to working were largely ignored, the possible exception being the apprehension that working part-time during the school year might be detrimental to school performance. Current studies of the influences of working on the adolescent's development are focused on both the positive and negative consequences of entering the work force.

The most extensive research on the influences of working on adolescent development has been done by Ellen Greenberger and Laurence Steinberg and their associates. They studied 531 tenth and eleventh graders, 212 of whom were employed part-time on their first job and 319 of whom had never worked (cf. Greenberger & Steinberg, Final Report). Only adolescents working in "naturally occurring" part-time jobs were studied. Adolescents working in career education or government sponsored youth training programs were specifically excluded from the study because the intent was to study employment as experienced by the large majority of adolescents.

Unlike previous researchers, who studied primarily long-term influences (for example, increased employability) of adolescent part-time work experiences, Greenberger and Steinberg studied short-term effects of working part-time during the school year. Short-term effects include the impact of

TABLE 9–4 **Presumed Benefits of Adolescent Work Experience**

Increase self-reliance
Promote intergenerational harmony
Increase social responsibility
Teach personal autonomy
Increase employability
Increase feelings of integration into adulthood
Learn mature work attitudes
Learn role flexibility
Enhance and broaden the self-concept
Learn to live with boring routines
Obtain relevant vocational training
Enhance educational experiences
Smooth the transition to adulthood

working on learning new skills and utilizing previously learned skills, the development of views and attitudes about work, changes in family and peer relations, personal development, and the like (Greenberger, Steinberg, & Vaux, 1981; Steinberg, Greenberger, Vaux, & Ruggiero, 1981b; Greenberger, Steinberg, & Ruggiero, 1982; Steinberg, Greenberger, Garduque, Ruggiero, & Vaux, 1982b).

A unique aspect of Greenberger and Steinberg's research was that they studied not only potential benefits but also potential detriments of adolescent part-time employment. They (Greenberger & Steinberg, Final Report) note three reasons that part-time employment may have negative influences on adolescent development. First, time spent working may be taken away from time spent with the family, friends, or on school work. As a result, family and peer relationships and school performance may suffer. Second, the routine and often boring work available to adolescents may foster negative attitudes toward work and working. As a result, as youth enter the full-time labor force, they may do so with attitudes that will make them poor employees, which may hinder their possibilities for career advancement. Third, health and behavioral problems may result from the added stress placed on the adolescent who works.

The adolescents involved in the study worked in a variety of jobs typical of those available to tenth and eleventh graders (see Table 9–5). On the average, the students had been working about nine months, at about 20 to 24 hours per week. They came from a variety of ethnic groups and social classes. Because these individual different characteristics were not related to the findings, that is, the findings applied to adolescents from all subgroups, no further mention is made of them. The information came from questionnaires, observations of adolescents' performance on typical tasks at work, and interviews with the adolescents and their parents.

TABLE 9–5 **Job Types Held by Adolescents**

Job	Percent
Food Service	35
Manual labor	15
Retail sales	13
Cleaning	10
Clerical	9
Skilled labor and operatives	6
Recreation aides and ushers	3
Hucksters	3
Child care	2
Newspaper delivery	2
Health aides	1
Educational aides	1

(Source: Derived from Greenberger, E., & Steinberg, L. [Final Report]. *Part-time employment of in-school youth: An assessment of costs and benefits.* Washington, DC: National Institute of Education.)

Positive Aspects of Part-Time Work. Adolescents who work part-time do indeed experience an increased sense of responsibility and autonomy (Steinberg, Greenberger, Garduque, Ruggiero, & Vaux, 1982b; Steinberg et al., 1982a), particularly if they work in a sales position or other setting that places them into contact with other people (Steinberg, 1982). The majority of adolescents take job requirements, such as punctuality, quite seriously, and about half feel that the way they do their job is important for the well-being of others (Steinberg et al., 1982a, 1982b). However, working adolescents do not develop a greater sense of social responsibility (Greenberger, Steinberg, & Vaux, 1981) than their nonworking peers.

The workplace also provides opportunities for some adolescents to acquire practical knowledge, such as dealing with consumer concerns and business practices (Greenberger, Steinberg, & Ruggiero, 1982; Steinberg et al., 1982a, 1982b), and some facility in dealing with the needs of others, such as might occur in retail sales jobs (Steinberg, Greenberger, Vaux & Ruggiero, 1981b; Greenberger et al., 1982; Steinberg, Greenberger, Jacobi, & Garduque, 1981a). These skills may well stand the adolescent in good

stead in the long run, but few adolescents work in jobs teaching these skills.

Learning of cognitive skills, or the use of basic skills learned in school, however, is very uncommon in the adolescent work place (Steinberg et al., 1982b; Greenberger et al., 1982). Most adolescents' work time is spent on tasks that have no particular cognitive component, for example, manual labor, cleaning, and other non-problem-solving activities. Even adolescents who work in clerical jobs spend less than 10 percent of their time using school-taught skills. In part, these trends reflect the lack of on-the-job training in adolescent work activities, and in part they reflect the fact that most adolescents do not work in cooperative activities with other workers, especially adults, from whom learning could occur (Steinberg, 1982, 1984). Contact with adults is limited to very minimal instruction; adults in the work place do not become the adolescent's friend or confidant (Greenberger et al., 1982). Few adolescents report a close relationship with an adult with whom they work.

Adolescents who work develop better skills in dealing with distraction, task persistence, and gaining pleasure from a job well done than do their nonworking peers (Steinberg, Greenberger, Vaux, & Ruggiero, 1981b; Steinberg et al., 1982b). When considering desired career and characteristics of specific jobs there are also some effects of working. Boys become more interested in exercising authority in an adult job, girls become more interested in job security and making a good living, and both boys and girls indicate that being able to be creative is an important job criterion. Nonetheless, working does not alter adolescents' expectations for career attainment or occupational prestige. The effects of working on long-range career and educational planning, then, are minimal.

Negative Aspects of Part-Time Work. Working part-time during the school year has several detrimental effects on school performance (Greenberger et al., 1981; Steinberg et al., 1982a, 1982b; Wirtz et al., 1988). Compared to their nonworking peers, working adolescents spend less time on homework, are absent more, and say they enjoy school less. Adolescents who work more than 15 to 20 hours per week also perform less well academically, probably because they simply are less involved in school. As you might guess, working adolescents also are less involved in extracurricular activities, likely because they simply don't have the time for them.

Greenberger and Steinberg (Final Report) also reported that part-time work entailed some health costs associated with the added stress placed on the working adolescent. Adolescents who work are more prone to using cigarettes, alcohol, and marijuana, and those in more stressful working conditions use these more (Greenberger et al., 1981; Steinberg et al., 1982b). These effects appear to be more closely associated with stress in the work place, for example, feeling one's job is meaningless, conflicts between the various roles one plays, and poor working conditions, than with income. Working *per se*, however, was not associated with decreased psychological or physical well-being, the negative influences being related to stress on the job.

About 60 percent of working adolescents reported that they had engaged in some form of deviance on the job—stealing goods, giving their friends a monetary break, stealing from co-workers, or calling in sick when not ill (Steinberger et al., 1981b, 1982b; Greenberger & Steinberg, Final Report). Working adolescents also develop cynical attitudes about working, including feeling work is meaningless and that there is little satisfaction to be gained from working hard.

Working adolescents spend less time with the family, and girls feel less close to the family, and spend less time with peers than do nonworking adolescents (Greenberger & Steinberg, 1981; Greenberger et al., 1980; Steinberg et al., 1982b). Although time spent with peers decreases, feelings of closeness to peers does not.

Adolescent Part-Time Work: Conclusions. In Table 9–6 we summarize Greenberger and Steinberg's major findings regarding the positive and negative effects of naturally occurring part-time employment during the adolescent years. The findings are not only enlightening but also sobering. One conclusion that cannot be denied is that the benefits of part-time work have been far overestimated. Although some gains in practical knowledge and the ability to take responsibility are evidenced, they are offset by the failure of adolescent jobs to teach new skills or utilize existing skills, both presumed benefits of working. Largely, this results from the types of jobs that are open to adolescents (Steinberg, 1982, 1984; Greenberger & Steinberg, 1981). The minimal skills taught are learned quickly and the benefit of that learning is reaped after a very short time. Although some work settings are more or less prone to this description (Steinberg, 1982, 1984), even those settings that may be characterized more positively do not teach or allow the use of higher-level cognitive skills.

A second indisputable conclusion is that the negative influences of part-time work have been underestimated. Parents, teachers, and others have always been concerned about working interfering with school performance. Unfortunately, this fear is borne out in the data, at least for adolescents who work more than 15 to 20 hours per week. More importantly, however, the other negative influences shown in Table 9–6 point to areas in which historically there has been no concern. Part-time work clearly entails costs in terms of substance abuse, the development of poor attitudes about working, and the acceptance of deviant work practices. In addition, because adolescents do not interact much with adults on the job, working does not really act to facilitate intergenerational understanding or promote an easier tran-

TABLE 9–6 **Positive and Negative Effects of Adolescent Part-Time Employment**

Positive	*Negative*
Develop autonomy and personal responsibility	Feel work does not contribute to overall effort
Feel work benefits others	Limited contact with adults
Learn some practical skills	No significant use of school-taught skills
In some jobs, learn how to deal more effectively with people	No learning of new cognitive skills
Enhanced work orientation	No effect on long-range occupational/educational plans
Development of job values and characteristics felt important	Lower involvement in school
	More school absences
	If work long hours, lower school performance
	Job stress increases use of cigarettes, alcohol, and marijuana
	Increased acceptance of deviant business practices
	Increased materialism
	Develop cynical attitudes about work
	Less time with family
	Less time with peers

(Source: Summarized from Greenberger, E., & Steinberg, L. D. [Final Report]. *Part-time employment of in-school youth: An assessment of costs and benefits.* Washington, DC: National Institute of Education.)

sition to adulthood. Rather, it appears to be simply an extension of the adolescent society (Greenberger & Steinberg, Final Report; Steinberg, 1982, 1984).

Greenberger and Steinberg (Final Report; see also Steinberg, 1982, 1984) make some suggestions for promoting the values and alleviating the detriments of adolescent work experiences. One suggestion is that work experiences be tailored to make use of school-taught skills and be designed to teach other skills, an effort that will require the cooperation of both school personnel and private industry. A second suggestion is to look at the issue of adolescent work in a manner similar to that used to examine the effects of working on adults.

For example, examining how adolescents react to job stresses (Greenberger et al., 1981) demonstrates that they react in a manner very similar to adults. Adult models on the job may be able to teach adolescents effective means of coping with stress that do not involve increases in substance abuse. Finally, it appears that the benefits of working are enjoyed after relatively minimal time working, with a longer time working, or working longer hours, contributing little.

In turn, some of the negative effects of working, such as lower school performance, increase with increased work time. Perhaps more attention should be given to just how much work an adolescent should do. This is a problem that must be faced by employers, who find adolescents attractive employees because of the minimal wages and benefits they provide to part-time workers, by parents, and by adolescents.

THEORIES OF VOCATIONAL CHOICE

Theories of vocational choice outline the critical factors in vocational determination. The various theories that attempt to describe how people make vocational choices have diverse approaches and emphases. Some stress personality characteristics, and others state that situational determinants are more critical than personality factors. Although the influences on vocational choice may be too numerous and too complex for any single existing theory, the group of theories reviewed below presents a comprehensive view of vocational determinants.

Components of Vocational Theories

Super (1953) listed a number of factors that should be considered in any theory of vocational choice. First, and perhaps most important, theories of vocational choice must recognize individual differences. People differ in abilities, interests, and personalities, and these differences are related to the vocational choices people make. Any theory of vocational development, then, must be able to relate individual difference characteristics to vocational decision making.

Similarly, an adequate theory of vocational development must account for the fact that one individual is capable of successful performance in a range of occupations. There is no one occupation uniquely suited to the competencies, interests, and personality of any one person. Hence, specific jobs in such groupings as clerical occupations or health sciences all have certain underlying similarities and various intragroup skill-level requirements. Someone interested in medicine need not become a doctor in order to work with medical issues and problems. Being a nurse, technician, or medical social worker may provide the same degree of satisfaction. A successful and useful theory of vocational development must be able to sort the individual difference factors mentioned above into the various suitable occupational groupings.

Each occupation requires some core set of abilities, such as social skills, cognitive skills, and personality attributes, to which the potential employee must adapt. Some individuals will be better suited to a given set of job skills than will others. The theory must be able to account for an appropriate match in individual characteristics and job-required skills.

Vocational theories should also account for growth within an occupation once it is chosen. Super favors a developmental stage theory in which one explores oneself and one's vocation within the occupational setting. In other words, Super views the development of vocational behavior as a process of adjustment which the individual must make by growing and changing with changing job requirements and opportunities. These adjustments maintain a balance between capabilities, job demands, and other factors that influence occupational enjoyment and value. This is best seen in job-change decision making and promotion to jobs requiring higher levels of decision making or personnel supervision. Each person must decide if the added requirements are "worth it" and if the competencies he or she possesses are likely to lead to successful performance. If the answer is yes, the person will have to adjust to the changes.

Accounting for the degree of satisfaction that one obtains from work and the reason some succeed while others fail at their work is another important aspect of vocational theory. Super feels this can be accomplished by relating vocational adjustment to the self-concept. If the job allows the individual to make good use of his talents, abilities, and interests, he is more likely to enjoy the work, do a good job, and gain from it.

Osipow (1968) states that current theories of vocational choice are too broad in scope. He argues that we need miniature theories describing relatively specific aspects of vocational choice and decision making. Once we understand these smaller segments of the problem, we can weave our explanations into more global theories. A second criticism Osipow levels against current vocational theories is that they tend to be male-oriented. Female career choice and development have been generally ignored. With increasing numbers of women entering the full-time job market, this issue must be addressed.

Third, and quite interestingly, Osipow suggests that theories of vocational choice must also include the possibility of no choice. In other words, Osipow questions the notion that everyone wants to work.

Finally, Osipow would like to see theories of a developmental nature. Current theories tend to be focused on adolescent decision making, or on how and why some individuals elect an alternative or second vocation, and do not necessarily focus on growth and development within vocations.

Psychoanalytic Theories

Erikson (1963) and Roe (1953, 1956, 1968) have each formulated psychoanalytic theories of vocational decision making. The psychoanalytic theorists believe that being happy and contented in one's vocation is a positive aspect of good psychological adjustment.

Erikson (1963) has related his version of psychoanalytic theory to the vocational world. The fourth stage of development in Erikson's model, learning industry as opposed to inferiority, begins in childhood, at about 6 or 7 years of age, and extends into adolescence and young adulthood. Resolving this conflict in favor of industry allows the individual to take pleasure in a job well done and in meeting tasks that challenge the individual's abilities. However, Erikson gives us very little, if any, clue to how vocational decisions are made. He argues that the well-adjusted person will gain satisfaction from employment because it will satisfy his or her basic need to be industrious.

Roe's (1968) is the most specific attempt to relate vocational choice to psychoanalytic theory. Roe's basic notion is that an individual will seek out and do well in a vocation that satisfies the demands and needs of his personality, as developed through early childhood experiences. Of major importance in this formulation are parent-child relationships, for Roe believes that these relationships orient people toward specific career types. This conclusion is based on Roe's early research (1951a, 1951b, 1953) on personality differences among research scientists in various fields. Roe thinks that the differences that are important to occupational choice deal with orientations toward people and a general lifestyle. Some children will be reared in such a way that they will seek out interactions with people, whereas others will be reared in ways that will cause them to avoid interaction as much as possible. Children who are reared by avoiding parents, for example, should have preferences for occupations involving minimal contact with people, such as research scientist, forest ranger, or technician. People-oriented individuals will likely be happiest in service occupations, business, or perhaps entertainment.

A direct implication of Roe's theorizing is that people should perform well and be satisfied in occupations that satisfy their lifestyle needs. Lack of intellectual capabilities, or lack of the economic assets necessary to prepare for a specific vocation, should be the only major deterrents to entering a vocation that will satisfy one's basic lifestyle needs.

Research based on Roe's hypothesis has, at best, produced equivocal evidence. The weight of the evidence suggests Roe's hypothesized relationship between vocational choice and child-rearing is faulty (Roe, 1964; Borow, 1966); a reasonable possibility is that the relationships are not as direct as she anticipated. Nachmann (1960) and Segal (1961), for example, reported personality trait differences between groups of law and social work students, the former having dominant fathers and the latter weak or absent fathers. Furthermore, law students were reared in homes more accepting of aggressive behaviors than were dental students. Personality traits, then, do relate to vocations. When research on this relationship is conducted with reference to the many other factors affecting vocational development, the relationship may become more clear.

The basic tenet of the psychoanalytic explanation of vocational choice, then, is that people choose occupations that satisfy basic personality needs. Generally speaking, this appears to be a useful concept, for satisfaction of needs is certainly an important aspect of vocations. Psychoanalytic theories do not take into account chance occupational encounters or environmental demands that prevent one from entering a specific occupation. In addition, psychoanalytic theories do not describe specifically how vocational choices are made, except to point out that the individual's personality is an important factor in such choices. Of course, this argument is completely circular and does little for explaining vocational choice. Furthermore, with the exception of Roe's emphasis on child-rearing processes, psychoanalytic theories do not discuss the developmental processes that lead to a particular occupational choice. Rather, they skirt that issue in favor of the more simple notion that vocational choice reflects satisfaction of the individual's basic personality needs, the development of which is explained. In the case of Roe's theory it is clear that the multitude of problems involved in assessing early parent-child relationships make the theory difficult to test. One could probably do as good a job of predicting vocational choice by relating current demands placed on the individual to the vocational decision processes.

Holland's Trait Measurement Theory

The earliest systematic attempts to explain vocational choices were made from a trait measurement perspective. The basic notion in this approach is that people entering the job market seek occupations that fit their particular interests and abilities. Hence, a popular approach to vocational choice, best exemplified by use of such inventories as the Strong Vocational Interest Blank (Strong, 1943, 1955), is to assess an individual's interests, vocation-related competencies, and personality characteristics, and then match those with similar measures on individuals successfully and happily engaged in various professions. The basic assumption in this approach is that traits are stable differences, and therefore can be used to remove some of the haphazard guessing involved in occupational guidance and choice. This is one commonly used strategy

Using interest inventories is a convenient means of beginning to explore potential vocations.

for helping high school or college students pick a vocation. The logic involved in the approach is straightforward and simple, and it is an easy procedure to assess one's interests and match them with those possessed by people in particular kinds of jobs.

Holland (1959, 1971, 1973) extended and refined the trait measurement approach in his notion that people use occupational titles to form conceptualizations of the work involved in any particular occupation. The person's views of occupations presumably reflect the ways in which the world is organized. This is what Holland calls a "modal personal style." From examining large amounts of data, Holland developed a scheme consisting of six modal personal orientations: realistic, intellectual, social, conventional, enterprising, and artistic. Each of these is described in some detail in Table 9–7. Each orientation reflects a complex set of personality, ability, and aspiration traits assessed by tests. Corresponding to each personal orientation is a comparable set of vocational environments requiring specific kinds of adjustments and skills. Theoretically, each of these vocational environments requires a particular life-style and personal orientation for optimal level of success. Choosing a suitable career involves seeking

TABLE 9–7 **Holland's Modal Personal Orientations**

Realistic	Concrete orientation toward physical skill and masculinity with a de-emphasis on social, interpersonal, and verbal skills
Intellectual	Orientation toward understanding and working with ideas rather than people
Social	Orientation toward working with people and avoidance of intellectual or physical pursuits
Conventional	Orientation toward a structured environment, following set regulations, and power and status identification
Enterprising	Orientation toward success through manipulation of others
Artistic	Orientation toward the self and creative expression; avoidance of structure and social interaction; artistic expression predominates

(Source: Adapted from Holland, J. L. [1964]. Major programs of research on vocational behavior. In H. Borow [Ed.], *Man in a world at work*. Boston: Houghton Mifflin. Reprinted by permission of American Association for Counseling and Development.)

out vocational environments that mesh with one's personal orientation toward the world.

The intent of Holland's theory is to spell out the relationships that exist between occupational environments and personal orientations toward life. Theoretically, it should be possible to determine an individual's personal orientation through the Vocational Preference Inventory (Holland, 1958) and use that information to guide vocational choice by suggesting suitable vocational environments. But, as with the psychoanalytic approach, the developmental aspects of career preferences are not addressed. In this regard, then, Holland's theory is somewhat incomplete as an explanation for the mechanics of vocational choice, although its practical value in vocational counseling may turn out to be quite high.

There are, however, several limitations to trait measurement theories (Borow, 1966). First, it is difficult to relate personal char-acteristics to the large number of occupational settings that exist today. Second, these models are based on the assumption that traits are static, which eliminates the possibility of investigating them from a developmental viewpoint. Third, there is no attempt to examine antecedent-consequent relationships in vocational development. Finally, the trait measurement approach ignores completely the exciting new developments in cognitive-developmental, learning, and social-learning theory.

Developmental Theories

The two theories to be reviewed in this section, those of Eli Ginzberg (1972) and Donald Super (1957), are developmental in nature. Each theorist takes a stage approach to the study of the development of vocational choices, although Ginzberg does so in a much more direct way than Super. As a result, it is possible to examine vocational choices within various age groupings and discuss the important parameters of vocational choice and development in children, preadolescents, adolescents, and young adults.

The critical factor in Super's theory is the relationship of the self-concept to vocation. Ginzberg's theory highlights the continual compromises one makes between vocations that are desired and those that are possible. Both theorists argue that the individual is continually forced to make adjustments in vocation-related choices that limit, to some degree, future choices of vocations.

The developmental aspects of these two theories make it possible to investigate the processes underlying vocational choice and decision making across the childhood, adolescent, and adulthood years. Rather than merely describing or making passing references to developmental processes, then, these theorists point out the important aspects of vocational choice and decision making that occur at various points in the life of the individual.

Ginzberg's Stage Theory. Ginzberg and his associates (Ginzberg, 1972; Ginzberg et al., 1951) proposed a stage theory of vocational choice conceptualized as the resolution of a series of conflicts between what is wished and what is possible. For most individuals these decision processes take place during adolescence, over a six- to twelve-year time span.

There are four stages in Ginzberg's theory. In the first, or *fantasy*, stage, which lasts until about age 10 or 11, the young person makes arbitrary vocational choices with no real consideration of the realities of the situation. During this stage children want to be cowboys, movie stars, astronauts, jet pilots, lawyers, or doctors.

The second, or *tentative*, stage begins when the young adolescent begins to take into account his own interests and capabilities when thinking about future vocational choices. There are four substages during this period. In the first, or *interest*, period, choices are made on the basis of personal likes and dislikes. This is a transition period between the fantasy and tentative stages. The second, or *capacities*, period begins at about age 13 or 14, coinciding with the onset of formal operations; the individual begins to assess his capabilities with respect to particular kinds of vocations. At about 15 or 16, personal values, orientations, and goals become an important part of vocational considerations (the *value* substage). The individual begins to realize that specific vocations have particular relationships to personal value structures, and that some vocations may be more suited to one's value structure than others. The fourth substage is a transition between the tentative period and the realistic stage. This *transition* period, which begins about age 17, is a period of consolidation during which interests, capabilities, and values are focused on particular vocational alternatives.

Ginzberg's third stage in vocational choice, the *realistic stage*, begins about age 18. It is during this time that reality testing be-

comes critically important as the individual tests his tentative vocational choices against the reality of vocational demands, and comes up with a vocational pattern that satisfies both his personal values and the demands of a particular occupation or group of occupations. These compromising aspects of vocational choice occur primarily during the exploration substage of the realistic period. During the crystallization substage, the individual develops a clear vocational goal with specific satisfactory occupations identified. In other words, a crystallization of the realities of vocational demands and the individual's personal capabilities, interests, and values has taken place.

The fourth stage is *specification*. It is reached when the individual makes a commitment to a specific vocation either by entering it or by beginning to train for it. Although there is considerable individual variation, most people enter this stage by the early twenties.

Ginzberg and his associates suggest that four specific psychological processes are essential to the vocational choice process. *Reality testing, ability to defer gratification, sensitivity to compromise,* and the *development of time perspective* help the individual develop the perspective to make optimal vocational choices. Educational background, emotional makeup, and personal values are also important determinants of vocational opportunities and outlook.

Although Ginzberg's theory was developed primarily from observations on boys, girls are assumed to progress through the fantasy and tentative periods of vocational choice in much the same way. During the reality stage, however, many girls also consider the vocational alternative of marriage and child rearing (Borow, 1976). As women's role in society changes, we will undoubtedly see a change in women's approach to vocational choices.

Another individual difference variable considered by Ginzberg and his associates is social class. The same general progression of the stages is evident in both middle- and lower-class adolescents, although the lower-class adolescents move through the realistic stage more quickly than the middle-class adolescents. In large part this is because middle-class adolescents tend to consider a wider variety of vocational alternatives than lower-class adolescents (Borow, 1976) and because middle-class adolescents take a longer educational preparation period than do their lower-class counterparts.

Ginzberg's theory, then, states that optimal career decisions come from a compromise between individual capabilities and vocational task demands. In his more recent formulations Ginzberg (1972) notes that the process of occupational choice may extend beyond the realistic period, as exemplified by mid-career vocational changes by men and women in their forties.

Research on Ginzberg's theory has produced somewhat equivocal evidence. Some research has produced evidence that there is a stage sequence in adolescent vocational maturity and choice which generally follows the process outlined by Ginzberg and his colleagues. Other research, however, indicates that vocational aspirations do not become more realistic during the high school years, suggesting the stage theory notions may not be entirely correct.

Super's Vocational Self-Concept Theory. Super (1953, 1957, 1969, 1985) and his colleagues (Super et al., 1957) have developed the most comprehensive developmental theory of vocational choice. The basic concept in Super's theory is that vocational choices are made in such a way as to allow the greatest opportunity for the expression of the developing self-concept of the individual. Individuals are viewed as continually developing their self-concept *vis-à-vis* career choices and performance, a form of reality testing. Vocational development, then, is a process involving changes in vocational choices that reflect changes in the individual's developing self-concept. In the earlier

stages of development, the self-concept is not fully developed; as a result, the vocational choices of younger and older adolescents will differ considerably.

From this perspective, it follows that the vocations picked will be the ones that allow the greatest expression of the self-concept. As the self-concept changes, the adolescent's vocational choices will become more narrowly defined. Super also realizes that, in addition to the individual's own competencies, there are environmental contingencies that affect vocational choices. For some, such as minority-group members, these limiting factors make some vocations extremely difficult to attain even though they might mesh well with the self-concept.

A second developmental aspect of Super's theory is that the adjustments one makes at any given stage in development can be used to predict adjustments at subsequent stages. As a result, Super believes people develop identifiable patterns of vocational and career outlooks. In the *stable* pattern, a career choice is made relatively early and is permanent. For example, some decide very early in life to become doctors, and they do so. The *conventional* pattern, so named because it is an apt description of vocational decision making for a wide variety of people, is exemplified by those who attempt several, perhaps interrelated, vocations and finally pick one as a permanent choice. The *unstable vocational* pattern is exemplified by the individual who is continually changing jobs. Career choices for this individual fluctuate as both the individual's own development and circumstances change. There is no single permanent or long-lasting career choice. The last pattern identified by Super and his colleagues is the *multiple* pattern, exemplified by the individual who moves horizontally within the occupational hierarchy from one employer to another at the same job level.

These occupational patterns reflect people's lifestyles, which, in turn, are related to their self-concept in general and their vocational self-concept in particular. There is, then, a continuous and ongoing process of adjustment and change. Changes in personality, interests, competencies, and the like, cause changes in vocational outlooks.

In making vocational choices the individual must deal with five developmental-vocational tasks, each of which is divided into two major stages: the exploratory and the establishment. The first task is *crystallization*, the integration of the notion of work into the self-concept. This occurs between the ages of 14 and 18. The second developmental-vocational task, *vocational preference specification*, involves narrowing the range of possible vocational choices and making appropriate preparations for those vocations; for example, entering vocational training programs, becoming a trainee, or enrolling in a college program. The age range for this task is 18 to 20. The third task is *implementation of a vocational preference*. During this period (roughly, 21 to 24) the individual either undergoes extensive training, for example, in an apprenticeship or advanced study program, or takes a job. At about age 25 *stabilization*, the fourth developmental-vocational task, occurs. The individual is now settled into a particular job and is testing it to see if the right choice was made. The final developmental-vocational task is *consolidation*, the period in which the individual advances in his or her chosen career and attains some degree of success and status. This period usually occurs after the age of 35.

One obvious implication of Super's theory is that the individual is continually testing potential vocational choices. Courses studied in school, independent study programs, work-study programs, and the like, are all helpful as he or she tries out various work roles. When the person finds a work role that meshes with ones self-concept (that is, one that is in harmony with one's abilities, interests, and personality), the individual is more likely to stay with that role than with one where the fit is not as good.

Super's theory suggests that vocational guidance courses and counselors should help individuals understand the self, particularly as it relates to the world of work. The better people understand themselves, and how they will function in the vocational setting, the greater the likelihood that the vocation people choose will satisfy them and benefit society as a whole.

Finally, Super's theory has a number of implications for exceptional adolescents. The retarded, the physically handicapped, or the learning-disabled adolescent is likely to have a different self-concept orientation and outlook on vocational and career opportunities than nonexceptional adolescents. Different kinds of training programs and guidance procedures might be implemented to ensure that these special students receive the right kind of vocational help.

Developmental theories focus on the processes underlying the development of vocational behavior. As a result, they play down the overstressed issue of specific vocational choice (Borow, 1976). As we gain greater insights into vocational behavior, we will understand more about how choices are made. Of course, this is a major advance over the trait measurement approach.

Implications of Theories of Vocational Choice

As you may surmise from the above theories, vocational decision making is a complex and not well understood process (Super & Hall, 1978). It entails a meshing of our personality, abilities, interests, and needs to vocational demands. Most of us do this without really thinking about what we are doing. It is as if we have our own personal theory of vocational choice that guides our decisions. Perhaps this is indicated in our statements that we are entering a particular vocation because it is interesting or because we like it. In effect, we choose vocations haphazardly. It is therefore to our credit that we do this so well.

Although the vocational theories tell us something about how long-term vocational plans are (should be) made, they tell us little about adolescents' choosing of part-time jobs, as you no doubt discerned. In all likelihood, this is because adolescents' primary reason for working is to make money. Adolescents are not highly interested in finding a job that will satisfy self-concept needs or suit basic interests. Hence, they are willing to take jobs that they well might not consider for careers. This may in part explain why they state that they rarely do more than expected on the job (Greenberger & Steinberg, Final Report). And it may explain their lack of satisfaction with becoming workers (Box 9–3).

INDIVIDUAL DIFFERENCES AND VOCATIONAL CHOICE

In the remainder of this chapter we discuss factors that relate to long-range vocational planning and decision making. A number of individual difference characteristics are important in the vocational decision making process. Intellectual capabilities, socioeconomic background, gender, and one's particular interests all relate both to the processes underlying vocational decision making and to the actual vocational choice made.

Intellectual Capabilities

Intellectual ability is the single most important personal competency related to vocational choice. In part, this is because some occupations require higher levels of intellectual ability than do others, although other factors, such as drive and motivation to succeed, are also important for success (Borow, 1976). Other things being equal, however, the greater the intellectual ability of an individual, the greater the chances for success in many different occupations.

A second, and very important, reason for the link between intellectual ability and vocational success is that intellectual ability is highly related to educational achievement. Hence, jobs requiring high levels of education, such as professional positions, upper-level management, and the like, are open only to those with many years of graduate and postgraduate education, and therefore are more likely to attract only highly intelligent and highly motivated individuals. This is not to say that a high level of intellectual ability is necessary for all occupations. Some jobs that are tedious, or involve repetitive routines, are better handled by those who do not have a high need for intellectual stimulation or creative thinking. We should also mention here that not all or even most individuals in jobs requiring little formal education are of average or below average intelligence. Many highly intelligent individuals may be in these types of jobs because of discrimination or because the job characteristics suit their needs (O'Leary, 1974).

Moreover, although those with higher intellectual capabilities are more likely to succeed in any given vocation than those with lower capabilities, sheer intellectual ability is no guarantee of success. As noted above, motivation and the fit of the job characteristics with the needs and personality of the individual are important factors in career success.

There is also some evidence to suggest that intellectual capabilities are related to the manner in which decisions about vocations are made (Borow, 1976). Adolescents who are brighter make vocational decisions that are more in line with their capabilities, interests, and probabilities of employment in that occupation than do less bright adolescents (Gribbons & Lohnes, 1966). The vocational choices of bright adolescents are more realistic than those of less bright adolescents. The latter group tends to have vocational aspirations that are unrealistically high and require competencies and skills they do not possess. Brighter adolescents also tend to be somewhat less dependent on

BOX 9–3   **Work Adjustment**

The study of the adjustment to work is relatively new (Lambert & Mounce, 1987). And there are no data about adolescent adjustment to work.

Work adjustment entails the worker's ability to adjust to his or her work environment. That is, it reflects the relation between the satisfaction of the worker (the degree to which the worker's job meets personal needs) and the satisfactoriness of the worker's performance (the degree to which the worker performs the job well). The greater the correspondence between measures of these two components of work adjustment—that is, the greater the correspondence between needs and abilities of the worker and the job—the greater the adjustment to work. The greater the work adjustment the lower the likelihood the person will leave the job, or be fired from the job.

Two aspects of this theorizing are important for our purposes. One is that adolescents generally find that their jobs do not meet their needs and expectations, as noted in the text. Given that only about 20 percent of adolescents find that their jobs meet expectations, it is not surprising that they develop somewhat negative perspectives of employment and may come to view work as an onerous task.

Second, this perspective has important implications for career counseling (Lambert & Mounce, 1987). Helping students match their needs, interests, and abilities to the demands of various jobs should help them more readily adapt to the world of work and of becoming a worker.

This latter perspective has been aided by the computer (Lambert & Mounce, 1987). Computer-assisted guidance systems are used by over a quarter of public secondary schools, although nearly half the students who could use these systems don't. The general advantages of these systems include (1) ease of use by the student, (2) the ability to match student work needs with job requirements, and (3) availability to large numbers of students with relatively little increase in staff time commitment.

By helping more adolescents make wiser career decisions we not only provide a service to the community but we also enhance the likelihood that workers will be more productive. In addition, we may go far in helping future adults find more satisfaction in their employment.

the opinions of family and peers and less susceptible to social pressure in general when they make occupational choices.

Vocational guidance counselors typically administer or acquire IQ test scores in order to be in a better position to counsel students about vocational choices. An especially important task is guiding less bright adolescents to vocations matching their intellectual ability, not because these adolescents are incapable of succeeding at a job that would require a higher level of ability, but because success at such a job would require the expenditure of a tremendous amount of energy, time, and effort, quite probably at the expense of their general lifestyles. The brighter adolescent would be more likely to succeed without neglecting other aspects of living.

Role of Socioeconomic Status

A number of investigators (e.g., Sum, Harrington, & Goedicke, 1987) have researched and discussed the relationship of social class to vocational aspirations and attainment. Generally speaking, social class relates to vocations in three ways. First, to some degree it determines the occupations that will be familiar to, and therefore considered by, the individual. Since middle-class adolescents are aware of a wider variety of vocations than lower-class adolescents, they have a wider variety to pick from.

Second, to some degree social class determines the acceptability of a particular vocation for a specific individual. The lower-class adolescent who wants to become a doctor, or the middle-class adolescent who wants to work on a production line, is likely to meet with considerable criticism from parents, peers, and family members because the aspirations are considered too high in the one case and too low in the other.

Third, social class determines in a very real way what jobs will be open to individuals. The bright, motivated lower-class adolescent may find that being a doctor is impossible because he or she does not have the money to go to school. A middle-class black adolescent may have the money to attend college, but may find that some professions are closed to him or her because of prejudice.

The relationship between social class and occupational aspirations has been investigated by a number of researchers (e.g., Sum et al., 1987). Generally speaking, lower-class adolescents have lower vocational aspirations than middle-class adolescents. Some (see Hollings-head, 1949) have argued this is because lower-class adolescents have a "class horizon" view of occupational goals; that is, they aspire to the same occupational level held by their parents. Some support for this notion comes from research by Elder (1971) and Grigg and Middleton (1968). As Elder points out, adolescents tend to choose jobs that they know about, jobs in which their parents and parents' friends are employed. As a result, the lower-class youth, who sees a great many people employed as unskilled or semiskilled workers, may set lower goals than the middle-class youth. Others have argued that lower-class youths view the opportunities for entering upper status occupations as small, and as a result set lower vocational goals than middle-class adolescents.

As we mentioned earlier, social class is related to the jobs that are actually available to young people, both because of the educational requirements for high prestige occupations and because social class is still associated with race. As Conger (1973) points out, employers tend to hire those who come from backgrounds similar to theirs,

perhaps because they feel they can work more easily with these people. However, Conger also notes that in some instances this may be simply a disguise for prejudicial judgments about people who may not hold the same sets of values as the employer.

The Influence of Gender

One of the major social tragedies of our times has been the view that women should be housewives and mothers and only secondarily, if at all, be allowed to achieve personal satisfaction and growth through a career. This personal loss is only one aspect of the tragedy; the loss of the contribution these women could have made to science, business, and the professions is another. Although the value of women in the labor force was amply demonstrated during World War II (L. Hoffman, 1979, 1980), it is only in more recent times that women have been allowed to enter the labor force freely and in high-prestige, high-level occupations (Borow, 1976; L. Hoffman, 1980).

The percentage of women who work outside the home is increasing. In 1980, 45.1 percent of married women with children under the age of 6 were employed, and 61.7 percent of married women with children between the ages of 6 and 17 were employed (U.S. Bureau of the Census, 1987). The comparable percentages for separated and divorced women are even higher. At present, then, approximately 60 percent of women aged 18 to 64 work outside the home. And, there is every reason to believe that the percentage will increase in the future. In other words, as adolescent women leave secondary schools we can expect increasing proportions of them to enter the work force, even if they elect to have children. It is important, therefore, to look at the vocational prospects for these women.

Although improvements in earnings have been made in recent years, women still earn substantially less than men (U.S. Bureau of the Census, 1987). In part, this differential occurs because women still tend to be employed in traditional female vocations, such as secretarial, clerical, and nursing jobs, and not employed in professions that pay more and are typically male dominated, such as legal, managerial, and medical. The future, however, continues to look bright. Businesses have seen the large pool of talent represented by women and substantial changes in the percentage of women employed in traditionally high-prestige, high-paying, male-dominated vocations have occurred. The trends toward greater employment opportunities for women, and toward equal pay for equal work, bode well for today's adolescent females. They will have more opportunities and career choices than previous generations of adolescent women had.

Another reason for the lower pay achieved by women, including those who are well trained for high-paying vocations, concerns differences in male and female career patterns. Many women choose to rear children during their late 20s through their 30s and into their 40s. They then choose to reenter the work force. However, they are, in effect, new workers and cannot command the wages of those males or females who have had that 15 to 20 years of experience. They have lost their relative position vis-à-vis their cohort of workers, and they likely can never make up the ground.

Several researchers have compared the occupational aspirations of adolescent males and females. Douvan and Adelson (1966) reported that the girls in their study aspired to a more restricted range of occupations than did the boys. Most of these girls saw themselves in stereotyped female occupational roles: teachers, nurses, secretaries, and so forth. Few indicated any interest in traditionally masculine occupational roles like engineer or business executive.

Angrist (1972) identified five career types or occupational orientations among college women. The *careerists* aspired to a full-time career in conjunction with the role of wife, mother, and home-maker. More so than in any of the other career types, women of this orientation aspired to enter the traditionally male-dominated vocations. In addition, these women indicated that child-care responsibilities and homemaking chores could be taken care of by others if they were unable to do so in conjunction with a career. At the other career extreme are *noncareerist* women, those who want to be full-time wives and mothers. For these women, preparing for an occupation was seen as a form of insurance against the possibility of having to work to support themselves or their children. A third group of women, the *shifters*, were inconsistent in their orientations toward a career. These women tended to have traditional family-oriented role expectations that were in conflict with their views about careers and their need to express their competency in areas outside the home. The two other types identified by Angrist were the *converts*, those who entered college without any career aspirations and changed their orientation toward a career some time during their college years, and the *defectors*, who entered as career-oriented freshmen but later decided that they really wanted to be full-time wives and mothers.

These data point up the underlying value conflict faced by many young women. Even many of the women who work full-time do so in the helping professions, which tends to reinforce the sex stereotype of women as nurturant people. Young men, on the other hand, tend to enter occupations that promise independence, power, and financial gain, in line with the traditional stereotype of men as assertive. Data such as these suggest that girls are trained during early and middle childhood to view their future lives in ways very different from boys (Maccoby & Jacklin, 1974), and that this rearing interferes with girls' career orientations.

This is not to say that all girls should be career-oriented, but rather that those who are, and the percentage of these girls is increasing (Borow, 1976), should have this option made clear to them both by parents in early childhood and by counselors in school. This is likely to be difficult in view of the importance of parental modeling for children's future development (Gewirtz, 1969; Bandura, 1969b). Boys see the father go to work, and, although it is lessening, a large percentage of girls see mother stay at home and take care of the children. Most boys have a same-sex model who works and many girls do not. More likely than not, the father who goes away to work will appear to lead a more exciting life than the mother who stays home. It is not difficult to conclude that girls reared by mothers who stay home are likely to have a different view of sex roles vis-à-vis work than girls reared by mothers who are also employed.

There is evidence (L. Hoffman, 1974, 1979) suggesting that girls whose mothers work have a less restricted view of the female sex role and are more career- and achievement-oriented. In part, this seems to be a result of the mother providing a model of a female who can work outside the home. Working mothers provide a role model for their daughters that in many ways is comparable to that provided by fathers for their sons (see Chapter 10 for a more complete discussion). Working mothers also may train their daughters to be more independent (L. Hoffman, 1979, 1980) and may encourage that independence. As a result, the daughters of working mothers may grow up in an atmosphere in which independence is not sex-typed male, or sex-typed at all, especially if the father accepts his daughter as feminine and expresses this while at the same time not limiting her independence (L. Hoffman, 1979).

Career-oriented girls are distinguishable from their non-career-oriented counterparts on several other personality dimensions that suggest career-oriented girls have a more achievement-oriented, masculine view of work roles.

Non-career-oriented college girls hold to the more traditional female sex roles, whereas career-oriented girls expand their sex role to include a career. Astin's (1968) data indicated that, compared to non-career-oriented females, career-oriented women have higher mathematical and mechanical interests and aptitudes, more frequently have interests in the physical sciences, and more frequently choose a college preparatory curriculum in high school. Almquist (1974) reported that career-oriented college girls tend to come from homes with a working mother, were not social isolates, had a wider variety of working experiences than non-career-oriented girls, wanted to use their special abilities, modeled career-oriented people, and were more oriented toward meeting their needs than suiting their parents. Although, as some note, career-oriented girls have a more masculine, achievement orientation, these girls still experience a degree of role conflict (Almquist, 1974; Astin, 1968). Considered in terms of Super's theory about the relationship of vocational choices and the self-concept, it is apparent that many career-oriented girls are at a disadvantage because their self-concept is less likely to include a traditional (that is, non-child-rearing) vocational component. Or, it may include factors that work directly against a vocational orientation.

As we noted above, jobs and the demands inherent in them are socially sex-typed. This has been true in the past and is true now. Oppenheimer (cited in Van Dusen & Sheldon, 1976) has identified the reasons for this continued stereotyping. His listing of factors includes: (1) women are willing to work in traditionally feminine jobs for low pay; (2) "women's jobs" don't require long-term commitments; (3) since such jobs exist all over the country, women can work anywhere their husbands' jobs take them; (4) "women's jobs" are women's jobs because they have traditionally been held by women. We may reasonably add the possibility that women have been conditioned psychologically to have certain attitudes and feelings that force them into specific jobs and keep them out of others. Societal expectations, then, affect female vocational choices both directly, through sex-role vocational stereotypes, and indirectly, through the conditioning of psychological traits related to vocational decision making. This last fact should lead to exciting new insights into female vocational choice.

Interests and Vocational Choices

As several theorists (for example, Holland, 1971, 1973; Super et al., 1957) have pointed out, people receive greater satisfaction and experience more success in occupations that are consistent with their interests and competencies than in occupations that are not consistent with them. This does not mean that simply because interest in a particular career is high, the individual will do well in it. As was pointed out above, intellectual competency and a host of other factors are also important.

The most extensive and exhaustive research on the relationship of interests to vocations has been done with the various vocational interest inventories that use the trait measurement approach discussed earlier in the chapter. The most commonly used of these instruments are the Kuder Occupational Interest Survey and the Strong Vocational Interest Blank (Strong, 1943, 1955). Since most adolescents at one time or another will come in contact with these scales, either as part of being interviewed for a specific job or in general guidance and counseling situations, a brief review of their utility is in order.

The basic theory behind these instruments is that an individual should be happy and successful in a job if his or her interests match the interests of people who have been successful in that particular job. Interest inventories are constructed by assessing the interests of successful people in various vocations and using these assessments as a reference group. In most instances, the inventories require one to make a forced choice between various alternatives, the choice being like, dislike, or uninterested, or some variant of this sort. The vocations recommended to a person are those in which current employee's interests match those of the individual. For example, a person with interests similar to those of the engineers in the reference group would be encouraged to consider engineering as an occupation.

Strong (1955) presented convincing evidence that the interests of college men accurately predict the vocations in which they will be engaged 18 years after graduation. Those who scored high (had A ratings) in particular occupational interest subgroupings tended to enter and remain in the vocations associated with those interest ratings. Conversely, men who had C ratings in those interest categories were employed in some other field. Other data (Cronbach, 1970) indicate that the vocational inventories are reasonably accurate predictors of the vocations that men will enter. Unfortunately, little research has been done with women, and it is difficult to assess the degree to which the vocational interest inventories are successful with women. It may be that, for women, the home versus career issue negates the relationship of interests to occupations. With regard to predicting success in a particular occupation, Cronbach, in reviewing the literature, indicates that the inventories are limited predictors of success in a vocation. However, they do provide guidance counselors with objective and useful data, and therefore serve a useful purpose.

SOCIAL INFLUENCES ON VOCATIONAL ASPIRATIONS AND CHOICE

A number of social influences affect adolescent vocational choices and aspirations. Parents, peers, siblings, and teachers are among those socializing agents that significantly affect adolescents' views of vocations.

Parental Influences

As we noted above, one way parents influence the vocational aspirations and choices of their offspring is through modeling (Vangelisti, 1988). Boys who identify strongly with their fathers tend to have traditional sex-typed interests and tend to use the father as a role model for vocational expression.

The most extensive study of parental role modeling on vocational development was conducted by A. P. Bell (1969). In a longitudinal study, Bell examined the importance of parental, and especially paternal, modeling as related to vocational choices in male adolescents. The subjects were interviewed first at about age 15 and again at about age 25. The interviews were designed to assess role models both in general and in specific life spheres. A variety of measures of occupational fulfillment were obtained, including job stability, job competence and success, and job satisfaction. Bell reported that the father was the primary role model during early adolescence but that other role models, for example, peers and adult relatives, became more important later. In other words, as the adolescent matured, others became important role models. However, of all the models, the father's role was the only one related to vocational adjustment in early adulthood. Adolescents who viewed their fathers as strong and positive role models tended to have higher vocational levels than adolescents whose fathers were weak or negative role models.

Finally, moderate use of the father as a role model in adulthood was more strongly associated with successful vocational adjustment than either strong and positive, or negative, modeling. This pattern of results is not surprising, since the young adult is likely to have less strong ties to the family and develop stronger ties to age-mates, who become significant in a variety of decision-making processes. Moreover, once in an occupation, co-workers can become models for that particular occupation and organization, something the father is less likely to be able to do.

Parents are important, too, because children tend to "follow in their footsteps." As we noted above, adolescents tend to enter vocations that they know about, and they certainly know more about their father's or mother's occupation than they do about any others. Werts (1968) compared fathers' and sons' occupations for 76,015 high school students and reported that for a number of occupations, particularly medicine, law, and science, sons entered the same profession as their fathers at a greater probability than would be expected by chance. Werts attributed this to familiarity with father's occupation, pressure from the parents to enter the specific vocation that has been satisfying to them, and to identification with the parents. In some instances, such as farming, it is also quite simple to take over the business from the father, and hence the large majority of individuals who entered farming had fathers who were also farmers.

Mortimer's (1974, 1976) research investigated similar issues and extended our understanding of the role of father's occupation because prestige of the father's occupation was included as a variable. Sons who had a close relationship to the father and whose fathers had high-prestige occupations were more likely to follow their father's vocation than sons in other groups. Of the two factors, closeness to father and prestige of father's occupation, the former was the more important. Feeling close to the father led to more choices of the father's vocation for business and professions than did feeling less close to the father. As more women become full-time workers, we may find similar trends for mothers and daughters.

A related issue is one of occupational status levels. Young people generally choose a vocation that is on the same level as, or a step above, their father's occupation (Kerckhoff & Huff, 1974). Partly this is because parents wish to have offspring who will do better than they did (Bordua, 1960), and partly it is because parents provide the support and means for attaining higher vocational levels than they themselves have attained. As we noted above, socioeconomic status and vocational aspirations are related, and it is unlikely that an individual will enter a vocation that will place him or her in a lower socioeconomic status than the one that the person came from. Similar data on girls are lacking. As more and more women are entering high-status, as well as low-level occupations (Borow, 1976), it should be possible to study more definitively the relative influence of the parents on female vocational choices as well.

In some ways, parental influences on adolescents' vocational choices are unfortunate. Few parents are capable of giving the right kind of vocational advice to their offspring, and those who do may often do so for the wrong reasons. Some parents wish to relive their own lives through their children. Clearly, this may not be best for the child. Also, parents are poor judges of the capabilities of their offspring and their offspring's interests. Overestimating the capabilities of the adolescent and recommending a vocation for which the individual is ill-suited can be devastating to the individual's vocational self-concept.

Peer Influences

Bell's (1969) data indicate that ninth-grade boys rank peers relatively low as influential role models for vocational choice, but at about age 25, peers achieve a ranking second only to the boy's father and other adult relatives. Kandel and Lesser (1969) studied peer and parent influences on vocational aspirations and choices. They report that girls have vocational aspirations more closely related to those their mother held for them than do boys, but that adolescents of both sexes have aspirations that are in line with both their mother's and best friend's. Friends apparently reinforce parental aspirations, most likely because friends come from backgrounds similar to the adolescent's.

The influence of peers on vocational aspirations and choices is also dependent upon social class. As Conger (1973) reports, lower-class adolescent boys who attend middle-class schools tend to have higher aspirations than lower-class boys attending lower-class schools. Partly this is a function of the school, since middle-class schools tend to be superior to lower-class schools, and partly it is due to associating with others who have high aspirations. In a sense, middle-class values rub off on the lower-class adolescent who associates with students from the middle class, increasing the individual's vocational aspirations. A similar but reverse set of operations exists for middle-class boys who associate primarily with lower-class boys (Conger, 1973). In this instance, the middle-class boys have lower aspirations than their middle-class counterparts who associate primarily with middle-class boys.

Sibling Influences

Siblings, and their sex status relative to the adolescent, are also important to vocational aspirations and views (Borow, 1966; Vangelisti, 1988). Boys with all-male siblings hold highly masculine vocational interest patterns, and girls with all-female siblings hold highly feminine ones. Of some interest are data indicating that girls with older brothers have highly masculine vocational interests. One explanation of this finding, which is consistent with O'Leary's (1974) theorizing regarding sex differences in vocational planning, is that older brothers act as significant role models. Hawley (1972) reports that women entering traditionally masculine professions indicate that the significant men in their lives have endorsed their lifestyles. The older brother, then, may encourage a lifestyle that is not traditionally feminine.

School Influences

Generally speaking, schools prepare students best for vocations that involve working with ideas, for obvious reasons (Vangelisti, 1988). In some ways, schools are getting away from this orientation and are becoming more interested in vocational training for specific occupations. This represents a shift from the philosophy of the 1960s, which was strongly influenced by industry's desire to have more highly educated employees. The school influences most directly affecting the vocational choices, aspirations, and training of the individual adolescent are the classroom teacher and the guidance counselor.

One way teachers affect their students' choices is by personal influence. The teacher's personality, warmth, knowledge, and advice are important and influential in students' vocational decision making. One study indicates that 39 percent of college students regard their high school teachers as the major influence in occupational choice.

There are a number of other direct, but less personal, ways that teachers can influence vocational choice. The teacher who is ill prepared, who denigrates students, or who is a poor teacher can damage the career plans of students, particularly marginal college-bound students, who may come to believe they are incapable of competing successfully at the college level. Of course, this shuts them off from a number of potential occupations.

Within the school framework, the guidance or vocational counselor is the person most directly responsible for helping students select appropriate vocations and curricula designed to prepare for the vocation. In effect, the vocational counselor's main job is to see that the student makes a realistic choice given the match between the student's personal characteristics and the job demands, the projected employment possibilities in the chosen vocation, and the adequacy of the planned curriculum of the student.

Some evidence indicates guidance counselors are not doing as good a job as they should be. It is well documented that high school students are quite ignorant about the world of work and the best or even available procedures for making vocational decisions (Borow, 1976). Significant percentages of students say they get little or no help from their school's guidance counselors (Noeth, Roth, & Prediger, 1975). In their study of 32,800 students in grades 8, 9, and 11, Noeth and colleagues reported that 20 percent of eleventh graders had only a low level of involvement in career planning and 50 percent indicated they got no help from their guidance counselors. In another large-scale study involving 5,225 males aged 14 to 24, Kohen and Breinich (1975) reported data indicating that degree of availability of guidance counselors did not relate to the student's knowledge of the work world.

One hopes that new guidance techniques, such as courses in the "how to" of career planning and computerized vocational choice systems (see Box 9–3), will help students become more capable of helping themselves and will aid counselors in their task.

SUMMARY

In the early history of the United States, children and adolescents were expected to work and contribute to the welfare of the family. Hence, adolescents worked on farms, or as apprentices, and did not enjoy the freedom from work that most current day adolescents may choose. With the passage of child labor laws, the nature of adolescent vocational training and decision making changed. Adolescents no longer had to work, and the work they could do was limited by the labor laws. We began to view working, and vocational decision making, in a discontinuous manner.

Recent years have seen a change in this perspective. Emphasis has been placed on the benefits of employment to the adolescent and the society. It has been argued that working will build self-esteem, teach valuable skills, and help integrate the adolescent into the society, thereby alleviating the barriers between generations. Currently, about 80 percent of adolescents will work part-time before they leave high school. The work experiences of adolescents do have some benefits: increases in personal responsibility; for some, the learning of valuable skills; and feeling that the work done is of benefit to others. However, there is no evidence that adolescents' working experiences make them more employable, consolidate school-taught skills, or teach other cognitive skills. Indeed, there is evidence to the contrary. Adolescents who work more than 15 to 20 hours per week spend less time with peers and family and on homework, enjoy school less, and do less well in school. The stresses associated with working in conjunction with other pressures on the adolescent result in increased use of alcohol, cigarettes, and marijuana. These findings have renewed interest in the nature and importance of adolescent part-time work and are cause for concern. It appears that the benefits of adolescent employment have been overestimated and the detriments underestimated.

Long-range vocational planning is an important task of adolescence. Theories of vocational development emphasize the important role played by personality characteristics, self-concept, interests, and abilities in career planning. In general, long-range career planning should take each of these factors into account and match the needs and abilities of the individual with job characteristics. The better the match, the more likely the individual will be successful and happy in the vocation.

A number of individual difference characteristics relate to vocational decision making processes. Girls with working mothers tend to be more career-oriented than girls whose mothers do not work. With the increased opportunities for vocations at all levels, and with the increasing percentage of working women with children, this is an important consideration. Parents act as peer models for the role of one's vocation, and there is some evidence that adolescents, and especially boys, do indeed emulate their parents' vocational choices. Intellectual competence is another individual characteristic that relates positively to vocational satisfaction, although motivation and the willingness to work hard are important to vocational success. Peers, siblings, school personnel, and coworkers also are important in the determination of vocational attitudes and choices.

GLOSSARY

Work. Any activity that places the adolescent in the role of worker and removes the individual from student or family roles.

Vocational identity. One's identity as a worker and contributor to society; one's view of the self in a vocation.

SUGGESTED READINGS

LAMBERT, B. G., & MOUNCE, N. B. (1987). Career planning. In V. B. Van Hasselt & M. Hersen (Eds.), *Handbook of adolescent psychology*. New York: Pergamon Press.

The authors provide an overview of the major theories of career decision making. In addition, major conceptual issues in describing the impact of adolescent work experiences are explored.

STEINBERG, L. D. (1984). The varieties and effects of work during adolescence. In M. Lamb (Ed.), *Advances in developmental psychology* (Vol. 3). Hillsdale, NJ: Lawrence Erlbaum.

Steinberg assesses the costs and benefits of adolescent work experiences in both school/government sponsored and naturally occurring circumstances. He also addresses the issue of the context (type) of work and how that context contributes to the benefits and detriments of working.

SUM, A. M., HARRINGTON, P. E., & GOEDICKE, W. (1987). One-fifth of the nation's teenagers: Employment problems of poor youth in America, 1981–1985. *Youth and Society, 18,* 195–237.

The authors explore the factors that influence the career planning of disadvantaged youth. In particular, they focus on those influences that are most important in understanding how adolescents from impoverished backgrounds make career decisions.

VANGELISTI, A. L. (1988). Adolescent socialization into the workplace: A synthesis and critique of current literature. *Youth and Society, 19,* 460–484.

The author details the impact of family, peer, and school influences on vocational decision making. In addition, other major influences on career planning, such as social class and race, are addressed.

Parent and Family Influences on Adolescent Socialization

10

CHAPTER OUTLINE

MAJOR ISSUES ADDRESSED

Changes in the Family Unit
Methods of Rearing and Disciplining Adolescents
Adolescent's Perceptions of Parental Child Rearing
The Influence of a One-Parent Home
How Children and Adolescents Adjust to Divorce
The Influence of the Working Mother
Adolescent Strivings for Independence and Autonomy
Siblings and the Adolescent

INTRODUCTION

For several reasons, our discussion of family influences on the adolescent is focussed primarily on the role of the parents. First, the role of the peer group, siblings, or any other socialization agent is supplemental to the major impact of the parents. Second, only little is known about the impact of other family members on the adolescent's development. There is a lack of research on sibling, grandparent, and stepparent effects, for example. In this context we will pay special attention to child-rearing techniques. These techniques, which will have been in use for many years before adolescence, are an important reflection of parent-adolescent interaction.

We also focus on several specific aspects of family life, because knowledge about their effects on the adolescent has accrued sufficiently to allow meaningful deductions about their impact on the adolescent. Specifically, we examine the impact of growing up in a single-parent family and the effects of maternal employment on the adolescent's development. Research on issues such as these provides insight into the importance of family structure for understanding adolescent development.

CHANGES IN THE FAMILY UNIT IN THE UNITED STATES

Changes in the structure of the family have occurred at an extremely rapid rate since the turn of the century. As a consequence, successive generations of adolescents have matured in circumstances often quite different from those of their parents' adolescence. Some of the important changes have been in the setting of the family and others have been in family composition.

Family Setting

Urban vs. Rural. In 1900, approximately two-thirds of the American population lived in rural areas. Today only about a fifth of the American population lives in rural areas (U.S. Bureau of the Census, 1989). The population shift has been mainly from the rural parts of the Midwest and the South to the large metropolitan areas on the Great Lakes and the East and West Coasts, and to the Southwest and the Sunbelt. Over the course of this century, then, increasing numbers of adolescents grew up in environments very different from those of their parents, both with regard to the general setting (such as smaller towns versus larger metropolitan areas) and with respect to the demands placed on the adolescent (such as adapting to larger schools).

Mobility. Other kinds of movement have taken place and changed the nature of the impact of the family on the adolescent. It is estimated that approximately 20 percent of the families in the United States changed residence each year during the past decade. Largely, this is a function of our corporate-oriented society. With such movement comes the need to hone adaptation skills. For the adolescent, the difficulties of frequent movement include the problems of making new friends, the inability to establish meaningful long-term friendships, adjustment to new schools, and the like. For older adolescents, movement may mean breaking long-established friendships, some of which may include very strong emotional ties.

Frequent movement also impacts on the nature of the family. Families develop less strong ties to the community in which they live (Campbell, 1969). These weakened ties to the community may contribute to adolescents' feeling alienated (e.g., Durkheim, 1951; Merton, 1961), and may contribute to the increase in delinquency and other adolescent behavioral problems. In addition, frequent moves and loosened community ties may produce changes in political and life philosophies as the family tries to adapt to new community and regional standards. The instability caused by these changes may affect the adolescent who is trying to sort through these issues in the process of forming an identity.

Family Composition

The composition of the American family has changed substantially since the turn of the century (see Box 10–1). The changes have been in terms of size of the family and family type.

Family Size. The size of the family in which adolescents are growing up has gotten smaller for more recent generations of adolescents. This has been the result of two major influences. First, we have become a nation of nuclear (parents and their offspring), as opposed to extended (families with other relatives in residence), families. Second, the size of the nuclear family is shrinking as parents are deciding to have fewer children.

Mead (1970) has discussed the importance of shrinking family size, particularly in the context of the change from extended to nuclear families, for understanding adolescent development. Instead of having strong ties to extended family members, such as grandparents, aunts, uncles, and cousins, today's adolescents tend to have significant family ties only to the parents. Therefore, the advantages of having intergenerational models for various adulthood roles are lost to the majority of today's adolescents. Mead (1970) argues that this situation has contributed to a lack of understanding between the generations because of lowered intergenerational contact. In an extended family, the adolescent has (1) daily models for adult social behaviors, manners, and roles, and (2) models for adult intergenerational interactions, for example, parents interacting with grandparents. These models may facilitate learning social skills and promoting intergenerational understanding. In today's modal family these advantages are lost.

Mead (1970) suggests that the change to a nuclear family has contributed to the development of what she terms a *cofigurative* culture, a culture in which the peers act as the basic model for the members. In a cofigurative culture, change is accepted as part

Increasingly, families have changed from extended to nuclear.

BOX 10–1 **Family Composition of the U.S.**

Adolescents grow up in family units that influence their development. The nature of these influences is detailed in the body of the chapter. It is therefore interesting to note the demographic characteristics of the family and changes in those characteristics over the last decade.

According to statistics provided by the U.S. Bureau of the Census (1989), there have been a number of changes in the nature of the family and its structure during the past decade. For example, the median age of first marriage has been increasing since 1980, when it was 21.8 for females and 23.6 for males. In 1985 it was 23 for females and nearly 25 for males. This increase translates into increased ages for child-bearing, which, in turn, means an increase in the age of parents when their offspring become adolescents. In addition, the divorce ratio, the number of divorced persons per 1,000 married persons living with their spouses, increased substantially during the 1980s. It was 79 for males and 120 for females in 1980; in 1987 it was 107 for males and 154 for females.

The increase in the divorce rate is directly related to the increase in the percentage of children involved in divorces, which has risen from 12.5 per 1,000 in 1970 to 17.3 per 1,000 in 1985. Finally, the percentage of children living in single-parent families increased dramatically since 1970. In 1970, 12 percent of children under the age of 18 lived with one parent; 3 percent lived with a divorced mother. In 1987, 24 percent of children under 18 lived with one parent; over 8 percent lived with a divorced mother. (Three percent of children under age 18 lived with neither parent. The remainder lived with their father, whether a result of divorce or death of their mother.) Putting it a different way, in 1987 only 73 percent of those under age 18 lived with both parents—the comparable figure for 1970 was about 85 percent.

The major determinant of living with a single parent is divorce. As noted in the text and above, the percentage of adolescents living with a divorced parent has increased sharply in the last two decades. This has raised a number of very important questions that researchers have been trying to answer. We know something of the importance of being a male or female when being raised in a single-parent family; and we know that older adolescents adjust better than do younger ones. But we do not know all the reasons why; that will take further research. We know little about what it means to be raised in a father-headed home (as a result of the father being given custody of his children). Given that we are likely to see further increases in the percentage of adolescents who spend time in a single-parent family these are very important questions.

Similarly, we need to know more about how experiencing a divorce affects adolescents' perceptions of their own likelihood of having successful relationships with those of the opposite sex, and how they perceive their own chances of having a happy marriage. These "long-term" effects of being an adolescent who has experienced the divorce of parents are virtually unresearched. Yet they may be the most important questions we can ask.

of the cultural heritage. The passing on of a consistent, unchanged set of cultural standards does not take place.

Family Type. At the turn of the century, and until relatively recently, the modal family involved only a single working parent, usually the father. As we elaborate below, today over 65 percent of women with children under 18 are in the work force. In other words, the modal family of today has two parents who work outside the home.

This change in family type has important implications for the growing child and adolescent. One of the more important is that it presents a generational change in family experiences of adolescents. Today's adolescents tend to mature in families with two working parents but their parents' adolescence was spent in a family with one working parent. In this sense, the parents of today's adolescents do not understand some of the stress associated with being a contemporary adolescent. This may be a contributor to parent-adolescent conflict. Adolescents today may be more capable of handling independence at an earlier age than their parents were, because they have more experience at doing so earlier.

Family type has changed in another important way, namely, the percentage of adolescents growing up in single-parent homes. As may be seen in Box 10–1, over a fifth of adolescents are currently living in single-parent homes. Current estimates are that approximately a third of adolescents will spend some portion of their adolescence in a single-parent home. These estimated figures are even higher for the economically disadvantaged and black adolescents. In fact, over 60 percent of black school-age children live in a single-parent home (U. S. Bureau of the Census, 1989). The comparable percentages are 21 for white and 35 for Hispanic school-aged children. Given that living in a single-parent home is highly likely to reduce economic resources (McLoyd, 1989a, 1989b), a large percentage of black youth are exposed to the consequences of poverty.

Another increasingly prevalent family type is that involving a stepparent. Of the adolescents experiencing the divorce of their parents, over half will experience the remarriage of one or both of their parents (Furstenberg, Petersen, Nord, & Zill, 1983), although this is *less* likely to occur to black youngsters. Living in a stepparent family may help alleviate poverty, but it also requires adjustment and changes in family interaction patterns, as we discuss below.

THE PARENTAL ROLE IN ADOLESCENT SOCIALIZATION

As noted above, the parents are the primary socialization influence on the adolescent. Certainly other members of the nuclear family, and extended family, influence the adolescent. However, because of the parents' long-standing association with the adolescent, their influence is greater than that of any other family member. In this section we explore models of parent-offspring interactions in order to highlight the ways in which the parents are influential models for, and shapers of, adolescent development.

Parental influences on adolescent socialization do not begin when the child is judged to be an adolescent. Rather, research demonstrates that parental child-rearing practices exert a continuous influence across the childhood and adolescent years. In fact, parents are extremely influential in determining the quality and duration of their child's adolescence because of their reactions toward their child and their perceptions of what an adolescent is and when adolescence begins.

The general thrust of research on parent effects on development has been two-pronged. One line of research has been focused on examinations of parental disciplinary techniques and their impact on personality and other aspects of development. A second line

Estimates are that about a third of adolescents today will spend some time in a single-parent family situation.

of research has focused on the offspring's perceptions of child-rearing techniques and the relation of these perceptions to aspects of development.

Parental Disciplinary Techniques

Research on the relationship between parental disciplinary techniques was spurred by Sigmund Freud (1924, 1950), who suggested that children who have extremely punishing parents may not identify with them and, in fact, may learn to hate them. A failure to identify with the parent, according to Freud, would result in poor socialization. Hence, it became important to study the degree to which various disciplinary techniques promoted or were antagonistic to the identification process.

The social-learning theorists (for example, Sears, Maccoby, & Levin, 1957; Sears, Rau, & Alpert, 1965; also see Chapter 2) also emphasize the importance of parental disciplinary techniques in social development. They note that parents not only shape the behaviors of their children directly, but also that children adopt values and behaviors similar to those of their parents through observational learning. Hence, the study of disciplinary techniques used by parents to train children becomes important to understanding children's and adolescents' behavior.

Before we discuss the varieties of disciplinary techniques parents employ, we must point out that the issue of causation in the relation of parent-child interactions is a complicated one. Historically, the study of relationships between child-rearing techniques and offspring behavior has been interpreted in a parent-causation framework (Crouter & McHale, 1989; Maccoby & Martin, 1983). In other words, it has been assumed that parental child-rearing techniques *cause* child behavior. This approach has proven to be too simplistic. More recent perspectives conceptualize child rearing as occurring in an entire family system. In this family-process-oriented approach,

child-rearing techniques are considered to be just one factor among many (e.g., number of working parents, number of parents in the home, the effects of siblings) that influence the adolescent's development *in an interacting fashion*. The focus is on how these multiple influences interrelate to affect the adolescent's development. By considering the process of family interaction it is also possible to examine the influence of the adolescent on the parent, which can help explain the parent's behavior.

Types of Discipline and Parenting. Hoffman (1970; see also Maccoby & Martin, 1983) has noted that there are at least three types of discipline techniques that are frequently used by parents. **Power assertion** is exemplified by the use of physical punishment, the deprivation of privileges or possessions, or the threat of any of these. By capitalizing on the relative weakness of the child, the parent is able to control the child's behavior. It is well documented that children will do things to avoid punishment and gain rewards (for example, Martin, 1975). Although we tend to associate the use of this type of discipline with younger children, the threat to withdraw privileges from the adolescent, for example, use of the car, is a form of power-assertive discipline. Ironically, the use of this type of discipline may teach the adolescent that the use of power and physical abuse is a way in which to control the world. As a result, the parent may rear a child or adolescent who will use this form of discipline in future child rearing as well as within everyday life contexts.

Non-power-assertive disciplinary techniques make up the second major class of punishments parents use. M. Hoffman has identified two that are frequently used. **Love withdrawal** refers to the expression of parental anger or disapproval by means of nonphysical displays of dissatisfaction and punishment. Ignoring the child, isolating the child from friends or siblings, and verbally expressing dislike or disappointment are examples of this form of punishment. Because these techniques involve implicit threats of abandonment and explicit expressions of disapproval, which may undermine the child's feelings of self-worth, they may in fact be more punitive than physical abuse. By producing guilt in the child, these forms of punishment may be very effective in controlling behavior. Of course, from the parental point of view, this is an ideal situation because it should teach children to monitor their own behavior. In addition, this form of punishment may be relatively long-term: the guilt that is built up may be much more long-lasting than the memory of physical punishment.

The other non-power-assertive technique identified by M. Hoffman is **induction**. The parent who uses induction techniques provides the child with a reason for not behaving in some particular way; for example, he or she explains the dangerous consequences of touching a hot stove, playing with matches, or becoming a drug user. In addition, the parent presents acceptable alternative means of behaving. Induction techniques, then, attempt to convince children to alter their behavior by appealing to their ability to understand that certain situations require specific forms of behavior. Neither physical nor emotional punishment is involved in induction techniques. Rather, induction represents a form of direct training of desired behavior within the context of what would normally be considered a punishment situation.

In general, of course, parents use a variety of disciplinary techniques in their rearing of children and adolescents. Few parents use exclusively one or another of the types of discipline. This makes the study of the importance of disciplinary effects difficult. To help alleviate this difficulty, researchers have attempted to identify parent types, that is, various groups of parents who may be characterized as being homogeneous in their child-rearing practices. By identifying various types of parents, it is possible to ex-

amine combinations of rearing practices related to development.

Becker (1964; see also Martin, 1975, and Schaefer, 1959) has summarized attempts to identify parent types and has determined that alternative patterns of child rearing may be identified by examining combinations of rearing techniques that vary on three dimensions. The three dimensions are: *restrictive versus permissive, anxious emotional involvement versus calm detachment*, and *warmth versus hostility*. The end point of each dimension is described by a constellation of parental behaviors. For example, the warmth pole of the *warmth versus hostility* dimension is characterized by acceptance, positive response to dependency bids, infrequent use of physical punishment, frequent use of praise, and approving behaviors. The hostility end of the dimension is defined by the opposite constellation of behaviors. As another example, the restrictive pole of the *restrictive versus permissive* dimension is defined by demands (and enforcement of demands) for modesty, table manners, quiet behavior, obedience; the permissive pole is defined by the opposite set of descriptors. Similarly, *anxious emotional involvement* refers to behaviors such as babying and overprotectiveness.

Becker (1964) identified different parent types by examining the combination of behaviors relative to the three dimensions. For example, democratic and indulgent parents are characterized as high on the dimensions of warmth and permissiveness; the only essential difference between them is that the indulgent parent is high in emotional involvement while the democratic parent is low on this dimension. Such a classification scheme, then, allows one to identify parents with different kinds of characteristics and then examine the effects of these differing characteristics on the personality development of children and adolescents (Elder, 1962, 1963).

A more simplified means of characterizing parent types has been suggested by others (e.g., Maccoby & Martin, 1983). It is focused on just two dimensions of child rearing: **parental responsiveness** and **parental demandingness**. Parental responsiveness is similar to Becker's warmth/hostility dimension in that it refers to the degree to which the parent interacts with the adolescent in a warm, supportive, and accepting manner. Parental demandingness refers to the extent to which parents expect and demand mature and responsible behavior; it is related to Becker's restrictive/permissive dimension. Maccoby and Martin note that four parent types can be identified by looking at the combinations of high and low for each dimension. These four parent types are: Authoritative, Authoritarian, Indulgent, and Indifferent (see Table 10–1). Parents who are high on each dimension, that is, those who not only respond warmly but demand mature and appropriate behavior, are labeled *authoritative*. Those who are low on each dimension, that is, those who respond in a cold or more cool manner and who make few demands for mature and appropriate behavior, are labeled *indifferent*. The other combinations are shown in Table 10–1.

Authoritative parents are high in both warmth and demandingness. Although they expect their children and adolescents to behave in a mature and responsible manner, their expectations are consistent with the child's maturity level. They teach autonomy and self-directedness, but they do not abdicate their responsibility for their offspring. They tend to use high levels of inductive discipline and to talk matters over with their offspring.

Indifferent parents behave toward their offspring in a manner consistent with the label. They spend little time with their children, and they deal with them in a manner designed to minimize the time they must interact with them. They use no particular view of what might be best for the child when rearing children and have a strong adult orientation—they arrange their lives for their own benefit and not for that of their children. As a result, they have little knowledge of their children's interests, friends, and the like. They tend to use little induction discipline, relying instead on power-assertive techniques.

Authoritarian parents tend to use power-assertive discipline techniques to force conformity and obeyance from their children. They tend to believe that children should obey parents simply because they are parents, and therefore are "right" in what they say and demand. They tend to be somewhat intrusive in their children's lives and restrict their autonomy.

Indulgent parents, while accepting, warm, and supportive, place few demands on their children because they view such demands as intrusive in the child's life. Indulgent parents view themselves as a "secure base" from which the child may explore the world. As a result, the children have a high degree of freedom—perhaps too much—to act as they choose.

A number of researchers have studied the effects of these various parent types on the child's and adolescent's development (see Baumrind, 1978; Elder, 1962, 1963; Maccoby & Martin, 1983). The most extensive investigation was conducted by Elder; it involved 7,350 adolescents in grades 7 through 12. Although Elder's classification system for parents was more elaborate than our four-group system, some of his groups overlap those discussed above. Hence, we can draw some generalizations from them.

First, fathers were rated as more authoritarian than were mothers (35 percent vs. 22 percent), who were rated as more indulgent (24 percent vs. 17 percent for fathers). In addition, parents in large families were rated

TABLE 10–1   **Types of Parental Disciplinary/ Rearing Techniques**

Parent Type	Demandingness	Responsiveness
Authoritative	High	High
Authoritarian	High	Low
Indulgent	Low	High
Indifferent	Low	Low

as more authoritarian than were parents in smaller families.

Second, Elder (1962) investigated how these adolescents reacted to these differing parenting styles by asking the adolescents if they thought their parents' ideals, rules, and principles about behavior were fair and reasonable or not. The authoritative parents were rated as being more fair than were parents in the other groups. This finding suggests that parents can be controlling as long as they are warm and listen to the adolescent's point of view. They are viewed as unfair if they don't allow the adolescent to express an opinion or engage in verbal interchange. Apparently, as in other family interactions, communication is a critical factor.

Finally, the adolescents were asked if their parents made them feel unwanted. Adolescents whose parents could be characterized as authoritative or indulgent were much less likely to indicate they felt unwanted than adolescents whose parents were of the other types. It appears that the acceptance, support, and warmth shown by these parents communicate to their adolescents that they are wanted and valuable in their parents' eyes. As we shall see, the dimension of parental warmth and acceptance may be the most important in terms of rearing relatively happy, self-confident, and identity-achieved adolescents.

Other research (see Maccoby & Martin, 1983) demonstrates the virtues of authoritative parenting over the other three types. Adolescents reared in authoritative home environments tend to have better self-concepts, to be more intellectually curious, and more socially skilled. They tend to be more active, vibrant, and creative individuals. In contrast, adolescents from authoritarian parenting backgrounds are more passive and less prone to try new things. They lack self-assurance and are more dependent. Parental indulgence often leads to irresponsible behavior and to social immaturity. Finally, delinquency is linked to indifference, as is drug and alcohol use. Although

there are exceptions to these sweeping generalizations, the evidence is convincing that authoritative parenting styles generally lead to better psychosocial adjustment.

There are a number of reasons why authoritative parenting seems to promote psychosocial development. First, authoritative parents engage in substantial amounts of inductive discipline. This entails a give-and-take that promotes reasoning about right and wrong, empathy, and identification with the parent. Also, it is done in the context of a warm, affectionate relationship. The adolescent learns that mistakes are tolerable and feels freer to try new things and to explore competencies. These discussions also teach the adolescent about the consequences of behavior and the interrelatedness of one's actions to others.

Authoritative parents also place limits, but they are appropriate to the adolescent's competencies. Moreover, authoritative parents are flexible, allowing rules to bend and change as situations dictate and as the adolescent matures. An example comes from the realm of independence and autonomy. Authoritative parents are more likely to grant increasing autonomy as the adolescent becomes capable of handling more independence.

To understand more fully the effects of these parent types, it is instructive to examine specific child-rearing behaviors and relate them to aspects of adolescent psychosocial development. Parents who express unconditional love for their adolescent help their offspring develop constructive and appropriate relationships with others, a sense of confidence in their own identity, and a relatively positive self-esteem (Coopersmith, 1967; Elder, 1963, 1968). Academic and intellectual difficulties, poor social relationships with peers and adults, psychosomatic disorders, and delinquency are related to parental hostility and rejection (Weiner, 1970; Kagan & Moss, 1962; Sears et al., 1957; Becker, 1964). As you might expect, parental restrictiveness produces offspring who are inhibited in terms of curiosity, creativity, and flexibility in solving intellectual, academic, and practical problems (Kagan & Moss, 1962; Becker, 1964; Sears et al., 1957, 1965). Warm but restrictive home atmospheres are related to children who are polite, neat, dependent, and conforming, and who are less aggressive and competitive with their peers. In contrast, when parents express warmth but also permit a high degree of age-appropriate autonomy, the child tends to be socially assertive, independent, more aggressive, and less conforming (Becker, 1964; Elder, 1968; Kagan & Moss, 1962; M. Hoffman, 1970), as noted earlier.

The most widely studied aspect of child-rearing influences during the adolescent years has been focused on the precursors of aggression and delinquency (Martin, 1975). It is quite clear that the use of power-assertive disciplinary techniques is a correlate of aggression and delinquency (Glueck & Glueck, 1950; Hetherington, Stouwie, & Ridberg, 1971). It appears that the modeling effects of aggressive disciplinary techniques outweigh the suppressive effects on the adolescent's aggressive behavior. The parent provides a model of control based on aggression and the adolescent learns to behave in a similar manner.

The acceptance-rejection and permissiveness-restrictiveness dimensions of child rearing also are related to aggressive and delinquent behavior on the part of adolescents. Parental rejection may frustrate the child's nurturance needs and feelings of being wanted. In turn, the child may lash out aggressively. This seems especially to be the case when both parents are rejecting (McCord, McCord, & Zola, 1959). Lack of discipline and inconsistent discipline are also positively correlated with delinquency (see McCord et al., 1959). The failure to provide consistent discipline and supervision apparently fails to teach the child appropriate social behaviors and sometimes allows aggressive or inappropriate behavior to be done with no negative consequences.

Perceptions of Child Rearing

In the research reviewed in this section, children's perceptions of their parents' child-rearing techniques are assessed and related to aspects of child development. Schaefer (1965a, 1965b) has outlined the philosophy underlying this approach. In general, the notion is that the study of child-rearing effects on the development of the child or adolescent should focus on the child's perspective of the parents' disciplinary techniques. It is the child's interpretation (perception) of the parents' behavior that is important for the child, not the objective behavior or the parents' view of the behavior.

In order to measure children's perceptions of parental child-rearing techniques, Schaefer (1965a, 1965b) developed the Children's Report of Parental Behavior Inventory (**CRPBI**). The CRPBI is a questionnaire designed to tap aspects of child rearing. After reading a brief statement or question, the respondent indicates whether it is like, somewhat like, or not like the parent. The questionnaire is completed once for the mother and again for the father. In this way it is possible to relate the child's perceptions of both the mother's and the father's child-rearing patterns to the child's behavior.

The CRPBI measures three dimensions (see Table 10–2 for example items) of child rearing. The first dimension is labeled **Acceptance versus Rejection** and reflects the degree to which the parents' attitude toward the child is one of acceptance and warmth or rejection and hostility. It is similar to the parental responsiveness dimension. The second dimension is called **Psychological Autonomy versus Psychological Control**. Scores on this dimension reflect the degree to which respondents feel their parents use psychological methods, for example, guilt, hostility, and intrusiveness, to control their behavior. Schaefer (1965a) argues that such methods of control do not permit the child to develop autonomously, as an individual apart from the parent. The third dimension

TABLE 10–2 **Example Items from the CRPBI**

Acceptance versus Rejection	Psychological Autonomy versus Psychological Control	Firm Control versus Lax Control
Enjoys talking things over with me	Feels hurt when I don't follow advice	Is easy with me
Is able to make me feel better when I am upset	Feels hurt by the things I do	Usually doesn't find out about my misbehavior
Makes me feel like the most important person in his (her) life	Tells me of all the things he (she) has done for me	Excuses my bad conduct
Comforts me when I'm afraid	Will talk to me again and again about anything bad I do	Can be talked into things easily

is labeled **Firm Control versus Lax Control** and reflects the degree to which the parent limits the child's activities by making rules and regulations and rigidly enforcing them. It is similar to the parental demandingness dimension.

At the present time, relatively little research relating adolescent perceptions of child rearing as measured with the CRPBI to other aspects of adolescent development has been conducted. Litovsky (Litovsky & Dusek, 1985) had seventh, eighth, and ninth graders complete the CRPBI and Coopersmith's (1967) Self-Esteem Inventory, a measure of self-concept. The only developmental trend in the analyses of the CRPBI scores was for the Acceptance versus Rejection dimension. The seventh and eighth graders viewed both their mothers and their fathers as more accepting than did the ninth graders. Litovsky suggested that, by ninth grade, the parents might feel compelled to restrict the adolescent's behavior more, or might be perceived to do so, because of increases in adolescent independence strivings. The analyses relating perceptions of child rearing to self-concept were interesting and enlightening. More positive self-concepts were associated with higher acceptance and lower use of psychological control by both mother and father, and with lower firm control by father. Scores on the Firm Control-Lax Control dimension for mother were not related to self-concept, perhaps because fathers are viewed as making more rules and being more rigid in enforcing them than are mothers. Providing a warm and accepting home atmosphere, which makes the adolescent feel wanted, fosters a healthy self-concept and feelings of self-worth.

Ziegler (Ziegler & Dusek, 1985) had adolescents in grades 6, 8, 10, and 12 complete the CRPBI and the Bem Sex Role Inventory (1974), which measures the degree to which the respondent views the self as masculine and feminine. As in the Litosky (Litovsky & Dusek, 1985) study, the younger adolescents (grades 6 and 8) viewed both the mother and the father as more accepting than did the older adolescents (grades 10 and 12). Adolescents (male or female) who viewed themselves as Feminine (possessing feminine traits to a high degree and masculine traits to a low degree) or as Androgynous (possessing both masculine and feminine traits to a high degree) viewed their mothers and their fathers as more accepting than did adolescents in the other sex-role classifications. The other dimensions of perceptions of parenting behavior were not related to sex roles.

In a study of adolescent females' identity development, Adams and Jones (1983) had their participants complete a brief measure of perceptions of child rearing and a measure assessing identity development. They reported that higher identity status, namely, achieved or moratorium (in an identity crisis), was associated with perceptions of the mother not being controlling or regulating and as encouraging free and independent behavior. These girls also perceived their fathers as fair in discipline. These perceived child-rearing techniques apparently encourage autonomy and enhance the identity process, perhaps because they allow the adolescent sufficient security to explore and discover the self. Mothers who were perceived as controlling and regulating their daughter's behavior had adolescents whose identities were diffuse. These girls also saw their fathers as unfair in disciplinary actions.

Interestingly, girls in the foreclosure identity status (those who made a commitment to an identity based on the wishes of others and not their own sorting through of the issues) perceived their mothers as warm and supportive but as not allowing much independence. They saw their fathers as fair in discipline and as highly praising. Adams and Jones suggest the foreclosed identity status was a result of parenting styles that do not grant sufficient freedom and autonomy.

Finally, Litovsky and Dusek (1988) examined the role of perceptions of child rearing on adolescent adjustment by looking at combinations of parents who differed in the degree to which they were perceived as high or low on each of the dimensions of the CRPBI. For each CRPBI dimension four parent combinations were identified: both high, both low, mother high/father low, father high/mother low. For example, for the Acceptance/Rejection dimension four groups of adolescents were identified: those who perceived both their parents as highly accepting and warm; those who perceived both parents as not very warm and accepting; those who perceived mother as warm and father as not very warm; and those who perceived father as warm and accepting but perceived mother as less so. The advantage of this approach is that it takes into account the fact that there are two parents in the home and they may use different disciplinary techniques, or at least be perceived to do so by the adolescent. Hence, it is possible to determine if one parent (for example, mother) exerts a greater influence than the other on adjustment, or if various

combinations result in different levels of adjustment.

The results indicated that adolescents who perceived both parents as highly accepting, warm, and supportive were better adjusted than were adolescents in the other three groups. In addition, perceiving the mother high on this dimension compensated for perceiving the father low, but the reverse was not the case—perceiving father as accepting did not compensate for perceiving mother as more cool and aloof. Similar findings were found for the Psychological Autonomy vs. Psychological Control dimension. In this case, perceiving both parents as using less psychological control (guilt, intrusiveness) resulted in better adjustment, with no compensation by either parent being evident. There were no effects for the Firm Control vs. Lax Control dimension.

One conclusion from this study is that adolescent adjustment is best when both parents are accepting and warm and perceived as not using guilt and other psychological means of controlling the adolescent. The findings are similar to those reviewed above for authoritative parents and to those reported by Adams and Jones (1983). Adolescents who perceive their parents as warm and nonintrusive may well be better able to develop high self-esteem, autonomy, independence, and the like, as we noted above. They will not be afraid to try new experiences to test their limits, knowing that if they are less than successful or if they get into trouble they will nonetheless be dealt with fairly and accepted by their parents.

Second, it appears that some compensatory effects exist, at least with regard to perceiving mother as supportive and accepting. This finding is quite in line with traditional sex-role stereotypes and shows the importance of maternal acceptance for adolescent adjustment.

The results of these studies point to the importance of perceptions of child-rearing for the adolescent's development. More specifically, the importance of feeling accepted and wanted seems to be an important aspect of adolescent development. Feeling accepted fosters a sense of self-worth and aids the development of a more flexible self-concept. It is also clear that feeling a degree of independence is necessary for optimal development.

Parent Personality and Adolescent Adjustment

One of the more recent trends in the study of parental influences on adolescent development has been to focus on the effects of the parents' personality. This research is guided by the family systems approach discussed above. As such, the intent is to examine parental and adolescent characteristics in combination as they influence adolescent development.

One line of research has been aimed at investigating the role of parents on adolescent drug use (Brook, Whiteman, & Gordon, 1983; Brook, Whiteman, Gordon, & Brook, 1984; Brook, Whiteman, Gordon, & Cohen, 1986). Brook and her colleagues have examined the role in adolescent drug use of the adolescent's personality, the parents' personality, and parental child-rearing techniques. In general, it appears that the adolescent's personality is the more important factor in drug use. Adolescents who have a high tolerance of deviancy, are rebellious, lack responsibility, and who have low expectations for academic achievement are prone to use drugs. These traits seem to result from parental child-rearing techniques and personality.

More specifically, adolescents reared by parents who are not child-centered (the indifferent parents noted above) and who have difficulty granting autonomy are more prone to becoming drug users. Distant and cold relationships with the father also contribute to drug use, as does having overly permissive parents. Having appropriately restrictive parents, and having a father who is warm and accepting, seems to insulate ad-

olescents from drug use. Finally, having parents who are drug users and having one or both parents being highly tolerant of drug use contributes to adolescent drug use.

More recent research has focused on maternal personality, more specifically, maternal depression (Dodge, 1990a, 1990b; Hops, Sherman, & Biglan, in press). The effects of growing up in a home with a depressed mother have recently been studied extensively. As is noted in Box 10–2, mother's personality, in this case a depressed personality, can have deleterious effects on the adolescent. However, as also noted, the father may dilute these effects if he is highly warm and accepting.

What this research shows is that there is a complex interplay between the characteristics of the parents, including personality and child-rearing techniques, and the adolescent that must be considered when trying to understand aspects of adolescent behavior. An important component is the general predisposition, that is, personality, of the parents.

FAMILY COMPOSITION AND ADOLESCENT SOCIALIZATION

Although examination of child-rearing patterns helps us gain some understanding of parental and family influences on adolescent development, such research examines only part of the picture because the focus is on only the parents. Other family factors no doubt impact on the adolescent and influence development. In this section, we examine two such factors, namely, living in a single-parent home and living in a home with two working parents. As was shown in Box 10–1, a substantial percentage of adolescents live in single-parent homes, typically with the mother. We explore below the impact of death and divorce, the primary causes of living in a single-parent home, on development during the adolescent years.

The second family composition factor of importance is maternal employment. The

BOX 10–2   Effects of Maternal Depression on the Adolescent: Example of the Family Systems Approach to Development

Historically, psychologists and others who have studied the effects of family members and family structure on the adolescent's development have focused on aspects such as child-rearing techniques, economic conditions, the effects of divorce, maternal employment, and the like. Research into these factors has provided considerable insight into the conditions that influence development of both the child and the adolescent.

As this research has progressed, investigators have developed increasingly more sophisticated questions and means of answering them. This has been especially clear in the study of the effects of divorce. As you will discover later in this text, the initial examinations of divorce simply focused on father absence as the critical feature. Researchers then proceeded to examine family structure (single parent, remarried parent, intact family) and viewed it is the determinant of the effects of divorce. Today, the focus is on the nature of family interactions and how they are similar and different in various family types. Again, as you will soon discover, it is this that is critical, not the family structure, in understanding the effects of divorce on the adolescent.

Recently, researchers have focused on parental temperament as a potentially important factor influencing the adolescent's temperament and family interactions. More specifically, concern has focused on the effects of growing up in a family with a depressed mother. Hops, Sherman, and Biglan (in press) have summarized the findings of this research. In comparison to children of nondepressed mothers, the children of depressed mothers are more irritable, depressed themselves, prone to suicide, and at increased risk for emotional problems and school difficulties. In addition, depressed mothers report more behavior problems in their children, as do the teachers of these children (Richters & Pellegrini, 1989). These negative influences of having a depressed mother are increased if there is marital discord in the home environment. Adolescent females are especially prone to show increases in depressive symptoms, and adolescent males increase in aggressive behavior, the difference perhaps being the result of sex typing of these behaviors.

Although an entire understanding of the causes of these effects of having a depressed mother is not possible at present, some suggestive evidence is available (Hops et al., in press). Depressed mothers may lack sound parenting skills that lead them to be less capable of looking out for the welfare of their children (Dodge, 1990a). They tend to use physical punishment and have deficits in responding to their children with affection. As noted in the text, these modes of responding have substantial negative effects on the adolescents' self-feelings and behavior.

The deleterious influence of the mother is attenuated if the husbands of depressed wives engage in higher rates of nurturant and caring behavior toward their children. It seems that having a good relationship with one parent can act to offset the harmful effects of the other parent to some degree.

Research such as this comes from a family systems model of development (Hops et al., in press). From this perspective, development is influenced not only by individuals but also by the family atmosphere (e.g., marital discord) and the interactions among all members of the family. The general perspective, for example, is that it is not simply the fact that the mother is depressed that causes aberrant development in adolescents. Rather, it is the nature of her parenting skills and social interactions that shape family patterns of behavior that is causal factor (Dodge, 1990a, 1990b). Research discovering these more fundamental causal paths leads not only to greater understanding but also to the possibility of remedial treatment.

modal family in the United States now involves a working mother. We shall also examine the impact of maternal employment on adolescent development.

Divorce and Living in a Single-Parent Family

As the information in Box 10–1 indicated, there has been a steady increase during the last two decades in the number of children affected by the divorce of their parents. At present, over 1 million children are affected annually. It is estimated that during the 1990s about a third of all American children under the age of 18 will have lived some amount of time with a divorced parent (Glick, 1979).

With the increase since 1960 in the number of children involved in divorce has come increased research on the effects of divorce on the child's and adolescent's development. Early research had a number of conceptual and methodological flaws that severely limited its utility for our understanding of the impact of divorce on the child's development (Hetherington, 1979). For example, early researchers focused on the negative influence of father absence without regard for the reason (death, divorce, military service, etc.) or permanency of the absence. In addition, the tendency was to attribute aberrant development directly to father absence—a single variable, unidirectional causal approach. Of course, absence of the father is only one of many variables that impact on the adolescent in single-parent families. Finally, there was a general tendency to treat all father-absent families as homogeneous, regardless of other differences, such as social class, the reason for the absence, or the child's relationship to both parents and the parents' relationship to each other.

In addition, the majority of the studies were not longitudinal in nature. The study of children or adolescents only once, usually relatively soon after the divorce, precluded studying how they adapted as time passed. Finally, early researchers often failed to study or even consider the relationship between the divorced father and the child, a relationship we now know is very important (Box 10–3).

Fortunately, as is usually the case, as more researchers became interested in the impact of divorce, methodological sophistication increased. We now have longitudinal research findings, studies in which control groups of children in intact families are included, and research on the importance of the father after divorce. As a result, some myths about the influence of divorce on the development of children and adolescents have been dispelled. In addition, current studies are multivariable in approach, recognizing that growing up in a father-absent family is a complex situation. Because the vast majority of high-quality extant research is with children, we review that material along with findings for adolescents.

Stress and Divorce. In considering divorce, we often view it as a unitary event, something that occurs relatively quickly and then is over. And, we tend to associate the stress of divorce with the short time period involved when separation happens. Of course, this is not a veridical picture.

Current conceptualizations view divorce as a course of events, each with various stresses. Hetherington (1979, 1989) points out that one must consider divorce as involving a sequence of events, each component with its own stresses, to which children—and adults—must adapt. There is the family situation prior to divorce, which often exposes the child to conflicting loyalties, hostilities between the parents, and, perhaps, doubts about their feelings toward one or both parents. In general, the home atmosphere tends to be conflict-ridden, which does not promote the child's development and may even retard it (Wallerstein, 1983). The preponderance of the evidence indicates that children's development may be better when living with one parent in a relatively harmonious home atmosphere, as opposed to living with two parents in a home characterized by fighting, hostility, bitterness, and all of the negative emotions associated with two adults who live together but are unhappy doing so. Children from single-parent homes have fewer psychosomatic illnesses, lower delinquency rates, and better

BOX 10–3 Joint versus Sole Custody

Historically, in the event of a divorce the courts awarded custody of children to the mother. Although fathers were granted visitation rights, the children were seen as living with their mothers. Mothers had primary (and majority) physical as well as legal custody of the children. In other words, the children not only physically resided with the mother but she had primary responsibility for making decisions about their schooling, health, and general welfare.

More recently, the concept of joint custody has gained in popularity. In joint *legal* custody both parents share the responsibility of decisions concerning the child's well-being. In joint *physical* custody the concept is that the child will live with each parent for substantial amounts of time. The latter is at times referred to as *co-parenting*. Indeed, in some areas of California this physical arrangement is decreed in nearly 20 percent of divorce settlements (Kline, Tschann, Johnston, & Wallerstein, 1989).

The concept of joint custody raises a number of issues both pro and con. Advocates point out that this arrangement increases contact with the "other" parent, which, as noted in the text, is important to children's and adolescent's adjustment to divorce. Those opposed note that co-parenting entails some amount of moving, the possible uprooting of friendships, and confusion about having a "psychological parent," that is, a parent and caretaker to whom the child has constant access. In addition, opponents argue that joint physical custody may cause the child to be continually involved in parental conflict, which may be detrimental to the child's development.

The most thoughtfully conducted study to examine the impact of joint custody on the child's social, behavioral, and emotional adjustment was conducted by Kline et al. (1989). They examined the social, behavioral, and emotional adjustment of children and adolescents aged 3 to 14 at the time of their parents' divorce some two years after the divorce. Some lived in sole-custody homes; others were involved in joint-custody arrangements. The researchers assessed the child's social and emotional growth, amount of contact with each parent, and number of times the child switched between care-taking parents each week. In addition, they had several measures of parental conflict and adjustment.

The findings were enlightening and informative. Type of custody did not relate to measures of psychological or social/emotional adjustment. In other words, those in sole vs. joint custody did not differ in their psychological growth. What was important—aside from age and sex of the child, as is elaborated in the text—was parental anxiety, which likely led to lowered parenting skills, and intraparental hostility and aggression. Parents who did not get along, who placed their children in the middle of their disagreements, who were aggressive toward each other, and who provided a home atmosphere of turmoil with regard to the other parent had children who were less well adjusted. The type of custody, the number of times the child "moved" and lived with one parent and then the other, and the like, were unrelated to how well the child coped with parental divorce.

Other researchers (Glover & Steele, 1988/89; Peck, 1988/89; Schnayer & Orr, 1988/89) have reported similar findings for self-esteem, social competence, and behavior problems. In addition, joint custody may facilitate adjustment to divorce and increase positive feelings toward both mother and father. On the negative side, it may produce feelings of conflict over loyalty toward parents (Peck, 1988/89). It now appears, however, that joint custody is at least as beneficial as single custody and that the mother is not necessarily the parent who should have custody.

Should these findings be replicated in further research they would have considerable impact on the other findings concerning contact with the noncustodial parent (see text). The important factor may not be time with the noncustodial parent, but rather the quality of relationship between the custodial and noncustodial parent that is important to how the child adapts to parental divorce.

emotional adjustment than do children from intact but unhappy homes.

Current research (Feldman, Wentzel, Weinberger, & Munson, 1989; Rossman & Rosenberg, 1989; Sarigiani, 1989) demonstrates that the quality of the marital relationship is generally more important than family structure in determining adolescent adjustment, and this is important both before and after parental separation (Hetherington, 1989). Those adolescents in less conflict-ridden homes show fewer behavioral, social, and cognitive problems in general and in coping with divorce.

A second period of stress is evidenced in the disorganization associated with the separation and divorce and the subsequent period of adjustment and coping experienced by the family members. Stress associated with loss of a parent, change in family structure, and uncertainty about the future tends to be greatest during the first year or so following separation and divorce.

The change in the structure of the family has a number of consequences: living in a female-headed household, which may be more stressful than a dual-parent household (McLanahan, 1983); developing changing relationships to both parents; perhaps mother going to work for the first time, and all that entails (more responsibility, more time without parent supervision); and, finally, a changed economic situation.

This latter circumstance is especially critical. In general, lower social status, which is related to lower income, is associated with poorer psychological adjustment (Lempers, Clark-Lempers, & Simons, 1989) for both male and female adolescents (Flanagan, 1989). The median family income of female-headed divorced families is only about 50 percent that of two-parent, married families (U.S. Bureau of the Census, 1989). As a result, approximately four times as many divorced families as intact families are below the poverty level and are subject to the harmful effects of poverty and the stresses associated with it. The numbers are even larger for black adolescents (McLoyd, 1989a, 1989b), who are not as well off as white adolescents to begin with.

Finally, within five years after the divorce, most children must adjust to living in a reconstituted family (Hetherington, 1979).

Some research indicates that homes involving a stepparent may have more stress and lower cohesiveness than original homes, especially if the stepparent is a stepmother. Glueck and Glueck (1962) reported higher delinquency rates in stepmother than stepfather families. Added stress comes from readjustments to the family routine, which may have been established only recently, the (at times) addition of stepsiblings, and the disciplinary techniques of the stepparent. We explore adapting to stepparents in detail below.

As you may surmise, the currently prevailing view of adapting to divorce is one of continually having to cope with the stress of a sequence of changes. Wallerstein (1983) has noted that the need to cope with these added stressors significantly adds to the normal crises faced when growing up. She has identified six tasks in this coping process that highlight the issues faced by the child from the time of the parents' separation to the child reaching adulthood. These are listed in Table 10–3. Wallerstein notes that the first two tasks are of immediate concern because of their relationship to continued healthy development. Resolving them within a year is optimal, then, for it will allow the child to continue to grow personally, cognitively, and socially. The next three tasks may take many years to resolve, depending on the age of the child. The last task, which is confronted during the adolescent years, deserves some elaboration.

Successful resolution of the sixth task, Achieving Realistic Hope Regarding Relationships, entails developing a sense that one has the capacity to love others and to be loved by them. In order to resolve this task, the adolescent must integrate the coping efforts directed at the earlier tasks. How the adolescent faces these issues will have important consequences for his or her view of marriage, heterosexual relations, and the like. It also will impact on the adolescent's resolution of the identity and intimacy crises discussed by Erikson. Indeed, the added

TABLE 10–3   **Psychological Tasks in Adapting to Parental Divorce**

1. *Acknowledging the reality of the marital rupture.* The child must come to grips with fears and fantasies about how difficult things will be and must learn that the parents will not live together again. This is especially difficult for young children.
2. *Disengaging from parental conflict and distress and resuming customary pursuits.* Children must learn to distance themselves from the parental difficulties, often with little help from the parents, and go about living a normal life conducive to healthy growth. Child also must not let the parental separation be completely consuming. As children get older this task does not get easier.
3. *Resolution of loss.* The child, who at this point may feel "unlovable," must come to grips with feelings of rejection and worthlessness. This may be especially difficult to do if mother is the one who leaves the house. This task is the most difficult and may take many years to resolve.
4. *Resolving anger and self-blame.* The child must overcome anger over the parents' decision to separate rather than stay together as the child wishes. The younger child especially must come to realize that he or she was not responsible for the divorce.
5. *Accepting the permanence of the divorce.* Children must overcome fantasies and hopes about parental reconciliation. This may be more difficult for younger children because of their lack of mature understanding of the nature and meaning of divorce.
6. *Achieving realistic hope regarding relationships.* This is primarily a task of the adolescent years. The adolescent must learn to trust others in intimate relationships and to develop the capacity to love, and be loved by, others.

(Source: Wallerstein, J. S. [1983]. Children of divorce: The psychological tasks of the child. *American Journal of Orthopsychiatry, 53*, 230–243. Reprinted by permission of American Orthopsychiatric Association.)

stress of having to deal with this final task, along with the psychosocial crises of adolescence, may make resolution of the intimacy crisis especially difficult.

To resolve the sixth task optimally, the individual must have resolved the other tasks in a relatively optimal manner as well. Although little research evidence is available, it does appear that, by the time of young adulthood, males from divorced families are as able to form strong, intimate re-

lations with girlfriends as are males from intact families (Guttman, 1988/89). They do not break up or reconcile any more frequently than do males from intact families.

Coping with divorce, then, is a developmental process involving the resolution of a series of tasks of a social and personal nature. It requires adjustment, and readjustment, over an extended period of time, and it often must be done with relatively little help from the parents, who are going through their own period of adjusting to new relations with each other, their children, and their general lives. Hence, successful adaptation will depend on the age of the child, the nature of the parent-child interactions, and the coping skills and supports the child can muster.

To research and discuss the impact of divorce on the child, then, is a complicated matter. Depending on where in the sequence of events one enters the situation, one may find very differing results. Thus, it is important to conduct longitudinal studies so as to map the course of adjustment to divorce and to gain a fuller picture of the impact of divorce and its many facets on the child and adolescent.

Reactions to Divorce. Hetherington and her colleagues (Hetherington, 1989; Hetherington, Cox, & Cox, 1976, 1979a, 1979b, 1979c) studied the adjustment of preschool children during the first two years following the divorce of the children's parents. Measures included interviews with parents, observation of the child in peer relations in nursery school, personality tests, and self-report ratings by parents. In addition to the 48 families in the divorcing sample, a control group of 48 families, matched on a number of variables to the divorcing sample, also was tested. Although the study was not concerned with the effects of divorce on adolescents, we report some of the findings because they describe aspects of the course of divorce in general.

One of the major findings of the study

was that the disruption of the divorce exerted a longer and more pervasive impact on boys than on girls. Although both boys and girls showed disturbances in play and social relations at home and at school initially, by the end of the second year after the divorce, the girls showed almost complete recovery. Despite the boys' showing improvement in these areas, their recovery was not on a par with that of the girls. It also was common for both boys and girls to show high dependency needs initially after the divorce and to show less socially and cognitively mature play behavior. Again, by two years after divorce, the girls had made up much of the loss but the boys had not (Hetherington et al., 1979a). The experience of divorce, then, was more traumatic and long-term for the preschool boys than for the preschool girls.

Hetherington (1979) suggests that these sex differences result from greater stress on the boy than on the girl involved in divorce. Boys are more likely than girls to be viewed more negatively by the mother, teachers, and peers. In addition, a greater degree of stress and depression is expressed by divorced mothers of boys than by divorced mothers of girls. The boy in a divorced family, then, may be exposed to greater frustration and aggression, and may respond with acting-out, aggressive, and noncompliant behavior.

There also is evidence (Hetherington 1979) that the mother-son relationship in divorce is a troublesome one. During the initial year after divorce, parenting skills decline for both the mother and the father. The decline in the mother's parenting skills is associated with increased aggression and noncompliant behavior in her son. This child behavior in turn prompted greater coercive behavior on the part of the mother, which in turn led to greater noncompliance by the son, and so forth. Although by two years after the divorce the mother-son relationship had improved, it was still a troublesome one.

Although Hetherington finds these differences, others do not (Allison & Furstenberg, 1989). It may be that such differences are present initially for some period of time, as Hetherington found for her young sample, or that they emerge only with children in certain age ranges and dissipate as time passes.

Hetherington (1989) has reported on the adjustment of her sample at age 10, six years after the divorce. Mother-son relations were still problematic in families where the mother did not remarry. These mothers still used more ineffectual rearing behaviors (nagging, complaining, lower ability to control the child's behavior), had a relatively high proportion of negative interchanges with their sons, and the like. Nonetheless, Hetherington cautions that these relations were not hostile, but rather were best characterized as intense and ambivalent. The mothers did show considerable warmth toward their preadolescent sons.

Six years after the divorce few differences between divorced and intact families were found for mother-daughter relations. The one major contributing factor in finding differences favoring intact families was the maturity rate of the daughter. In divorced families with early maturing daughters there was increased conflict between mother and daughter and an early distancing of the daughter from the mother—that is, the distancing that normally happens occurred when the daughters were younger.

In some ways preadolescents, both male and female, residing with a divorced mother "grew up" sooner than those living in intact families. They had more responsibility, but at the same time greater independence and input into decision making. Hetherington notes that for some this resulted in more equal and mutually supportive relationships with mother, but that for others it was detrimental because it interfered with other activities or involved maternal expectations for behavior that were beyond the competencies of the preadolescent. Finally, compared to mothers in intact families, divorced mothers were less knowledgeable about the lives of their preadolescent children—where they were and with whom, what they did in a daily sense, who their best friends were, and the like.

The findings of the Hetherington studies point out the complexities in family adjustment to divorce. Although we have focused here on parent-child relations, it is important to note that each parent must adapt to a changed adult role. Mothers tend to feel trapped by their children and their role as a single parent; fathers report feelings of being shut out of their children's lives (Hetherington et al., 1976). As a result, their behavior toward their children changes dramatically after divorce, with fathers becoming more indulgent and mothers somewhat overly strict yet inconsistent in their child-rearing patterns. The confluence of the widespread changes affecting all members of the family makes divorce a difficult period, especially during the first year. In the words of Hetherington and colleagues there is no such thing as a "victimless" divorce.

Hetherington's extensive research points out many of the factors involved in coping with divorce and the family relationships related to more successful coping. One implication of her findings is that the effects of divorce may attenuate over time—children recover. Another is that there may be age differences in adapting to divorce. Preadolescents and adolescents have coping resources that are unavailable to preschoolers and children, and they have a more mature understanding of the divorce situation (Kurdek, 1989), which may result in their coping more effectively. To examine these possibilities we need to review research in which the age of the child at the time of the divorce was investigated.

The most extensive study of developmental trends in adaptation to divorce was done by Wallerstein and Kelly (1976, 1979, 1980; Kelly & Wallerstein, 1975, 1976, 1977).

They have reported the reactions of 131 children and adolescents ranging in age from 3 to 19 at the start of the study. Families were referred by attorneys, school psychologists, teachers and others to the Children of Divorce Project. The intent of the project was to study adaptation of parents and children to divorce. Interviews were conducted with the children and the parents at the time of parental separation and one and four years later. The interviews were semistructured and obtained information on family life, the feelings toward divorce, the relationship of the parent to the child, parental perceptions of how well the child was coping with the divorce, and the like. Although there was no control group in the study, it is valuable because of its longitudinal design and study of coping by children over a wide age range.

As in the Hetherington studies, Wallerstein and Kelly found that the first year after the separation was the most difficult and stressful. It was less difficult for children who had lasting contact with the noncustodial father, again an indication of the positive mediating effect of the father on the child's adjustment to divorce. Results were reported for children in varying age groups. We summarize here some of the more salient findings.

The most common reactions of the preschool children (age 3–4 at the time of the separation) were regression, diffuse aggression, irritability, and separation anxieties. They experienced a good deal of cognitive confusion, such as continually expecting their father to come home, or believing that, since their parents were no longer living together, they were no longer their parents. They also tended to blame themselves for the divorce and promised to be better children if their parents would get together again. Kelly and Wallerstein (1975) suggest this may be their way of trying to master the situation and gain some kind of control over it. As might be expected, these children suffered loss in self-esteem. In general, the behavior of these children was much as that described by Hetherington et al. (1979a) in their study.

The 5- to 6-year-olds behaved in much the same way as the younger children, including having a tendency to blame themselves for their parents' divorce. However, this was the age group in which *some* of the children did not experience a slowing or retardation in developmental progress, self-confidence, or the like (Wallerstein & Kelly, 1974). This finding is reminiscent of Hetherington's (1966, 1972) suggestion that the age of 6 may be a critical period in divorce for boys. Those 5- to 6-year-olds who were less home-oriented, that is, those who enjoyed activities outside the home, were less adversely affected by the divorce than those who were highly home-oriented.

The 7- to 8-year-olds had considerable difficulty coping with the divorce. They were unable to use self-blame as a control and, unlike the older children, were not able to engage in behaviors designed to provide other types of mastery over the situation (Kelly & Wallerstein, 1976). As a result, these children tended to be pawns in their parents' battles with each other. In addition, because of their greater dependency needs relative to those of the older children, they were more likely to align with the care-taking parent against the other parent (Kelly & Wallerstein, 1976), even though they had strong loyalty ties to both parents. This situation, of course, caused these children great anguish and, at times, they appeared psychologically immobilized by their parents' separation.

The preadolescent (age 9–10) sample was composed of 31 children. They were characterized as actively trying to master their feelings and fears. They took active steps to deal with their feelings of rejection and sense of loss. Some tried to badger their mothers into re-establishing the previous relationship with the fathers. Others used different strategies to cope. Wallerstein and Kelly (1976) report that one girl translated the difficulties

of divorce into feelings of achievement and accomplishment by designing and selling a magazine announcing her parents' divorce.

Another important characteristic of these children was their anger toward their parents. This anger at separation occurred despite previously witnessed scenes of violence between the parents. These children simply did not want to see their parents divorced. Some of the preadolescents even had a sense of moral indignation that their parents were divorcing, and believed they were behaving in an irresponsible fashion. This group showed an increase in temper tantrums, demandingness, and nuisance behavior. Some of these children feared being forgotten or abandoned. Other fears included the emotional health of the custodial parent, concern that their needs would be overlooked, and concern that reliance on only one parent put them in a tenuous position.

Identity and self-esteem difficulties also arose in this group. Because the family group is important in the emerging sense of identity, identity development was ruptured with the separation of the parents. Self-esteem and identity issues had to be faced on the basis of a new family structure. These children also felt alone and lonely, hurt, and humiliated by parental separation. In part, this seems to stem from a sense that they must take sides, which leads to feelings of betrayal if a choice between the parents is made. To avoid this, many of the preadolescents simply refused to make a choice.

About half the preadolescents experienced difficulties in school and a decline in school performance. There was also a concomitant decline in peer relations, and increased aggression in play activities was common.

The follow-up interviews a year after the separation indicated considerable improvement. The sense of shame, loneliness and loss, intense worries, and the like dissipated. Adjustments to the new family structure, including stepparents in some cases, were progressing well. There was still some anger about the events in the divorce, but the divorce itself seemed to be accepted as a fact. This was not the case for some of the preadolescents, however, who showed a chronic depressive personality, low self-esteem, and difficulties in school and with peers. This latter minority engaged in some delinquency, sexual assertiveness that was age-inappropriate, continued feelings of isolation, and withdrawn behavior.

Clearly, the divorce experience was very difficult for the preadolescents. Nearly half had continued difficulty adjusting to the divorce a year after separation.

The adolescents (ages 13–19) also reacted with anger and feelings of moral indignation toward the parents (Wallerstein & Kelly, 1974). The more independent adolescents were less affected by the divorce than the more dependent or parent-oriented adolescents. A typical reaction of some of the adolescents was to withdraw from both parents and assume an aloof and uninvolved position in the family. They seemed to be interested only in themselves, exhibiting a wide range of self-centered behavior.

This behavior pattern was associated with better adjustment to the parents' divorce (Wallerstein & Kelly, 1974). The adolescents who were aloof tended to appear more sophisticated and to have a more mature attitude about divorce on the one year follow-up interview. They also showed some capacity for empathy and compassion toward the parents. The withdrawal seemed to be a mechanism that allowed the adolescents to continue their own development and subsequently to bring to the situation a more mature understanding of divorce in general, and their family situation, specifically. They were able to deal with divorce on their own terms.

As a group, the adolescents tended not to align with either parent. Those few who did, however, experienced developmental difficulties with independence attainment and autonomy. When they behaved independently or autonomously, the custodial parent felt threatened and deprived and tried to force further dependency on the adolescent.

Although sex differences in adjustment were evident in the younger age groups, with girls faring better than boys, no sex differences appeared in the adolescents' adjustment to divorce. The adolescents' greater psychological and cognitive maturity seems to mediate the sex differences occurring in the younger age groups.

Adolescent school-related behavior was best described as bimodal. Some showed accelerated social and academic growth; others viewed school as an intolerable drain on their meager coping resources. The latter adolescents experienced deteriorating grades, poor social relations, and fantasies about dropping out of school.

Divorce was difficult for the adolescents, in general, although not as difficult as it was for the preadolescents. More importantly, it appears that the more psychologically mature adolescents coped better, and may even have grown, in terms of independence, for example, with the divorce. For others, however, the divorce seemed to be a very destructive experience of some duration.

Wallerstein (1984) interviewed 30 of the original 34 preschool children, and 40 of their parents, 10 years after the divorce. The intent of the interview was to obtain retrospective information of how the children, now early adolescents, viewed the divorce. Wallerstein was interested in how they remembered the experience and the degree to which it was still a central concern to them. Further, she was interested in the nature of family relationships at the 10-year mark and how close the children felt toward their parents. Finally, Wallerstein was interested in discovering how these young adolescents dealt with interpersonal relations, whether they planned to marry, and the like.

These subjects claimed to have little memory of the divorce. What they did recall most frequently were scenes of parental conflict. Few recalled their own reactions. It appears that the children were too young for long-term memories of the experience. Nonetheless, nearly a third of these children evidenced that the divorce and subsequent change in family living situations remained a central concern a decade later. About a fourth of the children still strongly disapproved of the divorce, and about half indicated they wished they had an intact family. A majority indicated close, open, and trusting relationships with their mothers, as evidenced, in part, by their knowledge of their fathers' payment of child support and their concern over economic issues. In addition, they expressed concern for their mothers' loneliness. The children generally maintained strong psychological ties to their fathers, regardless of how frequently they saw and interacted with them. Some made strong efforts to contact their fathers at early adolescence even if they had not heard from them for many years. Finally, most were hopeful and optimistic about their own future marriages and family prospects. Interestingly, one recurrent theme involved knowing a prospective spouse as completely as possible, perhaps by living with the person, prior to getting married.

Wallerstein suggests that these children, who were very young when their parents divorced, may not experience long-term psychological consequences of the divorce. They have fewer unhappy memories than do children who were older, which may account for their optimism about the future, even though their experience with the divorce was more difficult than that of the older children. Wallerstein suggests that these youngsters may have been spared by their own immaturity at the time of their parents' divorce.

Several other researchers have focused their investigations specifically on the adjustment of adolescents to separation and divorce of their parents. Thomes (1968) interviewed 47 children and adolescents from single-parent homes (by divorce or separation) and 37 children and adolescents from intact families. All were asked about themselves and about their ideas of parental duties and the family. Both groups indicated that the mother performed parental duties to a greater degree than the father. Only four children from the single-parent homes did not include the father in their description of a home. Approximately a third of the subjects in each group indicated that they would discuss problems with their fathers first.

In addition, both groups were comparable in terms of hostility toward the father. This information suggests that Hetherington's notions about the importance of the age of the child in the effects of one-parent families are true. Moreover, Thomes's findings suggest that children and adolescents adjust well to paternal absence, since the fathers of these subjects had been absent from the home for at least two years prior to the study. These children and adolescents, then, may have had an initial adjustment experience that was difficult, but they subsequently became well adjusted and had feelings about parents and the home similar to children from intact homes.

In an extensive study, Burchinal (1964) examined the characteristics of adolescents from intact, single-parent, and **reconstituted families**. Like Thomes, Burchinal reported that the immediate effects of divorce were emotionally distressing for adolescents, but that within a relatively short time the adolescents recovered psychologically. Adolescents from single-parent or reconstituted homes did not differ in personality characteristics or social relationships from adolescents from intact homes.

This latter finding regarding personality characteristics suggests that self-concept development during the adolescent years may not be adversely affected by parental divorce and separation. This possibility has been extensively studied by Parish and his associates (Parish, 1981; Parish & Taylor, 1979; Parish, Dostal, & Parish, 1981). Children and adolescents in grades 3 through 8 and college students completed the Personal Attributes Inventory, a listing of positive and negative descriptive words. The subject first circled the words most descriptive of him or her, then completed the inventory again for mother, father, and family. In general, self-descriptions did not differ for children or adolescents in divorced versus intact families.

Indeed, it now appears that family structure, in and of itself, is of little importance to adolescent adjustment. The key factor seems to be parental discord (Long, 1986; Kurdek, 1988). Daughters' self-esteem is unaffected by family structure—those in single-parent and intact households have equivalent self-esteem. However, parental conflict is negatively related to self-esteem. That is, regardless of family structure, a daughter's self-esteem is lower if her parents have a discordant relationship. In a similar vein, a cooperative, working relationship not only helps the daughter—and likely the son—maintain a healthy self-esteem but it also helps the child cope with divorce more successfully (Kurdek, 1988), and maintain

cognitive and social competence (Long, Forehand, Fauber, & Brody, 1987).

This review of the effects of the divorce on the adolescent reveals the complexity of the issues. Divorce does have negative influences, although these seem to be less tied to family structure than to interpersonal relations between the child and both parents. Having an absent father need not be a negative influence on development, and, indeed, continued and sustained meaningful contact with the father can attenuate much of the negative impact of divorce. In turn, it is difficult to discern any real positive influences on divorce, *per se*, other than the improvement of home atmosphere, which relate to increases in personal growth.

In summarizing her research on children's coping with divorce, Hetherington (1989) noted that she could identify three groups of preadolescents distinguished by their means of adapting: aggressive-insecure, opportunistic-competent, and caring-competent.

The *aggressive-insecure* preadolescents had a number of behavior problems, both at

Family structure is less important to adjustment than living in a warm, happy home atmosphere.

home and at school. They had poor self-esteem, and 70 percent had no close friends. They were unhappy, angry, and insecure. Most, but not all, were boys.

This mode of adapting is associated with homes characterized by conflict and parental use of the power-assertive and love-withdrawal disciplinary techniques typical of authoritarian parenting. The boys had no close male role models, either because they were rejected by their fathers or stepfathers, or because their mothers had not remarried. Their relations with their mothers were ones of conflict and alienation, and the mothers tended to work full time. The girls also had poor relations with their mothers, but their relations with their fathers were not related to their problems. It appears that the preadolescents in this group were in a family situation that, regardless of family structure, was not conducive to sound behavioral and mental growth.

The preadolescents in the *opportunistic-competent* and *caring-competent* groups shared a number of similarities. In general, they coped well—they had good self-esteem, few behavior problems, performed well academically, were vibrant, skillful in interpersonal relations, and had sound relationships with peers.

The opportunistic-competent preadolescents tended to be manipulative in interpersonal relations; even as younger children they tried to play one parent against the other. They had good relations with at least one parent, often the same-sex parent; the alternative parent tended to be somewhat rejecting. Their friendships with peers often were short-lived, perhaps because they "used" them, a reflection of their egocentrism. Perhaps these patterns of adjustment occur because of the relations with the two parents—one more caring and the other more rejecting or neglecting. If parents do not reject this ploy early and prevent the child from succeeding in manipulative techniques, the child may learn to use these techniques as an interpersonal interaction style.

The striking aspect of the preadolescents in the caring-competent group is that they were nearly all girls. Only five of the 23 were boys. In general, they had good relations with their mother. In addition, Hetherington notes that these girls often assumed a caring role for others, often a younger sibling, but also a poorly coping mother, or even other extended family members. After reading Hetherington's summary of these preadolescents, one is tempted to conclude that they are simply "just good kids." It seems that this is a result of a strong, close mother-daughter bond in a home that is not characterized by rejection or conflict.

The distinctions among the three groups of preadolescents are clearly related to family atmosphere and interaction patterns. They point out that the parents play a pivotal role in their children's adjustment to divorce. If the parents play their role poorly, the negative effects of divorce can be very long-term; they can result in behavioral and interpersonal patterns that will be carried into the later adolescent and, likely, adulthood years.

Of course, the parents are not the only people or circumstances to which the child or adolescent experiencing divorce is exposed. Adjusting to stepparents, encountering changing relations with siblings, and dealing with other adults and social institutions also impact on adjustment.

Adjusting to Stepparents. Within five years of their parents' divorce, a substantial proportion of children must adapt to the remarriage of one or both of their parents. Some research has shown that this adaptation is more difficult for girls during both childhood (Hetherington, Cox, & Cox, 1985) and preadolescence (Santrock, Warshak, Lindbergh, & Meadows, 1982). Girls become more anxious, hostile, and less warm as a result of mother's remarriage. Although these effects dissipate over time, residues were present two years after the remarriage

(Hetherington, 1989) for those who were children when their mother remarried.

In contrast to the findings for girls, stepfathers seem to play a beneficial role on stepsons, both during childhood (Hetherington et al., 1985) and preadolescence (Santrock et al., 1982). Although some initial problem may occur, by two years after remarriage the boys did not show more aggressive or disruptive behavior than did boys in intact families. It is important to note that in one study (Hetherington, 1989) remarriage during early adolescence was associated with sustained, long-term behavior problems for both sons and daughters.

Other researchers have not found such strong sex differences in adjustment due to family structure or remarriage (Allison & Furstenberg, 1989; Kurdek & Sinclair, 1988). In these studies it was found that family structure was less important to adjustment, in general, and specifically adjustment to remarriage, than was the general interaction pattern in the family. Successful psychological adjustment in any family structure is associated with high family cohesion, a supportive family environment, the use of positive coping skills such as strong social supports, and the like. The family atmosphere that is conducive to providing these characteristics will foster psychological adjustment. Family structure, in and of itself, is unrelated to adolescent adjustment (Kurdek & Sinclair, 1988).

It appears that the studies reporting sex differences in male and female adaptation to stepfathers may not have accounted for the impact of family atmosphere. Hetherington (1989) has suggested how the process may operate.

For about the first two years after remarriage, stepfathers spend time trying to establish relationships with stepchildren, but they feel little affection for them. They tend to be somewhat distant, expressing neither considerable positive nor negative feelings toward stepchildren. When they did use authoritative stepparenting, which is the preferred mode of child rearing, it resulted in increased behavior problems in both stepsons and stepdaughters during the first two years of the marriage. Although these problems diminished for stepsons later, this was not the case for stepdaughters. Hetherington suggests that initially any attempt at control by the stepfather is viewed as adverse. She suggests that, initially, the stepfather should not try to shape and mold the child's behavior, but should (1) support the mother's child rearing and (2) attempt to establish a meaningful and workable relationship with the child. Authoritative parenting may be introduced later, when stepfather and stepchildren know each other better.

The stepchild's reactions to the stepfather represent the other aspect of the interaction. Initially, stepfathers may be viewed as intruders who compete for time, care, and affection from mother. Stepchildren may feel their relationship with their mother is threatened; this may especially be the case for daughters. Hence, initial reactions may be one of rejection and hostility, and of anger toward the mother for remarrying. It is as though no matter what the stepfather does, he "can't win." These reactions may be greater during early adolescence owing to increased independence strivings and identity concerns.

These reactions on the part of the stepfather and stepchildren result in an interaction style that will have a degree of tension, and could result in lower family cohesion, especially if there is a deterioration in the mother-child relationship. Hence, initial adjustment to stepfathers may be difficult and these difficulties may carry over to other areas of daily behavior. One could expect that where these problems are less evident, adolescent adjustment will be easier and occur more quickly. The key to successful adolescent adjustment to remarriage, then, lies in family interactions that promote cohesion, warmth, and a supportive environment devoid of threats to the self and to the child's relations with the mother.

Sibling Relations in Divorce. The effect of divorce on sibling relations has not been the central focus of research efforts. This is somewhat surprising because siblings could act as significant buffers and social supports in dealing with the stress of divorce, as occurred in some of Hetherington's caring-competent preadolescents. Alternatively, there could be increased hostility and rivalry as siblings vie for decreased family resources in the spheres of parental attention, care-giving, and affection. Unfortunately, the findings seem to indicate the latter is more common than the former.

Both Hetherington (1989) and Mac-Kinnon (1989) report that sibling pairs involving a boy (boy-girl or boy-boy) showed greater hostility, aggression, and sibling rivalry than the other combinations of siblings. This was especially the case when there was an older brother and a younger sister. Siblings in stepfamilies, in general, also had more negative interactions.

There are two important exceptions to this general finding (Hetherington, 1989). First, the relationships between siblings in stepfamilies improved over time, although by two years after the divorce they were still not on a par with the interactions of siblings in intact families. Second, older daughters in stepfamilies engaged in more care-taking, nurturing, and supportive interactions with their younger sisters, perhaps because they had a more realistic understanding of divorce (Kurdek, 1989).

The bases of these findings are not well understood at this time. MacKinnon (1989) suggests that boys may be modeling an assertive father, a father involved in conflict with a spouse prior to divorce. It may be, too, that the girls in boy-girl dyads are modeling more submissive behavior because that is how the mother behaved prior to the divorce. In other words, it may be that siblings

model the style of interaction of their parents prior to the divorce when they face the stress of the divorce situation.

Other Potential Supports. Other social and institutional supports are available to the child and adolescent coping with parental divorce. Hetherington (1989) mentions in this regard grandparents, schools, and peers.

Grandparents seem to provide important social and emotional roles with their divorced or remarried children, but they exert little control or influence on their grandchildren's adjustment unless they live in the home with them. Although this may benefit the grandchildren, it seems to produce a stifling effect on the grandparents' own children—the mothers felt as though they were children again, as though they had lost independence by living with their own parents again. In addition, conflicts between mother and grandparents arose over parenting issues, which made for difficulties. As Hetherington put it, grandparents are useful in emergencies, as with problem children, but otherwise provided little influence on the child's adjustment to divorce.

In contrast, the school environment seems to afford a much needed stable atmosphere of authoritativeness. Children in school when divorce occurred profited from the routine, regularized schedule. The school environment, with its structure, seemed a "safe haven" for the children that attenuated the adversity found at home. In addition, academic success was associated with enhanced coping, and for boys athletic achievement functioned in a similar manner. It appears that the routine and structure found in the school environment can buffer the child and adolescent in much the same manner that a supportive home environment can.

With increasing age of the child experiencing the divorce, peers play an increasingly important buffering role.

Hetherington notes that a single close, good friend was beneficial—children without such friendships had a more difficult time adjusting to divorce. This may be especially important for adolescents who disengage more readily from the divorce situation, as we noted earlier. Strong friendships and school affiliations provide support and structured activities that allow the adolescent to continue to deal in adoptive ways with not only the typical aspects of development faced by youngsters but also with the consuming aspects of parental divorce.

Maternal Employment and Adolescent Development

One of the most widespread structural changes in the American family has been the increase in the employment of mothers. As can be seen in Table 10–4, there has been a steady increase since 1970 in the percent of mothers who work outside the home. And the increase applies to both mothers with school-age children and those with younger ones. This trend is present for both married and divorced mothers, although the latter already were highly represented in the work force in 1970, resulting in the increases being less for them. Whether the increases will continue is a matter for the future. What is clear, however, is that the modal family in the United States involves a mother who works outside the home.

There are a variety of reasons for mothers increasingly entering the work force. For some it is an economic necessity. The increase in single-parent homes attests to this fact in family life. For many women, working is seen as a form of achievement for which they were trained. The increase in educational level of women supports this argument (L. Hoffman, 1979, 1980, 1989). The greater efficiency of household management techniques, including modern appliances and food-processing techniques, has resulted in less time being needed to manage everyday household activities. Finally, working mothers seem generally to be more satisfied with their lives (Gold & Andres, 1978a, 1978b), which makes work and the feelings of achievement even more attractive and satisfying. It is not surprising, then, that studies of the influence of maternal employment on the child's development have increased in the past decade. Although much less is known about the impact of maternal employment on the adolescent, some information is available, and it reveals that maternal employment may exert a positive influence on various aspects of adolescent development.

Unraveling the precise effects of maternal employment is difficult for many of the same reasons that discovering the effects of divorce is problematic. When the mother begins to work outside the home, the nature of the family structure and responsibilities

TABLE 10–4   **Percentage of Mothers Who Work Outside the Home by Age of Children, Marital Status, and Year**

| | Children (birth–5) | | Children (6–17) | |
	Married	*Divorced*	*Married*	*Divorced*
1970	30.3	63.3	49.2	82.4
1980	45.1	68.3	61.7	82.3
1985	53.4	67.5	67.8	83.4
1988	57.1	70.1	72.5	83.9

(Source: U.S. Bureau of the Census. [1989]. *Statistical abstract of the United States, 1988*. [109th ed.] Washington, DC: Government Printing Office.)

changes (L. Hoffman, 1979, 1980, 1989). Children take on more responsibility around the home and husbands do more house-work. Family income rises in two-parent families. Mothers spend less time with their children. And, many women experience a happier life because they are working out-side the home. Of course, many other changes occur, too.

One of the major concerns in the earlier research was the negative effects of maternal employment on the socialization of children and adolescents (L. Hoffman, 1974, 1977, 1979, 1980). A general rule that has emerged from research findings seems to be that, if appropriate care is provided for the child, no particular socialization problems seem to occur (for example, L. Hoffman, 1979); the same general rule holds for ad-olescents during after-school hours (L. Hoffman, 1979). The critical feature, here, seems not to be that mothers spend less time with their children, but rather that the time spent is of a higher quality, as measured, for example, by time spent in direct interaction with children. Although some mothers may overcompensate for time away from the child, the higher quality time many mothers spend with their children seems to be ben-eficial (L. Hoffman, 1979, 1989). In this re-gard, Richards and Duckett (1989), in their study of adolescents in grades 5 through 9, found that older adolescent females spent *more* time with the family when mother worked and younger adolescents spent no less time with the family when mother worked. In addition, maternal employment did not affect the quality of the time spent with the family. In part, this resulted because the adolescents spent more time with father when mother worked.

A second major issue concerns a mother's reasons for working and her job satisfaction. Each is important because of its relationship to family harmony and the degree of conflict in the home. Mothers who are not happy with their work tend to have poorer rela-tionships with their children than mothers who are happily employed (L. Hoffman, 1989). In addition, research (see Glasser & Navarre, 1965) demonstrates that mothers ill prepared for satisfying jobs may make in-appropriate demands on their children with respect to accepting responsibility for home management and care. This may make ma-ternal employment a difficult situation for the child.

Some research on child-rearing practices supports the importance of considering ma-ternal satisfaction with working when judg-ing the effects of maternal employment on the child. Working mothers who are happily employed and nonworking mothers who are happy staying home use very similar child-rearing practices. However, mothers who want to work but stay home because they feel it is their duty, report they have diffi-culty controlling their children and feel less confident in themselves as mothers (L. Hoff-man, 1974, 1979). Moreover, mothers who are not working but wish to work report rel-atively poor marital adjustment, which may lead to an unhappy home atmosphere not conducive to good psychological growth for the child. (L. Hoffman, 1989).

Adolescents' perceptions of their parents' child-rearing methods also are related to maternal employment (Litovsky & Dusek, 1988). Up to about the tenth grade, adoles-cents perceive their parents as more warm and accepting when mother does not work, or works only part time. Older adolescents perceive their parents as more accepting and supportive when mother works full time. It may be that younger adolescents require (and want?) more parental contact than do older adolescents, who in turn have stronger independence needs and may find being around parents to be stifling and an in-fringement on their freedom. As L. Hoff-man (1979) has argued, families in which both parents work may be especially con-ducive to meeting older adolescents' needs for developing autonomy because they are better able to relinquish tasks that promote the developing of autonomy and competence. When mother is home it may be more difficult to do so because a substantial component of mother's self-worth revolves around family care, the giving-up of which could damage her own feelings of self-worth. These findings, then, point to the benefits to the adolescent when mother works, largely through family context conditions that allow the development of self-reliance.

Studies of the impact of maternal employment on the adolescent's development are complicated by the fact that researchers have not studied large samples of adolescents whose mothers started work when they were adolescents. Hence, the available information is based only on whether the mother of the adolescent is working at the time of adolescence, not on when she started. Nonetheless, some very interesting findings have emerged.

One interesting consequence of maternal employment deals with the adolescent's conception of traditional sex roles. If both parents work, offspring develop a broader notion of sex roles. Since the husbands of working mothers tend to participate in household chores to a greater extent than the husbands of nonworking mothers, the adolescent may develop sex-role concepts that view both sexes as earner/achievers and caretakers of the home (L. Hoffman, 1989). Adolescent daughters of working mothers also have a less negative view of femininity than daughters of nonworking mothers (Broverman et al., 1972). The adolescent daughters of working mothers tend to be more independent, motivated, and to do better on measures of achievement (L. Hoffman, 1974, 1979). They also appear to be better adjusted socially and personally. Maternal employment is also related to better adjustment to social relations at school and better family relationships at home for both adolescent males and females (Gold & Andres, 1978a). The daughters of working mothers also tend to be more career-ori-

ented and to be interested in less conventionally feminine careers.

The findings for sons of working mothers are more complicated. Some evidence (Gold & Andres, 1978a, 1978b, 1978c) suggests that, although the elementary school-age sons of working mothers are better adjusted socially, they have lower IQ scores than the sons of nonworking mothers. This finding did not occur for the adolescents studied (Gold & Andres, 1978a). Social class also was important for sons. Despite the finding for the younger students, maternal employment did not relate to the middle-class sons' liking for school, grades, or occupational aspirations. A negative relationship between these latter measures and maternal employment was found for 10-year-old boys of working-class families. Sex-role attitudes and stereotypes of sons are also influenced by maternal employment. Sons of working mothers view women as more competent and see men as warmer than do sons of nonworking mothers.

Unlike the data for girls, however, the data for boys are influenced by social class. Lower-class sons of working mothers may have higher educational goals and aspirations, and grades, but they also seem to admire their fathers less (L. Hoffman, 1974). The strain in the father-son relationship may reflect the son's view of the father as somewhat of a failure because the mother often *has* to work to supplement family income (Gold & Andres, 1978b). This denigration of the father did not occur in the middle-class boys.

Maternal employment, then, has both beneficial and detrimental effects on the adolescent, although the positive influences seem to far outweigh the negative effects (L. Hoffman, 1979, 1980). It is important to note that the difficulties involved with maternal employment need not be viewed as arguments against maternal employment (L. Hoffman, 1980). Rather, they simply indicate situations to which solutions must be found. As the nature of the modal family changes, the natural course of events may deal with some issues, such as the feelings of the lower-class boys. Other problems may have to be dealt with in more active ways.

PARENT-ADOLESCENT RELATIONS AND ADOLESCENT INDEPENDENCE STRIVINGS

The adolescent years are marked by increases in independence strivings and autonomy (Hill, 1980). The attainment of increased independence from parents is, at times, filled with conflict, particularly during the early part of the pubertal cycle. Later, conflict is at a lower level as the adolescent and parent adapt to the issues involved in adolescent independence.

Several studies of parent-adolescent interaction illustrate the course of independence attainment. Jacob (1974) asked 11- to 16-year-old boys and their mothers and fathers to discuss emotionally charged situations that face families and come to a family decision about the situation. The interactions between the family members were observed and audio-recorded. The results indicated that both social class and age of the child were important to understanding the nature of the interactions. Parental influence in decision making was lower in families with 16-year-olds. In middle-class families, mothers were more influential than 11-year-olds, but 16-year-olds were more influential than mothers. In middle-class families, fathers were more influential than sons. The older adolescent son in middle-class families gained influence in the family at the expense of the mother. In the lower-class family, fathers were more influential than 11-year-old sons but less influential than 16-year-old sons. Mothers were more influential than 11-year-old sons but equal in influence to 16-year-old sons. In lower-class families, then, the influence of the father wanes with an increase in the age of the son.

Steinberg and Hill (1978) and Steinberg (1981) studied parent-child interactions in families with 11- and 14-year old sons. They were interested in both age and pubertal status as precursors of changes in parent-offspring interactions. The procedures were similar to those used by Jacob (1974). This set of studies provided longitudinal data on changes in family interaction as a function of age and physical maturity, each family being observed three times during the course of 1½ years.

In general, conflict between the son and the mother increased during the early period of the growth spurt, and then declined. During the early maturity period, sons and mothers interrupted each other with increasing frequency, sons showed less deference to their mothers, both mothers and sons explained their views less frequently, and there were rigid patterns of family interaction best characterized as strained and tense. Fathers tended to become more assertive with their sons, but the reverse was not the case. Sons generally showed increased deference toward their fathers and fathers deferred to their sons less frequently over the course of maturity. In general,

With increasing age, adolescents gain greater independence in decision making.

mothers and fathers had approximately equal positions greater than the sons in the dominance hierarchy during the early part of the maturity period. During the later part of the maturity cycle, the son was more influential than the mother but less influential than the father.

Steinberg (1981) suggests that both adolescents and parents respond to the son's physical development as an indication of entrance into adulthood, because these differences occurred regardless of age; that is, they occurred solely as a function of physical characteristics.

These studies illustrate the nature of adolescent independence strivings and gaining of autonomy as they occur within the family. Although they hint at conflict between the parents, which some may interpret as a generation gap (Mead, 1970), this is not the case. In general, adolescents appreciate their parents' way of life and find it satisfying (Yankelovich, 1969; Meissner, 1965). As Hill (1980) and others (for example, Yankelovich, 1969) point out, adolescent-parent conflict is less likely to reflect big differences in basic values and beliefs than in more superficial preferences toward music, dress, slang, and the like. Indeed, research (see Meissner, 1965; Meisels & Canter, 1971–72; Yankelovich, 1969) shows that adolescents generally enjoy their parents' company and have basic values closer to those of their parents than of their peers.

Adolescent independence strivings, then, do not necessarily signify a breaking away from the parents. Rather, they relate to changes in the role the adolescent plays in the family interaction system (Hill, 1980). Adolescents must learn to rely less on the parents in making personal decisions, adopting values, and the like (Douvan & Adelson, 1966; Elder, 1968) in order to become prepared for the adult world. In turn, the parents must adapt by allowing their adolescents to gain independence (Campbell, 1969). This may be particularly difficult be-

cause, just as the adolescent is undergoing developmental changes, so too are the parents (Hill, 1980). Although some of the maturing adult's concerns overlap parallel concerns of the adolescent, for example, changing physical characteristics and occupational achievements, others, such as children leaving the home, are very different. During adolescence, then, we should expect changes in family interactions because both the parent and the adolescent are undergoing developmental changes that relate to their interpersonal interactions. To be sure, some degree of conflict no doubt will arise but, as Hill (1980) points out, families still tend by and large to be supportive atmospheres for the adolescent. Just as adolescents must learn to accept responsibility for their autonomy, so must parents learn to reduce their feelings of personal responsibility for the adolescent and grant greater independence.

Independence strivings, then, reflect a joint effort on the part of the parent and the adolescent (Ryan & Lynch, 1989). Throughout the process, adolescents maintain an emotional closeness to their parents, as evidenced in their feeling secure in the family unit, being loved, and using their parents as valuable resources for growth and development.

Theoretical Explanations of Independence Strivings

Ausubel (Ausubel, Montemayor, & Svajian, 1977; see Berzonsky, 1978, for a brief overview of the major aspects of the theory) has presented the most comprehensive theoretical formulation of adolescent independence strivings. As you might suspect, the theory is steeped in the nature of transitions in parent-offspring interactions across the childhood and adolescent years. His general contention is that alterations in rearing patterns foster a change from the high dependency of infancy to the relative independence of late adolescence.

The infant, of course, is completely dependent on the parents for care. As the infant grows into early childhood the realization of this dependency becomes evident. Children realize that they need the parents and are dependent on them for their general well-being. Ausubel suggests that, as children are maturing, they begin to take this dependency on their parents as a threat to their self-concept, and that this initiates a crisis which the child may solve in one of several ways.

One solution Ausubel et al. (1977) note is called **satellization**, by which they mean the child comes to accept dependency on the parents, being a satellite revolving around the parents. Both the child and the parent accept the fact that the parent is the power in the relationship, and each is satisfied with the relationship. The parents value the child and treat the child with respect and the child, in turn, tries to live up to parental expectations.

Of course, not all children and parents establish a satellization relationship. There are two forms of nonsatellization: **undervaluation** and **overvaluation**. Undervaluation reflects a rejecting attitude by the parent toward the child. Although the parent meets the child's needs, this is done in a rather cold manner, because the child is seen as a burden. Because the child comes to realize this state of affairs, comformity to parental demands and wishes is done not out of a desire to please the parents, but to avoid punishment.

Overvaluation may result when parents are highly accepting of the child out of a wish to vicariously relive their lives in their child's life. Often, the parents overindulge their child and spoil him or her because the child could become what they were not. The parents tend to plan the life of the child in such a way as to relive that which they wished to be.

During adolescence, desatellization occurs. This is evidenced by a severing of ties to the parents as independence strivings increase. Secure feelings about the self and the self's ability to cope develop. The desatellized individual is able to function in an autonomous manner, behaving in a way consistent with his or her own needs and values. Behaviors no longer necessarily reflect an attempt to please the parents.

Clearly, Ausubel's (Ausubel et al., 1977) theory leads one to believe that satellization may lead to optimal adolescent development. Satellization allows the individual to develop feelings of self-worth based on feelings of competence and value. Nonsatellization threatens this aspect of development and may lead to difficulties during the adolescent years, such as insecurity in independence strivings.

The nature of our culture exacerbates insecurities in independence attainment because there are no formal rites of passage into adulthood and its independent status (Benedict, 1938; Kett, 1977). Other social systems do have formal rites of passage marking entrance into full adult status (cf. Mead, 1970). Such rites of passage clearly define the demarcation between the roles associated with childhood (or adolescence) and adulthood. Achieving independence is not a personal struggle in these societies; it is a clearly defined role expectation. Hence, independence attainment is easier than it is in our culture (Benedict, 1938).

Adding to this general confusion are the legal definitions of adulthood status, many of which vary from state to state. After the age of 16 or 18, the adolescent (or young adult) is expected to assume complete responsibility for various aspects of behavior, for example, accept responsibility for being an informed voter or user of alcohol. Because many aspects of legally defined adulthood do not occur at the same ages, added stress is placed on independence strivings. It is no wonder, then, that many adolescents find some degree of stress associated with independence strivings.

Factors Affecting Independence Attainment

Age and Cognitive Development. Initially, adults tend to extend independence and autonomy to adolescents in a relatively haphazard and perhaps inconsistent manner; responsibilities and privileges are generally based on age. This is evidenced in a number of different ways, such as the age at which the adolescent is allowed to date, changes in the time when he or she is expected home, changes in the nature and number of chores he or she is expected to do.

Physical developmental aspects interact with age trends in granting independence (Steinberg, 1981; Steinberg & Hill, 1978). As we noted above, adolescents become more influential in family decision making as a function of physical maturity. And, we pointed out earlier that adolescents who are bigger or grow more rapidly than their peers tend to be treated more like adults and to be given more adultlike responsibilities than smaller or later-maturing adolescents. Since adolescents mature earlier now than in previous generations, one may expect that certain kinds of adultlike privileges will be granted earlier now than in previous generations.

Cognitive development (Chapter 4) also enters into adolescent independence strivings by allowing the adolescent to reevaluate social circumstances. As we noted previously, adolescents are capable of understanding that some social rules are flexible and, therefore, are also capable of demanding answers to questions about why they are treated the way they are. The parents must now justify the way they treat their son or daughter. If this justification appears rational and reasonable, the adolescent may accept it with relatively little debate. Conflict may arise, however, if the parent is autocratic and unreasonable.

Gold and Douvan (1969) investigated, in a longitudinal study, changes in autonomy behavior in girls from age 11 to 18. Their data indicate that both behavioral and emotional autonomy increases with age. The trends toward independence from the family demonstrate that girls rely less on their families as they grow older.

Adolescents want and need independence, but in gradual amounts. That is, they wish to have only the amount of autonomy they can deal with successfully. The data of Douvan and Gold suggest that this is the case because the increases in autonomy are not dramatic in the sense that they occurred over a seven-year period, and in many instances showed only a 10 to 20 percent increase.

Sex Differences in Independence. Douvan and Adelson (1966) reported that boys were more interested in establishing independence from parental control, sought more responsibility for their own behaviors, and were more preoccupied with self-control than were girls. In general, these strivings and demands created some conflict between the boys and their parents. Girls, on the other hand, generally felt that the ways their parents treated them and the rules that were set down for them were relatively fair and honest. As a result, girls tended to have an easier time in strivings for independence. These data are in direct contrast to data (for example, Barry, Bacon & Child, 1957) indicating that in many tribal societies both boys and girls experience about the same degree of conflict, which is relatively low, even though there are considerable sex differences in independence training, with boys being socialized toward self-reliance and achievement, and girls toward nurturance, obedience, and dependence. Sex-role differences do not lead to differing degrees of difficulty in learning independence in these cultures, perhaps because the roles are well defined and generally accepted.

Kagan and Moss (1962) give some clues about the reasons for sex differences in independence strivings reported in American culture. They found that dependency was a more stable personality trait in girls from childhood into adolescence than it was in boys. In other words, girls who were dependent as young children tended to remain dependent as adolescents and adults. In contrast, dependence and independence were much less stable for boys through adolescence and into adulthood. Kagan and Moss attribute this sex difference to cultural training. Dependent boys are assumed to receive pressure to become more independent as they grow older, and independent boys are assumed to be allowed to remain that way in adolescence and adulthood. Girls, on the other hand, are trained to be relatively dependent and compliant in childhood as well as in adolescence and are reinforced for behaving that way (see Bardwick, 1971). The continuity in role expectations across childhood and adolescence for girls contrasts sharply with the discontinuity in male roles (dependency in childhood and independence later in life) and probably accounts for many of the sex differences. As we pointed out in discussing theories of adolescent socialization, adult reinforcement as well as modeling of particular sex-typed behaviors are important influences on the behaviors that will be exhibited by adolescents. The data of Kagan and Moss are consistent with this theorizing.

Although this explanation has a good deal of appeal, Bardwick (1971) and others point out that a number of other factors may be important in understanding sex differences in adolescent dependence and independence. For example, dependency may take any of several forms, including instrumental dependence, which is a seeking of help from an outside source, emotional dependence, which is seeking affection and comfort, and aggressive dependence, which includes manipulations of people or motives. In other words, dependency is not a one-dimensional trait; it has a number of different behavioral outlets that the girl may use to achieve the

same goals that the boy achieves in an independent fashion. In effect, males and females may achieve the same end by different means, and the sex difference in means may be irrelevant.

In other words, the sex differences in dependence and independence that we have reported in this section should not be exaggerated. Excessive stereotyping of boys and girls in terms of independence and dependence should be avoided. As with many other sex-typed characteristics, there are wide individual differences and variations within each sex and considerable overlap between the sexes. To argue that girls should all become independent or boys dependent is to defeat the individuality of the person and the developmental aspects that shape and mold that person. As sex roles become less rigidly defined, we will probably find fewer sex-related differences in dependence and independence.

Child Rearing and Independence Attainment. Elder's (1962, 1963, 1968, 1971) research has gone far in explaining the important role that child-rearing techniques play in adolescent independence strivings. Elder found that adolescents who reported that their parents used inductive discipline rated the highest in autonomy. Authoritarian parents had adolescents who were lower in autonomy and self-confidence; authoritative parenting was related to greater feelings of independence, probably because these parents allowed their adolescents to express their opinions.

These data very clearly indicate that parental roles and types of child-rearing practices can influence independence strivings in adolescents in several ways. First, parents can do a lot to help their children learn to become independent by giving them appropriate privileges and responsibilities at the appropriate age. Second, children can learn independent behaviors by observing the adults or parents who model these behaviors. In addition, certain parental types make adolescents feel that they are wanted, which should increase identification with, and modeling of, the parent (e.g., Elder, 1963). Baumrind (1966, 1968), particularly, has addressed this set of issues and has pointed out that it is extremely important for the adolescent to be given models of independence behaviors, as well as age-graded experiences in behaving independently, in order for appropriate degrees of autonomous and independent behavior to develop:

Strivings for independence in adolescence, then, mirror an extremely complex process of identification, modeling of parental roles, and reactions to parental child-rearing techniques. There are sex differences involved in these strivings as well as age and cognitive-developmental differences, the latter not being very well spelled out at this time. With this multitude of influences, it is no wonder that independence strivings in adolescents are problematical for adolescents as well as their parents.

The Family and Life-Span Development. Hill (1980) has pointed out a very important, if ill-researched, aspect of understanding parent-adolescent relations: parents are undergoing developmental changes just as are adolescents. In order to understand more fully the nature of parent-adolescent relationships, then, we should take a life-span view of development.

The life-span view includes the study of continuity in behavior across the life span as well as the study of changes in behavior from one period of development to another. In addition, the life-span approach recognizes the importance of studying the interaction of one generation of individuals with another. By taking a life-span perspective, then, greater insights into parent-adolescent interaction will be gained.

Hill (1980) notes that, unfortunately, we know but little of the nature of developmental influences on the adult with respect to their influence on parent-adolescent interaction. However, in an excellent paper

that should be read by anyone interested in family influences on adolescents, Chilman (1968) has attempted to define some factors that may be important. His major point is that the parents themselves are at a particularly vulnerable developmental period at about the same time that adolescents in the family begin to strive for independence. The parents have been married about 20 years and must face up to the fact that in a very short time their children will be gone from the home, leaving them without the responsibilities and daily duties that have consumed so much of their previous life together. The husband is in his early forties and has probably gone about as far as he ever will in his business or profession. The wife is faced with the prospect of a home empty of children and with considerably more leisure time than she has had in the past, particularly if she has been a full-time wife and mother.

For these, as well as other reasons, one might well expect parents to react to adolescent independence striving with ambivalence, confusion, and reluctance. Parents derive not only power but also great satisfaction from having their sons and daughters dependent upon them. Giving up this power and satisfaction may be extremely difficult for some parents, especially those who have drifted apart from each other and share their homelife activities primarily with their children. On the other hand, those who have been successful in their vocation, marriage, and development of outside interests, tend, as we would expect, to look forward to living a full life after their children leave home (Chilman, 1968).

SIBLING INFLUENCES ON THE ADOLESCENT

The effects of siblings on the adolescent's development depend on the number and sex of the siblings, the relationship they have with the adolescent, and the way they are

Siblings can act as effective socializing agents for each other because of their similiar experiences.

treated by the parents. Perhaps most importantly, sibling effects seem to relate to birth order.

One of the general findings about sibling effects on adolescent development is that first-born children tend to achieve better in academic spheres than their siblings (see Oberlander et al., 1970). This effect apparently increases with increases in family size (Oberlander et al., 1970), and is the same for both males and females. Although not well researched, this birth-order effect can be devastating if the first-born child is somewhat brighter than the second- or third-born. The older child will clearly stand out above the others in academic peformance. As a result, the younger child may be exposed to influences that are damaging to the self-concept. This, in turn, may lead to favoritism by the parents of one of their offspring. The result may be a considerable degree of sibling rivalry, including moments in which the siblings have a great deal of fondness for each other and others in which there is a good deal of ill will. In such instances, it is quite possible that the parents will reinforce the ill will by continually holding up one of the siblings as an example for the others. Obviously, this is not a happy state of affairs for the nonfavored sibling. The effects of such favoritism can even carry

over toward the relationships of the parents with the other adolescents.

Age differences between the siblings can also be important. Older brothers or sisters may be expected to acquire dates for their younger siblings, or to let them "tag along" on excursions with their friends. In such instances, older siblings may build up avoidance responses toward the younger siblings, and these, in turn, may lead to a good deal of ill will.

Obviously, there are a number of benefits in having siblings in the family: someone to play with as a child and, during adolescence, someone with whom interpersonal problems and family disputes can be discussed with the assurance of an understanding ear.

Indeed, some researchers (e.g., Cicirelli, 1972) have argued that siblings are at times better socializers than parents. Because they are closer in age and developmental experience to the adolescent, they may better understand his or her problems and growing pains. This may make it easier for the adolescent to discuss problems of growing up and difficulties with the parents. Older siblings may serve as useful models for aspects of social behavior; for example, peer group interactions, dating, getting along with parents, and the like. Siblings, then, may make a unique contribution to the adolescent's development.

Of course, there can be detrimental influences due to siblings. For example, Longstreth, Longstreth, Ramirez, and Fernandez (1975) reported that independent of sex, social class, and race, older siblings who are not effective in dealing with peers, parents, and the like may provide poor models for a younger sibling.

Finally, there is a tendency to view siblings as "growing up in the same environment." Of course, this is not true; siblings experience their environment very differently (Plomin & Daniels, 1987). Siblings are treated differently by both the parents and others (other siblings or relatives, for example), and, because they are different ages, they grow up in different stages of the family life cycle.

SUMMARY

The nature of the family has changed considerably since the turn of the century. The modal family is now urban, mobile, nuclear, smaller, and composed of two working parents. In addition, an increasing number of children and adolescents are growing up in single-parent families, either by the choice of the mother or as a result of the increasing divorce rate. Although the parents remain the single most important socialization influence on the adolescent, the changes in family living circumstances and in family composition mediate the influence of the parents.

Researchers have identified three major dimensions of child rearing that relate to various aspects of child and adolescent behavior. Parents who are rejecting (as opposed to accepting) frustrate adolescents' nurturance needs and feelings of being wanted. These children tend to be more aggressive and engage in more delinquency. Lax and inconsistent discipline also induces delinquency in adolescents. In general, power-assertive disciplinary techniques teach the adolescent control through force and aggressive behavior. Parents who are accepting, who do not overly use psychological means of controlling the adolescent's behavior, and who do not try to rigidly control the adolescent's behavior, rear adolescents with more positive self-concepts. This constellation of rearing techniques also leads to a more androgynous sex role.

Researchers have identified four types of parents based on their use of various types of disciplinary techniques: Authoritative, Authoritarian, Indulgent, and Indifferent. The evidence is convincing that the authoritative style of child rearing is more optimal than the others because it not only makes the adolescent feel wanted and loved but also provides for appropriate restrictions on behavior without ignoring the adolescent's input into decision making.

Divorce is a disruptive event for the entire family, in part because of the emotional aspects of the circumstance, and in part because of the disruption to family composition and daily routine. There are many factors to which the adolescent must adjust, including living with only one parent—usually the mother—and, perhaps, the remarriage of one or both of the parents. Adolescent reactions to parental divorce generally include anger and moral indignation toward the parents. Many adolescents withdraw from both parents and only a few take sides with one parent. Some adolescents experience difficulty in school, but many do not. The more psychologically mature and independent adolescents adapt better to parental divorce. In general, it appears that, although divorce is difficult for the adolescent, it is not as difficult as it is for preadolescents or preschool children.

It is now recognized that family structure in and of itself is not the critical feature in adolescent development. Whether growing up in a single-parent, stepparent, or intact family, the adolescent's psychological health is most affected by family atmosphere. The freer from conflict, the more cohesive, and the warmer the family atmosphere, regardless of family structure, the happier and more psychologically healthy the adolescent will be.

The majority of mothers with children under 18 years of age now work. There are a number of benefits to the adolescent of a working mother. Adolescents, both male and female, of working mothers develop more flexible views of sex roles. Adolescent females have a less negative view of femininity, and they tend to be more independent, motivated, and career-oriented. These aspects of maternal employment may be lost if the mother is unhappy because she is working or if the mother's going to work disrupts the family routine too much.

Independence strivings increase during

the adolescent years. In part, this seems to reflect the physical development of the adolescent. More physically mature adolescent males tend to exert greater influence in family decision making. As secure feelings about the self develop, the adolescent becomes desattelized, that is, less reliant on the parents and more autonomous. Although some conflicts between parent and adolescent occur over independence strivings, these tend not to be particularly serious for most adolescents. Communication between parent and adolescent fosters better adjustment of both the parent and the adolescent to independence.

Little research is available on the influences of other family members on the adolescent. Siblings can have both positive and negative influences. Modeling an effective sibling can promote peer group interactions, and siblings provide a sounding board for dealing with parents. However, siblings who are ineffective in social situations or who exhibit deviant behavior may provide poor models.

GLOSSARY

CRPBI (Children's Report of Parental Behavior Inventory). A questionnaire that assesses children's perceptions of their parent's rearing styles.

Dimensions of child rearing:

Acceptance versus rejection (Schaefer). A dimension of the CRPBI that reflects how accepting, warm, and supportive—versus cold, hostile, and rejecting—the child perceives the parents to be.

Psychological autonomy versus psychological control (Schaefer). A dimension of the CRPBI reflecting the degree to which the child perceives the parents as using guilt and other psychological means to control his or her behavior.

Firm control versus lax control (Schaefer). On the CRPBI, the dimension of child rearing reflected by the making and enforcing of many rules and regulations as opposed to

allowing greater freedom and spontaneity on the part of the child.

Induction. A form of discipline involving explanations for why some behavior was wrong and providing alternative forms for behaving under those conditions.

Love withdrawal. A form of punishment involving ignoring or isolating the child and verbally expressing dislike and disappointment toward the child.

Non-power-assertive. A form of discipline involving love withdrawal or induction.

Overvaluation. Parental overacceptance and overindulgence of their offspring in an attempt vicariously to relive their own childhood.

Parental demandingness. The extent to which parents expect and demand mature and responsible behavior.

Parental responsiveness. The degree to which the parent is warm, supporting, and accepting.

Parent types

Authoritative. High-demanding, high-responsive parents.

Authoritarian. High-demanding, low-responsive parents.

Indifferent. Low-demanding, low-responsive parents.

Indulgent. Low-demanding, high-responsive parents.

Power assertion. A disciplinary technique involving the use of physical punishment or the threat of it.

Reconstituted family. A family in which there is a stepparent.

Satellization. The perception of children that they are not independent of their parents but are like a satellite, revolving around their parents and dependent upon them.

Undervaluation. Parental rejection of the child, causing the child to conform to parental wishes out of a fear of punishment.

SUGGESTED READINGS

DODGE, K. A. (Ed.), (1980). Special section: Developmental psychopathology in children of depressed mothers. *Developmental Psychology, 26,* 3–67.

This special issue is devoted to research and theory on the effects of growing up in a home with a depressed mother. Research presented touches on the adverse effects on infants, children, and adults.

HETHERINGTON, E. M. (1979). Divorce: A child's perspective. *American Psychologist, 34,* 851–858.

In a very readable essay, Hetherington reviews the course of divorce and points out many of the difficulties involved in studying the impact of divorce on the child and adolescent. She reviews existing literature and highlights the important findings.

HETHERINGTON, E. M. (1989). Coping with family transitions: Winners, losers, and survivors. *Child Development, 60,* 1–14.

Hetherington discusses the nature of family relations related to the child adapting to parental divorce. The role played by the parents as well as other family members and social institutions is explored.

HOFFMAN, L. W. (1979). Maternal employment: 1979. *American Psychologist, 34,* 859–865.

Hoffman reviews both the positive and negative aspects of maternal employment as they impact on the child and adolescent. In her brief review she points out both sex differences and social class effects on the impact of maternal employment on the child.

Journal of Divorce, 12, 1988/89.

The special issue of this journal contains a number of reviews as well as original research reports on a variety of topics related to divorce: custody concerns, clinical aspects of adaptation, facilitating children's coping, etc.

Peer-Group Influences on Adolescent Development

11

CHAPTER OUTLINE

MAJOR ISSUES ADDRESSED

Factors Related to Peer-Group Formation
Ways That Peers Affect the Individual
The Role of Intimate Friends in Development
Variables Related to Peer Popularity
The Development of Heterosexual Friendships
Adolescent Marriage
Peer versus Parent Influences

INTRODUCTION

One of the popular stereotypes concerning adolescents is that they are much more peer-oriented than children. A second popular stereotype is that adolescent values, likes and dislikes, and views of society are much more akin to peer than parent perspectives. In this chapter we examine evidence relevant to these stereotypes as we explore the importance of peers on the adolescent's socialization.

WHY STUDY PEER RELATIONS?

Aside from the popular stereotypes, there are a number of reasons for studying peer relations during the adolescent years. As children slowly become emancipated from their parents, they spend increasing amounts of time with their peers (for example, Hartup & Laursen, 1989). This increasing time spent with peers serves a variety of functions.

It is with peers that adolescents may try out various roles, picking and choosing those that seem to "fit" with few long-term consequences of failure in role acquisition (Thornburg, 1971). For example, if the role of leader is comfortable, the peer group is likely to make this obvious. Adult peer groups are unlikely to be so kind in the reverse case.

Peer interaction also allows contact with age mates who share similar problems, conflicts, likes, and dislikes. In this way, peers serve the useful function of promoting adaptation to intergenerational conflict and adaptation to those with differing values (Armsden & Greenberg, 1987; Hartup & Laursen, 1989; Berndt, 1989). Hence, peers help adolescents learn to tolerate individual differences.

Of course, studying peer relations allows us to assess the relative importance of peers and parents on the adolescent's development. The most current evidence (for example, Berndt, 1989; Krosnick & Judd, 1982; Montemayor, 1982; O'Brien & Bierman, 1988) suggests that susceptibility to peer influence increases during adolescence, but that it does not surpass the impact of the parents (Buhrmester & Furman, 1987). There are, then, developmental trends in the relative influence of parents and peers on the adolescent, but the influence of parents does not wane (Krosnick & Judd, 1982; Montemayor, 1982). Rather, it appears that the relative influence of peers and parents on the adolescent depends on the domain of behavior being studied (Hunter & Youniss, 1982; Reid, Landesman, Treder, & Jaccard, 1989).

In contrast to the unisexual childhood peer groups, the heterosexual adolescent peer groups provide training grounds for adult peer interactions, which also are heterosexual in nature. In this way childhood and adolescent peer groups perform different functions. Contrasting peer interactions in childhood and adolescence helps us better understand the social forces that promote growth toward adulthood roles and behaviors.

Techniques in the Study of Peer Relations

Psychologists have used both experimental and observational research techniques in the investigation of peer effects on adolescent development. As often happens with research in socialization, there are a number of problems that limit the kind of research that can be done, and that at times lead to confusion about the interpretation of findings (for example, Campbell, 1964; Dunphy, 1963; Thornburg, 1971). One such problem is that findings are often based on questionnaires or interviews that may produce data that are faulty (for example, the interviewees may either intentionally or unintentionally distort their recollections), incomplete, or open to bias by the interviewer. If interviewees distort their responses, it is impossible to obtain accurate data about the importance of the peer group. In addition, the findings are often reported in terms of group means or percentages of people responding, which means that we lose the individuality of the interviewee's responses. These wide individual variations should not be forgotten, because they shed considerable light on the effects of the peer group on adolescents.

The alternative to the questionnaire or interview approach is to observe the natural formation of adolescent groups and assess their effects on the individual. If one chooses this technique, it is necessary to determine what behaviors are to be observed, and in what circumstances or settings. Should the study be conducted on the playground, in the classroom, at the neighborhood hangout, or on the Little League practice field? In addition, one must always question the degree to which the presence of an observer, especially an adult, may alter the frequency with which certain critical behaviors occur. Given the sensitivity of adolescents to the presence of adults, this is no minor problem. In addition, it is unclear to what degree group formation processes for one type of group adequately and appropriately describe group formation processes for other types of groups.

Another problem that may arise in assessing data on peer-group relationships is the problem of select or biased samples. If one studies select or biased samples of adolescents, it is impossible to determine adequately the general nature of peer-group formation and effects on development. Although some instances of such select group studies are obvious, for example, the study of campus radicals, other biasing factors may not be quite so obvious. Studying group formation in middle-class adolescents and then generalizing the findings to adolescents across the social-class spectrum is probably inappropriate because different factors may influence group formations in middle-class and lower-class adolescent populations. Similarly, the study of group formation and effects in boys may not reflect the factors operating in group formation among girls.

PEER-GROUP FORMATION AND FUNCTION

Most of the research on peer relations was done from the late 1920s through the early 1950s (Hartup, 1989). The establishment of university schools during the 1930s was largely responsible for these investigations. Major issues investigated included the formation of peer groups, development changes in the influence of peers on the child or adolescent, and the nature of social interactions with peers. More contemporary research has focused on the relative influence of parents versus peers, the factors influencing friendship choices, why isolation from peers occurs, and methodological advancements in the study of peer relations.

Defining Peer Groups

The term *peer* usually connotes an age mate. In general, when we consider peers, we refer to groups of children or adolescents who are about the same age. The reference to age with respect to defining peers probably is quite suitable when discussing children, because children largely associate with those who are of the same age (Hartup, 1989). However, adolescents often associate with individuals from a relatively wide age range. For example, adolescent girls tend to date somewhat older boys; earlier maturers tend to associate with somewhat older adolescents, because they find such interactions more rewarding than interactions with their less developed age mates. We must be cautious, then, not to limit our conception of peers during the adolescent years by considering them only to be age mates. In many situations (such as school clubs and athletic teams) peers may well be older or younger than the adolescent.

The term *group* also is somewhat elusive. A group is not simply a crowd; it is more than a simple aggregation of individuals who happen to be in one place at the same time (Dunphy, 1963). Psychologists generally agree that groups are composed of *interacting individuals who possess a common goal and norm structure* (Sherif, Harvey, Hood, & Sherif, 1961; Sherif & Sherif, 1953). Groups have leaders and followers and usually a division of labor. They are formed for some purpose and generally have sets of rules, implicit or explicit, that govern the behavior of the members. This is true of long- or short-term groups and of spontaneous as well as *ad hoc* groups.

The formation and influence of peer groups obviously does not begin in adolescence. Children have peer groups and are subject to their influence. Indeed, in many ways, the functions of childhood and adolescent peer groups are very similar (see Box 11–1). The influence of adolescent peer groups on the individual, then, is an extension of peer influences during the childhood years (Furman, 1989).

BOX 11—1   Peer Influences on Children and Adolescents

Some of the functions served by peer contact are similar during the childhood and adolescent years. Peer contact provides the opportunity to interact with age mates and to develop age-appropriate social skills. One of the more important such skills learned is simply how to get along with others in various situations, including cooperation and competition. In both childhood and adulthood, peers provide someone with whom to do things of mutual interest. Peers also provide the opportunity to develop age-related intellectual and physical skills.

In some ways, the role of peer contact during the adolescent years is more important than it is during the childhood years. Peer relations during adolescence become much more like adult peer relations. The peer group becomes heterosexual, for example (Connolly, 1989). Learning how to interact with peers of the opposite sex is an important aspect of adolescent, but not childhood, peer groups. Some adolescent peer groups (clubs, for example) are also very similar to adulthood groups, and provide the opportunity to learn the social skills involved in being a member of a formal organization. Adolescent peer groups also provide the opportunity to share ideological values and ideals and help the adolescent develop a sustained sense of morality.

Another important aspect of adolescent, but not childhood, peer groups involves social comparison and self-evaluation. The peer group provides the adolescent with a natural environment for social comparison, particularly with respect to norms and values for appropriate appearance, likes and dislikes, and behavior (Coleman, 1980). In addition, adolescence is a time for self-evaluation as the self-concept and identity are being developed (Connolly; White, Stevens, & Burstein, 1987; Gavin & Furman, 1989). The common sense view holds that social comparison with peer group norms and values leads to self-evaluation and attempts to change the self in ways deemed desirable (Ausubel, Montemayor, & Svajian, 1977). Eisert and Kahle (1982) suggest that the reverse causal direction may be more correct. They argue that self-evaluation provides a framework for assessing social information and, therefore, mediates social comparison. In their study, they had junior high school boys judge physical (strength, appearance) and role (being a friend, being liked) self-evaluation, and physical (strength) and role (getting along with teachers) status at the start of the junior year and then a year later. They reported that self-evaluation was causally predominant over social comparison. In other words, during late adolescence, self-attitudes temper the nature of social comparisons with the peer group. As a result, they conclude that adolescence is not a time of extreme dependence on the peer group for social comparison and, hence, self-evaluation.

Peer group influences show a continuity from childhood through adolescence, then, but there are important differences. Adolescent peer groups provide a model for adult peer relations that is not provided by childhood peer groups.

Group Formation in Childhood

The first peer group to which the child belongs probably is based on sex, age, and neighborhood. From the preschool years to about seventh or eighth grade, children tend to associate almost exclusively with others of their own sex. It is not until early adolescence that it becomes acceptable to have close associations with members of the opposite sex (Hartup, 1989). In all likelihood, this reflects the types of activities in which children engage, which are largely sex typed.

Age is also an important determinant of peer group formation during the childhood years, as noted above. Children's peer groups have a much narrower age range of members than do adolescents' peer groups. This probably reflects age differences in interests and physical competencies related to the types of games and other activities in which children engage. Older children find the activities of younger children boring, and younger children may not comprehend the rules of games played by older children (Piaget, 1932, 1952). Because these factors are not so limiting during adolescence, adolescent peer groups may have a wider age range of members (Connolly, 1989; O'Brien & Bierman, 1988).

Children tend to associate with those who live in the relatively immediate vicinity of their own residence because these are the initial peers readily available to the child. As children become more mobile, they may associate with others who live some distance away, especially during the school hours, but still maintain considerable contact with neighbors. Because the adolescent is more mobile and is more likely to come in contact with other adolescents living in different areas, adolescent groups tend not to be limited by neighborhood as much as children's groups.

The factors leading to the formation of friendships and groups have been the subject of numerous investigations (Hartup, 1970a; Coleman, 1989; Berndt, 1982; Gottman, 1983). Later, we will examine factors related to the forming of friendships. Here we discuss how groups form.

In a series of creatively designed and excellently conducted researches, Sherif and his co-workers detailed the formation of children's peer groups. Sherif and Sherif (1953) studied group formation in white middle-class boys in a camp setting. To allow intragroup friendships to develop, two groups of boys were kept separate from each other for three days. In the second phase of the experiment, the two groups were split in half and recombined (that is, one-half of group A and one-half of Group B became group C, and the remaining halves became group D). The two new groups were observed for five days. These two groups, which were carefully matched in terms of personalities and abilities, were also kept apart. In the third phase of the experiment, the two groups were placed in competitive situations with each other.

In phase one of the experiment, clear friendship and status patterns emerged; in phase two these patterns changed and new friendship and status patterns emerged (even though half of each group was composed of children who knew each other from the first phase). During phase two there was clear evidence of a hierarchical structure in both groups; that is, each group produced leaders and followers. The leaders tended to be the more popular members of the group, but there was not a perfect correlation between leadership status and popularity. Each group also formed its own norms during the five days of the second phase of the experiment. In phase three (the competitive situation between the groups) a moderate degree of hostility broke out between the groups, and the one group that consistently lost in competition began to break up and lose its solidarity.

Sherif et al. (1961) replicated this experiment with a group of fifth-grade boys. During the competitive phases of the experiment there were changes in the group's structure as new leaders came to the fore, primarily as a function of their excellence in competition. In these groups, leadership roles depended upon the group's immediate goal. Intergroup conflict was lessened during an added fourth phase in which forced cooperation between the groups was necessary in order to complete a task.

These studies show that during childhood gradual shifts occur in the nature of peer groups toward the structure found in adolescent groups. In late childhood, groups evolve into leaders and followers, with leadership being based primarily on popularity. In competitive situations, however, there is a tendency for leadership to be determined by the skills and expertise one can bring to the group task and goals. During later childhood, intense loyalty to the group is evident. This may result from a "need" to feel that one belongs to something, which emerges from the initial stages of egocentrism. By belonging and conforming the individual may reduce feelings of anxiety caused by the imaginary audience (Chapter 4). Finally, groups develop standards and norms guiding behavior and fostering a sense of group identity, which may act to facilitate the individual's identity development and feelings of belonging to, and fitting into, the larger social structure.

Adolescent Group Formation

Dunphy (1963) made one of the most comprehensive and extensive studies of the nature and development of the adolescent peer group. Using diaries that were kept by the subjects, questionnaires, and interviews, Dunphy discovered that the adolescent belongs to two basic kinds of groups: the *crowd* and the **clique**. The major distinction between these two groups was in terms of size. Approximately 80 percent of the youths in Dunphy's study belonged to one of these two kinds of groups. The remaining 20 percent

tended not to get involved with groups even if offered the opportunity to do so. It should be pointed out that peer-group membership is not necessary, in all cases, for proper growth and maturation (Grinder, 1969).

The crowd is the larger of the two groups and is composed of a collection of cliques. In Dunphy's investigations, crowds contained from 15 to 30 members, with an average size of 20.2 members. These crowds were roughly three times the size of cliques, which ranged from three to nine members in size, with an average of 6.2 members per clique. The average crowd, then, was made up of two to four cliques.

The first stage in Figure 11–1 is the precrowd stage, which describes the late childhood peer groups discussed above. Stage 2 cliques are made up of young adolescents of similar age and maturity. Dunphy suggests that the unisexual stage 2 cliques provide their members with support and security for the relatively new experience of dealing with members of the opposite sex. Boys and girls are willing to interact, but generally only within the security afforded by their respective unisexual cliques.

During stage 3, heterosexual cliques begin to develop. Individual heterosexual interaction (dating) is begun by the upper status members of the unisexual cliques (Dunphy, 1963). The adolescents in stage 3 maintain dual membership in a sex-appropriate unisexual clique and a heterosexual clique. There is no longer the high level of support provided by the stage 2 type of unisexual clique, but there is still the security that comes from belonging to a unisexual clique.

Between stage 3 and stage 4, the adolescent peer group undergoes a transition and emerges as a constellation of fully developed heterosexual cliques that interact rather closely with each other. The cliques now form what Dunphy calls a fully developed crowd. From middle adolescence onward the number of opposite-sex friends in the individual's network increases, as does the

Late adolescence

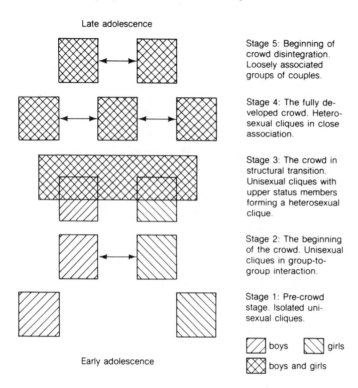

Stage 5: Beginning of crowd disintegration. Loosely associated groups of couples.

Stage 4: The fully developed crowd. Heterosexual cliques in close association.

Stage 3: The crowd in structural transition. Unisexual cliques with upper status members forming a heterosexual clique.

Stage 2: The beginning of the crowd. Unisexual cliques in group-to-group interaction.

Stage 1: Pre-crowd stage. Isolated unisexual cliques.

Early adolescence

boys   girls
boys and girls

FIGURE 11–1   **Stages of Group Development in Adolescence**
(Source: Dunphy, D.C. [1963]. The social structure of urban adolescent peer groups. *Sociometry*, 26, 230–246.)

likelihood of having a romantic friend (Connolly, 1989).

In stages 3 and 4, the cliques are composed of boys who are between 3 and 22 months older than the girls, with an average age difference of approximately 10 months. The crowd, then, is composed of heterosexual cliques in which the boys tend to be slightly older than the girls.

During stage 5, the crowd begins to disintegrate slowly, and cliques consisting of couples begin to emerge. Stage 5, then, represents the completion of the cycle from the pre-crowd, unisexual cliques of late childhood and early adolescence to the cliques composed of heterosexual couples, a pattern that is typical of adulthood cliques. The need for emotional support and comfort from the unisexual clique no longer exists, because individuals have developed the interpersonal skills necessary in heterosexual relationships.

Functions of a Clique.   The major function of a clique is talking about and planning crowd activities (Dunphy, 1963). The dissemination of information about crowd activities and the evaluation of past activities are other major functions of cliques. The relatively small number of members in a clique permit a high degree of cohesion, which is reflected in the similar interests and backgrounds of its members. Cliques function primarily during weekdays; only about a third of their activities occur on the weekends. As with any group, cliques have leaders as well as followers. The leaders tend to date more often and to form steady heterosexual relationships sooner than the other members of the group. In a sense, they tend, by their example, to push the other members toward more advanced levels of development. Another major function of the clique leader is to represent the clique within the crowd setting.

There are a number of advantages and disadvantages to belonging to a clique (Coleman, 1961; Dunphy, 1963; Horrocks & Benimoff, 1967). A clique offers security and a feeling of importance as well as a buffer for social transition situations, for example, adjustments to college. The clique may also promote the acquisition of socially acceptable behaviors by demanding that its members conform to group behavior norms. The disadvantages of clique membership are obvious. By encouraging conformity, the clique suppresses individuality. Because of its close-knit nature and small size, the clique may promote snobbishness and stifle opportunities to get to know others from different backgrounds. Moreover, rejection of attempts to penetrate the clique can be damaging to the rejected individual's self-concept. Nevertheless, it seems that the advantages of the clique as a socializing agent outweigh its disadvantages.

An important function of adolescent cliques is the planning of larger group activities.

The Function of a Crowd. The crowd is the center of organized group activities, such as parties or other social activities, and serves the function of introducing adolescents to heterosexual interaction situations. Crowd activities take place primarily on weekends. All crowds tend to be heterosexual in composition, with the boys, on the average, approximately 10 months older than the girls. Not all members of a clique belong to a crowd, but everyone in a crowd belongs to a clique. Because of its size and its composition (a collection of cliques), a crowd is considerably less intimate than a clique. Crowds and cliques also differ in function. The crowd acts as a facilitator in the adolescent's transition from same-sex cliques to heterosexual cliques. This does not mean that unisexual cliques do not continue into adulthood: fraternities, sororities, and community groups such as the Lions are examples of adult unisexual cliques.

Crowds, like cliques, have advantages and disadvantages (Dunphy, 1963). Crowds provide opportunities to interact with, learn to understand, and adapt to others with differing values and backgrounds. As we noted above, crowds influence and promote heterosexual contact. Crowds have disadvantages, too; they encourage snobbishness, cause friction with parents, and in some cases, cause members to neglect school and home life.

The transitions noted above for childhood and adolescent groups reflect the continual evolutions of group formation and membership toward adulthood types. Similar trends exist for the role of groups. During the childhood and adolescent years, peers become increasingly important for companionship (Buhrmester & Furman, 1987; O'Brien & Bierman, 1988; Reid et al., 1989) and for emotional support and intimacy (Buhrmester & Furman, 1987; Reid et al., 1989). Finally, a similar trend is evident when examining the bases on which groups are formed (O'Brien & Bierman, 1988).

Children and preadolescents define groups through common activities and social behaviors, and indicate that these are the areas in which the group exerts its strongest influence. Adolescents perceive the group as exerting more global and far-reaching influences, extending to dress codes, attitudes, and values. In addition, adolescents, like adults, view peer groups as important indicators of their own self-worth, with peer rejection interpreted as a sign that one is not worth very much. Given that social acceptance is associated with higher self-esteem and social engagement, and peer rejection with social withdrawal (Connolly et al., 1987; Killeen & Frame, 1989), this suggests that adolescence is when the peer group becomes important for psychological adjustment.

Conformity to Peer-Group Norms

Adolescents are often stereotyped as conformists. Whether this stereotype is used in connection with group preferences for certain tastes in music or clothing, or whether

Conformity to peers, as in dress codes, increases up to mid-adolescence and then declines.

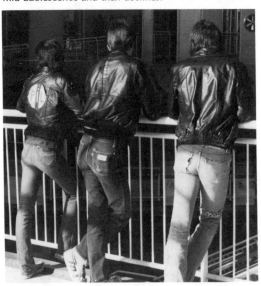

it relates to more global concepts, such as group togetherness, it suggests that adolescents do not think or act independently. What of conformity in childhood? Is it lower than conformity at adolescence, and, if so, why?

Conformity refers to the degree to which the individual follows the behavior patterns deemed appropriate by the group. There is considerable research and theorizing on children's conformity behavior, largely viewed within the framework of imitation and social-learning theories. According to social-learning theory, conformity to peer behaviors should depend on, and vary according to, peer reinforcement, increasing and decreasing with increases and decreases in reinforcement for conformity behavior.

Hence, we might expect the degree of conforming behavior to increase during adolescence if it can be demonstrated that there is greater reinforcement for conforming behavior in adolescent peer groups than in childhood peer groups. Some evidence (for example, Meyer, 1959) supporting this view is discussed below.

Piaget, discusses conformity behavior during childhood and adolescence within the context of learning to understand the rules of social behavior (1932). During the first, or egocentric, stage the child has neither a clear conception of social rules nor much understanding of why people behave the way they do. Although the child may imitate adults, it is rote imitation and does not entail underlying conceptualizations of rules for behavior. During the second stage, labeled extreme conformity (ages 6–11), the child develops an understanding of social rules and begins to conform to them; this stage is also marked by an increase in social interactions with peers. At about 11 years, the child's conception of rules begins to change, from one that views rules as coming from outside or supernatural forces, to one that views rules as the product of social consensus.

According to Piaget, peer conformity

should begin to decline gradually as the adolescent gains an adult perspective of rules. Age changes in conformity to group norms, then, are seen as resulting from developing cognitive abilities that allow qualitatively different understandings of the nature of norms. As a result, Piaget's theory allows for the prediction of age changes in conformity. The available research evidence tends to support predictions based on Piaget's theory, and therefore lends credence to the notion that conforming behavior in children is partially a function of the child's cognitive abilities.

A classic investigation of conformity behavior in childhood and adolescence was carried out in several experiments reported by Berenda (1950). In these experiments, conformity to peers was measured by the subject's agreement with peers' inaccurate estimates of the length of a line drawn on a card. In one experiment conformity behavior in 7- to 10-year-olds was compared to conformity behavior in 11- to 13-year-olds under conditions of peer pressure exerted by the eight brightest children in the child's school class. The child was exposed to incorrect judgments by these bright peers, and conformity was measured by the number of times the child agreed with the peer group and gave an inaccurate estimate of line length. For both age groups, the number of incorrect answers was greater when the child was exposed to incorrect peer information than when the child gave judgments alone. The younger subjects conformed to the false judgments more than the older subjects, but the difference was not statistically significant. On the basis of other similar experiments, Berenda reported significant age differences in conformity to peer judgments between the 7- to 10-year-olds and the 11- to 13-year-olds only when the peers gave a variety of different overestimates of line length. When the peer overestimates were all the same, no significant age difference occurred.

Other investigators (e.g., Brownstone & Willis, 1971; Iscoe, Williams, & Harvey, 1963, 1964) have found similar results and report an increase in conformity to peer judgments to mid-adolescence, followed by a decline through the later adolescent years. Similarly, early and mid-adolescents perceive greater conformity to peers than do older adolescents (Gavin & Furman, 1989; Urberg & Degirmencioglu, 1989), and, younger adolescents report that peers exert a greater influence on them than do older adolescents.

The developmental trend in conformity is similar to that reported for egocentrism (Chapter 4). It may be that adolescents conform in order to avoid being different and "sticking out" in front of the imaginary audience. As egocentrism increases, then, it may result in increased conformity. Both egocentrism and conformity may decline from mid- to late adolescence as a result of the adolescent's developing identity. As the adolescent begins to develop a set of personal values—that is, an identity—there will be less need to conform, and there will be an increase in expressing the unique aspects of the self. Increased satisfaction from individual relations with peers will also result in decreased conformity.

Some researchers (e.g., Douvan & Adelson, 1966; Douvan & Gold, 1966) have also pointed out that conformity helps adolescents define themselves in ways different from adults, which may facilitate gaining independence from the family (Gavin & Furman, 1989). Dressing similarly, enjoying the same music, and sharing a common value structure help adolescents define a culture different from the dominant adult culture. To use Coleman's (1961) terms, conformity results in an adolescent society.

The adolescent society has been most extensively investigated by Coleman (1961). Perhaps the most useful and important concept to come out of his work is his finding that there is no such thing as a single adolescent society. There are certain common cultural or behavioral expressions, but there are also a number of differences in the way adolescents think, behave, and view the world. Nevertheless, there are ascertainable patterns of behavior which are followed by adolescents and which make it quite reasonable to talk about the adolescent society.

Coleman has noted that the adolescent society exists primarily within the school setting, where adolescents, set apart from the larger adult culture, develop their own lifestyles. Dunphy's (1963) research on adolescent peer groups bears this out. Coleman would argue that the value structures and systems set up by adolescents are quite different from those in the larger adult society. As we have already seen, social group structures and behavioral customs do differ considerably from those of adults. However, as we shall explore further, these differences tend to be superficial in nature, dealing with such aspects of everyday life as slang language, modes of dress, and music likes and dislikes. In most other respects, adolescents share the value structure of adults.

FRIENDSHIP DEVELOPMENT AND INFLUENCE

Friendships represent a very special case of peer influences. With increasing age, children and adolescents spend increasing amounts of time with friends. In this section we examine several aspects of adolescent friendships and compare them with childhood friendships.

Stability in Friendships

Investigations of peer group popularity have provided evidence indicating relatively stable patterns of friendship during the childhood years (for example, Hartup, 1989). Stability correlations for popularity ranged from .41 to .76 for various subgroups of nursery school children over a 20-day interval (Hartup, Glazer, & Charlesworth, 1967) and may stay at these levels over even longer periods of time. Although other investigators have reported somewhat lower correlations, the general consensus seems to be that popularity is reasonably stable in early childhood.

There is some evidence that friendship patterns in late adolescence fluctuate even less. Horrocks and Thompson (1946) reported that, over a two-week test-retest time period, popularity was more stable for older (16- to 18-year-olds) than younger (11- to 15-year-olds) adolescents. Skorepa, Horrocks, and Thompson (1963) have presented data on friendship fluctuations from ages 5 through 21. Childhood friendships, which are quite unstable to begin with, show a gradual decrease in fluctuation until about ages 12 or 13, the onset of puberty, when there is again a slight increase in fluctuation; the fluctuation slowly declines until age 18. After 18 there is again an increase in fluctuations of friendships, probably because the individuals are in situations where new friends are readily available (for example, college or the work force) or because old friends are getting married or moving away. The data of Skorepa and his colleagues indicate some sex differences in fluctuations of friendships and, along with the research of Douvan and Adelson (1966), demonstrate that girls' friendships fluctuate somewhat more than boys'.

Roles Played by Friends

In childhood, friends are, for the most part, simply someone with whom to do things. During adolescence the nature of friendships changes (Douvan & Adelson, 1966). During early adolescence (ages 11–13), friendships are still focused on activities, and friends are chosen on the basis of activities, with little notion of long-term mutuality (O'Brien & Bierman, 1988). From about age 14 to 16, friendships are based on the concepts of loyalty and security, more so for females than males (Berndt, 1982; Buhrmester & Furman, 1987; O'Brien &

Bierman, 1988). Friends must be trustworthy and loyal, for the individual is highly dependent on friends for identity and value development. From age 17 onward, friendships are based on concepts of mutuality and shared experiences. Friends are chosen on the basis of personality and their contribution to a mutually rewarding friendship.

Douvan and Adelson (1966) and Osterrieth (1969) clearly spelled out both the advantages and disadvantages associated with the kinds of friendships formed during adolescence. Adolescents need friends who are loyal and trustworthy because they rely on them for emotional support. Adolescents who have such friends need not fear that the innermost feelings they share with their friends will be laughed at or talked about with others. By sharing feelings of disappointment as well as happiness with close friends, the adolescent is able to deal better with the emotional ups and downs of adolescence. In addition, friends are an important source of social and emotional support in stressful situations (Buhrmester & Furman, 1987; Moran & Eckenrode, 1989; Reid et al., 1989).

Douvan and Adelson also point out that close friendships play an important role in helping the adolescent define the self. By being able to share his or her innermost feelings and beliefs with another, the adolescent is able to come to a greater realization of who and what he or she is. Exploring new ideas and opinions with a close friend, with the idea that personal change is possible (Douvan & Adelson, 1966), allows the individual to grow and develop a sense of the self that might not otherwise be possible (Berndt 1982; Coleman, 1980; Gavin & Furman, 1989).

Because of the intensity and intimacy involved in adolescent friendships, a friend's betrayal can be devastating. To be "put down" or ridiculed by someone to whom you have revealed your innermost feelings is a bitter pill to swallow. Adolescents may interpret such behavior as meaning that their

Because adolescent friendships are based on trust and loyalty, close friends can hurt the adolescent emotionally.

own self-worth has declined and may begin to develop negative feelings about themselves (O'Brien & Bierman; 1988; Coleman, 1980).

The intensity and passion involved in adolescent friendships declines during the later adolescent years (O'Brien & Bierman, 1988), when friendships become based more on the compatibility of personal characteristics than on the need to have someone to share confidences with. In turn, there is an increasing tendency to appreciate and even seek out people with widely differing characteristics. Douvan and Gold (1966) suggest that this trend may be due to a declining need for dependence and support. The breakup of crowds and cliques in later adolescence (the fifth stage of group development) reflects this change in friendship patterns.

Friends exert a substantial influence on the adolescent. Recently, Berndt (1989) has pointed out two mechanisms by which this influence operates. The first deals with the friend's characteristics, attitudes, values, and behaviors. If these are appropriate, positive, and healthy the friend may exert beneficial influences on the adolescent. If they are not, the influence may be detrimental, as in inducing the friend into delinquent behavior.

The second mechanism involves the nature and quality of the friendship. If it is based on mutual respect and trust, intimacy, and **prosocial behavior** the friend will have a positive influence, as in helping the adolescent cope with stressful situations such as parental divorce. If these positive qualities are lacking then the benefits will not accrue—the friend will not have the ability to act as a buffer to stress, for example.

Peer influence does not just happen automatically, as the various catch phrases describing adolescent peer relations seem to suggest. Rather, the nature of peer influences depends upon the characteristics of the peer and the qualities of the relationship. Indeed, in extremely poor circumstances, peers can actually abuse adolescents (Box 11–2) or be a primary source of comfort.

Intimate Friendships

The most influential peers are intimate friends. It is these peers to whom the adolescent is most likely to confide personal and intimate feelings, to turn to for social and emotional support, and to derive the greatest feelings of acceptance and warmth. Thus one is hardly likely to confide sensitive, highly personal feelings to anyone other than an intimate friend. In the research literature, *intimate friendships* are defined as those involving the sharing of personal and private thoughts and feelings (Berndt, 1982). They also involve factual knowledge of a friend's feelings, worries, and personality (Berndt, 1982).

The development of intimate friendships during the adolescent years was the focus of a study by Sharabany, Gershoni, and Hof-

man (1981). These researchers had students in grades 5, 7, 9, and 11 rate their friendship with either a same- or opposite-sex friend. The ratings involved measures of intimate disclosure (for example, feeling free to talk about anything with the friend) and intimate knowledge of the friend (knowing how the friend feels without being told). The results showed that there is an increase in intimacy with same-sex friends during the later adolescent years, a finding replicated by Buhrmester and Furman (1987) for students in grades 2, 5, and 8. Intimacy in opposite-sex friendships increased across the adolescent years and was somewhat higher for female-to-male than male-to-female friendship patterns. In general, adolescent females seek intimate friendships sooner than do adolescent males (Buhrmester & Furman, 1987). The findings of these researchers indicate that intimacy with opposite-sex friends is an added type of intimate friendship during adolescence but it does not replace intimacy with same-sex friends.

A number of researchers have investigated the characteristics of intimate friendships. Adolescents with intimate friends tend to score higher than those without intimate friends on measures of affective perspective taking, the ability to be socially sensitive and infer others' feelings, and altruism, sharing, showing concern for others, helping others, and the like. They also tend to base friendships on interpersonal understanding to a greater degree than do children who do not have intimate friendships. Intimate friends also engage in more mutual interactions that are beneficial to each other; for example, they exchange helpful information when working on a task jointly.

Finally, intimate friends have relatively extensive knowledge of each other's personalities and share similar views of schooling, music and clothes preferences, and interests.

The picture one gets is that those adolescents who are sensitive to others and to interpersonal relations in general are better able to achieve intimate relations with peers.

BOX 11–2 The Victims of Peer Abuse

The study of aggression during the childhood and adolescent years has focused on the nature of the aggressive individual and the circumstances that relate to that person behaving in an aggressive manner. It has been found that a vast majority of children and adolescents do not prefer an aggressive mode of interaction and that those who do become rejected by peers and may experience long-term adjustment problems. In contrast, there have been but few studies of the victims of peer aggression.

A number of interesting questions come to mind in this regard. Are some children or adolescents "picked out" to be victims? Do victims behave in ways, for example, aggressively, that prompt others to make them victims? Do victims provide reinforcement to those who are aggressive against them, thereby making themselves targets for aggression? If so, what is the nature of the reinforcement?

These and similar questions are behind the research of David Perry and his colleagues (Perry, Kusel, & Perry, 1988; Perry & Williard, 1989) on the dynamics of being a victim of peer abuse during the childhood and early adolescent years. In one study they developed a questionnaire to assess one's standing as a victim of peer physical and verbal abuse and used it to investigate victimization with students in grades 3 through 6. One finding was that victims tended to be rejected children, that is, children who had been rated by their peers as more frequently disliked than liked. In other words, a minority of children (about 10 percent) receive the bulk of peer aggression. Second, although being aggressive was related to being rejected and therefore increasing one's likelihood of being a victim, not all rejected children were highly aggressive. Aggression and victimization are not related; they are independent.

In a second study, Perry and his colleagues (Perry & Williard, 1989) examined the consequences that victims were perceived to provide those who were aggressive against them. Possible consequences included tangible rewards (e.g., money), showing signs of pain and suffering, and retaliation. In addition, the researchers sought to determine whether the perceived rewards were different for children known to be high vs. low in victimization.

The results indicated that children were more likely to expect tangible reinforcers and victim suffering, and less likely to expect retaliation, when aggressing against another child who was a typical target of peer abuse. In addition, they cared more about obtaining tangible rewards and were less concerned about victim suffering and the potential for retaliation.

Becoming a victim of peer aggression is no doubt a complicated process, but some evidence (reviewed by Perry et al., 1988) suggests it may be related to the formation of insecure attachments to parents during the infancy years, resulting in the youngster behaving in a vulnerable manner and projecting a vulnerable personality. Because victims are rejected by their peers they are in a group of youngsters and adolescents who are more prone to dropping out of school, becoming delinquents, and experiencing psychological maladjustment, such as depression. Being able to determine those who are most prone to becoming victims of peer abuse early may allow remediation and improved peer relations.

It is likely that this is a result of their ability to get along well with their peers, although research has not directly addressed this issue.

Factors Affecting Popularity

Considerable research has been directed toward discovering the characteristics of popular and less popular children and adolescents.

Children's Popularity with Peers. Popularity with peers has been assessed by a number of sociometric instruments, for example, the Guess Who technique, preferences for play partners, and best friends. The approach used by most investigators is to correlate sociometric ratings of popularity with scores from personality or cognitive tests, social class, or physical factors in order to determine the factors that relate to popularity. The resulting sets of correlations are then examined to determine the variables positively and negatively associated with popularity. It is difficult, however, to determine the causality relationship for each set of correlates. For example, assume that peer popularity ratings and school grades are positively correlated. It is just as likely that being popular causes one to do better in school, perhaps by making one more relaxed and comfortable in the school setting, as it is that doing well in school causes one to be popular. It is important to note at the outset, too, that even though some children are rated low in popularity, they are not necessarily rejected or actively avoided. Low-popular children may be simply ignored by their peers. Popularity and rejection are not the end-points of a single dimension.

Among childhood groups, IQ and social class are perhaps the two most important correlates of popularity. The correlation between IQ and peer popularity ranges from a low (about .20) to a moderate (about .65) level (for example, Davis, 1957; Wardlow & Greene, 1952). Although these correlations are as we might expect, they are difficult to interpret because IQ and social class are positively correlated. As a result, it is not clear whether the positive correlations reported are due to IQ or social class.

Roff and Sells (1965) clarified this relationship in their study of 2,800 fourth-grade students who were divided into four social-class levels on the basis of parental income and education levels. In each classroom of fourth graders, each child picked the four most liked and two least liked peers, with boys picking boys and girls picking girls. Within each social-class level the IQ scores of the most and least liked peers were examined, and it was found that for every socioeconomic level, the high-popular peers had a higher average IQ score than the low-popular peers. In other words, among childhood groups there is a rather strong relationship between IQ and popularity independent of social-class level. Other evidence (Vosk, Forehand, Parker, & Richard, 1982) shows a strong positive relationship between school performance, which is correlated with IQ, and popularity.

Although the evidence is scarce, the research suggests that in socially mixed peer groups, the lower-class child is less popular than the middle- or upper-class child (Grossman & Wrighter, 1948). It appears, then, that social class and popularity are correlated in much the same manner as IQ and popularity. The higher the child's social class, the higher the popularity ratings by peers.

There are a number of possible explanations for the relationship of social class to popularity. The results of a study by Feinberg, Smith, and Schmidt (1958) suggest that different values held by male adolescents from the lower, middle, and upper classes may account for bias. At all social-class levels, the accepted peers were characterized as intelligent, fair, athletic, good company, and honest. At the lower- and middle-class levels, the boys also stressed common interests, minding one's own business, and the ability to talk well as important in describing popular peers. The boys from the high-income groups stressed leadership, scholarship, cooperativeness, and participation in activities as critical for peer acceptance. These data strongly suggest that friendship patterns in childhood and adolescence are related to social class, and that the basis for this relationship is in the value systems of the different classes.

The research, then, suggests that in childhood peer groups, the less bright, the less affluent, and the less academically successful are not as popular as their brighter or more academically successful peers. Although, as we mentioned earlier, it is difficult to be exact about the causal chain involved in these relationships, it appears that intellectual level or school achievement is the major factor relating to popularity at all social-class levels (Roff & Sells, 1965). To the extent that this is true, it is important for teachers, school administrators, and parents to become aware of this and help the child deal with any problems that may arise, for example, relative isolation from highly desired peers (Killeen & Frame, 1989).

Peer Popularity in Adolescence

Acceptance by the peer group depends largely upon having certain qualities and behaving in ways condoned by the peer group. A number of researchers (for example, Coleman, 1961; Hartup, 1970a, 1970b, 1989) have investigated the characteristics possessed by liked and disliked peers. Liked peers are those who are good-looking, well-groomed, fun, and outgoing; who possess good social skills, act their age, are cooperative, are cheerful and happy, have a good sense of humor, are more self-confident, and are more committed to their own best friends (Clark & Ayers, 1988). Disliked peers are viewed as being homely, sloppy, shy and withdrawn, rude, childish, having a bad reputation, quarrelsome, inconsiderate, conceited, and irresponsible. Liked peers tend to make others feel accepted and comfortable. Disliked peers have just the opposite effect. In general, adolescents like peers who are similar to themselves and hold values similar to theirs. They dislike peers with highly different values, or those who have different backgrounds and personality characteristics.

Adolescents also like peers who are bright and who come from the culturally dominant groups in society (Clark & Ayers, 1988). Intelligence and social class, then, are positively correlated with peer popularity and acceptance. An adolescent who is below average in ability and is doing poorly in school, and is aware that others know this, may behave in ways that cause others to exclude the individual from the peer group; for example, being defensive about school performance, being shy, and being irresponsible are all traits that are disliked by the peer group.

Similarly, lower-class adolescents are less likely to be accepted in the peer group than are middle- or upper-class adolescents. Closely related to this issue is the importance of ethnic identity. Although there is still a trend toward same ethnic group friendships, there is some evidence (see Hraba & Grant, 1970) that increases in ethnic group pride and identity are leading to increasing friendship choices across ethnic and social-class lines. There is some tendency, then, for friendship patterns to be based more on individual personality characteristics and less on global background traits. If this trend continues, the individual adolescent will become exposed to more individuals with widely differing backgrounds, thereby overcoming some of the current limitations of clique and crowd membership.

The findings of Coie, Dodge, and Coppotelli (1982) clarify some of these findings because the relationship of a number of characteristics to popularity ratings was assessed in a single study. The third, fifth, and eighth graders indicated three best liked and three least liked children in their class. They then listed the name of a person who best fit each of 24 behavioral descriptions. Popular children were viewed as cooperative, achievers, and attractive, while unpopular children were viewed as aggressive, disruptive, snobbish, and unattractive.

One important determinant of the adolescent's acceptance and popularity is physical attractiveness (Clark & Ayers, 1988). The research of Cavoir and Dokecki (1973) with fifth and eleventh graders indicates that there are developmental trends in this relationship as well as effects dependent upon degree of popularity. The subjects ranked black and white photographs of their classmates from least to most attractive. They also rated the degree to which they liked the people pictured in the photo. Each child ranked and rated both boys and girls.

The boys' and girls' ratings of physical attractiveness were nearly identical (average correlation of ranking was .91). There was

Physical attractiveness is an important aspect of peer popularity during adolescence.

istics of accepted, neglected, and rejected seventh- and eighth-grade boys and girls. The 10 boys and 10 girls in each of the three categories were identified by asking students to name those most favored as work and play companions and those most and least liked as seating neighbors. Each pupil then indicated the student who best fit each of a series of personality traits, such as tidy, friendly, enthusiastic, having humor about the self, active in games, likable, etc. The number of times a student was positively or negatively mentioned was algebraically scored. The data for accepted peers bear out the research we discussed earlier. The neglected students, whether male or female, were generally not mentioned on any of the traits. They were neither liked nor disliked by their peers. The socially rejected students, whether male or female, received a preponderance of negative mentions. They attract attention through negative means and are described differently from both the accepted and neglected peers.

some evidence that physical attractiveness was more strongly related to popularity for fifth than for eleventh graders. The other major finding relevant to our discussion is that the discrepancy between physical attractiveness ratings and popularity ratings was generally greater for those in the middle range of popularity than for those at either extreme. These data indicate that physical attractiveness is an important determinant of peer acceptance and popularity primarily at the extremes of popularity. Extremely good-looking or unattractive adolescents are likely to have popularity judgments based on their physical attractiveness, but the majority of adolescents will be judged on other bases.

Other personality characteristics of liked and disliked peers have been investigated in several studies (for example, Gronlund & Anderson, 1957; Kuhlen & Lee, 1943). As we noted above, high-accepted peers are viewed as enthusiastic, cheerful, and friendly, whereas low-accepted peers are viewed as restless and hostile. Gronlund and Anderson went one step further and investigated the perceived personality character-

HETEROSEXUAL PEER RELATIONS

As we have pointed out several times above, during late childhood and early adolescence, close friends are generally of the same sex. Same-sex friendship and peer group patterns help the individual develop the self-assurance and social skills necessary for the heterosexual friendships of mid-adolescence.

The first heterosexual friendships are often awkward and sometimes even antagonistic relationships (Douvan & Adelson, 1966; Douvan & Gold, 1966), but they do present an opportunity to learn to relate and adjust to opposite-sex peers. When the adolescent begins to take part in heterosexual group activities (look again at stage 3 in Figure 11–1), he or she still has the support of a same-sex peer group. As the adolescent becomes more comfortable with opposite-sex relationships (stage 4), he or she no longer needs the support of a same-sex peer group. A major impetus for this type of development in the United States is the dating system.

Developmental Sequences in Heterosexual Friendships

A number of investigators have studied the developmental course of opposite-sex friendships and relations. Moreno (1934) studied children in kindergarten through eighth grade. The data indicated more opposite-sex choices for friendships at the lower and upper grade levels; there was a decline in opposite-sex friendships during the middle grades. Kanous, Daugherty, and Cohn (1962) found that this pattern held true for upper-class but not lower-class children and adolescents. Moreover, they reported that lower-class adolescents seemed to have opposite-sex friends at an earlier age. This social-class difference is probably due to differences in socialization experiences, such as degree of contact with the peer groups.

More recent information (e.g., Buhrmester & Furman, 1987; Connolly, 1989) shows similar increases in opposite-sex friendships from mid- to later adolescence. From middle to later adolescence, opposite-sex friends are more likely to be listed in the friendship network, and they become more important to the individual (Buhrmester & Furman, 1987). In addition, some evidence (Buhrmester & Furman, 1987) indicates that adolescent females seek out these types of intimate friendships at earlier ages than do adolescent males.

Kuhlen and Houlihan (1965) presented data indicating that the choice of opposite-sex people to do things with increased over the 20-year period from 1942 to 1963. In 1942, approximately 300 boys and 300 girls in grades 6, 9, and 12 were administered a questionnaire on which they indicated a first and second choice of companions for a number of activities, including "occupying the next seat in the classroom," "playing games

with," and "studying with" (Kuhlen & Lee, 1943). In 1963, the same questionnaire was administered to 1,034 boys and 1,027 girls in grades 6 through 12 in four of the same schools. The percentage of boys choosing girls and girls choosing boys showed an increase over the 20-year time span for grades 6, 9, and 12. The increases were generally more dramatic for girls than for boys (see Table 11–1). In other words, the evidence indicates that opposite-sex choices were greater in 1963 than 20 years earlier, and may mean that there is a trend toward increased heterosexual friendships occurring at earlier ages.

Perhaps the most comprehensive study of heterosexual friendships was done by Broderick (1966). Approximately 1,000 middle- to upper middle-class adolescents between the ages of 10 and 17 were involved in the research. Broderick's data spell out age and sex differences in adolescent opposite-sex friendships in terms of the nature, structure, and perception of the appropriateness of opposite-sex friendships during adolescence. Same-sex friendships were still the mode for 10- and 11-year-olds, with only a few individuals engaging in relatively nonintimate opposite-sex relationships. Interest in the opposite sex tended to be unilateral in nature and unreciprocated. There were also certain situations when it was and was not appropriate to be in the company of an opposite-sex peer. For example, it was not acceptable to sit with opposite-sex peers in the school cafeteria. But it was acceptable to go to the movies with an opposite-sex peer. Generally speaking, girls were more ready to cross the sex barrier than boys.

The 12-year-olds and, to only a slightly lesser degree, the 13-year-olds, evidenced the most extreme social segregation. When cross-sex choices were made, girls tended to choose older boy friends, and boys tended to choose younger girl friends. Social sanctions on when it was appropriate and inappropriate to be with an opposite-sex peer declined somewhat, but were still evident.

TABLE 11–1 **Percentages of Boys and Girls Choosing Opposite-Sex Peers in 1942 and 1963** *(The top entry is the percentage; the entry in parentheses is the sample number.)*

		GRADE						
		6	7	8	9	10	11	12
Boys choosing girls								
	1942	45.0			72.5			75.0
		(109)			(120)			(108)
	1963	48.8	68.9	69.2	79.9*	81.6	83.3	91.0†
		(167)	(120)	(182)	(194)	(148)	(119)	(104)
Girls choosing boys								
	1942	39.2			59.7			63.0
		(120)			(124)			(119)
	1963	52.8*	46.7	69.6	72.9*	68.3	72.7	82.7*
		(159)	(135)	(147)	(180)	(159)	(137)	(110)

*1942–1963 difference significant at the .05 level.

†1942–1963 difference significant at the .01 level.

(Source: Adapted from Kuhlen, R. G., & Houlihan, N.B. [1965]. Adolescent heterosexual interest in 1942 and 1963. *Child Development, 36,* 1049–1052.)

The 14- and 15-year-olds in Broderick's study had markedly broken down the sex barriers. Both boys and girls had opposite-sex friends, although girls had more. There was now a clear preference for opposite-sex friends in small group situations, such as going out on dates and going for walks, but in large group situations, for example, the school cafeteria, there was still a preference for same-sex companionship.

Broderick points out that the 16- to 17-year-olds showed a restructuring of basic friendship patterns. Negative feelings about the opposite sex had almost entirely disappeared. Approximately 50 percent of the boys and 75 percent of the girls indicated friendship patterns that crossed sex lines. Trust and security tended to be components of these opposite-sex relationships. In general, they were quite similar to adulthood opposite-sex friendships.

These data on the development of heterosexual friendships indicate both intergenerational and intragenerational development sequences. Heterosexual relationships seem to be acceptable at an earlier age now than they were during the previous generation (Kuhlen & Houlihan, 1965). In addition, the data indicate that, as one learns behavior appropriate to heterosexual relationships, and thus becomes more comfortable with them, the relationships become deeper and more gratifying (Broderick, 1966; Douvan & Adelson, 1966; Coleman, 1961).

Although normative data of the sort discussed above provide a good description of the changing nature of adolescent friendship patterns, we must look elsewhere for explanations of why the patterns change as they do. It might well be that cognitive evaluations of the social environment change (see Kohlberg, 1969; Piaget, 1972) and produce changes in overt behaviors. If true with respect to friendship patterns, it would suggest that, as the adolescents' interests and abilities become broader and less sex-stereotyped, there is a reevaluation of the role of heterosexual friendships. This may be particularly true with respect to interest in sexuality, an obvious area for the development of heterosexual friendships. The biological changes that accompany the onset of adolescence are often felt to produce an increase in the sex drive (see Chapter 8), which may be reflected in a cognitive restructuring of the appropriateness of heterosexual friendships. Although this sequence of events may be reasonable, data bearing on the issue are quite rare. Therefore, our evaluation of the role of cognition in heterosexual friendship formation must await future research.

An alternative explanation of the developmental trends discussed above comes from the social-learning approach (for example, Gewirtz, 1969; Bandura, 1969a, 1969b). From this perspective, we could predict that adolescents will seek out those who provide positive reinforcement and avoid those who are negatively reinforcing. It would be expected, therefore, that crowds and cliques would be composed of individuals who have similar interests and values, because the members would positively reinforce each other. Dunphy's (1963) research and model certainly fit this description, as does the research of others on peer group formation. If changes in heterosexual affiliations can be explained in the same manner, then the changes in group formation reported by Dunphy will also be explainable from a social-learning-theory perspective.

Meyer (1959) investigated the perceived reinforcement aspect of heterosexual friendships in a sample of boys and girls in grades 5 through 12. Each child rated, and was rated by, every other child according to the degree he or she satisfied succorance (sympathy) or play-mirth needs. Both boys and girls rated same-sex peers higher than opposite-sex peers, indicating that same-sex peers met these social needs to a greater degree than opposite-sex peers. Moreover, these trends did not change over grade levels, indicating little change in boys' and girls' perceptions of their peers' ability to satisfy their needs. These data clearly indicate greater reinforcing value in same rather than opposite-sex peers. There was a developmental trend toward boys picking girls, and vice versa, starting at about eighth grade, for play-mirth needs.

The data of Dunphy and Meyer are consistent with the social-learning view of the development of peer relationships. As social encounters lead to reinforcing opposite-sex affiliations, friendship patterns change toward greater heterosexuality. This, in turn, leads to changes in the nature of adolescent groups and cliques. Ultimately the crowd breaks up when couples, who find themselves mutually reinforcing, seek out other couples who meet their social needs.

Dating Patterns during Adolescence

Dating is the most common expression of heterosexual relationships in adolescence. Some adolescents begin to date relatively early, for example, by 12 years of age (Broderick, 1966), although some data suggest that the modal age for dating is approximately 14 for girls and 15 for boys (Douvan & Adelson, 1966; Douvan & Gold, 1966). To return to Broderick's data for a moment, it appears that the earliest age at which dating begins is 10 or 11, when about 25 percent of both the boys and girls say that they have had a date. In most instances, these dates occur less than once a month and with a very small number of partners. In the 12- to 13-year-old bracket there are very sharp increases in the proportion of students who have had a date. About half of the boys and 60 percent of the girls who are 12 have had at least one date; about 75 percent of each sex have had a date by age 13. Again, dates are relatively infrequent, still only about once a month. By 14 to 15 years of age, more than 80 percent of the adolescents are dating. And dating tends to increase in frequency, with about 25 percent of adolescents dating once a week. By 16 to 17 years of age, 95 percent or more of the boys and girls indicate that they are dating. Both the frequency of dating, which is now typically once a week, as well as the number of dating partners, increased.

An interesting question concerns the etiology of dating, that is, why adolescents begin to date when they do. On the surface this seems a simplistic question: dating be-

One aspect of heterosexual friendships is dating, which involves learning new social roles.

gins because of biological and physiological changes (Dornbusch et al., 1981). The increase in the sex drive (see Chapter 3) and other biological changes (for example, physical maturity) are given precedence in the initiation of dating. Others (for example, Ausubel et al., 1977) note the importance of social influences, such as peer group norms, in the initiation of dating.

Dornbusch et al. (1981) conducted an investigation to determine the relative influence of biological/maturational and social influences on dating. Over 6,700 adolescents, representing a national probability sample of 12- to 17-year-olds, were subjects in the study. As part of a larger study, they were asked if they had ever had a date, their age was determined, and an examining physician indicated by reference to standardized pictures their degree of sexual development. The correlations between age and having had a date were .56 for males and .62 for females. The correlations between sexual maturity and having had a date were .49 for males and .38 for females. Other more sophisticated analyses also revealed stronger relationships between age and dating than between sexual maturity and dating. The authors concluded that, although biological maturity is an aspect of initiating dating, social factors, including peer pressure, institutionalized expectations, and social ma-

turity are more important in determining when adolescents start to date.

Because the dating system is the primary vehicle for mate selection in the United States, and may be partly responsible for the high divorce rate, it is important to try to understand its nature, development, and function. Unfortunately, our understanding of the nature of dating is somewhat limited by the atheoretical and descriptive nature of research on dating. Nevertheless, these data do tell us something about the way dating affects the adolescent.

Stages in the Dating Process. A number of researchers have investigated the values looked for in a dating partner. Social characteristics, for example, prestige (belonging to the "correct" fraternity or sorority), popularity, personality characteristics, disposition, and manners are important in date selection. Although adolescents may express the view that personality characteristics outweigh prestige factors in date selection, some data clearly indicate that, in actual dating situations, prestige factors outweigh personality characteristics. This is, in part, a result of the artificial and superficial nature of the American dating system. Of considerable importance, however, is Christensen's (1950) finding that prestige factors are somewhat less important than personality dimensions in mate selection. Hence, although dating may be done on a superficial basis, mate selection may be done on bases more conducive to long-term, satisfying heterosexual relationships, at least with respect to these dimensions, if not others.

As Herold (1973, 1974) points out, however, both prestige and personality traits are important in date selection, but at different times in the relationship. Prestige factors, especially physical appearance, are initially important in determining potential dating partners. Following an initial dating exposure, social sophistication factors become more important. Self-confidence, ease in meeting people, and being able to carry on a conversation are important determinants for the beginning of a long-term relationship. Personality traits become more important during the third stage of dating. Honesty, reliability, and the like, determine whether or not one will continue the relationship. At all three stages, each partner in the dating process must weigh the prestige and personality factors in determining the desire to continue the relationship.

Functions of Dating. Dating serves a number of functions besides that of courtship and mate selection, especially during early and middle adolescence (Douvan & Adelson, 1966; Douvan & Gold, 1966). Although dating is certainly relevant to, and may lead to, courtship and mate selection it is, for most adolescents, a social experience that involves learning how to get along with and manipulate others. There are a number of functions served by the dating process. These are listed in Table 11–2.

The socialization function of dating allows the adolescent to develop both personally and socially. From dating, adolescents learn a number of social skills related to interacting with persons of the opposite sex; they also get to know persons who, by virtue of their sex, are simply different from themselves. The value of the socialization function, of course, is that it helps the individual learn appropriate adult forms of behavior.

Dating also provides recreation and entertainment opportunities. "It's fun." Dating is and can be viewed as a form of diversion. In this sense, it is an end in itself.

Participative eagerness and independence assertion are closely allied functions of dating, in that they allow the individual to behave in ways that are independent of the adult world (Grinder, 1966). *Participative eagerness* refers to dating in order to avoid boredom, responsibility, or doing things with the family. *Independence assertion* refers to the sometimes flagrant flouting of adult social norms; for example, using a false I.D. to obtain drinks in a bar, or racing cars on public streets. In this sense, dating is an opportunity for the individual to strike out against adult authority (Grinder, 1966) with the support of a date and the peer group.

Dating can also be a way to achieve status. Being seen with highly desirable peers may help one achieve membership in the "in" group or enhance one's own social standing. In this sense, dating is a mechanism for manipulating one's social status.

Dating is obviously a source of legitimate sexual gratification. In fact, for some, dating may be no more than an opportunity to engage in heterosexual behavior, with no intention of having any kind of a long-term relationship.

Of course, courtship and mate selection are an important part of dating. Through dating, individuals come to know each other and to respond as a pair, particularly if they date over a relatively long period of time. They learn to anticipate each other's behavior, and hence to guide their own behavior. Although physical attractiveness is a primary

TABLE 11–2 **Functions of Dating**

1. Socialization	Dating allows one to get to know the opposite sex and learn how to interact with them.
2. Recreation	Dating is a source of fun and pleasure.
3. Participative eagerness	Dating helps one avoid boredom, loneliness, anxiety, or work.
4. Independence assertion	Dating allows independence from the family and its rules.
5. Status seeking	Dating allows one to associate with prestigious peers and the "in group," which enhances one's status.
6. Sexual gratification	Dating is an appropriate and acceptable means for sexual contact.
7. Courtship	Dating allows one to get to know members of the opposite sex and select a mate.

(Source: Compiled from Grinder, R. E. [1966]. Relations of social dating attractions to academic orientation and peer relations, *Journal of Educational Psychology, 57*, 27–34; and Skipper, J. K., Jr., & Nass, G. [1966]. Dating behavior: A framework for analysis and an illustration, *Journal of Marriage and the Family, 28*, 412–420.)

initiator in the dating relationship, this quality becomes less important as individuals come to know each other better. As noted above, personality traits then become more important. This function of dating involves what Skipper and Nass have called a high degree of instrumental orientation and emotional involvement. In other words, in the instance of courtship and mate selection, dating involves a means to a larger goal (instrumental involvement) as well as a high degree of emotional involvement. When both dating partners feel this way the relationship is likely to continue.

The selection of a mate is not only a decision of monumental importance but it also represents the culmination of an exceedingly arduous process. Although many believe that the self-selection process allows one complete freedom in choosing a mate, the evidence indicates that people do not make use of this freedom. People choose mates who are like them, presumably because of the reciprocal reward value provided by those who hold similar beliefs. Adolescents marry those from similar educational and socioeconomic backgrounds. The vast majority of people choose mates who are neither too different nor too threatening—someone like themselves.

Douvan and Adelson (1966) spelled out several consequences related to these functions of dating. First, they note that for middle-class adolescents dating seems to fulfill many of these functions. The experience gained by interacting with a variety of opposite-sex peers tends to make the individual feel comfortable in heterosexual situations. However, Douvan and Adelson also point out that dating can lead to a series of superficial and empty relationships because of the role-playing that goes on in dating relationships.

According to the dating code, a good date is one who is cheerful, well mannered, and fun, no matter what the situation. Certainly this is not how people are all the time, but if they act that way because it is expected of them, they may never get to the point where they can be completely honest with their dating partner. Douvan and Adelson note that this is particularly likely to occur if dating is begun too early. Perhaps this is because early dating cuts the individual off to a certain degree from same-sex relationships, which are helpful and perhaps necessary for the development of self-identity.

Beginning to date too late may also be a problem (Douvan & Adelson, 1966; Douvan & Gold, 1966). Adolescents who begin to date late tend to lag behind their peers in social development and tend to become more dependent on adults and parents for security. These people may feel cut off from their peers and may develop into loners or isolates who become absorbed in themselves and do not learn how to rely on others for companionship, friendship, and self-assurance.

Husbands (1970) has severely criticized the dating system, primarily because of the superficiality of the relationships that develop. Multiple dating (dating a number of people at one time) entails a relatively low degree of involvement in the relationship, which, on the one hand, makes it easier to terminate, but which, on the other hand, impedes the development of meaningful emotional relationships. Playing the dating game leads to role-playing and de-emphasizes the importance of basic human values in interpersonal relationships. Making a good impression becomes the mode and motivation of behavior. It also makes it difficult for game players to make a commitment to a long-term relationship. Husbands (1970) suggests that this sequence of events may produce conflict in the dating relationship and ultimately instability in marriage. Less superficial dating norms should be beneficial to the development of meaningful heterosexual relationships.

The material discussed in this section suggests that the optimal developmental course for heterosexual relationships is for the individual to have close and intimate same-sex relationships during late childhood and early adolescence, and to develop healthy heterosexual relationships during mid- and late adolescence. In this way the individual should develop the self-security and self-identity necessary for successful adult heterosexual relationships.

Going Steady: A Special Dating Circumstance

Broderick (1966) pointed out that both the frequency of dating as well as the number of dating partners increase during the adolescent years. Recent research by Bell and Chaskes (1970) indicates that the decade between 1958 and 1968 evidenced no decline in frequency of dating among college coeds. However, coeds in 1968 dated only half the number of people that coeds in 1958 did. Although there seems to be an increasing trend toward going steady (77 percent of the 1968 coeds vs. 68 percent of the 1958 coeds), there is no concomitant trend toward a lower frequency of dating.

Poffenberger (1964) made a comprehensive study of steady dating. He found that adolescents who went steady spent a larger proportion of their time dating than those who did not. Approximately two-thirds of the boys and girls who were going steady dated three or more nights a week, with approximately 15 to 20 percent dating five to seven nights a week. A high percentage of those who were going steady said that they planned to marry the person with whom they were going steady. Interestingly, over 40 percent of the boys and 25 percent of the girls involved in this study indicated that they had never gone steady. Hence, a relatively high percentage of adolescents do not go steady at all. Moreover, approximately 40 percent of the boys and girls who had gone steady had done so with three or more different persons, indicating that going steady does not necessarily result in a long-term relationship.

These figures on going steady are, in a sense, somewhat disheartening, because there is research evidence that marital success is related to the number of friends (both male and female) one has before marriage (Udry, 1971). Since steady dating limits the number of friendships that one may develop, particularly with opposite-sex friends, it may be that, in the long run, going steady is detrimental to marital happiness.

Going steady has both advantages and disadvantages. Security, feeling popular, feeling loved and wanted, and having assured companionship are among the advantages of going steady. Disadvantages include being cut off from other friends, conflict with parents who do not approve of the steady or feel the relationship is too serious, and a feeling of being tied down.

Another disadvantage to going steady is the accompanying change in expectations with regard to sexual behaviors. Going steady is closely related to the expectation of petting and intercourse (Reiss, 1967).

Going steady also may involve breaking up. The most extensive study of the social and psychological aspects of breaking up was done by Hill and his associates (Hill, Rubin, & Peplau, 1979). They studied 231 couples over a two-year period, at the end of which 103 (45 percent) ended in a breakup. Those couples who remained together had higher levels of love and intimacy at the start of the relationship, and had a relationship that involved equal commitment to each other as opposed to one person being more committed to the other. Those couples that remained together also were more similar with respect to age and educational plans than those who broke up.

The reasons for breaking up typically involved boredom, a growing difference in interests, and the female's desire for independence. One partner being romantically involved with someone else was not mentioned with a high frequency.

Breaking up was psychologically difficult for both partners. The one rejected, particularly if the male, showed more depression and difficulty adapting. Nonetheless, the one initiating the breakup remained somewhat lonely and depressed even a year after the relationship ended.

Finally, the most serious long-term disadvantage to going steady is that it may lead to an early marriage for which both people may be ill prepared (Poffenberger, 1964). The couple may develop bitter feelings about marriage, and may be confronted with the trauma of divorce before they are socially mature adults.

Adolescent Marriage

Marriage involves the formal acceptance of a number of responsibilities. It also involves a dramatic change from a previous lifestyle. For adolescents, adjustment to marriage is likely to be even more difficult than it is for adults because of their relative immaturity, their desire for post-secondary education, and the financial burdens of marriage (Burchinal, 1960, 1965). Coping with restrictions on personal freedom and learning to be considerate of the needs and desires of another person require a degree of maturity and willingness to sacrifice that few adolescents possess. Entering marriage with a romantic and idealistic view, as adolescents tend to do, makes adjustment difficult, if not impossible.

Although there is no general consensus on the definition of an early marriage, there is at least a tacit agreement in the research literature that early marriage refers to marriage between individuals who are 20 years of age or younger (Burchinal, 1965).

One reason for concern about early marriage is that there is a positive correlation between early marriage and failure in marriage, as indexed by either divorce or marital maladjustment. Adolescents who marry tend to experience a greater amount of dissatisfaction than do persons who marry at a later age, with the peak of instability occurring for those who are between 14 and 18 years of age when they marry. Those who

wed during adolescence feel that their marriages are less satisfactory and less satisfying than those who marry later. They express feelings of regret about having been married as early as they were, especially if they are girls who were premaritally pregnant (Burchinal, 1965).

Divorce statistics indicate that early marriages are relatively unsuccessful. Those who marry during the adolescent years have a divorce rate that is between two and four times greater than those who marry in their twenties (Monohan, 1963). Landis and Landis (1968) presented data indicating that marriages for those under 20 have about a 20 percent divorce rate, whereas the divorce rate is only half of that if both people are between 20 and 25 and only about 8 percent if both people are over 30. From this perspective, the evidence that there is a slight upturn in the average age at first marriage is encouraging. For males, the current median age at first marriage is 25 years, and for females it is 23 years. These increases in age at first marriage are related to changing social concepts, such as trial marriages (Mayer, 1971), as well as continued and longer attendance in school and college (Burchinal, 1965).

An important issue in adolescent marriage and its success is the reason for the marriage. The primary reason for adolescent marriage is pregnancy (Burchinal, 1960). Approximately 71 percent of premaritally pregnant brides are under the age of 18 and 95 percent are under the age of 21. Burchinal (1960) presented data indicating that in any marriage involving one high school student, 57 percent of the girls were pregnant. If both participants were in high school, 87 percent of the girls were pregnant. Marriages that are due to premarital pregnancy tend to be those in which at least one participant is not marrying the person he or she would have ultimately chosen; such marriages often involve couples who do not really know each other very well. As a result, these marriages are often un-

Adolescent marriages, which often result from an unexpected pregnancy, are fraught with many difficulties.

erally must work at relatively low-paying jobs.

Burchinal (1965) points out another reason for financial problems: adolescents do not save money in anticipation of unexpected expenses. They want many of the material things our society has to offer, but they don't have the financial resources to pay for them. They may go into debt, which will aggravate the problems caused by their already relatively inflexible budget. Even though parents may wish to alleviate the financial problems of their married sons or daughters, the adolescents may refuse the offer of help in an attempt to maintain independence from the parent. The combination of a low income and a lack of experience in managing finances, then, produces financial problems that can become a primary conflict area for the adolescent husband and wife. In all likelihood, unless the couple is capable of sacrificing a great deal for education, their lifestyle will not change significantly, because they will always be faced with limited job opportunities and, hence, income.

Another significant and important problem in adolescent marriages is early parenthood. As already noted, premarital pregnancy is a major reason for adolescent marriages. The younger the adolescents are at the time of marriage, the sooner they are likely to have a family. Since early pregnancy can often lead to a number of medical problems for both the future infant (for example, prematurity) and the mother (complications of pregnancy), added strain is placed on a family situation that is already somewhat unstable.

Although the picture we are painting here is not a happy one, some adolescent marriages do work. Burchinal (1965) has investigated a number of factors that relate to success or failure in adolescent marriages. Aside from age, the most optimal factors related to marriage are delayed pregnancy, knowing the partner for several years with at least a six-month formal or informal engagement, flexibility in interpersonal rela-

happy and, as we noted above, often end in divorce. And there are other serious, long-term consequences of adolescent marriage and pregnancy (see Box 11–3). Adolescents are aware of these trends and often cite them as reasons for not getting married; the marriage rate for adolescents has declined from one in 10 in the 1960s to about one in 20 currently. And, as we noted in Chapter 8, there has been a substantial decline in adolescent marriage due to pregnancy.

Some adolescents marry to get away from an unpleasant home atmosphere or to become involved in what they view as a happier life. This is especially true for those whose friends are getting married and who, as a result, feel lonely and left out.

Those who marry early have lower intelligence test scores and poorer school achievement records (Burchinal, 1965). These characteristics have obvious implications for financial security. Financial problems are one of the most important concerns faced by adolescent marriages. Young people with only a high school education gen-

BOX 11–3 **Long-Term Consequences of Adolescent Marriage, Childbirth, and Their Co-Occurrence**

As is noted in the text, females who give birth during their adolescent years suffer a number of negative consequences that occur relatively immediately. Many do not complete school, and when they enter the labor market most qualify only for entry-level jobs. In addition, they tend to have low birth-weight babies, who are difficult to care for, and they tend to lack mothering skills. As noted in Chapter 8, being an adolescent mother is not desirable. Similar negative experiences impact on the adolescent father.

Although these relatively immediate consequences of adolescent pregnancy have been recognized for some time, very little effort has been aimed at investigating and understanding the long-term consequences of adolescent marriage, childbirth, or both on the socioeconomic and marital history of the parties involved. Interesting questions concern the potential alleviation of initial difficulties, marital stability, and potential long-term differential effects for both males and females.

Questions such as these were at the center of research conducted by Teti and Lamb (1989; Teti, Lamb, & Elster, 1987). They were interested in discovering the effects, in adulthood, of having been married, parented a child, or both during the adolescent years. They surveyed both males and females ages 30 to 55. Some had never married, some had married during adolescence, and some had married during adulthood. Within each of these three groups, some had never become parents, some had become parents during adolescence, and some had become parents during adulthood. The survey concerned schooling, employment and income, and marital stability.

For females, both adolescent marriage and having a child during adolescence were detrimental to socioeconomic status and marital stability. Females who had their first child during adolescence had lower educational levels and economic status than those who had their first child during adulthood or who never had a child. Women who married during adolescence were somewhat better off, but they still did not match the attainments of those who married during adulthood. Both adolescent marriage and adolescent childbirth were associated with lowered marital stability.

For males, the critical factor was not whether or not they became fathers during adolescence but rather whether or not they married during their adolescent years. Those who married during adolescence completed less schooling, had lower-status occupations, and earned less money than those who married during adulthood. In addition, marriage during adolescence was associated with increased marital discord, divorce, and remarriage.

The consequences of adolescent marriage on employment and socioeconomic status for both males and females, and for adolescent childbirth for females, are relatively easy to understand. Marriage entails economic realities that force adolescents to leave school. Lower educational levels result in lower-paying jobs, which in turn relates to lower socioeconomic status.

Teti and Lamb suggest that, for females, the relation of adolescent marriage and childbearing to marital stability may be a result of failure to resolve adequately the identity and intimacy crises discussed by Erikson (Chapter 2). Because these crises are entered into, and resolved, during the adolescent years, early marriage may have a disruptive influence resulting from the individual's inability to explore relationships with a variety of people. These researchers go on to suggest that failure to establish satisfying relations during adolescence results in a continued failure to do so during adulthood.

These studies demonstrate that not only are there immediate, short-term consequences to adolescent marriage and childbearing, but that there are also long-term consequences. During the later adolescent and early to mid-adulthood years, those who marry or give birth during adolescence do not recover from their earlier circumstances.

tionships, having supportive parents, having an assured income, and maintaining an independent residence. Because of their immature psychological status, relatively low-income production, and likelihood of not knowing their partner long enough, adolescent marriages are a poor choice.

Alternative Living Experiences

As we noted earlier, one of the reasons for the increasing median age of first marriage is the changing social standards with respect to heterosexual living arrangements. Trial marriages, communes, and alternative marriage styles allow individuals to engage in marital-like relationships without the legal complications and responsibilities of formalized marriage.

Trial marriage is one form of living together without the constraints of formalized marriage. Typically this does not involve plans for parenthood (Mead, 1966). In such a relationship, the couple lives together in an attempt to get to know each other and adapt to each other's idiosyncrasies, to "try out" each other before entering into formalized marriage. Increasing numbers of couples are engaging in this form of cohabitation, which allows one to experience a marital-type relationship and, in effect, try marriage out to see if *it* fits.

Companionate marriage is the true alternative to marriage; as such, it differs from trial marriage. In trial marriage, the couple may intend to marry someday. Companionate marriage involves no such intent.

Companionate marriage grew out of concerns that marriage forced people to stay together for the wrong reasons, legal reasons, as opposed to the right reasons, commitment and love for one another. If the couple wishes to separate, it is less costly than divorce or legal separation. However, what to do with any children that may be involved remains a problem, just as it is in legalized marriage. Hence, although a good deal of individual freedom may be gained, the re-

sponsibilities for offspring, and the problems that arise during separation when offspring are involved, are the same as they are in a legalized marriage. In fact, legalized marriage may provide a better vehicle for ensuring the welfare of offspring.

Communal living is the other major alternative lifestyle in the United States. Communes sprang up in the 1960s and continued to grow slowly in size and number during the 1970s. Otto (1971) characterized communal living as having a high degree of concern for meaningfulness and openness but with strong individual ties and commitments. Although problems of leadership, economics, and division of labor can be extremely disruptive to communal living, a number of communes have succeeded in providing a true alternative lifestyle for their members.

Although we have not discussed alternative living styles in detail, one can easily see that there is strong sentiment, particularly among adolescents, for alternatives to the traditional marriage style. In some ways, this is probably a good thing, because it allows adolescents to engage in meaningful heterosexual relationships without the serious consequences of early marriage. In a sense, alternative lifestyles may present new opportunities for adolescents to become more familiar with both themselves and the responsibilities and concerns that are involved in a lifelong commitment to another person.

However, there are disadvantages to these alternative living styles as well. They do not solve the problems that are inherent in traditional marriage, except at the level of providing more freedom to the individual. Children of couples involved in these alternative living arrangements still suffer when their parents separate and still end up being reared by only one parent. It is unclear, then, whether or not these alternative lifestyles prepare one for the realities of marriage. One might even suspect that the forced adaptations required by marriage are useful for helping the individual develop a sense of self, and that having complete freedom to abandon a relationship without "really trying to make it work" may be detrimental to the development of the individual.

These alternative living experiences raise the interesting possibility that living together prior to marriage may lead to increased marital stability and happiness. Research (see Macklin, 1978) shows that this is not the case. The interactions of nonmarried partners are very similar to those of married couples; the same problems are present, as are the same types of joys. Moreover, living together prior to marriage does not predict marital success.

PEER VERSUS PARENT INFLUENCE

Generally speaking, differences between parents and their adolescent children tend to be rather superficial. Parents, more than anyone else, are responsible for their child's social values, morals, and code of behavior. Although there is a heightened conformity to peer group values during early to mid-adolescence, the influences of the adolescent peer group tend to be much more superficial, narrowly defined, and short term than parental influences. In addition, as we pointed out above, adolescents collect in peer groups that are composed of individuals with backgrounds and values similar to their own. In effect, this means that the peer group may act to reinforce the basic values the parent has taught the adolescent. As a result, the influences of parents and peers will be more often complementary than conflicting.

It should also be pointed out that neither the parent nor the peer group has an overriding influence on all aspects of the adolescent's life. The adolescent evaluates and weighs the opinions and beliefs of each group, and is influenced by each to a greater or lesser degree according to the content area being considered. As we have already noted, peer influences and opinions are likely to dominate in the realms of fads, music, dress, language, and some aspects of social behavior. Parental influences will generally be predominant in basic social values and morals.

A study by Floyd and South (1972) specifically investigated the adolescent's orientation to parents and peers in a sample of 409 sixth-, eighth-, tenth-, and twelfth-grade males and females. One questionnaire assessed the degree to which the students were peer- or parent-oriented. The subjects indicated the degree to which they agreed or disagreed with statements such as, "I prefer to grow up to be more like my friends rather than my parents." The subjects were divided into peer (27 percent), parent (30 percent), and mixed orientation (43 percent) groups. The subjects then indicated the degree to which parents, as opposed to peers, met their needs for a series of items previously rated as high, medium, or low in importance.

Generally speaking, parent orientation decreased and peer orientation increased, though somewhat less, with increasing age. There was also an increase in the mixed orientation category over age. Males were slightly more peer-oriented then females. When parents were viewed as the better source of need satisfaction, adolescents were parent- as opposed to peer-oriented. The reverse was also true. These results demonstrate developmental trends in parent and peer orientation and support the notion that each influence has its place in adolescent socialization. The data also indicate that adolescents are aware of these areas of influence. There are areas in which parents are seen as better able than peers to meet the adolescent's needs, and parents are sought out. The converse is also true. Neither parents nor peers are omnipotent influences in the adolescent's development.

Some research (see Montemayor, 1982) suggests this may be a result of differing experiences adolescents have with peers and parents. Hunter and Youniss (1982) found that parents were viewed as more controlling

Parents and peers influence and satisfy the adolescent, but in different types of ways and activities.

than peers, particularly at the seventh and tenth grade. In turn, peers were viewed as providing greater intimacy and nurturance than parents. Hunter and Youniss conclude that parents and peers are viewed by the adolescent as fulfilling different needs.

Montemayor's (1982) study lends further insight into these issues. He studied the activities in which adolescents engage with parents and peers and when alone. He found that adolescents were equally involved with parents and peers, but in different activities. Time spent with parents was much more likely to be task-oriented, time with peers recreation-oriented. It appears that parents and peers satisfy differing needs—parents

exerting necessary controls and teaching aspects of responsibility, and peers providing more personal need satisfaction and necessary recreational outlets. More recent research (e.g., Connolly, 1989; Moran & Eckenrode, 1989; Reid et al., 1989) further clarifies these differences. Adolescents seek information from parents but social and emotional support from peers, the latter showing increases with the age of the adolescent. These differences in the roles played by parents and peers are related to the types of conflicts—and conflict resolutions—that adolescents have with parents and peers (see Box 11–4).

We also should keep in mind the role individuality plays in the adolescent's need to conform to either the parents or the peer group (Douvan & Adelson, 1966). Children and adolescents who are raised by democratic parents, and those who are more self-confident, need not be dominated by either group because they have learned the skills that are necessary for making appropriate decisions. This may be why Floyd and South found such a large mixed orientation group.

Nevertheless, real difficulties can arise when there is conflict between parental values and those of the peer group. This will occur primarily when there is a homogeneous peer group with a set of values that are quite different from those of the parent, and when there is a tendency on the part of the adolescent to be highly conforming to the peer group. In such an instance, the adolescent is torn between two sets of values that may be at bipolar positions. Although such occurrences are rare, they are particularly likely to occur when parent-child relationships are poor, because the parent shows a lack of interest in the child and an unwillingness to become involved in his or her life. With an especially deviant peer group, it is critical that the parents provide appropriate models for the adult world and help the adolescent acquire a set of values that will stand the adolescent in good stead during adulthood.

BOX 11-4 Differences in Adolescents' Conflicts and Conflict Resolution with Parents, Siblings, and Peers _____

One consequence of developing close relationships is that conflict arises. Recently, psychologists have begun to study the similarities and differences in the nature of conflicts that adolescents have with parents, siblings, and peers, and the ways in which these conflicts are resolved (Hartup & Laursen, 1989; Laursen, 1989; Raffaelli, 1989).

As you might suspect, conflicts with parents tend to concern issues of autonomy and parental control. These conflicts reflect the adolescent's increasing need to explore the boundaries of self-competence and to express one's individuality. They seem to mirror not only the growing independence of the adolescent but also the closeness that adolescents feel toward their parents. As Laursen (1989) notes, conflict is integral to close relationships, and adolescents are closer to their parents than anyone else. Conflict resolution is achieved through compromise, which allows the relationship to remain close and intact.

Conflicts with peers are dependent upon whether or not the peer is a friend (Hartup & Laursen, 1989). Conflicts with friends involve sharing of personal problems, being ignored or left out, and telling secrets. With nonfriends, conflicts tend to involve put-downs and criticisms. In general, conflicts with peers are interpersonal in nature. Raffaelli (1989) notes that with friends, conflicts tend to be avoided or constrained and resolution of conflicts is done in such a manner as to allow the relationship to continue. In addition, conflicts with friends seem to be more prominent when they concern self-esteem issues, with resolution not strongly revolving around winner/loser dimensions.

Siblings engage in conflict more readily and allow conflict to escalate to substantial degrees, often to the point where parental intervention is necessary to terminate the conflict. Conflicts may involve many issues, but they often relate to "turf" concerns and privacy. Siblings resolve conflicts less readily than do friends.

Raffaelli (1989) suggests that these differing types of conflict provide different forums for expressing opinions and engaging in social interactions of an antagonistic nature. By having these opportunities, adolescents are able to explore more fully the boundaries of their selves and their competencies. It is interesting to note, however, that conflict resolution with those to whom the adolescent has close ties is generally done in a manner that allows the close relationship to continue.

SUMMARY

In many ways, peer interactions serve the same functions for adolescents and children, including the teaching of age-appropriate skills. However, because of its heterosexual composition, the adolescent peer group setting provides a much better training ground for adult peer interactions. In adolescence, the peer group provides the opportunity for trying out various social roles, and sets standards for adolescent behavior.

Adolescents typically belong to two types of groups, the clique and the crowd. The clique is a small (3–9) group, serving the primary function of conversation and planning of group activities. Crowds, the second group, are made up of cliques, and provide the initial opportunity for heterosexual interaction. The crowd is the center of organized social activities.

During the earlier years of adolescence, there is an increase in conformity to peer group norms and standards, perhaps as a result of increasing egocentrism and the need to develop an identity. During the later high school years conformity declines as egocentrism abates and identity develops.

Intimate friendships develop during the adolescent years. These friends tend to show high levels of empathy and social perspective-taking ability. It is demanded that intimate friends be loyal and trustworthy because of the very close ties the adolescent has to the intimate friend. Of course, betrayal by an intimate friend can be very devastating to the adolescent.

Popularity during the adolescent years is largely dependent on being at least moderately attractive, having acceptable social skills, behaving in accord with group norms, and the like. Disliked peers are viewed in the opposite ways. In addition, adolescents tend to like more those peers who are from their own social standing.

It is during adolescence that heterosexual peer relations are begun. These intimate relations do not supplant same-sex intimate relations. With increasing age, there is an increase in the number of opposite-sex friends. This is most readily seen in the initiation of dating, which seems more closely tied to social expectations than to biological maturity. Through dating, adolescents acquire social skills for interacting with the opposite sex, are able to exert independence needs, achieve status, and, of course, engage in recreational activities. Although mate selection can occur through dating during the adolescent years, adolescent marriages are more prone to end in divorce than marriages occurring during the adulthood years.

Although adolescents spend increasing amounts of time with peers, resulting in an increase in the influence of peers, parents remain highly influential on the adolescent. This occurs because parents and peers fulfill different needs of the adolescent. Parents provide needed guidance and skill training, and peers provide recreational outlets. The peer group, then, does not become omnipotent for most adolescents.

GLOSSARY

Clique. A small, tightly knit group of people who share common interests.

Conformity. Willingness to allow external events or people to govern one's behavior.

Prosocial behavior. Moral behaviors involving helping, sharing, and other behaviors for which the individual expects no reward.

SUGGESTED READINGS

AUSUBEL, D. P. (1954). *Theory and problems of adolescent development*. New York: Grune & Stratton.

Ausubel discusses the basic functions of the adolescent peer group. These functions (for example, builder of self-esteem and replacement for the family) are related to general aspects of adolescent development.

BERNDT, T. (1982). The features and effects of friendship in early adolescence. *Child Development, 53,* 1447–1460.

Berndt reviews the literature on friendship development during the adolescent years and compares it to friendship influences during childhood. The specific focus is on intimate relationships during the early adolescent years.

COLEMAN, J. (1980). Friendship and the peer group in adolescence. In J. Adelson (Ed.), *Handbook of adolescent psychology*. New York: John Wiley & Sons.

Coleman explores the impact of friends on the adolescent. In doing so, he uses common examples to demonstrate how peers influence aspects of adolescent behavior. He also addresses issues of peer-parent conflict and interest.

HARTUP, W. W. (1989). Social relationships and their developmental significance. *American Psychologist, 44,* 120–126.

The author reviews material concerning the formation and function of peer groups with a focus on the importance of friendship relations. In addition, material on parents vs. peer influences is presented.

IRWIN, C. E., Jr. (Ed.). (1987). *Adolescent social behavior and health. New directions for child development.* San Francisco Jossey-Bass.

In this edited book, prominent researchers explore the nature of adolescent social interactions with parents and peers; developmental transitions such as changing schools; and adolescent adjustment in relations to the various social relationships that adolescents experience.

School Influences on Adolescent Development

12

CHAPTER OUTLINE

MAJOR ISSUES ADDRESSED

The Functions of Schooling

Adolescents' Views of Schools and Schooling

The Role of Athletics in the School Environment

Family Influences on School Performance

The Characteristics of Schools

Student Characteristics Related to Academic Success

Causes of Dropping Out of School

School Transitions

INTRODUCTION

The school is the one social institution to which virtually all adolescents are exposed. From the time the child begins school until the school years are ended, more time is spent in the school and in engaging in school-related activities than is spent in any other single function.

Moreover, the school represents the meeting ground for the peer group and is the setting in which many peer group functions occur. As a result, the school represents both a formal and informal mechanism that is highly influential in the socialization of the adolescent. The formal aspect of the school's socialization function is the transmission of the knowledge and skills that will allow the individual to be a successful member of society. The informal aspects relate to the physical setting of the school, including neighborhood, classmates, friends, and peer groups.

As we explore the various aspects of the school situation and its influence on the adolescent's development, we shall attempt to assess the importance of the quality of schools and the degree to which schools meet the needs of the adolescent. Our discussion will be addressed to such questions as: What are the functions of schools? How well do schools do their job? How do the views of parents, adolescents, and teachers compare on these issues? In what ways do schools prepare the individual to be a happy, adequately functioning, contributing member of society?

THE FUNCTIONS OF SCHOOL

The school serves two primary functions: maintenance-actualization and skills training/cultural transmission (Linney & Seidman, 1989; Murphy, 1987). These two functions can also be described respectively as individual-oriented and community-oriented functions. In general, the **mainte-** **nance-actualization function** of the school is aimed at giving the student an opportunity to grow socially and emotionally. This is as true for those who are high on measures of these traits as it is for those who, because of personal circumstances, are poorly developed in these areas. Similarly, the **skills-training/cultural-transmission function** of schools is aimed at providing the individual with the skills and knowledge necessary to become an economically independent and productive member of the society. The former set of skills should enhance the individual's self-esteem and self-concept, and the latter should make the individual capable of functioning within our social system.

The Maintenance-Actualization Function

The role of the school in the psychological development of the individual is often neglected in discussions of school effects on the adolescent. If not actually neglected, it has been regarded with suspicion because of its role as a socializer of "good" (that is, conforming) citizens. In a sense, this common criticism of school objectives is not very different from Silberman's (1970) notion that schools educate individuals for docility. As McCandless (1970) describes it, the maintenance-actualization function of schools revolves around the notion of enriching the individual's personal, psychological, and emotional development. The intent here is that the individual should come out of school feeling better about himself than he did before, even if the individual was relatively secure at the time of entrance into school.

In some ways schools achieve this function, but in other ways they do not. For example, schools generally do relatively little with regard to the quality of the students' school experience, social or academic (Johnston & Bachman, 1976). Although school counselors may attempt to help students function better within the school setting, they are overloaded with students, and are typically more concerned with helping students gain entrance into institutions of higher learning than they are with helping students cope with current problems. Furthermore, little is done to try to teach students how to identify and deal with problems. As a result, they may continually fail and, ultimately, drop out of school, which, of course, hurts both the individual and society.

More directly, schools do attempt to teach competencies and skills to students, which should have some bearing on their views of their own capabilities and self-worth. We shall discuss below the degree to which schools are perceived as doing an adequate job in this regard.

In other ways, too, schools fail in their self-actualization function. In fact, the school setting and atmosphere may, in some ways, be detrimental to maintenance-actualization (for example, Wagner, 1970; Finger & Silverman, 1966). The prolonged period of time spent in the school setting lengthens the adolescent's dependence, both emotional and economic, on parents; and the school, as an agent of adult society, maintains control over the adolescent and at the same time tries to teach him independence (Wagner, 1970; Havighurst, 1972). This is especially true of college students, who may remain more or less economically dependent and under parental control for a significant number of years.

Finger and Silverman find that attitudes toward learning are related to changes in performance between elementary and junior high school. Those with positive attitudes increase, and those with negative attitudes decrease in performance, regardless of intellectual abilities. Since attitudes about learning are acquired in learning situations, these findings suggest that some aspects of the school experience turn off some students by altering their attitudes. The research of Walberg, House, and Steele (1973) suggests this may be especially critical in grades 9 and 10. Although a high degree of formal education is desirable, and perhaps

necessary, in our complex society, it is important to recognize that negative as well as positive consequences may result from time spent in the school setting. Future research on these issues is needed in order to spell out the critical mechanisms involved so that changes can be made in the school environment (for example, curriculum) to promote maintenance-actualization for all students.

The Skills-Training/Cultural-Transmission Function

The training-acculturation function refers to the school's traditional role of teaching skills and imparting information (McCandless, 1970). It is this function that has been most stressed, both historically and currently, within the American educational system. The school acts as a community organization that channels people into future educational and vocational areas, and to a large degree determines the future of every single adolescent. A diploma from a high school certifies that the person who holds it is qualified for entrance into college or a

One function of schooling is skills training.

vocation, or (minimally) possesses the skills necessary to function in a variety of job categories.

In a similar vein, schools serve to pass on the beliefs, values, and traditions of a culture from generation to generation (Johnston & Bachman, 1976). Students learn various role expectations by the examples that are set in school, and learn to fill those roles by the training they receive in school.

Recently, researchers have become interested in how various characteristics of schools relate to learning and achievement. This is especially important in light of students' views that school is of instrumental value and is useful for acquiring marks of adult status (Hurrelman, 1987). In this regard, effective schools are those with strong leadership, with orderly and nonoppressive atmospheres, frequency of monitoring of student performance, and teacher input into decision making (Linney & Seidman, 1989). It now appears that attending a single-sex versus coeducational school has no impact on achievement, college entrance, or post-high school work (Marsh, 1989). Another important variable is school size, which we discuss in detail below.

Another facet of adolescent school experience that has been investigated somewhat extensively is the transition from elementary to middle or junior high school. Because this occurs at a time when adolescents are experiencing other changes—such as physical growth, evolving parent and peer relationships, and other potential life changes, such as divorce of the parents—changing school may add more stress to the adolescent's life and may have deleterious effects on both personal growth and academic performance (Simmons, Burgeson, Carlton-Ford, & Blyth, 1987). Researchers have examined school transitions both with respect to the general development of the adolescent and with regard to specific academic performance (see Box 12–1).

It now seems clear that school transitions result in substantial changes in personal de-velopment. Girls evidence increases in depressive symptomology (Hirsch & Rapkin, 1987), for example. Also, students in general suffer from declines in self-esteem and motivation (e.g., confidence in one's academic ability, general interest in school; Eccles et al., 1989b). In addition, transitions from supportive to nonsupportive teachers, and vice versa, result in decreases or increases, respectively, in performance in mathematics (Midgley, Feldlaufer, & Eccles, 1989a, 1989b). These changes apparently are tied to sex-role behaviors (Box 12–1), which may account for their being of somewhat greater impact for females than for males. Researchers suggest that easing the transition by employing team-teaching, which allows for smaller classes and closer contact between students and teachers, structuring the middle school or junior high school around subunits called "houses," which results in a smaller reference group, and the like, can do much to reduce the strain of the transition and its negative impact on personal and academic performance (Fenzel, 1989b).

Other Functions of School

The school has a number of other functions. Child care is one; the child spends more time (five to six hours a day) with schoolteachers and school personnel than with his or her parents. As a result, teachers and staff members serve as important models for the child. In many ways, the models provided by school personnel reinforce the behaviors that parents wish their children to acquire. In some cases, however, school models present behaviors and points of view that differ from those of the parents.

We previously noted the importance of the school as a center for the peer group and its activities. The school also offers the individual the opportunity to achieve status within our social system, because status and extensive education are positively correlated. In addition, the individual who does well in the school setting will achieve a cer-

BOX 12–1   **The Transition to Junior High School** ⎯⎯⎯⎯⎯⎯⎯⎯⎯⎯

Early adolescence is a period involving a number of substantial transitions, including the biological, interpersonal, and social spheres of life. One of the transitions experienced by virtually every adolescent is that involving the change from elementary school to middle school or junior high school (Simmons & Blyth, 1987). Researchers recently examined the nature of this transition, including the stresses that adolescents perceive will be involved and the degree to which these perceived stresses dissipate, or increase, after the transition.

Specific concerns about stress and the transition to a different school environment center on changes in self-esteem, adjustment to the new school atmosphere, effect of the change on grades, and the influence of entering a new school on peer and teacher relations (Fenzel, 1989a, 1989b; Mekos, 1989). In addition, researchers have focused on how students adapt to the demands of the academic (e.g., homework) and social (e.g., older peers) environments of the new school and on whether these adaptations to the transition are different for males and females.

Mekos (1989) investigated this transition from grades 6 to 7 in a longitudinal study in which 100 students were interviewed and completed questionnaires near the end of sixth grade and later at the start and near the end of seventh grade. Concerns about peer relations (meeting new people, losing old friends) were high in sixth grade but declined shortly after starting seventh grade. Academic concerns (liking classes, having too much homework) were high after starting seventh grade and remained high near the end of seventh grade. Those for whom the transition ultimately created the greatest concern were the aggressive and disruptive students, who became increasingly negative about the transition to junior high school.

Fenzel (1989a, 1989b) investigated the effects of transition to middle school (grade 5 to grade 6 transition) on males and females. Her perspective was to look at the increase or decrease in role strain due to the transition. Her primary emphasis was on how changing roles from elementary to middle school might affect self-esteem, relations with teachers, and relations with parents. The findings indicated that the transition was not particularly stressful because of the team-teaching structure of the middle school, which allowed smaller classes and more intimate contact with teachers, and that boys reported greater declines in stress than did girls.

Research in this area suggests that preparation of students in elementary school can ready them for the transition to the middle or junior high school. Taking students to the new school, having them engage in a few days of the new curriculum, and using "houses" (more intimate groupings of students) can alleviate the stress associated with changing schools.

tain degree of respect and status from the peer group. These individuals are likely to be singled out by teachers for special programs and to be selected and recommended for higher educational opportunities.

The Pervasive Impact of Schooling

One may well wonder whether or not the school system is capable of successfully performing all these various functions. This is a critical question when one realizes the massive numbers of individuals exposed to elementary and secondary schooling in the United States. In 1985, the most recent year for which data are available (U.S. Bureau of the Census, 1989), there were over 110,000 public and private elementary and secondary schools in the United States. Approximately 43 million students were enrolled in these schools. Those enrolled represented 95.3 percent of 5- to 6-year-olds, 99.2 percent of 7- to 13-year-olds, 97.6 percent of 14- to 15-year-olds, and 92.3 percent of 16- to 17-year-olds.

There is no doubt that the school milieu touches upon nearly every child and adolescent in the United States. As a result, it is perhaps the most pervasively influential social institution to impact on the adolescent. In this regard, it is important to note that in 1980 only 74 percent of students in the cohort (those who would be eligible for graduation had they stayed in school) graduated. This statistic suggests that perhaps the school system is not meeting the needs of some, if not all, of the remaining 26 percent of students.

In the remainder of this chapter we shall examine a number of ways that schools influence adolescent development. In doing so, we shall examine evidence concerning the quality of education, the curriculum, the role of the teacher, and perceptions of the nature of education in the United States. Finally, we shall discuss a number of factors that relate to success and failure in the school setting.

THE CHARACTERISTICS OF SCHOOLS

We have been talking about the school in a rather general way. It is time to be more specific. The public school is a community organization. But, free public education was not always the case; it took a large number of court cases to establish our current concept of community-financed, community-run, primary and secondary schools.

Although a complete discussion of the evolution of the public education system in the United States is far beyond the scope of this text (the interested reader may consult Kett [1977] and Murphy [1987] for historical information with an emphasis on adolescence), it is enlightening to review briefly several major factors in the rise of the public education movement.

Initially, educational systems were privately financed by wealthy backers interested in keeping "young hoodlums" off the streets. With time, efforts to provide tax monies to support public education arose and, around 1850, began to become accepted. The large influx of immigrants was a major factor in the final approval of taxation for the support of public education for the masses. In 1851, compulsory education laws were being considered, debated, and passed in order to keep young people off the streets. In addition, because youth were not able to be employed, more jobs were created for adults. As Kett (1977) noted, this was the beginning of the establishment of childhood and adolescence as the school years slowly were lengthened. Today, compulsory attendance at school extends to at least the age of 16 in most states.

As with any social institution, it was necessary for the public school to establish a series of goals. Historically, the public high schools' primary goal was to provide instruction for students who wished to go to college (Murphy, 1987). Slowly, however, this concept has changed, and is still changing, toward the goal of providing an education for all young people, not just those who want a college education. More and more, the public is demanding that high schools, in particular, teach a variety of skills to adolescents of differing abilities and interests. As a result, there are special programs for the retarded, for the gifted, for the creative, for those who wish to enter college, and for those who want job-specific skills.

Along with changes in curriculum, there have been changes in the character of the school. In this section, we shall examine a number of these characteristics, for example, school size, in order to discern how these variables affect the adolescent. In particular, we shall focus on the issue of school size and the degree to which it hinders or helps the acquisition of skills. We shall also focus on the school curriculum. Although these two school characteristics are related, the relationship is neither as strong nor as broad as one might think.

The Middle-Class Nature of Schools

Ever since they began, American public schools have been middle-class institutions. Schools still fail to meet the needs of a substantial number of adolescents from other sectors of society (Silberman, 1970). School board members tend to come from the middle and upper-middle classes; the majority of them are professionals who hold college and graduate degrees (Dejnozka, 1963). The lack of representation from the lower socioeconomic groups in the community may limit both knowledge and concern about the needs of less advantaged students.

Schoolteachers, too, have tended to come from the middle classes (Groff, 1962), although current trends indicate that this tendency is changing. As a result, teachers are becoming more aware of the needs and concerns of students from the lower socioeconomic strata and are perhaps better capable of dealing with their problems.

Traditionally, schools have been characterized as feminine in nature. At the most obvious level, elementary school teachers in any given school are much more likely to be women than men. As a result, schools succeed quite well with middle-class children, particularly girls who are attentive and hold middle-class values and traditions (Combs & Cooley, 1968).

Social versus Academic Orientation

Considerable research has been conducted to investigate how adolescents view the school. The evidence clearly points out that the school is viewed as a social rather than an academic situation (for example, Linney & Seidman, 1989). This is a somewhat disheartening, but hardly surprising, conclusion when we consider that the school is the center of peer group activity.

J.S. Coleman (1960, 1961, 1965) conducted the initial extensive studies of the social nature of schools. He interviewed students in midwestern high schools varying in size from slightly more than 100 students to about 2,000 students. One question asked how the student would most like to be remembered. Only 31 percent of the boys and 28 percent of the girls wished to be remembered as bright students. Forty-five percent of the boys wished to be remembered by their peers as athletic stars, and 72 percent

of the girls wanted to be remembered as being popular. Academic success, then, was not generally viewed as a major factor in the legacy the students wished to leave behind them. This finding suggests that reinforcement for academic work was not as high as it was for being athletic or popular. Some support for this notion comes from the answers to the question about what it takes to be a member of the leading crowd.

Again, although there were differences across the various schools, athletic prowess, liking to have fun, being a good date, and other social factors were considered more important than academic success. The nonacademic qualities result in greater reinforcement from peers, and probably teachers, school administrators, parents, and the community. As a result, they become the preferred and more important qualities for adolescents.

The importance of athletics in the status system of the high school is not surprising. Successful performance in athletics brings pride to the community, school, students, and individuals in our society, because we value the qualities involved in athletics. Given our penchant for heros, athletics historically have provided the opportunity for boys to gain status and provide pride to many others. With the passage of Title IX of the 1972 Educational Amendments Act, which prohibits federal funds if sex discrimination is practiced in athletics, the opportunity for girls to gain status through athletic achievement is expanded.

Snyder (1972) reported findings similar to Coleman's in his study of high school juniors. Academic achievement was listed by only a small percentage of students as being important in determining popularity and leadership. This was true for both boys and girls. Friesen (1968) reported similar data for a Canadian sample of students. Boys in Friesen's study viewed athletics as more important than popularity, and girls viewed popularity as more important than athletics. In this sample, however, the students indicated that academic skills were more important for the future than either athletics or popularity. Although the sample of Canadian students seemed to stress academics somewhat more than the samples of American students, athletics and social encounters still played a very strong role.

Perhaps the most extensive study of the academic and social nature of the school has been conducted by Bachman and his associates (for example, Bachman, Green, & Wirtanen, 1971; Bachman et al., 1967; Johnston & Bachman, 1976). In their multifaceted project, Bachman and his co-workers surveyed over 2,000 boys and 2,000 teachers. Teachers and students filled out a questionnaire rating the degree to which they felt a number of objectives were actually emphasized in the school setting and the degree to which they felt each should be emphasized.

The data showed that both the boys and the teachers indicated athletics were the area receiving the greatest amount of emphasis in the school setting. Maintaining order and quiet also received a great deal of emphasis. Emphasis on academic achievement received somewhat lower ratings, and socialization and transmission of cultural values were rated lowest. Although the teachers' rankings were somewhat higher than those of the boys', the agreement between them was extremely high (the rank-order correlation equaled .94). Clearly, both the teachers and the boys were aware that differential weights were given to these objectives.

The boys' and teachers' ideal rankings of school objectives differed considerably from their rankings of perceived objectives. Both groups felt that motivating students to learn, transmitting subject matter, responding to individual needs, and preventing dropouts *should* be among the major objectives of the school. Johnston and Bachman argue that these data indicate that students and teachers would like to see more emphasis on teaching and socialization and less emphasis on athletics and maintenance of order and

quiet. Again, the rankings of the teachers and the boys for the ideal distribution of school objectives were very similar (the rank-order correlation equaled .73).

Athletics and the School

The above data reveal that both the boys and the teachers in the Bachman study felt that athletics was overemphasized. Specific research on interscholastic athletics has been conducted by a number of people (see Coleman, 1965). Solberg (1970), in particular, argues that the emphasis placed on interscholastic athletics far overshadows the emphasis placed on academic programs in American high schools. Indeed, he has gone so far as to say that sports have "become the tail that wags the dog," and that athletic activities take up much more than their fair share of time and concern on the part of students and faculty alike. Partially this occurs because communities support successful athletic events. As Coleman (1965) notes, it is easier to get money to build a new gymnasium for a successful athletic team than it is to get money to support academic programs. A successful athletic program reflects favorably on the entire community. In some smaller communities, in fact, the high school football or basketball team may be the major focus of community interest for several months a year.

Athletics play a positive role in the high school. First, as we noted above, athletes tend to be popular among their peers (Watkins, 1989; Watkins & Montgomery, in press). As a result, the successful athlete is likely to be looked up to and emulated more than someone who is not in the athletic limelight. Of course, the latter group will be much larger than the former, so that one advantage to being successful in interscholastic athletics is that one can become a model for other students. This, in turn, should enhance the athlete's self-esteem and self-confidence, and perhaps force him (or her) to live up to the expectations of other people by learning more mature behavior patterns than fellow classmates (Watkins & Montgomery, in press). Hence, participation in interscholastic athletics may contribute to the furthering of one's socialization.

Participation in interscholastic athletics and academic achievement are not necessarily mutually exclusive endeavors. Rehberg (1969) has identified several ways in which the two spheres of influence may go hand in hand. One way in which the two go together was mentioned above: an increase in self-esteem due to the reinforcement received for successful sports competition from people who are important to the individual. This increase in self-confidence may transfer to academic situations and help the individual improve academic performance.

The second way that academics and athletics are positively related is that the athlete may receive a greater degree and a higher quality of counseling from career counselors and teachers than other students do. As a result, the athlete may be able to crystalize future goals and deal with current academic problems in a more successful manner than the non-athlete.

Third, achievement in athletics and

Although athletic competition has many positive benefits for the athlete and the community, many argue that it has become too emphasized.

achievement in academics are not completely independent. The same qualities that lead to success on the playing field may also bring success in the classroom. Fourth, participation in athletics with other achievement-oriented peers may reinforce the athlete's high aspirations and may act as a cohesive influence to push him to higher levels of academic performance.

Finally, the athlete may try hard to perform well in the classroom in order to present a consistent picture of the self; that is, a picture of an individual who is successful in a number of different areas of his life. To be known as a "dumb jock" may be extremely damaging to the adolescent's self-concept. As a result, striving toward high academic achievements often goes hand in hand with success in athletics.

The Role of School Size

In the United States today, bigness is often equated with goodness. Translating this general statement to the situation under discussion, we might say that bigger schools offer significantly more opportunities to students than do small schools. These advantages are thought by some to outweigh the claim that large schools are cold and impersonal. On the other hand, there are those who say that small schools are better because they give each student more individual attention and a sense of belonging (Linney & Seidman, 1989).

One assumption underlying work on school size is that participation is necessary for behavioral settings to exist and maintain themselves. In the school context, behavioral settings refer to sports, language clubs, student councils, as well as cliques and crowds. One of the major findings is that students in small schools engage in a greater number of activities than do students in large schools (Barker, 1964). In fact, students in small schools engage in more than twice the number of activities, although there are only approximately a quarter of the number of different activities available. Students spend more time and effort in school-related activities in the small school in part because they are pressured to do so to maintain these activities for the school. This leads to a somewhat lower criterion for entrance into certain of the activities, for example, sports activities, because the sample from which students can be selected is more limited than it is in larger schools.

Wicker (1968) reports that students coming from small schools feel that the involvement they have had in school activities has helped them develop skills and self-confidence. As you can see in Table 12–1, in a variety of different activities, students in small schools received a greater degree of satisfaction and feeling of accomplishment from their involvement in various kinds of activities than did students from larger schools. As Gump (1966) points out, these data are consistent with other information indicating that all students, both those from large and those from small schools, who participate in school activities report greater satisfaction and feelings of accomplishment than those who do not.

What this demonstrates, then, is that in smaller schools, a larger number of the students participate in a greater number of activities than students in larger schools do.

TABLE 12–1 **Examples of Activities That Affected Students in Small Schools More Positively Than Students in Large Schools**

Attribute Affected	Activity
Skill development	Games, play, dances
Build confidence	Games, play, projects
Test one's abilities	Play, dances, projects
Feel needed by others	Games, play
Feeling of accomplishment	Play
Work closely with others	Games, play, projects

(Source: Derived from Wicker, A. W. [1968]. Undermanning, performance, and students' subjective experience in behavioral settings of large and small high schools. *Journal of Personality and Social Psychology, 10,* 255–261.)

These students derive a high degree of satisfaction from participation in school-related activities (Linney & Seidman, 1989). In larger schools, students tend to receive more satisfaction from observing the behavior of others and from feelings of school spirit that are built up through association and identification with the participation of other people. This vicarious kind of participation apparently does not lead to the kinds of individual satisfaction that is gained from actual participation. Again, however, it is worth emphasizing that when degree of participation is equated, students from large and small schools do not differ on these dimensions of satisfaction.

Willems (1967) came to a similar conclusion in his study of potential dropouts compared to students with average capabilities. He examined "sense of obligation" with respect to participation in extracurricular activities in these two groups of students. In smaller schools the marginal students, the potential dropouts, indicated that they had a sense of obligation similar to that of their peers who were successful students. In larger schools, however, the potential dropouts reported little or no sense of obligation toward participation in the activities. This was true both in 1961 and again in 1965. These data, in a dramatic way, provide support for the notion that in smaller schools students feel pressure to participate in school activities.

When speaking of large and small schools, the issue of curriculum variety inevitably comes up. To what degree are the curricula in large and small schools different, and how important is this difference?

In reviews of studies investigating the effect of school size on the individual, the teachers in large schools tend to be better qualified academically, are required to teach fewer courses outside of their major area of interest, and are better at preparing students to go on to college than teachers in smaller schools. The advantage of smaller schools seemed to lie in the greater degree to which teachers cooperated with each other, which seemed to lead to a greater degree of student confidence in the teacher.

Gump's (1966) research on school size and curriculum, however, indicates that bigness does not necessarily correlate perfectly with variety of academic offerings. Generally speaking, a 100 percent increase in the size of the school produces only about 17 percent increase in the variety of the curriculum. In addition, Gump notes that many of the opportunities available to students in larger schools are taken advantage of by only a small proportion of the students. This led him to conclude, quite interestingly, that although big schools may offer their students greater opportunities for participation in a larger number of activities, smaller schools do a better job of actually translating these opportunities into profitable experiences for the individual student.

One might summarize the effects that we have discussed above in the following way. Larger schools do, indeed, offer both a greater variety of courses and more outside activities. However, the percentage of students who participate in outside activities is smaller in large schools than in small schools. In smaller schools, nearly everyone is expected to, and in fact does, participate in one or more of the social and extracurricular activities of the school. Given the kinds of effects that participation in school activities has on the individual student (that is, gains in self-confidence and feelings of self-worth), small schools certainly offer one advantage that larger schools do not, except to a smaller number of their students. Indeed, even the potential dropout is less likely to become a real dropout in the smaller school because of pressure exerted by peers, teachers, and others for completing the school curriculum.

Although there are advantages to participation in school activities, there also are disadvantages, which may be greater in a small school setting. Grabe (1981) studied the effects of participation in high school activities,

such as clubs, athletics, fine arts, and social situations, on students in grades 9 to 12. He replicated Gump's (1966) findings of an advantage of participation on self-concept development. Moreover, participation was more strongly related to self-concept in small than in large schools. Going beyond the work of Gump, Grabe also investigated the effects of poor performance in an activity. He found that in both small and large schools, poor performance led to feelings of alienation, but that these negative feelings were much stronger in small schools.

Perhaps we can summarize best by noting that both large and small schools offer benefits to adolescents through extracurricular activities. Participants who are competent benefit. Those who are less competent may experience some psychological distress.

What, then, might we do to try to capture the "best of both worlds" for the adolescent? Linney and Seidman (1989) suggest that dividing large schools into "houses" or "schools within schools" can reduce deviancy, help develop a sense of identity, and provide greater opportunities for student involvement.

The Role of School Curricula

As we noted above, larger schools do a better job, academically at least, of preparing their students for college. This is true for at least two reasons. First, the teachers seem to be somewhat better qualified in larger schools. Second, the curriculum in a larger school offers the students a wider variety of academic experiences. Next to the influence of the teacher, the curriculum has perhaps the greatest impact on the adolescent's academic development. The curriculum is largely responsible for skill and knowledge acquisition, which in turn affects the future educational and career opportunities that will be available to the student.

Havighurst (1978) has analyzed the nature of school curricula since 1955 and has pointed out some of the major changes that have occurred. In his analysis, Havighurst notes that, during the decade from 1955 to 1965, schools flourished, with wide-ranging support from parents, the community, and government officials. There was a change in perspective, such that programs aimed at a variety of students with differing characteristics were instituted. In addition, a strong emphasis on science and mathematics education prospered as the "space race" impact became felt by those responsible for educating our youth.

During the decade from 1965 to 1975 there was a change in the philosophy of education. Educators and curricula became more concerned than previously with the educational needs of low-income and minority students. Alternative curricula, including a decrease in required courses, sprang up. And, there was an emphasis on educating students to understand their history, role, and identity as members of a pluralistic society (Linney & Seidman, 1989). Hence, for example, courses on black studies or women's studies became popular and replaced other elective or required courses.

As you are aware, there have been numerous recent criticisms of the nature of the educational system, and there has been a concomitant move to return "to the basics" (Murphy, 1987). Citing declining average scores on standardized tests such as the Scholastic Aptitude Test, critics argue that schools are not doing the job of educating youngsters adequately. As a result, we hear much of lengthening school days or the school year, increasing requirements for graduation, increasing homework assignments, which increases learning (Keith, 1982; Chen & Stevenson, 1989), competence learning, and the like. Hence, we likely will be seeing changes in the nature of school curricula.

Many high schools today offer three major curricula. The *college preparatory* curriculum is aimed at preparing students to attend colleges and universities. The *vocational* curriculum is employment-oriented.

In addition to studying basic subjects such as English and mathematics, students enroll in specialized courses teaching specific vocational skills and, in some instances, engage in on-the-job training. Finally, there is the *general* curriculum, which usually is characterizable as a less stringent form of the college preparatory curriculum. Its goal is to provide a general education for students not interested in attending college or making a commitment to a vocational training program. Through the offering of these alternative curricula, schools attempt to provide educational opportunities to the majority of their students.

One specific area of curricular concern is the degree to which the curriculum may be revised to maintain the dropout in the school setting. Both Fantini (1973) and Gorman (1972) discuss the kinds of curricular changes that are needed to make the schools more responsive to the needs of students, including the potential dropout. Both agree that there is a great need to devise innovative programs of study to meet the specific needs and interests of students from different socioeconomic and ethnic backgrounds. More self-guidance and independent study are also considered desirable. Independent study, for example, may also include the possibility of the student's devising, in consultation with an adviser, a curriculum that is focused on his or her own career aspirations. Finally, the use of computers in instruction has been suggested as a means of improving learning (see Box 12–2).

HOW GOOD A JOB DO SCHOOLS DO?

Evaluating the quality of the American educational system, or any other for that matter, is extremely difficult. In part, this difficulty stems from a lack of agreement about what measures ought to be used in such evaluations. We expect the schools to be all things to all students. We tend to neglect the fact that some students may not (or

BOX 12–2 **Computers and Learning/Instruction**

One of the most dramatic current technological advances to affect the educational system in the past generation has been the advent of the tabletop computer. Over the past 10 years or so researchers and educators have been conversing about a variety of issues involved in the use of computers in the instructional processes of the school system. Issues center on the use of the computer as a tutor, as a means of teaching skills, as a tool for achieving academic goals, and the virtue of the computer in making learning more fun and intrinsically motivating. As Lepper and Gurtner (1989) note, there are pros and cons, hopes and fears, in each of these areas. Many research studies have been done to address some of these issues. For others, little or no research is available, or the current findings are contradictory or not convincing.

One area in which substantial research has accumulated is that assessing the computer as a tutor. As a tutor, the computer provides instantaneous feedback, is a facilitator of learning, is highly individualistic in that programs can be tailored to the specific needs of students, and requires the student's participation. Those who are skeptical of computer applications to the classroom contend that using the computer to "teach" students may lead to regimentation in the classroom; increase inequality rather than equality in schooling because some students will have greater access to hardware, software, and adult guidance; fail to meet the needs of those students who do not learn as well when given autonomy in progressing at their own pace, and dehumanize learning.

Ever since the 1970s, over 200 studies have examined the utility of the computer as a tutor (Lepper & Gurtner, 1989), with mixed results. Evidence indicates that over 66 percent of students learning with computer-assisted instruction (CAI) would score at or above the median of those in traditional classrooms as assessed by various achievement measures, particularly in cases in which the students were lower as opposed to average in ability, and younger as opposed to older. Lepper and Gurtner point out, however, that in a number of studies showing substantial benefits of CAI there may have been greater instructional time, for example, in the CAI classes compared to the regular classes. Hence, the benefit of CAI may in part be due to the greater instructional time, not the proposed advantages of CAI. Hence, whether CAI is a benefit as a tutor remains an open question.

A newer area of research involves the computer as a means of teaching thinking and creative skills. The general idea is that computers can be used to simulate laboratory experiments, particularly dangerous ones, for example, or provide opportunities to engage in intellectual skills not addressed in the standard curriculum. Critics of computer use in the classroom fear that computers may "shape" the curriculum because some areas of instruction, such as mathematics or science, are more readily adapted to the computer than others, such as history or art. In addition, opponents note that computers may not allow the development of social and interpersonal skills and may foster an attitude of the purely rational and logical as a means of assessing competence and achievement (Lepper & Gurtner, 1989).

In the area of computer use in the classroom the evidence for benefits is equivocal. Some studies demonstrate little transfer of skills out of the computer environment. Other research, employing younger children and more contact with adults for consultation, shows some benefits, particularly if the projects involve very specific requirements (Lepper & Gurtner, 1989).

There is little doubt that computers will play an increasing role in the classroom. In order for that role to be most effective, Lepper and Gurtner (1989) suggest that more attention be paid to individual differences among children, particularly in regard to their motivational needs and learning styles. Further, they suggest that special attention must be given to ensuring that what is learned at the computer terminal is transferable to other contexts. Finally, they suggest that computer programs be written to emulate "expert" teachers and tutors, those who are sensitive to the individual needs of students.

may) do well regardless of the quality of the school experience; we also tend to neglect the interaction among the school, its curriculum and teachers, and the individual student.

Dropout Rate as a Measure of School Success

One measure used to assess the quality of American educational institutions is the dropout rate. The considerable information that has been accumulated on the dropout rate is at the same time both encouraging and discouraging. Silberman's data (1970) indicate that the dropout rate is approximately 25 percent. This trend is true for both the white majority and the various minority groups. For example, Burton and Jones's (1982) data indicate that the decline in the dropout rate is greater for blacks than for whites. That is, the reduction in the dropout rate is greater for black students, especially younger black students, than for white students. More recent information (U.S. Bureau of the Census, 1989) for 1985 indicates that of 16- to 17-year-olds, 6.1 percent (455,000) dropped out of school. The greater percentage was for white (6.5 percent of the population) than black (4.7 percent of the population) students.

The problem with using the dropout rate as a measure of school success is that it does not take into account the schools that simply push students through, that give diplomas for time served. Although students may be staying in school longer, they may be receiving no better education than the students who spend less time in school. Silberman notes, however, that in a large number of situations in which similar or identical tests were administered to high school populations at two different times, over 90 percent of the comparisons revealed that the later-tested group scored higher than the earlier-tested group. This would lead to the conclusion that, in general, the more time a student spends in school, the

more the student does in fact learn. Students are staying in school longer now than ever before and are learning more as a result.

Criticisms of the School System

A number of observers have been rather critical of the job the American school system is doing (for example, Murphy, 1987). As Silberman (1970) points out, some of the criticisms come from people who feel that everything was better in the past than it is now. Clearly, the data indicate this is not the case. Then there are those who know that the schools have been improving but wish them to improve at an even greater rate.

Silberman (1970) criticizes the schools for teaching students to be docile and accepting, for giving them what he calls an "education for docility." He believes that schools tend to overemphasize discipline and conformity to rules at the expense of allowing students to develop sensitivity, curiosity, self-initiative, and involvement in their own education. Students apparently agree; remember Bachman's finding that students felt that maintenance of order was emphasized too much in the public schools. One cause of this emphasis, according to Silberman, is that schools make decisions about curriculum and instructional methods as a matter of convenience and efficiency. They tend to ignore the research, which suggests that alternative educational programs may be even more productive to the development of student competencies. They view education as something to be done to students and not something that students can do for themselves. According to Silberman, students in traditional schools view school as something to put up with, not as an exciting opportunity for learning. This is unfortunate, because the schools fail to take advantage of the cognitive changes that occur during adolescence, changes that could open up new possibilities for the education of adolescents. Indeed, even middle-class schools often fail to challenge their students because of the

Increasing percentages of students feel the need and have the desire to gain further education upon graduation from high school.

regimented routine and the emphasis on discipline and order that follows from that routine. Indeed, it may be the school's failure to appeal to the new intellectual competencies of its students that leads students to place greater emphasis on the social aspects of the school.

Student Views of the School Situation

The view of the school as an institution that students must suffer through is in part responsible for student concerns about the curriculum. Hoy and his co-workers (Hoy, 1972; Hartley & Hoy, 1972) came to the conclusion that student behavior reflects students' feelings of normlessness, powerlessness, and meaninglessness in the school environment.

The student's feeling that the academic requirements are meaningless is perhaps the easiest of these student perceptions to understand. A student who feels that school work is irrelevant to his own future will find school a meaningless experience. Rewards from the school situation will be relatively low, and the individual may feel left out and may engage in behaviors that are disruptive and perhaps aimed at changing the existing school environment. In effect, powerless-

ness gives rise to normlessness, which in turn gives rise to behaviors reflecting the meaninglessness of the school situation for some individuals. Ultimately some students will drop out, and large numbers of others will simply muddle through, docilely playing the game (Silberman, 1970).

Two interesting questions arise from this analysis. First, to what degree are these views prevalent among adolescents in the high school situation? Second, if these views do exist for a large number of adolescents, do students feel they should have a greater degree of control in determining curricula?

Although there is no doubt that a strong minority of students feel that they should have a greater say in policy-making, curriculum development, and other aspects of the school situation, the majority of students apparently have quite different feelings. The data from Harris's (1969) survey of student views on policy-making indicate that 58 percent of the students felt that they should have a greater participation in policy-making and that 54 percent felt that student participation should be of greater importance than it is currently perceived to be. Only a minority of students felt that they should have more to say about discipline, the conduct of classes, and the determination of grading procedures. Parents and teachers, as you might suspect, had views that were considerably more conservative than those of the students. These groups generally felt that the degree of student involvement in these affairs of the school was about right.

Harris's data show that the majority of the students (81 percent) felt that the schools and teachers were doing an excellent to a good job. These data support Bachman's survey and indicate that student attitudes toward school are generally positive and that as a group, they are relatively satisfied with the school situation. This suggests that schools are, indeed, doing a satisfactory job and that the critics of the system are overemphasizing the negative points.

More recent surveys show that adolescents in the 1970s generally were approving of their education. Less than a third felt their education was poor preparation for the life they wished to live (Yankelovich, 1974), and nearly 75 percent indicated they wanted to obtain further education. Miller (1976) surveyed a select sample (all were listed in *Who's Who Among High School Students*) of over 22,000 students and reported that, in characterizing their education, 84 percent said it was important, 73 percent said the subjects were relevant, nearly 40 percent said it was challenging, and 55 percent said the teachers were good. Despite these "good" views, these very capable students also had some criticisms of their school years. A fifth felt the subjects they studied were irrelevant, nearly 40 percent felt their teachers were just adequate, and half felt that school was routine. Finally, Hurrelman (1987) reported that adolescents in the 1980s viewed school as having instrumental value (skill learning) and as useful for acquiring the marks of adult status. Across the last three decades, then, there is substantial consistency in student views that schools and the educational system serve a valuable and important function.

The views of parents concerning the role of the school are noteworthy. According to

Harris's 1969 survey, the major area of parental concern is discipline. Sixty-two percent of parents said that "maintaining discipline is more important than student self-inquiry," and 63 percent believed the school should crack down on unruly students. These views contrast sharply with those of the students; apparently parents and children have different concerns about school.

The views and concerns of teachers are generally more similar to those of the students than those of the parents, although they are in between the two. As a result, teachers tend to become caught in the middle, between parents and students, in debates about the philosophy of education. In this sense, teachers become mediators in a generation-gap type of situation.

FACTORS INFLUENCING SCHOOL SUCCESS

Clearly, the teacher exerts a significant influence on the degree of success that the adolescent will experience in the school situation. Through teaching methods, curriculum development, grading procedures, as well as personal characteristics, the teacher exerts a tremendous influence on student attitudes in the school. Since degree of success in school is related to delinquency and other forms of antisocial behaviors, it is important to examine some of the factors that are critical to success in the school, in addition to the role of the teacher.

The Role of the Parents

Parental influences on school performance begin long before the adolescent years. Such influences include general views about education, parental involvement in their child's education, family structure (see Box 12–3), and child-rearing techniques. Moreover, as parents change in these regards their influences on school perfor-

BOX 12–3 **Family Structure and Adolescent School Achievement**

Recently, researchers have become interested in studying family structure as it relates to adolescents' school achievement (see Kurdek & Sinclair, 1988; Zimiles & Lee, 1989). This is an important subject because of the large number of adolescents who will live for some period of time in a single-parent or stepparent family. Researchers have been concerned not only about school performance, such as grades earned, but also school behavior, such as absences and misconduct. Research with children has shown that those from intact families not only perform somewhat better academically but have fewer behavioral problems related to school, although the differences between the groups diminish when social class is controlled (see Kurdek & Sinclair, 1988). Does family structure relate to adolescent school achievement and behavior?

Kurdek and Sinclair (1988) studied eighth-grade males and females from each family structure. They found that students from intact families had higher year-end grades than did students in the other two family structures. In addition, those from intact families had higher quantitative achievement test scores than did those from stepfather families and fewer absences than did those from where the mother had custody. Amount of contact with the noncustodial father was not related to school achievement for those students not living with their biological father. This finding indicates that the differences in school grades are not the result of the lack of a male model.

Zimiles and Lee (1989) studied over 13,000 high school sophomores from intact, single-parent, and stepparent (reconstituted) families. Those from intact families had higher grades than those from the other two groups, both as sophomores and as seniors. In general, students from intact families were less likely to drop out of school. Males from single-parent families were more likely to drop out than were males from stepfamilies. The reverse was true for the females. The differential dropping out of school by students in the three family types seemed not to be a result of differential levels of achievement, as assessed by either achievement tests or school grades.

Several points should be noted. First, the differences in grades and achievement test scores, while statistically reliable, are not large. As a group, students from single-parent and reconstituted families are not failing school. Second, the group differences, as is always the case, mask individual differences among students. Just as some students from intact families are excellent and others are not, some students from single-parent and stepparent families are excellent and others are not. These differences among students seem more related to other factors, such as parental involvement in school and an authoritative parenting style (see text), than to the type of family structure.

Finally, these differences seem unrelated to social class; that is, the differences are not simply a result of reduced economic circumstances. The causes of these differences, then, lie in how the adolescent adjusts to parental divorce, in general, and in the nature of family interaction patterns. At present, we know virtually nothing of the specific nature of the causes of the differences.

mance may change (Bradley, Caldwell, & Rock, 1988). Hence, it is the parents' contemporary attitudes and behaviors, not those of the past, that are most important to the adolescent's school achievement.

Educational Attainment and Adolescent Success in Schools. As Sewell and Shah (1968a, 1968b) have demonstrated, parental educational attainment shows a high degree of relationship with the aspirations and success of adolescents in the school setting. Ad-

olescents who come from families with highly educated parents are more likely to attend college than adolescents who come from less educated families. Generally speaking, the educational level reached by the father has a more significant influence on adolescents of both sexes than the educational level of the mother. Partially, these effects are due to the fact that educated parents tend to stress the importance of education.

Moreover, parental educational level correlates highly with social class as measured by occupation or income. In effect, educational attainment and social class are such closely related variables that it is difficult to tell which might be the more important. Middle- and upper-class parents are also more likely to encourage and take active roles in their child's educational achievement than are lower-class parents.

These social-class differences are probably also partly due to the high costs of a college education. Parents in the lower economic strata are less likely than their middle-class counterparts to be able to afford to send their children to college. As a result, they may tend to stress the importance of nonacademic skills for their children. To these parents, "doing well" in school may seem relatively unimportant.

Parental Encouragement and Rewards for Academic Success. As we all know from our own personal experience, parental encouragement and rewards generally lead to better school performance (Stevenson & Baker, 1987). It appears that parental encouragement reflects parental attempts to develop mature behavior in their children. When parents spell out a definable set of expected behaviors, adolescents know what is expected of them in school and attempt to perform at this level, particularly when they have rewarding parents who are actively involved in their education. In support of this notion, Morrow and Wilson (1961), in their study of family relations of high-achieving and underachieving boys, demonstrated that high achievers have parents who give more praise and approval for school performance and encourage more identification with themselves than do underachievers (see Table 12–2).

These data suggest that parental child-rearing techniques may be related to school performance. The evidence reveals that for a wide variety of social classes and ethnic groups, authoritarian and permissive parenting styles are negatively related to the

TABLE 12–2 **Examples of Parent and Family Behaviors That Distinguish High- and Low-Achieving Boys**

Parent/Family Activity Positively Related to High Achievement
More family recreation
Family sharing of confidences
Parental approval
Family morale
Parental appropriate restrictiveness
Reasonable parental discipline
Having trusting parents
Respect and affection for one's parents

(Source: Based on Morrow, W. R., & Wilson, R. C. [1961]. Family relations of bright high achieving and underachieving high school boys. *Child Development, 32*, 501–510.)

adolescent's academic achievement (Dornbusch et al., 1987; Elder, 1965; Pratt, Sebastian, & Bountrogianni, 1989). In turn, an authoritative parenting style is associated positively with school achievement. Authoritative parents engage in a variety of behaviors that promote school success (Pratt et al., 1989). For example, they have more contact with the school and teachers, and more positive attitudes about homework. In addition, they promote autonomy and independence, both of which are positively related to school success (Grolnick & Ryan, 1989; Stevenson & Baker, 1987; Wentzel, 1989).

We might summarize this section in the following way. Parents who have attained a relatively high level of education tend to value it either as a means to an end (a high-level job) or as security insurance. For whatever reasons, these attitudes seem to be reflected in their child-rearing techniques; these techniques in turn seem to prepare their children for success in the school, probably by giving them positive attitudes toward school. By training their children to be relatively autonomous and independent and by giving them a degree of achievement motivation and respect for knowledge, these parents, who come primarily from the middle and upper classes, tend to produce offspring who are successful in school and view it in positive ways. On the other hand, authoritarian and rigid parents tend not to pass these values on to their children.

Peer Influences on School Achievement

In Chapter 11 we outlined a number of important peer-group influences on the adolescent's development. Peer-group influences very clearly carry over into the realm of academic achievement, with those who are well liked by their peers tending to be scholastically more successful than those who are less well liked or rejected by their peers (Schmuck, 1963; Alexander & Campbell, 1964; Rigsby & McDill, 1972). These influences stem from making plans together about going to college (Alexander & Campbell, 1964), from being liked by peers (Schmuck, 1963), and also from social-class differences in views toward future education (Pavalko & Bishop, 1966).

The primary etiology of this close relationship between friends and educational aspirations, as well as the influence of the peer group in general on educational plans and aspirations, involves the notion of reciprocity of friendship. If there is a high degree of closeness between friends, and if this relationship is reciprocal, then peers have a strong effect on educational planning and aspirations. This has been demonstrated in several studies. Rigsby and McDill (1972) investigated peer relationships and educational aspirations in a sample of 20,345 students. The students were asked a series of questions. One question asked them to give the number of their friends who were in or planned to attend college. A second asked which students in their school they went around with most often. In addition to responses to these two questions, Rigsby and McDill measured the percentage of friends who came from families where the father had some college education. They also measured the academic values of the friends.

The peer group apparently exerts a con-

Close friendships foster similarity between peers' educational aspirations and achievements.

siderable influence on academic aspirations. The perceived proportion of friends with college plans and the actual percentage of friends with college plans related highly to the adolescents' educational plans. The other measures did not. Reciprocity of friendship, then, is strongly related to educational plans.

Kandel and Lesser (1969) also demonstrated the importance of reciprocity in the correlation between friendship patterns and educational aspirations. Where friendships were reciprocal, there was a greater degree of agreement on educational aspirations and goals than in friendships that were unreciprocated. In addition, friends who saw each other frequently outside the school setting were in greater agreement on academic goals than were friends who saw each other only infrequently outside of school. Finally, when the school friend was also the overall best friend, the degree of agreement on academic objectives and aspirations was higher than when the individual school friend was not the overall best friend.

These data indicate a very strong relationship between friendship status and academic aspirations. The basis of this relationship seems to lie in the reciprocity with which the individuals view the friendship. Peers can provide an environment which is conducive to academic competence and in which the individual is expected to conform to the norms and expectations of others. Given this conformity, those who are able to succeed in school are more likely to hold similar views and higher aspirations than those who are not able to be successful. It appears, then, that the influence of the peer group is mediated by mutual reinforcement of a relatively common basic set of notions about the value of education.

Parent versus Peer Influences

We have presented data indicating that the educational aspirations of adolescents are highly similar both to those of their close friends and to those of their parents. The popular stereotypes of adolescents would have us believe that peers exert a stronger influence on the development of educational goals and aspirations than parents. As we noted above, parents tend to be more influential than peers with respect to long-term educational goals and views. In addition, parents and peers, because of their similar backgrounds, tend to reinforce each other's objectives.

Additional data on this point come from Kandel and Lesser's (1969) study. They reported that 57 percent of adolescents had educational views that agreed with those of their parents as well as their friends, and that those who agreed with the values of their parents were also very likely to agree with the values of their peers (76 percent). Those who disagreed with parental values were considerably less likely to agree with their friends' values (59 percent). As Kandel and Lesser point out, then, there is little if any conflict between the adolescent's parents and peers vis-à-vis the adolescent's future educational goals.

Socioeconomic Status and Educational Aspiration and Success

Social class is a global variable that includes a number of different dimensions, such as the neighborhood in which one lives, the income level of the family, the child-rearing practices of the parents, the attitudes of family members and friends toward education, and a host of other characteristics that influence the views the adolescent holds about life. As a result of these and other differences, middle-class students start school with an advantage over lower-class students, but the exact reasons are unclear. Therefore, to make broad generalizations about social-class differences related to educational aspirations or achievements is not very satisfying because it tells us little about individual differences (see Box 12–4). Indeed, the multitude of the dimensions underlying social class makes it difficult to investigate social class in relation to any psychological variable. In order to be as precise as we can in our presentation of social class and its relationship to school achievement and aspirations, we have broken the discussions down into several subcategories.

The Influence of the Neighborhood. Neighborhood characteristics are strongly related to social class as well as to academic aspirations and achievement (Boyle, 1966). Students from more prosperous areas have higher educational aspirations and do better in school than students from poorer neighborhoods, even when age, measurement procedures, intellectual levels, and family background factors are adjusted. The neighborhood is an important factor in school achievement because the schools students attend are generally determined by the neighborhood in which they live. As a result, the students in a school tend to be of relatively homogeneous backgrounds. In fact, if high schools are classified according to the socioeconomic status of the majority of individuals in the school, the aspirations of any one student will lie in the direction of the aspirations of the majority of the students in the school. In other words, middle-class students attending a school in a lower-class neighborhood have lower educational aspi-

BOX 12–4   Is Socioeconomic Status Related to Academic Achievement?

As is pointed out in the text, there is a widely held belief that socioeconomic status (SES) and academic achievement are strongly related. Hence, the prevalent view is that the impact of schooling on the child must be assessed within the general context of the child's SES (Coleman et al., 1966). The stereotypic view is that students from economically and socially advantaged backgrounds will have higher grade point averages, achievement test scores, and the like. Much data support this stereotype, but a substantial number of studies do not reveal this pattern of relationships.

In a thorough review of 101 studies producing 636 correlations between measures of SES and achievement, White (1982) pointed out some of the complexities involved in understanding the relationship between SES and school achievement. One very important issue involved the specific measure of SES employed in any given study. A variety of measures of SES have been used in various research projects:

> Family income
> Parent education
> Occupation of household head
> Atmosphere of home
> School SES rating
> Value of house
> Resources available to the school

Of the various measures employed, the one that has the strongest correlation with school achievement is home atmosphere. White argues that this measure takes into account a variety of factors that might well relate to school achievement, for example, reading to children, encouraging children to complete homework assignments, emphasizing the value of education, and providing educational opportunities outside the school setting. This finding indicates that it is *how* parents rear their children, not issues of family economics or general educational level, that is important in the relationship between SES and school achievement. In other words, the simplistic approach to studying the relationship between SES and achievement is likely not a productive or important one.

A second important issue concerned the measure of academic achievement employed. In some studies, standardized achievement test scores were used as the measure of achievement. In other studies, teacher-assigned grades represented the measure of achievement. Finally, in other studies, IQ was the criterion measure. The results of White's review indicate that use of achievement measures or IQ yield the higher correlations with SES.

White's review points out several difficulties involved in assessing the relationship between SES and school achievement. First, the strength of the relationship depends on the measures of SES and school achievement that are used. It is not possible to state the relationship in an unqualified manner. Second, the relatively high correlations between measures of home atmosphere and measures of school achievement highlight the difficulties of unraveling the cause-effect directions in the relationship. Does the home atmosphere described above cause the child to do better on school achievement measures, or does the child who does well cause alterations in the home atmosphere, making it the sort noted above? The tendency is to believe the former. However, the evidence is more properly interpreted as indicating a likely reciprocal causal relationship.

rations than do middle-class students attending a middle-class school.

The reverse is also the case, with lower-class students who attend middle-class schools having higher educational aspirations than do lower-class students who attend lower-class schools. This is very clearly indicated in a study by Wilson (1959), in which schools were grouped as either "upper white collar," "lower white collar," or "industrial." In the upper white-collar schools, about 65 percent of the fathers of the boys who were studied were upper white-collar or college educated; only 14 percent of the fathers of the boys in the industrial schools had any college education. This should give you some idea of the degree of difference in the composition of the student bodies in the two types of schools. Wilson's data indicated that 80 percent of the students in the upper white-collar schools, 57 percent in the lower white-collar schools, and 38 percent in the industrial schools wanted to go to college. Wilson attributed these differences to the neighborhood influence.

To highlight these differences in a slightly different way, 93 percent of the boys who came from families where the father was a professional man and 50 percent of the boys whose fathers were manual workers intended to go to college *if they also attended an upper white-collar school.* In the industrial school, these percentages were two-thirds and one-third, respectively. The atmosphere of the school, which reflects the values, attitudes, and expectations of the neighborhood, is a determinant of student educational aspirations.

Social-Class Differences in Attitudes Toward School. People from different socioeconomic classes have different attitudes about the value of education. Upper middle-class and upper-class adolescents view education as more intrinsically rewarding than do lower-class adolescents. Bachman and others (1967) present convincing data indi-

cating that the individual's view of his or her own school ability is highly related to socioeconomic status even when school-related factors such as intelligence are controlled. Boys from higher socioeconomic levels have more positive attitudes and fewer negative attitudes toward school than do boys from lower socioeconomic levels. In addition, at any given level of education, the middle-class and upper middle-class child or adolescent is likely to achieve higher grades and standardized test scores than the lower-class peer.

There are a number of obvious as well as subtle reasons for these differences. Economic situation is an example of an obvious factor that relates to school aspirations. Students from the lower economic levels are less likely to have money for further education, and indeed may be forced to quit school to help support the family. Even though loans are available for attending school, a young person is likely to be ambivalent about accepting money that must be paid back in the future. Less obvious are factors intrinsic to the school situation. Lower-class schools are less likely to have funds for ancillary personnel, supplies, and equipment, and probably don't do as good a job of preparing the students academically as do middle-class schools.

Social Class and Parental Views. As we noted above, parental views of the value of school also differ across social classes. Middle-class parents tend to value school and promote school success to a greater degree than do lower-class parents. Lower-class parents tend to be less involved in the schooling of their children and tend to view it more as a vocational than an academic experience. These views of parents, in some ways, are not unrealistic. Schools tend to be geared to the needs and desires of middle-class students and to be aimed primarily at preparing people for middle-class society.

We should not lose sight of the fact, however, that there are widely varying attitudes toward school within, as well as between, social classes. The parents of lower-class adolescents are concerned about the education their children get, but perhaps their concerns are somewhat different from those of middle-class parents. Indeed, in one study (Simpson, 1962) it was demonstrated that middle-class and lower-class boys who had parents who rewarded achievement in school had higher educational aspirations than middle-class boys whose parents were not as involved or concerned about the school success of their children.

These values may be handed down to the individual adolescent through parental modeling and may explain why school success is more valued by middle-class than lower-class adolescents. As a result, middle-class and upper-class adolescents may hold higher aspirations and strive harder to do better in school than their lower-class counterparts. This analysis may explain why lower-class students in middle-class schools have higher educational aspirations than their peers in the lower-class schools. Part of the change that is being experienced in public school curricula is due to pressure on the part of the lower-class parents to have the schools meet the needs of their children. These parents express the view that schools should offer a wide range of curricula aimed at meeting diverse student needs. To the extent that schools do this, we may see a corresponding increase in the school's interest in students from lower socioeconomic levels.

The Disadvantaged Minority. As Silberman (1970) notes, although the schools are beginning to take into account the needs of minority-group students such as blacks, Indians, and Chicanos, they still do not give them the kind of education they could profit from most. As a result, the individual who comes from an ethnic minority is not likely to be well prepared for further academic work, at least not at the college level.

These differences were dramatically supported in research by Coleman et al. (1966) and Whiteman and Deutsch (1968). In both these studies, it was demonstrated that the degree of deprivation experienced by an individual was related to school performance. Indeed, over time, the deprived individuals "lose" (fail to improve) basic cognitive, intellectual, and language capabilities. The minority groups performed less well than white middle-class subjects at all grade levels, and the disparity in the performance was either maintained or increased across school grades.

For example, first-grade white students scored 54 on tests of nonverbal abilities and 53 on tests of verbal skills. Puerto Ricans scored 46 and 45, American Indians 53 and 48, and blacks 43 and 45 on these two tests. The twelfth-grade white students scored 52 on each test, the Puerto Ricans 43 on each, the American Indians 47 and 44, and the blacks 41 on each test. These differences are indeed distressing because at each grade level the number of students who drop out of school is likely to be greater for the nonwhite than for the white population. In effect, the grade-level differences in the Coleman data may be even larger than they appear to be were the performance of all adolescents who entered school, those who remained as well as those who dropped out, assessed.

Whiteman and Deutsch report similar data from IQ tests, ratings of self-concept, and tests assessing the development of language skills and capabilities. It appears that, as minority adolescents continue in the school situation, they learn less and less and their relative standing continually drops. In other words, poor education at the beginning of the school experience is compounded by a lack of progress later on.

Individual Characteristics and Academic Success

The most obvious individual difference characteristic that is related to school success is intelligence, as measured by the IQ test.

As you know from our previous discussion of intellectual and cognitive development (Chapter 4), the IQ test was devised in order to predict success in the normal school curriculum. Examination of the correlation between IQ and tests of academic achievement reveal that this relationship is about .5 to about .8, depending upon the IQ test that is used and the achievement area being considered in the correlation.

Generally speaking, the correlation is higher for areas that stress verbal skills. This is in keeping with the general nature of IQ tests, which tend to be highly verbal.

Correlations between IQ scores and school grades tend to be somewhat lower, ranging from about .4 to .6 for boys and about .7 to .8 for girls (McCandless, Roberts, & Starnes, 1972). This is in contrast to the kinds of correlations that are obtained with standardized achievement test scores, in which there are typically no sex differences. In all likelihood, this reflects different expectations on the part of the teacher for student performance depending upon sex (McCandless et al., 1972). Boys are traditionally more assertive and restless in school, whereas girls are more conforming and disciplined, a difference that undoubtedly affects the way teachers perceive boys and girls enjoying, and profiting from, the school environment. In addition, teachers are well aware that in the early grade levels boys are "less ready" to enter the school situation than are girls. As a result, teachers may expect differential performances from boys and girls and, consciously or unconsciously, may grade girls more favorably than boys in line with their expectations.

A number of other, more general, personality characteristics have also been related to success in the school. Those who achieve in school have good study habits, are usually interested in school, tend to be grade conscious, have a relatively high degree of self-confidence and self-acceptance, are highly motivated for academic achievement, and set realistic goals for themselves. On the other hand, those who do poorly, or who are underachievers, tend to have difficulty in many of these areas; they tend to be impulsive, pleasure seeking, and incapable of delaying rewards. They tend not to like school, to derive relatively little satisfaction from it, and to have a good deal of pessimism about their future.

It is often difficult in these research areas to determine the causal factor; that is, does doing poorly in school produce the attitude differences that we noted above, or do the attitude differences cause the school failure? Whatever the cause and effect relationship is, it is clear that a relationship between attitudes and performance in school does exist.

The Impact of the Teacher and the School

There is no doubt that the single most important aspect of the school situation in terms of influencing adolescent attitudes as well as success in school is the teacher (Linney & Seidman, 1989). Through individual teacher-student interactions, as well as through curriculum presentation and attitudes about students, the teachers exert a good deal of control over how adolescents view school and how well they will do there. If there is a good match between teacher characteristics and student characteristics, then the student will probably do better than if there is a poor match. Although there are those who criticize teachers as being incompetent, there are relatively few in the profession who do a poor job (Silberman, 1970). The majority of teachers are well-trained and competent people who are concerned about the education of young people and work hard to promote a suitable educational environment. Unfortunately, many of the problems for which teachers are blamed are beyond their control. Shortages of money, teaching materials, support staff, and equipment lead to feelings of dissatisfaction that may be centered, unfairly, on the teacher.

All of us have had our favorite teachers, and, if we worked at it, we could probably identify certain characteristics that somehow distinguish our favorite teachers. Jersild (1963) investigated the characteristics of adolescents' best-liked and least-liked teachers. Generally speaking, teachers who behave as human beings and show emotional involvement with students tend to be liked best. Kindness and friendliness were considered more important by the students than academic competencies. Perhaps the students view all teachers as having roughly equivalent academic competencies, and therefore ignore competency as a variable in discriminating between teachers, preferring instead to look at human qualities. As Jersild notes, teaching ability does not relate to whether or not the teacher is liked or disliked. A number of other investigators have reported similar data indicating that warmth and friendliness are highly valued traits in teachers.

For a teacher to be effective the school environment must be supportive of teacher efforts and conducive to student learning. The effective school must have strong leadership from the principal, but in an orderly and nonoppressive manner (Linney & Seidman, 1989). Teachers need to be involved in decision making and curriculum planning. These conditions foster pride in the teacher and relate to teachers holding high expectations for the adolescent's performance. This, in turn, helps adolescents have high expectancies for their performance and produces an atmosphere conducive to learning.

THE SCHOOL DROPOUT

As noted above, about one-fourth of students drop out of high school (U.S. Bureau of the Census, 1989). In this section we explore several aspects of dropping out.

The disadvantages to the high school dropout are many. First, there are few job opportunities for the dropout. Although many jobs do not require a high school diploma, these jobs nevertheless often go to those with a high school diploma or even more education. This puts the high school dropout at the bottom of the economic ladder. This is particularly a problem for those who come from minority group backgrounds. There are large numbers of young nonwhite dropouts who have very bleak employment prospects. Partially as a result of these employment possibilities, inner-city youths may turn to delinquency, criminal behavior, and drug addiction (Cervantes, 1965a, 1965b), and inner-city neighborhoods become hotbeds of antisocial behavior. These individuals make up a disproportionate share of those who engage in socially unapproved behaviors, and at present there seems to be little that can be done to help them.

Dropping out of high school is in part a function of the curriculum, as we noted above. Curricula that are ill suited to the needs of certain segments of the population are unlikely to maintain student interest and attendance in the school. In part, then, dropping out of high school reflects a general dissatisfaction with courses that are not designed to prepare these students for a future vocation.

It is often felt that the primary reason for dropping out of high school is economic. As Cervantes (1965a, 1965b) has noted, however, only about 3 percent of the students who drop out of high school do so for financial reasons. Clearly, the primary reasons for dropping out of high school are noneconomic.

Characteristics of High School Dropouts

There are various reasons for dropping out of school. Some dropouts leave school because of circumstances beyond their control. Others leave school because they cannot perform at a satisfactory level. Finally, there are some who are capable of dealing with the school curriculum, but who leave because the curriculum is boring or otherwise distasteful to them, or because they cannot compete successfully in a middle-class school system. These latter students often feel that the curriculum has nothing to do with their life goals and that attending school is therefore a waste of time. However, the large majority of school dropouts are those who have only a low probability of graduating (Cervantes, 1965a, 1965b; Silberman, 1970). As Voss, Wendling, and Elliott (1966) demonstrated, approximately one-third of dropouts but only one-tenth of graduates have IQs below 85. However, nearly half (48 percent) of the dropouts had IQs in the normal range and approximately 6 percent were above average in IQ score. These data very strongly suggest that intellectual capability *per se* is not the sole cause of dropping out of school. However, in analyzing their data for early versus late dropouts, Voss and his colleagues did note that early dropouts were very likely to have below minimal IQ levels (three-quarters had IQs lower than 85), whereas only a third of later dropouts had IQ scores below 85. It seems, therefore, that for early dropouts, intellectual capabilities are a more important determinant than for later dropouts.

In addition to raw intellectual capabilities (as assessed by IQ tests), school performance is related to dropping out. Voss and his co-workers demonstrated that, by the seventh grade, the average dropout is two years below grade level in reading and arithmetic ability and has probably failed one or more years of school. As the individual continues in the academic setting, it is highly likely that future failures will occur and the individual will fall even further behind (Voss, Wendling, & Elliott, 1966; Silberman, 1970).

Because neither intellectual skills nor school performance are perfect predictors of dropping out of high school, other factors, such as family background, motivation for performance in the school, and attitudes toward the school setting, must have some

prediction value (Elliott, Voss, & Wendling, 1966). The gross social-class measure relates to the attitudes one has toward school; and lower-class students, Elliott and his co-workers suggest, can't or won't compete in the middle-class milieu of the school. Hence, they are more likely than middle-class students to drop out.

Cervantes (1965a, 1965b) also focused on the importance of family antecedents as a cause of dropping out of school. It is Cervantes's contention that family support for remaining in school is relatively low in lower-income families. Given that income is a relatively unimportant reason, as we noted above, for leaving school, it appears that attitudes of family members toward school are the more critical factor. Cervantes's research demonstrates that home atmosphere, as exemplified by communication between parents and adolescents, seems to be a critical factor. Over 80 percent of dropouts felt that they were not accepted or understood by their family, whereas over 80 percent of graduates felt that they were accepted and understood. Dropouts also felt to a very high degree that there was little communication in the home. Cervantes went on to relate this kind of information to family activity. Dropouts participated in joint family activities only infrequently, whereas half of the students who graduated from high school indicated they either frequently or very frequently participated in family activities. These data indicate a very strong degree of association between family antecedents and dropping out of school.

Combs and Cooley (1968) also investigated home issues related to dropping out of school. These investigators reported that global home factors related to socioeconomic status (family income, books in the home, educational level of the parents) did not relate to dropping out of high school for boys, although there was a relationship for girls at the lower socioeconomic levels. These data support the notion that it is family attitudes and not status *per se* which relate

Dropouts cut themselves off from higher-paying jobs and are more often unemployed than those who graduate from high school.

to dropping out of school. As we noted above, parents in lower-income groups are less likely to encourage their children to do well in school or to insist that they stay there until they graduate. Many of these parents do not see the relationship between education and future success. The parents' negative attitude about the advantages of schooling and their child's feelings of alienation from the middle-class values taught by the school have considerable impact on whether or not the adolescent will remain in school.

Some research goes a step further and identifies personality characteristics and views of the world that separate dropouts from graduates (Combs & Cooley, 1968; Cervantes, 1965b). Dropouts tend to be lower in self-confidence, emotional maturity, and sociability, and tend to score higher on impulsiveness, than nondropouts. Dropouts tend to resent authority and to have

lower self-esteem than nondropouts. Which is the cause and which is the effect is a difficult problem to assess. Does dropping out produce the kinds of changes that are observed, or do the kinds of changes precede dropping out of school? Whatever the answer, it appears that these differences are symptomatic of the kinds of behaviors that separate dropouts from nondropouts.

Combs and Cooley (1968) presented additional data indicating that the dropout is most likely enrolled in a general course of studies. At the ninth-grade level, dropouts and nondropouts of both sexes are approximately equally represented in the various school curricula. At the time of dropping out, however, dropouts are overrepresented in the general, as opposed to college-preparatory or commercial-business, curricula. Approximately 75 percent of the dropouts are in the general school curriculum, although only 60 percent of boys and 36 percent of girls are in the general curricula. Combs and Cooley speculate that perhaps the general curriculum is insufficient to deal with the vocational needs and desires of dropouts and may well influence their decision to leave school.

As we can see from the above, dropping out of school has a number of antecedents. Parental and family influences are certainly important. All adolescents need support and encouragement for continuing and performing well in the school setting. Parents who do not provide this kind of support may be encouraging their sons and daughters to view school in a negative fashion. Peers, too, play an important role. To the degree that the individual feels accepted by peers, he or she is more likely to remain in school. The school, however, also plays an important role. School curricula that reflect and foster middle-class values do not meet the needs of a relatively large segment of the population, with the result that adolescents from that segment tend to think of themselves as inadequate and school as irrelevant. All these factors combine and contribute to the decision of the individual to leave school. Unfortunately, the outlook for dropouts is not very good. The relatively lower level of academic competencies and the lack of a high school diploma leave these individuals with an uncertain occupational future and a poor outlook for advancement.

Consequences of Dropping Out of School

Perhaps the most extensive research on the consequences of dropping out of high school was Bachman's study of 2,213 tenth-grade boys (Bachman, Green, & Wirtanen, 1972). In comparing those who dropped out with those who didn't drop out but did not go to college, Bachman substantiated earlier research indicating that dropouts (1) were more likely to have lower levels of aspirations and higher delinquency rates, (2) tended to come from lower economic levels, and (3) had generally lower self-esteem than nondropouts. Their unemployment records were also much higher than those of the nondropouts. One finding of considerable interest was that some of the students actually gained in self-esteem and self-concept after dropping out of school. Bachman suggests that dropping out of school allows the individual to get out of a situation in which there were very few rewards, which, in turn, produces an increase in self-concept.

One may well ask what can be done to help alleviate the dropout situation. Unfortunately, it appears that current efforts are not very helpful. As you might suspect from our previous discussions, work on reducing the number of dropouts must begin at the elementary school level. The dropout has a tendency to fall behind at that level, and continues to fall further behind as school progresses (Combs & Cooley, 1968). By introducing remedial treatment early, and perhaps even altering the curriculum to reflect the needs of these students, it may be possible to keep substantial numbers of potential dropouts in school. However, simply keeping students in school is no guarantee

they will learn, or profit from their education.

Furthermore, as was noted above, keeping them in school may be forcing them to remain in an environment that is relatively unrewarding. Therefore, it will be necessary to program the environment in such a way as to provide the rewards necessary to maintain an appropriate level of interest in the school. In all likelihood, this will have to be done through curriculum revisions aimed at making education more relevant for these students. Bachman suggests that dropping out is not a problem but only a symptom of previously existing problems. In that case, one would have to alter the family behaviors and attitudes that are presumably at the root of these problems. Unfortunately, this is much easier said than done.

SUMMARY

Broadly speaking, schools serve two functions for the 43 million children and adolescents enrolled in them. The maintenance-actualization function involves the enrichment of the individual's personal life, psychological well-being, and emotional development. In general, schools do not meet this function very well. The second major goal of schools involves skills-training/cultural transmission. This function, which involves imparting information and teaching skills, is performed relatively well by the public and private schools.

Schools are characterized by a middle-class orientation. Teachers and administrators tend to come from middle-class backgrounds and schools tend to teach middle-class values. Hence, the school system tends to succeed best with students who hold these values. Schools also have a strong social orientation. Students view the social and athletic activities of the school as the primary means of gaining acceptance, leadership, and popularity. They downplay the importance of academic excellence, and relatively few wish to be remembered as outstanding students.

One concern that has stimulated considerable research is school size. It is clear that there are both advantages and disadvantages in large and small schools. Small schools allow a greater percentage of students to participate in various extracurricular activities. Large schools offer greater academic opportunities. However, it must be remembered that a doubling of school size translates into only a 17 percent increase in curricular options. In both large and small schools, participation in extracurricular activities facilitates self-concept and self-confidence development. And, in both types of schools, failure in activities chosen for participation leads to some feelings of alienation.

A very important concern is how well schools meet their functions. This is an especially salient issue today, given the criticisms of the school system and the declining mean SAT scores of students. One way of examining this problem is by looking at dropout rates. These are declining for both black and white students. A greater percentage of students are completing high school, and they are learning more by staying in school longer. Although there are problems with the schooling of children and adolescents, there is no evidence that schools are doing a poor job.

Another way to examine the issue of success of the school system is to ask students to evaluate their school experience. In general, students are approving of their education. A large majority felt the subjects studied were relevant. Most students felt their teachers were at least "good," and three-quarters indicated they wanted to obtain further education. On the other hand, nearly half felt school was routine and about 40 percent felt their teachers were just adequate. Although the students' ratings indicate they feel there are some difficulties, the general consensus is that schools are seen as providing a relevant educational experience.

A variety of factors influence success in the school environment. Parental influences are important, particularly with respect to the attitudes they espouse toward schooling. Parents who encourage academic excellence, who are not authoritarian in their child-rearing practices, who encourage autonomy and independence, have children who perform better in school. Peers also exert important influences on school achievement. Adolescents who are generally liked and accepted by their peers do better. In addition, if the peer group and close friends have strong academic orientations, the individual adolescent is likely to hold a similar perspective of schooling and do better.

Another important factor is the socioeconomic background of the student. The important issue here is general home atmosphere. Students from backgrounds in which education is encouraged, in which parents provide a suitable atmosphere for learning, and in which the student is allowed to pursue education, do better.

Despite the general feelings about the value of schooling, some adolescents still choose to drop out of school. Few do so because they need to help support the family. In addition, most dropouts have the intellectual competence to complete a high school curriculum. These data suggest that, although some students drop out because of lack of ability, many others do so for a variety of other reasons. One of these other reasons is lack of feeling accepted by the family. Many dropouts tend to be insecure and lacking in self-confidence. Finally, some drop out because the curriculum simply is irrelevant to them. Unfortunately, at the present time, there appears to be little we can do to keep some students from dropping out of school.

GLOSSARY

Maintenance-actualization function. The function provided by schools to enhance student social and emotional growth.

Skills-training/cultural transmission function. The function of schools involving transmission of the skills and knowledge allowing the individual to become an economically independent and productive member of society.

SUGGESTED READINGS

COLEMAN, J., HOFFER, T., & KILGORE, S. (1981). *Public and private schools*. Washington, DC: U.S. Department of Education.

In this report, the authors address a number of aspects of the school environment, mission, and practices. A particularly interesting discussion centers on the role of homework in student achievement and how public and private schools differ in meting out homework.

GRABE, M. (1981). School size and the importance of school activities. *Adolescence*, 16, 21–31.

Grabe examines involvement in school activities as a function of size of school and relates involvement in activities to student's personal growth. An interesting aspect of the study is the investigation of the impact of successful versus unsuccessful performance and how that differs between large and small schools.

LEPPER, M. R., & GURTNER, J-L. (1989). Children and computers: Approaching the twenty-first century. *American Psychologist, 44*, 170–178.

The authors discuss a number of educationally relevant issues relating to the use of computers in schools. They view concerns from both the practical and the theoretical perspective.

LINNEY, J. A., & SEIDMAN, E. (1989). The future of schooling. *American Psychologist, 44*, 336–340.

The authors present a readable and interesting discussion of the major factors affecting school performance, including the role of the teacher and alternative educational environments.

Deviant Behavior during Adolescence

13

CHAPTER OUTLINE

MAJOR ISSUES ADDRESSED

The Definition of Deviant Behavior

The Incidence of Delinquent Behavior

The Causes of Delinquent Behavior

Suicide during the Adolescent Years

Adolescent Drug Use—What and Why?

Eating Disorders during the Adolescent Years

Psychological Disorders Experienced by Adolescents

Parent Influences on Delinquency and Other Disorders

INTRODUCTION

In the previous chapters, the focus was on typical, or "normal," aspects of adolescent development. Our intent was to provide information about the many facets of development experienced by most adolescents. In a sense, we attempted to describe the adolescent experience with which we all are familiar.

In this chapter we focus on the most prevalent types of deviant behavior that occur during the adolescent years. The deviant behaviors we shall discuss include conduct disorders, such as delinquency and running away from home, some of which have legal overtones, and disorders of social functioning, such as eating disorders, suicide, and mental disturbances. In a sense, this material rounds out our earlier discussions by highlighting the difficulties some adolescents experience. As we noted in Chapter 2, although adolescence in general is not especially stressful, for a minority of youngsters it is a very difficult developmental epoch.

DEFINITION OF DEVIANCY

Deviant development is perhaps one of the most difficult concepts to define. In everyday usage, deviancy usually implies that some aspect of development is not normal, and is therefore probably bad. We immediately place a value judgment, typically negative, on deviant behavior. In addition, for most of us, deviancy usually refers to some aspect of social behavior; that is, we relate it to the socialization process. However, deviancy may occur in a number of different realms of development and be of several sorts (See Box 13–1).

Intellectual deviance exists in the form of mental retardation or extremely high IQ scores; it also exists when a child is very precocious with regard to level of cognitive functioning (see Chapter 4). Biological deviance, specifically with regard to being an extremely early or extremely late maturer, was discussed in Chapter 3. Of course, as noted above, another form of deviancy is evidenced by behaviors that fall into the category of those considered illegal by the society; these may be termed *culturally deviant behaviors*.

Two aspects of deviancy are illustrated by these examples. First, our general tendency to place a negative connotation on the term "deviant" is not justified. Indeed, at times there are advantages to being deviant—consider the early maturing male we discussed in Chapter 3, for example. The advantages of being deviant far outweigh the disadvantages in this case. Second, it should be clear that deviancy is defined with respect to some concept of a norm or average. The norm may be stated in terms of theoretical averages, as is the case with respect to IQ; cultural standards, such as expressed in the legal code; or general averages, such as found in growth rates. Nonetheless, in each instance, deviance is considered within the context of a norm. An individual's behavior is considered deviant if it departs in a substantial way from the norm.

As the above examples demonstrate, some forms of deviance involve engaging in inappropriate or unacceptable forms of behavior *as defined by the norm*. However, it is important to note that the norm typically is defined by some majority, or by some group (for example, lawmakers) representing the majority opinion or acting to promote the benefit of all. As is discussed below, however, some deviant behaviors are reinforced by subgroups acting outside the generally accepted norms. Hence, delinquent behaviors, for example, may be considered deviant by the society at large, and may be punished by the broader society, but may also be rewarded by subgroups within the larger society. In other words, some types of deviant behaviors are learned, and they are learned and maintained by the same psychological mechanisms as those behaviors deemed appropriate.

BOX 13–1 **The Diagnostic and Statistical Manual of Mental Disorders**

The defining of various mental disorders is, perhaps, even more difficult than the defining of deviance, although the two clearly are similar. Because the American Psychiatric Association recognized both the theoretical and applied/practical importance of being able to define mental disorders in an accurate, appropriate manner, a Task Force on Nomenclature and Statistics was established in 1974 to wrestle with the issues. The Task Force was charged with developing a set of diagnostic criteria, a glossary of terms, and a well-articulated classification scheme of mental disorders. The result of the effort was published in 1987: *The Diagnostic and Statistical Manual of Mental Disorders*, or *DSM-III-Revised*.

Early in the planning and writing of **DSM-III**, it was recognized that no simple, acceptable definition of mental disorder existed. Hence, it was decided that behavioral descriptions of symptoms would provide the most useful guide. As a result, in *DSM-III-R*, mental disorders are considered to be clinical syndromes with either a painful symptom, such as distress, or as involving an interruption of normal functioning, that is, a disability or impairment.

The purpose of the *DSM-III-R* is to facilitate identification and treatment of clinical disorders. In order to accomplish this goal, the Task Force established a reliable set of diagnostic criteria for 16 different broad categories of disorders, and numerous subcategories. The use of commonly accepted and standardized criteria, and the clear definition of terms, is of benefit to patients, to those who train health care professionals, to those who administer treatment, and to researchers.

As an example, consider the eating disorder anorexia nervosa, which we discuss in detail below. The behaviors defining the disorder include a disturbance of body image, a weight loss of at least 25 percent, an intense fear of becoming obese, a refusal to maintain a normal body weight, and no physical illness causing the weight loss. This set of symptoms (behaviors) defines the disorder. Other constellations of symptoms define other disorders.

The Task Force took great care to classify disorders, not people. Hence, in *DSM-III*, people are not classified as schizophrenic, for example; rather, a set of behavioral symptoms is identified as schizophrenia. Although this is a subtle point for the layperson, it is an important one, for all individuals with a similar disorder may differ in ways important for their treatment. Labeling the disorder and not the person helps maintain the individuality of the disorder any given patient may have.

JUVENILE DELINQUENCY

Defining Delinquency

Juvenile delinquency, a form of antisocial behavior, is a term typically applied to the criminal behaviors of those who are under 16 or 18 years of age, depending on the laws of the particular state in which the individual resides. Hence, delinquency is a legal term used to denote lawbreaking by those who are not considered adults (Patterson, DeBaryshe, & Ramsey, 1989).

The term juvenile delinquency, and its associated connotations, was developed to protect young offenders from being labeled criminals with police records, and to allow them to be treated differently from adults by the legal system (Binder, 1988). Hence, juvenile courts were established, and laws were passed prohibiting the publication of juvenile offenders' names. All this was done with the hope of rehabilitating young offenders and reducing the risk of social stigma that might contribute to their becoming adult criminals. Current estimates are that it costs about $1 billion per year to maintain our juvenile justice system (Patterson et al., 1989).

Delinquent acts include all the crimes that apply to adults, such as burglary, robbery, car theft, murder, and the like, but also include behaviors that, if performed by adults, would not be considered illegal, such as truancy, running away from home, and violating a curfew. Because these laws vary from state to state, what is delinquent in one community may not be considered delinquent in another. Similarly, some communities enforce the laws more vigorously than others. Finally, many juvenile delinquent acts are never discovered, or illegal acts are not known to be done by delinquents. For all these reasons, official statistics on delinquency are likely underestimations of the degree to which it is a problem.

There is another issue which is pertinent here. Delinquent behaviors, although outside the norms of society in general, may be common, and sometimes acceptable, within a particular social, age, or ethnic subgroup. In other words, the same behaviors that violate the norms of the society may be reinforced by the norms of the particular peer group and subculture to which the adolescent belongs. Hence, delinquency has both a cultural and a legal basis, and may generally be viewed as a conflict between the norms of society and the behaviors of the individual given a particular culture-norm reference (Patterson et al., 1989).

Incidence of Juvenile Delinquency

Studying the incidence of juvenile delinquency is difficult because, for the most part,

Auto theft is one of the more prevalent crimes committed by delinquents.

we must rely on recorded incidences of delinquency as opposed to actual rates of occurrence (Gold & Petronio, 1980). As we point out below, actual incidences of juvenile delinquency may be much higher. Moreover, there are multiple measures of incidence—**adjudicated** cases, number of arrests, the percentage of adolescents who engage in delinquency, types of crimes committed, and self-reports.

Despite the difficulties caused by these vagaries, it is clear that, through at least the mid-1970s, juvenile delinquency increased. It then seemed to level off and, as we show below, began to decrease. It is important to note that the increase in delinquency occurred at a greater rate than the increase in the juvenile population. Hence, not only were there more delinquent acts, but apparently more adolescents were engaging in delinquency and were doing so at higher rates than previously.

The percent of persons arrested who were under age 18 is shown in Table 13–1. Since 1974 this percentage has progressively declined, and the decline applies to both males and females. In addition, the decline is present for both serious crimes (e.g., murder, forcible rape) and nonserious crimes (e.g., vandalism, running away from home). Nonetheless, in 1987 over 1.12 million minors were arrested for nonserious crimes and over 650,000 for serious crimes (U. S. Bureau of the Census, 1989).

A word of caution is necessary in interpreting these data. First, they likely are underestimates of actual delinquency rates, as noted above. Second, these data come from arrest records, not adjudicated cases. As we all are aware, being arrested does not necessarily mean one is guilty of the crime of which one is accused. Given that arrests do represent one measure of delinquent behavior, and that the confounding factors likely were the same in 1978 and later, the data in Table 13–1 probably reflect a decline in actual delinquency.

TABLE 13–1   **Percentage of Those Arrested Who Were Under Age 18, by Year**

1974	1976	1978	1980	1982	1987
27.2	24.9	23.3	20.9	17.9	16.5

(Source: Adapted from U.S. Bureau of the Census [1989]. *Statistical abstract of the United States: 1989*. Washington, DC: Government Printing Office.)

Sex Differences in Juvenile Delinquency

The incidence rates of delinquency are somewhat higher for males than females, and the kinds of delinquent acts engaged in by the two sexes also are different.

Sex Differences in Incidence. Historically, male juvenile offenders have outnumbered female offenders on the order of 4 or 5 to 1. We should note, at this point, that in all likelihood, the delinquency rates for girls have historically been underestimated. Wise (1967) collected self-report survey data from a sample of middle-class high school sophomore and junior males and females under conditions of complete anonymity. The results indicated that, overall, the girls had lower delinquency rates than the boys, but that their rates were notably higher than might be expected on the basis of official records. In contrast to the data in the *Uniform Crime Reports* the girls equaled the boys in the areas of alcohol offenses and sexual misconduct. Wise suggested that part of the reason for such discrepancies is that girls are less likely than boys to recommit an illegal act, thus lowering the probability that they will get caught. Hence, official records for delinquency will be higher for boys than for girls. Since Gold's (1970) data indicate a definite relationship between frequency of delinquent behavior and probability of getting caught, Wise's explanation seems quite reasonable.

Sex Differences in Delinquent Behaviors. The kinds of delinquent behaviors engaged in by males and females differ.

This difference is no doubt due in part to sex-role training. Boys are expected to be aggressive and assertive, whereas girls are expected to be passive. For example, boys most frequently engage in burglary, larceny, theft, and other forms of crimes that involve aggressive behavior (Gold, 1970). Girls are more likely to be reported for being incorrigible, for engaging in illicit sexual behavior, or for running away from home. Generally speaking, boys are considerably more delinquent than are girls, and engage in delinquent behaviors that involve higher degrees of aggression and assertiveness than do girls. The exceptions revealed nearly identical percentages for boys and girls. Of some interest, the current data indicate that, overall, boys and girls engaged in similar kinds of delinquent behaviors but at much different rates.

Social Class and Delinquency

The degree to which social class and delinquency are related is a matter of great debate. The importance of the issue resides in more than our better discovering the causes of delinquency and crime. It also is critical to theorizing about delinquency, because virtually every sociological theory of delinquency rests on there being a strong link between poverty, poor living conditions, parental neglect, and other conditions associated with social class background. Discovering clear answers to the question, however, is hampered by differences in the measures used—self-report or official statistics—to assess delinquency. The answer also may well be related to the types of delinquency assessed, and the frequency with which delinquent behaviors are shown.

In general, official rates of delinquency are higher for lower-socioeconomic-status adolescents than for those from the middle classes (Gold & Petronio, 1980:), partly because lower-class adolescents are more likely to get caught and prosecuted for delinquent acts (cf. Gold & Petronio, 1980). Some researchers (cf. Braithwaite, 1981; Elliott & Ageton, 1980) also suggest that social class differences reflect inaccuracies in reporting of juvenile delinquency data. They go on to note that, in all likelihood, there are virtually no differences in delinquency as a function of social class. Those who support this argument tend to rely on studies of self-reported delinquency, which may, they argue, provide more accurate information because substantial amounts of delinquency never get reported or else go undetected.

Although there is considerable appeal in the self-report method of measuring delinquency, the technique has been criticized on a number of grounds, including the difficulty of making up the measures, owing to unrepresentativeness of the items and item overlap (Elliott & Ageton, 1980); the tendency to use small, nonrepresentative samples (Elliott & Ageton, 1980; Braithwaite, 1981); the tendency to call relatively minor acts, such as disobeying parents, delinquency (Braithwaite, 1981); and other problems (Elliott & Ageton, 1980; Braithwaite, 1981). Were these problems handled in sufficient ways, the use of self-report instruments to assess social class differences in delinquency might, indeed, provide more accurate assessments of delinquency as related to social class.

The most carefully conducted study of this type to date is that done by Elliott and Ageton (1980). They conducted a self-report study of delinquency with 1,726 adolescents aged 11 to 17. The sample was a representative national probability sample, meaning it included proportionate numbers of males and females, races (blacks and whites were analyzed in the data reported), and social class levels. The interview contained 47 items assessing a variety of categories of criminal behavior (e.g., crimes against people, hard drug use, crimes against property). The respondents indicated how many times during the past year they had committed each of the behaviors and, if more than 10, the frequency (once a week, once a month, etc.). All respondents were assured of confidentiality and protection from legal subpoena by the U.S. Department of Health, Education, and Welfare.

The findings indicated social class differences in delinquency for crimes against people (sexual assault, aggravated assault, robbery); there were no differences for the other categories. Hence, lower-class adolescents engaged in over 3.5 times the crimes against people as did middle-class adolescents.

Other major findings showed that the social class differences were only evident at the higher overall levels of delinquency. For those reporting the highest total number of delinquent acts (200 or more) the ratio of lower- to middle-class delinquency was again over 3 to 1. Social class differences in delinquency, then, seem to be restricted to crimes against people and are present only for those engaging in a great deal of delinquent behavior. The social classes do not differ in most forms or at most levels of delinquency.

Elliott and Ageton (1980) point out that these data are actually quite consistent with official records showing social class differences. It is well established (cf. Gold, 1970; Gold & Petronio, 1980) that the more frequently one engages in delinquent behavior, the more likely one is to get caught, booked, and appear in court. Because lower-class adolescents admit to engaging in more delinquency, they probably do, thus making it more likely that they will get caught. As a result, one must conclude that the official records showing social class differences in delinquency do not reflect only biases in police arrests and differential treatment of the delinquent as a function of social class, although these things may occur. The differences also reflect real social class differences in rates and types of delinquency. Although the data demonstrate a link between social class and delinquency, however, they also make it clear that social class is not the sole determinant of delinquency (Pine, 1966).

Data on middle-class juvenile delinquency support the notion that poverty and poor living conditions are not the strong determinants of delinquency one might suspect. Sebald (1968), for example, presented data indicating significant and large increases in juvenile crime among middle-class adolescents. In a further investigation, Vaz (1969) collected data on both middle-class and upper-class boys enrolled in either private or public institutions. The results of the study were similar to those reported above, but the upper-class boys in private institutions engaged in the highest degree of delinquency. There were no differences between the upper- and middle-class boys' delinquency rates when both groups were enrolled in a public institution.

Developmental Trends in Delinquency

Just as there are social class factors related to delinquency, so too are there developmental trends. Gold and Reimer (1975) collected self-report data from a representative sample of 1,395 adolescents aged 11 to 18. They reported data on the frequency of offenses and the seriousness of offenses as a function of age. For both males and females, frequency of nontrivial delinquent acts increased from age 11 to age 18. For boys, the increase was from 2.25 to 10.5; for girls it was from 1.25 to 6.5. In each case, there is an approximate fivefold increase. Males showed an increase in serious crimes from age 11 (2.25) to age 15 (8.25), after which there was little change. Incidence of serious

crimes by females remained relatively low (1 to 2) at all age levels.

Other data (see O'Malley, Bachman, & Johnston, 1977) demonstrate that relatively serious crimes against people and property decline from age 16 to age 18, but rise again at age 19 before declining into early adulthood (age 23). The general trend, then, is for delinquent behaviors to be associated most strongly with the mid adolescent years, especially about age 15, and to decline thereafter, although it is unclear that it reaches zero for any representative group thus far tested. At the present time, it is not possible to determine why age 15 or so is when delinquency seems to peak.

The Causes of Delinquency

No simple way exists to determine the causal factors involved in delinquency. No doubt many factors determine whether or not a given adolescent will engage in delinquent behavior. For any single causal factor, one can find some adolescents who possess that characteristic and who are delinquent, and others who possess it and are not. Delinquency, clearly, is caused by *multiple* determinants.

The Peer Group and Delinquency. Studies of peer-group effects on delinquency have been centered on the role of peer pressure and the influence of gang membership.

Peer pressure and involvement with peers is one way in which adolescents are socialized into delinquent behavior (cf. Patterson et al., 1989).

Eisenthal and Udin (1972) asked 89 boys and 90 girls ranging in age from 14 to 19 about their involvement in drug and alcohol use. Both the boys and girls indicated that indirect peer-group pressure had a strong effect on whether or not they would use alcohol or drugs, with direct social pressure to use these drugs being much less important. Fear of being rejected by the group, particularly among the girls in the study, was an

Peer pressure and influences can be strong socializers of delinquent behavior.

important motivational influence on drug and alcohol use.

Polk (1971) investigated the relationship between the amount of involvement with the peer group and delinquency in adolescent males. The males who were highly peer-oriented tended to engage in high as opposed to low or medium amounts of delinquency. Other researchers (cf. Gold & Petronio, 1980) also report that adolescents whose friends are delinquent are more likely to be delinquent themselves.

Although these relationships exist, it is difficult to determine directions of causation. Do strong peer relationships lead to delinquency, or vice versa? Does associating with delinquents cause one to become delinquent, or do delinquents seek out each other for companionship? Perhaps each direction is true to some degree. This seems to be the case when one looks at evidence from the study of juvenile gangs.

For some adolescents, the gang represents a family substitute. The gang can provide excuses and justifications (for example, appeals to gang loyalty) for delinquent behavior that allow the adolescent to deny psychologically that he or she is engaging in

delinquent acts. In effect, the adolescent is socialized into delinquency by peers (Patterson et al., 1989). The most extensive studies of juvenile gangs were conducted by Miller (1966). Although his research is much too extensive to present in detail, some of his findings are important for an understanding of the etiology of juvenile delinquent behaviors.

From his research Miller concludes that it is the atypical gang member who engages in violent or extreme forms of antisocial behavior. Moreover, violence is not a primary motive for the formation of adolescent gangs. When violent gang behavior did occur in the gangs Miller studied, it was not motivated by a desire to hurt innocent people, but rather by a need to secure status, masculinity, and honor. The *delinquent gang* engages in delinquency primarily as a way of securing money for material possessions. A second type of gang, the *violent gang*, engages in delinquent activities that are primarily centered around the members' need for prestige and personal satisfaction.

Gangs of both types exert a considerable influence on the behavior of the individual gang member, because they provide mutual support as well as a feeling of belonging. Gang membership also confers prestige; in fact, for some individuals, it may be the only way to achieve status and increase self-esteem (Patterson et al., 1989, Wells, 1989).

Social Structure and Delinquency. Historically, one of the more popular views of delinquency has been that it is born and nurtured in city slums, in general, and high-crime areas, in particular. If that were indeed the case, and if the conditions surrounding poverty could be alleviated, there would be no delinquency. However, there is a slowly growing literature indicating that juvenile delinquency is increasing more in suburban than in inner-city areas (Conger, 1971; Sebald, 1968). Moreover, delinquency is on the rise in rural areas as well. One factor that seems to contribute to these increases in suburban and rural juvenile delinquency is the high degree of geographic mobility and the corresponding lessening of ties to the community.

One view that sheds some light on the problem has been proposed by a number of individuals from diverse fields of study (for example, Cloward, 1968; Cloward & Ohlin, 1966; Merton, 1966; Simons & Gray, 1989). Generally speaking, all of these writers point out that an understanding of the community's values is necessary for an understanding of delinquent behavior. In one form or another, each of these researchers noted the importance of the match between social values that are esteemed by the community and the availability of means for the individual to achieve these values. In addition, these writers point out the importance of the individual's perception of his chances of reaching socially sanctioned and valued goals, and how this perception might influence his behavior.

Cloward and Ohlin (1960) systematically studied the relationship between communities and the opportunities they offered to residents for achieving success. They suggest that deviant behavior will continue to exist and increase if there is a marked discrepancy between the goals the community feels are desirable and the opportunities it offers its citizens to achieve those goals. Successful communities are those that offer their citizens ample legitimate opportunities to engage successfully in tasks that will lead to highly esteemed rewards.

Cloward and Ohlin characterize the unsuccessful community as one that does not provide legitimate opportunities for people to achieve what the community at large regards as desirable and good. In such communities delinquency arises because of the lack of opportunities for young people to gain success in legitimate ways. When legitimate opportunities are lacking, or fail to produce the desired outcome, young people engage in illegitimate activities in order to acquire what is viewed by the society as good.

In other words, when legitimate opportunities are lacking, young people will engage in illegitimate activities to try to gain the prestige, status, and material possessions that society says are good, but they will be able to do that only to the degree that opportunities to act illegally present themselves.

Durkheim (1951) and Merton (1961, 1966) discussed the notion of *anomie* (translate as *alienation*) as it relates to the impact of the community on the individual. Anomie refers to feelings of powerlessness and isolation from society. Durkheim postulated that anomie leads to deviance because the individual is overwhelmed by unrealistically high aspirations for success. The discrepancy between society's goals, those that society says one should attain, and the structure provided by the society for reaching these goals is the critical issue. As a result, anomie is likely to be high particularly among the poor, the objects of prejudice, and those who live in rural or remote areas where legitimate opportunities are limited. In such instances, one is likely to see a high degree of deviant behavior, although there is some evidence to indicate that delinquency is not a necessary outcome of alienation and anomie (Glueck & Glueck, 1968).

Cloward and Ohlin (1960) described three kinds of delinquent groups that may arise when there are no legitimate opportunities for success and achievement. The *criminal group* engages in illegal behaviors to obtain income. For this group, crime is a profession, and some juvenile gangs are a training ground for organized crime. The *conflict group* engages in delinquent acts in order to obtain and maintain status. Finally, the *retreatest group* of delinquents is, in effect, a drug subculture aimed at providing its members with an escape from the existing realities of the world. These groups of delinquent adolescents represent different attempts by lower-class youngsters to deal with the discrepancy between the middle-class values and goals they hold and the lack of opportunity to achieve these goals.

The set of views presented above highlights the importance of community and cultural factors in delinquency. Similar processes may operate for middle-class adolescent as well. If so, these views will help us better understand increases in middle-class delinquency and delinquency among girls.

Child-Rearing and Delinquency. The single best predictor of adolescent delinquency, particularly for boys, is the relationship the adolescent has with the parent (Ahlstrom & Havighurst, 1971; Conger & Miller, 1966). The better the relationship the boy has with his parents, the less likely he is to engage in delinquent behavior. The more strained, hostile, and rejecting the relationship between the parent and the adolescent, the greater the likelihood of delinquency (Glueck & Glueck, 1950). This conclusion is based on considerable research into the child-rearing patterns and family relationships that exist in homes of delinquent and nondelinquent adolescents.

Generally speaking, research has demonstrated that the early disciplinary techniques employed by parents of delinquents tend to be erratic, overly strict, involving both physical punishment and a high degree of hostility toward the child (Patterson et al., 1989). The home atmosphere of delinquents tends to be characterized by a greater degree of parental rejection and a relatively lower degree of cohesiveness than that of nondelinquents. It should not be surprising, then, to note that parents of delinquent children have minimal aspirations for their offspring. They also express little interest in their child's school performance and may have a host of personality and adjustment problems of their own (Patterson et al., 1989).

Paternal absence is one aspect of the father-son relationship that has been demonstrated to be related to delinquency (Lynn & Saurey, 1959; Kelly & Baer, 1969; Farnworth, 1984). Paternal absence may produce an overcompensating masculine personality in the adolescent male, particularly if the father leaves home before the child is about 5 years of age (Lynn & Saurey, 1959). In addition, paternal absence is related to recidivism rates for males. Kelly and Baer reported recidivism rates for juvenile delinquents whose fathers were in the home as well as for a group coming from mother-only homes. The recidivism rate was 12 percent for those adolescents coming from intact homes. Among those coming from nonintact homes, however, the recidivism rate was 39 percent if the father left home before the child was 7 years old, but if the father left after the child was 7, the recidivism rate dropped to 10 percent. As we have noted elsewhere, the effects of a one-parent home are most dramatic if the father leaves when the child is very young. These data are consistent with our previous discussion and indicate the importance of parents as role models for learning appropriate social behavior.

The critical feature of paternal absence is its relation to maternal parenting skills and family functioning, as we pointed out in Chapter 10. Following divorce, for example, parenting skills of both the custodial parent and noncustodial parent decline. Thus, home atmosphere, oversight of children's activities, and home routine are disrupted. These disruptions in parenting and family atmosphere can lead the child to engage in problem behavior and make him or her more vulnerable to engaging in delinquent acts (Patterson et al., 1989). This may be an especially serious problem if the child is relatively young when the father leaves. It is well documented that the younger the child is when first arrested the greater the recidivism rate. These "early starters" average about twice the convictions as those who are "late starters" (Patterson et al., 1989), perhaps because the late starters have had a longer period of more adequate child rearing and a happier home life that teaches the importance of prosocial behavior (Patterson et al., 1989).

Generally speaking, adolescent delinquents report hostility toward their parents and have poor relationships with them. Given social class differences in child-rearing techniques, it is not surprising that lower-class adolescents engage in more delinquent behaviors than do middle-class adolescents. In addition, Elder's research (1963, 1968, 1971) suggests that certain kinds of parental child-rearing techniques will be more likely to produce delinquency than others.

More recent research on parental influences on delinquency has taken a systematic approach to analyzing family interaction patterns that may predispose the child toward antisocial behavior (Patterson et al., 1989). As noted above, the families of delinquents tend to be harsh, with the parents having little positive involvement with the child. In addition, the parents do not monitor the child's behavior or supervise youngsters' activities. The interaction between parent and child can be characterized as one of continually intensifying coercion, which may result in the child employing antisocial behaviors to escape unpleasant interactions with family members. When successful, the coercive means of controlling social interactions through antisocial behavior is reinforced.

Patterson and colleagues (1989) suggest, then, that parents teach their children to behave in antisocial ways in social interactions. They train their children for deviant behavior. This is often accompanied by little training for prosocial behavior, the child's positive social behaviors often being ignored or responded to inappropriately. In addition, children in homes such as these often to not learn proper social skills—they don't know the right way to behave in a variety of social situations.

Other evidence supports the notion that delinquents perceive and define social situations differently from nondelinquents (see Lee & Prentice, 1988; Slaby & Guerra, 1988). Compared to nondelinquents, delinquents have relatively immature role-taking and moral-reasoning ability. They define social problems in hostile ways and see few consequences for behaving in an aggressive manner. Moreover, they believe aggression is a legitimate means for dealing with social problems and do not see suffering to others resulting from their actions. It seems reasonable to presume that this is the result of a long developmental history of learning from family interactions.

The aggressive and antisocial behavior learned in the home life of the person results in social rejection by normal peers (Patterson et al., 1989). Antisocial children do not have the proper social skills to become part of groups that do not perceive the same degree of legitimacy of aggressive interactions. Hence, the child becomes further rejected and more subject to joining deviant peer groups, from whose members the child may gain positive acceptance.

The chain of events leading to delinquency is illustrated in Figure 13–1. As you can see, the key underlying event is the nature of parental child rearing and the home environment, including parent-child interactions. And, the process begins with the home environment of the parents when they were themselves children.

The fathers of delinquent adolescents also tend to be cruel, neglecting, and less warm and affectionate than the fathers of nondelinquent adolescents (Glueck & Glueck, 1950; Lang, Pampenfus, & Walter, 1976). In our discussion of social-learning theory (see Chapter 2) we pointed out the importance of adult models for children. It is not surprising, then, to note that delinquents tend to come from homes where the parents may well have police records of their own (Cressey & Ward, 1969). The delinquent adolescent may simply be modeling a set of role behaviors that lead to acts of delinquency because these are the only role behaviors available. The parents, and particularly the father, may, in effect, teach their offspring to be delinquent (Neapolitan, 1981).

Somewhat less research has been done on

FIGURE 13–1 **The Roots and Consequences of Antisocial and Delinquent Behavior**

Grandparenting of parents ⟶	Parent Characteristics ⟶	Abnormal Development ⟶
	Child-rearing philosophy	Moral reasoning
	Social class	Social skills
	Education	Social role taking
	Family status	Antisocial behavior
	Income	
Failures ⟶	Vulnerability to Deviant Groups ⟶	Undesirable outcomes
Academic/		Delinquency
Peer relations		Adjudication
		Recidivism
		Poor future parenting skills

the role of the mother. What research is available suggests that mothers of delinquents may be characterized as hostile or indifferent toward their offspring (McCord, McCord, & Zola, 1959). Other evidence demonstrates that mothers of delinquent boys tend to be domineering and aggressive (Ackerly, 1933).

Correlates of Delinquency

Since juvenile delinquency is a form of deviancy, one would expect that a number of aspects of the behavior as well as personality formation of juvenile delinquents will be different from those of adolescents who are not delinquent.

Self-Concept and Delinquency. Some researchers (for example, Bynner, O'Malley, & Bachman, 1981) have investigated self-concept development in delinquent adolescents. Generally speaking, delinquents have poor self-concepts. They view themselves negatively and feel that they are undesirable people. They have little self-respect and place little value on their own contributions to society. In general, too, they feel that society views them in this way. Thus, self-concepts of delinquent adolescents may be

characterized as uncertain, confused, and quite variable. This contrasts sharply with the self-concepts of nondelinquent adolescents, who tend to have positive and much more stable self-concepts.

One of the dangers of this negative view of the self is that delinquent adolescents begin to believe the labels that society places on them and begin to behave in ways that make those labels come true. Of some interest, black boys who get into trouble see delinquents more positively, that is, as stronger, smarter, and tougher, than do delinquent white boys. It appears that the young blacks have, in effect, defined a reward hierarchy that is based upon values not typically considered desirable by the larger society. Given the fact that the black delinquent adolescent is likely to have come from a subculture in which opportunities for achieving socially desirable goals are few, this is not to be unexpected. It may, in fact, be a highly adaptive mode of behavior for black adolescents. Because they view legitimate opportunities for success as closed to them, they create a new reward hierarchy that will give them some aspects of success and the good life (Cloward, 1968; Cloward & Ohlin, 1966).

The importance of the relationship between self-concept and delinquency has been perhaps best spelled out by Dinitz, Scarpitti, and Reckless (1962). In their research, 101 12-year-old boys from high delinquency areas were nominated by their elementary school teachers as potentially delinquent. These boys were matched to a control group of 125 12-year-olds who were expected by their teachers to stay out of trouble. When the boys were 16, 70 of the "vulnerable boys" and 103 of the "good boys" were tested for factors relating to delinquent behavior. Although 27 of the vulnerable boys had had serious and frequent contact with the courts during the four years of the study, only four of the 103 good boys had been involved in delinquent kinds of behavior, and these were but minor offenses. Examination of the self-concepts of the two groups revealed that the vulnerable boys viewed themselves more negatively than did the good boys. From these findings, the authors argue that a good self-concept acts as an inner buffer against deviancy. A poor self-concept, on the other hand, is believed to be a major contributing factor to delinquency because it develops from, and then reinforces, the individual's feelings of being cut off from society. In other words, the self-concept is a reflection of the degree to which the individual views the likelihood of succeeding within the social structure of the society in which the person is living.

Other evidence (see Patterson et al., 1989; Wells, 1989) indicates that delinquents may enhance their self-esteem by engaging in delinquent behavior. Those who engage in serious crimes, and those with the lowest self-esteem initially, enhance self-esteem by behaving in a delinquent manner. For those who engage in nonserious crimes or who do not have very low self-esteem, engaging in delinquent acts does not enhance self-esteem. Hence, it appears that self-esteem enhancement is limited to those delinquents with pathologically poor self-esteem.

Personality Correlates of Delinquency. Researchers have compared a number of personality characteristics of delinquents and nondelinquents in an attempt to elucidate the personal consequences of delinquency. Although no single personality type can be associated with delinquency, delinquents tend to be defiant, resentful, hostile, and lacking in self-control. They also lean toward an external locus of control (Parrott & Strongman, 1984), which leads them into feeling they are at the mercy of forces outside their sphere of influence. In turn, as elaborated above, they develop poor self-concepts.

Moral development is another area of psychological functioning in which delinquents and nondelinquents have been compared. Generally speaking, delinquents score lower than nondelinquents on tests of moral development (Lee & Prentice, 1988; Slaby & Guerra, 1988). The importance and implication of this finding are discussed by Swendinger and Swendinger (1967), who asked 54 delinquent and 54 nondelinquent boys to role-play gang members and make judgments about the gang's behavior, such as beating someone up or ripping off a rich person. In each role-playing sequence, there was an objector who gave reasons why the gang should not act in deviant ways. When nondelinquent boys were the objectors they gave relatively appropriate moral reasons for not beating up or stealing from someone, such as "it's wrong," or "we don't have the right to do that." When delinquent boys were the objectors, they focused on such reasons as the possibility of getting caught. The delinquent boys apparently see the world as an amoral jungle in which everyone is a potential victim, and they seem to feel that they must grab whatever they can before someone else gets it or gets them. In addition, they expressed little guilt over what they were doing because they feel that people deserve what they get. Again, then, we see that juvenile delinquents lack inner controls or a highly developed superego, and have their behaviors guided more by social or external controls (Slaby & Guerra, 1988).

The most extensive longitudinal study of personality development in delinquent and nondelinquent children and adolescents was carried out by Conger and his colleagues (Conger & Miller, 1966; Conger, Miller, & Walsmith, 1965). These investigators followed two groups of children (delinquent and nondelinquent) from kindergarten or first grade through the adolescent years, to investigate personality development. Differences between the two groups emerged during the early school years and increased during the middle school and high school years. It is important to note that the two groups, delinquent and nondelinquent, were matched in terms of neighborhood, IQ, social class, and minority group membership, as well as on a number of other variables. Hence, the differences discovered cannot be attributed to the differential influences of these variables.

The delinquents tended to be viewed as less well adapted and as less willing to accept responsibility than the nondelinquents. Delinquents were further characterized as having poor attitudes toward authority, as exhibiting socially inappropriate behaviors with adults as well as their peers, as not getting along well with their peers, and as being less well liked than the nondelinquents. Of some interest, the delinquents also rated themselves in a similar way, reminiscent of the notion that labeling individuals as delinquent may be related to their behaving in ways consistent with the labels (Rachin, 1975).

In the school situation, the two groups also differed. The delinquents were more easily distracted, had short attention spans, gave up easily when challenged, had a number of academic problems, and tended to be absent from school more than the nondelinquents. The delinquents often were viewed as underachievers who had poor work habits and came from home atmospheres that were not conducive to academic learning. This is

not surprising since parents of delinquents often do not become involved in school or believe in the value of education. They were viewed as less well adjusted and cheerful, not only by the teachers and their peers, but also by themselves. Of some interest, Conger and his colleagues reported that the delinquents were resentful of authority and environmental pressures to conform, another illustration of the notion that external control may be necessary to guide the behavior of delinquents but that it is resented by them.

Although this is but a brief sketch of Conger's research, it demonstrates broad-ranging personality differences between delinquent and nondelinquent adolescents, both male and female, which begin to emerge in the first few grades of the elementary school, are highly visible between the third and sixth grades, and become even more dramatic by ninth grade. Although the research does not tell us much about the etiology of the personality differences between the two groups, the investigators suggest that an important factor is the home environment. In addition, delinquent adolescents tend to be shut off from a variety of people because of their antisocial behaviors and, as a result, seek comfort and security from other delinquents who no doubt reinforce their antisocial behavior. Partly because of their generally poor self-concept, delinquents are less well adjusted, and furthermore know that other people believe they are not well adjusted. As a result, they tend to denigrate themselves even more.

Granick's (1966) research on 328 black and 142 white juvenile delinquents between the ages of 16 and 18 revealed that the delinquents visualized themselves as having considerable emotional problems, more so than in the control group of 367 nondelinquent adolescents. This is particularly true for the white delinquents or for those with lower IQs or younger ages. Perhaps this results from stress that comes from the knowledge that one is engaging in inappropriate or unacceptable behaviors. As the individual gets older, greater amounts of reinforce-ment are available for the inappropriate be-havior and, furthermore, the discrepancies between what society says one should have and the means for obtaining it become larger, partially because the adolescent has built a lifestyle that forces this to be the case. Hence, inappropriate behaviors continue.

Barndt and Johnson (1955) examined the future orientation of delinquents and non-delinquents, and reported that delinquents tend to live for the here and now and have problems orienting toward the future. This was evidenced in their lack of planning for the future and their ideas about the future, which tended to be rather unrealistic. The nondelinquent group, on the other hand, was quite future-oriented, and engaged in planning and behaviors that would prepare them for the future.

The picture that emerges from these re-searches is not a pretty one. Delinquent youths suffer not only because they are pun-ished by society if they are caught, but also because they pay a heavy personal price for their delinquency. Although it is difficult to tell whether or not delinquency causes ad-justment problems, or whether the reverse is the case, the price is paid nonetheless.

Delinquency and School Performance. A number of investigators have researched the relationship between delinquency and school behavior. This research has focused on several interrelated issues, including de-linquency as it relates to absenteeism and dropping out of school, as well as adjustment upon returning to school.

Generally speaking, juvenile delinquents do poorly in school, as assessed both by teacher ratings and by achievement mea-sures (Patterson et al., 1989). Some have sug-gested that doing poorly in school is a cause of delinquency because the adolescent then drops out of school and takes up delinquent behaviors. The rationale for this argument is based upon the legitimate opportunity no-tion of Cohen (1961) and Cloward and Ohlin

(1960). In turn, those who are academically successful are much less likely to engage in delinquent behaviors. Alternatively, Patter-son and colleagues (1989) suggest that it is the child's learning of antisocial behavior and difficulty with following rules and deal-ing with authority that results in poor school performance. Antisocial children have poor attentional skills and, perhaps because of poor monitoring by the parents, do not com-plete homework assignments. They seem to lack those basic skills necessary to compete succesfully in an academic environment.

School absenteeism is perhaps one of the first instances of a direct relationship be-tween school problems and delinquency (Tennent, 1971). Tennent notes that there are three possible reasons for this relation-ship. First, truancy may lead to delinquency because the adolescent has too much idle time and seeks delinquent behaviors for stimulation and excitement. Second, delin-quency may lead to truancy because peer or social pressures may make the adolescent hesitant about returning to school. Finally, truancy and delinquency may simply be in-dicative of some other maladjustment that manifests itself in each of these ways. Sil-berberg and Silberberg (1971) note that frustrating experiences in the school might force the adolescent to avoid the school set-ting. Traditional teaching methods may not be suited to these individuals and, when school failure is coupled with the kinds of family problems we have discussed above, these adolescents may look to delinquency as the only way to achieve a measure of suc-cess in the world.

A similar set of reasons may account for the relationship between dropping out and delinquency. Does the individual who is a delinquent drop out of school because he is a delinquent, or does dropping out of school cause him to become a delinquent? There is some evidence in favor of the latter alter-native: the high school dropout is unlikely to become employed and therefore has the time to get in trouble. The most extensive study of the relationship between dropping out and delinquency was done by Glueck and Gleuck (1968). In the delinquent sub-sample, 62 percent dropped out of high school before the age of 16, and 96 percent dropped out at 16, compared with a total of 52 percent for those who were nondelinquent. In other words, the delinquents tended to drop out of school at the earliest possible opportunity. That they are not doing this to go to work is indicated by the fact that, of the 62 percent who dropped out before 16 years of age, only 2.5 percent were gainfully employed. The relationship between dropping out and delinquency is further highlighted by the authors' findings that in the delinquent sample, 39 percent of the dropouts were removed from school and placed into correctional institutions, but in the nondelinquent sample none was expelled.

One of the problems faced by a delinquent removed from school is readjustment to the school situation after release from a correctional institution. Novotny and Burstein (1974) found that of the 94 teen-age boys in their studies, 72 percent returned to school in the community, but over three-quarters of these students ultimately dropped out of school. Compared to those who dropped out, those who finished high school had a much more supportive environment, particularly in the form of people interested in helping them and seeing them finish high school. None of these graduates was involved in antisocial behaviors during the school years, with only two of them getting into serious difficulties during the three-year follow-up study. In contrast, 40 percent of those who dropped out and 50 percent of those who did not reenter school after being released from the correctional institution were involved in serious legal problems during the follow-up years. Clearly, returning to the school situation is a difficult task for the juvenile delinquent, perhaps because the school environment, with its middle-class values, gives such an

adolescent little opportunity to experience success (Tennent, 1971). Vocational training programs may be a useful alternative, as might other less traditional school programs (Silberberg & Silberberg, 1971).

As these and other researchers have noted, the school situation presents so many difficulties for the adolescent delinquent that special programs or procedures might have to be implemented to ensure these adolescents a measure of success in school.

Senna and his colleagues (1974–75) examined the relationship between juvenile delinquent behaviors and school behaviors in 296 high school students in the 14- to 18-year-old age range. In contrast to most previous research, this study was conducted in a white middle-class suburban area. Delinquency was assessed by a questionnaire completed by the respondents; the items on the questionnaire included stealing, damaging property, using drugs or alcohol, gambling, breaking and entering, and fighting. School behavior was also assessed by a self-report instrument which included items such as cheating on tests, coming late to class, cutting school, and failing course work.

The relationship between the two types of scores was negative. Those who did well in school engaged in fewer delinquent behaviors than those who did less well. Some of the individual relationships are worth noting. For example, classroom misconduct is highly correlated with crimes against property, indicating a general lack of concern and respect for others. Absenteeism is highly correlated with drinking and using drugs, activities common to adolescents with time on their hands.

The data on the relationship between delinquency and school performance support the data on the relationship between delinquency and parental relations, peer relations, and social relations. In all these areas the delinquent comes off second best. The general adjustment problems that were discussed above pervade the life of the adolescent.

TREATING AND PREVENTING DELINQUENCY

The data presented above are rather depressing. First, the crimes of the delinquent are often fairly serious crimes. Assault, theft, vandalism, and the time consumed in dealing with such problems all represent losses of human and material resources. But the most important loss of all is the loss of thousands of young people who might have made substantial contributions to the growth and development of the social order. The delinquent adolescent, especially if put away in an institution, is probably lost forever.

Unfortunately, the incarceration of delinquents has done little to lower delinquency rates (Wheeler & Cottrell, 1966). Adolescents themselves believe that frustrating experiences with their parents, poor home atmospheres, and boredom are the major contributors to delinquent behavior, and that it is these factors that must be changed if their lives are going to change.

The major approach to dealing with the problem of delinquency has been to treat identified delinquents. Traditionally this has meant working with adolescents who have police records and ignoring significant numbers of other adolescents. Unfortunately, few preventative measures have been taken, although this is probably the approach that would be most successful. A comprehensive program aimed at helping young children who are potential delinquents learn to cope better with their home lives, school problems, and psychological problems is probably the most intelligent approach to treating delinquency.

Treatment for juvenile delinquents has typically fallen into two categories: psychoanalytic and related kinds of therapy and behavior modification programs. Although there is some evidence to suggest that probation and even incarceration may help the juvenile delinquent, those favoring a therapeutic approach to the treatment of delinquency point out that institutions cannot be successful in dealing with delinquents because they are not designed to deal with the individual problems of each delinquent. Therapy is viewed as a way to help the individual adolescent deal with the specific problems confronting him. For example, teaching acceptance of responsibility might be necessary for some delinquents, while teaching higher levels of moral thinking and the building of a strong superego might be necessary for others.

In addition, it is highly likely that different forms of treatment may be necessary to deal with individuals with different personalities or with differing needs (Jacobsen & Wirt, 1968).

Although the above arguments appear rational and reasonable, the success of various therapeutic programs has not been very great. There is evidence (Patterson et al., 1989) that adolescents in therapy have lower recidivism rates, but when the therapy sessions are stopped, recidivism rates increase. Hence, therapy helps reduce delinquent behaviors, but only for a short time after it is completed. Permanent changes in behavior are much more difficult to obtain. It now appears that there is no especially successful treatment that reduces recidivism more than any other kind (Whitehead & Lab, 1989).

As noted in Box 13–2, the traditional method of treating delinquency and other behavioral and social problems has been to wait until they occur and then treat the symptoms, the undesirable behaviors. An alternative to this approach is a preventative model. As applied to delinquency, Patterson and others (1989) note that a key is to teach parents better family management techniques that will help the child to learn more socially appropriate behaviors. When this type of intervention is done with preadolescents it has shown success in reducing antisocial and delinquent behavior. In addition, teaching the child sound academic and social relationship skills is of benefit. Patterson and colleagues (1989) now believe we are able to identify children at risk for antisocial be-

BOX 13–2 Treatment vs. Prevention of Behavioral and Psychological Disorders

The way we deal with behavioral and psychological disorders is to treat them after the fact. In other words, when a behavioral or psychological problem is evidenced by certain symptoms we identify the nature of the disorder and then prescribe some means of treatment aimed at reducing the symptoms. When the symptoms disappear we presume the problem is gone. Rarely do we go to the causes of the symptoms and alter the situation. Moreover, we do not engage in preventative care—dealing with the underlying causes of the problem before the problem emerges.

This means of dealing with psychological disorders is based on the medical model of treatment for physical disorders. In the latter, the patient exhibits certain symptoms that lead to a diagnosis which, in turn, results in some form of treatment. Consider the following example:

Antecedents ⟶	Symptoms ⟶	Treatment
In the rain	Sniffles	Rest
Get wet	Cough	Aspirin
Cold	Sore throat	Decongestant

Certain antecedent conditions lead to specific symptoms calling for a standard treatment. The person has contracted a cold, or the flu, and takes drugs and other treatment that basically aleviate the symptoms until they are gone. None of the treatment is aimed at altering the antecedent conditions. Admittedly, this is an oversimplified example, but it represents the typical means of dealing with common medical disorders.

We treat psychological disorders in much the same manner. Consider the following example for delinquency:

Antecedents ⟶	Symptoms ⟶	Treatment
Poor family relations	Learn antisocial behavior	Incarceration
Academic failure	Aggressiveness	Work program
		Therapy

Again, albeit a simplified version of the material presented in the text, it makes the point that we deal with the symptoms rather than the causes of psychological problems. Hence, when the individual reenters the environment that caused the problem, the treatment's successful effects are eroded, just as going out improperly dressed can again lead to respiratory symptoms.

An alternative model would deal with prevention. In the field of medicine, preventative care is popular and the public is encouraged to use it. Maintaining a diet low in saturated fat and animal fat, not smoking, not drinking if one is pregnant, and similar health measures are examples of preventative medicine. The intent is to eliminate the antecedents of disease.

Patterson et al. (1989) suggest that preventative measures might be used to help children "at risk" for delinquency. Such measures would include forms of parent training with regard to child management, teaching children appropriate social relationship and academic skills, and teaching the parent about child-rearing techniques. By making the early home atmosphere conducive to proper prosocial development it may be possible to reduce delinquency and, thereby, criminal activity when the child becomes an adult.

havior sufficiently early in the school years to institute intervention techniques aimed at preventing delinquency.

EATING DISORDERS

As we noted in Chapter 3, adolescence is a time of very rapid physical growth. Adolescents' bodies change not only in shape, as they develop a mature physique, but also in size. Adolescents worry about being too tall or too short, too skinny or too heavy. Throughout recent history, Americans, and especially adolescents, have been preoccupied with body weight—thin is in! This concern with body weight, and particularly the preoccupation of female adolescents with weight management, is related to several disorders that occur largely during the adolescent years: obesity, anorexia nervosa, and bulimia.

Obesity

Maintenance of normal body weight for the adolescent's height and bone structure is very difficult for some adolescents. Surprisingly, however, underweight is as prevalent as **obesity**. Approximately 10 to 15 percent of all adolescents are truly obese, as defined by skinfold measures that involve determining the thickness of the fat layer underneath the skin (subcutaneous fat). Skinfold thickness is usually measured by calipers applied to the triceps, the muscle on the underside of the upper arm. Obesity, as opposed to simple overweight, is an abnormal state characterized by excessive deposits of unused fat throughout the body. Overweight usually involves stored fluids. Excess fat is also involved, but not to the degree seen in obese individuals.

Obesity is classified into two etiological groups. Simple, or exogenous, obesity is due to eating too much food, getting too little exercise, or both. Endocrine, or endogenous, obesity is due to irregularities of glandular secretions, such as in diabetes or Cushing's disease. In addition to the skinfold measures already cited, both these forms of obesity show similar symptoms, including excessive perspiration, irritation of the skin, joint discomforts, menstrual disorders, and reduced physical ability.

Obesity is more prevalent in girls than in boys, probably because boys are generally more active than girls. Another factor that contributes to the sex difference in obesity is that the increased estrogen output of puberty fosters an increase in the size rather than the number of cells. This makes a transient "plumpness" an invariable part of adolescence for adolescent girls as well as boys. Obesity in adolescence presents current and future problems for the obese individuals. It can affect social relationships, school performance, and emotional adjustment in such diverse areas as dependency and sex identification.

Obesity is not necessarily related to poor eating habits, but may be related to biological conditions.

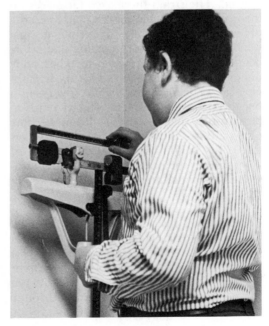

Obese individuals are not necessarily big eaters; as a matter of fact, they may take in the same amount or a smaller amount of calories than individuals of normal build (Insel & Moss, 1974). However, they are relatively sedentary, whereas lean adolescents are usually more active. Lean adolescents may compensate for their overeating with overactivity. This overactivity rapidly depletes available proteins, carbohydrates, and fats, and forces the individual into a vicious circle where weight gain is virtually impossible.

Obesity also presents a future health hazard. It is related to cardiovascular disease, hypertension, joint disease, and gynecological disorders. Even during adolescence, a certain amount of abnormality exists in obese youngsters in terms of timing of growth. They are usually taller and exhibit skeletal development and urinary steroid output corresponding to children a year or so older. In other words, obese children tend to demonstrate an accelerated growth trend over their normal weight peers.

Nevertheless, obese individuals are not normal. The strain the excess fat places on their metabolic system merely speeds up the processes that would occur in their normal weight peers. We must remember that, while being overweight is relative to other body dimensions, obesity is not. Obesity is pathological. Furthermore, while overweight may be a passing problem, obesity tends to be chronic—most obese children become obese adults. If an individual has not reduced his weight to normal by the end of adolescence, the odds are against that individual's *ever* attaining a normal adult weight (Epstein, 1987).

The roots of obesity are complex and, as noted above, may include both biological and psychological factors. It is the latter which present the greatest problem for treatment. The specific problem seems to be the obese adolescent's view that his or her life is directed by others, perhaps through extreme dependence on parents. As a result,

they feel they do not or cannot control their own eating urges. Although behavioral training, such as teaching discrimination of eating patterns and changing those patterns, can be effective in altering eating behavior (Epstein, 1987), the long-term prognosis is not good until the individual is brought to realize his or her own competency and separateness as a human being and develops a self-directed view of life. Hence, treatment of obesity involves not only the alteration of eating patterns but also the alleviation of psychological symptoms.

Anorexia Nervosa

Anorexia nervosa is characterized by a relentless pursuit of a thin body despite hunger, help from others, and threat of starvation (Halmi, 1987). Most anorexics are females (90 percent to 95 percent), most come from the upper middle and upper social classes, and most are highly preoccupied with thoughts of food (Howat & Saxton, 1988). Available evidence suggests that anorexics tend to be rather model children and adolescents, experiencing few if any developmental difficulties. Although in the past anorexia could lead to death due to starvation (in about 10 percent of anorexics), that is rare today.

Examination of the family background and precipitating conditions of anorexics leads to some similarities with the obese individual (cf. Hood, Moore, & Garner, 1982). Parents of anorexics often do not allow the development of independence and a sense of self-determined identity. Rather, they often try to control the adolescent's life and encourage dependence, both of the adolescent on them and of them on the adolescent. As a result, the adolescent prone to become anorexic, like the obese adolescent, comes to feel that outside forces are in control of his or her life.

Anorexics also have a disturbed body image. They tend to overestimate body size and individual body parts. They see themselves

Anorexics have a poor body image and see themselves as fat even when they are severely underweight.

as fat even when they are nearly emaciated. They tend to deny, or not recognize, hunger pangs, and feel full after very meager meals. As a result, they keep dieting, inducing vomiting, and the like in attempts to lose yet more weight.

The syndrome may have roots in an inability, or unwillingness, to grow up. The extreme dependence sought by the parents, and especially the mother, may get translated into an inability to handle sexual maturity, a fear of becoming independent, and the like. Some have interpreted anorexia as an attempt to "reverse" the growth process.

Because of the physical as well as psychological factors involved in anorexia, treatment is two-pronged. One aspect of treatment is aimed at dealing with the physical stress on the individual. Behavior modification programs aimed at increasing food intake have proven somewhat useful (Halmi, 1987).

The second aspect of treatment is focused on the psychological causes underlying the anorexia. This includes developing a personality that feels in control, a strong self-concept, appropriate relationships with family members, who may also be involved in treatment, and a sense of being able to take responsibility for one's life. Estimates are that about half of anorexics recover, the remainder either experiencing somewhat extreme weight fluctuations, not recovering, or committing suicide.

Bulimia

Bulimia is characterized by periods of binge eating—eating as much as 4,800 calories in one sitting, mostly in the form of sweets—and purging, through self-induced vomiting, the use of laxatives, or both (American Psychiatric Association, 1980).

Bulimics are nearly exclusively females (99 percent), many of whom have difficulty relating to, and communicating with, their mothers. For most, binge eating begins at about 18 years of age. Because most bulimics have had some college, which begins at about 18 years of age, it has been speculated that one factor in bulimia is a lack of ability to adapt to living away from home.

Johnson, Lewis, Love, Lewis, and Stuckey (1984) surveyed 1,268 high school females. They found that nearly 5 percent met the *DSM-III* criteria for bulimia. Other estimates of incidence put it at between 3 and 9 percent (Halmi, 1987). Some interesting contrasts between the bulimic and nonbulimic women were observed. Even though the weight of the two groups was equal, the bulimics were prone to viewing themselves as overweight. They also showed less satisfaction with their body image and were more frequent dieters. Sixty-eight percent of the bulimics, but only 35 percent of the non-bulimics, were on diets.

Aside from the demographic characteristics of bulimics, little is known of the nature of the disorder and virtually no information is available on the effectiveness of various treatments.

SUICIDE

In absolute terms, suicide does not account for a large number of deaths (currently about 5,000 per year). However, it is the second leading cause of death among adolescents, outranked only by deaths due to accidents. Although adolescents account for only about 7 percent of suicides, they account for about 12 percent of attempts. Thus, approximately 100,000 adolescents, or 1 in 1,000, attempt suicide every year (Weiner, 1982). As a result, in recent years there has been an increased concern about adolescent suicide and suicide prevention.

Incidence of Suicide

Interest in adolescent suicide has increased dramatically in recent years (Petti & Larson, 1987). In large part this is because suicide is the fifth leading cause of death for those under age 15 (accidents, heart disease, cancer, and pneumonia head the list) and the second leading cause of death for those ages 15 to 24 (accidents are first). Because suicide is a tragic event for both the victim and the family, and because it is presumably preventable, attention has focused on trying to better understand the etiology of suicide and the means that might be effective in prevention.

The prevalence rate for those 15 to 24 was 13.1 per 100,000 in 1986 (U. S. Bureau of the Census, 1989), and it was much higher for males (21.7 per 100,000) than for females (4.4 per 100,000). The prevalence rates for the adolescent years are presented in Table 13–2. As you can see, for both

Suicide, the second leading cause of death among adolescents, claims about 5,000 young people each year.

younger and older adolescents there was nearly a doubling of the rate from 1970 to 1986. This incidence rate translates into relatively few deaths (Table 13–3), especially when considered in comparison to the leading cause of death, namely accidents, for these age groups. Nonetheless, preventing suicide would save thousands of adolescent lives.

For obvious reasons, suicide is difficult to identify for statistical purposes, but the classification of attempted suicide is an even bigger challenge. At present, it is not possible to state with assurance how many attempted suicides there are. Estimates (Halmi, 1987) are that the ratio of attempted to successful suicides may be as high as 50 to 1. Females attempt suicide at higher rates that males; males are successful in suicide attempts at higher rates than females. Moreover, the means of committing suicide differ between the sexes. Males are much more likely than females to use aggressive and violent means, such as stabbing, hanging, and shooting, to commit suicide. Females are more likely than males to use passive means to commit suicide; for example, the use of poisons or

TABLE 13–2 **Rate of Suicide per 100,000 for Early and Late Adolescents, 1970–1986**

Age	1970	1980	1986
10–14	.6	.8	1.5
15–19	5.9	8.5	10.2

(Source: Adapted from U.S. Bureau of the Census [1989]. *Statistical abstract of the United States: 1989*. Washington, DC: Government Printing Office.)

drugs is more prevalent among females than males. For both sexes, however, the use of violent means of attempting suicide is more likely to be successful than the use of passive means.

Other factors make the identification of attempted suicide difficult. An individual may actually only attempt suicide, with no intent of being successful, but because of some unforeseen circumstance succeed. Others may actually be attempting to succeed at suicide but, for one reason or another, do not, their actions then being labeled attempted suicide. For example, not taking enough pills, or pulling away just as the gun goes off, may cause the otherwise intended suicide to be unsuccessful.

The Causes of Suicide

The causes of suicide are difficult to determine (Halmi, 1987). One factor that seems clearly related to adolescent suicide is poor family relationships (Blumenthal & Kupfer, 1988; Ruben-Stein et al. 1989). A large majority of adolescent suicide attempters come from families in which home harmony is lacking. The parents may be fighting, a divorce may be impending or apparently impending, and the parents may not get along well with the adolescent. The major disciplinary mode tends to be power-assertive. As a result, the adolescent often feels neglected, unwanted, and alienated from the family. And, of course, communication between the parents and the adolescent is poor, at best. In turn, the adolescent may come to feel socially isolated, which may be the single most important factor in decisions to attempt suicide.

Other factors also contribute to adolescent suicide. A sizeable proportion of adolescent suicide attempts follow the breakup of a romance. **Depression**, perhaps caused by romantic entanglements, also is related to adolescent suicide (Hulmi, 1987). In all these instances, however, the suicide seems to be the result of a relatively long-term set of precipitating events, the most recent simply being the last straw. It is as though the ad-

TABLE 13–3 **Deaths from Accidents and Suicides in 1986 for Males and Females from Two Age Groups**

Sex	Age	CAUSE	
		Accidents	Suicide
Male	<15	5,200	200
	15–24	15,200	4,300
Female	<15	2,900	100
	15–24	4,500	800

(Source: Adapted from U.S. Bureau of the Census [1989]. *Statistical abstract of the United States: 1989*. Washington, DC: Government Printing Office.)

olescent is punishing not only the self but all others, who must live with the fact that someone they know has committed suicide.

In part, the picture one gets is that those who attempt suicide—both adolescents and others—have insufficiently developed coping skills (Halmi, 1987). They may be isolated from other people, an important social support system, and may not have effective means of coping with daily hassles and important but stressful life events (see Box 13–3). As a result, they see suicide as the "only way out."

Treatment of Potential Suicides

Of course, there can be no treatment for the individual who has been successful in

---

BOX 13—3 Psychosocial Development and Adolescent Coping Styles

One focus of research on coping with stress has been the investigation of the relation between coping styles and psychological adjustment. Some research demonstrates that general psychological adjustment is related to coping styles. More well-adjusted adults employ coping strategies aimed at changing the stressful event, whereas less well-adjusted adults tend to employ avoidant, or emotion-focused, coping strategies (e.g., Holahan & Moos, 1987; McCrae & Costa, 1986). Among adolescents, those with better self-esteem tend to be more likely to use active as opposed to avoidant coping strategies (Compas, 1987; Compass & Phares, in press; Ebata & Moos, 1989).

Jorgensen and Dusek (in press) investigated the relation between resolution of Erikson's psychosocial crises and the use of various coping strategies by a group of college students. Those students who had more successfully resolved the crises reported that when stressed they were more likely to employ strategies that were aimed at altering the stressful event. Hence, they would seek information and advice, talk to friends, and try to do something to alter the stressful situation. Those who less successfully resolved the crises were more likely to use avoidant coping strategies; they would vent their frustration in certain ways, avoid doing things to alter the stressful situation, and sleep more. Of course, the difference between the two groups of students is relative—everyone may cry or avoid dealing with stressful events, and everyone may tackle stressful events. The differences that Jorgensen and Dusek found were, first, that by late adolescence, general coping styles develop. Second, there are clear preferences for the modal manner of dealing with stress that relate to psychological adjustment.

It appears, then, that adolescents and adults have general styles of coping with stress. Jorgensen and Dusek suggest that these general styles may develop during infancy and childhood as the individual resolves the various crises discussed by Erikson. For example, optimal resolution of the Basic Trust vs. Mistrust, and Intimacy vs. Isolation crises may result in the individual trusting his or her own judgment and feeling comfortable seeking social support from others when under stress. As noted in the text, social support is a very important coping mechanism.

Successful resolution of the Autonomy vs. Shame and Doubt; Initiative vs. Guilt; Industry vs. Inferiority; and Identity vs. Identity Diffusion crises generally results in the acquisition of instrumental traits—having the confidence in one's ability and desire to make choices, having a sense of the ability to achieve through self-initiated plans and actions, and viewing the self as active and as taking charge of one's life. Those who more successfully resolve these crises seem to have developed the psychological resources necessary to confront stressful situations actively, and they seem to have the feeling that they can deal with those situations successfully. Hence, they are more prone to employing active coping strategies.

As further research is conducted on the determinants of coping strategies we no doubt will be able to fill in the picture of how we develop coping styles. Research on the importance of learning coping strategies from parents, siblings, peers, and the role of child-rearing practices in coping will be important in this regard committing suicide. However, we can treat those who are suicide prone or those who have attempted suicide unsuccessfully. Perhaps the single best predictor of suicide proneness is talking about committing suicide. It simply is not true that if a person talks about committing suicide he or she will not attempt it. Although it is common to contemplate suicide (Bolger et al., 1989), ignoring someone who threatens to commit suicide is very risky, for many who threaten ultimately attempt to take their own lives.

Virtually all treatment programs involve therapy for both the long-term problems making one prone to suicide attempts and for the immediate situation. In order to be maximally successful, especially with adolescent suicide attempters, the therapy should involve not only the adolescent but the parents as well. Relationships with parents must be changed in order to make the adolescent feel less alienated and worthless. In addition, skills necessary for coping with frustrations and depression must be taught.

DRUG USE

In this section we focus on adolescent drug use, including adolescent use of cigarettes (nicotine) and alcohol. Although in everyday discourse we may not consider these latter two drugs to be in the same category as the illicit drugs adolescents use, they are the two drugs adolescents most frequently use. Moreover, adolescents may develop both physical and psychological addiction to these drugs, just as may occur with the illicit drugs and, again as with the illicit drugs, they present health hazards to the adolescent.

Sex Differences in Drug Use

In general, adolescent males admit to more drug use than adolescent females. And, males admit to more regular (daily) use of drugs. However, these sex differences tend to be related more strongly to illicit drugs, such as marijuana, heroin, and cocaine, for example. A greater percentage of females used, or are using, stimulants and tobacco (Newcomb & Bentler, 1989). The percentage of males and females admitting to alcohol use is nearly equal (93.4 percent of males and 91.8 percent of females in 1981 and declined to 88.5 and 85.3 in 1982), although males are more likely to have used alcohol recently.

Developmental Trends in Drug Use

The use of drugs must be considered from the standpoint of their legality. Some drugs, such as alcohol and cigarettes, are licit. Others, such as marijuana and cocaine, are illicit. There is substantial evidence that, although about a third of adolescents have tried at least one illicit drug, most drug use involves licit drugs (Newcomb & Bentler, 1989).

Some examples of both licit and illicit drug use are shown in Table 13–4 for both adolescents and young adults. As you can see, use of illicit drugs increased from the mid-1970s to the mid-1980s. The same was true for alcohol, but a reverse occurred for cigarettes. In general, there was a decline in

Adolescent drug use, including cigarette smoking, is on the decline.

TABLE 13–4   **Drug Use Statistics**

| | Percent of Those Aged 12–17 | | | | Percent of Those Aged 18–25 | | | |
| | *Ever Used* | | *Current User* | | *Ever Used* | | *Current User* | |
	1974	*1985*	*1974*	*1985*	*1974*	*1985*	*1974*	*1985*
Marijuana	23.4	23.7	12.0	12.3	52.7	60.5	25.2	21.9
Cocaine	3.6	5.2	1.0	1.8	12.7	25.2	3.1	7.7
Alcohol	54.0	55.9	34.0	31.5	81.6	92.8	69.3	71.5
Cigarettes	52.0	45.3	25.0	15.6	68.8	76.0	48.8	37.2

(Source: U.S. Bureau of the Census [1989]. *Statistical abstract of the United States: 1989.* Washington, DC: Government Printing Office.)

drug use across the 1980s (Newcomb & Bentler, 1989).

Etiology of Drug Use and Abuse

Newcomb and Bentler (1989) distinguish between drug *use* and drug *abuse*. Abuse involves negative consequences to the self and others, and to property. Abuse also involves using drugs known to have a high probability of dependence. Occasional use of a drug, such as alcohol or tobacco, is simply use. Although a "fuzzy" distinction, it is an important one for it helps us to distinguish levels of drug users.

Drug use seems most closely tied to social influences, such as peer pressure and social class, and psychological factors, such as family relations, poor self-esteem, and stressful life events. These factors may cause the adolescent to on occasion use various drugs in order to gain acceptance, to relieve stress (see Box 13–3), or to escape unpleasant feelings. Drug abuse, as with alcohol, may have a genetic basis (Newcomb & Bentler, 1989). As with other disturbances in normal development, family factors are an important determinant.

Prevention and Treatment

Although the current trend is to educate adolescents about the problems that can arise from drug use and abuse, the evidence that such programs are successful is mixed (Newcomb & Bentler, 1989). Attempts to prevent the availability of drugs also do not solve the problem. The upshot of these efforts is that for drug use there are some benefits, but for drug abuse there are none. The latter situation involves unhappiness that is ingrained, limited life opportunities, and psychological distress not addressed by current prevention programs. Helping those who are at risk for drug abuse will require much more extensive and personally tailored programs.

There is a growing industry for drug treatment. Successful programs focus on improving social functioning, eliminating drug use, continuing school enrollment, and staying in treatment. These procedures help the individual integrate the self into the social fabric of those who are more well adjusted and to help the individual gain in self-esteem.

OTHER DISORDERS

Adolescence is a time of relatively rapid change in many spheres of development, as we have noted many times in earlier chapters. The changes in biological and cognitive development, social, peer, and parent relationships, and the like, all produce a degree of stress on the adolescent (see Chapter 2; Weiner, 1980). Although most adolescents cope with the changes in an adaptive manner, for some the added stress may lead to one or another psychological disorder. We review below some of the more common psychological disorders affecting adolescents.

Weiner (1980) has identified the major behavioral problems faced by adolescents, including school attendance and achievement, delinquent behavior, and suicide, topics we have discussed previously in this or other chapters. In addition, he has noted that schizophrenia and depression are two of the major psychological/behavioral disorders that are prevalent among disturbed adolescents.

Schizophrenia

Those who experience schizophrenia are most likely to exhibit the symptoms initially during the adolescent or early adulthood years (Weiner, 1980, 1982). Weiner notes that about a quarter to a third of adolescents seeking professional help for psychological problems exhibit schizophrenic symptoms. The symptoms of the disorder include a reduced ability to think logically and coherently, variability in moods, hallucinations (visual and aural), deteriorating social relationships, decreases in energy, withdrawal, and hostile or impulsive behavior.

Researchers (e.g., Pogue-Geile & Harrow, 1987) have identified several means of distinguishing adolescent schizophrenia from other adolescent disorders, including depression, which we discuss below. First, persistence and pervasiveness of exhibiting the symptomology is a key. An adolescent who may experience depression but who, when not depressed, still shows symptoms of schizophrenia is a likely candidate for actually having the disorder. Second, adolescents who exhibit little concern for normal development in peer and other social relations may be exhibiting schizophrenic symptoms. Immaturity of interests and attitudes may reflect a lack of interest in the typical aspects of adolescent life and be indicators of withdrawal. Finally, the pervasiveness of the showing of symptoms is a key. For example,

the inability to deal with ordinary thoughts in logical and nonambiguous ways may indicate schizophrenic symptomology.

Treatment of schizophrenia during adolescence is difficult, as it is during any other part of the life span. More importantly, the earlier the disorder occurs, the less successful treatment tends to be, which means that when it occurs during adolescence as opposed to adulthood, the prognosis is mediocre, at best. Only about 23 percent of adolescents showing schizophrenic symptoms recover completely (Weiner, 1982), and about half permanently display schizophrenic tendencies (Veck, 1978).

Treatment of schizophrenic symptoms varies a great deal. Hospitalization is common, at least for short periods of time. Individual, family, or group therapy is aimed at building social relationships in an attempt to build self-esteem and reduce withdrawal. In some instances, drug therapy, which reduces considerably the hallucinogenic features of schizophrenia, is used. This apparently has the benefit of facilitating other forms of therapy (Siris, Van Kammen, & Docherty, 1978).

Depression

Depression, in varying degrees, has been experienced by virtually all of us. In the usual case, it occurs when we feel a loss of some type, for example, through death, a broken relationship with someone important to us, or through separation (Halmi, 1987). Although we all have felt this way on one occasion or another, we have tended to adapt well to the separation. For some adolescents, or adults, the adaptation is not effective. Weiner (1980, 1982) estimates that about 10 percent of adolescents may at one time or another exhibit symptoms of primary depression, including self-deprecation, crying spells, suicidal thoughts, and the like.

The symptoms of depression, and indeed the disorder itself, seem to depend on age.

Younger adolescents, up to about age 16 or 17, do not exhibit the same signs of depression as do older adolescents or adults (Weiner, 1980, 1982). The reasons for this are related to the developmental tasks (see Chapters 1 and 2) faced by adolescents of different ages. Younger adolescents face tasks that challenge self-esteem (for example, independence from parents, heterosexual friendship patterns), which make them less likely to admit self-critical attitudes and feelings of helplessness. Second, they are more likely to express feelings and emotions through doing rather than thinking. Hence, they are much less likely than older adolescents or adults to express and feel the brunt of depression through cognitive functions such as introspective preoccupation.

During adolescence there are some other symptoms of depression. Extreme fatigue, even after adequate rest, difficulty in concentrating, as on school work, even after adequate study, and extreme occupation with physical development, may be signals of impending or existent depression (Weiner, 1980, 1982). Older adolescents and adults may manifest depression through drug abuse, alienation from others, or other means of cutting the self off from the social world. This seems to reflect a view that there is little point in doing anything constructive.

The causes of depression may be many, and it is unclear if any is more important than others. Seligman (1975) argues that learned helplessness—the view that one has very little control over life events, which are determined by others or by forces outside one's control—is a key to depression. Others argue that depression results from a poor self-esteem and negative view of the self resulting from earlier poor rearing and experiences. Each of these beliefs about the etiology of depression is tied to various therapeutic approaches, including individual, family, or group therapy, drug therapy, and behavior therapy. Which, if any, is most successful is completely open to debate (Weiner, 1982).

SUMMARY

Deviancy is a very difficult term to define. In general, it refers to development, or behavior, that is outside some norm. Hence, one may be deviant in terms of biological growth, intellectual development, or social behavior. The most prevalent forms of deviancy in adolescence are juvenile delinquency, various eating disorders, suicide, drug use and abuse, and other psychological disorders such as schizophrenia and depression.

Juvenile delinquency is the term used to describe illegal behaviors of those who are minors (usually those under 16 or 18 years of age, depending on the state of residence). The incidence of delinquency increased until the mid-1970s and then leveled off. Boys engage in more delinquency than do girls; boys also engage in more violent forms of delinquency. The incidence of delinquency peaks at about 15 years of age and then levels off, so older adolescents engage in more delinquency than do younger adolescents.

A number of factors presumably fostering delinquency have been investigated. One of the more salient characteristics is social class. Whether working with official police and court records, or with adolescent self-reports, it is clear that there is a social class difference in delinquency. Adolescents from poorer socioeconomic backgrounds engage in more delinquency than their middle-class peers. However, in recent years, there has been an increase in middle-class delinquency, and in delinquency in suburban areas. Although social class is in part a determinant of delinquency, then, it is not the sole or overriding factor it once was thought to be.

Other factors involved in socializing an adolescent into delinquency are the peer group and the relationship with the parents. Peers not only teach delinquent behavior but also reinforce it. This might be especially true in some types of adolescent gangs. For boys, the single most important factor involved in delinquency is the relationship with the parents. Delinquents, both boys and girls, view their relationships with their parents in very poor ways. They see their fathers as neglecting, hostile, and rejecting. In addition, the parents of delinquents tend to use considerable physical punishment, and to be erratic and overly strict in child rearing.

Although no single personality type can be identified as a "delinquent personality," some characteristics of delinquents can be identified. In general, delinquents develop poor self-concepts and see themselves as cut off from society. In part, then, they view society in a hostile manner. Delinquent adolescents also have an external locus of control, which means they see things as happening to them rather than seeing themselves in control of their own destiny. Delinquents also tend to do poorly in school, which may lead to their engaging in some specific forms of delinquency, such as truancy, and to their dropping out of school.

At the present time, there is no evidence to suggest that one form or another of treatment is best to use with delinquents. Because we identify delinquents after the fact, that is, after they already have engaged in delinquent behavior, we seem to treat the symptom and not the cause.

There are three main eating disorders that occur with high frequency in the adolescent population. Obesity is the most common. Obesity may result from eating too much or from metabolic disorders. However, obese adolescents tend to be more sedentary than their leaner peers. Obesity is a serious problem because of the health hazards it poses, including hypertension, heart disease, and joint disease. Treatment usually involves changing eating patterns and dealing with psychological factors predisposing one to obesity.

Anorexia nervosa is also a health hazard. The anorexic tends to eat very little, despite hunger, and to lose considerable body weight. Most anorexics are females and most become anorexic during the adolescent years. One factor that seems to predispose the adolescent to anorexia nervosa is the failure of parents to allow the individual to become independent. Anorexics also have a poor body image, seeing themselves as fat even though they are emaciated. Treatment often involves behavior modification to increase food intake and therapy to deal with psychological problems.

Bulimics eat huge amounts of food (up to nearly 5,000 calories) and then purge their systems through the use of laxatives, induced vomiting, or both. Bulimics are nearly all females, the disorder appearing usually around 18 years of age or so. The causes of the disorder, and the best treatment, are not yet determined.

Although the absolute number of adolescents who commit suicide is not large, it is a tragedy. Nearly 7 percent of all suicides are adolescents, and estimates are that 1 in 1,000 adolescents attempts to commit suicide. The one factor that is clearly associated with suicide is poor family relations, which make the adolescent feel neglected and isolated. These feelings lead to depression, which may predispose the adolescent to suicide. Treatment typically involves building better family and peer relationships.

Drug use by high school adolescents seems to have peaked in the late 1970s. Since then, there has been a slight decline in the use of most drugs. Nonetheless, 7 percent of adolescent high school students daily use marijuana and 6 percent daily use alcohol. About 20 percent of adolescents smoke daily. Males admit to using more drugs, and to more regular use of drugs. Whether it be marijuana, nicotine, or alcohol, the most frequently used drugs, there are serious physical effects associated with drug use. In addition, some drugs, such as nicotine, are physically addicting.

An important factor in drug use is parent behavior and parent attitudes about drug use. Adolescents whose parents model drug use are more likely to use drugs, as are adolescents whose parents do not convey messages about the ills of drug use. In addition, feelings of isolation and alienation from parents contribute to drug use. Finally, peer drug use is related to the adolescent's use of various drugs.

Schizophrenia and depression are the two most prevalent psychological disorders during the adolescent years. At the present time, we know little of the precipitating causes for these disorders. Treatment usually involves dealing both with the symptoms, perhaps through drug therapy, and with family relationships, which seem to be primary causes in the disorders.

GLOSSARY

Adjudicate. To bring a case before a judge or jury.

Anorexia nervosa. A psychological eating disorder characterized by a failure to eat, causing a dangerous drop in body weight.

Bulimia. A psychological eating disorder characterized by binge eating and then purging.

Depression. A psychological disorder characterized by lowered self-esteem, feelings of inferiority, and sadness.

DSM-III (Diagnostic and Statistical Manual-III). A manual listing the psychological and behavioral criteria for the classification of psychological disorders.

Juvenile delinquency. Illegal acts performed by juveniles.

Obesity. A condition of overweight characterized by high levels of subcutaneous fatty tissue.

SUGGESTED READINGS

RUTTER, M., GILLER, H. (1984). *Juvenile delinquency: Trends and perspectives.* New York: The Guilford Press.

The authors discuss a variety of issues involved in delinquency. Developmental trends and so-

cial class influences are stressed, especially in a cross-cultural perspective. There is also an excellent discussion of correlates of delinquency, precipitating factors, and treatment approaches.

JOHNSTON, L. D., BACHMAN, J. G., & O'MALLEY, P. M. (1981). *Student drug use in America: 1975–1981.* Rockville, MD: National Institute on Drug Abuse.

The authors discuss not only the physical and psychological effects of drug use, but also a variety of trends over the recent past in high schooler's use of drugs. The comprehensiveness of the report, and the use of national random samples, makes the information very useful for those interested in adolescent drug use.

PATTERSON, G. R., DeBARSYSHE, B. D., & RAMSEY, E. (1989). A developmental perspective on antisocial behavior. *American Psychologist, 44,* 329–335.

In this article, the authors present a comprehensive view of how various aspects of family life relate to juvenile delinquency.

PETTI, T. A., & LARSON, C. N. (1987). Depression and suicide. In V. B. Van Hasselt & M. Hersen (Eds.), *Handbook of adolescent psychology.* New York: Pergamon Press.

The authors discuss the etiology of both depression and suicide and the relation between the two. They present a very readable discussion of the many complicated factors involved in each of these issues.

WEINER, I. B. (1980). Psychopathology in adolescence. In J. Adelson (Ed.), *Handbook of adolescent psychology.* New York: John Wiley & Sons.

Weiner discusses a variety of adolescent psychological disturbances. He reviews precipitating causes and treatment patterns, as well as identifying syndromes of behavior.

APPENDIX

Methods of Research in the Study of Adolescence

CHAPTER OUTLINE

MAJOR ISSUES ADDRESSED

INTRODUCTION

The intent of this appendix is not to make researchers or statisticians out of you, but rather to give you some idea of how research studies are designed and conducted. We also want you to become familiar with some of the terms used in discussing research projects. Equally importantly, we would like you to become aware of the limitations of various research designs in order to evaluate the relevancy of various research studies to the theory discussed in the text. To accomplish these goals we shall provide some examples of various kinds of studies.

THE FUNCTION OF RESEARCH

One function of research is to test hypotheses derived from a theory. If the research findings support the hypothesis, the theory gains in truth value and validity as an adequate representation of the real world. If the research does not support the hypothesis, we have a right to question either the theory, the design of the research, or the appropriateness of that kind of research as a test of the hypothesis. This function of research is also important in determining the generalizability of a theory, that is, the degree to which the theory can explain behavior in more than one situation or for more than one population.

A second major function of research is to generate new hypotheses about behavior. In this sense, research acts to help develop and define the limits of a theory. Research may produce new constructs that relate to the particular theory or theories being tested. Hence, research can aid the development of a theory by making it broader and better defined. In this way, research is a critical tool for pointing directions in which theories should or may be expanded or changed.

Another function of research is to explain and predict behavior. It permits us to make predictions or statements that help us determine the conditions necessary to bring about a particular kind of behavior. Hence, research tools are necessary for testing whether theories are capable of predicting behavior.

As we also mentioned in Chapter 2, research is used to test alternative theories of the causes for some kinds of behavior. A theory is tested by accumulating evidence that either supports it or indicates that an alternative theory is better. Without research it would be impossible to test alternative theories and, therefore, we would have no objective means of determining which of several theories is better or more useful.

With particular reference to adolescent psychology, research must be focused in several directions; it must address itself to the biological, cultural, and intellectual factors underlying adolescent development. Hence, in the remainder of this appendix, we shall focus on research aimed at understanding the complexities of these factors in the investigation of adolescent development.

Finally, developmental research, including adolescent research, focuses on changes in behavior. Therefore, we shall discuss research methods aimed at investigating changes in behavior in order to highlight the particular methodological problems encountered when one wishes to study development.

RESEARCH ON ADOLESCENT DEVELOPMENT

We shall now examine some specific aspects of research in adolescent psychology. First, we shall discuss several ways in which research designs differ. Every research project may be described in terms of certain dimensions which we will discuss below. Second, we shall look at the mechanics, uses, advantages, and disadvantages of the kinds of research designs discussed in this text.

Dimensions of Research

Psychological research projects may differ from each other in a number of ways. In Table A–1 we list four classification dimensions of research projects and summarize the major aspects of each dimension. Although these dimensions are probably not all-inclusive, they will serve to demonstrate the different focuses that an investigation may have. The end points of these four dimensions are not necessarily mutually exclusive: a single research design may contain elements from both end points of a single dimension.

Laboratory versus Naturalistic. Laboratory research is typically conducted in an artificial situation, and the tasks presented are usually unfamiliar to the subject. This is done because it is necessary to control extraneous variables in order to assess the effects of the particular variable under study. The artificial situation eliminates distracting and extraneous influences on performance, and unfamiliar tasks are chosen because they are equally novel to all those tested. Thus, in studies of classical conditioning, for example, the subject is not studied in his or her own living room, but is more likely to be placed in a quiet and unfamiliar room.

Naturalistic observation is conducted "in the field," and usually entails simply observing and recording what people do in certain kinds of real-life circumstances, for exam-

ple, how people behave after or while viewing an automobile accident. Another example of naturalistic observation is the kind of research that is done in astronomy. It is not possible to create a functional replica of the universe in the laboratory. Therefore, the astronomer's only laboratory is a post from which he or she can observe the kinds of behaviors that go on in the heavens. Other examples of observational research include assessments of social behaviors, for example, the behaviors of street gangs, and surreptitious observations of individuals in any kind of a naturalistic situation.

Manipulative versus Nonmanipulative. Manipulative research involves a manipulation of some variable by the experimenter in an attempt to determine whether or not that variable will produce differences in the behavior of the subjects in an experiment. The variable that is manipulated is called the *independent variable.* The logic of the manipulative strategy states that subjects receiving one level (manipulation) of the independent variable should perform better (or worse) than subjects receiving a different level. For example, subjects drinking four ounces of alcohol immediately before a driving test should perform more poorly than subjects taking no alcohol before the test. Typically, manipulative research is conducted in the laboratory, although it may be done in a natural setting. In nonmanipulative research,

TABLE A–1   **Classification Dimensions of Research Projects**

1. Laboratory	versus	Naturalistic
artificial situation;		natural environment
control of extraneous variables		loose control of extraneous variables
2. Manipulative	versus	Nonmanipulative
cause-effect-oriented		discover relationships among variables—not cause-effect
usually experimental		usually correlational
3. Theoretical	versus	Atheoretical
test theories		answer immediate questions of applied nature
laboratory/manipulative		naturalistic/observational
4. Age change	versus	Age difference
longitudinal		cross-sectional
growth-oriented		behavior-difference-oriented

the experimenter simply observes and records the behavior of the subjects. This research is usually done in a naturalistic setting, although some kinds of nonmanipulative research are done in the laboratory.

The advantage of the manipulative research approach is that it is a very reliable way to discover how a variable relates to behavior. That is, cause and effect relationships may be determined in manipulative research. One might, for example, manipulate the amount of practice that people have in some particular situation, and then assess their performance on a related kind of task. In this way it is possible to determine the degree to which practice relates to performance. On the other hand, one may go into naturalistic settings and find people who, in the normal course of events, have varying degrees of practice at some particular skill, and assess their performance on some criterion task. In this case, the experimenter is not performing any particular manipulation. Observational research of this sort is particularly necessary when it is not feasible to use manipulation; for example, in many instances it would not be ethical (or legal) to conduct manipulative research on hormonal factors relating to human behavior because of potential adverse effects.

Although developmental research has generally been nonmanipulative in the past, manipulative studies have become more and more popular. The reasons are obvious and we have discussed some of them above. There is still a large amount of nonmanipulative research conducted, especially questionnaire studies, but the disadvantage of not being able to demonstrate a cause and effect relationship directly by the manipulation of variables has produced a decline in the use of the nonmanipulative research strategies and has limited their use to those areas in which manipulative research would be either impossible or a breach of professional ethics.

Theoretical versus Atheoretical. The third dimension listed in Table A–1 is labeled *theoretical versus atheoretical.* A good deal of research is conducted to test theories, for the reasons noted above. However, some research is conducted simply to satisfy the curiosity of the investigator or to collect data to begin to formulate a theory. The latter kinds of research studies are atheoretical in the sense that no particular theory is being tested.

Most developmental psychologists, including those who are interested in adolescent development, primarily do theory-oriented research. However, atheoretical research is often used to define certain kinds of problems and to generate data that may be used as a base on which to build a theory about behavior. In addition, atheoretical research is often conducted in order to answer questions of immediate concern; for example, much of the research on classroom behavior and teaching methods has been atheoretical.

Age Change versus Age Difference. The fourth dimension is a very important one for developmental research projects. Developmental researchers are typically interested in changes in behavior that occur with increases in the age of the subjects. This kind of research is represented by the longitudinal research strategy discussed below. Age-change research is truly developmental because it produces growth curves of behavior in a single group of subjects tested and retested over a period of time. In other words, repeated measurements on a group of subjects as they mature permit direct developmental assessments.

Age-difference research refers to research in which data on age-related differences in behavior are obtained from subjects of different ages in a single experiment. Because subjects in age-different research studies are of different ages, and because they are tested only one time, it is impossible to demonstrate growth (change) trends in behavior.

A good deal of developmental research, including that in adolescent psychology, is of the age-difference sort, partly because it is cheap to do in terms of time, personnel, and money, whereas age-change research presents a number of problems that are sometimes extremely difficult to solve. We must always be somewhat suspect of growth trends derived from age-difference research, especially when we wish to use them to interpret developmental behavior. This is not to say that no valuable information is gained from age-difference research. Such findings can be valuable, especially when there is no reason to suspect that environmental factors are causing differences in the psychological functioning of the various age groups. There are some research studies, although not many, that involve components of both age-change and age-difference research. We shall discuss several of these below because they are the ones that we will see in increasing numbers in the future.

These four dimensions are not so much a system for classifying research projects as they are a means of assessing the contribution of a research project to knowledge about development. For example, laboratory research that is manipulative, theoretical, and age-change-oriented should tell us something of the theoretical basis for developmental changes in the effects of some variable on behavior. Certainly, this kind of information is desirable and necessary for a clear understanding of development. Similarly, naturalistic, correlational, and atheoretical research that involves several age groups may be of the sort that contributes to our understanding of age differences in the relationship(s) between two or more variables in the natural setting. Both types of research, different as they are, contribute to our knowledge of development.

Research Designs in Adolescent Psychology

We shall now discuss four research designs that are commonly employed in developmental psychology and present their limitations, advantages, and disadvantages. We shall also discuss examples of each kind of research in order to highlight the particular strategy involved in each.

Cross-Sectional Research. A cross-sectional experiment is defined as the systematic assessment of several groups of people at approximately the same point in time. One major characteristic of a cross-sectional study is that all groups of subjects involved in the study are tested only once and over a relatively short period of time. A second characteristic is that manipulations of variables are usually involved, allowing the assessment of cause and effect relationships. With reference to the dimensions listed in Table A–1, the cross-sectional study is, in most instances, theoretical and manipulative. In developmental research it is also age-difference-oriented, although only one age group need be involved. Most cross-sectional research is conducted in the laboratory, but it may also be conducted in naturalistic settings. The major contribution of cross-sectional research to our understanding of adolescent development, then, lies in testing theories and providing data on the causes of behavior. Age differences in the effects of various manipulations may also be investigated.

There are both advantages and disadvantages to the cross-sectional experiment. A major advantage is that it is relatively economical in terms of time, money, and personnel. An experiment involving many hundreds of people might be conducted in only a few days.

The economy of the cross-sectional study makes it an ideal method for conducting research to test hypotheses derived from theories. Therefore, one often sees cross-sectional experiments that are aimed at assessing the theoretical statements of one versus another particular theory about behavior. However, a cross-sectional experiment may tell us little about age changes in behavior because the subjects are tested only once and are of different ages. Another disadvantage to the cross-sectional study is that some kinds of problems, for example, those involving assessments of growth, cannot be investigated.

The typical cross-sectional experiment is, as we noted above, manipulative in nature. In other words, the independent variable is manipulated to test whether or not it relates to behavior in the predicted ways. Some subjects in the experiment will form the *experimental group*; that is, that group of subjects on which the manipulation is performed. The remainder of the subjects will form the *control group*, the group of subjects on which no manipulation is performed. The behavior of all the subjects is measured on some task; the score derived is the *dependent variable*. In other words, the independent variable is the variable manipulated in the experiment, and the dependent variable is the measure that is taken. The particular manipulations that are performed are called the *treatment conditions*; the experimenter determines which particular treatments, or manipulations of the independent variable, produce changes in the behavior of the subjects. In this way it is possible to make cause and effect statements about the relationships of particular manipulations to particular magnitudes of the dependent variable.

Within a developmental research framework, one particular independent variable of interest is age. In many instances treatments are assumed to affect subjects differently according to age. By assessing the different effects of a manipulation on various age groups, one may gain insights into various developmental processes. For example, Dusek (Dusek, Kermis, & Mergler, 1975; Dusek, Mergler & Kermis, 1976) demonstrated that labeling to-be-remembered information facilitated subsequent recall more for preadolescents (grades 3, 4, 5, and 6) than for adolescents (grades 7 or 8). This research suggests that adolescents use more efficient methods to remember material than do children, a piece of information that

is of interest to those who are investigating the development of memory processes.

Not all cross-sectional studies involve age manipulations. There are cross-sectional studies in which the investigator is primarily interested in assessing the behavior of subjects within a given age level or examining behavior in a particular kind of setting.

Longitudinal Studies. A longitudinal experiment may be defined as the systematic study of the same group or groups of individuals at regular intervals over time. In a longitudinal study there is more than one measurement of the behavior of the individuals under study. Because the behaviors of the same group or groups of subjects are assessed at different points in time, the longitudinal study is truly developmental, that is, it permits the assessment of uniformity and diversity in patterns of growth over time. For example, we could study growth in IQ test performance, problem-solving ability, or physical traits, and discuss developmental (age-change) trends as opposed to simple age differences. With respect to the four dimensions listed in Table A–1, the longitudinal study is always an age-change study. It may fall at either pole on the remaining three dimensions.

The longitudinal study has several additional advantages. First, it is ideal for investigating the effects of cultural factors that may influence behavior but whose influence is not revealed until months or even years later. Second, longitudinal studies demonstrate continuities and commonalities in behavior over time. Longitudinal studies also have certain limitations. As we noted above, they are expensive in terms of time, money, and personnel. Not only are there limits to the amount of time that a single individual might wish to devote to a longitudinal study, but there are also limits to the amount of money available to keep track of subjects, establish and maintain testing procedures, and continue the interest of the subjects in the experiment.

Sample attrition is also a severe problem in longitudinal studies, particularly when older people are involved. Subjects move, die, and lose interest in continuing with the experiment. As a result, at each point one is essentially testing a different sample, and therefore the generality of the developmental findings might be in question. Another drawback to the longitudinal study is that it is relatively hard to replicate. Since replication is one way of being sure that the results obtained in the original experiment are reliable, this is a very serious limitation. Finally, introducing new testing procedures into a longitudinal study once it has started is often difficult. For example, we cannot conduct a longitudinal study on the growth of IQ using the Stanford-Binet and then change to the Wechsler Adult Intelligence Scale, because IQ is not measured in the same way in each of the two tests. Therefore, our IQ scores would not be comparable from one testing to the next.

Combined Longitudinal and Cross-Sectional Designs. Cross-sectional and longitudinal designs have certain drawbacks that make them at times inadequate for assessing developmental phenomena. In the traditional cross-sectional design, in which several different age groups are tested at the same time, age effects may be confounded with cohort effects. (Schaie uses the term *cohort* to describe a group of subjects born in the same year.) In other words, subjects of different ages may behave in the experiment in ways that are different but cannot be attributed solely to differences in age. What may appear in the results to be an age difference in performance may in reality be a cohort (time of birth) difference. Because effects are perfectly confounded, we cannot logically conclude that one and not the other is responsible for the differences observed in the experiment. It is particularly difficult to assess cohort effects in cases where a significant cultural factor might have influenced development. For example, certain differences in attitudes between samples of 50-year-olds and 20-year-olds might be as much a function of cultural influences (the 50-year-olds were born before World War II) as of age.

In a longitudinal study, age and time of measurement are perfectly confounded. In other words, the age of the subjects is related directly to the time at which measurements are taken. To the extent that significant cultural events intervene between one testing and another, the changes that one observes might or might not be due to the intervening cultural events. Take our 50-year-olds again. If they are Americans born in the 1930s, they have experienced one global and two limited wars. One might well expect that their attitudes toward war would be as much affected by history as by maturing psychological processes. As with the confoundings in the cross-sectional study, only rarely can the effects be separated.

If no significant cultural factors intervene, there is no difficulty with the traditional designs. But in our fast-paced, technological culture this is unlikely. Hence, in a cross-sectional study it is very dangerous to generalize age differences from one time of measurement to another. In a longitudinal design, it is risky to generalize age differences over time from one cohort (those born in one given year) to another.

Since Schaie's (1965) original article, a great deal of discussion has focused on alternative research designs that might be used in order to separate true age differences and changes from cohort and time-of-measurement effects. The following example will illustrate that it is possible to arrange research designs that will isolate age and cohort effects. We shall draw on Schaie and Strother's research (1968a) on cognitive change during the adult years.

Schaie and Strother tested 500 subjects ranging in age from 20 to 70 years with a variety of tests of intellectual abilities, including verbal meaning, spatial ability, reasoning, and number and word fluency.

Twenty-five males and 25 females within each five-year interval (20–24, 25–29, and so forth) were tested. Seven years later, 302 of the same subjects were retested with the same instruments. Taken separately, the first and second testings each represent a cross-sectional study of intellectual abilities at different ages. Taken jointly, the two testings represent a longitudinal study of the development of intellectual abilities. However, because subjects from 10 different cohorts were tested twice at the same two times, this is called a cross-sequential study, a design that permits isolation of age effects.

Case Study Research. The case study may be defined as the systematic assessment of one individual at regular intervals over time. The case study, then, is a special case of longitudinal assessment. Typically the case study is naturalistic, correlational, and atheoretical, although, as always, there are exceptions.

There are several benefits to the case study approach, including the fact that it is inexpensive in terms of the amount of data collected, and it is quite practical for treatment purposes. In fact, case studies are most common in therapy situations. Case studies allow the examination of intraindividual changes in behavior. By studying stability of performance in a single individual, we can gain some notion about the stability of psychological traits. For example, case studies of IQ development reveal wide variations in the tested IQ, leading to the conclusion that IQ test performance is not very stable (for example, Honzik, Macfarlane, & Allen, 1948; Dearborn & Rathney, 1963).

There are some disadvantages to case studies, however. First, the data are quite probably biased because they represent growth and development for one individual. As a result, the information obtained cannot (usually) be generalized to other cases and certainly will not lead to the formulation of general laws of development and behavior. A second problem with the case study is that

it becomes quite difficult, although not impossible, to manipulate variables and make clear interpretations of the results. For example, one might manipulate reinforcement contingencies and study their effects on behavior with a single individual. Indeed, operant research is often conducted in this fashion. However, certain personal variables cannot be manipulated. For instance, an individual cannot be both low and high anxious, or low and high IQ, or male and female.

Although case studies are popular for demonstrating and illustrating certain aspects of development, psychologists are more concerned with general laws of development derived from research on groups of adolescents than with the particular development of a single adolescent. This is not to deny the importance of individual differences, but rather to emphasize the more general aspects of adolescent development.

Interview-Survey Research. Certainly the most frequently used research technique in the study of adolescence is the survey or questionnaire approach. When the questionnaire asks the adolescent to state views about some topic, for example, political or moral behavior, the questionnaire is called an *opinionnaire*, since the subjects are expected to respond on the basis of their own feelings and opinions. When the subjects are asked to respond to a questionnaire that is about themselves, the questionnaire is often called an *inventory*. In this instance, individuals may be asked to describe something about themselves, such as self-concept. When a questionnaire is administered in person by an examiner, it is often called an *interview*. When it is sent through the mail or administered to a large group of people at once, it is often called a *survey*. Interviews and surveys usually are administered in the natural setting and most often are correlational in nature. They may have characteristics at either end of the other two dimensions.

There are a number of advantages to this

approach, which is why it has become so popular. First, a great deal of information may be collected from large numbers of people in a very short period of time. For example, the author and his assistants have administered as many as 800 questionnaires to large groups of adolescents in just a few days. In that time, approximately 300,000 pieces of data were collected. In addition, adolescents may give more honest answers on sensitive items (for example, those dealing with sexual behavior and feelings about parents) when they can respond anonymously to a written questionnaire.

The most serious limitation of the questionnaire method is that it is normative and descriptive in nature. Hence, it reveals no information about cause and effect relationships. Issues dealing with whether or not subjects are lying when they respond to the questionnaire, whether the interviewer is somehow biasing the subjects' responses, and the reliability of retrospective reports are other problems that enter into an evaluation of the utility of data collected by the questionnaire method.

STATISTICAL CONCEPTS

Throughout the text reference is made to experiments of the sorts described in the previous section. All observations, whether made in the laboratory or in a naturalistic setting, must be organized, categorized, and summarized before any meaning can be attibuted to them. This process of *data compression* produces numerical measures; for example, scores on a performance measure or a listing of heights and weights for the sample studied. These numerical measures describe the data collected; therefore they belong in the realm of *descriptive statistics*. Testing of hypotheses is done through the use of *inferential statistics*. In this section we shall discuss some concepts related to both descriptive and inferential statistics.

TABLE A–2   **Statistical Concepts**

Descriptive Statistics summarize and describe data.
Measures of central tendency:
mean—average of the scores
median—the middle score (50% of the scores are higher and 50% are lower)
mode—the most frequently occurring score
Measures of variability:
range—the difference between the lowest and the highest score
standard deviation—square root of the variance
variance—the sum of the squared deviations of the scores from the mean divided by the number of scores
Measures of association:
correlation coefficient—a measure of association between two variables
a factor—a cluster of test scores or items that are highly related to each other and not related to scores or items in other factors
Inferential Statistics are used to test hypotheses.
Random sample: a sample drawn from a population in such a way that every member of the population has an equal chance of being picked
Experimental group: the subjects receiving the experimental treatment
Control group: the subjects receiving no experimental treatment
Significance level: the probability that differences between the experimental and control groups at the end of the experiment are due to chance
t-test: technique used to assess differences between experimental and control groups in a two-group experiment
F-test: technique used to assess differences when more than two groups are tested or more than one variable is manipulated
Independent variable(s): the variable(s) manipulated in the experiment
Dependent variable(s): the variable(s) measured in the experiment

Descriptive Statistics

Descriptive statistics techniques are used to summarize the data that are collected in an experiment and to communicate the findings of the experiment to the scientific community. A listing of various techniques employed in both descriptive statistics and inferential statics is given in Table A–2. Since many of these terms are probably familiar to you, we shall review them only briefly to refresh your memory.

Measures of Central Tendency. One way to summarize data is through various measures of central tendency, each of which reflects to some degree the "typical" score. There are several such measures, including the mean, the median, and the mode. The *mean* is commonly employed to communicate differences between groups of subjects who vary according to age, sex, or experimental treatment. However, the mean may also be employed in a naturalistic experiment. Hence, by looking at the mean one is able to speak of scores increasing or decreasing as a function of age level, sex, or some other variable of interest. Recall the results of the Schaie and Strother (1968a) experiment discussed above.

The median and the mode are less frequently employed. The *median*, which is used for dividing a distribution of scores into two equal groups of scores, is most frequently used to separate subjects into two groups for experimental purposes. For example, in a number of experiments children and adolescents have been divided into low-anxious and high-anxious groups by taking a median split on anxiety level. The investigators conducting these experiments wish to find out if the problem-solving strategies of low- and high-anxious subjects differ, and if these differences exist at various age levels.

The *mode* is used primarily to describe a distribution of scores in order to highlight scores that are obtained relatively frequently.

Measures of Variability. Just as there are measures of central tendencies, or similarities, in the scores obtained in an experiment, so too are there measures of variability. One measure of variability is simply the range of the scores, the highest to the lowest score. Obviously, this statistic provides some information about the scores but it doesn't tell us very much.

To describe more completely the nature of the distribution of scores, psychologists use two measures: the *standard deviation* and the *variance*, the latter being the square of the former. The standard deviation and the variance are direct measures of the variability of all the scores within the distribution from the mean score. The smaller the standard deviation or variance, the more compact (closer to the mean) the distribution of scores, and the larger the standard deviation or variance, the more disparate the scores. In a bell-shaped distribution, 68 percent of the scores fall within plus or minus one standard deviation from the mean. For example, IQ tests are designed to have a mean score of 100, and a standard deviation of either 15 or 16. By knowing this information we know that a score of 116 is one standard deviation above, and a score of 84 one standard deviation below, the mean IQ. By knowing the mean of the distribution and the standard deviation of the scores, then, we are able to discern the relative position of any given score within the distribution.

The final descriptive statistic we shall discuss is the *correlation coefficient*, denoted by r, which is a measure of the relationship between two scores derived from each subject. For example, we might wish to know the relationship between intelligence and school performance. In order to calculate this relationship we would need to have an IQ score on each subject as well as some measure of school performance. The correlation coefficient, then, allows us to determine how closely the two sets of scores, the IQ score and the school performance measure, are related.

The correlation coefficient may take on any value from -1 to $+1$. The larger the absolute value of the number, that is, the number irrespective of the sign attached to it, the stronger the relationship. The smaller the absolute value of the number, the weaker the relationship. A correlation of 0 demonstrates that there is no relationship between the two sets of scores. A correlation of +1 indicates that there is a perfect positive relationship between the scores. In our example of IQ scores, this means that the highest score on IQ is matched with the highest score on the school measure, and the lowest score on IQ is matched with the lowest score on the school measure, with all the intermediate scores falling in a perfect rank ordering. A correlation of −1 indicates that the highest IQ score goes with the lowest school performance score and the lowest IQ score with the highest school performance score, with all of the other intervening scores having the same perfect *inverse* relationship. In psychology, it is extremely rare to find correlations that are +1.0 or −1.0. We are much more used to dealing with correlations on the order of .5 or .6. These correlations indicate that there is some degree of relationship between the two scores but also that the two scores are somewhat independent.

The major reason for calculating correlation coefficients is to use them for purposes of prediction. To continue with our IQ and school performance example, it is very helpful to know a child's IQ score in terms of predicting school performance because we know that IQ and school performance scores correlate approximately +.6 or +.7 (for example, Bond, 1940). If an adolescent is having problems dealing with a school curriculum, but the youngster's IQ is in the normal or better-than-normal range, we may wish to examine factors other than intelligence to try to discover why the student is having a problem.

There are a number of cautions involved in interpreting correlation coefficients. First, one must be careful *not* to infer that simply because two variables are related (correlated), one somehow causes the other. Correlations are not measures of causation; they are simply measures of relationship. For example, if we give the same group of adolescents an IQ test at the age of 12 and then again at 18, we will find a correlation of about .76 (Honzik, Macfarlane & Allen,

1948). None of us would suggest that the IQ test given at 18 caused the performance at age 12. Nor is the reverse the case. Rather a certain set of abilities, motivating conditions, and other factors, perhaps unknown, cause the correlation.

Second, the absolute value of the correlation coefficient, not its sign, determines its strength. The sign attached to the correlation coefficient simply tells the direction of the relationship. Correlations of −.6 and +.6 are equally strong, but in opposite directions.

Finally, one must take care in interpreting the correlation coefficient in terms of its "realness." To clarify this point, let us take up again our example of IQ and school achievement. If we square the correlation coefficient, we have an estimate of the variability in school performance that is accounted for by IQ test performance. In our example, this variability will range somewhere between .36 (.6 × .6 = .36) and .49 (.7 × .7 = .49). In other words, only 36 to 49 percent of school performance can be accounted for by knowledge of the IQ. The remainder of the variability in school performance must be accounted for by other factors. Hence, although knowing the adolescent's IQ test score will help us deal with issues about the ability to handle school tasks, it is not a perfect predictor of performance. Unless the correlation is extremely high, for example, .95 to 1.0, one should look for other factors that might be related to the adolescent's ability to perform on some given task. A number of examples of correlational data are found in the text.

Factor Analysis. Factor analysis is a tool frequently employed by investigators who want to describe a large number of measures by a smaller number of factors. Therefore, we shall try to explain briefly what factor analysis is and how it works.

Suppose we administer a test containing nine items. We tabulate the scores and compute the correlations shown in part *a* of Ta-

TABLE A–3 **Item Intercorrelation Matrix**

	1	2	3	4	5	6	7	8	9
	\multicolumn{9}{c}{Intercorrelations for the nine items}								
1	1.0	.1	.8	.2	.9	.2	.0	.1	.0
2		1.0	.1	.7	.1	.2	.8	.0	.1
3			1.0	.0	.1	.2	.1	.0	.1
4				1.0	.1	.0	.0	.1	.2
5					1.0	.1	.1	.3	.2
6						1.0	.0	.8	.7
7							1.0	.3	.2
8								1.0	.8
9									1.0

Factors produced by grouping related correlations

I	II	III
1	2	6
3	4	8
5	7	9

ble A–3. The entries in the bottom diagonal are all 1.0 because scores correlated with themselves always produce a perfect positive correlation. Examination of the remaining correlations indicates that the items show a high correlation in some instances and a low or zero correlation in others. Imagine a matrix with 50 or more items, producing 1,225 correlations. How could one possibly absorb that much information? In such cases, factor analysis can be used to reduce information to a more manageable size by grouping together those items that are highly related. The items in each group correlate only minimally with items from other groups.

In part *b* of Table A–3 we have listed three factors for the matrix in part *a*. As you can see, the items in each cluster show high intercorrelations among themselves and low intercorrelations with items from the other clusters. Although we have oversimplified the procedure, the example does illustrate the basic purpose and technique of factor analysis. By examining the contents of the items included in each factor we can often label the factor.

As you can see, factor analysis is a powerful tool. An important thing to keep in mind is that factors are not "real." They exist only in our data. As you read factor analytic research in this or other texts, it is important to keep in mind that factors simply reduce information to a manageable size or amount.

Inferential Statistics

Although the techniques of descriptive statistics are useful for categorizing and summarizing the data collected in any kind of study, they are not useful, in most cases, for testing hypotheses about the causes of behavior. Therefore, it is important to have some understanding of inferential statistics, which are used for this purpose. As with descriptive statistics, we shall make this discussion relatively brief.

Inferential statistics permit us to go beyond a mere description of data and infer cause and effect relationships between the dependent variables we measure and the independent variables we manipulate. Consider, for example, a simple experimental design that involves only two groups of subjects. One group will be the experimental group, the group that will be subject to some kind of manipulation. The other group will be a control group, the group that will receive no manipulation. Let us further assume that we are interested in a group of adolescents, say, tenth graders. Therefore, we go to a large school, take the names of all the tenth graders in the school, put them in a hat, and then randomly draw 50 names for each of our two groups.

We have now selected a *random sample* of subjects; that is, a sample of subjects picked from a given population in such a way that everyone in the population has an equal chance of being selected. The population we are talking about is the population of tenth graders in a single school; it is not the population of all tenth graders in the United States. Nevertheless it is, to some extent, representative of the larger population.

When we pick two random samples in this fashion, we may assume logically that if we were to measure them at the start of the experiment on any of a number of variables, the two groups would be very similar. For example, each group will have about the same number of males and females, each should have the same number of good and poor students, and each should have roughly equivalent average height, weight, and intelligence levels. The larger the random sample, the more likely this is to be the case. Moreover, each random sample drawn from a given population will be representative of the larger population from which it is drawn, again with the proviso that the larger the random sample, the greater the degree to which it will reflect characteristics of the larger population.

Since we have two comparable random samples at the start of the experiment, we may assume that any differences in their performance at the conclusion of the experiment must be due to our experimental manipulation and nothing else. If this is the case, then, we have through our manipulation identified a cause of behavior or a factor that underlies performance in some given task. To the extent that our random samples accurately reflect the larger population, we may generalize the results of the experiment to the larger population.

As we noted above, the factor that we manipulate is called the independent variable. The measure that we take is on the dependent variable. Our interest, then, is in the performance of the experimental group and the control group on the dependent variable. Do they perform similarly or differently?

Following the completion of the experiment, inferential-statistics techniques are used to evaluate the difference between the experimental and the control group. The logic of inferential statistics says that if the results of our experiment demonstrate a difference in performance between the experimental and control groups, we may assume that a true cause and effect relationship exists between the independent and dependent variables. Also inherent in the logic of inferential statistics is the concept of error

—that because of chance factors, the samples we have selected are not exactly representative of the larger population, and therefore will yield erroneous data. In general, we are willing to accept the results obtained if we can prove (mathematically)* that there is only a 5 percent chance that the independent variable had no effect. Obviously, with a probability of error of 5 in 100, we may be incorrect in our assumption. However, since we have conducted only one experiment, we will accept this error level and rely on replication of the results to demonstrate if we are wrong.

When we talk about significant differences, or levels of significance, we are talking of differences that would occur by chance only 5 percent of the time. Sometimes the mathematical formula reveals an even smaller probability-of-error statistic. You will see such statistics on the tables in this text ($p = .01, p = .02$). This means that there is only a very small probability (1 out of 100 or 2 out of 100) that the results are erroneous.

The important point to understand is that by manipulating potential causes of behavior (independent variables) in an experiment, and then demonstrating that the manipulation produced differences in the performance (dependent variable) of the experimental and control groups, we are able to determine the causes of behavior.

PROBLEMS IN EVALUATING AND CONDUCTING RESEARCH

Thus far we have talked about research in a fairly positive way, in a way that makes it seem straightforward, simple, and unbelievably clear. In reality, however, this is not the

---

*By applying the appropriate formula to the data from the experiment, we can calculate a statistic that will tell us if the difference between the control and experimental groups is so large that we may attribute it to our manipulation.

case. There are a number of potential pitfalls in any research project, some obvious and some not so obvious, and one should be aware of these when evaluating research results. In this final section, we will discuss some of these issues.

Experimenter Bias Effects

When an investigator designs and conducts research, he or she is trying to prove or disprove a hypothesis. Therefore, there is always the danger that the experimenter may bias the results to come out as desired. The basic notion is that the experimenter may either intentionally or (more likely) unintentionally cue subjects to respond in ways that are consistent with his or her expectations. The more ambiguous the situation and the less objective the scoring of the dependent variable, the greater the chances for an experimenter bias effect. This is particularly important in adolescent research environments, such as surveys or interviews, that are frequently used in studying adolescent development. By slanting questions in certain ways, or by using particular tonal inflections or facial expressions, an interviewer may cue respondents to answer questions in ways that are consistent with what the investigator wishes to believe. Clearly this is not desirable because the information gleaned from such experiments is not necessarily representative of how the real world functions.

Another kind of experimenter bias enters into the scoring of data. An investigator may make errors in categorizing or scoring responses, particularly on ambiguous kinds of tests. We must stress here that we are not saying researchers intentionally bias the data they collect. Rather, we are saying that because it is so easy for bias to slip in, one must take considerable precautions to ensure that it does not.

Another, more subtle, form of bias is the expectations that we hold for a given adolescent's behavior when we know something about the adolescent's background. For example, we might expect school performance, intelligence test performance, moral values, sexual behavior, and a host of other measures to be different in an inner-city lower-class adolescent and a suburban middle-class adolescent. But our expectations may not reflect reality. The good scientist tries to be objective in these areas. We do not want our biases, however subtle, to determine the outcomes of experiments or to force us into a theoretical stance that is incorrect. We do want our research findings, and the theories they generate and substantiate, to reflect the real world.

Problems of Sampling

There are a number of problems encountered in obtaining samples of adolescents. One is simply the practical difficulty of obtaining random groups of adolescents for experiments or for filling out questionnaires. The problem here is one of generalizability, about which we will have more to say later.

Another problem, somewhat peculiar to studies of adolescent development, is how to define or measure adolescence. In Chapter 1, we noted that adolescence begins with the onset of puberty and ends with maturity, a socially defined measure. We also noted that there is some discussion about the validity of that particular definition because it is somewhat arbitrary. By using a simple age criterion we will certainly make some errors, classifying some potential subjects as adolescents when in fact they are not, particularly at the younger age levels. However, classifying adolescents on measures other than age is extremely difficult. One can hardly imagine a school allowing an investigator to ask girls if they have reached menarche or to ask boys to reveal their secondary sex characteristics. Clearly this problem of measurement will cause us to have some random error in our research findings. In turn, this will mean that our results will be somewhat limited. Although in some research this may not be a serious problem, in normative studies it is an important issue.

In a similar vein, any sample that we take from a normal school classroom will necessarily leave out some types of adolescents. For example, adolescents who are chronically ill or who are severely handicapped are unlikely to be found in a normal classroom. To the extent that our sample does not reflect students in these special categories, it will limit the generalizability of our research findings.

A third sample problem arises when one uses volunteers or paid subjects as opposed to a captive population. There are clear data (Rosenthal & Rosnow, 1975) indicating that volunteer subjects differ in a number of personality dimensions from nonvolunteer subjects. Again, to the extent that a sample is composed entirely of volunteer subjects, it will be biased and will not allow us to make general statements about the adolescent population with as much certainty as we would have with a completely random sample. The most obvious way in which volunteer subjects differ is in terms of their cooperativeness, which means they may be more willing to discuss certain matters, for example, drug use, sexual behavior, parental child-rearing techniques, or to reveal certain kinds of behavior about themselves than nonvolunteer subjects. Therefore, by using only volunteer subjects, we obtain inflated values on certain kinds of information and, perhaps, deflated values on others. Obviously, such a bias will influence the conclusions that we derive about adolescent development. Replication of an experiment with nonvolunteer subjects is of some help in determining whether or not our results are biased, but because of other factors, such as a different sample drawn from a slightly different population, it is not conclusive either. At present it is difficult to determine how big a problem this may be.

Retrospective Report

As we have noted several times, the most popular research technique used in studying adolescence is the survey, questionnaire, or interview. In many instances, these techniques require the adolescent to reconstruct or recall information from the past. For example, an investigator may wish to relate adolescent moral development to parental child-rearing techniques. This will require both a measure of current moral development as well as measures of child-rearing techniques used by the parents. If both the adolescent and the parents are interviewed, the investigator will find that there is relatively little agreement on what child-rearing techniques were used. In part, this will be due to forgetting or incorrect recall by both the parents and the adolescent. In part, it will be due to the respondents' desire to give answers that are "socially acceptable." None of us enjoys discussing the "bad" or "incorrect" things we do with someone in an authority position. Necessarily, then, these data must be regarded with some degree of skepticism.

Another problem involved in survey and questionnaire studies is the degree of frankness with which adolescents will answer the questions. As we noted above, it is possible that adolescents will give answers they think the investigator wants or answers that will make them look good. On the other hand, the respondent may refuse to answer some questions or may forget an answer. About all we can do is hope that the individual neither forgets nor answers the questions dishonestly.

Problems of Reliability and Validity of Measuring Instruments

A common problem encountered in adolescent research deals with the reliability and validity of measuring instruments, whether IQ tests, questionnaires of moral development, or scales that measure self-concept or attitudes. *Reliability* is the degree to which the instrument measures whatever it measures in consistent ways. In other words, if I were to give you IQ tests today and tomorrow, the reliability of the test would be indicated by the closeness of your scores. *Validity* is the degree to which the test measures what it purports to measure. If a test is both reliable and valid, our confidence in the results of research employing the test is increased because we know the test measures what it claims to measure and it does it in a consistent way.

Generalization of Research Findings

There are a number of problems related to the generalization of research findings. One such problem is the tendency to regard research findings as more significant or clear-cut than they actually are. Our discussion of the use of the correlation between IQ and school achievement falls within this vein. Too often teachers, parents, or counselors interpret a correlation between IQ and achievement as much stronger and more important than it actually is. Many children have been victimized by this kind of misuse or misinterpretation of the correlation coefficient.

A second problem, more important for our understanding of adolescent development generally, is to apply research findings gathered in one situation and under one set of circumstances to another situation that differs from the original in one or more critical characteristics. For example, a primarily Catholic population might give a very different set of responses in a research study testing attitudes on birth control, abortion, and sexual behavior than another religious population. Generalizing experimental results from one population to the larger population requires great care.

Inappropriate generalization also occurs in case studies. As we noted above, case studies are popular in adolescent development, and indeed are useful for highlighting certain aspects of development. Naive readers too often generalize from a given case study to the adolescent population in general or to themselves. However, because a case study involves a single individual, it is unlikely to reflect general laws of development. Furthermore, most, but certainly not all, case studies evolve from the study or treatment of some form of abnormal behavior. The bulk of the published case studies in adolescent psychology deals with adolescents who have had some sort of personality disorder or problem. To derive notions of general laws of adolescent development from them is unfair both to the individual involved in the case study and to those who wish to discover general laws of development.

This is not to say that there is no value in case studies or in intensive studies of a single individual. However, caution is necessary in reading case studies and generalizing them to yourself or to your friends. Like you, the individual in the case study has a unique developmental history. Therefore, the developmental influences that shaped that particular individual may or may not accurately reflect the influences that were a part of your particular development.

It is, of course, perfectly legitimate to generalize research results, but one must first consider the population on which the study was done and the characteristics of the population to which one wishes to generalize. The closer the characteristics of the two groups, the more reasonable the generalization. In addition, if experimental findings are replicated with different samples of people having different characteristics, then we can be relatively sure of the stability of the particular findings from the experiment. In this case, we can generalize those results to broader spectrums of the adolescent population.

Special Problems in Studying Adolescents

Researchers have become increasingly aware that it is a subject's right to refuse to participate in an experiment. Therefore, we are faced with a dilemma: on the one hand, we must recognize the rights of the individual; on the other hand, we wish to advance science. Jeopardizing one value for the other is surely not beneficial to either. Moreover, the ethical guidelines of the American Psychological Association insist that a subject be informed of the nature of the experiment, the uses to which the information will be put, and any kinds of stress under which the subject may be placed before the subject performs in the experiment. The subject may refuse to participate and should not be penalized for not participating.

Because of the nature of many areas of interest in the study of adolescence, this issue is an extremely important one. Adolescents may not want to discuss aspects of their sexual behavior, sexual development, relationships with their parents and siblings, or a host of other factors of interest to those of us who study adolescent development. This is not so much a problem with adults because adults are generally more aware of the value of research. It is also not so much an issue with children, because teachers and principals and others in the school organization are capable of reviewing the research and making judgments on participation based on the value of the research. Adolescents, on the other hand, are old enough to make the decision for themselves. Their right to information about the study and their right to refuse to participate should be guaranteed.

Another issue, related more to adolescent development than to the study of development in childhood or adulthood, is the notion of frankness. There are a number of studies of adolescent development (see Chapter 8) in which aspects of sexual behavior have been investigated with adolescents who were quite candid and open in their responses to the questionnaires. A guarantee of anonymity helps one gain the confidence of adolescent subjects. However, more often than not, it is probable that this degree of frankness occurs only in a select group of adolescents, and we may not know the exact characteristics of that group. In this case, as we discussed above, the generalizability of the research findings is difficult and problematical.

SUMMARY

In this appendix on methodology we have tried to make you more aware of a number of issues that are involved in conducting research projects so that you may become a more sophisticated and knowledgeable student of adolescent development. The various research designs we have discussed, and the problems associated with them, are common in all areas of developmental psychology. Some of them are particularly important in adolescent development; for example, in the longitudinal study, because of the transitional nature of adolescence.

The information on statistics is important in the sense that some rudimentary understanding of statistics is necessary for reading and understanding psychological research. We do not want you to be handicapped by lack of relevant knowledge as you read through the text, but we also do not want you to become so involved with statistics that you lose sight of the fact that we are talking about people. If you understand the statistical terms and concepts presented in this appendix, you will be able to understand and evaluate the research discussed in the text.

As with any endeavor, there are problems involved in using research to understand behavior. We discussed a number of these in the last section. In spite of these drawbacks, there have been a substantial number of useful research projects in the field of adolescent development. We should be able to gain considerable information from these projects as we go through the text. You, as a more sophisticated reader, should also be able to profit from your increased understanding of the role of research and theory in explaining behavior.

References

ABRAHAMS, B., FELDMAN, S., & NASH, S. (1978). Sex role self-concept and sex role attitudes: Enduring personality characteristics or adaptations to changing life situations? *Developmental Psychology, 14*, 393–400.

ACKERLY, S. (1933). Rebellion and its relation to delinquency and neurosis in 60 adolescents. *American Journal of Orthopsychiatry, 3*, 147–160.

ADAMS, G., & FITCH, S. (1982). Ego stage and identity status development: A cross-sequential analysis. *Journal of Personality and Social Psychology, 43*, 574–583.

ADAMS, G., & JONES, R. (1983). Female adolescents' identity development: Age comparisons and perceived child-rearing experience. *Developmental Psychology, 19*, 249–256.

ADAMS, J. F. (1980). Adolescents in an age of acceleration. In J. F. Adams (Ed.), *Understanding adolescents: Current developments in adolescent psychology* (4th ed.). Boston: Allyn & Bacon.

ADELSON, J. (1971, Fall). The political imagination of the young adolescent. *Daedalus*, 1013–1050.

ADELSON, J. (1975). The development of ideology in adolescence. In S. Dragastin & G. Elder (Eds.), *Adolescence in the life cycle.* (pp. 63–78). New York: John Wiley & Sons.

ADELSON, J., & DOEHRMAN, M. (1980). The psychodynamic approach to adolescence. In J. Adelson (Ed.), *Handbook of adolescent psychology.* New York: John Wiley & Sons.

ADELSON, J., & O'NEIL, R. (1966). The development of political thought in adolescence: A sense of community. *Journal of Personality and Social Psychology, 4*, 295–308.

AHAMMER, I. M. (1973). Social-learning theory as a framework for the study of adult personality development. In P. B. Baltes & K. W. Schaie (Eds.), *Life-span developmental psychology: Personality and socialization.* New York: Academic Press.

AHLSTROM, W. M., & HAVIGHURST, R. J. (1971). *400 losers.* San Francisco: Jossey-Bass.

ALBRECHT, S., BAHR, H., & CHADWICK, B. (1979). Changing family and sex roles: An assessment of age differences. *Journal of Marriage and the Family, 41*, 41–50.

ALEXANDER, C. N., JR., & CAMPBELL, E. Q. (1964). Peer influence on adolescent educational aspirations and attainments. *American Sociological Review, 29*, 568–575.

ALLEN, C. (1958). *Homosexuality: Its nature, causation and treatment.* London: Staples Press.

ALLEN, C. (1962). The problems of homosexuality. *International Journal of Sexology, 15*, 40–42.

ALLISON, P. D., & FURSTENBERG, F. F., JR. (1989). How marital dissolution affects children: Variations by age and sex. *Developmental Psychology, 25*, 540–549.

ALMQUIST, E. M. (1974). Sex stereotype in occupational choice: The case for college women. *Journal of Vocational Behavior, 5* (1), 13–21.

AMERICAN PSYCHIATRIC ASSOCIATION. (1980). *Diagnostic and statistical manual of mental disorders* (3rd ed.). Washington, DC: American Psychiatric Association.

ANDRE, T., FREVERT, R. L., & SCHUCHMANN, D. (1989). From whom have college students learned what about sex? *Youth and Society, 20*, 241–268.

ANGELINO, H., & MECH, E. (1955). Some "first" sources of sex information as reported by sixty-seven college women. *Journal of Psychology, 39*, 321–324.

ANGRIST, S. S. (1972). Variations in women's adult aspirations during college. *Journal of Marriage and the Family, 34*, 465–467.

ANSHEL, M. H., MULLER, D., & OWENS, V. (1986). Effect of a sports camp experience on the multidimensional self-concepts of boys. *Perceptual and Motor Skills, 63*, 363–366.

ANTILL, J. (1983). Sex-role complementarity versus similarity in married couples. *Journal of Personality and Social Psychology, 45*, 145–155.

ARBUTHNOT, J. (1975). Modification of moral judgment through role playing. *Developmental Psychology, 11*, 319–324.

ARCHER, S. (1982). The lower age boundaries of identity development. *Child Development, 53*, 1551–1556.

ARMSDEN, G. C., & GREENBERG, M. T. (1987). The inventory of parent and peer attachment: Individual differences and their relationship to psychological well-being in adolescence. *Journal of Youth and Adolescence, 16*, 427–454.

ARO, H., & TAIPALE, V. (1987). The impact of timing of puberty on psychosomatic symptoms among fourteen- to sixteen-year-old Finnish girls. *Child Development, 58*, 261–268.

ASTIN, H. S. (1968). Career development of girls during the high school years. *Journal of Counseling Psychology, 15*, 536–540.

AUSUBEL, D. P. (1954). *Theory and problems of adolescent development.* New York: Grune & Stratton.

419

AUSUBEL, D., MONTEMAYOR, R., & SVAJIAN. P. (1977). *Theory and problems of adolescent development* (2nd ed.). New York: Grune & Stratton.

BABER, K. M., & MONAGHAN, P. (1988). College women's career and motherhood expectations: New options, old dilemmas. *Sex Roles, 19,* 189–203.

BACHMAN, J. G., GREEN, S., & WIRTANEN, I. (1971). *Youth in transition: Vol. 3. Dropping out—problem or symptom?* Ann Arbor: University of Michigan, Institute for Social Research.

BACHMAN, J. G., GREEN, S., & WIRTANEN, I. (1972). *Dropping out—problem or symptom?* Ann Arbor: University of Michigan, Institute for Social Research.

BACHMAN, J. G., & JOHNSTON, L. D. (1979). *Fewer rebels, fewer causes: A profile of today's college freshmen.* Ann Arbor: University of Michigan, Institute for Social Research.

BACHMAN, J. G., JOHNSTON, L. D., & O'MALLEY, P. M. (1980). *Monitoring the future: Questionnaire responses from the nation's high school seniors, 1980.* Ann Arbor: University of Michigan, Institute for Social Research.

BACHMAN, J. G., KAHN, R. L., MEDNICK, M. T., DAVIDSON, T. N., & JOHNSTON, L. D. (1967). *Youth in transition: Vol. 1. Blueprint for a longitudinal study of adolescent boys.* Ann Arbor: University of Michigan, Institute for Social Research.

BACHMAN, J. G., & O'MALLEY, P. (1977). Self-esteem in young men: A longitudinal analysis of the impact of educational and occupational attainment. *Journal of Personality and Social Psychology, 35,* 365–380.

BACHMAN, J., & O'MALLEY, P. (1986). Self-concepts, self-esteem, and educational experiences: The frog pond revisited (again). *Journal of Personality and Social Psychology, 50,* 35–46.

BANDURA, A. (1964). The stormy decade: Fact or fiction? *Psychology in the Schools, 1,* 224–231.

BANDURA, A. (1969a). *Principles of behavioral modification.* New York: Holt, Rinehart & Winston.

BANDURA, A. (1969b). Social-learning theory of identificatory processes. In D. A. Goslin (Ed.), *Handbook of socialization theory and research.* Chicago: Rand McNally.

BANDURA, A. (1973). *Aggression: A social learning analysis.* Englewood Cliffs, NJ: Prentice-Hall.

BANDURA, A., & MACDONALD, F. J. (1963). Influence of social reinforcement and the behavior of models in shaping children's moral judgments. *Journal of Abnormal and Social Psychology, 67,* 274–281.

BANDURA, A., & WALTERS, R. H. (1959). *Adolescent aggression.* New York: Ronald Press.

BANDURA, A., & WALTERS, R. H. (1963). *Social learning and personality development.* New York: Holt, Rinehart, & Winston.

BARDWICK, J. M. (1971). *The psychology of women: A study of biocultural conflicts.* New York: Harper & Row.

BARKER, R. G. (1964). Ecological units. In R. G. Barker & P. V. Gump (Eds.), *Big school, small school.* Stanford CA: Stanford University Press.

BARNDT, R. J., & JOHNSON, D. M. (1955). Time orientation in delinquents. *Journal of Abnormal and Social Psychology, 51,* 343–345, 374.

BARRY, H., III, BACON, M. K., & CHILD, I. L. (1957). Cultural survey of some sex differences in socialization. *Journal of Abnormal and Social Psychology, 3,* 327–332.

BASKIN, W., & POWERS, G. (1969). *Sex education: Issues and directives.* New York: Philosophical Library.

BAUCOM, D. H., BESCH, P. K., & CALLAHAN, S. (1985). Relation between testosterone concentration, sex role identity, and personality among females. *Journal of Personality and Social Psychology, 48,* 1218–1226.

BAUMRIND, D.(1966). Effects of authoritative parental control on child behavior. *Child Development, 37,* 887–907.

BAUMRIND, D. (1968). Authoritarian vs. authoritative control. *Adolescence, 3,* 255–272.

BAUMRIND, D. (1978). Parental disciplinary patterns and social competence in children. *Youth and Society, 9,* 239–276.

BAUMRIND, D. (1982). Are androgynous individuals more effective persons and parents? *Child Development, 53,* 44–75.

BAUMRIND, D. (1986). Sex differences in moral reasoning: Response to Walker's (1984) conclusion that there are none. *Child Development, 57,* 511–521.

BAYLEY, N. (1955). On the growth of intelligence. *American Psychologist, 10,* 805–810.

BAYLEY, N., & ODOM, M. H. (1955). The maintenance of intellectual ability in gifted adults. *Journal of Gerontology, 10,* 91–107.

BEACH, F. (1958). Neural and chemical regulation of behavior. In H. F. Harlow & C. N. Wolsey (Eds.), *Biological and biochemical bases of behavior.* Madison: The University of Wisconsin Press.

BECKER, W. C. (1964). Consequences of different kinds of parental discipline. In M. L. Hoffman & L. W. Hoffman (Eds.), *Review of child development research* (vol. 1). New York: Russell Sage Foundation.

BELL, A. P. (1969). Role modeling of fathers in adolescence and young adulthood. *Journal of Counseling Psychology, 16,* 3–35.

BELL, A., WEINBERG, M., & HAMMERSMITH, S. (1981). *Sexual preference: Its development in men and women.* Bloomington: Indiana University Press.

BELL, R., & COUGHEY, K. (1980). Premarital sexual experience among college females, 1958, 1968, 1978. *Family Relations, 29,* 353–357.

BELL, R. Q. (1968). A reinterpretation of the direction of effects in studies of socialization. *Psychological Review, 75,* 84–88.

BELL, R. R. (1966). Parent-child conflict in sexual values. *Journal of Social Issues, 22,* 34–44.

BELL, R. R., & CHASKES, J. B. (1970). Premartial sexual experience among coeds, 1958 and 1968. *Journal of Marriage and the Family, 32,* 81–84.

BEM, S. (1974). The measurement of psychological androgyny. *Journal of Consulting and Clinical Psychology, 42,* 155–162.

BEM, S. (1975). Sex role adaptability: One consequence of psychological androgyny. *Journal of Personality and Social Psychology, 31,* 634–643.

BEM, S. (1977). On the utility of alternative procedures for assessing psychological androgyny. *Journal of Consulting and Clinical Psychology, 45,* 196–205.

BEM, S. (1981). Gender schema theory: A cognitive account of sex typing. *Psychological Review, 88,* 354–364.

BENE, E. (1965). On the genesis of female homosexuality. *British Journal of Psychiatry, 111,* 815–821.

BENEDICT, R. (1938). Continuities and discontinuities in cultural conditioning. *Psychiatry, 1*, 161–167.

BERENDA, R. W. (1950). *The influence of the group on the judgments of children.* New York: King's Crown Press.

BERKOWITZ, M. W., & GIBBS, J. C. (1983). Measuring the developmental features of moral discussion. *Merrill Palmer Quarterly, 29*, 399–410.

BERNDT, T. (1982). The features and effects of friendship in early adolescence. *Child Development, 53*, 1447–1460.

BERNDT, T. J. (1989, April). *Two pathways of friends' influence: Description and developmental changes.* Paper presented at the Biennial meetings of the Society for Research in Child Development, Kansas City, MO.

BERNSTEIN, R. (1980). The development of the self-system during adolescence. *Journal of Genetic Psychology, 136*, 231–245.

BERTI, A. M. (1988). The development of political understanding in children between 6–15 years old. *Human Relations, 41*, 437–466.

BERZONSKY, M. (1978). Formal reasoning in adolescence: An alternate view. *Adolescence, 13*, 279–290.

BINDER, A. (1988). Juvenile delinquency. In M. R. Rosenzweig, & L. W. Porter (Eds.), *Annual review of psychology.* Palo Alto, CA: Annual Reviews Inc.

BLASI, A. (1980). Bridging moral convention and moral action: A critical review of the literature. *Psychological Bulletin, 88*, 1–45.

BLOCK, J. (1973). Conceptions of sex role: Some cross-cultural and longitudinal perspectives. *American Psychologist, 28*, 512–527.

BLOS, P. (1962). *On adolescence.* New York: Free Press.

BLOS, P. (1967). The second individuation process of adolescence. In R. Eissler, A. Freud, H. Hartman, & M. Kris (Eds.), *Psychoanalytic study of the child* (Vol. 22). New York: International Universities Press.

BLOS, P. (1972). The function of the ego ideal in late adolescence. In R. Eissler, A. Freud, M. Kris & A. J. Solnit (Eds.), *Psychoanalytic study of the child* (Vol. 27). New York: International Universities Press.

BLOS, P. (1974). The genealogy of the ego ideal. In R. Eissler (Ed.), *Psychoanalytic study of the child* (Vol. 29). New Haven, CT: Yale University Press.

BLUMENTHAL, S. J., & KUPFER, D. G. (1988). Overview of early detection and treatment strategies for suicidal behavior in young people. *Journal of Youth and Adolescence, 17*, 1–23.

BOLDIZAR, J. P., WILSON, K. L., & DEEMER, D. K. (1989). Gender, life experiences, and moral judgment development: A process-oriented approach. *Journal of Personality and Social Psychology, 57*, 229–238.

BOLGER, N., DOWNEY, G., WALKER, E., & STEININGER, P. (1989). The onset of suicidal ideation in childhood and adolescence. *Journal of Youth and Adolescence, 18*, 175–190.

BOND, E. A. (1940). *Tenth-grade abilities and achievements.* New York: Columbia University Press, Teachers College, Bureau of Publications.

BORDUA, D. J. (1960). Educational aspirations and parental stress on college. *Sociological Forces, 38*, 262–269.

BORING, E. G. (1950). *A history of experimental psychology.* New York: Appleton-Century-Crofts.

BOROW, H. (1966). Development of occupational motives and roles. In L. W. Hoffman & M. L. Hoffman (Eds.), *Review of child development research* (Vol. 2). New York: Russell Sage Foundation.

BOROW, H. (1976). Career development. In J. F. Adams (Ed.), *Understanding adolescence: Current developments in adolescent psychology.* Boston: Allyn & Bacon.

BOTELLA-LLUSIA, J. (1973). *Endocrinology of women.* Philadelphia: W. B. Saunders.

BOURNE, E. (1978a). The state of research on ego identity: A review and appraisal (Pt. 1). *Journal of Youth and Adolescence, 7*, 223–251.

BOURNE, E. (1978b). The state of research on ego identity: A review and appraisal (Pt. 2). *Journal of Youth and Adolescence, 7*, 371–392.

BOYES, M. C., & WALKER, L. J. (1988). Implications of cultural diversity for the universality claims of Kohlberg's theory of moral reasoning. *Human Development, 31*, 44–59.

BOYLE, R. P. (1966). The effect of the high school on students' aspirations. *American Journal of Sociology, 71*, 628–639.

BRADLEY, R. H., CALDWELL, B. M., & ROCK, S. L. (1988). Home environment and school performance: A ten-year follow-up and examination of three models of environmental action. *Child Development, 59*, 852–867.

BRAINERD, C. (1978). The stage question in cognitive developmental theory. *Behavioral and Brain Sciences, 2*, 173–213.

BRAITHWAITE, J. (1981). The myth of social class and criminality reconsidered. *American Sociological Review, 46*, 36–57.

BRIM, O. G., JR. (1966). Socialization through the life cycle. In O. G. Brim, Jr., & S. Wheeler (Eds.), *Socialization after childhood.* New York: John Wiley & Sons.

BRIM, O. G., JR. (1975, July). Life span development of the theory of oneself. Invited address to the International Society for the Study of Behavioural Development Biennial Conference. University of Surrey, Guildford, Surrey.

BRODERICK, C. B. (1966). Socio-sexual development in a suburban community. *Journal of Sex Research, 2*, 1–24.

BRONFENBRENNER, U. (1960). Freudian theories of identification and their derivatives. *Child Development, 31* 15–40.

BROOK, J., WHITEMAN, M., & GORDON, A. (1983). Stages of drug use in adolescence: Personality, peer, and family correlates. *Developmental Psychology, 19*, 269–277.

BROOK, J., WHITEMAN, M., GORDON, A., & BROOK, D. (1984). Paternal determinants of female adolescent's marijuana use. *Developmental Psychology, 20*, 1032–1043.

BROOK, J., WHITEMAN, M., GORDON, A., & COHEN, P. (1986). Dynamics of childhood and adolescent personality traits and adolescent drug use. *Developmental Psychology, 22*, 403–414.

BROOKS-GUNN, J. (1986). Pubertal processes and girls' psychological adaptation. In R. M. Lerner, & T. T. Foch (Eds.), *Biological psychosocial interactions in early adolescence: A life-span perspective.* Hillsdale, NJ: Lawrence Erlbaum.

BROOKS-GUNN, J. (1987). Pubertal processes: Their relevance for developmental research. In V. B. Van Hasselt, & M. Hersen (Eds.), *Handbook of adolescent psychology.* New York: Pergamon Press.

BROOKS-GUNN, J., & RUBLE, D. (1982). The development of menstrual-related beliefs and behaviors during early adolescence. *Child Development, 53*, 1567–1577.

BROOKS-GUNN, J., & WARREN M. P. (1988). The psychological significance of secondary sexual characteristics in nine- to eleven-year-old girls. *Child Development, 59,* 1061–1069.

BROOKS-GUNN, J., & WARREN, M. P. (1989). Biological and social contributors to negative affect in young adolescent girls. *Child Development, 60,* 40–55.

BROUGHTON, J. (1982). Cognitive interaction and the development of sociality: A commentary on Damon and Killen. *Merrill Palmer Quarterly, 28,*369–378.

BROVERMAN, I., BROVERMAN, D., CLARKSON, F., ROSENKRANTZ, P., & VOGEL, S. (1970). Sex-role steroeotypes and clinical judgments of mental health. *Journal of Consulting and Clinical Psychology, 34,* 1–7.

BROVERMAN, I., VOGEL, S., BROVERMAN, D., CLARKSON, F., & ROSENKRANTZ, P. (1972). Sex-role stereotypes: A current appraisal. *Journal of Social Issues, 28,* 59–78.

BROWNSTONE. J. R. & WILLIS R. H (1971). Conformity in early and late adolescence. *Developmental Psychology, 4,* 334–337.

BUHRMESTER, D., & FURMAN, W. (1987). The development of companionship and intimacy. *Child Development, 58,* 1101–1113.

BURCHINAL, L. G. (1960). School policies and school age marriages. *Family Life Coordinator, 8,* 45–46.

BURCHINAL, L. G. (1964). Characteristics of adolescents from unbroken, broken, and reconstituted families. *Journal of Marriage and the Family, 26,* 44–51.

BURCHINAL, L. G. (1965). Trends and prospects for young marriages in the U. S. *Journal of Marriage and the Family, 27,* 243–254.

BURTON, N., & JONES, L. (1982). Recent trends in achievement levels of black and white youth. *Educational Researcher, 11,* 10–17.

BURTON, R. V. (1963). The generality of honesty reconsidered. *Psychological Review, 70,* 481–499.

BYNNER, J., O'MALLEY, P., & BACHMAN, J. (1981). Self-esteem and delinquency revisited. *Journal of Youth and Adolescence, 10,* 407–441.

BYRNE, D. (1974). The development of role taking in adolescence. *Dissertation Abstracts International, 34* (11), 5647B.

CALSYN, R., & KENNY, D. (1977). Self-concept of ability and perceived evaluation of others: Cause or effect of academic achievement? *Journal of Educational Psychology, 69,* 136–145.

CAMPBELL, E. Q. (1969). Adolescent socialization. In D. A. Goslin (Ed.), *Handbook of socialization theory and research.* Chicago: Rand McNally.

CAMPBELL, J. D. (1964). Peer relations in childhood. In M. L. Hoffman & L. W. Hoffman (Eds.), *Review of child development research* (Vol. 1). New York: Russell Sage Foundation.

CAPLAN, P. (1978, August). *Erikson's concept of inner space: A data-based reevaluation.* Paper presented at the Annual Meetings of the American Psychological Association, Toronto.

CAPLOW, T., & BAHR, H. (1979). Half a century of change in adolescent attitudes: Replication of a Middletown survey by the Lynds. *Public Opinion Quarterly, 43,* 1–17.

CARLSON, R. (1965). Stability and change in the adolescent's self-image. *Child Development, 36,* 659–666.

CARTER, D. B. (1987). The roles of peers in sex role acquisition. In D. B. Carter (Ed.), *Current conceptions of sex roles and sex typing.* New York: Praeger.

CARTER, D. B., & PATTERSON, C. (1982). Sex roles as social conventions: The development of children's conceptions of sex-role stereotypes. *Developmental Psychology, 18,* 812–824.

CAVOIR, N., & DOKECKI. P. R. (1973). Physical attractiveness, perceived attitude similarity and academic achievement as contributors to interpersonal attraction among adolescents. *Developmental Psychology, 9,* 44–54.

CENTERS FOR DISEASE CONTROL(1980). *Abortion survival.* Washington, DC: Department of Health, Education, and Welfare (Centers for Disease Control).

CERVANTES, L. F. (1965a). Family background, primary relationships, and the high school dropout. *Journal of Marriage and the Family, 5,* 218–223.

CERVANTES, L. F. (1965b). *The dropout: Causes and cures.* Ann Arbor: University of Michigan Press.

CHEN, C., & STEVENSON, H. W. (1989). Homework: A cross-cultural examination. *Child Development, 60,* 551–561.

CHILMAN, C. S. (1968, October). Families in development at mid-stage in the family life cycle. *Family Coordinator,* 297–313.

CHILMAN, C. S. (1973). Why do unmarried women fail to use contraceptives? *Medical Aspects of Human Sexuality, 7,* 167–168.

CHRISTENSEN, H. (1950). *Marriage analysis.* New York: Ronald Press.

CICIRELLI, V. (1972). The effect of sibling relationship on concept learning of young children taught by child-teachers. *Child Development, 43,* 282–287.

CLARK, M. L., & AYERS, M. (1988). The role of reciprocity and proximity in junior high school friendships. *Journal of Youth and Adolescence, 17,* 403–411.

CLAUSEN. J. A. (1975). The Social meaning of differential physical and sexual maturation. In S E Dragastin & G. H. Elder, Jr. (Eds.) *Adolescence in the life cycle.* New York: Halsted.

CLOWARD, R. (1968). Illegitimate means, anomie, and deviant behavior. In J. Short (Ed.), *Gang delinquency and delinquent behavior.* New York: Harper & Row.

CLOWARD, R., & OHLIN, L. E. (1960). *Delinquency and opportunity: A theory of delinquent gangs.* Glencoe, IL: The Free Press.

CLOWARD, R., & OHLIN, L. E. (1966). Illegitimate means, differential opportunity and delinquent subcultures. In R. Giallombardo (Ed.), *Juvenile delinquency: A book of readings.* New York: John Wiley & Sons.

COADY, H., & SAWYER, D. (1986). Moral judgment, sex, and level of temptation as determinants of resistance to temptation. *Journal of Psychology, 120,* 177–181.

COHEN, A. (1961). *Delinquent boys: The culture of the gang.* New York: The Free Press.

COIE, J., DODGE, K., & COPPOTELLI, H. (1982). Dimensions and types of social status: A cross-age perspective. *Developmental Psychology, 18,* 557–570.

COLBY, A., KOHLBERG, L., GIBBS, J., & LIEBERMAN, M. (1983). A longitudinal study of moral judgment. *Monographs of the Society for Research in Child Development, 48,* Serial No. 200.

COLEMAN, J., HOFFER, T., & KILGORE, S. (1981). *Public and private schools.* Washington, DC: U.S. Department of Education.

COLEMAN, J. C. (1978). Current contradictions in adolescent theory. *Journal of Youth and Adolescence, 7,* 1–11.

COLEMAN, J. C. (1980). Friendship and the peer group in adolescence. In J. Adelson (Ed.), *Handbook of adolescent psychology*. New York: John Wiley & Sons.

COLEMAN, J. C. (1989). *The nature of adolescence*. New York: Routledge, Chapman, & Hall, Publishers.

COLEMAN, J. S. (1960). The adolescent subculture and academic achievement. *American Journal of Sociology, 65,* 337–347.

COLEMAN, J. S. (1961). *The adolescent society*. New York: The Free Press.

COLEMAN, J. S. (1965). *Adolescents and the schools*. New York: Basic Books.

COLEMAN, J. S., CAMPBELL, E. Q., HOBSON, C. J., McPARTLAND, J., MOOD, A. M., WEINFIELD, F. D., & YORK, R. L. (1966). *Equality of educational opportunity*. Washington, DC: Government Printing Office.

COMBS, J., & COOLEY, W. W. (1968). Dropouts: In high school and after high school. *American Educational Research Journal, 5,* 343–363.

COMPAS, B. E. (1987). Coping with stress during childhood and adolescence. *Psychological Bulletin, 101,* 393–403.

COMPAS, B. E., & PHARES, V. (in press). Stress during childhood and adolescence: Sources of risk and vulnerability. In E. M. Cummings, A. L. Green, & K. H. Karraker (Eds.), *Lifespan developmental psychology: Perspectives on stress and coping*. Hillsdale, NJ: Lawrence Erlbaum.

CONGER, J. J. (1971, Fall). A world they never knew: The family and social change. *Daedalus,* 1105–1138.

CONGER, J. J. (1973). *Adolescence and youth: Psychological development in a changing world*. New York: Harper & Row.

CONGER, J. J., & MILLER, W. C. (1966). *Personality, social class, and delinquency*. New York: John Wiley & Sons.

CONGER, J. J., MILLER, W. C., & WALSMITH, C. R. (1965). Antecedents of delinquency, personality, social class and intelligence. In P. H. Mussen, J. J. Conger, & J. Kagan (Eds.), *Readings in child development and personality*. New York: Harper & Row.

CONNELL, E. B., DAVIS, J. E., GOLDZIEHER, J. W., & WALLACE, E. Z. (1971). *Hormones, sex, and happiness*. Chicago: Cowles.

CONNOLLY, J. (1989, April). *The adolescent peer group: Age-related changes in size, membership, and context*. Paper presented at the Biennial Meetings of the Society for Research in Child Development, Kansas City, MO.

CONNOLLY, J., WHITE, D., STEVENS, R., & BURSTEIN, S. (1987). Adolescent self-reports of social activity: Assessment of stability and relations to social adjustment. *Journal of Adolescence, 10,* 83–95.

CONSTANTINOPLE, A. (1969). An Eriksonian measure of personality development in college students. *Developmental Psychology, 1,* 357–372.

COOLEY, C. H. (1902). *Human nature and the social order*. New York: Scribner's.

COOLEY, C. H. (1909). *Social organization*. New York: Scribner's.

COOPERSMITH, S. (1967). *The antecedents of self-esteem*. San Francisco: W. H. Freeman.

CRESSEY, D. R., & WARD, D. A. (1969). *Delinquency, crime and social process*. New York: Harper & Row.

CRONBACH, L. J. (1970). *Essentials of psychological testing*. New York: Harper & Row.

CRNIC, L. S., & PENNINGTON, B. F. (1987). Developmental psychology and the neurosciences: An introduction. *Child Development, 58,* 533–538.

CROUTER, A. C., & McHALE, S. M. (1989, April). *Childrearing in dual- and single-earner families: Implications for the development of school-age children*. Paper presented at the Biennial Meetings of the Society for Research in Child Development, Kansas City, MO.

CULP, R. E., CULP, A. M., OSOFSKY, J. D., & OSOFSKY, H. J. (April, 1989). *Adolescent and older mothers: Comparison of their interaction with their six-month-old infants*. Paper presented at the Biennial Meetings of the Society for Research in Child Development, Kansas City, MO.

CURNEY, P. (1987). Self-esteem enhancement in children: A review of research findings. *Educational Research, 29,* 130–136.

CUTLER, JR., G. B., COMITE, F., RIVIER, J., VALE, W. W., LORIAUX, D. L., & CROWLEY, JR., W. F. (1983). Pituitary desensitization with a long-acting luteinizing-hormone-releasing hormone analog: A potential new treatment for idiopathic precocious puberty. In J. Brooks-Gunn & A. C. Petersen (Eds.), *Girls at puberty*. New York: Plenum Press.

DAMON, W., & HART, D. (1982). The development of self-understanding from infancy through adolescence. *Child Development, 53,* 841–864.

DAMON, W., & HART, D. (1988). *Self understanding in childhood and adolescence*. New York: Cambridge University Press.

DAMON, W., & KILLEN, M. (1982). Peer interaction and the process of change in children's moral reasoning. *Merrill Palmer Quarterly, 28,* 347–367.

DARWIN, C. R. (1859). *On the origin of species by means of natural selection*. London: J. Murray.

DAVIDSON, R. B., & HAVILAND, J. M. (1989a). *A review of the adolescent contraception literature: A developmental perspective on age and gender*. Unpublished manuscript, Rutgers University.

DAVIDSON, R. B., & HAVILAND, J. M. (April, 1989b). *A developmental approach to understanding and predicting adolescent contraception*. Paper presented at the Biennial Meetings of the Society for Research in Child Development, Kansas City, MO.

DAVIS, J. A. (1957). Correlates of sociometric status among peers. *Journal of Educational Research, 50,* 561–569.

DEARBORN, W. F., & RATHNEY, J. W. M. (1963). *Predicting the child's development* (2nd ed.). Cambridge, MA: Sci-Art.

DEJNOZKA, E. L. (1963). Schoolboard members: Their opinions, status, and financial willingness. *Journal of Educational Sociology, 36,* 193–199.

DeLAMATER, J., & MacCORQUODALE, P. (1979). *Premarital sexuality: Attitudes, relationships, behavior*. Madison: University of Wisconsin Press.

DELLA SELVA, P., & DUSEK, J. (1984). Sex role orientation and resolution of Eriksonian crises during the late adolescent years. *Journal of Personality and Social Psychology, 14,* 204–212.

DEMO, D., & SAVIN-WILLIAMS, R. (1983). Early adolescent self-esteem as a function of social class: Rosenberg and Pearlin revisited. *American Journal of Sociology, 88,* 763–774.

de VRIES, B., & WALKER, L. J. (1986). Moral reasoning and attitudes toward capital punishment. *Developmental Psychology, 22,* 509–513.

DICKSTEIN, E. (1977). Self and self-esteem: Theoretical foundations and their implications for research. *Human Development, 20,* 129–140.

DiCLEMENTE, R. J., PIES, C. A., STOLLER, E. J., STRAITS, C., OLIVIA, G. E., HASKIN, J., & RUTHERFORD, G. W. (1989). Evaluation of school-based AIDS education curricula in San Francisco. *Journal of Sex Research, 26,* 188–198.

DINITZ, S., SCARPITTI, F., & RECKLESS, W. (1962). Delinquency vulnerability: A cross group and longitudinal analysis. *American Sociological Review, 27,* 517–525.

DODGE, K. A. (1990a). Developmental psychopathology in children of depressed mothers. *Developmental Psychology, 26,* 3–6.

DODGE, K. A. (1990b). Special section: Developmental psychopathology in children of depressed mothers. *Developmental Psychology, 26,* 3–67.

DONENBERG, G. R., & HOFFMAN, L. (1988). Gender differences in moral development. *Sex Roles, 18,* 701–717.

DORNBUSCH, S., CARLSMITH, J., GROSS, R., MARTIN, J., JENNINGS, D., ROSENBERG, A., & DUKE, P. (1981). Sexual development, age, and dating: A comparison of biological and social influences upon one set of behaviors. *Child Development, 52,* 179–185.

DORNBUSCH, S. M., RITTER, P. L., LEIDERMAN, P. H., ROBERTS, D. F., & FRALEIGH, M. J. (1987). The relation of parenting style to adolescent school performance. *Child Development, 58,* 1244–1257.

DOUVAN, E. (1970). New sources of conflict in females at adolescence and early adulthood. In J. M. Bardwick (Ed.), *Feminine personality and conflict.* Belmont, CA: Brooks/Cole.

DOUVAN, E., & ADELSON, J. (1966). *The adolescent experience.* New York: John Wiley & Sons.

DRAGASTIN, S., & ELDER, G. (1975). *Adolescence in the life cycle.* New York: John Wiley & Sons.

DUDGEON, J. A. (1973). Breakdown in maternal protection: Infections. In L. J. Stone, H. T. Smith, & L. B. Murphy (Eds.), *The competent infant.* New York: Basic Books.

DULIT, E. (1972). Adolescent thinking a la Piaget: The formal stage. *Journal of Youth and Adolescence, 1,* 281–301.

DUNCAN, P. (1971). Parental attitudes and interactions in delinquency. *Child Development, 42,* 1751–1765.

DUNCAN, P., RITTER, P., DORNBUSCH, S., GROSS, R., & CARLSMITH, J., (1985). The effects of pubertal timing on body image, school behavior, and deviance. *Journal of Youth and Adolescence, 14,* 227–236.

DUNPHY, D. C. (1963). The social structure of urban adolescent peer groups. *Sociometry, 26,* 230–246.

DURKHEIM, E. (1951). *Suicide: A study of sociology.* New York: The Free Press. (J. A. Spaulding and G. Simpson Translation.) (Original work published 1897.)

DUSEK, J. B. (1971). Experimenter bias in performance of children at a simple metor task. *Developmental Psychology, 4,* 55–62.

DUSEK, J. B. (1975). Do teachers bias children's learning? *Review of Educational Research, 45,* 661–684.

DUSEK, J. B. (1978). *The development of the self-concept in adolescents.* (Final Report, Contract No. HD-09094). Washington, DC: National Institute of Education.

DUSEK, J. (1987). *Adolescent development and behavior.* Englewood Cliffs, NJ: Prentice-Hall.

DUSEK, J. B. (1987). Sex roles and adjustment. In D. B. Carter (Ed.), *Current conceptions of sex roles and sex typing.* New York: Praeger.

DUSEK, J. B., CARTER, D. B., & LEVY, G. (1986). The relationship between identity development and self-esteem during the late adolescent years: Sex differences. *Journal of Adolescent Research, 1,* 251–265.

DUSEK, J. B., & FLAHERTY, J. (1981). The development of the self-concept during the adolescent years. *Monographs of the Society for Research in Child Development, 46* (4, Whole No. 191), 1–61.

DUSEK, J. B., KERMIS, M., & MERGLER, N. (1975). Information processing in low- and high-test-anxious children as a function of grade level and verbal labeling. *Developmental Psychology, 11,* 651–652.

DUSEK, J. B., KERMIS, M., & MONGE, R. H. (1979). The hierarchy of adolescent interests: A social-cognitive approach. *Genetic Psychology Monographs, 100,* 41–72.

DUSEK, J. B., KLEMCHUK, H. P., HUTCHINSON, C. B., & BOCK, B. (1989). *Correlates of adjustment during the late adolescent years: Masculinity, femininity, and motivational needs.* Manuscript submitted for publication.

DUSEK, J. B., MERGLER, N., & KERMIS, M. (1976). Attention, encoding, and information processing in low- and high-test anxious children. *Child Development, 47,* 201–207.

DUSEK, J. B., & MONGE, R. H. (1974). *Communicating population control facts to adolescents.* (Final Report, contract No. R01-HD 06724). Washington, DC: National Institute of Child Health and Human Development, U.S. Department of Health, Education, and Welfare.

DYK, P. A., & ADAMS, G. R. (1987). The association between identity development and intimacy during adolescence: A theoretical treatise. *Journal of Adolescent Research, 2,* 223–235.

EASTMAN, W. F. (1972). First intercourse. *Sexual Behavior, 2,* 22–27.

EBATA, A. T., & MOOS, R. H. (1989; April). *Coping and adjustment in distressed and healthy adolescents.* Paper presented at the Biennial Meetings of the Society for Research in Child Development, Kansas City, MO.

ECCLES, J. S. (1987). Adolescence: Gateway to gender-role transcendence. In D. B. Carter (Ed.), *Current conceptions of sex roles and sex typing.* New York: Praeger.

ECCLES, J. S., JACOBS, J., HAROLD-GOLDSMITH, R., JAYARATNE, T., & YEE, D. (1989a). *The relations between parents' category-based and target-based beliefs: Gender roles and biological influences.* Paper presented at the Biennial Meetings of the Society for Research in Child Development, Kansas City, MO.

ECCLES, J., MIDGLEY, C., FELDLAUFER, H., WIGFIELD, A., REUMAN, D., & MACLVER, D. (1989b, April). *Student and classroom environment mismatch: Junior high school transition effects.* Paper presented at the Biennial Meetings of the Society for Research in Child Development, Kansas City, MO.

ECCLES, J., & WIGFIELD, A. (1985). Teacher expectations and student motivation. In J. Dusek (Ed.), *Teacher Expectancies* (pp. 185–226). Hillsdale, NJ: Lawrence Erlbaum.

EHRHARDT, A., & BAKER, S. (1973). *Hormonal aberrations and their implications for the understanding of normal sex differentiation.* Paper presented at the Biennial Meetings of the Society for Research in Child Development, Philadelphia.

EHRHARDT, A., & BAKER, S. (1974). Fetal androgens', human central nervous system differentiation, and behavior sex differences. In R. C. Friedman, R. M. Richart, & R. Vande Weile (Eds.), *Sex differences in behavior.* New York: John Wiley & Sons.

EHRHARDT, A., & MONEY, J. (1967). Progestin-induced hermaphroditism: IQ and psychosocial identity. *Journal of Sexual Research, 3,* 83–100.

EHRMANN, W. (1960). *Premarital dating behavior.* New York: Bantam Books.

EICHORN, D. (1963). Biological correlates of behavior. In H. W. Stevenson (Ed.), *Child psychology.* Chicago: University of Chicago Press.

EISEN, M., & ZELLMAN, G. L. (1987). Changes in incidence of sexual intercourse of unmarried teenagers following a community-based sex education program. *Journal of Sex Research, 23,* 527–533.

EISENTHAL, S., & UDIN, H. (1972). Psychological factors associated with drug and alcohol usage among neighborhood youth corps enrollees. *Developmental Psychology, 7,* 119–123.

EISERT, D., & KAHLE, L. (1982). Self-evaluation and social comparison of physical and role change during adolescence: A longitudinal analysis. *Child Development, 53,* 98–104.

ELDER, G. H., JR. (1962). Structural variations in the child-rearing relationship. *Sociometry, 25,* 241–262.

ELDER, G. H., JR. (1963). Parental power legitimation and its effects on the adolescent. *Sociometry, 26,* 50–65.

ELDER, G. H., JR. (1965). Family structure and educational attainment: A cross-national analysis. *American Sociological Review, 30,* 81–96.

ELDER, G. H., JR. (1968). Parent-youth relations in cross-national perspective. *Social Science Quarterly, 49,* 216–228.

ELDER, G. H., JR. (1971). *Adolescent socialization and personality development.* Chicago: Rand McNally.

ELDER, G. H., JR. (1974). *Children of the great depression.* Chicago: University of Chicago Press.

ELDER, G. H., JR. (1980). Adolescence in historical perspective. In J. Adelson (Ed.), *Handbook of adolescent psychology.* New York: John Wiley & Sons.

ELIAS, J., & GEBHARD, P. (1969). Sexuality and sexual learning in childhood. *Phi Delta Kappan, 50,* 401–406.

ELKIND, D. (1967a). Cognitive structure and adolescent experience. *Adolescence, 2,* 427–434.

ELKIND, D. (1967b). Egocentrism in adolescence. *Child Development, 38,* 1025–1034.

ELKIND, D. (1968). Cognitive development in adolescence. In J.F. Adams (Ed.), *Understanding adolescence.* Boston: Allyn & Bacon.

ELKIND, D. (1969). Piagetian and psychometric conceptions of intelligence. In *Environment, heredity and intelligence. (Harvard Educational Review).* 171–189.

ELKIND, D. (1970). *Children and adolescents: Interpretive essays on Jean Piaget.* New York: Oxford University Press.

ELKIND, D. (1978a). *The child's reality: Three developmental themes.* Hillsdale, NJ: Lawrence Erlbaum.

ELKIND, D. (1978b). Understanding the young adolescent. *Adolescence. 13,* 127–134.

ELKIND, D. (1985). Egocentrism redux. *Developmental Review, 5,* 218–226.

ELKIND, D., & BOWEN, R. (1979). Imaginary audience behavior in children and adolescents. *Developmental Psychology, 15,* 38–44.

ELLIOTT, D. S., & AGETON, S. S. (1980). Reconciling race and class differences in self-reported and official estimates of delinquency. *American Sociological Review, 45,* 95–110.

ELLIOTT, D. S., VOSS, H. L., & WENDLING, A. (1960). Capable dropouts and the social milieu of the high school. *Journal of Educational Research, 60,* 180–186.

ELSTER, A. B., LAMB, M. E., & TAVARE, J. (1987). Association between behavioral and school problems and fatherhood in a national sample of adolescent youths. *The Journal of Pediatrics, 111,* 932–936.

EMMERICH, W. (1973). Socialization and sex-role development. In P. B. Baltes & K. W. Schaie (Eds.), *Life-span developmental psychology: Personality and socialization.* New York: Academic Press.

EMMERICH, W. (1974). Developmental trends in evaluations of single traits. *Child Development, 45,* 173–183.

EMPEY, L. T. (1956). Social class and occupational aspiration: A comparison of absolute and relative measurement. *American Sociological Review, 21,* 703–708.

ENGEL, M. (1959). The stability of the self-concept in adolescence. *Journal of Abnormal and Social Psychology, 58,* 211–215.

ENRIGHT, R., LAPSLEY, D., & SHUKLA, D. (1979). Adolescent egocentrism in early and late adolescence. *Adolescence, 14,* 687–695.

ENRIGHT, R., & SUTTERFIELD, S. (1980). An ecological validation of social cognition development. *Child Development, 51,* 156–161.

EPPERSON, D. C. (1964). A reassessment of indices of parental influence in "the adolescent society." *American Sociological Review, 29,* 93–96.

EPSTEIN, L. H. (1987). Behavioral treatment of childhood obesity. *Psychological Bulletin, 101,* 331–342.

EPSTEIN, S. (1973). The self-concept revisited: Or a theory of a theory. *American Psychologist, 28,* 404–416.

ERIKSON, E. (1951). Sex differences in the play configurations of preadolescents. *American Journal of Orthopsychiatry, 21,* 667–692.

ERIKSON, E. (1959). Identity and the life cycle. *Psychological Issues, 1,* 1–71.

ERIKSON, E. (1963). *Childhood and society* (2nd ed.). New York: W. W. Norton & Co., Inc.

ERIKSON, E. (1964). *Insight and responsibility.* New York: W. W. Norton & Co., Inc.

ERIKSON, E. (1968). *Identity, youth, and crisis.* New York W. W. Norton & Co., Inc.

ERLENMEYER-KIMLING, L., & JARVIK, L. F. (1963). Genetics and intelligence. *Science, 142,* 1477–1479.

ERON, L., HUESMANN, L., BRICE, P., FISCHER, P., & MERMELSTEIN, R. (1983). Age trends in the development of aggression, sex-typing, and related television habits. *Developmental Psychology, 19,* 71–77.

FAGOT, B. I., & LEINBACH, M. D. (1987). Socialization of sex roles within the family. In D. B. Carter (Ed.), *Current conceptions of sex roles and sex typing.* New York: Praeger.

FAGOT, B. I., & LEINBACH, M. D. (1989). The young child's gender schema: Environmental input, internal organization. *Child Development, 60,* 663–672.

FANTINI, M. (1973). Alternatives within public schools. *Phi Delta Kappan, 54,* 444–449.

FARNWORTH, M. (1984). Family structure, family attributes, and delinquency in a sample of flow-income, minority males and females. *Journal of Youth and Adolescence, 13,* 349–364. 227

FAUST, M. S. (1977). Somatic development of adolescent girls. *Monographs of the Society for Research in Child Development, 42* (169).

FEATHER, N. (1975). *Values in education and society.* New York: The Free Press.

FEATHER, N. (1980). Values in adolescence. In J. Adelson (Ed.), *Handbook of adolescent psychology* (pp. 247–294). New York: John Wiley & Sons.

FEINBERG, M. R., SMITH, M., & SCHMIDT, R. (1958). An analysis of expressions used by adolescents of varying economic levels to describe accepted and rejected peers. *Journal of Genetic Psychology, 93,* 133–148.

FEINGOLD, A. (1988). Cognitive gender differences are disappearing. *American Psychologist, 43,* 95–103.

FELDMAN, S. S., WENTZEL, K. R., WEINBERGER, D., & MUNSON, J. A. (1989, April). *Marital satisfaction of parents of preadolescent boys and its relationship to family and child functioning.* Paper presented at the Biennial Meetings of the Society for Research in Child Development, Kansas City, MO.

FENZEL, L. M. (1989a, April). *The transition to middle school: Longitudinal trends and sex differences in student role strains.* Paper presented at the Biennial Meetings of the Society for Research in Child Development, Kansas City, MO.

FENZEL, L. M. (1989b, April). *An ecological study of changes in student role strains during the transition to middle school.* Paper presented at the Biennial Meetings of the Society for Research in Child Development, Kansas City, MO.

FILSINGER, E. (1980). Difference between own and friend's social status as a predictor of psychological differentiation. *Psychological Reports, 45,* 187–195.

FILSINGER, E., & ANDERSON, C. (1982). Social class and self-esteem in late adolescence: Dissonant context or self-efficacy? *Developmental Psychology, 18,* 380–384.

FITZGERALD, T. H. (1973, November). Career education: An error whose time has come. *School Review,* 91–105.

FLAHERTY J., & DUSEK, J. (1980). An investigation of the relationship between psychological androgyny and components of self-concept. *Journal of Personality and Social Psychology, 38,* 984–992.

FLANAGAN, C. (1989, April). *Economic stress in the family: Do the effects for daughters and sons differ?* Paper presented at the Biennial Meetings of the Society for Research in Child Development, Kansas City, MO.

FLAVELL, J. H. (1963). *The developmental psychology of Jean Piaget.* Princeton, NJ: Van Nostrand Reinhold.

FLAVELL, J. H. (1977). *Cognitive psychology.* Englewood Cliffs, NJ: Prentice-Hall.

FLAVELL, J. H. (1982). On cognitive development. *Child Development, 53,* 1–10.

FLOYD, H. H., JR., & SOUTH, D. R. (1972). Dilemma of youth: The choice of parents or peers as a frame of reference for behavior. *Journal of Marriage and the Family, 34,* 627–634.

FODOR, E. M. (1972). Delinquency and susceptibility to social influence among adolescents as a function of level of moral development. *Journal of Social Psychology, 66,* 257–260.

FORD, C. S., & BEACH, F. A. (1951). *Patterns of sexual behavior.* New York: Harper-Hoeber.

FORD, M. (1982). Social cognition and social competence in adolescence. *Developmental Psychology, 18,* 323–340.

FREEBERG, N. E., & ROCK, D. A. (1973). Dimensional continuity of interests and activities during adolescence. *Human Development, 16,* 304–316.

FREEMAN, D. (1983). *Margaret Mead and Somoa: The making and unmaking of an anthropological myth.* Cambridge, MA: Harvard University Press.

FREUD, A. (1948). *The ego and the mechanisms of defense* (C. Baines, Trans.). New York: International Universities Press.

FREUD, A. (1958). Adolescence. In R. Eissler, A. Freud, H. Hartman, & M. Kris (Eds.), *Psychoanalytic study of the child* (Vol. 13). New York: International Universities Press.

FREUD, S. (1924). The passing of the Oedipal complex. In *Collected papers* (Vol. 2). London: Hogarth Press.

FREUD, S. (1930). *Three contributions to the theory of sex.* New York: Nervous and Mental Disease Publishing Co.

FREUD, S. (1935). *A general introduction to psychoanalysis.* New York: Liveright.

FREUD, S. (1950). *The ego and the id.* London: Hogarth Press. (Original published work in 1923).

FRIEDMAN, W. J., ROBINSON, A. B., & FRIEDMAN, B. L. (1987). Sex differences in moral judgments? A test of Gilligan's theory. *Psychology of Women Quarterly, 11,* 37–46.

FRIESEN, D. (1968). Academic-athletic-popularity syndrome in the Canadian high school society. *Adolescence, 3,* 39–52.

FRISH, R. E. (1974). Critical weight at menarche, initiation of the adolescent growth spurt, and control of puberty. In M. M. Grumbach, G. D. Grave, & F. E. Mayer (Eds.), *Control of the onset of puberty.* New York: John Wiley & Sons.

FRISH, R. E. (1983). Fatness, puberty, and fertility: The effects of nutrition and physical training on menarche and ovulation. In J. Brooks-Gunn & A. C. Petersen (Eds.), *Girls at puberty.* New York: Plenum Press.

FRISK, M., TENHUNEN, T., WIDHOLM, O., & HORTLING, H. (1966). Psychological problems in adolescents showing advanced or delayed physical maturation. *Adolescence, 1,* 126–140.

FURMAN, W. (1989). The development of children's social networks. In D. Belle (Ed.), *Children's social networks and social supports.* New York: John Wiley & Sons.

FURTH, H., & McCONVILLE, K. (1981). Adolescent understanding of compromise in political and social arenas. *Merrill Palmer Quarterly, 27,* 413–427.

FURSTENBERG, F., JR., BROOKS-GUNN, J., & MORGAN, S. (1987). *Adolescent mothers in later life.* New York: Cambridge University Press.

FURSTENBERG, F., PETERSON, J., NORD, C., & ZILL, N. (1983). The life course of children of divorce: Marital disruption and parental contact. *American Sociological Review, 48,* 656–668.

GAGNON, J. H., & SIMON, W. (1969). They're going to learn in the street anyway. *Psychology Today, 3,* 46–47.

GALLATIN, J. (1980). Political thinking in adolescence. In J. Adelson (Ed.), *Handbook of adolescent psychology* (pp. 344–382). New York: John Wiley & Sons.

GALLUP, G., & POLING, D. (1980). *The search for America's faith.* New York: Abington.

GALTON, F. (1883). *Inquiries into human faculty and its development.* London: Macmillan.

GAVIN, L. A., & FURMAN, W. (1989). Age differences in adolescents' perceptions of their peer groups. *Developmental Psychology, 25,* 827–834.

GERRARD, M. (1987). Sex, sex guilt, and contraceptive use revisited: The 1980s. *Journal of Personality and Social Psychology, 52,* 975–980,

GEWIRTZ, J. L. (1969). Mechanisms of social learning: Some roles of stimulation and behavior in early human development. In D. A. Goslin (Ed.), *Handbook of socialization theory and research.* Chicago: Rand McNally.

GEWIRTZ, J. L., & STINGLE, K. G. (1968). The learning of generalized imitation as the basis for identification. *Psychological Review, 75,* 374–397.

GILLIGAN, C. (1982). *In a different voice.* Cambridge, MA: Harvard University Press.

GILLIGAN, C., & ATTANUCCI, J. (1988). Much ado about . . . knowing? Noting? Nothing? A reply to Vasudev concerning sex differences and moral development. *Merrill Palmer Quarterly, 34,* 451–456.

GINZBERG, E. (1972). Toward a theory of occupational choice: A restatement. *Vocational Guidance Quarterly, 20,* 169–176.

GINZBERG, E., GINZBERG, S. W., AXELROD, S., & HERMAN, S. L. (1951). *Occupational choice.* New York: Columbia University Press.

GLASSER, P., & NAVARRE, E. (1965). Structural problems of the one-parent family. *Journal of Social Issues, 21,* 98–109.

GLAZER, C., & DUSEK, J. (1985). The relationship between sex-role orientation and resolution of the Eriksonian developmental crises. *Sex Roles.*

GLICK, P. (1979). Children of divorced parents in demographic perspective. *Journal of Social Issues, 35,* 170–182.

GLOVER, R. J., & STEELE, C. (1988/89). Comparing the effects on the child of post-divorce parenting arrangements. *Journal of Divorce, 12,* 185–201.

GLUECK, S., & GLUECK, E. T. (1950). *Unraveling juvenile delinquency.* New York: Commonwealth Fund.

GLUECK, S., & GLUECK, E. T. (1962). *Family environment and delinquency.* Boston: Houghton Mifflin.

GLUECK, S., & GLUECK, E. T. (1968). *Delinquents and non delinquents in perspective.* Cambridge, MA: Harvard University Press.

GOLD, D., & ANDRES, D. (1978a). Developmental comparisons between adolescent children with employed and nonemployed mothers. *Merrill Palmer Quarterly, 24,* 243–254.

GOLD, D., & ANDRES, D. (1978b). Developmental comparisons between 10-year-old children with employed and nonemployed mothers. *Child Development, 49,* 75–84.

GOLD, D., & ANDRES, D. (1978c). Relations between maternal employment and development of nursery school children. *Canadian Journal of Behavioural Science, 10,* 116–129.

GOLD, J. J. (1968). *Textbook of gynecologic endocrinology.* New York: Harper & Row.

GOLD, M. (1970). *Delinquent behavior in an American city.* Belmont, CA: Brooks/Cole.

GOLD, M., & DOUVAN, E. (1969). *Adolescent development.* Boston: Allyn & Bacon.

GOLD, M., & PETRONIO, R. J. (1980). Delinquent behavior in adolescence. In J. Adelson (Ed.), *Handbook of adolescent psychology* (pp. 495–535). New York: John Wiley & Sons.

GOLD, M., & REIMER, D. J. (1975). Changing patterns of delinquent behavior among Americans 13 through 16 years old: 1967–1972. *Crime and Delinquency Literature, 7* 483–517.

GOLDBERG, S., BLUMBERG, S., & KRIGER, A. (1982). Menarche and interest in infants: Biological and social influences. *Child Development, 53,* 1544–1550.

GORMAN, B. W. (1972). Change in the secondary school: Why and how. *Phi Delta Kappan, 53,* 565–568.

GOSLIN, D. A. (1969). Introduction. In D. A. Goslin (Ed.), *Handbook of socialization theory and research.* Chicago: Rand McNally.

GOTTMAN, J. (1983). How children become friends. *Monographs of the Society for Research in Child Development, 48* (Whole No. 201).

GRABE, M. (1981). School size and the importance of school activities. *Adolescence, 16,* 21–31.

GRANICK, S. (1966). *Emotional distress in ghetto delinquents. A report from comparison of three treatment models in delinquency* (Project D-282 DHEW). Washington, DC: Department of Health, Education, and Welfare.

GREEN, R. (1980). Homosexuality. In H. Kaplan, A. Freedman, & B. Sadock (Eds.), *Comprehensive textbook of psychiatry* (Vol. 2) (3rd ed.). Baltimore: Williams & Wilkins.

GREEN, R. (1987). *The 'sissy boy' syndrome and the development of homosexuality.* New Haven, CT: Yale University Press.

GREENBERGER, E., & STEINBERG, L. D., (Final Report). *Part-time employment of in-school youth: An assessement of costs and benefits.* Washington, DC: National Institute of Education.

GREENBERGER, E., & STEINBERG, L. D. (1981). The workplace as a context for the socialization of youth. *Journal of Youth and Adolescence, 10,* 185–211.

GREENBERGER, E., & STEINBERG, L. D. (1983). Sex differences in early labor force experience: Harbinger of things to come. *Social Forces,* 467–486.

GREENBERGER, E., & STEINBERG, L. D., & RUGGIERO, M. A. (1982). A job is a job is a job . . . or is it? *Work and Occupations, 9,* 79–96.

GREENBERGER, E., STEINBERG, L., & VAUX, A. (1981). Adolescents who work: Health and behavioral consequences of job stress. *Developmental Psychology, 17,* 691–703.

GREENBERGER, E., STEINBERG, L. D., VAUX, A., & McAULIFFE, S. (1980). Adolescents who work: Effects of part-time employment on family and peer relations. *Journal of Youth and Adolescents, 9,* 189–202.

GREENBERGER, J. W., GERVER, J. M., CHALL, J., & DAVIDSON, H. H. (1965). Attitudes of children from a deprived environment toward achievement-related concepts. *Journal of Educational Research, 59,* 57–62.

GREENWALD, H. (1970). Marriage as a non-legal voluntary association. In H. A. Otto (Ed.), *The family in search of a future.* New York: Appleton-Century Crofts.

GREIF, E., & ULMAN, K. (1982). The psychological impact of menarche on early adolescent females: A review of the literature. *Child Development, 53,* 1413–1430.

GRIBBONS, W. D., & LOHNES, P. R. (1966). Occupational preferences and measured intelligence. *The Vocational Guidance Quarterly, 14*, 211–214.

GRIFFITHS, T., DUSEK, J. B., & CAREY, M. P. (1988, April). *Masculinity and femininity ratings of items from the Beck Depression Inventory.* Poster presented at the meting of the Eastern Psychological Association, Buffalo, NY.

GRIGG, C. M., & MIDDLETON, R. (1968). Community of orientation and occupational aspirations of ninth-grade students. *Social Forces, 38*, 303–308.

GRINDER, R. E. (1966). Relations of social dating attractions to academic orientation and peer relations. *Journal of Educational Psychology, 57*, 27–34.

GRINDER, R.E. (1969). Distinctiveness and thrust in the American youth culture. *Journal of Social Issues, 25*, 7–20.

GROFF, P. J. (1962). The social status of teachers. *Journal of Educational Sociology, 36*, 20–25.

GROLNICK, W. S., & RYAN, R. M. (1989). Parent styles associated with children's self-regulation and competence in school. *Journal of Educational Psychology, 81*, 143–154.

GRONLUND, N. E., & ANDERSON, L. 1957). Personality characteristics of socially accepted, socially neglected, and socially rejected junior high school pupils. *Educational Administration and Supervision, 43*, 329–338.

GROSSMAN, B., & WRIGHTER, J. (1948). The relationship between social rejection and intelligence, social status, and personality among sixth-grade children. *Sociometry, 11*, 346–355.

GROTEVANT, H. D. (1986). Assessment of identity development: Current issues and future directions. *Journal of Adolescent Research, 1*, 175–182.

GROTEVANT, H. D. (1987). Toward a process model of identity formation. *Journal of Adolescent Research, 2*, 203–222.

GROTEVANT, H., SCARR, S., & WEINBERG, R. (1977). Patterns of interest similarity in adoptive and biological families. *Journal of Personality and Social Psychology, 35*, 667–676.

GROTEVANT, H., & THORNBECKE, W. (1982). Sex differences in styles of occupational identity formation in late adolescence. *Developmental Psychology, 18*, 396–405.

GROTEVANT, J. THORNBECKE, W., & MEYER, M. (1982). An extension of Marcia's identity status interview into the interpersonal domain. *Journal of Youth and Adolescence, 11*, 33–47.

GRUMBACH, M. M., GRAVE, G. D., & MAYER, F. E. (Eds.), (1974a). *Control of the onset of puberty.* New York: John Wiley & Sons.

GRUMBACH, M. M., ROTH, J. C., KAPLAN, S. L., & KELCH, R. P. (1974b). Hypothalamic-pituitary regulation of puberty: Evidence and concepts derived from clinical research. In M. M. Grumbach, G. D. Grave, & F. E. Mayer (Eds.), *Control of the onset of puberty,* New York: John Wiley & Sons.

GUARDO, E., & BOHAN, J. (1971). Development of a sense of self-identity in children. *Child Development, 42*, 1909–1921.

GUILFORD, J. P. (1966). Intelligence: 1965 model. *American Psychologist, 21*, 20–25.

GUILFORD, J. P. (1967). *The nature of human intelligence.* New York: McGraw-Hill.

GUMP, P. V. (1966). *Big schools, small schools.* Moravia, NY: Chronicle Guidance Publications.

GUTTMAN, J. (1988/89). Intimacy in young adult males' relationships as a function of divorced and non-divorced family of origin status. *Journal of Divorce, 12*, 253–261.

HAAS, A. (1979). *Teenage sexuality.* New York: Macmillan.

HALL, G. S. (1904). *Adolescence* (2 Vols.). New York: Appleton.

HALLWORTH, H. J., DAVIS, H. & GAMSTON, C. (1965). Some adolescents' perceptions of adolescent personality. *Journal of Social and Clinical Psychology, 4*, 81–91.

HALMI, K. A. (1987). Anorexia nervosa and bulimia. In V. B. Van Hasselt & M. Hersen (Eds.), *Handbook of adolescent psychology.* New York: Pergamon Press.

HAMBURG, D., & TAKANISHI, R. (1989). Preparing for life: The critical transition of adolescence. *American Psychologist, 44*, 825–827.

HAMILTON, S. F., & CROUTER, A. C. (1980). Work and growth: A review of research on the impact of work experience on adolescent development. *Journal of Youth and Adolescence, 9*, 323–338.

HARRIS, C. (1963). *Problems in measuring change.* Madison: University of Wisconsin Press.

HARRIS, D. (1959). Sex differences in the life problems and interests of adolescents. *Child Development, 30*, 453–459.

HARRIS, L. (1969). What people think of their high school (a survey). *Life, 66*, 22–23.

HARRIS L. (1971). Change, yes—upheaval, no. *Life, 70*, 22–27.

HARTER, S. (1986). Processes underlying the construction, maintenance, and enhancement of the self-concept in children. In J. Suls. & A. G. Greenwald (Eds.), *Psychological perspectives on the self* (Vol. 3). Hillsdale, NJ: Lawrence Erlbaum.

HARTER, S. (1989). Processes underlying adolescent self-concept formation. In R. Montemayor (Ed.), *Advances in adolescent development: Vol. 2. The transition from Childhood to adolescence.* New York: Russel Sage Foundation.

HARTLEY, M. C., & HOY, W. K. (1972). Openness of school climate and alienation of high school students. *California Journal of Educational Research, 23*, 17–24.

HARTSHORNE, H., & MAY, M. S. (1928–1930). *Studies in the nature of character: Vol. 1, Studies in deceit: Vol. 2, Studies in self-control: Vol. 3, Studies in the organization of character.* New York: Macmillan.

HARTUP, W. W. (1970a). Peer interaction and social organization. In P. H. Mussen (Ed.), *Carmichael's manual of child psychology.* New York: John Wiley & Sons.

HARTUP, W. W. (1970b). Peer relations. In T. D. Spencer & N. Kass (Eds), *Perspectives in child psychology.* New York: McGraw-Hill.

HARTUP, W. W. (1989). Social relationships and their developmental significance. *American Psychologist, 44*, 120–126.

HARTUP, W. W., GLAZER, J. A., & CHARLESWORTH, R. (1967). Peer reinforcement and sociometric status. *Child Development, 38*, 1017–1024.

HARTUP, W. W., & LAURSEN, B. (1989, April). *Contextual constraints and children's friendship relations.* Paper presented at the Biennial Meetings of the Society for Research in Child Development, Kansas City, MO.

HAVIGHURST, R.J. (1951). *Developmental tasks and education.* New York: Longmans, Green.

HAVIGHURST, R. J. (1964). Youth in exploration and man emergent. In H. Borow (Ed.), *Man in a world at work.* Boston: Houghton Mifflin.

HAVIGHURST, R. J. (1972). *Developmental tasks and education* (3rd ed.). New York: David McKay.

HAVIGHURST, R. J. (1978). Common experience versus diversity in the curriculum. *Educational Leadership, 36,* 118–121.

HAWLEY, P. (1972). Perceptions of male models of femininity related to career choice. *Journal of Counseling Psychology, 19,* 308–313.

HAY, D., & O'BRIEN, J. (1983). The La Trobe twin study: A genetic approach to the structure and development of cognition in twin children. *Child Development, 54,* 317–330.

HEBBELINCK, M. (1977). Biological aspects of development at adolescence. In J. P. Hill & F. J. Monks (Eds.), *Adolescence and youth in prospect.* Surrey, England: IPC Science and Technology Press.

HELLER, K., & PARSONS, J. (1981). Sex differences in teachers' evaluative feedback and students' expectancies for success in mathematics. *Child Development, 52,* 1015–1019.

HENSHAW, S. K. (1987). Characteristics of U.S. women having abortions, 1982–1983. *Family Planning Perspectives, 19,* 5–9.

HEROLD, E. S. (1973). A dating adjustment scale for college students. *Adolescence, 8,* 51–60.

HEROLD, E. S. (1974). Stages of date selection: A reconciliation of divergent findings on campus values in dating. *Adolescence, 9,* 113–120.

HETHERINGTON, E. M. (1966). Effects of paternal absence on sex-typed behaviors in Negro and white predolsecent males. *Journal of Personality and Social Psychology, 4,* 87–91.

HETHERINGTON, E. M. (1972). Effects of father absence on personality development in adolescent daughters. *Developmental Psychology, 7,* 313–326.

HETHERINGTON, E. M. (1979). Divorce: A child's perspective. *American Psychologist, 34,* 851–858.

HETHERINGTON, E. M. (1989). Coping with family transitions: Winners, losers, and survivors. *Child Development, 60,* 1–14.

HETHERINGTON, E. M., Cox, M., & Cox, R. (1976). Divorced fathers. *Family Coordinator, 25,* 417–428.

HETHERINGTON, E. M., Cox, M., & Cox, R. (1979a). The development of children in mother headed families. In D. Reiss & H. Hoffman (Eds.), *The American family: Dying or developing.* New York: Plenum Press.

HETHERINGTON, E. M., Cox, M., & Cox, R. (1979b). Family interactions and the social emotional and cognitive development of children following divorce. In V. C. Vaughan & T. B. Brazelton (Eds.), *The family: Setting priorities.* New York: Science and Medicine.

HETHERINGTON, E. M., Cox, M., & Cox, R. (1979c). Stress and coping in divorce. A focus on women. In J. Gullahorn (Ed.), *Psychology and women in transition.* New York: B. H. Winston & Sons.

HETHERINGTON, E. M., Cox, M., & Cox, R. (1985). Long-term effects of divorce and remarriage on the adjustment of children. *Journal of the American Academy of Child Psychiatry, 24,* 518–530.

HETHERINGTON, E. M., STOUWIE, R., & RIDBERG, E. (1971). Patterns of family interaction and child-rearing attitudes related to three dimensions of juvenile delinquency. *Journal of Abnormal Psychology, 78,* 160–176.

HIGGINS, A., POWER, C., & KOHLBERG, L. (1983, April). *Moral atmosphere and moral judgment.* Paper presented at the Biennial Meetings of the Society for Research in Child Development, Detroit.

HIGHAM, E. (1980). Variations in adolescent psychohormonal development. In J. Adelson (Ed.), *Handbook of adolescent psychology.* New York: John Wiley & Sons.

HILL, J. (1980). The family. In M. Johnson (Ed.), *Toward adolescence: The middle school years. The 79th yearbook of the National Society for the Study of Education: Part I.* Chicago: University of Chicago Press.

HILL, J., & MONKS, F. (1977). *Adolescence and youth in prospect.* Surrey, England: IPC Science and Technology Press.

HILL, C., RUBIN, Z., & PEPLAU, L. (1979). Breakups before marriage: The end of 103 affairs. In G. Levinger & O. Moles (Eds.), *Divorce and separation.* New York: Basic Books.

HILL, J., HOLMBECK, G., MARLOW, L., GREEN, T., & LYNCH, M. (1985a). Pubertal status and parent-child relations in families of seventh-grade boys. *Journal of Early Adolescence, 5,* 31–44.

HILL, J., HOLMBECK, G., MARLOW, L., GREEN, T., & Lynch, M. (1985b). Menarcheal status and parent-child relations in families of seventh-grade girls. *Journal of Youth and Adolescence, 14,* 301–316.

HIRSCH, B. J., & Rapkin, B. D. (1987). The transition to junior high school: A longitudinal study of self-esteem, psychological symptomatology, school life, and social support. *Child Development, 58,* 1235–1243.

HODGSON, J., & FISCHER, J. (1979). Sex differences in identity and intimacy development in college youth. *Journal of Youth and Adolescence, 8,* 37–50.

HOFFERTH, S. L., KAHN, J. R., & BALDWIN, W. (1987). Premarital sexual activity among U.S. teenage women over the past three decades. *Family Planning Perspectives, 19,* 46–53.

HOFFMAN, L. (1961). Mothers' enjoyment of work and effects on the child. *Child Development, 32,* 187–197.

HOFFMAN, L. (1974). Effects of maternal employment on the child—A review of the research. *Developmental Psychology, 10,* 204–228.

HOFFMAN, L. (1977). Changes in family roles, socialization, and sex differences. *American Psychologist, 32,* 644–657.

HOFFMAN, L. (1979). Maternal employment: 1979. *American Psychologist, 34.* 859–865.

HOFFMAN, L. (1980). The effects of maternal employment on the academic attitudes and performance of school-aged children. *School Psychology Review, 9,* 319–335.

HOFFMAN, L. W. (1989). Effects of maternal employment in the two-parent family. *American Psychologist, 44,* 283–292.

HOFFMAN, M. L. (1970). Moral development. In P. H. Mussen (Ed.), *Carmichael's manual of child psychology* (Vol. 2, 3rd ed.). New York: John Wiley & Sons.

HOFFMAN, M. L. (1977). Sex differences in empathy and related behaviors. *Psychological Bulletin, 28,* 295–321.

HOFFMAN, M. L. (1980). Moral development in adolescence. In J. Adelson (Ed.), *Handbook of adolescent psychology.* New York: John Wiley & Sons.

HOFFMAN, M. L. & SALTZSTEIN, H. D. (1967). Parent discipline and the child's moral development. *Journal of Personality and Social Psychology, 5,* 45–57.

HOLAHAN, C. J., & MOOS, R. H. (1987). Personal and contextual determinants of coping strategies. *Journal of Personality and Social Psychology, 52*, 946–955.

HOLLAND, J. L. (1958). A personality inventory employing occupational titles. *Journal of Applied Psychology, 42*, 336–342.

HOLLAND, J. L. (1959). A theory of vocational choice. *Journal of Counseling Psychology, 6*, 35–45.

HOLLAND, J. L. (1964). Major programs of research on vocational behavior. In H. Borow (Ed.), *Man in a world at work.* Boston: Houghton Mifflin.

HOLLAND, J. L. (1971). *A counselor's guide for use with the Self-Directed Search: A guide to educational and vocational planning.* Palo Alto, CA: Consulting Psychologists Press.

HOLLAND, J. L. (1973). *Making vocational choices: A theory of careers.* Englewood Cliffs, NJ: Prentice-Hall.

HOLLINGSHEAD, A. B. (1949). *Elmtown's youth.* New York: John Wiley & Sons.

HONZIK, M. P., MACFARLANE, J. W., & ALLEN, L. (1948). The stability of mental test performance between two and eighteen years. *Journal of Experimental Education, 17*, 309–324.

HOOD, J., MOORE, T. E., & GARNER, D. (1982). Locus of control as a measure of ineffectiveness in anorexia nervosa. *Journal of Consulting and Clinical Psychology, 50*, 3–13.

HOPS, H., SHERMAN, L., & BIGLAN, A. (in press). Maternal depression, marital discord, and children's behavior: A developmental perspective. In G. R. Patterson (Ed.), *Depression and aggression in family interactions.* New York: Lawrence Erlbaum.

HORN, J. L. (1968). Organization of abilities and the development of intelligence. *Psychological Review, 75*, 242–259.

HORN, J. L., & CATTELL, R. B. (1966). Age differences in primary ability factors. *Journal of Gerontology, 21*, 210–220.

HOROWITZ, H. (1967). Prediction of adolescent popularity and rejection from achievement and interest tests. *Journal of Educational Psychology, 58*, 170–174.

HORROCKS, J. E., & BENIMOFF, M. (1967). Isolation from the peer group during adolescence. *Adolescence, 2*, 41–52.

HORROCKS, J. E., & THOMPSON, G. A. (1946). A study of the friendship fluctuations of rural boys and girls. *Journal of Genetic Psychology, 69*, 189–198.

HOWARD, L. (1960). Identity conflicts in adolescent girls. *Smith College Studies in Social Work, 31*, 1–21.

HOWAT, P. M., & SAXTON, A. M. (1988). The incidence of bulimic behavior in a secondary and university school population. *Journal of Youth and Adolescence, 17*, 221–231.

HOY, W. K. (1972). Dimensions of student alienation and characteristics of public high schools. *Interchange, 3*, 38–52.

HRABA, J., & GRANT, G. (1970). Black is beautiful: A reexamination of racial preference and identification. *Journal of Personality and Social Psychology, 16*, 398–402.

HUNT, M. (1970, July). Special sex education survey. *Seventeen,* 94ff.

HUNTER, F., & YOUNISS, J. (1982). Changes in functions of three relations during adolescence. *Developmental Psychology, 18*, 806–811.

HURRELMAN, K. (1987). The importance of school in the life course: Results from the Bielefeld study on school-related problems in adolescence. *Journal of Adolescent Research, 2*, 111–125.

HUSBANDS, C. T. (1970). Some social and psychological consequences of the American dating system. *Adolescence, 5*, 451–462.

HYDE, J., & PHILLIS, D. (1979). Androgyny across the life-span. *Developmental Psychology, 15*, 334–336.

INHELDER, B., & PIAGET, J. (1958). *The growth of logical thinking from childhood to adolescence.* New York: Basic Books.

INSEL, P. M., & MOSS, R. H. (1974). *Health and the social environment.* Lexington, MA: D. C. Heath.

IRWIN, C. E., JR. (Ed.). (1987). *Adolescent social behavior and health: New directions for child development.* San Francisco: Jossey-Bass.

ISCOE, I., WILLIAMS, M., & HARVEY, J. (1963). Modification of children's judgments by a simulated group technique. A normative developmental study. *Child Development, 34*, 963–978.

ISCOE, I., WILLIAMS, M., & HARVEY, J. (1964). Age, intelligence, and sex as variables in the conformity behavior of Negro and white children. *Child Development, 35*, 451–460.

JACOB, T. (1974). Patterns of family conflict and dominance as a function of child age and social class. *Developmental Psychology, 10*, 1–12.

JACOBSEN, J. L., & WIRT, R. D. (1968). *MMPI profiles associated with outcomes of group therapy with prisoners.* Minneapolis: University of Minnesota.

JAMES, W. (1890). *The principles of psychology.* New York: Holt.

JANSSENS, J. M. A. M., GERRIS, J. R. M., & JANSSEN, A. W. H. (1989, April). *Childrearing, empathy and prosocial development.* Paper presented at the Biennial Meetings of the Society for Research in Child Development, Kansas City, MO.

JENSEN, A. R. (1969). How much can we boost IQ and scholastic achievement? *Harvard Educational Review, 39*, 1–123.

JERSILD, A. T. (1963). *The psychology of adolescence* (2nd ed.). New York: Macmillan.

JOHNSON, C., LEWIS, C., LOVE, S., LEWIS, S., & STUCKEY, M. (1984). Incidence and correlates of bulimic behavior in a female high school population. *Journal of Youth and Adolescence, 13*, 15–26.

JOHNSON, L. D., & BACHMAN, J. G. (1976). Educational institutions. In J. F. Adams (Ed.), *Understanding adolescence.* Boston: Allyn & Bacon.

JOHNSTON, L. D., BACHMAN, J. G., & O'MALLEY, P. M. (1981). *Student drug use in America: 1975–1981.* Rockville, MD: National Institute on Drug Abuse.

JONES, K. L., SHAINBERG, L. W., & BYER, C. O. (1975). *Human sexuality.* New York: Harper & Row.

JONES, M. (1965). Psychological correlates of somatic development. *Child Development, 36*, 899–911.

JONES, M. C. (1957). The later careers of boys who were early and late maturing. *Child Development, 28*, 113–128.

JONES, M. C., & BAYLEY, N. (1950). Physical maturing among boys as related to behavior. *Journal of Educational Psychology, 41*, 129–148.

JONES, M. C., & MUSSEN, P. H. (1958). Self-conceptions, motivations and interpersonal attitudes of early and late maturing girls. *Child Development, 29* 491–501.

JORGENSEN, R. S., & DUSEK, J. B. (in press). Adolescent adjustment and coping strategies. *Journal of Personality.*

JURKOVIC, G. J. (1980). The juvenile delinquent as a moral philosopher: A structural-developmental perspective. *Psychological Bulletin, 88*, 709–727.

Juvenile court statistics 1970. (1972). Washington, DC: National Center for Social Statistics. U.S. Department of Health, Education, and Welfare.

KACERGUIS, M., & ADAMS, L. G. (1980). Erikson stage resolution: The relationship between identity and intimacy. *Journal of Youth and Adolescence, 9*, 117–126.

KAGAN, J., & MOSS, H. A. (1962). *Birth to maturity: The Fels study of psychological development,* New York: John Wiley & Sons.

KALLEN, D., & STEPHENSON, J. (1982). Talking about sex revisited. *Journal of Youth and Adolescence, 11*, 11–23.

KANDEL, D. B., & LESSER, G. S. (1969). Parental and peer influences on educational plans of adolescents. *American Sociological Review, 34*, 213–223.

KANE, F., MOAN, C., & BOLLING, B. (1974). Motivational factors in pregnant adolescents. *Diseases of the Nervous System, 34*, 131–134.

KANOUS, L. E., DAUGHERTY, R. A., & COHN, T. S. (1962). Relation between heterosexual friendship choices and socio-economic level. *Child Development, 33*, 251–255.

KANTNER, J., & ZELNIK, M. (1973). Contraception and pregnancy: Experience of young unmarried women in the United States. *Family Planning Perspectives, 5*, 21–35.

KAPLAN, H. (1975). *Self attitudes and deviant behavior.* Pacific Palisades, CA: Goodyear.

KATCHADOURIAN, H. (1977). *The biology of adolescence.* San Francisco: W. H. Freeman.

KAUFMAN, A. S., & FLAITZ, J. (1987). Intellectual growth. In V. B. Van Hasselt & M. Hersen, (Eds.), *Handbook of adolescent psychology.* New York: Pergamon Press.

KAYE, H. (1967). Homosexuality in women. *Archives of General Psychiatry, 17*, 626–634.

KEASEY, C. B. (1971). Social participation as a factor in the moral development of preadolescents. *Developmental Psychology, 5*, 216–220.

KEATING, D. (1980). Thinking processes in adolescence. In J. Adelson (Ed.), *Handbook of adolescent psychology.* New York: John Wiley & Sons.

KEITH, T. (1982). Time spent on homework and high school grades: A large-sample path analysis. *Journal of Educational Psychology, 74*, 248–253.

KELLY, F. J., & BAER, D. J. (1969). Age of male delinquents when father left home and recidivism. *Psychological Reports, 25*, 383–388.

KELLY, J., & WALLERSTEIN, J. (1975). The effects of parental divorce: I. The experience of the child in early latency. II. The experience of the child in late latency. *American Journal of Orthopsychiatry, 45*, 253–255.

KELLY, J., & WALLERSTEIN, J. (1976). The effects of parental divorce: Experiences of the child in early latency. *American Journal of Orthopsychiatry, 46*, 20–32.

KELLY, J., & WALLERSTEIN, J. (1977). Brief interventions with children in divorcing families. *American Journal of Orthopsychiatry, 47*, 23–39.

KENYON, F. E. (1968). Studies in female homosexuality. *British Journal of Psychiatry, 35*, 1337–1350.

KERCKNOFF, A. C., & HUFF, J. L. (1974). Parental influence on educational goals. *Sociometry, 37*, 307–327.

KERMIS, M., MONGE, R. H., & DUSEK, J. B. (1975, April). *Human sexuality in the hierarchy of adolescent interests.* Paper presented at the Biennial Meetings of the Society for Research in Child Development, Denver.

KESSEN, W. (1965). *The child.* New York: John Wiley & Sons.

KESSEN, W. (1970). "Stage" and "structure" in the study of children. In W. Kessen & C. Kuhlman (Eds.), *Thought in the young child.* Chicago: University of Chicago Press.

KESTENBERG, J. (1967a). Phases of adolescence with suggestions for a correlation of psychic and hormonal organization. Part I: Antecedents of adolescent organizations in childhood. *Journal of the American Academy of Child Psychiatry, 6*, 426–463.

KESTENBERG, J. (1967b). Phases of adolescence with suggestions for a correlation of psychic and hormonal organization. Part II: Prepuberty, diffusion, and reintegration. *Journal of the American Academy of Child Psychiatry, 6*, 577–614.

KESTENBERG, J. (1968). Phases of adolescence with suggestions for a correlation of psychic and hormonal organizations. Part III: Puberty, growth, differentiation, and consolidation. *Journal of the American Academy of Child Psychiatry, 7*, 108–151.

KETT, J. (1977). *Rites of passage.* New York: Basic Books.

KILLEEN, M. R., & FRAME, C. L. (1989, April). *Peer relations and social self-concept.* Paper presented at the Biennial Meetings of the Society for Research in Child Development, Kansas City, MO.

KILMANN, P., WANLASS, R., SABALIS, R., & SULLIVAN, B. (1981). Sex education: A review of its effects. *Archives of Sexual Behavior, 10*, 177–205.

KIM, Y., & ZELNIK, M. (1982). Sex education and its association with teenage sexual activity, pregnancy, and contraceptive use. *Family Planning Perspectives, 14*, 117–119, 123–126.

KIMBROUGH, R. (1969). SOS for junior high school students. In W. Baskin & G. Powers (Eds.), *Sex education: Issues and directives.* New York: Philosophical Library.

KINSEY, A. C., POMEROY, W. B., & MARTIN, C. E. (1948). *Sexual behavior in the human male.* Philadelphia: W. B. Saunders.

KINSEY, A. C., POMEROY, W. B., MARTIN, C. E., & GEBHARD, P. H. (1953). *Sexual behavior in the human female.* Philadelphia: W. B. Saunders.

KLINE, M., TSCHANN, J. M., JOHNSTON, J. R., & WALLERSTEIN, J. S. (1989). Children's adjustment in joint and sole physical custody families. *Developmental Psychology, 25*, 430–438.

KOENIG, M., & ZELNIK, M. (1982). The risk of premarital first pregnancy among metropolitan-area teenagers: 1976–1979. *Family Planning Perspectives, 14*, 239–241, 243–247.

KOHEN, A. I., & BREINICH, S. C. (1975). Knowledge of the world of work: A test of occupational information for young men. *Journal of Vocational Behavior, 6*, 133–144.

KOHLBERG, L. (1963a). The development of children's orientations toward a moral order: I. Sequence in the development of moral thought. *Vita Humana, 6*, 11–33.

KOHLBERG, L. (1963b). Moral development and identification. In H. Stevenson (Ed.), *Child psychology. 62nd yearbook of the National Society for the Study of Education.* Chicago: University of Chicago Press.

KOHLBERG, L. (1966). A cognitive developmental analysis of children's sex-role concepts and attitudes. In E. E. Maccoby

(Ed.). *The development of sex difference.* Stanford: Stanford University Press.

KOHLBERG, L. (1969). Stage and sequence: The cognitive-developmental approach to socialization. In D. A. Goslin (Ed.), *Handbook of socialization theory and research.* Chicago: Rand McNally.

KOHLBERG, L. (1976). Moral stages and moralization. In T. Lickona (Ed.), *Moral development and behavior: Theory, research, and social issues.* New York: Holt, Rinehart & Winston.

KOHLBERG, L. (1980). *Recent research in moral development.* New York: Holt.

KOHLBERG, L., & ZIGLER, E. (1967). The impact of cognitive maturity on sex-role attitudes in the years four to eight. *Genetic Psychology Monographs, 75,* 89–165.

KOOCHER, G. (1974). Emerging selfhood and cognitive development. *Journal of Genetic Psychology, 125,* 79–88.

KREBS, D., & GILLMORE, J. (1982). The relationship among the first stages of cognitive development, role-taking abilities, and moral development. *Child Development, 53,* 877–886.

KREIPE, R. E., & STRAUSS, J. (1989). Adolescent medical disorders, behavior, and development. In G. R. Adams, R. Montemayor, & T. P. Gullotta (Eds.), *Biology of adolescent behavior and development.* Newbury Park, CA: Sage Publications, Inc.

KROSNICK, J., & JUDD, C. (1982). Transitions in social influence at adolescence: Who induces cigarette smoking? *Developmental Psychology, 18,* 359–368.

KUHLEN, R. G., & ARNOLD, M. (1944). Age differences in religious beliefs and problems during adolescence. *Journal of Genetic Psychology, 64,* 291–300.

KUHLEN, R. G., & HOULIHAN, N. B. (1965). Adolescent heterosexual interest in 1942 and 1963. *Child Development, 36,* 1049–1052.

KUHLEN, R. G., & LEE, B. J. (1943). Personality characteristics and social acceptability in adolescence. *Journal of Educational Psychology, 34,* 331–340.

KUPFERSMID, J., & WONDERLY, D. (1980). Moral maturity and behavior: Failure to find a link. *Journal of Youth and Adolescence, 9,* 249–261.

KURDEK, L. A. (1988). A 1-year follow-up study of children's divorce adjustment, custodial mother's divorce adjustment, and post-divorce parenting. *Journal of Applied Developmental Psychology, 9,* 315–328.

KURDEK, L. A. (1989). Siblings' reactions to parental divorce. *Journal of Divorce, 12,* 203–219.

KURDEK, L. A., & SINCLAIR, R. J. (1988). Adjustment of young adolescents in two-parent nuclear, stepfather, and mother-custody families. *Journal of Consulting and Clinical Psychology, 56,* 91–96.

KURDEK, L. A., & SINCLAIR, R. J. (1988). Relation of eighth graders' family structure, gender, and family environment with academic performance and school behavior. *Journal of Educational Psychology, 80,* 90–94.

LAMBERT, B. G., & MOUNCE, N. B. (1987). Career planning. In V. B. Van Hasselt & M. Hersen (Eds.), *Handbook of adolescent psychology.* New York: Pergamon Press.

LANDIS, J. T., & LANDIS, M. G. (1968). *Building a successful marriage* (5th ed.). Englewood Cliffs, NJ: Prentice-Hall.

LANG, D., PAMPENFUHS, R., & WALTER, J. (1976). Delinquent females' perceptions of their fathers. *Family Coordinator, 25,* 475–481.

LAPSLEY, D. K. (1985). Elkind on egocentrism. *Developmental Review, 5,* 227–236.

LAPSLEY, D. K., JACKSON, S., RICE, K., & SHADID, G. E. (1988). Self-monitoring and the "new look" at the imaginary audience and personal fable: An ego developmental analysis. *Journal of Adolescent Research, 3,* 17–31.

LAPSLEY, D. K., MILSTEAD, M., QUINTANA, S. M., FLANNERY, D., & BUSS, R. (1986). Adolescent egocentrism and formal operations: Tests of a theoretical assumption. *Developmental Psychology, 22,* 800–807.

LAPSLEY, D. K., & MURPHY, M. N. (1985). Another look at the theoretical assumptions of adolescent egocentrism. *Developmental Review, 5,* 201–217.

LAURSEN, B. (1989, April). *Interpersonal conflict during adolescence.* Paper presented at the Biennial Meetings of the Society for Research in Child Development, Kansas City, MO.

LAVOIE, J. (1974). Type of punishment as a determinant of resistance to deviation. *Developmental Psychology, 10,* 181–189.

LAVOIE, J. (1976). Ego identity formation in middle adolescence. *Journal of Youth and Adolescence, 5,* 371–385.

LAZAR, I., & DARLINGTON, R. (1982). Lasting effects of early education: A report from the consortium for longitudinal studies. *Monographs of the Society for Research in Child Development, 47,* (Whole No. 195).

LEAHY, R. (1981). Parental practices and the development of moral judgments and self-image disparity during adolescence. *Developmental Psychology, 17,* 580–594.

LEARY, M. R., & SNELL, W. E., Jr. (1988). The relationship of instrumentality and expressiveness to sexual behavior in males and females. *Sex Roles, 18,* 509–522.

LECKY, P. (1945). *Self-consistency: A theory of personality.* Shelter Island, NY: Island Press.

LEE, L. C. (1971). The concomitant development of cognitive and moral modes of thought: A test of selected deductions from Piaget's theory. *Genetic Psychology Monographs, 83,* 93–146.

LEE, M. (1952). Background factors related to sex information and attitudes. *Journal of Educational Psychology, 43,* 467–485.

LEE, M., & PRENTICE, N. M. (1988). Interrelations of empathy, cognition, and moral reasoning with dimensions of juvenile delinquency. *Journal of Abnormal Child Psychology, 16,* 127–139.

LEFURGY, W. G., & WOLOSHIN, G. W. (1969). Immediate and long-term effects of experimentally induced social influence in the modification of adolescents' moral judgments. *Journal of Abnormal and Social Psychology 12,* 104–110.

LEIDERMAN, P. H., MELDMAN, M. A., & RITTER, P. L. (1989). *Parent and peer influences on adolescent self-esteem in a multiethnic high school population.* Paper presented at the Biennial Meetings of the Society for Research in Child Development, Kansas City, MO.

LEIGH, B. C. (1989). Reasons for having sex: Gender, sexual orientation, and relationship to sexual behavior. *Journal of Sex Research, 26,* 199–209.

LEIZER, J. I., & ROGERS, R. W. (1974). Effects of method of discipline, timing of punishment, and timing of test on resistance to temptation. *Child Development, 45,* 790–793.

LEMPERS, J. D., CLARK-LEMPERS, D., & SIMONS, R. L. (1989). Economic hardship, parenting, and distress in adolescence. *Child Development, 60,* 25–39.

LEPPER, M. R., & GURTNER, J-L. (1989). Children and computers: Approaching the twenty-first century. *American Psychologist, 44*, 170–178.

LEVITZ-JONES, E., & ORLOFSKY, J. (1985). Separation-individuation and intimacy capacity in college women. *Journal of Personality and Social Psychology, 49*, 156–169.

LEVY, G. D., & CARTER, D. B. (1989). Gender schema, gender constancy, and gender-role knowledge: The roles of cognitive factors in preschoolers' gender-role stereotype attributions. *Developmental Psychology, 25*, 444–449.

LEWIN, K. (1935). *A dynamic theory of personality.* New York: McGraw-Hill.

LEWIN, K. (1939). Field theory and experiment in social psychology: Concepts and methods. *American Journal of Sociology, 44*, 868–897.

LEWIN, M., & TRAGOS, L. M. (1987). Has the feminist movement influenced adolescent sex role attitudes? A reassessment after a quarter century. *Sex Roles, 16*, 125–135.

LIBBY, R. (1970). Parental attitudes toward high school sex education programs. *The Family Coordinator, 19* 234–247.

LINDZEY, G. (1965). Morphology and behavior. In G. Lindzey & C. S. Hall (Eds.), *Theories of personality.* New York: John Wiley & Sons.

LINN, M. C., & PETERSON, A. C. (1985). Emergence of characterization of sex differences in spatial ability: A meta-analytic analysis. *Child Development, 56*, 1479–1498.

LINNEY, J. A., & SEIDMAN, E. (1989). The future of schooling. *American Psychologist, 44*, 336–340.

LITOVSKY, V. G., & DUSEK, J. B. (1985). Perceptions of child rearing and self-concept development during the early adolescent years. *Journal of Youth and Adolescence, 14*, 373–387.

LITOVSKY, V. G., & DUSEK, J. B. (1988). Maternal employment and adolescent adjustment and perceptions of child rearing. *International Journal of Family Psychiatry, 9*, 153–167.

LIVSON, N., & PESKIN, H. (1980). Perspectives on adolescence from longitudinal research. In J. Adelson (Ed.), *Handbook of adolescent psychology.* New York: John Wiley & Sons.

LONG, B. (1986). Parental discord vs. family structure: Effects of divorce on the self-esteem of daughters. *Journal of Youth and Adolescence, 15*, 19–27.

LONG, N., FOREHAND, R., FAUBER, R., BRODY, G. (1987). Self-perceived and independently observed competence of young adolescents as a function of parental marital conflict and recent divorce. *Journal of Abnormal Child Psychology, 15*, 15–27.

LONGSTRETH, L., LONGSTRETH, G., RAMIREZ, C., & FERNANDEZ, G. (1975) The ubiquity of big brother. *Child Development, 46*, 769–772.

LONKY, E., REIHMAN, J., & SERLIN, R. (1981). Political values and moral judgment in adolescence., *Youth and Society, 12*, 423–431.

LOOFT, W. R. (1972). Egocentrism and social interaction across the life span. *Psychological Bulletin, 78*, 73–92.

LOOFT, W. R. (1973). Socialization and personality throughout the life span: An examination of contemporary psychological approaches. In P. B. Baltes & K. W. Schaie (Eds.), *Lifespan development psychology: Personality and socialization.* New York: Academic Press.

LORENZ, K. Z. (1965). *Evolution and modification of behavior.* Chicago: University of Chicago Press.

LOWRIE, S. H. (1961). Early and late dating: Some conditions associated with them. *Marriage and Family Living, 23*, 284–291.

LOWRIE, S. H. (1965). Early marriage: Premarital pregnancy and associated factors. *Journal of Marriage and the Family, 27*, 48–57.

LUCKEY, E., & NASS. G. (1969). A comparison of sexual attitudes and behavior in an international sample. *Journal of Marriage and the Family, 31*, 364–379.

LUTWAK, N. (1984). The interrelationship of ego, moral, and conceptual development in a college group. *Adolescence, 19*, 675–688.

LYNN, D., & SAUREY, W. L. (1959). The effects of father-absence on Norwegian boys and girls. *Journal of Abnormal and Social Psychology, 59*, 258–262.

MA, H. K. (1988). Objective moral judgment in Hong Kong, mainland China, and England. *Journal of Cross Cultural Psychology, 19*, 78–95.

MCADAMS, D., BOOTH, L., & SELVIK, R. (1981). Religious identity among students at a private college: Social motives, ego stage, and development. *Merrill Palmer Quarterly, 27*, 219–239.

MCCALL, R. (1979). The development of intellectual functioning in infancy and the prediction of later IQ. In J. Osofsky (Ed.), *Handbook of infant development.* New York: John Wiley & Sons.

MCCALL, R., APPLEBAUM, M., & HOGARTY, P. (1973). Developmental changes in mental performance. *Monographs of the Society for Research in Child Development, 38*, (No. 150).

MCCALL, R. B., EICHORN, D. H., & HOGARTY, P. S. (1977). Transitions in early mental development. *Monographs of the Society for Research in Child Development, 43* (1–2, Whole No. 174).

MCCANDLESS, B. R. (1970). *Adolescents: Behavior and development.* Hinsdale, IL: The Dryden Press.

MCCANDLESS, B. R., ROBERTS, A., & STARNES, T. (1972). Teachers' marks, achievement test scores, and aptitude relations with respect to social class, race, and sex. *Journal of Educational Psychology, 63*, 153–159.

MCCARTHY, J., & HOGE, D. (1982). Analysis of age effects in longitudinal studies of adolescent self-esteem. *Developmental Psychology, 18*, 372–379.

MCCORD, W., MCCORD, J., & ZOLA, I. K. (1959). *Origins of crime.* New York: Columbia University Press.

MCCRAE, R. R., & COSTA, P. T., Jr. (1986). Personality, coping, and coping effectiveness in an adult sample. *Journal of Personality, 54*, 385–405.

MCDOUGALL, W. (1908). *An introduction to social psychology.* London: Methuen.

MCLANAHAN, S. (1983). Family structure and stress: A longitudinal comparison of two-parent and female-headed families. *Journal of Marriage and the Family, 45*, 347–357.

MCLOYD, V. C. (1989a, April). *Facing the future in hard times: Choices, perceptions, and behavior of black adolescents.* Paper presented at the Biennial Meetings of the Society for Research in Child Development, Kansas City, MO.

MCLOYD, V. C. (1989b, April). *Individual, familial, and external factors influencing the mental health of children in low-income female-headed families.* Paper presented at the Biennial Meetings of the Society for Research in Child Development, Kansas City, MO.

MACCOBY, E. E., & JACKLIN, C. (1974). *The psychology of sex differences.* Stanford, CA: Stanford University Press.

MACCOBY, E. E., & JACKLINM, C. (1980). Sex differences in aggression: A rejoinder and reprise. *Child Development, 51,* 964–980.

MACCOBY, E., & MARTIN, J. (1983). Socialization in the context of the family: Parent-child interaction. In E. M. Hetherington (Ed.), *Handbook of child psychology: Socialization, personality, and social development* (Vol. 4). New York: John Wiley & Sons.

MACKINNON, C. E. (1989). An observational investigation of sibling interactions in married and divorced families. *Developmental Psychology, 25,* 36–44.

MACKLIN, E. (1978). Review of research on nonmarital cohabitation in the United States. In B. Murstein (Ed.), *Exploring intimate life styles.* New York: Springer-Verlag.

MAGNUSSON, D., SATTIN, H., & ALLEN, V. (1986). Differential maturation among girls and its relation to social adjustment in a longitudinal perspective. In P. Baltes, D. Featherman, & R. Lerner (Eds.), *Life span development and behavior* (Vol. 7). Hillsdale, NJ: Lawrence Erlbaum.

MALINA, R. M. (1979). Secular changes in size and maturity: Causes and effects. In A. F. Roche (Ed.), Secular trends in human growth, maturation, and development. *Monographs of the Society for Research in Child Development, 44* (Whole No. 3–4).

MARCIA, J. (1966). Development and validation of ego identity status. *Journal of Personality and Social Psychology, 3,* 551–558.

MARCIA, J. (1967). Ego identity status: Relationship to change in self-esteem, "general maladjustment," and authoritarianism. *Journal of Personality, 35,* 119–133.

MARCIA, J. (1976). Identity six years after: A follow-up study. *Journal of Youth and Adolescence, 5,* 145–160.

MARCIA, J. (1980). Identity in adolescence. In J. Adelson (Ed.), *Handbook of adolescent psychology.* New York: John Wiley & Sons.

MARKUS, H., & NURIUS, P. (1986). Possible selves. *American Psychologist, 41,* 954–969.

MARSH, H. W. (1987). The big-fish–little-pond effect on academic self-concept. *Journal of Educational Psychology, 79,* 280–295.

MARSH, H. W. (1989). Effects of attending single-sex and coeducational high schools on achievement, attitudes, behaviors, and sex differences. *Journal of Educational Psychology, 81,* 70–85.

MARSH, H. W., BYRNE, B. M., & SHAVELSON, R. J. (1988). A multifaceted academic self-concept: Its hierarchical structure and its relation to academic achievement. *Journal of Educational Psychology, 80,* 366–380.

MARTIN, B. (1975). Parent-child relations. In F. D. Horowitz (Ed.), *Review of child development research* (Vol. 4). Chicago: University of Chicago Press.

MARTIN, C., & HALVERSON, C. (1981). A schematic processing model of sex typing and stereotyping in children. *Child Development, 52,* 1119–1134.

MARTIN, C. L., & HALVERSON, C. F. (1987). The roles of cognition in sex role acquisition. In D. B. Carter (Ed.), *Current conceptions of sex roles and sex typing.* New York: Praeger.

MARTINEAU, P. (1966). Adulthood in the adolescent perspective. *Adolescence, 1,* 272–280.

MASTERS, W. H., & JOHNSON, V. E. (1966). *Human sexual response.* Boston: Little, Brown.

MASTERS, W. H., & JOHNSON, V. E. (1970). *Human sexual inadequacy.* Boston: Little, Brown.

MATTESON, D. (1977). Exploration and commitment: Sex differences and methodological problems in the use of identity status categories. *Journal of Youth and Adolescence, 6,* 353–374.

MAYER, L. A. (1971, February). New questions about the U. S. population. *Fortune,* 82–85.

MEAD, G. H. (1934). *Mind, self, and society.* Chicago: University of Chicago Press.

MEAD, M. (1939a). *From the south seas. Part 3: Sex and temperament in three primitive societies.* New York: Morrow.

MEAD, M. (1939b). *Male and female,* New York: Morrow.

MEAD, M. (1950). *Coming of age in Samoa.* New York: Morrow.

MEAD, M. (1953). *Growing up in New Guinea,* New York: Mentor Books.

MEAD, M. (1966). Marriage in two steps. *Redbook, 127,* 48–49.

MEAD, M. (1970). *Culture and commitment: A study of the generation gap.* New York: Doubleday.

MEILMAN, P. (1979). Cross-sectional age changes in ego identity status during adolescence. *Developmental Psychology, 15,* 230–231.

MEISELS, M. M., & CANTER, F. M. (1971–72). A note on the generation gap. *Adolescence, 6,* 523–530.

MEISSNER, W. W. (1965). Parental interaction of the adolescent boy. *Journal of Genetic Psychology, 107,* 225–233.

MEKOS, D. (1989, April). *Students' perceptions of the transition to junior high: A longitudinal perspective.* Paper presented at the Biennial Meetings of the Society for Research in Child Development, Kansas City, MO.

MELGES, F. T., & HAMBURG, D. A. (1977). Psychological effects of hormonal changes in women. In F. A. Beach (Ed.), *Human sexuality in four perspectives.* Baltimore: The Johns Hopkins University Press.

MEREDITH, H. V. (1963). Change in the stature and body weight of North American boys during the last 80 years. In L. P. Lipsitt & C. C. Spiker (Eds.), *Advances in child development and behavior* (Vol. 1). New York: Academic Press.

MEREDITH, H. V. (1976). Findings from Asia, Australia. Europe and North America on secular change in mean height of children, youths, and young adults. *American Journal of Physical Anthropology, 44,* 315–326.

MERTON, R. K. (1961). *Social theory and social structure.* New York: The Free Press.

MERTON, R. K. (1966). Social structure and anomie. In R. Giallombardo (Ed.), *Juvenile delinquency: A book of readings.* New York: John Wiley & Sons.

MEYER, W. J. (1959). Relationships between social need strivings and the development of heterosexual affiliations. *Journal of Abnormal and Social Psychology, 59,* 51–57.

MIDGLEY, C., FELDLAUFER, H., & ECCLES, J. S. (1988a). Change in teacher efficacy and student self- and task-related beliefs in mathematics during the transition to junior high school. *Journal of Educational Psychology, 81,* 247–258.

MIDGLEY, C., FELDLAUFER, H., & ECCLES, J. S. (1989b). Student/teacher relations and attitudes toward mathematics before and after the transition to junior high school. *Child Development, 60,* 981–992.

MILANI-COMPARETTI, M. (1977). Genetics and adolescent development: Perspectives for the future. In J. P. Hill, & F. J. Monks (Eds.), *Adolescence and youth in prospect*. Surrey, England: IPC Science Technology Press.

MILLER, D. (1976). What do high school students think of their schools? *Phi Delta Kappan, 57*, 700–702.

MILLER, J. P. (1975). Suicide and adolescence. *Adolescence, 10*, 11–24.

MILLER, L., & BIZZELL, R. (1983). Long-term effects of four preschool programs: Sixth, seventh, and eighth grades. *Child Development, 54*, 727–741.

MILLER, P., & SIMON, W. (1980). The development of sexuality in adolescence. In J. Adelson (Ed.), *Handbook of adolescent psychology* (pp. 383–407). New York: John Wiley & Sons.

MILLER, P. Y., & SIMON, W. (1979). Do youth really want to work: A comparison of the work values and job perceptions of younger and older men. *Youth and Society, 10*, 379–404.

MILLER, W. B. (1975). Lower class culture as a generating milieu of gang delinquency. *Journal of Social Issues, 14*, 5–19.

MILLER, W. B. (1966). Violent crimes in city gangs. *Annals of the American Academy of Political and Social Science, 364*, 96–112.

MILLSTEIN, S. G. (April, 1989). *Behavioral risk factors for AIDS among adolescents*. Paper presented at the Biennial Meetings of the Society for Research in Child Development, Kansas City, MO.

MINUCHIN, P., & SHAPIRO, E. K. (1983). The school as a context for social development. In P. H. Mussen & E. M. Hetherington (Eds.), *Handbook of child psychology* (4th ed.). New York: John Wiley & Sons.

MITCHELL, J. J. (1975). Moral growth during adolescence. *Adolescence, 10*, 221–222.

MIZNER, G. L., BARTER, J. T., & WERME, P. H. (1970). Patterns of drug use among college students. *American Journal of Psychiatry, 127*, 15–24.

MOHR, D. (1978). Development of atrributes of personal identity. *Developmental Psychology, 14*, 427–428.

MOIR, D. J. (1974). Egocentrism and the emergence of conventional morality in preadolescent girls. *Child Development, 45*, 229–304.

MONAHAN, T. (1966). Family status and the delinquent child: A reappraisal and some new findings. In R. Giallombardo (Ed.), *Juvenile delinquency: A book of readings*. New York: John Wiley & Sons.

MONEY, J. (1961). Sex hormones and other variables in human eroticisms. In W. C. Young (Ed.), *Sex and internal secretions* (Vol. 2). Baltimore: Williams and Wilkins.

MONEY, J., & EHRHARDT, A. (1972). *Man and woman, boy and girl*. New York: Mentor.

MONEY, J., EHRHARDT, A., & MASICA, D. N. (1968). Fetal feminization induced by androgenic insensitivity in the testicular feminizing syndrome: Effect on marriage and maternalism. *John Hopkins Medical Journal, 123*, 105–114.

MONEY, J., HAMPSON, J. L. (1955). An examination of some basic sexual concepts: The evidence of human hermaphroditism. *Bulletin of Johns Hopkins Hospital, 97*, 301–319.

MONGE, R. H., DUSEK, J. B., & LAWLESS, J. (1977). An evaluation of the acquisition of sexual information through a sex education class. *Journal of Sex Research, 13*, 170–184.

MONOHAN, T. P. (1963). Does age at marriage matter in divorce? *Social Forces, 32*, 81–87.

MONTEMAYOR, R. (1982). The relationship between parent-adolescent conflict and the amount of time adolescents spend alone and with parents and peers. *Child Development, 53*, 1512–1519.

MONTEMAYOR, R., BROWN, B., & ADAMS, G. (1985). *Changes in identity status and psychological adjustment after leaving home and entering college*. Paper presented at the Biennial Meetings of the Society for Research in Child Development, Toronto.

MONTEMAYOR, R., & EISEN, M. (1977). The development of self-conceptions from childhood to adolescence. *Developmental Psychology, 13*, 314–319.

MOORE, K., PETERSON, J., & FURSTENBERG, F., Jr. (1986). Parental attitudes and the occurrence of early sexual activity. *Journal of Marriage and the Family, 48*, 777–782.

MORAN, P., & ECKENRODE, J. (1989, April). *Gender differences in the costs and benefits of social relationships among adolescents*. Paper presented at the Biennial Meetings of the Society for Research in Child Development, Kansas City, MO.

MORENO, J. L. (1934). *Who shall survive: A new approach to the problems of human interrelations*. Washington, DC: Nervous and Mental Disease Publishing Co.

MORROW, W. R., & WILSON, R. C. (1961). Family relations of bright high-achieving and under-achieving high school boys. *Child Development, 32*, 501–510.

MORTIMER, J. (1974). Patterns of intergenerational occupational movements: A smallest-space analysis. *American Journal of Sociology, 79*, 1278–1299.

MORTIMER, J. (1976). Social class, work, and the family: Some implications of the father's occupation for familial relationships and sons' career decisions. *Journal of Marriage and the Family, 38*, 241–256.

MUNRO, G., & ADAMS, G. (1977). Ego-identity formation in college students and working youth. *Developmental Psychology, 13*, 523–524.

MURPHY, J. (1987). Educational influences. In V. B. Van Hasselt & M. Hersen (Eds.), *Handbook of adolescent psychology*. New York: Pergamon Press.

MUSSEN, P. H., & JONES, M. C. (1957). Self-concepts, motivations, and interpersonal attitudes of late and early maturing boys. *Child Development, 28*, 243–256.

MUUSS, R. E. (1988). *Theories of adolescence* (5th ed.). New York: Random House.

NACHMAN, B. (1960). Childhood experience and vocational choice in law, dentistry, and social work. *Journal of Counseling Psychology, 7*, 243–250.

NATIONAL OPINION RESEARCH CENTER(1980). *High School and beyond: A national longitudinal study for the 1980s*. Chicago: Author.

NEAPOLITAN, J. (1981). Parental influences on aggressive behavior: A social learning approach. *Adolescence, 16*, 831–839.

NEIMARK, E. (1975). Intellectual development during adolescence. In F. D. Horowitz (Ed.), *Review of child development research* (Vol. 4). Chicago: University of Chicago Press.

NESSELROADE, J. R., & BALTES, P. B. (1974). Adolescent personality development and historical change: 1970–1972. *Monographs of the Society for Research in Child Development, 39* (Whole No. 1), 1–80.

NEWCOMB, M. D., & BENTLER, P. M. (1989). Substance use and abuse among children and teenagers. *American Psychologist, 44*, 242–248.

Niles, W. (1986). Effects of a moral development discussion group on delinquent and predelinquent boys. *Journal of Counseling Psychology, 33*, 45–51.

Noeth, R. J., Roth, J. D., & Prediger, D. J. (1975). Student career development. Where do we stand? *The Vocational Guidance Quarterly, 23*, 210–218.

Nottelmann, E. (1987). Competence and self-esteem during transition from childhood to adolescence. *Developmental Psychology, 23*, 441–450.

Novotny, E. S., & Burstein, M. (1974). Public school adjustment of delinquent boys after release from a juvenile corrective institution. *Journal of Youth and Adolescence, 3*, 49–60.

Nunn, G. D., & Parish, T. S. (1987). An investigation of the relationships between children's self-concepts and evaluations of parent figures: Do they vary as a function of family structure? *Journal of Psychology, 121*, 563–566.

Oberlander, M., Jenkins, N., Houlihan, K., & Jackson, J. (1970). Family size and birth order as determinants of scholastic aptitude and achievement in a sample of eighth graders. *Journal of Consulting and Clinical Psychology, 34*, 19–21.

O'Brien, S. F., & Bierman, K. L. (1988). Conceptions and perceived influence of peer groups: Interviews with preadolescents and adolescents. *Child Development, 59*, 1360–1365.

O'Connell, L., Betz, M., & Kurth, S. (1989). Plans for balancing work and family life: Do women pursuing nontraditional and traditional occupations differ? *Sex Roles, 20*, 35–45.

O'Leary, V. E. (1974). Some attitudinal barriers to occupational aspirations in women. *Psychological Bulletin, 81*, 809–826.

Olejnik, A. (1980). Adult's moral reasoning with children. *Child Development, 51*, 1285–1288.

O'Malley, P., & Bachman, J. (1983). Self-esteem: Change and stability between ages 13 and 23. *Developmental Psychology, 19*, 257–268.

O'Malley, P. M., Bachman, J. G., & Johnston, J. (1977). *Youth in transition. Final report: Five years beyond high school: Causes and consequences of educational attainment.* Ann Arbor, MI: Institute for Social Research.

Orlofsky, J. L., & O'Heron, C. A. (1987). Development of a short-form sex role behavior scale. *Journal of Personality Assessment, 51*, 267–277.

Orlofsky, J., Marcia, J., & Lesser, I. (1973). Ego identity status and the intimacy vs. isolation crisis of young adulthood. *Journal of Personality and Social Psychology, 27*, 211–219.

Osipow, S. H. (1968). *Theories of career development.* New York: Appleton-Century-Crofts.

Osterrieth, P. A. (1969). Adolescence: Some psychological aspects. In G. Caplan & S. Lebovici (Eds.), *Adolescence: Psychosocial perspectives.* New York: Basic Books.

Otto, H. A. (1971), April). Communes: The alternative lifestyle. *Saturday Review*, 16–21.

Overton, W. F., & Reese, H. W. (1973). Models of development: Methodological implications. In P. B. Baltes & K. W. Schaie (Eds.), *Life-span developmental psychology: Personality and socialization.* New York: Academic Press.

Owens, W. A., Jr. (1953). Age and mental abilities. *Genetic Psychology Monographs, 48*, 3–54.

Parikh, B. (1980). Development of moral judgment and its relation to family environmental factors in Indian and American families. *Child Development, 51*, 1030–1039.

Parish, T. (1981). The impact of divorce on the family. *Adolescence, 16*, 577–580.

Parish, T., Dostal, J., & Parish, J. (1981). Evaluations of self and parents as a function of intactness of family and family happiness. *Adolescence, 16*, 203–210.

Parish, T., & Taylor, J. (1979). The impact of divorce and subsequent father absence on children's and adolescents' self-concepts. *Journal of Youth and Adolescence, 8*, 427–432.

Parrott, C. A., & Strongman, K. T. (1984). Locus of control and delinquency. *Adolescence, 19*, 459–471.

Parsons, J., Kaczala, C., & Meece, J. (1982). Socialization of achievement attitudes and beliefs: Classroom influences. *Child Development, 53*, 322–339.

Patterson, G. R., DeBarsyshe, B. D., & Ramsey, E. (1989). A developmental perspective on antisocial behavior. *American Psychologist, 44*, 329–335.

Pavalko, R. M., & Bishop, D. R. (1966). Peer influences in the college plans of Canadian high school students. *The Canadian Review of Sociology and Anthropology, 3*, 191–200.

Peck, J. S. (1988/89). The impact of divorce on children at various stages of the family life cycle. *Journal of Divorce, 12*, 81–106.

Peck R. F., & Havighurst, R. J. (1960). *The psychology of character development.* New York: John Wiley & Sons.

Peplau, L., Rubin, Z., & Hill, C. (1977). Sexual intimacy in dating relationships. *Journal of Social Issues, 33*, 86–109.

Pepper, S. C. (1942). *World hypotheses.* Berkeley: University of California Press.

Perlmutter, R., & Shapiro, E. R. (1987). Morals and values in adolescence. In V. B. Van Hasselt & M. Hersen (Eds.), *Handbook of adolescent psychology.* New York: Pergamon Press.

Perry, D. G., Kusel, S. J., & Perry, L. C. (1988). Victims of peer aggression. *Developmental Psychology, 24*, 807–814.

Perry, D. G., & Williard, J. C. (1989, April). *Victims of peer abuse.* Paper presented at the Biennial Meetings of the Society for Research in Child Development, Kansas City, MO.

Peskin, H. (1967). Pubertal onset and ego functioning. *Journal of Abnormal Psychology, 72*, 1–15.

Peskin, H. (1973). Influence of the developmental schedule of puberty on learning and ego development. *Journal of Youth and Adolescence, 2*, 273–290.

Petersen, A. C. (1985). Pubertal development as a cause of disturbance: Myths, realities, and unanswered questions. *Genetic, Social, and General Psychology Monographs, 111*, 205–232.

Petersen, A. C. (1988). Adolescent development. In M. R. Rosenzweig & L. W. Porter (Eds.), *Annual review of psychology.* Palo Alto, CA: Annual Reviews, Inc.

Petersen, A. C., & Taylor, B. (1980). The biological approach to adolescence: Biological change and psychological adaptation. In J. Adelson (Eds.), *Handbook of adolescent psychology.* New York: John Wiley & Sons.

Petronio, R. (1980). The moral maturity of repeater delinquents. *Youth and Society, 12*, 51–59.

Petti, T. A., & Larson, C. N. (1987). Depression and suicide. In V. B. Van Hasselt & M. Hersen (Eds.), *Handbook of adolescent psychology.* New York: Pergamon Press.

PFEFFER, C. (1986). *The suicidal child.* New York: Guilford Press.

PIAGET, J. (1932). *The moral judgment of the child.* Glencoe, IL: The Free Press.

PIAGET, J. (1952). *The origins of intelligence in children* (M. Cook trans.). New York: International Press.

PIAGET, J. (1968). *Six psychological studies.* New York: Vintage.

PIAGET, J. (1970). Piaget's theory. In P. H. Mussen (Ed.), *Carmichael's manual of child psychology* (Vol. 1, 3rd. ed.). New York: Basic Books.

PIAGET, J. (1972). Intellectual evolution from adolescence to adulthood. *Human Development, 15,* 1–12.

PIAGET, J. (1980). Intellectual evolution from adolescence to adulthood. In R. E. Muuss (Ed.), *Adolescent behavior and society: A book of readings* (3rd ed.). New York: Random House.

PIAGET, J., & INHELDER, B. (1969). *The psychology of the child.* New York: Basic Books.

PINE, G. (1966). The affluent delinquent. *Phi Delta Kappan, 48,* 138–143.

PINNEAU, S. R. (1961). *Changes in intelligence quotient.* Boston: Houghton Mifflin.

PLOMIN, R. (1983). Developmental behavioral genetics. *Child Development, 54,* 253–259.

PLOMIN, R., & DANIELS, D. (1987). Why are children in the same family so different from one another? *Behavioral and Brain Sciences, 10,* 1–60.

POLK, K. (1971). A reassessment of middle-class delinquency. *Youth and Society, 2,* 333–354.

POFFENBERGER, T. (1964). Three papers on going steady. *Family Life Coordinator, 13,* 7–13.

POGUE-GEILE, M. F., & HARROW, M. (1987). Schizophrenia: An evolving concept. In V. B. Van Hasselt & M. Hersen (Eds.), *Handbook of adolescent psychology.* New York: Pergamon Press.

PRATT, M. W., SEBASTIAN, T., & BOUNTROGIANNI, M. (1989, April). *Parental beliefs and practices regarding school and homework: Parenting style and ethnic differences at the junior high level.* Paper presented at the Biennial Meetings of the Society for Research in Child Development, Kansas City, MO.

QUADAGNO, D., BRISCOE, R., & QUADAGNO, J. (1977). Effect of perinatal gonadal hormones on selected nonsexual behavior patterns: A critical assessment of the nonhuman and human literature. *Psychological Bulletin, 84,* 62–80.

RABIN, J. S. (1987). Two-paycheck families: Psychological responses to social change. In D. B. Carter (Ed.), *Current conceptions of sex roles and sex typing.* New York: Praeger.

RACHIN, R. L. (1975). The male juvenile delinquent and his behavior. In R. F., Hardy & J. G. Cull (Eds.). *Fundamentals of juvenile criminal behavior and drug abuse.* Springfield, IL: C. C. Thomas.

RAFFAELLI, M. (1989, April). *Conflict with siblings and friends in late childhood and early adolescence.* Paper presented at the Biennial Meetings of the Society for Research in Child Development, Kansas City, MO.

RAMSEY, G. (1943). The sex information of younger boys. *American Journal of Orthopsychiatry, 3,* 347–352.

RAYMOND, C. L., & BENBOW, C. P. (1986). Gender differences in mathematics: A function of parental support and student sex typing? *Developmental Psychology, 22,* 808–819.

REES, J. M., & TRAHMS, C. M. (1989). Nutritional influences on physical growth and behavior in adolescence. In G. R. Adams, R. Montemayor, & T. P. Gullotta (Eds.), *Biology of adolescent behavior and development.* Newbury Park, CA: Sage Publications, Inc.

REESE, H. W., & OVERTON, W. F. (1970). Models of development and theories of development. In L. R. Goulet & P. B. Baltes (Eds.), *Life-span developmental psychology: Research and theory.* New York: Academic Press.

REHBERG, R. A. (1969). Behavioral and attitudinal consequences of high school interscholastic sports: A speculative consideration. *Adolescence, 4,* 69–88.

REID, M., LANDESMAN, S., TREDER, R., & JACCARD, J. (1989). "My family and friends": Six- to twelve-year-old children's perceptions of social support. *Child Development, 60,* 896–910.

REISS, I. L. (1967). *The social context of premarital sexual permissiveness.* New York: Holt.

RENSHON, S. A. (Ed.). (1977). *Handbook of political socialization: Theory and research.* New York: The Free Press.

REPINSKI, D. J., & WHITBECK, L. B. (1989, April). *Parental behavior and adolescent self-esteem: An assessment of measures.* Paper presented at the Biennial Meetings of the Society for Research in Child Development, Kansas City, MO.

REST, J. R. (1976). New approaches in the assessment of moral judgment. In T. Lickona (Ed.). *Moral development and behavior: Theory, research, and social issues.* New York: Holt.

REST, J. (1983). Morality. In J. Flavell & E. Markman (Eds.), *Handbook of child psychology; Volume III: Cognitive development.* New York: John Wiley & Sons.

RHEINGOLD, H. L. (1969). The social and socializing infant. In D. A. Goslin (Ed.), *Handbook of socialization theory and research.* Chicago: Rand McNally.

RICHARDS, M., & PETERSEN, A. C. (1987). Biological theoretical models of adolescent development. In V. B. Van Hasselt & M. Hersen (Eds.), *Handbook of adolescent psychology.* New York: Pergamon Press.

RICHARDS, M. H., & DUCKETT, E. (1989, April). *Maternal employment and young adolescents' daily experience with family.* Paper presented at the Biennial Meetings of the Society for Research in Child Development, Kansas City, MO.

RICHTERS, J., & PELLEGRINI, D. (1989). Depressed mothers' judgments about their children: An examination of the depression-distortion hypothesis. *Child Development, 60,* 1068–1075.

RIDDLE, M. A., & CHO, S. C. (1989). Biological aspects of adolescent depression. In G. R. Adams, R. Montemayor, & T. P. Gullotta (Eds.), *Biology of adolescent behavior and development.* Newbury Park, CA: Sage Publications, Inc.

RIGSBY, L. C., & McDILL, E. L. (1972). Adolescent peer influence processes: Conceptualization and measurement. *Social Science Research, 1,* 305–321.

ROBINSON, I. E., KING, K., & BALSWICK, J. O. (1972). The premarital sexual revolution among college females. *Family Coordinator, 21,* 189–194.

ROCHE, A. F. (1979). Secular trends in human growth, maturation, and development. *Monographs of the Society for Research in Child Development, 44* (Whole No. 179).

ROE, A. (1951a). A psychological study of eminent biologists. *Psychological Monographs, 65,* (14a).

ROE, A. (1951b). A psychological study of eminent physical scientists. *Genetic Psychology Monographs, 43,* 121–293.

ROE, A. (1953). A psychological study of eminent psychologists and anthropologists and a comparison with biological and physical scientists. *Psychological Monographs, 65,* 1–68.

ROE, A. (1956). *Psychology of occupations.* New York: John Wiley & Sons.

ROE, A. (1964). Personality structure and occupational behavior. In H. Borow (Ed.), *Man in a world at work.* Boston: Houghton Mifflin.

ROE, A. (1968). Early determinants of vocational choice. In D. G. Zytowski (Ed.), *Vocational behavior.* New York: Holt.

ROFF, M., & SELLS, S. B. (1965). Relations between intelligence and sociometric status in groups differing in sex and socioeconomic background. *Psychological Reports, 16,* 511–516.

ROGEL, M., ZUEHLKE, M., PETERSEN, A., TOBIN-RICHARDS, M., & SHELTON, M. (1980). Contraceptive behavior in adolescence: A decision-making perspective. *Journal of Youth and Adolescence, 9,* 491–506.

ROKEACH, M. (1973). *The nature of human values.* New York: The Free Press.

ROPER, B., & LeBEFF, E. (1977). Sex roles and feminism revisited: An intergenerational attitude comparison. *Journal of Marriage and the Family, 39,* 113–120.

ROSENBERG, F., & ROSENBERG, M. (1978). Self-esteem and delinquency. *Journal of Youth and Adolescence, 7,* 279–291.

ROSENBERG, M. (1965). *Society and the adolescent self-image.* Princeton, NJ: Princeton University Press.

ROSENBERG, M. (1986). Self-concept from middle childhood through adolescence. In J. Suls & A. G. Greenwald (Eds.), *Psychological perspectives of the self* (Vol. 3). Hillsdale, NJ: Lawrence Erlbaum.

ROSENKRANTZ, P., VOGEL, BEE, H., BROVERMAN, I., & BROVERMAN, D. M. (1968). Sex-role stereotypes and self-concepts in college students. *Journal of Consulting and Clinical Psychology, 32,* 287–295.

ROSENTHAL, R. (1966). *Experimenter effects in behavioral research.* New York: Appleton-Century-Crofts.

ROSENTHAL, R., & ROSNOW, R. L. (1975). *The volunteer subject.* New York: John Wiley & Sons.

ROSS, S. (1978). *The youth values project.* New York: State Communities Aid Association.

ROSSMAN, B. B. R., & ROSENBERG, M. S. (1989, April). *Children in violent and discordant families: Coping, conflict control beliefs, and outcome.* Paper presented at the Biennial Meetings of the Society for Research in Child Development, Kansas City, MO.

ROWE, J., & MARCIA, J. (1980). Ego identity status, formal operations, and moral development. *Journal of Youth and Adolescence, 9,,* 87–99.

RUBENSTEIN, J. L., HEEREN, T., HOUSMAN, D., RUBIN, C., & STECHLER, G. (1989). Suicidal behavior in "normal" adolescents: Risk and protective factors. *American Journal of Orthopsychiatry, 59,* 59–71.

RUBLE, D., & BROOKS-GUNN, J. (1982). The experience of menarche. *Child Development, 53,* 1557–1566.

RUSS-EFT, S., SPRENGER, M., & BEEVER, A. (1979). Antecedents of adolescent parenthood and consequences at age 30. *Family Coordinator, 18,* 173–178.

RUSSELL, C. (1980). Unscheduled parenthood: Transition to 'parent' for the teenager. *Journal of Social Issues, 36,* 45–63.

RUSSELL, G. (1978). The father role and its relation to masculinity, femininity, and androgyny. *Child Development, 49,* 1174–1181.

RUTTER, M., & GILLER, H. (1984). *Juvenile delinquency: Trends and perspectives.* New York: The Guilford Press.

RYAN, R. M., & LYNCH, J. H. (1989). Emotional autonomy versus detachment: Revisiting the vicissitudes of adolescence and young adulthood. *Child Development, 60, 340–356.*

SANTROCK, J., WARSHAK, R., LINDBERGH, C., & MEADOWS, L. (1982). Children's and parents' observed social behavior in stepfather families. *Child Development, 53,* 472–480.

SARIGIANI, P. (1989, April). *Ratings of the marital relationship and parent and adolescent adjustment.* Paper presented at the Biennial Meetings of the Society for Research in Child Development, Kansas City, MO.

SATTLER, J. (1982). *Assessment of children's intelligence and special abilities.* Boston: Allyn & Bacon.

SAVIN-WILLIAMS, R. C., & SMALL, S. A. (1986). The timing of puberty and its relationship to adolescent and parent perceptions of family interactions. *Developmental Psychology, 22,* 342–347.

SCALES, P., & KIRBY, D. (1983). Perceived barriers to sex education: A survey of professionals. *Journal of Sex Research, 19,* 309–326.

SCARR, S., & McCARTNEY, K. (1983). How people make their own environments: A theory of genotype—environment effects. *Child Development, 54,* 424–435.

SCARR, S., WEBBER, P., WEINBERG, R., & WITTIG, M. (1981). Personality resemblance among adolescents and their parents in biologically-related and adoptive families. *Journal of Personality and Social Psychology, 40,* 885–898.

SCARR, S., & WEINBERG, R. (1976). IQ test performance of black children adopted by white families. *American Psychologist, 31,* 726–739.

SCARR, S., & WEINBERG, R. (1977). Intellectual similarities within families of both adopted and biological children. *Intelligence, 1,* 170–191.

SCARR, S., & WEINBERG, R. (1978). The influence of "family background" on intellectual attainment. *American Sociological Review, 43,* 674–692.

SCARR, S., & WEINBERG, R. (1983). The Minnesota adoption studies: Genetic differences and malleability. *Child Development, 54,* 260–267.

SCHAEFFER, D. (1969). Environmental factors in homosexuality of adolescent girls. *Psychoanalytic Review, 56,* 283–295.

SCHAEFER, E. S. (1959). A circumplex model for maternal behavior. *Journal of Abnormal and Social Psychology, 59,* 226–235.

SCHAEFER, E. S. (1965a). Children's reports of parental behavior: An inventory. *Child Development, 36,* 413–424.

SCHAEFER, E. S. (1965b). A configurational analysis of children's reports of parent behavior. *Journal of Consulting Psychology, 29,* 552–557.

SCHAIE, K. W., ROSENTHAL, F., & PEARLMAN, R. M. (1953). Differential deterioration of functionally "pure" mental abilities. *Journal of Gerontology, 8,* 191–196.

SCHAIE, K. W., & STROTHER, C. R. (1968). A cross-sequential study of age changes in cognitive behavior. *Psychological Bulletin, 70,* 671–680.

SCHMUCK, R. (1963). Some relationships of peer liking patterns in the classroom to pupil attitudes and achievement. *The School Review, 71*, 337–359.

SCHNAYER, R., & OTT, R. R. (1988/89). A comparison of children living in single-mother and single-father families. *Journal of Divorce, 12*, 171–184.

SCHULENBERG, J., VONDRACEK, F., & CROUTER, A. (1984). The influence of the family on vocational development. *Journal of Marriage and the Family, 46*, 129–143.

SCHWEINHART, L., & WEIKART, D. (1978, July). *Perry preschool effects nine years later: What do they mean?* Paper presented at the NICHD Conference on Prevention of Retarded Development in Psychosocially Disadvantaged Children, University of Wisconsin-Madison.

SEARS, D. O. (1975). Political socialization. In F. I. Greenstein, & N. W. Polsby (Eds.), *Handbook of political science: Vol. 2. Micropolitical theory*. Reading, MA: Addison-Wesley.

SEARS, R. R. (1950). Personality. *Annual Review of Psychology, 1*, 105–118.

SEARS, R. R., MACCOBY, E. E., & LEVIN, H. (1957). *Patterns of child rearing*. Evanston, IL: Row, Peterson.

SEARS, R. R., RAU, L., & ALPERT, R. (1965). *Identification and child rearing*. Stanford CA: Stanford University Press.

SEBALD, H. (1968). *Adolescence: A sociological analysis*. New York: Appleton-Century-Crofts.

SEGAL, S. J. (1961). A psychoanalytic analysis of personality factors in vocational choice. *Journal of Counseling Psychology, 8*, 202–210.

SELIGMAN, M. E. (1975). *Helplessness: On depression, development, and death*. San Francisco, CA: W. H. Freeman.

SELMAN, R. (1976). Social-cognitive understanding: A guide to educational and clinical practice. In T. Lickona (Ed.), *Moral development and behavior: Theory, research, and social issues*. New York: Holt.

SELMAN, R. (1980). *The growth of interpersonal understanding*. New York: Academic Press.

SELMAN, R., & BYRNE, D. (1974). A structural-developmental analysis of levels of role taking in middle childhood. *Child Development, 45*, 803–806.

SENNA, J., RATHUS, S. A., & SIEGEL, L. (1974–75). Delinquent behavior and academic investment among suburban youth. *Adolescence, 9*, 481–494.

SETTLAGE, D., BAROFF, S., & COOPER, D. (1974). Sexual experience of younger teen girls seeking contraceptive assistance for the first time. *Perspectives, 6*, 21–23.

SEWELL, W. H., & SHAH, V. P. (1968a). Parents' education and children's educational aspirations and achievements. *American Sociological Review, 33*, 191–209.

SEWELL, W. H., & SHAH, V. P. (1968b). Social class, parental encouragement, and educational aspirations. *The American Journal of Sociology, 73*, 559–572.

SHAH, F., & ZELNIK, M. (1981). Parent and peer influence on sexual behavior, contraceptive use, and pregnancy experience of young women. *Journal of Marriage and the Family, 43*, 339–348.

SHANTZ, C. (1975). The development of social cognition. In M. F. Hetherington (Ed.), *Review of child development research* (Vol. 5). Chicago: University of Chicago Press.

SHARABANY, R., GERSHONI, R., & HOFMAN, J. (1981). Girlfriend, boyfriend: Age and sex differences in intimate friendship. *Developmental Psychology, 17*, 800–808.

SHAVELSON, R., & BOLUS, R. (1982). Self-concept: The interplay of theory and methods. *Journal of Educational Psychology, 74*, 3–17.

SHELDON, W. H. (1940). *The varieties of human physique*. New York: Harper & Row.

SHERIF, M., HARVEY, O. J., HOOD, W. R., & SHERIF, C. W. (1961). *Intergroup conflict and cooperation: The robbers cave experiment*. Norman: University of Oklahoma Press.

SHERIF, M., & SHERIF, C. W. (1953). *Groups in harmony and tension*. New York: Harper & Row.

SHERMAN, J., & FENNEMA, E. (1977). The study of mathematics by high school girls and boys: Related variables. *American Educational Research Journal, 14*, 159–168.

SHERMAN, S. J., JUDD, C. M., & PARK, B. (1989). Social cognition. In M. R. Rosenzweig & L. W. Porter, (Eds.), *Annual review of psychology* (Vol. 40). Palo Alto, CA: Annual Reviews, Inc.

SHIFFLER, N., LYNCH-SAUER, J., & NADELMAN, L. (1977). Relationship between self-concept and classroom behavior in two informal elementary classrooms. *Journal of Educational Psychology, 69*, 349–359.

SILBERMAN, C. E. (1970). *Crisis in the classroom: The remaking of American education*. New York: Random House.

SILBERBERG, N. E., & SILBERBERG, M. C. (1971). School achievement and delinquency. *Review of Educational Research, 41*, 17–33.

SIMMONS, R. G., & BLYTH, D. A. (1987). *Moving into adolescence: The impact of pubertal change and school context*. New York: Aldine de Gruyter.

SIMMONS, R. G., BLYTH, D. A., & McKINNEY, K. L. (1983). The social and psychological effects of puberty on white females. In J. Brooks-Gunn & A. C. Petersen (Eds.), *Girls at puberty*. New York: Plenum Press.

SIMMONS, R. G., BURGESON, R., CARLTON-FORD, S., & BLYTH, D. A. (1987). The impact of cumulative change in early adolescence. *Child Development, 58*, 1220–1234.

SIMON, W. (1969). Sex. *Psychology Today, 3*, 23–27.

SIMON, W., BERGER, A., & GAGNON, J. (1972). Beyond anxiety and fantasy: The coital experiences of college youth. *Journal of Youth and Adolescence, 1*, 203–222.

SIMON, W., & GAGNON, J. H. (Eds.), (1970). *The sexual scene*. Chicago: Aldine Publishing Co.

SIMONS, R. L., & GRAY, P. A. (1989). Perceived blocked opportunity as an explanation of delinquency among lower-class black males: A research note. *Journal of Research in Crime and Delinquency, 26*, 90–101.

SIMPSON, E. (1987). The development of political reasoning. *Human Development, 30*, 268–281.

SIMPSON, R. L. (1962). Parental influence, anticipatory socialization, and social mobility. *American Sociological Review, 27*, 517–522.

SIRIS, S. G., VAN KAMMEN, D. P., & DOCHERTY, J. P. (1978). Use of anti-depressant drugs in schizophrenia. *Archives of General Psychiatry, 35*, 1368–1377.

Sisson, L. A., Hersen, M. & Van Hasselt, V. B. (1987). Historical perspectives. In V. B. Van Hasselt & M. Hersen (Eds.), *Handbook of adolescent psychology*. New York: Pergamon Press.

Skipper, J. K., Jr., & Nass, G. (1966). Dating behavior: A framework for analysis and an illustration. *Journal of Marriage and the Family, 28*, 412–420.

Skorepa, C. A., Horrocks, J. E., & Thompson, C. G. (1963). A study of friendship fluctuations of college students. *Journal of Genetic Psychology, 102*, 151–157.

Slaby, R. G., & Guerra, N. G. (1988). Cognitive mediators of aggression in adolescent offenders: I. Assessment. *Developmental Psychology, 24*, 580–588.

Smith, E. A. (1989). A biosocial model of adolescent sexual behavior. In G. R. Adams, R. Montemayor, and T. P. Gullotta (Eds.), *Biology of adolescent behavior and development*. Newbury Park, CA: Sage Publications, Inc.

Smith, E., Udry, J., & Morris, N. (1985). Pubertal development and friends: A biosocial explanation of adolescent sexual behavior. *Journal of Health and Social Behavior, 26*, 183–192.

Smith, T. L. (1986). Self-concepts of youth sport participants and nonparticipants in grades 3 and 6. *Perceptual and Motor Skills, 62*.

Smollar, J., & Ooms, T. (1987). Young unwed fathers: Research review, policy dilemmas and options. Summary report. Washington, D. C.

Snarey, J. R., Reimer, J., & Kohlberg, L. (1985). Development of social-moral reasoning among Kibbutz adolescents. A longitudinal cross-cultural study. *Developmental Psychology, 21*, 3–17.

Snel, D. L., Carey, M. P., & Dusek, J. B. (1988, April). *Sex roles and the diagnosis of depression and substance abuse.* Poster presented at the meeting of the Eastern Psychological Association, Buffalo, NY.

Snel, D. L., Carey, M. P., & Dusek, J. B. (1989, April). *Gender biases related to psychodiagnosis among mental health professionals.* Poster presented at the meeting of the Eastern Psychological Association, Boston.

Snyder, E. E. (1972). High school student perceptions of prestige criteria. *Adolescence, 6*, 129–136.

Snygg, D., & Combs, A. W. (1949). *Individual behavior.* New York: Harper & Row.

Soares, A. T., & Soares, L. M. (1969). Self-perceptions of culturally disadvantaged children. *American Educational Research Journal, 6*, 31–45.

Soares, A. T., & Soares, L. M. (1971). Comparative differences in the self-perceptions of disadvantaged and advantaged students. *Journal of School Psychology, 9*, 424–429.

Soares, A. T. & Soares, L. M. (1972). The self-concept differential in disadvantaged and advantaged students. *Proceedings of the Annual Convention of the American Psychological Association, 7*, Pt. 1, 195–196.

Sobesky, W. (1983). The effects of situational factors on moral judgments. *Child Development, 54*, 575–584.

Solberg, J. R. (1970). Interscholastic athletics–tail that wags the dog? *Journal of Secondary Education, 45*, 238–239.

Sorensen, R. C. (1973). *Adolescent sexuality in contemporary America.* New York: World.

Spearman, C. (1927). *The abilities of man.* New York: Macmillan.

Spence, J. (1982). Comments on Baumrind's "Are androgynous individuals more effective persons and parents?" *Child Development, 53*, 76–80.

Spence, J., & Helmreich, R. (1978). *Masculinity and femininity: Their psychological dimensions, correlates, and antecedents.* Austin: University of Texas Press.

Spence, J., & Helmreich, R. (1979). Comparison of masculine and feminine personality attributes and sex-role attitudes across age groups. *Developmental Psychology, 15*, 583–584.

Spence, J., & Helmreich, R. (1981). Androgyny versus gender schema: A comment on Bem's gender schema theory. *Psychological Review, 88*, 365–368.

Spence, J., Helmreich, R., & Stapp, J. (1974). The Personal Attributes Questionnaire: A measure of sex role stereotypes and masculinity-femininity. *JSAS: Catalog of Selected Documents in Psychology, 4*, 43.

Stechler, G. (1973). Newborn attention as affected by medication during labor. In L. J. Stone, M. T. Smith, & L. B. Murphy (Eds.), *The competent infant.* New York: Basic Books.

Steinberg, L. (1981). Transformations in family relations at puberty. *Developmental Psychology, 17*, 833–840.

Steinberg, L. (1989). Pubertal maturation and parent-adolescent distance: An evolutionary perspective. In G. R. Adams, R. Montemayor, & T. P. Gullotta (Eds.), *Biology of adolescent behavior and development.* Newbury Park, CA: Sage Publications, Inc.

Steinberg, L., & Hill, J. (1978). Patterns of family interaction as a function of age, the onset of puberty, and formal thinking. *Developmental Psychology, 14*, 683–684.

Steinberg, L. D. (1982). Jumping off the work experience bandwagon. *Journal of Youth and Adolescence, 11*, 183–205.

Steinberg, L. D. (1984). The varieties and effects of work during adolescence. In M. Lamb (Ed.), *Advances in developmental psychology* (Vol. 3). Hillsdale, NJ: Lawrence Erlbaum.

Steinberg, L. D., Greenberger, E., Garduque, L., & McAuliffe, S. (1982a). High school students in the labor force: Some costs and benefits to schooling and learning. *Educational Evaluation and Policy Analysis, 4*, 363–372.

Steinberg, L. D., Greenberger, E., Garduque, L., Ruggiero, M., & Vaux, A. (1982b). Effects of working on adolescent development. *Developmental Psychology, 18*, 385–395.

Steinberg, L. D., Greenberger, E., Jacobi, M., & Garduque, L. (1981a). Early work experience: A partial antidote for adolescent egocentrism. *Journal of Youth and Adolescence, 10*, 141–157.

Steinberg, L. D., Greenberger, E., Vaux, A., & Ruggiero, M. (1981a). Early work experience: Effects on adolescent occupational socialization. *Youth and Society, 12*, 403–422.

Stevenson, D. L., & Baker, D. P. (1987). The family-school relation and the child's school performance. *Child Development, 58*, 1348–1357.

Strong, E. K. (1943). *Vocational interest of men and women.* Stanford CA: Stanford University Press.

Strong, E. K. (1955). *Vocational interests 18 years after college.* Minneapolis: University of Minnesota Press.

Sullivan, E. V. (1970). Political development during the adolescent years. In E. D. Evans (Ed.), *Adolescents: Readings in behavior and development.* Hinsdale, IL: Dryden.

Sum, A. M., Harrington, P. E., & Goedicke, W. (1987). One-fifth of the nation's teenagers: Employment problems of poor youth in America, 1981–1985. *Youth and Society, 18,* 195–237.

SUPER, D. E. (1953). A theory of vocational development. *American Psychologist, 8,* 185–190.

SUPER, D. E. (1957). *The psychology of careers.* New York: Harper & Row.

SUPER, D. E. (1969). Vocational development theory: Persons, positions, and processes. *Counseling Psychologist 1,* 2–9.

SUPER, D. E. (1985). Coming of age in Middletown. *American Psychologist, 40,* 405–414.

SUPER, D. E., CRITES, J., HUMMEL, R., MOSER, H., OVERSTREET, P., & WARNATH, C. (1957). *Vocational development: A framework for research.* New York: Teachers College, Columbia University.

SUPER, D. E., & HALL, D. T. (1978). Career development: Exploration and planning. In M. Rosenzweig & L. Porter (Eds.), *Annual review of psychology* (Vol. 29). Palo Alto, CA: Annual Reviews, Inc.

SWENDINGER, H., & SWENDINGER, J. (1967). Delinquent stereotypes of probably victims. In M. W. Klein (Ed.), *Juvenile gangs in context.* Englewood Cliffs, NJ: Prentice-Hall.

TANNER, J. M. (1970). Physical growth. In P. H. Mussen (Ed.), *Carmichael's manual of child psychology* (Vol. 1, 3rd ed.). New York: John Wiley & Sons.

TANNER, J. M., WHITEHOUSE, R. H., & TAKAISHI, M. (1966). Standards from birth to maturity for height, weight, height velocity, and weight velocity: British children. *Archives of Disease in Childhood, 41,* 454–471.

TENNET, T. G. (1971). School non-attendance and delinquency. *Educational Research, 13,* 185–189.

TETI, D. M., & LAMB, M. E. (1989). Socioeconomic and marital outcomes of adolescent marriage, adolescent childbirth, and their co-occurrence. *Journal of Marriage and the Family, 51,* 203–212.

TETI, D. M., LAMB, M. E., & ELSTER, A. B. (1987). Long-range socioeconomic and marital consequences of adolescent marriage in three cohorts of adult males. *Journal of Marriage and the Family, 49,* 499–506.

THOMES, M. M. (1968). Children with absent fathers. *Journal of Marriage and the Family, 30,* 89–96.

THORNBURG, H. (1970). Age and first sources of sex information as reported by 88 college women. *Journal of Health Issues, 40,* 156–158.

THORNBURG, H. (1970–71). Adolescence: A re-interpretation. *Adolescence, 5,* 463–484.

THORNBURG, H. (1971). Peers: Three distince groups. *Adolescence, 6,* 59–76.

THORNBURG, H. (1972). A comparative study of sex information sources. *Journal of School Health, 42,* 88–91.

TIEGER, T. (1980). On the biological basis of sex differences in aggression. *Child Development, 51,* 943–963.

TOBIN-RICHARDS, M. H., BOXER, A. M., & PETERSEN, A. C. (1983). The psychological significance of pubertal change: Sex differences in perceptions of self during early adolescence. In J. Brooks-Gunn & A. C. Petersen (Eds.), *Girls at puberty.* New York: Plenum Press.

TOMLINSON-KEASEY, C., & KEASEY, C. B. (1974). The mediating role of cognitive development in moral judgment. *Child Development, 45,* 291–298.

TRACY, D. M. (1987). Toys, spatial ability, and science and mathematics achievement: Are they related? *Sex Roles, 17,* 115–138.

TROWBRIDGE, N. (1972). Self-concept and socio-economic status in elementary school children. *American Educational Research Journal, 9,* 525–537.

TURIEL, E. (1974). Conflict and transition in adolescent moral development. *Child Development, 45,* 14–29.

TURIEL, E. (1977). Conflict and transition in adolescent moral development: II: The resolution of disequilibrium through structural reorganization. *Child Development, 48,* 634–637.

TURIEL, E., & ROTHMAN, R. (1972). The influence of reasoning on behavioral choices at different stages of moral development. *Child Development, 43,* 741–756.

UDRY, J. R. (1971). *The social context of marriage* (2nd ed.). Philadelphia: Lippincott.

UDRY, J. (1987). Hormonal and social determinants of adolescent sexual initiation. In J. Bancroft (Ed.), *Adolescence and puberty.* New York: Oxford University Press.

UDRY, J., TALBERT, L., & MORRIS, N. (1986). Biosocial foundations for adolescent female sexuality. *Demography, 23,* 217–230.

UNGER, R. (1979). Toward a redefinition of sex and gender. *American Psychologist, 34,* 1085–1094.

U. S. BUREAU OF THE CENSUS (1982). *Current population reports, Series P-20, "Marital status and living arrangement: March, 1981."* Washington, DC: Government Printing Office.

U. S. BUREAU OF THE CENSUS. (1989). *Statistical abstract of the U. S., 1989* (10th ed.). Washington, DC: Government Printing Office.

U. S. BUREAU OF THE CENSUS. (1987). *Statistical abstract of the U.S., 1987* (108th ed.). Washington, DC: Government Printing Office.

URBERG, K. (1979). Sex role conceptualizations in adolescents and adults. *Developmental Psychology, 15,* 90–92.

URBERG, K. A., & DEGIRMENCIOGLU, S. (1989, April). *Peer influence on adolescent values.* Paper presented at the Biennial Meetings of the Society for Research in Child Development, Kansas City, MO.

URBERG, K., & LABOUVIE-VIEF, Q. (1976). Conceptualizations of sex roles: A life span developmental study. *Developmental Psychology, 12,* 15–23.

VANDENBERG, D. (1968). Life-phases and values. *Education Forum, 32,* 293–302.

VAN DUSEN, R. A. & SHELDON, E. B. (1976). The changing status of American women: A life cycle perspective. *American Psychologist, 31,* 106–116.

VANGELISTI, A. L. (1988). Adolescent socialization into the workplace: A synthesis and critique of current literature. *Youth and Society, 19,* 460–484.

VAN HASSELT, V. B., & HERSEN, M. (1987). *Handbook of adolescent psychology.* New York: Pergamon Press.

VAZ, E. W. (1969). Delinquency and the youth culture: Upper- and middle-class boys. *Journal of Criminal Law, Criminology, and Police Science, 60,* 33–46.

VECK, J. C. (1978). Social Influences on the prognosis of schizophrenia. *Schizophrenia Bulletin, 4,* 86–101.

VEROFF, J., DEPNER, C., KULKA, R., & DOUVAN, E. (1980). Comparison of American motives: 1957 versus 1976. *Journal of Personality and Social Psychology, 39,* 1249–1262.

VIGOD, Z. (1972). The relationship between occupational choice and parental occupational. *Alberta Journal of Educational Research, 18,* 287–294.

VOSK, B., FOREHAND, R., PARKER, J., & RICKARD, K. (1982). A multimethod comparison of popular and unpopular children. *Developmental Psychology, 18,* 571–575.

VOSS, H. L., WENDLING, A., & ELLIOTT, D. S. (1966). Some types of high school dropouts. *Journal of Educational Research, 59,* 363–368.

VOSS, J. (1980). Sex education: Evaluation and recommendations for future study. *Archives of Sexual Behavior, 9,* 37–59.

WADSWORTH, B. J. (1971). *Piaget's theory of cognitive development.* New York: David McKay.

WAGNER, H. (1970). Adolescent problems resulting from the lengthened educational period. *Adolescence, 5,* 339–344.

WAGNER, H. (1971). The increasing importance of the peer group during adolescence. *Adolescence, 6,* 53–58.

WALBERG, H. J., HOUSE, E. R., & STEELE, J. M. (1973). Grade level, cognition, and affects: A cross-section of classroom perceptions. *Journal of Educational Psychology, 64,* 142–146.

WALKER, L. (1980). Cognitive and perspective-taking prerequisites for moral development. *Child Development, 51,* 131–139.

WALKER, L. (1982). The sequentiality of Kohlberg's stages of moral development. *Child Development, 53,* 1330–1336.

WALKER, L. (1983). Sources of cognitive conflict for stage transition in moral development. *Developmental Psychology, 19,* 103–110.

WALKER, L., DEVRIES, B., & RICHARD, S. (1984). The hierarchical nature of stages of moral development. *Developmental Psychology, 20,* 960–966.

WALKER, L. J. (1986). Sex differences in the development of moral reasoning: A rejoinder to Baumrind. *Child Development, 57,* 522–526.

WALKER, L. J. (1989). A longitudinal study of moral reasoning. *Child Development, 60,* 157–166.

WALKER, L. J., DE VRIES, B., & TREVETHAN, S. D. (1987). Moral stages and moral orientations in real-life and hypothetical dilemmas. *Child Development, 58,* 842–858.

WALLERSTEIN, J. S. (1983). Children of divorce: The psychological tasks of the child. *American Journal of Orthopsychiatry, 53,* 230–243.

WALLERSTEIN, J. S. (1984). Children of divorce: Preliminary report of a ten-year follow-up of young children. *American Journal of Orthopsychiatry, 54,* 444–458.

WALLERSTEIN, J., & KELLY, J. (1974). The effects of parental divorce: The adolescent experience. In E. Anthony & C. Koupernik (Eds.), *The child and his family.* New York: John Wiley & Sons.

WALLERSTEIN, J., & KELLY, J. (1976). The effects of parental divorce: Experiences of the child in later latency. *American Journal of Orthopsychiatry, 46,* 256–269.

WALLERSTEIN, J., & KELLY, J. (1979). Children and divorce: A review. *Social Work, 36,* 468–475.

WALLERSTEIN, J., & KELLY, J. (1980). *Surviving the breakup: How children and parents cope with divorce.* New York: Basic Books.

WARDLOW, M. E., & GREENE, J. E. (1952). An exploratory sociometric study of peer status among adolescent girls. *Sociometry, 15,* 311–318.

WATERMAN, A. (1982). Identity development from adolescence to adulthood: An extension of theory and a review of research. *Developmental Psychology, 18* 341–358.

WATERMAN, A., GEARY, P., & WATERMAN, C. (1974). A longitudinal study of changes in ego identity status from the freshman to senior year at college. *Developmental Psychology, 10,* 387–392.

WATERMAN, A., & GOLDMAN, J. (1976). A longitudinal study of ego identity development at a liberal arts college. *Journal of Youth and Adolescence, 5,* 361–369.

WATERMAN, A., & WATERMAN, C. (1971). A longitudinal study of changes in ego identity status during the freshman year at college. *Developmental Psychology, 5,* 167–173.

WATERMAN, A., & WHITBOURNE, S. (1982). Androgyny and psychological development among college students and adults. *Journal of Personality, 50,* 121–133.

WATKINS, B. (1989, April). *Conceptions of athletic excellence among children and adolescents.* Paper presented at the Biennial Meetings of the Society for Research in Child Development, Kansas City, MO.

WATKINS, B., & MONTGOMERY, A. B. (in press). Conceptions of athletic excellence among children and adolescents. *Child Development.*

WECHSLER, D. (1955). *Manual of the Wechsler Adult Intelligence Scale.* New York: The Psychological Corporation.

WEINER, I. B. (1970). *Psychological disturbance in adolescence.* New York: John Wiley & Sons.

WEINER, I. B. (1980). Psychopathology in adolescence. In J. Adelson (Ed.), *Handbook of adolescent psychology.* New York: John Wiley & Sons.

WEINER, I. B. (1982). *Child and adolescent psychopathology.* New York: John Wiley & Sons.

WEIR, M. W. (1967). Mental retardation. *Science, 157,* 576–577.

WEISS, R. (1982). Understanding moral thought: Effects on moral reasoning and decision making. *Developmental Psychology, 18,* 852–861.

WELLS, L. E. (1989). Self-enhancement through delinquency: A conditional test of self-derogation theory. *Journal of Research in Crime and Delinquency, 26,* 226–252.

WENTZEL, K. R. (1988). Gender differences in math and English achievement: A longitudinal study. *Sex Roles, 18,* 691–699.

WENTZEL, K. R. (1989). Adolescent classroom goals, standards for performance, and academic achievement: An interactionist perspective. *Journal of Educational Psychology, 81,* 131–142.

WERTS, C. E. (1968). Paternal influence on career choice. *Journal of Counseling Psychology, 15,* 48–52.

WHEELER, S., & COTTRELL, L. S. (1966). *Juvenile delinquency: Its prevention and control.* New York: Russell Sage Foundation.

WHITE, C. B. (1975). Moral development in Bahamian school children: A cross-cultured examination of Kohlberg's stages of moral reasoning. *Developmental Psychology, 11,* 535–536.

WHITE, K. (1982). The relation between socioeconomic status and academic achievement. *Psychological Bulletin, 91,* 461–481.

WHITEHEAD, J. T., & LAB, S. (1989). A meta-analysis of juvenile correctional treatment. *Journal of Research in Crime and Delinquency, 26,* 276–295.

WHITEMAN, M., & DEUTSCH, M. (1968). Social disadvantage as related to intellective and language development. In M. Deutsch, I. Katz, & A. Jensen (Eds.), *Social class, race, and psychological development*. New York: Holt.

WHITLEY, B. E., JR. (1988a). Masculinity, femininity, and self-esteem: A multitrait–multimethod analysis. *Sex Roles, 18,* 419–431.

WHITLEY, B. E., JR. (1988b). The relation of gender-role orientation to sexual experience among college students. *Sex Roles, 19,* 619–638.

WHITLEY, B. E. (1989, August). *College students' reasons for sexual intercourse: A sex role perspective.* Paper presented at the Annual Convention of the American Psychological Association, Atlanta.

WICKER, A. W. (1968). Undermanning, performances, and students' subjective experiences in behavior settings of large and small high schools. *Journal of Personality and Social Psychology, 10,* 255–261.

WILLEMS, E. P. (1967). Sense of obligation to high school activities as related to school size and marginality of student. *Child Development, 38,* 1247–1260.

WILSON, A. B. (1959). Residential segregation of social classes and aspirations of high school boys. *American Sociological Review, 24,* 836–845.

WINDMILLER, M. (1976). Moral development. In J. F. Adams (Ed.), *Understanding adolescence: Current developments in adolescent psychology.* Boston: Allyn & Bacon.

WIRTZ, P. W., ROHRBECK, C. A., CHARMER, I., FRASER, B. S. (1988). Employment of adolescents while in high school: Employment intensity, interference with schoolwork, and normative approval. *Journal of Adolescent Research, 3,* 97–105.

WISE, N. B. (1967). Juvenile delinquency among middle-class girls. In E. W. Vaz (Ed.), *Middle-class juvenile delinquency.* New York: Harper & Row.

WOHLWILL, J. (1973). *The study of behavioral development.* New York: Academic Press.

WOHLWILL, J. F. (1970). The age variable in psychological research. *Psychological Review, 77,* 49–64.

WOLFBEIN, S. L. (1964). Labor trends, manpower, and automation. In H. Borow (Ed.), *Man in a world at work.* Boston: Houghton Mifflin.

WOODS, M. B. (1972). The unsupervised child of the working mother. *Developmental Psychology, 6,* 14–25.

WYDEN, P. (1968a). How mothers raise homosexual sons. In *Growing up straight.* New York: Stein & Day.

WYDEN, P. (1968b). How fathers raise homosexual sons. In *Growing up straight.* New York: Stein & Day.

WYLIE, R. C. (1961). *The self-concept: A critical survey of pertinent research literature.* Lincoln: University of Nebraska Press.

WYLIE, R. C. (1974). *The self-concept: A review of methodological considerations and measuring instruments* (Vol. 1, rev. ed.). Lincoln: University of Lincoln Press.

WYLIE, R. C. (1979). *The self-concept* (Vol. 2). Lincoln: University of Nebraska Press.

YALOM, I., GREEN, R., & FISK, M. (1973). Prenatal exposure to female hormones: Effects on psychosexual development in boys. *Archives of General Psychiatry, 28,* 554–561.

YANCY, W. S., NADER, P. R., & BURNHAM, K. L. (1972). Drug use and attitudes of high school students. *Pediatrics, 50,* 739–745.

YANKELOVICH, D. (1969). *Generations apart.* New York: Columbia Broadcasting System.

YANKELOVICH, D. (1974). *The new morality: A profile of American youth in the 70s.* New York: McGraw-Hill.

YEE, D. K., & ECCLES, J. S. (1988). Parent perceptions and attributions for children's math achievement. *Sex Roles, 19,* 317–333.

YOUNG, E., & PARISH, T. (1977). Impact of father absence during childhood on the psychological adjustment of college females. *Sex Roles, 3,* 217–227.

ZELNIK, M., & KANTNER, J. (1972). Sexuality, contraception and pregnancy among young unwed females in the United States. In R. Parke, Jr., & C. Westoff (Eds.), *Demographic and social aspects of population growth.* Washington, DC: Government Printing Office.

ZELNIK, M., & KANTNER, J. (1974). The resolution of teenage first pregnancies. *Family Planning Perspectives, 6,* 74–80.

ZELNIK, M., & KANTNER, J. (1977). Sexual and contraceptive experience of young unmarried women in the United States, 1976, 1971. *Family Planning Perspectives, 9,* 55–71.

ZELNIK, M., & KANTNER, J. (1978). First pregnancies to women aged 15–19: 1976 and 1971. *Family Planning Perspectives, 10,* 11–20.

ZELNIK, M., & KANTNER, J. (1980). Sexual activity, contraceptive use and pregnancy among metropolitan-area teenagers: 1971–1979. *Family Planning Perspectives, 12,* 230–237.

ZELNIK, M., KIM, Y. J., & KANTNER, J. F. (1979). Probabilities of intercourse and conception among U.S. teenage women, 1971 and 1976. *Family Planning Perspectives, 11,* 177–183.

ZIEGLER, C., & DUSEK, J., (1985). Perceptions of child rearing and adolescent sex role development. *Journal of Early Adolescence, 5,* 215–227.

ZIEGLER, C., & DUSEK, J., & CARTER, D. (1984). Self-concept and sex-role orientation: An investigation of multidimensional aspects of a personality development in adolescence. *Journal of Early Adolescence, 4,* 25–39.

ZIGLER, E. (1967). Familial mental retardation: A continuing dilemma. *Science, 155,* 292–298.

ZIGLER, E. (1963). Metatheoretical issues in developmental psychology. In M. M. Marx (Ed.), *Theories in contemporary psychology.* New York: Macmillan.

ZIMILES, H., & LEE, V. E. (1989, April). *Adolescent family structure and educational progress.* Paper presented at the Biennial Meetings of the Society for Research in Child Development, Kansas City, MO.

ZUMPF, C. L. (1989). *Mirror, mirror on the wall: Gender differences in the link between appearance and self-worth in early adolescence.* Paper presented at the Biennial Meetings of the Society for Research in Child Development, Kansas City, MO.

Photo Credits

Name Index

Subject Index